Law and the Web of Society

Law and the Web of Society

Cynthia L. Cates

and

Wayne V. McIntosh

Georgetown University Press / Washington, D.C.

Georgetown University Press, Washington, D.C. 20007

© 2001 by Georgetown University Press. All rights reserved.

Printed in the United States of America

10 9 8 7 6 5 4 3 2 1

2001

This volume is printed on acid-free, offset book paper.

Library of Congress Cataloging-in-Publication Data
Cates, Cynthia L., 1950–
 Law and the web of society / Cynthia L. Cates, Wayne V. McIntosh.
 p. cm.
 Includes bibliographical references and index.
 ISBN 0-87840-860-6 (paper : alk. paper)
 1. Law—United States. 2. Sociological jurisprudence. I. McIntosh, Wayne V., 1950–. II. Title.

Kr379.C38   2001
301′.115—dc21   2001023262

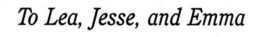

To Lea, Jesse, and Emma

Contents

List of Figures and Tables

Figures

Tables

Preface

Many outstanding books have been written on the subject of "law and society," a broad topic of interest to many and a popular course on hundreds of college campuses. This is yet another effort, with several useful differences, to shed some light on that matrix of relationships.

This book centers around two core themes. Like the spider's web, law is *ubiquitous* but it is *ambivalent*. Law is all around us. It is everywhere, and it is everywhere all the time. Though most of us do not see it—or at least do not recognize it most of the time—it shapes our lives from the weightiest moments to the most mundane tasks. Law can be terribly nebulous, charged with accomplishing competing, even sometimes seemingly contradictory, ends. Take one major example, the one that largely informs this book. On the one hand, law is what we use to achieve order, to make us safe and secure, and to make our lives run smoothly. At the same time, Americans prize individual liberty dearly, and we expect the law to defend our freedom. Thus, as Justice Cardozo first observed, we charge law with effecting a scheme of "ordered liberty" (*Palko v. Connecticut*, 302 U.S. 319, 325 (1937)). Liberty, however, can be, and sometimes is, the antithesis of order and so, our ambivalence about law.

The material for the book is a direct offshoot of these themes. The substance for most law and society tracts tends to be special-interest centered, focusing on law and its impact on various groups in society (i.e., law and racial groups, law and class groups, law and police interests, etc.). Clearly, this is very important, since segments of society both shape and are shaped by law in profound ways. The law, however, affects us not simply as members of discrete racial, class, or organizational entities but in a much more universal sense: It affects us as members of the broad social economic system at large, every minute of the day, from before birth until well after death. The material selected herein thus reflects the ubiquitous and universal nature of law.

The book is divided into two parts and eleven chapters. Part I (chapters 1 through 5) is a general overview of law and society and the judicial processes that undergird it. In this part we traverse the surface of the web. Chapter 1 explains the themes of the book generally, that law is both ubiquitous and ambiguous. Chapter 2 is a consideration of the forms and functions of law. Chapter 3 focuses this consideration particularly in the American context. Chapter 4 is a general overview of the American legal structure and judicial process. Chapter 5 is an examination of legal actors.

Part II (chapters 6 through 9) examines law from the perspective of life, so our analysis of the web in this section is based on the individual life cycle and on key aspects of our lives that we all share. In effect, we enter the web. Of course, we are all born, we all assume identities, most of us manage to traverse the difficult terrain from childhood to adulthood, and we all die. The vast majority of us form relationships—a few are close and loving, many more are simply casual or utilitarian. In all of this, law is heavily involved. We take the opportunity in chapter 10 to consider law in the context of the broader sociopolitical structure. Finally, in the concluding chapter, we return to our core themes, the ubiquitous and ambivalent nature of law, to again stress the interwovenness of law and society.

Acknowledgments

Much of the theme, structure, and research for this book has been developed over the past three years as we taught and refined a jointly offered, cross-campus, web-based course titled "Law On-Line" (www.bsos.umd. edu/gvpt/lawonline/). We wish to offer our most sincere thanks to our wonderful students who have made teaching such a joy and learning (ours) such a thrill.

In addition, we are immensely grateful to three law-*makers*, Governor Parris N. Glendening (D-MD), Congressman Benjamin L. Cardin (D-MD), and Congressman Robert L. Ehrlich, Jr. (R-MD), each of whom took time from his very busy schedule to provide us with a personal definition of law as a starting point for our reflection on this subject.

The research for this book inevitably took us into areas we had not anticipated, and we learned a great deal in the process. We also benefited significantly from the comments and suggestions of a number of colleagues. First and foremost, Douglas Reed (Government Department, Georgetown University) read the entire manuscript and offered a long list of constructive criticisms and suggestions. John Sprague is an old and dear friend. His comments on the parts he read were, as always, quite useful, and his remarks, challenging. A number of colleagues in the Department of Government and Politics at the University of Maryland—Mark Graber, Karen Kaufmann, Irwin Morris, and Eric Uslaner—also read portions of the text, and their suggestions and insights were extremely helpful as we redrafted and attempted to tie things together. Despite our best efforts, we no doubt made many mistakes and left some stones unturned. Responsibility for error, of course, rests entirely with us.

Part I

The Web of Law

1   Law and the Web of Society: An Introduction

The Law, wherein, as in a magic mirror, we see reflected not only our own lives, but the lives of all men that have been!

—Oliver Wendell Holmes, Jr., 1885[1]

Perhaps no one has ever said it more eloquently than Justice Holmes. For indeed, the march of law throughout history is a reflection of all the loftiest aspirations, deepest sorrows, and most mundane daily contrivances of humanity. It speaks to our great purposes when, as in the U.S. Constitution, it strives to create "a more perfect Union" dedicated to justice, peace, and liberty.[2] It speaks to our most profound anguish in documents such as the International Convention on the Prevention and Punishment of the Crime of Genocide.[3] And it speaks to our comparatively modest day-to-day needs in the thousands upon thousands of statutes and ordinances aimed at such commonplace matters as traffic speeds, garbage removal, and food safety. Law *is* the mirror of all that we want (and have ever wanted) to achieve and of all that we want (and have ever wanted) to avoid.

We could take Holmes a step further. His metaphor suggests a one-way reflection—law as mirror of us. But, surely, the reflection works both ways. For we as humans, collectively and individually, also mirror the law. Most everything we do reflects some consideration of law, and it does so whether we know it or not.

Indeed, the human life cycle and the law are inextricably intertwined from beginning to end, both in the broadest societal sense and in the six to eight decades that most of us are individually afforded here on earth. The law reaches us, and we it, from our genesis in the embryonic fluid to our final resting place six feet under. In that respect, law and life take on more than the smooth plane properties of a two-way mirror. To use a different metaphor, they form a continuous and exquisitely complex web, woven around and about all that we do and all that we are.

That metaphor—of law and society in a webbed relationship—is the one that informs our thinking, and, consequently, that of this book.[4] It is a particularly apt analogy in two respects. First, from the perspective of one deep within the interior of a web, the web itself, composed of all its many tangled threads, seems all-encompassing—it is ubiquitous. And so do we social creatures find ourselves embedded in a social/legal structure whose extensive threads reach back through the millen-

nia, forward through generations yet to come, back through our conceptions, and forward through our deaths.

Second, webs are meandering, mysterious objects—they are inherently ambiguous. But to the entomologist and the spider herself, they seemingly have no beginning nor end. Too, the relationship between law and society, although ubiquitous, is riddled with ambiguity, as law serves seeming cross-purposes in society, and society, in turn, demands contradictory deeds from the law.

Law and Society: The Ubiquitous Web

In this book, we take law to be ubiquitous—to be everywhere—in two distinct, but interrelated senses. It is pervasive in the very broadest sociohistorical sense. Thus, the LAW writ large, even as it informs and governs us today, threads back through the very furthest reaches of human history. Indeed, in one very important meaning, it actually precedes human history. Thus, as we discuss later in the book, classical liberal theories of natural law maintain that law is not produced by any government entity; rather it simply exists to be discovered as part of the natural order of the universe. The fact that such ideas are neither provable nor disprovable makes little difference. What *does* make a difference is the fact that the Founders relied heavily upon a theory of natural law in constructing the basic guarantes of the U.S. Constitution. Thus, whether we accept or doubt the existence of natural law, we are inextricably and significantly tied to this ancient idea.

Nor is our social relation to natural law the only filament that tethers us to a long line of ancient legal thought. So, the law, at the turn of the twenty-first century, is a complex web, the result of century upon century, layer upon layer, of customary principle, statutory enactment, regulatory fiat, and judicial interpretation, all linked to the delicate task of civilizing society and social relationships. This very broadest sense of ubiquity will be addressed in chapters 2 and 3.

Law, however, is ubiquitous in another, more ordinary sense. And it is this sense that informs the remaining chapters of the book. For law is both more and less than a grand, abstract web woven about all of human history. It is the stuff of everyday life, of the individual's everyday life, and of the individual's everyday life all day long and from cradle to grave. The web, in other words, envelops and binds not just law and society, but *you*, specifically, as a part of law and society.

The Law: From Cradle to Grave

Follow John Q. Public, ordinary American citizen, through just a few of the high points of his life. John is conceived. His mother's initial decision—whether to maintain or end the pregnancy—is taken under color of judgments made by the U.S. Supreme Court[5] and a tangle of regulations based in federal and state legislative statutes.[6] Depending upon which state his embryonic debut takes place, his mother's behavior—whether she drinks, takes drugs, gets prenatal care—may be governed by the law.[7]

John is born—a full-fledged human being after nine months in the womb. Like most of us, he makes his entrance in a state-regulated hospital, his birth immediately recorded for the purposes of obtaining a state-issued birth certificate. This certificate, required by law, will later be essential to his obtaining such other legally essential items as his federally mandated Social Security number and his state-allocated driver's license.

As a newborn, and on through his childhood, John will be required by law to obtain a series of immunizing vaccinations from a legally licensed medical practitioner, both for his own protection against deadly disease and for the protection of those around him. If John does not receive the mandatory shots, he will not be allowed to spend his earliest time away from home at a decent daycare center (one licensed by the law of the state), nor, later, will he be able to attend school—something he is required to do by law in most states until he is about sixteen years old.

As a typical middle-class American kid, John will receive, throughout the course of his childhood, hundreds of toys from his doting parents and relatives. These toys, his folks presume, meet certain safety standards, the product of regulations drawn up under color of law. Since the vast majority of his toys will be made in China, they are governed by a series of (very loosely enforced) laws designed to prevent the importation of goods made by child or forced-prison labor.[8]

John's parents also presume that the food he eats at home has been inspected by government agents to ensure its safety. They also assume that the hundreds of "Happy Meals" he will ingest over the course of his childhood have been cooked at legally established temperatures so that he never succumbs to *E. coli* bacteria.[9]

Of course, as we have said, John will spend most of his youth in school. There, he will be educated by teachers who must meet a number of requirements mandated by state law. The subjects he is taught are also the product of law. Increasingly, he will take one after another after another after another legally mandated competency tests to prove that he has learned all that the law requires him to be taught.[10]

When he graduates high school, John will decide whether to enter the workforce, or go on for more education. If he decides to go directly to work, his employment will be governed by layer upon layer of law—law that determines the minimum salary he can be paid,[11] whether and under what circumstances he may band together with other employees to demand better wages and conditions from his employer,[12] the level of safety he can expect on the job,[13] his rights to be free from discrimination[14] and harassment,[15] and the amount of his paycheck that he must fork over to the government, to name just a very few.

If he opts to prolong his educational experience, he no doubt will apply for any one or a number of grants and loans established over the years by federal and state lawmakers. He will expect, of course, that his college or university abides by the many civil rights laws promulgated over the past four decades—some aimed specifically at educational institutions.[16] And, he will complete his education only by complying with the many by-laws established by the school he attends; if he is one of the majority of students who attends a public institution, a lot of these will have been set by the state legislature.

Within his early adulthood, we can anticipate John falling head over heels in love. If he follows the normal course of events, he will want to get married. In a very significant respect, the law determines whom he can (or more appropriately, whom he can*not*) wed.[17] In order to be socially recognized, the law must license his nuptials. This is extremely important, for without the legal nod, John cannot expect his life partner to share in the economic benefits to which he will someday be entitled.

Later, if John is one of the unlucky "50 percent," he or his spouse will decide to call it quits. The end of his legal union, and his rights and duties thereafter, will have been spelled out by state law. His divorce will be finalized, his property divided, and the custody of his children determined by a court of law.

Remarried (and happy, we trust) later in life, John decides to spend his waning years in comfortable retirement. Presumably, he will receive benefits from the Social Security fund into which he has been required by law to put a portion of his paycheck throughout his working life. In addition, hopefully, the employer maintaining his private pension fund has abided by laws regulating the investment and disbursement of such monies.

Many years later, after John buries his second wife, according to state regulations, his own failing health forces his children to place him in a nursing home.[18] Their guilt is assuaged somewhat by the thought that this home meets the legal standards of adequate end-of-life care. Finally, ravaged by cancer and heart disease, John asks his caregivers to hasten the inevitable end through lethal injection. Whether they can honor his request is a matter of—guess what?—law.[19]

The Law: All Day Long

Having followed John Q. Public through a lifetime, we will now follow Jane Doe through a single day. Jane, let us say, is a typical American college student. Thus, when her alarm goes off at 7 A.M. to wake her for her first 8 o'clock class, she naturally shuts it off, rolls over, and goes back to sleep. When she does awake sometime around 11 (oh well, there's always the afternoon classes), she brushes her teeth, washes her hair, and scrubs herself, confident in her cleanliness because her toothpaste, shampoo, and shower soap all bear legally required labels listing their cleaning ingredients.[20]

Fresh and ready to learn, Jane jumps in her car. Although she resents the way it wrinkles her clothes, she fastens her seatbelt because that is what the law demands.[21] Her normal 80-mph cruise around the beltway headed toward school is slowed on three occasions—twice by the sight of a police car whose occupant might easily pull her over for exceeding the 55-mph limit set by law, and once by the road construction being funded by a recently passed congressional transportation act.[22]

Once on campus, and with an entire hour to go until her 2 P.M. class, Jane settles in at the Union with friends to drink coffee and grab a bite to eat. She is entirely confident that the food and drink she buys will not sicken her because she knows they must meet certain legal standards. In the middle of this pleasant repast, she panics, remembering that her professor has scheduled a quiz for today. She fumbles nervously for a cigarette, but must go outside to smoke it since hers is a state university and the legislature recently enacted a law banning lighted tobacco products in public buildings.[23]

Anxiously approaching her classroom, Jane is delighted by that which universally brings joy to college students: the "Class Canceled" sign. It seems her professor has been called to jury duty and must, by law, make an appearance at court. Jane and her classmates thus wander outdoors where a group of students is staging a protest. Fascinated, Jane watches as one of the protestors sets fire to an American flag. As campus police descend on the dissidents, they scream something about their free speech rights, presumably protected by the First Amendment to the Constitution. The police, as they haul the students off, cite several university and local ordinances aimed at preventing disturbances of the peace.[24]

After attending two late afternoon classes, Jane heads off to soccer practice. She feels lucky knowing that while her mother had very limited athletic possibilities, today the university must, by law, allocate resources to her team equal to those of the men's team (Title IX, *Civil Rights Act of 1964*). Although buoyed by this ideal of equality, Jane is disturbed when she learns that the university has instituted new rules requiring its student athletes to submit to periodic urine testing for drugs. When Jane and her colleagues protest this invasion of privacy, they are assured that such testing has been upheld by the courts—it's legal (see, e.g., *Vernonia School District 47j v. Acton*, 515 U.S. 646 (1995)).

Following practice, Jane hunkers down at the library for an evening of study. At 10 p.m., proud of the work she has accomplished, Jane would like to unwind with a beer. But, Jane is only twenty years old, and the law says she must be twenty-one to drink.[25] Thus, her decision is not simply whether to grab a brew, but whether to relax within or without the law. And so, Jane ends her day as she began it, wrapped in the complex web of law.

We live a life, and we live it day by day, in the web of law.

Law and Society: The Ambiguous Web

It would indeed make life easier—both in the broad societal sense and in the individualized sense faced by John and Jane—if the ubiquitous web of law and society were a simple, straightforward affair. But webs, by their nature, are complex things. And complex things are seldom easy things. We ask much of law, and much of what we ask is inherently contradictory. Thus, for example, as discussed in chapters 2 and 3, we demand that the law liberate us, and zealously protect our freedom and our individuality, while simultaneously directing it to control us, keep us safe, protect us, and tell us and others what we should do. As a social condition, we ask the law to accomplish two huge, contradictory tasks—to accomplish both liberty *and* order. We force it to be ambiguous.

Such cross-purposes, as discussed in chapters 5 through 9, permeate our lives as we live them day to day, and through the years. The law (the web of so many laws) surrounding our relationships, our births, our childhood, our identity, and our deaths—indeed, our entire sociopolitical economy—often attempts to achieve countervailing goals and contradictory ends. It is all one huge balancing act. We also very often resort to the courts as the legal balancers of last resort. Indeed, as explored in this book, in ways small and large, balancing legal conflicts arising in the course of lives lived is the great task of courts. So, a local court weighs John's modest claim against Jane after they meet, unhappily, during a parking lot fender-bender. That same day, perhaps, far away in its "marble palace" in Washington, the Supreme Court weighs two other competing claims, these with nationwide implications. Or, take, for example, one small slice of John's life and one minor event in Jane's day.

Suppose that John's mother had been an unfortunate addict of drugs, unable to shake the monkey from her back during pregnancy. Suppose, tragically, that John had been born a "cocaine baby." Depending upon the state of his birth, John's mother may have been subject to prosecution under any of numerous child abuse and endangerment statutes. It seems simple enough, but the law must then decide if John, in the womb, was indeed a "child" at all. As a mere fetus, and thus without specific constitutional protection, do his *potential* rights, or a state's interest in his potential rights, outweigh those of his mother to bodily autonomy? These are the kinds of difficult questions with which courts wrestle every day—seemingly caught between one legal rock and another legal hard place.[26]

Or, imagine Jane's chance encounter with the student protestors. The U.S. Supreme Court has unequivocally stated twice that flag burning is a legitimate form of political speech, fully protected by the First Amendment.[27] But, even this most fundamental of fundamental liberties, our right to engage in "fully protected" speech, is subject to a whole host of so-called "time, place, and manner" restrictions designed to maintain public order. If the protestors failed to get a proper permit for their demonstration, if they were blocking access to a campus building, or if they were being too raucous, they might well find themselves on the wrong side of the law in spite of their otherwise valid claims to free speech. Law constantly finds itself running into other laws, and running into itself.

the word "web" is still prevalent and still forms the benchmark for our visualizations—and metaphors.

But over the last several years, the word has ceased to be pegged exclusively to the endeavors of our eight-legged friends. Today, when we use the word, we are just as likely—and probably, in the environment of higher education, more likely—to be referring to the World Wide Web, that wonderful network that has made communication and research on the Internet so much easier and so much richer over the span of just a few short years. Today, using any one of an ever expanding number of search engines, an ever expanding wealth of information is at our fingertips. Part of this wealth (an ever expanding part) is the law. Sources for finding, accessing, analyzing, and critiquing the law have grown—and grown rapidly—over just the few short years of the web's existence. Law is on the Internet and it is there *en masse*.[28]

This book utilizes the word "web" in its new-age, technological sense as well. Much of our own research reported herein is the result of poring over web-based data. Like all who have dived head first into Internet research and writing over the past couple of years, we have experienced as much frustration as success; we have wasted as much time as we have effectively utilized. Yes, there's a world of data on the web, but vast portions of that world are composed of junk and drivel. Indeed, were one to eliminate advertisements, personal web pages, pornographic offerings, and the array of idiosyncratic chat rooms, most of the web would disappear. Still, what was left would offer the researcher an almost full platter of fascinating and even essential information, including much of law and society.

At the end of this, and each subsequent chapter, we provide a section titled, "Law on the Web." Within these sections, we offer a number of relevant and useful websites, along with hints for students of law and society interested in effectively utilizing the Internet. The World Wide Web has clearly become—and is becoming more so day by day—an integral part of the larger and more ancient web of law and society.

Law and Society: The World Wide Web

Once upon a time—actually, a time not so very long ago—the word "web" had a fairly unambiguous meaning. To those of us lucky enough to be born in the 1950s and after, no doubt the word "web" conjured up pleasant associations with the brightest, most loyal, and best writer among characters in children's literature (White 1952). But even to our progenitors, that unfortunate multitude of forebears who came of age before "Charlotte," the word "web" was clearly associated with the work of spiders, if not *the* spider. Of course, that sense of

Law on the Web

Helpful Hints

Many of you, we suspect, are already accomplished webmasters. We also would guess that many others have "surfed" around only occasionally, possibly for fun, and probably with some frustration. We know that at least some of you have never been on the Internet, either because you lacked access or because you were just plain afraid or turned off by the whole thing. Well, no matter which category you fall under, now's the time to give it a whirl.

In each chapter of this book, we direct you to a number of websites relevant to the material discussed in that chapter. Let's begin here with a few of the better, very general legal websites.

FindLaw

www.findlaw.com/

Findlaw is a wonderful site that links you to a huge array of legal resources including many court opinions, state and federal statutes and regulations, legal publications, law-related news, and law firms. You may also do legal searches using FindLaw's search function.

LawCrawler

www.lawcrawler.com/

LawCrawler, which may also be accessed through Find-Law, allows you to search the web for law-related information.

American Law Sources On Line (ALSO)

www.lawsource.com/also/

ALSO provides a compilation of links to all online sources of American, Canadian, and Mexican law that are available without charge.

The 'Lectric Law Library

www.lectlaw.com/

Another good general site (this one is also a lot of fun) that allows you to find and access law-related information and products. Among other things, the site features a "bookstore," a legal dictionary and encyclopedia, and a "forms room," featuring wills and other legal forms.

The House of Representatives Internet Law Library

law.house.gov/1.htm

A great site which, among other things, allows you to access U.S. federal laws (arranged by original published source and agency); U.S. state and territorial laws; laws of other nations; treaties and international law; laws of all jurisdictions (arranged by subject); law school, law library catalogues and services; attorney and legal profession directories; and law book reviews and publishers.

THOMAS, The Legislative Information System of the Library of Congress

thomas.loc.gov/

Allows you to search congressional bills, *The Congressional Record*, congressional committee activity, and a variety of historical documents.

Library of Congress

lcweb.loc.gov/homepage/1chp.html

Allows you to search the Library of Congress.

Legal Information Institute of the Cornell Law School

www.law.cornell.edu/

Possibly the best of the law school sites, Cornell's offers online its collection of recent and historic Supreme Court decisions, its hypertext versions of the full U.S. Code, U.S. Constitution, Federal Rules of Evidence and Civil Procedure, recent opinions of the New York Court of Appeals and commentary on them, the American Legal Ethics Library, and other important legal materials—federal, state, foreign and international.

Oyez Oyez Oyez

court.it-services.nwu.edu/oyez/

This is a good multimedia database about the U.S. Supreme Court. In addition to abstracts of key constitutional cases, it provides digital audio (RealAudio) of the oral arguments in many important cases, as well as several recordings of the announcement of the Court's opinion. It also links to the written opinions of the Court in all cases since 1893, provided by the FindLaw project. In addition to case resources, it provides brief biographies and portraits of all 108 justices who have served on the Supreme Court. The site recently added digital audio recordings of speeches made by several justices.

Legal Engine Search

www.legalengine.com/

A truly excellent catalog of law on the Internet.

CataLaw

www.CataLaw.com/

This is a catalog of law on the Internet. CataLaw arranges legal and government indexes on the net into one uniform and universal meta-index.

LawRunner

www.lawrunner.com/

Another legal search and index site.

Meta-Index for U.S. Legal Research

gsulaw.gsu.edu/metaindex/

Yet another good index site.

Law Street

www.lawstreet.com/

Contains a "journal" highlighting selected current legal news, a "find-a-lawyer" service, a law guide that provides a reference to the laws of all 50 states, and, for your lighter browsing moments, courtroom cartoons.

Court TV On Line

www.courttv.com/

Provides background and verdicts on cases spotlighted on Court TV. Also contains a legal dictionary, and some fun stuff, such as a page on "Wills of Famous People," including those of Jerry Garcia, John Lennon, Elvis Presley, Princess Di, Babe Ruth, Marilyn Monroe, Richard Nixon, and Chief Justice Warren Burger (www.courttv.com/legaldocs/newsmakers/wills/).

Internet Library of Law

www.phillipsnizer.com/internetlibrary.htm?internetlib2.htm

Provides court decisions by category.

AllLaw.com

www.AllLaw.com/

Provides law by topic. Also provides links to law schools, legal jobs, and a variety of legal forms.

*   *   *

Finally, if it doesn't already, you may want to bug your university library administrators into subscribing to **LEXIS-NEXIS**, an outstanding and easily searchable online database containing, among many other things, a vast number of judicial decisions, state and federal laws and regulations, and news stories from around the world. The web version, **LEXIS-NEXIS Academic Universe**, can be accessed at web.lexis-nexis.com/universe.

2 The Network of Law: General Considerations

Justice? You get justice in the next world, in this world you have the law.
—William Gaddis (1994, 11)

This is the opening line of an award-winning novel whose chief protagonist, Oscar Crease, devotes most of his time and energy to the law. Indeed, Oscar is constantly involved in litigation (usually as a plaintiff) and nearly always considers the potential for a lawsuit as he moves from one situation to the next. Gaddis wrote the novel as a satire on the "litigious society" we are constantly told we have become. Whether the United States has actually become overly litigious is a debatable question, and one that we will address, but Gaddis's broader point is not really debatable. Our lives are completely saturated by law. In one sense we are little more than agents involved in a hopefully long stream of action, called life, that can be broken down into bits, each one of which has a different set of rights and obligations associated with it, each one of which carries the potential for litigation.

For example, simply going to McDonald's for a cup of coffee with a group of friends might be considered a purely social activity, or we could think of it in purely economic terms—but it also involves a series of legal issues. How do we know that when we order coffee, we will get coffee, and not some chemical compound configured to give us a coffee sensation? How do we know that the four sugar packs we dump into our brew really contain sugar? Or, that the "cream" is really cream and that it is free of harmful bacteria? Or, that the styrofoam cup will not melt from the coffee's heat, or that, if we accidentally spill a bit of it, we won't suffer immediate third-degree burns? We make a lot of assumptions when we make such a transaction, and something other than a deep faith in humanity allows us to do so. The same can be said for everything else we do during the course of a day, from the time we shower and brush our teeth until we turn off our last light switch. Literally, everything we do has legal implications.

Ubiquity of Law

If law is so ubiquitous, how can we distinguish it from other things? One set of issues upon which we focus stems from the distinguishability of our laws and legal system from our social culture. Are law and society separate and distinct entities existing independently but which influence each other? Much research in the law and society field looks for cause-effect relationships. For example, compliance studies, attempting to determine the extent of and conditions under which compliance with various types of law occurs, begin with the notion that people's behavior is influenced by the law (e.g., Tyler 1990). This is also the premise underlying criminal law, that is, the law has a deterrent effect (e.g., Archer, Gartner, and Beittel 1983).

A second set of questions that guides our consideration and discussion revolves around the core relationship between law and politics. Our legal system holds out the promise of equal treatment under law, neutrality of decision making, fair consideration of issues. But much research suggests that the powerful, or the "haves," not only make the laws, but are usually able to use the legal system to great advantage, while those less powerful, the "have nots," cannot typically expect to see real benefit in the legal process (e.g., Galanter 1974).

Often, when we think of law, we think of it as pristine, driven by principle, or Lady Justice, bearing perfectly balanced scales. Some judges are called "justices" as if they actually embody the concept itself. Politics, on the other hand, is ugly. It is driven by expediency. Justice in politics seems irrelevant; one does what is necessary to win. Politicians are called all manner of scurrilous, insulting names, as if they embody the worst of human instincts. Indeed, when the public is asked to rate its government institutions, the U.S. Congress consistently ranks at the bottom (e.g., Asher and Barr 1994; Borman and Ladd 1994). These perceptual differences exist primarily in the realm of mythology, but they are important nonetheless. After all, the Founders purposely and carefully separated the judicial department of government from the other two branches, so that people involved in the former could make decisions in a principled environment free from the political pressures faced by the executive and legislature. However, Alexis de Tocqueville, a young lawyer commissioned by the French government to assess the American penal system, observed over 160 years ago that "[s]carcely any

9

political question arises in the United States which is not resolved, sooner or later, into a judicial question," (de Tocqueville 1945, 126) and if the Frenchman could return to the United States today, he would certainly repeat that observation without qualification. Indeed, law-focused advocacy groups have proliferated to unprecedented numbers and aggressively assert themselves at every conceivable decisional turn (e.g., Herrnson, Shaiko, and Wilcox 1998). In this regard, the judicial process is hardly distinguishable from the traditional political processes of governing. In fact, courts have come to be recognized as focal points to which interest groups devote considerable effort and resources. For example, advocacy groups not only file their own legal claims, but also frequently attach themselves to litigation filed by others as well (e.g., O'Connor 1980; Epstein 1985). Some cases literally draw a teeming crowd of advocacy organizations jockeying for position and aspiring to have a modicum of input into the process.[1] More generally speaking, we find many of the same issues, as well as the same constellations of parties and interest groups, involved in the judicial process that are observed elsewhere in our system of government. Perhaps it is impossible to understand law without understanding the politics surrounding it. In any event, there is a gap between the myth and perception of law, on one hand, and its realities, on the other.

Ambiguity of Law

Unraveling and understanding the connections between law and society is not as straightforward as it might seem to be at first blush. Indeed, "law" is a term that is used by us all literally everyday, but if you take a moment to think about it, we often take its meaning for granted. In actuality, "law" has a rather ephemeral meaning, suggesting different things to different people, and even different things to the same person. We also take the existence of law for granted, as if it were some kind of given. Of course, legislatures never cease to produce new law, but a lot of law has been around for a long time, long before any of us were born. If pressed, we could identify the source for some of it—such as, freedom of speech is probably mentioned in the First Amendment to the U.S. Constitution, and speed limits are probably state law set at some point by the state legislature. But most of us are oblivious to most of the laws that govern the bulk of our activities, and many of us are equally clueless about where these laws might have come from.

The U.S. governing system consists of layer upon layer of institutions, many of which possess lawmaking capability within their respective jurisdictions, including legislatures, administrative agencies, and courts. Each community produces an underlayer of local custom and common practice, an informal system that runs parallel to the formal written law. Things can become quite complex very quickly. Thus, we need to establish some common points of reference.

What Is Law?

Trying to define what law is can be a daunting task. Lawyers and judges have disagreed on a definition. One can say that it is what lawyers practice and what judges decide upon. However, this "lite" definition is too vague to be of real value. Indeed, much of what many lawyers do is unrelated to formal law (e.g., Seron 1996), and whether judges decide issues upon law or some other set of criteria is a matter of considerable scholarly debate (cf. Segal, Epstein, Cameron, and Spaeth 1995; Segal and Spaeth 1993; Halpern and Lamb 1982; Epstein and Knight 1998). U.S. Circuit Judge Jerome Frank, who wrote extensively about courts and the judging process, admitted that he "seriously blundered" in trying to define law because "that word drips with ambiguity," and he concluded that efforts at definition are futile (Frank 1930, xiii). Indeed, law is not a concrete object that exists out there in a form that we can sink our teeth into. By contrast, a table is a table. Although one can put a table to many different uses, we still recognize it, unambiguously, as a table. This is not the case with law. Law lies in a conceptual field, consisting largely of language, values, and purposes.

Moreover, at its most basic level, law gives expression to power relations, restricting behavior and steering activities in specified directions. There are things that we don't do simply because it is "against the law." If we do them anyway, we run the risk of confronting a force much larger than ourselves that is capable of delivering undesirable sanctions. For the average person, law consists of a vast set of official rules and regulations that are inextricably linked to public institutions.

What we generally give less thought to, however, is the equally vast informal system of law, some of which shadows the formal one in the form of off-the-record bargaining and negotiation, and some of which lies entirely in the private sphere, such as the conditions for employment at Microsoft Corporation, rules of academic dishonesty that govern university students, the assignment of responsibilities and obligations within a family, and the like.

Sources of Law

Law exists in a variety of forms and derives from a range of sources. Usually, when we talk about law it is in reference to a connection with the governing system—that is, the rules and regulations produced by public officials that carry the weight of government power. This is what is known as *positive law*. Such law derives, for example, from legislatures in the form of statutes (e.g., 55-mph speed limits), administrative agencies in the form of regulations (e.g., state and local rules governing the conduct of police officers when they pull motorists over for speeding), courts in the form of case law (e.g., judicial decisions covering vehicular searches and seizures), and judicial decisions interpreting statutes, regulations, constitutions, and sometimes common law. Positive law is thus created by a deliberate decision-making process, and it is written down for future reference.

In this book we shall be primarily concerned with positive law, and we will devote considerable attention to how that law is produced by our legal system and processed by those associated with it. The legal system consists of all government institutions—legislative, administrative, and judicial—involved in lawmaking. Our main focus is on activities, both formal and informal, in and around the judicial branch of that system. This alone encompasses a lot of activities, including those of judges, lawyers, law enforcement officials, and litigants. Having said that, law can derive from other sources, which we shall consider briefly before returning to a more general discussion of positive law. Natural law and customary law are often cited as exerting great influence on our formal legal processes. This is no doubt true; however, they are conceptual constructs with indefinite borders.

Natural Law

Charles Stuart purchased James Sommersett as a slave in Virginia and, in 1769, set sail to England. In 1771, Sommersett escaped only to be captured by Stuart's agents and held in chains on his ship anchored in the Thames River, awaiting a trip to Jamaica where Stuart intended to sell him to another master. Alerted to the situation, three English citizens filed for a writ of *habeas corpus* against Stuart demanding that he deliver Sommersett to court and justify his bondage. Thus, Chief Justice Lord Mansfield was presented with a complex set of legal issues.[2] Although it was not permitted in England, the international slave trade was quite brisk and highly profitable to a number of prominent English businessmen, and slavery was openly practiced and legally sanctioned across most of the British colonies. Relevant precedent regarding similar situations was ambiguous, and Lord Mansfield could have decided the issue either way. Because neither Stuart nor Sommersett was a British citizen, Virginia law might be applied. However, the incident in question took place on British soil, and the law of England, which did not recognize slavery, might apply.

In 1772 Mansfield ordered that Sommersett be released. He took the occasion to juxtapose natural law, imbued with a deep sense of morality, with positive law, which is merely instrumental:

The state of slavery is of such a nature, that it is incapable of being introduced on any reasons, moral or political, but only by positive law, which preserves its force long after the reasons, occasion, and time itself from whence it was created, is erased from memory. It is so odious, that nothing can be suffered to support it, but positive law. Whatever inconveniences, therefore, may follow from the decision, I cannot say this case is allowed or approved by the law of England; and therefore the black must be discharged. (*Sommersett v. Stuart*, 1 Lofft 1, 98 Eng. Rep. 499, 20 Howell's State Trials 1, 80–81 (KB 1772), quoted in Higgenbotham 1978, 352–53).

In other words, Lord Mansfield found slavery to be absolutely immoral and counter to the law of nature. Natural law can be superceded, but only by positive law. As Cover (1975, 17) notes, "*Somerset's Case* . . . held that there was nothing necessary or inevitable about the law's harmony with nature. Where positive law sanctioned slavery, Mansfield explicitly conceded the supremacy of such positive law. For the colonies *Somerset's Case* . . . portray[ed] a troublesome moral gap. Slave law is morally wrong, but it can exist."

Natural law has been a theoretical subject of considerable debate since well before our nation's founding (cf. Aquinas 1988; Blackstone 1765, 1769; Hume [1751] 1957). Natural law theorists have argued that the authority for some positive law necessarily derives, at least in part, from the moral standards that originate objectively from the natural order of the world and the inborn rationality of human beings. Thus, there is observable intersection between morality and law. According to natural law theorists, fundamental law is not produced by any government entity; rather it simply exists to be discovered as part of the natural order of the universe. Perhaps it is divinely ordained. The basic theory is neither provable nor disprovable, and it has been articulated in a number of versions with important supporters and detractors. The Founders relied heavily upon a variation of natural law in constructing the basic guarantees of the U.S. Constitution (see, e.g., Corwin 1929; Bailyn 1967). This included a belief in a "higher-order law," that the universe is governed by a rational order, and that through a deliberative, contemplative process humans can utilize their intelligence to understand that rational order. By considering the experience of civilized history, one can reach a general understanding of fairness and justice in human interactions.

The institution of slavery presented an obvious challenge to the Founders' basic philosophy (and Mansfield's *Sommersett* opinion was not unknown to them). But they were able rationalize it. As Higgenbotham (1978, 10) notes, "If blacks could be perceived as inferior, basically uneducable and inherently venal, it might be intellectually less self-condemnatory to relegate them because of their 'lower status' to a subordinate role—either for their 'own good' or, . . . for the good of the total society" (see, e.g., Jefferson 1787, 229–39).[3]

More broadly, historical example indicates clearly that those in positions of power attempt to accumulate more advantages for themselves at the expense of the less powerful. Thus, those who possess power by virtue of holding a government office must do so by the consent of, and be held accountable to, the governed. They should also be obligated to act in the general interest of all, rather than to further their own selfish purposes. This is precisely the point that Alexander Hamilton argued in *Federalist* #1: "Among the most formidable obstacles which the new Constitution will have to encounter may readily be distinguished the obvious interest of a certain class of men in every State to resist all changes which may hazard a diminution of the power, emolument, and consequence of the offices they hold under the State establishments."[4] As we discuss more fully in chapter 3, the Founders believed that one can observe ambition, a thirst for power and domination, in the very nature of humankind (natural law), and human intervention is required to ensure the greater good. These are the issues that James Madison addressed in his classic *Federalist* essays.

While the Founders relied upon their understanding of natural law to design the contours of constitutional government, on the other side of the scale, Justice Oliver Wendell Holmes, a century later, ridiculed the notion that natural law could serve a useful purpose in adjudicating conflicts as the "product of wishful thinking." Two quite rational people can, through individual reasoning, reach opposite conclusions about what is true or just.[5] "The jurists who believe in natural law seem to me," he wrote in 1918, "to be in that naive state of mind that accepts what has been familiar and accepted by them and their neighbors as something that must be accepted by all men everywhere" (Holmes 1918, 40–41).

Although Holmes was attacked by various scholars, particularly religious philosophers, for questioning the validity of natural law, it is difficult today not to accept his basic premise. Indeed, reasonable people reach opposite conclusions regarding legal issues every day. Like a good debater, a practiced lawyer might find herself able to present equally sound arguments on either side of a legal question. Some find this to be unprincipled, complaining that the law must provide us with a guiding sense of morality and values. "Every thoughtful law student or lawyer has had the disquieting sense of being able to argue too well or too easily for too many conflicting solutions," Unger (1976, 8) observes. "Because everything can be defended, nothing can; the analogy-mongering must be brought to a halt." If we view things from a communal level, however, our basic morals and values, upon which there is overwhelming consensus, contain internal contradictions, yielding inevitable conflict.

As a practical matter, most lawyers who litigate prefer to argue consistently on one side of the plethora of legal debates our society produces. However, good lawyering involves, among other things, the ability to anticipate contentions likely to be presented by the opposing side. Moreover, judges at all levels decide similar cases differently, and those on our appellate courts reach different conclusions from colleagues responding to precisely the same scenario and legal arguments. Appeals court panels are often splintered; judicial unanimity is not the norm.[6] Further, it is not unusual for judges and justices who agree with each other on the appropriate outcome to do so for clearly different reasons.[7] Members of the nation's highest court sometimes even disagree in interpreting the *Federalist Papers*. In 1995, for example, the Court heard a challenge to legislation enacted by the Arkansas state legislature, placing limits on the number of consecutive terms that U.S. Senators and House of Representatives members could serve (*U.S. Term Limits, Inc. v. Thornton*, 514 U.S. 779 (1995)). Both the majority and dissent devoted considerable space to their respective counterinterpretations of Madison's *Federalist* #52, in which he discussed qualifications for election to Congress and the states' role in that process. The justices were closely divided on this one. By a slim 5–4 margin, Madison is understood to have intended to fix the qualifications for election to the U.S. Congress in the Constitution so that standards are uniform across the nation. With a single justice's opinion shift, or with another mix of justices, the outcome would have been very different. Of course, scholars argue over the meaning of *The Federalist Papers* every day. However, this particular intellectual debate had real consequences.

Customary Law

On a more concrete plane, customary law springs from human experience of living together in communities, consisting of the unwritten laws that we inherit, being members of a longstanding group with a common history, set of traditions, and sense of morality. In other words, rules restricting certain behaviors and encouraging others that provide a sense of order to things often come from the mere act of communal living. Some legal theorists have difficulty distinguishing law from other by-products of human existence. Writing at the turn of the twentieth century, James Coolige Carter practically equated law with life experience: "Law, Custom, Conduct, Life—different names for almost the same thing—true names for different aspects of the same thing—are so inseparably blended together that one cannot even be thought of without the other" (Carter 1907, 320). More recently, Unger (1976, 49) notes that, "In the broadest sense, law is simply any recurring mode of interaction among individuals and groups, together with the more or less explicit acknowledgment by these groups and individuals that such patterns of interaction produce reciprocal expectations of conduct that ought to be satisfied."

This conception of law requires no central authority; indeed law in this form exists quite separate and independent from any governing regime. Nonetheless, customary law consists of a code of conduct, governs interactions among group members, and sets expectations for behavior, communications, and exchange.

Each of us has preferences, likes and dislikes, habits, quirks of personality, and so on, that evolve into routines of activities. This could be a morning or evening ritual, for instance. But in any case, our individual routines are threatened by taking on a roommate or spouse, or when a new family member arrives in our midst. In other words we make adjustments to accommodate the gain or loss of a group member, and individual routines accrete into a set of group expectations that are generally acknowledged. Successful communal living arrangements depend upon members' acceptance of the group's unspoken rules.

We can extend these concepts to the nation as a whole, where all of us are members of some group with special sets of norms and expectations to which we conform in order to retain our membership. Indeed, we likely confront a range of different "communities" in the normal course of conducting our daily business, and we might feel quite out of place as we move from one "neighborhood" to another. Moreover, we may try to alter our behavior accordingly to "fit in," as codes of local culture can often conflict (cf. Durkheim 1951; Barber 1996; Norgren and Nanda 1988; Redhead 1995; see chapter 10). What is acceptable within one circle might well be unacceptable, or even be considered patently offensive, within others. In the face of such a context, we each seek safe haven against a hard, cruel outer world, binding ourselves to a smaller community where we find comfort. The accompanying rules exert a powerful influence over our behavior, arguably a much more powerful influence than those that have been established by our governing regime. This can produce a group mentality in which identifiers adhere to informally created but shared norms and unwritten rules. For example, high school kids expend considerable energy trying to "fit in" with each other, but they must ultimately learn to accept norms of more encompassing groups if they are to navigate successfully through life as adults. The all-male corporate boardroom might breed a local norm that fosters bawdy jokes at the expense of women; however, when that norm spills into a more diverse occupational setting, the stage is set for sexual harassment litigation.[8] In 1996, Texaco was forced to admit that its executive culture needed rehabilitation when the contents of a series of audio tapes were released. The company had been fighting a race discrimination case for more than two years when the tapes, secretly recorded by one of those in attendance at managerial meetings, were made public. During the meetings, at least two long-term Texaco executives openly made disparaging remarks about African Americans and discussed destruction of internal documents that were being sought by the plaintiffs. Lawyers for the corporation immediately changed course to begin discussions leading to a settlement, and Texaco CEO Peter Bijur announced plans to address the problematic culture that permeated the company's higher ranks (e.g., Frankel 1997).

Finally, in these self-defined communities we individually inhabit, politics is an extremely important force. Every group has a pecking order; some individuals dominate everyone else. They are intimidating figures because they are big, or strong, or charismatic, or wealthy, or have some attribute or possession considered valuable by the group that converts into power. In a conflict situation, we have a good idea who will win and who will lose, and rights and obligations within the community are distributed accordingly. At a higher level, a similar dynamic of power relations is observable among groups, where one (or a few) dominates over the others and is able to exert disproportionate influence over law and policy produced by official institutions that govern the whole.[9]

All of this makes the business of understanding the role of law in our society more difficult. Laws with government sanction apply to everyone within specified institutional jurisdictions. Because of their breadth and range of coverage, positive laws are less efficient than tradition, custom, and other peer influences in terms of influencing behaviors. In fact, as we stated earlier, it is likely that we are unaware of many of them. We cannot, however, be unaware of the expectations and demands of our immediate primary communities.[10] Despite the fact that positive law may be less efficient than that which exists less formally, it does carry with it the full force and power of the government and official enforcement institutions.[11]

But what is the nature of the relationship between informal and formal systems of law? In many ways, formal law reflects informally created understandings of morality, right and wrong, and the like. Indeed, public decision makers do not (cannot, and probably should not) abandon their privately held conceptions of the "good society" when they navigate among home, religious assembly, private club meeting, and public office (see, e.g., Greenawalt 1995). The positive law that results, then, quite obviously will be heavily colored by the informal codes of communities inhabited by contemporary decision makers.[12] Despite the fact that judges, unlike legislators, are expected to make decisions based upon preexisting legal principles (and decidedly not on political considerations), it is unrealistic to expect that they can segregate their private convictions from their public decisional calculus. Moreover, judges make decisions in very small groups. Indeed, it only takes five like-minded justices to form a Supreme Court majority. Trial judges work alone. Thus, the likelihood that formal law will be embroidered by informal standards is quite high.[13]

In 1986, the U.S. Supreme Court decided such a case. At issue in *Bowers v. Hardwick* (478 U.S. 186, (1986)) was whether consensual homosexual sodomy can be criminalized by state statute and whether, by doing so, the state violates individual privacy rights under the Constitution. (Among other things, *Hardwick* presents a classic conflict between individual liberty and social order.) Writing for the majority, Justice White noted that condemnation of homosexuality has ancient roots and agreed with Georgia Attorney General Bowers' reliance upon the Old and New Testaments and the writings of St. Thomas Aquinas to show that "traditional Judeo-Christian values proscribe such conduct."[14] Moreover, Justice White argued that

Even if the conduct at issue here is not a fundamental right, respondent asserts that there must be a rational basis for the law and that there is none in this case other than the presumed belief of a majority of the electorate in Georgia that homosexual sodomy is immoral and unacceptable. This is said to be an inadequate rationale to support the law. The law, however, is constantly based on notions of morality, and if all laws representing essentially moral choices are to be invalidated under the Due Process Clause, the courts will be very busy indeed. Even respondent makes no such claim, but insists that majority sentiments about the morality of homosexuality should be declared inadequate. We do not agree, and are unpersuaded that the sodomy laws of some 25 States should be invalidated on this basis.[15]

Justice Stevens, one of the four *Hardwick* dissenters, disagreed:

The assertion that "traditional Judeo-Christian values proscribe" the conduct involved cannot provide an adequate justification for [the state statute]. That certain, but by no means all, religious groups condemn the behavior at issue gives the State no license to impose their judgments on the entire citizenry. The legitimacy of secular legislation depends instead on whether the State can advance some justification for its law beyond its conformity to religious doctrine. Thus, far from buttressing his case, petitioner's invocation of Leviticus, Romans, St. Thomas Aquinas, and sodomy's heretical status during the Middle Ages undermines his suggestion that [the statute] represents a legitimate use of secular coercive power. A State can no more punish private behavior because of religious intolerance than it can punish such behavior because of racial animus (478 U.S. 186, 211–212; notes and references deleted).

Positive Law

The most basic law in the United States is that expressed in the Constitution, which lays out in rather general terms the powers associated with the departments of government and the procedural rules by which the government may exercise its authorities, and limitations on those powers. State constitutions, which are usually much more specific and hence much longer, also provide similar fundamental baselines at that level. *Constitu-

tional law* is the highest form of positive law, because the various rule-making government agents and agencies derive their authority from it. The U.S. Congress, for example, has the authority under Article 1, Section 8, of the Constitution to enact legislation (*statutory law*) regulating commerce among the states. Accordingly, Congress usually writes broadly worded policy statutes to address specific forms of commerce, such as the broadcast industry, and allows an executive administrative agency (such as the Federal Communications Commission) to enact specific rules (*regulatory law*) that will carry out the policy. When there is conflict over the provisions in the statute and/or application of the rules, litigation brings the courts into action, and judges must interpret the meaning of the language of law. Eventually the controversy might be heard by the U.S. Supreme Court. The Constitution thus sets up a blueprint that is to be followed for providing for the general welfare, and when inevitable conflict arises, it is to be referred to an agency of government for resolution. Hence, as John Adams once said, "we are a nation of laws not men."

Common Law

Common law traces its roots to England. Unlike its European neighbors who adopted the Roman model of having the national legislative body write the fundamentals of rights and obligations into permanent statutory fixtures, or Civil Law Codes, the British monarchy preferred to rely upon the rationality of its agent judges. As conflicts filtered into the courts, judges rendered decisions based upon their understanding of events that led to the dispute, the local context in which it arose, and their sense of enduring concepts of right and wrong. In announcing his decision, a judge would also indicate the principle that guided his thinking. Eventually, such judicial opinions were recorded for future reference, and the body of written *case law* quickly became important resources to both lawyers and judges in constructing claims arguments and in justifying outcomes. The doctrine of *precedent*, that judges' thinking should be governed by the principles articulated in previously decided cases, then, is a common law precept.

The United States, like other former British colonies, inherited the common law system, and American judges, particularly at the state level, continued to cite common law precedents well into the nineteenth century.[16] Today, there are only a few remnants of common law that remain, as nearly every conceivable issue has been addressed by legislative statute or administrative regulation. Precedent, however, continues to play a key and central role in the judicial decision-making process, and as judges are called upon to interpret statutes and regulations, judicial case law is a critical component to understanding how a particular law should be applied.

Formal and Informal Law

Hence, law can be understood as either formal or informal. Formal law is manufactured through a decision-making process (deliberative, rational, and so on), in which concrete choices are made among competing alternatives. Formal law is written down to facilitate enforcement, compliance, and interpretation. Informal law either exists regardless of any human effort or occurs spontaneously as common understandings of how one should behave in various situations.

Informal Law	Formal Law
Natural law	Positive law
Custom	Constitution
	Statutes
	Regulations
	Common law
	Case law

If law is the product of cognitive human action, it is also a means to achieve specific goals.

Functions of Law

Stability and Law

Former Justice Benjamin Cardozo defines law as "a principle or rule of conduct so established as to justify a prediction with reasonable certainty that it will be enforced by the courts if its authority is challenged" (Cardozo 1924, 52). This way of looking at law and the legal system gets at the notions of purpose and function. Why do we have law? What functions does our legal system serve? The former justice argues in essence that the law is a stabilizing force in an otherwise unruly world. Social, political, economic, and technological changes occur all around us. While these forces sometimes proceed slowly, they often move quite rapidly. Legal principles, on the other hand, are relatively constant. They also can change, and we shall address that issue a bit later, but legal rules governing common interaction and exchange have a permanence, at least a perceived permanence, that other forces do not. Law, then, is a means by which people are put on notice that certain activities will be acceptable and others unacceptable. When a question of right and wrong occurs, there is a clear basis for predicting what the outcome will be and how our courts will respond.

When you think about it, most of our everyday decisions are based upon a series of predictions about how other people will behave. For instance, in the United States, we drive on the right side of the road. We always have, despite the stunning changes that have occurred since the first automobile puttered along the unpaved pathways that served as streets in those days.

Otherwise, we would not know what to expect, and we would have a most insecure basis for calculating our own moves. Law elevates this to a social level by creating a set of general expectations and providing a means for enforcing them. Thus, a person driving on the left side of the road can expect to pay a pretty hefty legal penalty.

Order and Law

However, this understanding of the role of law in our society only takes us so far; it is incomplete. Law, as we have been discussing, is a means by which the governing regime can maintain order, a quality upon which every society places a high value. An orderly society is also easier to govern, so it is always in the interest of government officials to enact laws aimed at accomplishing a greater degree of discipline.[17] Our entire criminal law regime, which seems to grow with each legislative session, has been enacted in pursuit of that purpose. On the other hand, the reach of government authority is restricted from encroaching upon the private affairs of individuals to the extent that liberty is unreasonably jeopardized. This means that we have law about law—that is, rules that govern the actions of government officials in their quest to fulfill the social order mandate.

Law as Balance

Thus, another way of looking at the role of law is that it involves a direct trade-off between individual freedom and social order, or the attempt to strike a balance between the two. We place high value on both of these concepts, and we have laws that promote both. The conflict between individual liberty and social order has been especially important in the structure of American law, a subject to which we shall devote considerable attention in chapter 3. But for now, consider the following: Driving a car is usually a highly individualized activity, and from the start, the automobile has held the allure of individual autonomy and freedom. Whether upon necessity or pure whim, we can travel distances that were unthinkable in the days before the mass availability of the car. Regardless of the personal freedom that the automobile has enabled, and regardless of how dearly we value it, it is far from absolute. At the community level, we have attempted to impose a degree of predictability and order on our streets and highways, and if we do not follow the rules we risk losing the privilege to drive. The same authority that accommodates our selfish desire to own and operate an automobile, with minimal threshold legal requirements, also imposes upon us a responsibility to behave selflessly, to act in the best interest of others, with an extensive regime of rules and regulations. Yet, at the same time, that same authority is obligated to respect our individual autonomy and freedom. This yields a significant area of ambiguity in the law, as the following case example from the State of New York illustrates.

The People of the State of New York, Plaintiff, v Petar Ilieveski, Defendant. JUSTICE COURT OF NEW YORK, TOWN OF BRIGHTON, MONROE COUNTY 670 N.Y.S.2d 1004

January 12, 1998, Decided

DISPOSITION: Defendant not guilty of the charge of violating V&T Law § 1120(b).

COUNSEL: Petar Ilieveski, defendant pro se.

Howard R. Relin, District Attorney of Monroe County (Karen Holt of counsel), for plaintiff.

OPINION: Karen Morris, J.

Defendant is charged with failing to keep right in violation of Vehicle and Traffic Law, § 1120(b). Under the circumstances, it appears he was charged with the incorrect section of the statute. As a result I find defendant not guilty.

Defendant is charged with violating subdivision (b) of V&T § 1120. That subdivision reads as follows:

Upon all roadways, any vehicle proceeding at less than the normal speed of traffic at the time and place and under the conditions then existing shall be driven in the right-hand lane then available for traffic ...

The defendant pled not guilty and a trial was held. The People's case consisted of the testimony of Trooper Rowe. He testified as follows: on July 3, 1997 at 3:00 p.m. he observed defendant's car heading southbound in the left lane of a three-lane expressway; the speed limit on the expressway was 55 miles per hour; using a calibrated speedometer, the Trooper paced defendant's vehicle for about a mile and a half; the speed of defendant's car was 55–56 miles per hour; defendant was travelling slower than other traffic on the expressway; defendant had many opportunities to move to other lanes during the time the officer paced the defendant; after stopping defendant the trooper asked Mr. Ilieveski if he knew why the trooper stopped him; defendant responded, "No, I know I wasn't speeding."

Defendant testified as follows: he was travelling at 55 miles per hour; while the Trooper was pacing defendant, the Trooper was positioned to defendant's right and therefore defendant could not move to either of the lanes to his right; if he accelerated to pass the Trooper and then move to the right, defendant feared he would be stopped for speeding; the officer, upon stopping defendant, inquired as to defendant's ethnicity leading defendant to believe that the issuance of the ticket was a discriminatory act.

Both parties agree that defendant was travelling at a legal rate of speed. To find defendant guilty of the violation charged— V&T Law § 1120(b)—when he was travelling within the speed limit, albeit at the maximum, would require that I interpret the statute to mandate an incongruous result: that law-abiding drivers risk a ticket and a fine for failing to move to the right to accommodate speeders in the passing lane. In response to my queries about the propriety of enforcing V&T Law § 1120(b) in this circumstance, the assistant district attorney argued that defendant's actions encouraged "**road rage**"[1] by those impeded from using the left-most lane for passing. The Trooper submitted copious articles, studies and related materials about driver aggression. These materials establish that **road rage** is a growing phenomenon of significant concern to

those charged with maintaining the safety of our highways. This phenomenon has resulted in the death of 218 people and injuries to 12,610 during a seven-year period beginning January, 1990.

One of the acknowledged causes of **road rage** is blocking of the passing lane. V&T Law § 1120(a) is relevant in this regard. That section reads as follows:

Upon all roadways of sufficient width a vehicle shall be driven upon the right half of the roadway, except as follows: (1) when overtaking and passing another vehicle proceeding in the same direction ...

Had the Trooper charged Mr. Ilieveski with a violation of this section the charge might well have been upheld. By charging defendant with violating V&T Law § 1120(b), additional factors are implicated. As a Town Justice I enforce the speeding laws on a regular basis. Those found guilty pay a minimum fine and surcharge of $ 55.00 (increasing to $ 60.00 for infractions occurring on or after January 1, 1998) and often are sentenced to pay more than the minimum, amounts not insignificant to many. I cannot believe that the legislature, when adopting V&T Law § 1120(b), intended that drivers traveling at a legal rate be punished for failing to clear the passing lane to make room for those exceeding the limit. I find that subdivision (b)'s mandate that "any vehicle proceeding at less than the normal speed of traffic at the time and place and under the conditions then existing be driven in the right-hand lane" must be interpreted to mean "any vehicle proceeding at less than the normal speed of traffic ... up to the applicable speed limit."

I am very concerned about the phenomenon of **road rage**. Safety on our roadways is critical to the wellbeing of virtually all members of our society. However, in our laudable efforts to avert **road rage** we cannot cower to those who violate the law by speeding or otherwise. Such would be a dangerous path that could lead to lawlessness. The remedy for aggression on our roads is not to ticket law-abiding drivers but to prosecute fully those who engage in **road rage**.

For the above reasons, I find defendant not guilty of the charge of violating V&T Law § 1120(b).

Concerning defendant's testimony that the officer inquired as to defendant's national origin, I make no finding as to what was or was not said. I am mindful of the challenges to police officers' safety that exist every time an officer stops a driver for a traffic infraction or otherwise. The officer, trained to detect violations of the law and schooled in security matters, is best situated to determine the necessary procedures to effectuate the issuance of a traffic ticket. I note, however, that questions about one's national origin can leave an impression in a motorist's mind that nationality affects how the officer treats that driver. The constitution provides that all people in this country are entitled to equal protection of the laws. All law enforcement officials should ensure that this constitutional right is a reality both in practice and perception. If there is no need for an officer to know a defendant's country of origin, which presumably is the case in most traffic stops, such question should not be asked.

January 12, 1998

Karen Morris, Brighton Town Justice

Footnotes

1. **Road rage** is defined in the materials submitted by the Trooper as, "The reaction to aggressive driving, which is defined as—Operating a motor vehicle in a selfish, bold or pushy manner, without regard for safety or the rights of other highway users. It involves traffic violations such as speeding, unsafe

lane changes, failure to keep right, following too closely, and failing to signal."

While criminal law offers a plethora of convenient examples of the inevitable conflicts between the exercise of individual freedom and the state's obligation to maintain social order, it represents only a small proportion of the total body of law in the United States. In fact, it is a small part of our public law system consisting of all sorts of rules and regulations that are overseen and enforced by a host of government agencies, all in the name of promoting social order and the common good. Just to name a few, there are federal treaties and other acts regarding international relations, state and federal environmental and taxation regulations, food and drug regulations, radio and television broadcast licensing requirements, fish and wildlife protections, regulations for hospitals and restaurants, and many communities have zoning laws to restrict and/or stimulate certain types of land usage. The promulgation of statutes and regulations via the legislative and administrative processes at all levels of government represents an attempt by the state to standardize activities, to create stereotypical templates that apply to all parties and transactions that fall under their umbrella. It also represents temporary outcomes of the quintessential game of high-stakes politics (e.g., Kerwin 1994).

Law as Referee

Not all activities, however, in a specified area of coverage fit the stereotype anticipated by the standard rule. Universal rules are unavoidably ambiguous. In the interest of fairness, the system must accommodate those who cry foul, or at least entertain their grievance claims. We also know that a system unable to make exceptions is particularly harsh, oppressive, and unfair. Thus, questions of fairness will arise in all aspects of legislative and administrative law, regarding scope of coverage, implementation, enforcement, and impact.

Moreover, cases of absolute agreement on the need for and specifications of new law are extraordinarily unlikely. Virtually nothing sails through the U.S. Congress or any of the state legislatures. In fact, debate is sometimes rancorous and lively, illustrative of the collision of significant interests involved. Even when decorum reigns and compromise solutions are crafted, some parties will perceive themselves as winners, and others as losers. Indeed, compromise might actually increase the pool of perceived losers. Not all political losers go home secure in the notion that the republican process has worked its magic and that we are all better off as a consequence. More likely, they begin to strategize for the next round and/or look for alternative decision points where they might channel their effort more effectively. The same logic applies to political "winners." They

must immediately begin to anticipate their adversaries' next moves. Our courts play host to much of this conflict. The judicial process, thus, is a crucial component of policy and lawmaking, and litigation is, in essence, political activity. For example, the *Communications Decency Act of 1996* met with litigation the day President Clinton signed it into law, and eventually parts were found to be unconstitutionally vague and overbroad by the U.S. Supreme Court. At issue in *Reno v. ACLU* (117 S. Ct. 2329 (1997)) were two provisions of the law that sought to protect minors from harmful material on the Internet. Specifically, the statute "criminalize[d] the 'knowing' transmission of 'obscene or indecent' messages to any recipient under 18 years of age [and] prohibit[ed] the 'knowing' sending or displaying to a person under 18 of any message 'that, in context, depicts or describes, in terms patently offensive as measured by contemporary community standards, sexual or excretory activities or organs.'" At the state level, Proposition 227 in California, ending bilingual education programs in public schools, passed overwhelmingly (61 percent to 39 percent) by voters in referendum on Tuesday, June 2, 1998. On June 3, the result was challenged as political losers filed suit arguing that the new law was unconstitutional.[18] The inseparability of politics and law is clear in such cases. As we shall see, although it might be less obvious in other contexts, it is also true more generally.

Law as Manager

Another way in which our legal system promotes order is by providing ways for people to manage their relationships with a massive network of private, or civil, law. People can look to the law for guidance, support, and expectations in the process of organizing their affairs and managing the complex and multidimensional web of relationships that define life in our world of interdependencies. The law provides a means of formalizing expectations, articulating them to a particular relational partner, and, if necessary, demanding authoritative clarification of mutual status. That relational partner might be a spouse, merchant, business associate, employee, creditor, medical doctor, or insurance company, and because the state is a major employer, contractor, and purchaser of goods and services, the other party might well be a government agency.

The law also assigns rights and obligations that accompany our multitude of relationships. The Constitution both obliges government to perform a set of general tasks for the entire community and grants rights to individual citizens that cannot be abridged by government authority in fulfilling those responsibilities. Moreover, individuals have a right to own property but are obligated not to put their property to uses that are detrimental or harmful to others. Indeed, one is obliged to consider the interests of others, such as the impact of your property use on the value of others' land, on water quality in the region, and so on.

The story of Jennings Osborne, an impulsive and wealthy businessman in Little Rock, Arkansas, offers a case in point. In 1986, in response to his then six-year-old daughter's request for outdoor Christmas lights to mark the holiday season, Mr. Osborne began what was to become a remarkable project. With each succeeding year, the display grew in proportion, drawing huge crowds from all over the state (even Bill Clinton paid a visit while he was governor) to view it. By 1994, Osborne had bought three adjacent houses to accommodate his massive six-acre exhibition that included over 3.5 million lights, with "illuminated angels, wise men, reindeer and trees, . . . an electric church steeple, . . . surrounded by electric choirboys and churchgoers," a simulated "locomotive, driven by Santa, . . . a gigantic electric globe with the words 'For God So Loved the World,'" and much more. Osborne even hired a full-time engineer to plan, implement, and oversee his effort "to make people happy" (Steinhauer 1994, 26). He did not, however, make his immediate neighbors happy. Six of them filed suit, seeking to enjoin him from flipping the switch that lit up the sky from dusk until midnight every evening for more than a month, that invited thousands of unwanted gawkers to trample through their yards, that brought nightly traffic jams into their otherwise tranquil residential streets, that literally made them "prisoners in [their] own homes" (Steinhauer 1994, 26). Osborne fought back, arguing that he should be allowed to do with his own private property whatever he wished. The courts ruled otherwise, however, declaring that he did not have the right to transform his house into a theme park over the objections of his neighbors.[19]

Generally speaking, people have the right to enter into various types of relationships, but when doing so they also must accept the legal responsibilities of those associations. This is equally true of the decision to get married, to borrow money, to rent an apartment, to hire an employee, to sell a product or service, or to purchase a home in a residential neighborhood.

Literally everything we do entails a relationship with at least one other party (often a number of other parties). In effect, life is little more than a series of relationships, and law governs them all. In this sense, law is ubiquitous. Far more often than not, all of this goes completely unnoticed. Things generally go relatively smoothly. However, when a problem does come up, we recognize that we are not alone.[20] Avoidance is a common strategy, but it is not always available as an option. In general, then, when a problem occurs, one or both parties will set in motion some plan of action designed to influence the outcome. The particular strategy a party deploys will depend upon a range of factors, such as expectations for the future (are the parties involved in an ongoing relationship or are they strangers?), relative

strengths and weaknesses (differences in raw power, financial resources, access to information, support from allies, and the like), and willingness to put forth the necessary effort (a psychological factor representing a barrier that many people are not prepared to cross; many prefer simply to "lump it" rather than assert themselves because it is just not worth it [e.g., Felstiner 1974]). All kinds of strategies are possible, but to invoke the law is an attempt to utilize the power of the state to achieve a favorable solution in one's private conflict. We could define politics in much the same terms. Hence, on this plane, law and politics are practically indistinguishable, and the use of law to manage one's affairs is a subset of the larger population of political activities. Moreover, the same resources that are translatable into political power are useful in the legal arena as well.

When we consider the totality of relationships and interactions, the potential for conflict is truly staggering. Most conflict, though, ends far short of the judicial arena. Usually the parties work among themselves to resolve it; often lawyers are brought into the mix; sometimes litigation is filed, and some of it evolves into full-blown court trials and appeals. The accumulation of judicial decisions (case precedents) in a given area carves out a set of referents, guiding the behavior of players in each field and becoming the background upon which participants can draw conclusions and extrapolate predictions. Among informed players, then, the judicial process enhances stability. As judge-crafted law is absorbed into a community of actors, private orderings are arranged relatively less often on the basis of ad hoc criteria. Prediction of likely outcomes, anticipating and short-circuiting conflict, and negotiating private solutions to those problems that do arise, are among the many services provided by the lawyer community.

The Legal System

The state has constructed an intricate legal system where grievances can be aired, claims lodged, and relevant decisions are made. This serves the interests of the community in a number of ways, not the least of which is to provide a relatively peaceful means for managing conflict. After all, managing conflict in the official arena at the very least generates perceptions of state responsiveness, enhances legitimacy of the governing regime at key intervals, and perhaps diffuses potentially troublesome grievances. Although there are a multitude of ways for dealing with conflict, and there are a wide range of institutions providing relevant service commodities, the state has a keen interest in dominating the market and seeing most significant problems channeled through its court system. From a sociopolitical perspective, if parties litigate a conflict, they are, in effect, obliged to consent to the norms of society in finding a solution. Much of the judicial ritual, especially in a public trial, serves to remind and reinforce that obligation. Placing a conflict in a court, where it will be compared with and judged by some preexisting general rules and to similar situations that have been resolved in the past, involves a social concern that transcends the parochial interests of the actual parties. This means that a sense of community is promoted through the litigation process.

Courts compete with other forms of conflict resolution. To the extent that they win the competition, they enhance government stability and general regime legitimacy. Indeed, litigation represents an affirmative sign that people perceive the process to be a legitimate one worthy of their support. When people do not utilize the courts and instead take the law into their own hands, then the governing system is jeopardized.

Our legal system, then, serves three broad purposes at once, each of which becomes a justification for having so much and so many layers of law. One of its purposes is *order maintenance*: Law is a stabilizing force, making actions predictable and providing a means for enforcing a minimal level of social order. Next is enhancement of *individual liberties*: Law also promises a certain level of individual rights against government or state authority. Finally, law serves a *conflict management* function: Law represents a set of references for deciding conflicts between people and provides a vast network of forums (courts) where those conflicts can be heard. With these broad functions in mind, we can make a number of additional observations regarding law and the legal system.

Legislative and executive law are representative of the current balance of political power and thus reflect the norms, sense of morality, and values that dominate in contemporary society. These laws may constitute a majority view, but given the structure of our governing system, not necessarily so. The law then serves as something like a value compass, whose poles are determined by the ruling group; behavior that is in conformity with the dominant morality is legitimized, and that which is out of sync is correspondingly stigmatized. This can be altered with a shift in the national balance of power or with a change in viewpoint among those in control. Either way, law is an evolutionary process rather than a revolutionary one; change is usually marginal rather than unequivocal. The same observations hold for law at the state level, thus producing variations around central themes at the same point in time across communities. In other words, we should expect state law on the same subject to be different from one state to another. Some states have death penalty statutes; others do not. Among those that do, some provide for lethal injection; some, electrocution; a few employ a firing squad; and still others, hanging.[21] Similarly, although abortion is legal across the entire country, state-imposed restrictions vary considerably.[22] Moreover, it is possible to try a juvenile as

an adult at age fifteen in most states, but some allow it at younger ages.

Because judges are primarily drawn from the same slice of the population as are legislators and chief executives, they are very much a part of the ruling group and likely share a similar sense of values and moral outlook with their other-branch cohort (e.g., Dahl 1957; Goldman 1995, 1989a, 1989b). Add to this the precedent-based decision structure in the courts, and we have the makings of a law-producing system, not just stable, but bent on stability, or stubbornly conservative. This, however, does not mean that it is stagnant. The law does change, even if very slowly.

It is tempting to say that judicial law also reflects the current balance of political power; however, this is an analytical question that judges and their observers have answered differently. The U.S. Constitution separates the judicial branch from the other two to provide insulation from pressure and constituency politics and to allow the judiciary a degree of independence from the general mood that other decision makers lack. The idea was that judges should be free to exercise sound judgment based upon preexisting principles of law, to serve as a "guard[ian of] the Constitution and the rights of individuals . . . against the effects of occasional ill humors in society."[23] Upon appointment, they are granted life tenure and are subject to removal only through the impeachment process. To the chagrin of some critics, federal judges, more than two centuries since the founding, remain relatively free from political constraints. During the 1996 presidential campaign, for example, a U.S. District Judge's ruling that evidence in a New York drug case was inadmissible at trial[24] was heavily criticized by candidate Robert Dole and Republican members of Congress, with many openly talking of impeachment.[25] Some Democrats, including President Clinton, suggested that the judge should either reverse his decision or resign. Judge Baer did eventually reverse himself (*U.S. v. Bayless*, 921 F. Supp. 211 (S.D.N.Y. 1996)) based on newly presented evidence not offered by the government at the initial hearing.[26] Although he was adamant in stating that he had not collapsed under the weight of pressure, he certainly was not immune to it (the outcry was intense), and even after he reversed his ruling, the attacks continued. By the fall of 1997, National Public Radio legal correspondent, Nina Totenberg, was reporting that, "Some [Republican members of Congress] have proposed doing away with life tenure for judges. They've proposed impeaching judges whose decisions they don't like. They've held hearings on judicial activism, singling out judges whose opinions they oppose. And they've introduced legislation to limit the authority and reach of the federal courts. Last week, House Republican Whip Tom DeLay told the *Washington Post* that federal judges 'need to be intimidated. If they don't behave, we're going to go after them in a big way.'"[27] Although most state judges face periodic elections of one type or another, as a practical matter they are also fairly well insulated from constituency politics.[28]

All of this means that the decision calculus of judges is different from that of legislators and executives. Although social scientists endlessly wrangle about political influences—including the personal preferences of individual judges—jostling and maneuvering within courts with multiple judges (appeals courts), and external forces—such as public opinion, interest groups, and the like—one thing is clear: Judges and justices are expected to reconcile their decisions today with those in similar cases that have arisen from the same community in the past (e.g., cf. Knight and Epstein 1996a, 1996b; Marshall 1989; Caldeira and Wright 1988).

Judicial Continuity

Our judicial system seeks continuity in the law and, to the extent possible, that purpose is promoted by structure and judicial decision rules. We consider the structure of the court system in greater detail in chapter 4, but for now suffice it to say that the courts are arranged in a hierarchical design that determines each court's jurisdiction. Jurisdictional rules govern the subject matter and geographic reach for each court. The most numerous, and the busiest, are the trial courts, which represent the forums where litigation is originally filed and, if the parties fail to negotiate a solution, trials are conducted. For example, the federal system has ninety-four U.S. District Courts distributed nationwide to cover every geographic area, with at least one per state. Decisions there can be reviewed, if either or both parties file an appeal to the U.S. Circuit Court of Appeals that has jurisdiction over the district court of origin. There are thirteen circuit courts, which are, again, distributed across the country. The Fourth U.S. Circuit, for example, is available to hear appeals from any of the district courts in North and South Carolina, Virginia, West Virginia, and Maryland. Similarly, the First Circuit includes Maine, Massachusetts, New Hampshire, Rhode Island, and Puerto Rico. At the top is the U.S. Supreme Court with authority, but no obligation, to review the decision of any other court, so it is the only court with national jurisdiction.[29] Every state and the District of Columbia has its own unique court system designed to address conflicts that arise under state law. While the actual structures offer many variations on the federal model, each represents a tiered arrangement with a court of final resort at the pinnacle having statewide jurisdiction. Like the U.S. Circuit Courts, the various state courts of final appeals are subject to review only by the U.S. Supreme Court.[30]

What this means is that every court (except the U.S. Supreme Court itself) is subject to some superior court's jurisdiction, and the authority of case precedent follows this jurisdictional hierarchy. In other words, judges are expected to abide by their own prior rulings as well as follow the principles delineated in cases previously decided by courts above them in the jurisdictional structure. This is the doctrine of precedent, or *stare decisis*.[31]

The doctrine of *stare decisis* serves as a constraint on judicial decision making, the expectation being that judges will follow precedent within their jurisdiction. According to Cardozo (1924, 20), "*Stare decisis* is at least the everyday working rule of our law. . . . It is a process of search, comparison, and little more." This brings continuity and stability to the general understanding of what the law means. That understanding can vary from one jurisdiction to the next, and it often does. The state courts of California, for instance, are free to ignore case precedents decided in the state courts of Idaho, Wisconsin, or Texas. Likewise, the Third U.S. Circuit Court and its included district courts are under no obligation to follow interpretations of law produced in the Eighth Circuit. Only the U.S. Supreme Court can attempt to impose uniformity of interpretation across the entire system. These institutional characteristics and expectations of court operations, even if presented in oversimplified form, have observable consequences for our system of law. They also fail to provide a satisfactory explanation for the judicial lawmaking process.

As early as 1835, de Tocqueville noted that the nature of our legal system not only enhances the stature and importance of the legal profession, but it renders lawyers essential to obtaining access to law. In fact, the superior knowledge held by practicing attorneys, in de Tocqueville's view, converts them into an American aristocracy.

This aristocratic character, which I hold to be common to the legal profession, is much more distinctly marked in the United States and in England than in any other country. This proceeds not only from the legal studies . . . but from the nature of the law. . . . The English and the Americans have retained the law of precedents; that is to say, they continue to found their legal opinions and the decisions of their courts upon the opinions and decisions of their predecessors. In the mind of an English or an American lawyer a taste and a reverence for what is old is almost always united with a love of regular and lawful proceedings . . .

[N]othing . . . can be more obscure and strange to the uninitiated than a legislation founded upon precedents. The absolute need of legal aid that is felt in England and the United States, and the high opinion that is entertained of the ability of the legal profession, tend to separate it more and more from the people and to erect it into a distinct class (de Tocqueville 1945, 276–77).

Although it is not clear that the American public today would consider lawyers to be an aristocracy, that they are essential is transparently clear. Two centuries of lawmaking has added considerable bulk and density to an already complex system. Lawyers play a variety of roles, and we shall take them up in greater detail in a subsequent chapter. Note also that de Tocqueville remarked upon the conservative influence embedded in a precedent-based legal structure.

Stare decisis is indeed oriented to history rather than the future. Judicial lawmaking thus connects current conflicts directly to the past. It is inherently conservative. Nonetheless, the law of precedent is of a dual nature. Although legal principles are relatively constant, they are not immutable. Again, Cardozo (1924, 20–21) lends some insight: "[O]f course, no system of living law can be evolved by such a process, and no judge of a high court, worthy of his office, views the function of his place so narrowly. If that were all there was to our calling, there would be little of intellectual interest about it. The man who had the best card index of the cases would also be the wisest judge." And, in his ill-fated Senate confirmation hearings, Judge Robert Bork characterized his potential role on the U.S. Supreme Court as participating in an "intellectual feast."[32] The words of these two prominent jurists make it very clear that there is much more to our judicial lawmaking process than applying precedent.

Judicial Legitimacy

In 1992, the justices of the U.S. Supreme Court issued a series of opinions that were rather remarkable. In addition to addressing the strictly legal issues involved, the justices engaged in a lengthy debate regarding the meaning of *stare decisis*, the role of legal principle, pressure politics and public opinion, and the appropriate posture the Court must present in order to maintain its legitimacy. At issue in *Planned Parenthood of Southeastern Pa. v. Casey* (505 U.S. 833 (1992)) were a number of abortion restrictions enacted by the Pennsylvania state legislature in 1989. Although the Court was seriously divided in its views, a majority did agree that *Roe v. Wade* (410 U.S. 113 (1973)) should not be overturned, preserving the central tenet that women have the right to choose whether to terminate a pregnancy in its early stages. Nonetheless, restrictions can be imposed without necessitating the heightened scrutiny demanded by *Roe* so long as they do not constitute an "undue burden" on women's free choice, and the trimester rationale of *Roe*, which neatly demarcated the point at which a state can intervene in the abortion decision, was discarded in favor of a "viability" threshold. In other words, a woman must not be unduly burdened in making her choice before the point at which her fetus has sufficiently developed so that it can survive outside the womb; beyond the moment of viability, the state has a greater interest in protecting the potential life that the fetus represents. As a result, much of the structure and rationale of the *Roe* opinion and mandate is significantly changed, leaving only the core notion of free choice early in pregnancy (although this too is changed,

now dependent upon the rather vague ideas of "undue burden" and "viability"). The lead opinion in *Planned Parenthood*, written by Justices O'Connor, Kennedy, and Souter, argued that, despite the significant revisions, the central principle articulated in *Roe* remains unaltered; to trash it outright would not only contradict the command of *stare decisis* but also jeopardize the Court's legitimacy. The four-member minority of Chief Justice Rehnquist and Justices White, Thomas, and Scalia found that logic unconvincing and disingenuous, arguing that a more principled position would be to go ahead and overturn the *Roe* precedent.

Justice O'Connor, Justice Kennedy, and Justice Souter on *Stare Decisis*[33]

Our analysis would not be complete … without explaining why overruling Roe's central holding would not only reach an unjustifiable result under principles of stare decisis, but would seriously weaken the Court's capacity to exercise the judicial power and to function as the Supreme Court of a Nation dedicated to the rule of law. To understand why this would be so, it is necessary to understand the source of this Court's authority, the conditions necessary for its preservation, and its relationship to the country's understanding of itself as a constitutional Republic.

The root of American governmental power is revealed most clearly in the instance of the power conferred by the Constitution upon the Judiciary of the United States, and specifically upon this Court. As Americans of each succeeding generation are rightly told, the Court cannot buy support for its decisions by spending money, and, except to a minor degree, it cannot independently coerce obedience to its decrees. The Court's power lies, rather, in its legitimacy, a product of substance and perception that shows itself in the people's acceptance of the Judiciary as fit to determine what the Nation's law means, and to declare what it demands.

The underlying substance of this legitimacy is of course the warrant for the Court's decisions in the Constitution and the lesser sources of legal principle on which the Court draws. That substance is expressed in the Court's opinions, and our contemporary understanding is such that a decision without principled justification would be no judicial act at all. But even when justification is furnished by apposite legal principle, something more is required. Because not every conscientious claim of principled justification will be accepted as such, the justification claimed must be beyond dispute. The Court must take care to speak and act in ways that allow people to accept its decisions on the terms the Court claims for them, as grounded truly in principle, not as compromises with social and political pressures having, as such, no bearing on the principled choices that the Court is obliged to make. Thus, the Court's legitimacy depends on making legally principled decisions under circumstances in which their principled character is sufficiently plausible to be accepted by the Nation.

The need for principled action to be perceived as such is implicated to some degree whenever this, or any other appellate court, overrules a prior case. This is not to say, of course, that this Court cannot give a perfectly satisfactory explanation in most cases. People understand that some of the Constitution's language is hard to fathom, and that the Court's Justices are sometimes able to perceive significant facts or to understand principles of law that eluded their predecessors and that justify departures from existing decisions. However upsetting it may be to those most directly affected when one judicially derived rule replaces another, the country can accept some correction of error without necessarily questioning the legitimacy of the Court. In two circumstances, however, the Court would almost certainly fail to receive the benefit of the doubt in overruling prior cases. There is, first, a point beyond which frequent overruling would overtax the country's belief in the Court's good faith. Despite the variety of reasons that may inform and justify a decision to overrule, we cannot forget that such a decision is usually perceived (and perceived correctly) as, at the least, a statement that a prior decision was wrong. There is a limit to the amount of error that can plausibly be imputed to prior Courts. If that limit should be exceeded, disturbance of prior rulings would be taken as evidence that justifiable reexamination of principle had given way to drives for particular results in the short term. The legitimacy of the Court would fade with the frequency of its vacillation.

That first circumstance can be described as hypothetical; the second is to the point here and now. Where, in the performance of its judicial duties, the Court decides a case in such a way as to resolve the sort of intensely divisive controversy reflected in Roe and those rare, comparable cases, its decision has a dimension that the resolution of the normal case does not carry. It is the dimension present whenever the Court's interpretation of the Constitution calls the contending sides of a national controversy to end their national division by accepting a common mandate rooted in the Constitution. The Court is not asked to do this very often, having thus addressed the Nation only twice in our lifetime, in the decisions of Brown and Roe. But when the Court does act in this way, its decision requires an equally rare precedential force to counter the inevitable efforts to overturn it and to thwart its implementation. Some of those efforts may be mere unprincipled emotional reactions; others may proceed from principles worthy of profound respect. But whatever the premises of opposition may be, only the most convincing justification under accepted standards of precedent could suffice to demonstrate that a later decision overruling the first was anything but a surrender to political pressure and an unjustified repudiation of the principle on which the Court staked its authority in the first instance. So to overrule under fire in the absence of the most compelling reason to reexamine a watershed decision would subvert the Court's legitimacy beyond any serious question. . . .

The country's loss of confidence in the Judiciary would be underscored by an equally certain and equally reasonable condemnation for another failing in overruling unnecessarily and under pressure. Some cost will be paid by anyone who approves or implements a constitutional decision where it is unpopular, or who refuses to work to undermine the decision or to force its reversal. The price may be criticism or ostracism, or it may be violence. An extra price will be paid by those who themselves disapprove of the decision's results when viewed outside of constitutional terms, but who nevertheless struggle to accept it, because they respect the rule of law. To all those who will be so tested by following, the Court implicitly undertakes to remain steadfast, lest in the end a price be paid for nothing. The promise of constancy, once given, binds its maker for as long as the power to stand by the decision survives and the understanding of the issue has not changed so fundamentally as to render the commitment obsolete. From the obligation of this promise, this Court cannot and should not assume any exemption when duty requires it to decide a case in conformance with the Constitution. A willing breach of it would be nothing less than a breach of faith, and no Court that broke its faith with the people could sensibly expect credit for principle in the decision by which it did that.

It is true that diminished legitimacy may be restored, but only slowly. Unlike the political branches, a Court thus weakened could not seek to regain its position with a new mandate from the voters, and even if the Court could somehow go to the polls, the loss of its principled character could not be retrieved by the casting of so many votes. Like the character of an individual, the legitimacy of the Court must be earned over time. So, indeed, must be the character of a Nation of people who aspire to live according to the rule of law. Their belief in themselves as such a people is not readily separable from their understanding of the Court invested with the authority to decide their constitutional cases and speak before all others for their constitutional ideals. If the Court's legitimacy should be undermined, then, so would the country be in its very ability to see itself through its constitutional ideals. The Court's concern with legitimacy is not for the sake of the Court, but for the sake of the Nation to which it is responsible. The Court's duty in the present case is clear. In 1973, it confronted the already-divisive issue of governmental power to limit personal choice to undergo abortion, for which it provided a new resolution based on the due process guaranteed by the Fourteenth Amendment. Whether or not a new social consensus is developing on that issue, its divisiveness is no less today than in 1973, and pressure to overrule the decision, like pressure to retain it, has grown only more intense. A decision to overrule Roe's essential holding under the existing circumstances would address error, if error there was, at the cost of both profound and unnecessary damage to the Court's legitimacy, and to the Nation's commitment to the rule of law. It is therefore imperative to adhere to the essence of Roe's original decision, and we do so today.

Justice Stevens on *Stare Decisis*[34]

The Court is unquestionably correct in concluding that the doctrine of stare decisis has controlling significance in a case of this kind, notwithstanding an individual Justice's concerns about the merits. The central holding of Roe v. Wade, 410 U.S. 113 (1973), has been a "part of our law" for almost two decades. It was a natural sequel to the protection of individual liberty established in Griswold v. Connecticut, 381 U.S. 479 (1965). The societal costs of overruling Roe at this late date would be enormous. Roe is an integral part of a correct understanding of both the concept of liberty and the basic equality of men and women. . . .

Justice Blackmun on *Stare Decisis*[35]

The Court's reaffirmation of Roe's central holding is also based on the force of stare decisis. [N]o erosion of principle going to liberty or personal autonomy has left Roe's central holding a doctrinal remnant. . . . Indeed, the Court acknowledges that Roe's limitation on state power could not be removed without serious inequity to those who have relied upon it or significant damage to the stability of the society governed by the rule in question. In the 19 years since Roe was decided, that case has shaped more than reproductive planning—[a]n entire generation has come of age free to assume Roe's concept of liberty in defining the capacity of women to act in society, and to make reproductive decisions. The Court understands that, having "call[ed] the contending sides . . . to end their national division by accepting a common mandate rooted in the Constitution," a decision to overrule Roe would seriously weaken the Court's capacity to exercise the judicial power and to function as the Supreme Court of a Nation dedicated to the rule of law. What has happened today should serve as a model for future Justices and a warning to all who have tried to turn this Court into yet another political branch. . . .

Chief Justice Rehnquist, Justice White, Justice Scalia, and Justice Thomas on *Stare Decisis*[36]

The joint opinion, following its newly minted variation on stare decisis, retains the outer shell of Roe v. Wade, 410 U.S. 113 (1973), but beats a wholesale retreat from the substance of that case. We believe that Roe was wrongly decided, and that it can and should be overruled consistently with our traditional approach to stare decisis in constitutional cases.

The joint opinion of Justices O'Connor, Kennedy, and Souter cannot bring itself to say that Roe was correct as an original matter, but the authors are of the view that the immediate question is not the soundness of Roe's resolution of the issue, but the precedential force that must be accorded to its holding. Instead of claiming that Roe was correct as a matter of original constitutional interpretation, the opinion therefore contains an elaborate discussion of stare decisis. . . .

Stare decisis is defined in Black's Law Dictionary as meaning "to abide by, or adhere to, decided cases." Black's Law Dictionary 1406 (6th ed. 1990). Whatever the "central holding" of Roe that is left after the joint opinion finishes dissecting it is surely not the result of that principle. While purporting to adhere to precedent, the joint opinion instead revises it. Roe continues to exist, but only in the way a storefront on a western movie set exists: a mere facade to give the illusion of reality. In our view, authentic principles of stare decisis do not require that any portion of the reasoning in Roe be kept intact. "Stare decisis is not . . . a universal, inexorable command," especially in cases involving the interpretation of the Federal Constitution. Burnet v. Coronado Oil & Gas Co., 285 U.S. 393, 405 (1932) (Brandeis, J., dissenting). Erroneous decisions in such constitutional cases are uniquely durable, because correction through legislative action, save for [505 U.S. 833, 955] constitutional amendment, is impossible. It is therefore our duty to reconsider constitutional interpretations that "depar[t] from a proper understanding" of the Constitution. Garcia v. San Antonio Metropolitan Transit Authority, 469 U.S., at 557; see United States v. Scott, 437 U.S. 82, 101 (1978) ("'[I]n cases involving the Federal Constitution, . . . [t]he Court bows to the lessons of experience and the force of better reasoning, recognizing that the process of trial and error, so fruitful in the physical sciences, is appropriate also in the judicial function'" (quoting Burnet v. Coronado Oil & Gas Co., supra, at 406-408 (Brandeis, J., dissenting))). Our constitutional watch does not cease merely because we have spoken before on an issue; when it becomes clear that a prior constitutional interpretation is unsound, we are obliged to reexamine the question.

The joint opinion discusses several stare decisis factors which, it asserts, point toward retaining a portion of Roe. Two of these factors are that the main "factual underpinning" of Roe has remained the same, and that its doctrinal foundation is no weaker now than it was in 1973. Of course, what might be called the basic facts which gave rise to Roe have remained the same—women become pregnant, there is a point somewhere, depending on medical technology, where a fetus becomes viable, and women give birth to children. But this is only to say that the same facts which gave rise to Roe will continue to give rise to similar cases. It is not a reason, in and of itself, why those cases must be decided in the same incorrect manner as was the first case to deal with the question. And surely there is no requirement, in considering whether to depart from stare decisis in a constitutional case, that a decision be more wrong now than it was at the time it was rendered. If that were true, the most outlandish constitutional decision could survive forever, based simply on the fact that it was no more outlandish later than it was when originally rendered.

Nor does the joint opinion faithfully follow this alleged requirement. The opinion frankly concludes that Roe and its progeny were wrong in failing to recognize that the State's interests in maternal health and in the protection of unborn human life exist throughout pregnancy. But there is no indication that these components of Roe are any more incorrect at this juncture than they were at its inception. In the end, having failed to put forth any evidence to prove any true reliance, the joint opinion's argument is based solely on generalized assertions about the national psyche, on a belief that the people of this country have grown accustomed to the Roe decision over the last 19 years and have "ordered their thinking and living around" it. As an initial matter, one might inquire how the joint opinion can view the "central holding" of Roe as so deeply rooted in our constitutional culture when it so casually uproots and disposes of that same decision's trimester framework. Furthermore, at various points in the past, the same could have been said about this Court's erroneous decisions that the Constitution allowed "separate but equal" treatment of minorities, see Plessy v. Ferguson, 163 U.S. 537 (1896), or that "liberty" under the Due Process Clause protected "freedom of contract," see Adkins v. Children's Hospital of District of Columbia, 261 U.S. 525 (1923); Lochner v. New York, 198 U.S. 45 (1905). The "separate but equal" doctrine lasted 58 years after Plessy, and Lochner's protection of contractual freedom lasted 32 years. However, the simple fact that a generation or more had grown used to these major decisions did not prevent the Court from correcting its errors in those cases, nor should it prevent us from correctly interpreting the Constitution here. See Brown v. Board of Education, 347 U.S. 483 (1954) (rejecting the "separate but equal" doctrine); West Coast Hotel Co. v. Parrish, 300 U.S. 379 (1937) (overruling Adkins v. Children's Hospital, supra, in upholding Washington's minimum wage law).

Apparently realizing that conventional stare decisis principles do not support its position, the joint opinion advances a belief that retaining a portion of Roe is necessary to protect the "legitimacy" of this Court. Because the Court must take care to render decisions "grounded truly in principle," and not simply as political and social compromises, the joint opinion properly declares it to be this Court's duty to ignore the public criticism and protest that may arise as a result of a decision. Few would quarrel with this statement, although it may be doubted that Members of this Court, holding their tenure as they do during constitutional "good behavior," are at all likely to be intimidated by such public protests. But the joint opinion goes on to state that, when the Court "resolve[s] the sort of intensely divisive controversy reflected in Roe and those rare, comparable cases," its decision is exempt from reconsideration under established principles of stare decisis in constitutional cases. This is so, the joint opinion contends, because, in those "intensely divisive" cases, the Court has call[ed] the contending sides of a national controversy to end their national division by accepting a common mandate rooted in the Constitution, and must therefore take special care not to be perceived as "surrender[ing] to political pressure" and continued opposition. This is a truly novel principle, one which is contrary to both the Court's historical practice and to the Court's traditional willingness to tolerate criticism of its opinions. Under this principle, when the Court has ruled on a divisive issue, it is apparently prevented from overruling that decision for the sole reason that it was incorrect, unless opposition to the original decision has died away. The joint opinion agrees that the Court's stature would have been seriously damaged if, in Brown and West Coast Hotel, it had dug in its heels and refused to apply normal principles of stare decisis to the earlier decisions. But the opinion contends that the Court was entitled to overrule Plessy and Lochner in those cases, despite the existence of opposition to the original decisions, only because both the Nation and the Court had learned new lessons in the interim. This is at best a feebly supported post hoc rationalization for those decisions.

There is also a suggestion in the joint opinion that the propriety of overruling a "divisive" decision depends in part on whether "most people" would now agree that it should be overruled. Either the demise of opposition or its progression to substantial popular agreement apparently is required to allow the Court to reconsider a divisive decision. How such agreement would be ascertained, short of a public opinion poll, the joint opinion does not say. But surely even the suggestion is totally at war with the idea of "legitimacy" in whose name it is invoked. The Judicial Branch derives its legitimacy not from following public opinion, but from deciding by its best lights whether legislative enactments of the popular branches of Government comport with the Constitution. The doctrine of stare decisis is an adjunct of this duty, and should be no more subject to the vagaries of public opinion than is the basic judicial task.

There are other reasons why the joint opinion's discussion of legitimacy is unconvincing, as well. In assuming that the Court is perceived as "surrender[ing] to political pressure" when it overrules a controversial decision, the joint opinion forgets that there are two sides to any controversy. The joint opinion asserts that, in order to protect its legitimacy, the Court must refrain from overruling a controversial decision lest it be viewed as favoring those who oppose the decision. But a decision to adhere to prior precedent is subject to the same criticism, for, in such a case, one can easily argue that the Court is responding to those who have demonstrated in favor of the original decision. The decision in Roe has engendered large demonstrations, including repeated marches on this Court and on Congress, both in opposition to and in support of that opinion. A decision either way on Roe can therefore be perceived as favoring one group or the other. But this perceived dilemma arises only if one assumes, as the joint opinion does, that the Court should make its decisions with a view toward speculative public perceptions. If one assumes instead, as the Court surely did in both Brown and West Coast Hotel, that the Court's legitimacy is enhanced by faithful interpretation of the Constitution irrespective of public opposition, such self-engendered difficulties may be put to one side.

The internal debate among the justices here demonstrates several key points. Principle is clearly important to judicial decision making; however, principle does not decide cases. Judges do. As early as 1803, Chief Justice Marshal argued, "It is emphatically the province and duty of the judicial department to say what the law is" (*Marbury v. Madison*, 5 U.S. 137, at 177 (1803)). To this task, each individual judge brings a specific menu of policy preferences. Having said that, it is also the case that judicial decisions cannot be expressed in terms of policy preferences outright. The opinion writing process translates those preferences into more palatable legalistic phraseology, justified with ample references to preexisting precedent and steeped in principles of prior case law. As Justice Scalia stated succinctly in a 1991 concurrence, "I am not so naive (nor do I think our forebears were) as to be unaware that judges in a real sense 'make'

law. But they make it as judges make it, which is to say as though they were 'finding' it" (*James B. Beam Distilling Co. v. Georgia*, 501 U.S. 529, at 549 (1991) (Scalia, J., concurring)). To do otherwise would foster the perception that decisions are unprincipled and threaten the Court's legitimacy. If the logic of this seems circular, it is; but it is something that the justices take quite seriously. It also makes it difficult for researchers to reach definitive conclusions regarding motivations behind individual judges' and justices' decisions (e.g., George and Epstein 1992; Segal and Spaeth 1996a, 1996b).

It is clear that the justices realize that they are not just deciding legal issues; they are also making national policy. This means that they address a national political audience of other decision-making elites and interest group representatives who pay close attention to what they have to say. The *Planned Parenthood* conflict, for example, attracted a large number of outside parties, who filed separate *amicus curiae* (friend of the court) briefs in an attempt to persuade the justices in one direction or the other. The list of interested third parties is impressive, including the U.S. Solicitor General for the U.S. government, governors of two states, attorneys general representing fifteen states and the District of Columbia, the City of New York, a number of members of the U.S. Congress, a range of state legislators, and a host of interest groups. Judges on other courts find themselves in a similar position, the primary difference being the geographic reach of their policy statements. In each case the cast of participants parallels that which is registered in the legislative process at each level. Hence the legal and political are closely intertwined; politics in the courts simply dresses itself in legal garb.

Delivery and style of a judicial opinion are equally as important as the content, so the language that judges employ is a crucial consideration. Indeed, as the justices noted in their *Planned Parenthood* opinions, the legitimacy of the Court hinges upon perceptions, which in turn are influenced by the authoritativeness conveyed in judicial rationales. No matter how clearheaded, rational, and practical a judge might be, her personal observations and preferences are not authoritative, nor are they considered legitimate criteria for decision making. Of course, no one can divorce oneself from one's personal preferences. But actual debate concerns appropriate application and interpretation of preexisting legal principles that can be found in case precedent, and these are the terms upon which judges must address the controversies before them. Consistency plays a large part in this as well. The general expectation is that the trajectory of judge-made law will be fairly predictable and stable, thus allowing relevant parties to make their own decisions with some degree of confidence that their actions are in conformance with the law. This is one of the major points of contention among the *Planned Parenthood* opinion writers. Four justices were prepared to overturn

Roe. However, the lead opinion authors argue that doing so would be a "breach of faith," and Justice Stevens concurs, suggesting that the "societal costs . . . would be enormous." Presumably, at times, a judge is compelled to reach a conclusion with which she personally disagrees in order to remain faithful to the institutionalized expectation of constancy.

On the other hand, there will always be considerable disagreement with an individual judge's or a full court's interpretation and application of precedent. This has certainly been the case with regard to the constitutional basis for the right to privacy and a woman's right to choose to have an abortion. Millions of dollars and enormous effort have been spent challenging and defending the legal foundation for the *Roe* rationale. One point upon which the *Planned Parenthood* Court agreed was that the law has changed. Even though a high premium is placed upon constancy, judicial conception of any particular legal principle is in a chronic state of development. As Cardozo (1924, 28) aptly observed, "the glacier still moves," despite the restrictions of *stare decisis*. In a way, this gives some comfort to those who disagree with contemporary judicial rationales. Today's understanding of law is always challengeable.

This is part and parcel of a political process. Some win and some lose, regardless of the arena where the confrontation takes place. Again, law and politics share the same bed. However, attention to institutional issues of authoritativeness and legitimacy in the opinion-writing process provides a basis for losing parties to support the system, even though they disagree with particular outcomes. The following comment by Justice Scalia in a 1990 concurring opinion was probably written with this in mind: "To hold a governmental act to be unconstitutional is not to announce that we forbid it, but that the Constitution forbids it. . . . [T]he Constitution does not change from year to year; . . . it does not conform to our decisions, but our decisions are supposed to conform to it."[37] Such remarks from the bench help to build and maintain a reservoir of support from the courts' constituencies, particularly within those circles where specific decisions are unpopular (see, e.g., Gibson, Caldeira, and Baird 1998; Hoekstra and Segal 1996). With these observations in mind, one can use a marketplace perspective to think about and assess what goes on in the legal system. Indeed, law can be understood as a political and economic marketplace, where influence, ideas, and precedent are all currency tendered in the effort to achieve preferred outcomes. Money is also a critical ingredient that allows parties to purchase information, expertise, and the services of influential advocates (see, e.g., Galanter 1974; Caldeira and Wright 1988). Moreover, individual markets display definite life cycles of ebb and flow as key commodities and players enter and exit. The law exhibits similar characteristics as particular legal issues grow and decline in prominence; the popularity of ideas, tests, principles, and the like, also come and go.

A second major constituency is the legal community relevant to the issue at hand. One segment consists of advocates in the field—in the *Roe-Planned Parenthood* instance, lawyers actively involved in abortion litigation. They look for any clues regarding future direction so that they can cast argumentation in their current case portfolio in the most advantageous terms. Just because the U.S. Supreme Court decides a set of issues, such as those presented in *Planned Parenthood*, does not mean that the controversy is ended. In 1992, when the Court decided *Planned Parenthood*, there were countless other abortion-related cases in various stages of litigation throughout the court system and many more potential ones not yet filed. The attorneys involved in those controversies, many of whom represent organized interests, adjusted their legal strategies in midstream in light of the latest Supreme Court precedent. Analogous modifications occur across the range of legal issues on the heels of opinions issued from the high court. Similarly, decisions by the U.S. Circuit Courts and state supreme courts produce comparable aftershocks, although their associated constituencies are comparatively smaller.

Another, and rather larger, portion of the legal community is also relevant to this equation. Here we would count those lawyers who advise individual clients regarding appropriate courses of action and those who prefer negotiation to adjudication (e.g., Auerbach 1984; Kritzer 1990; Sarat and Felstiner 1995). A primary objective among this group is to keep matters out of the court system, rather than maintaining constant surveillance for cases to bring in. Because their practice lacks the immediacy of the advocates discussed above, absorption of the latest precedents will likely occur more slowly and unevenly. Indeed, as a practical matter, life is much easier if one can assume that the law does not radically change. Another perspective for examining the legal system, then, is to consider law as, in essence, a communications process where law consists of a series of logically deduced linguistic constructions and transmission of information across a community with varying degrees of receptivity and absorption (e.g., Probert 1972).

A third major constituency addressed by the Supreme Court consists of other judges, who look to the Court for leadership. If the Court expects unwavering consistency among lower courts, they must be careful to set an appropriate example and to provide the system with a relatively clear template that other judges can use as a framework for their own decisions. One of the reasons most often cited by investigators to explain why the Supreme Court decides to hear an issue is to clarify points of law upon which lower courts have expressed divergent views (e.g., Ulmer 1984; Perry 1991; Provine 1980). Structurally, the Court sits at the pinnacle of the system, the only tribunal with nationwide jurisdiction, which speaks with a voice of authority that no other court can override. Justice Stevens, writing for the Court in 1994, states that "by the rules that necessarily govern our hierarchical federal court system . . . [i]t is this Court's responsibility to say what a statute means, and once the Court has spoken, it is the duty of other courts to respect that understanding of the governing rule of law" (*Rivers v. Roadway Express, Inc.*, 511 U.S. 298, at 312 (1994)). Although it does not always have "the final word" on the actual dispensations—most cases are remanded to a lower court for further proceedings—the Supreme Court does have the capacity to unify our understandings of law. This also suggests an alternative perspective for assessing the legal world. In other words, law represents and is structured as a system of power hierarchies (e.g., Kennedy 1983).

Conclusions

The dominant jurisprudence of the nineteenth century viewed law as autonomous from the social, economic, and political worlds around it (see, e.g., Horwitz 1977, 1992). Accordingly, law operated entirely upon a set of principles that were self-contained and self-referential. This view of an autonomous legal system also accommodates the idea of insulating courts and judges from ordinary politics and the idea that the majority will (even as reflected in legislative and executive actions) just might be wrong. At the very least, the masses cannot be trusted to act in accordance with legal principles.[38] The winds of politics do not allow for orderly lawmaking in a consistent and just manner. Jurisprudence and logic must prevail in judges' minds, and they are insulated from outside influences so that a body of neutral tenets can be protected from power plays and rash, illogical thinking.

Few today would hold onto the notion that law is completely autonomous, or that judges are totally isolated from the world.[39] There are those, however, who insist that autonomy of law is the model we should strive for (e.g., Bickel 1962; Wechsler 1961; Berger 1977; Bork 1990). In their view, legal autonomy is much preferable to a law/society symbiosis. Accordingly, the art of judging should be a principled one. That, after all, is what *stare decisis* is all about, and if judges are left to roam freely for justification of their decisions, our system of laws could deteriorate into a jumble of *ad hoc*, idiosyncratic statements offering little guidance to future generations of similar disputes. Moreover, statements of law would differ wildly from one jurisdiction to another, diverging according to "contemporary community standards" as judges from various jurisdictions understood them. Kairys (1990, 4), however, argues that this creates little more than a "myth of legal reasoning," which is a device used by judges to distance themselves from the nitty-gritty undesirable social relations that

produce litigation. Hence, *stare decisis* allows judges to avoid immersion in contaminated waters while appearing to be perfectly fair and evenhanded. Indeed, their decisions "are expressed and justified and largely perceived by judges themselves, in terms of 'facts' that have been objectively determined and 'law' that has been objectively and rationally 'found' and 'applied.'"

In realistic terms, strict segregation of law and society is difficult to envision, and most commentators have settled upon a semi-autonomous view of law (see, e.g., Lempert and Sanders 1986, 401–27). Judges do have to reconcile their own decisions with those that were rendered in the past. They are, in many ways, honor bound to recognize continuity as a high priority in the work they do. Much of their legitimacy hinges upon their ability to protect from erosive elements the sculpture they have inherited. But even in paying homage to history, judges must find ways to harmonize the past with the present. Social conditions change, commodity markets grow and decay, technological development races ahead toward some unknown destination, and, as these things happen, stress is placed upon the judicial lawmaking process with all of its internal braking mechanisms and external expectations of continuity.

In this chapter we have introduced law in a broad sense, and discussed a number of categorical concepts. The chapters that follow will look specifically at law within the American context. Chapter 3 considers some of the ideas that were important to the Founders and that continue to resonate through our law today, and chapter 4 discusses the structure, processes, and actors found in our legal system. Part II (chapters 5 through 8) addresses specific legal issues that arise over the various stages of life, that shadow the individual, literally, from before delivery to beyond the grave. Finally, we live out our lives within the contours created by the ebb and flow of forces at work in the larger political economy, with a primary agent being technological development. Indeed, the influence of technology in every aspect of our existence is transparent as we enter the twenty-first century. It has changed the ways in which we communicate with each other, our conception of quality of life, and even the definitions of life and death. In parallel, our entire lives are enveloped in a web of law, and we shall explore some of its dimensions in Part III.

Law on the Web

Helpful Hints

In this, and all subsequent chapters, we rely heavily on the research, ideas, and sometimes, even the words of others. Like all researchers and writers, we credit those others for what we have borrowed. Of course, you do this in writing your own papers, probably referring to a style guide, such as Kate Turabian's *A Manual for Writers* or the *Chicago Manual of Style*. Whatever manual we use as writers, we are all careful to give credit where credit is due because it is the right thing to do and because plagiarism can get a person into a lot of trouble.

While we are all amply familiar with methods for giving credit to hardcopy books, magazines, newspapers, and other information sources, the means for giving credit to online sources are much less clear, and, frankly a bit more cumbersome. Nevertheless, it is just as crucial to accurately cite Internet sources as it is to accurately cite the works you find on library shelves.

Some Internet citation rules are the same as those for citing hardcopy sources. For example, always provide the author of a work if her or his name is given and the title or top-level heading of the work being cited. Some citation rules, however, are different when working with online materials. For example, you must always give the uniform resource locator (URL) of the site. The URL is the address of the site provided at the top of your screen. A hypothetical address might read: yoursite.edu/. The URL must always and accurately be noted in the citation.

When referring to electronic journals and other publications, always provide the date of publication just like you would for a hardcopy source. A lot of what is on the Internet, however, is not obviously dated. If possible, in such cases, you should provide the date on which the document was last modified. You can find this information by going into "view" on your toolbar and clicking "Page info" or by using Ctrl+I. If even this information is not provided, you should provide the reader with the date of your visit to the site.

Finally, when citing hardcopy sources, you always provide the reader with the page on which you found the data, thought, or quote to which you are referring. Web documents do not have pages as such. Therefore, if you are dealing with lengthy documents, you should refer to the section or paragraph that you have borrowed. Appearing below are some citation illustrations:

- *Example 1*: Susan Schmidt and John F. Harris, "Lewinsky Is Questioned by Starr Team," 28 July 1998, available at www.washingtonpost.com/wp-srv/politics/special/clinton/stories/starr072898.htm.
- *Example 2*: In chapter 3, we made use of an online version of *The Federalist Papers*. An illustrative footnote reads: Madison, *Federalist* #51, para. 4, available at www.law.emory.edu/pub-cgi/print_hit_bold.pl/FEDERAL/federalist/feder51.html (accessed 4 July 1998).

In this chapter, we have talked about law in the most general terms. As you know, legal terms can often be very confusing to the layperson, particularly because many are in Latin or of Latin derivation. Thus, the following presents a compendium of some of the better legal and general reference sites on the web.

A Smattering of Legal Reference Sites

Introduction to Basic Legal Citation (1997–98 ed.), by Peter W. Martin (Cornell Law School)

www.law.cornell.edu/citation

This citation primer is based on the sixteenth edition of the "Bluebook." The document links, point by point, to the disk version of this material held on the Legal Information Institute's Folio web server.

The Harvard Law School Library 1L Dictionary

www.law.harvard.edu/library/research_guides/one_l_dictionary.html

A dictionary specifically designed to assist new law students the first few days of their law school experience.

Oran's Dictionary of the Law

www.wld.com/conbus/orans/Welcome.asp

From West's *Legal Dictionary* (The West Group); allows you to search for legal terms and definitions.

The 'Lectric Law Lexicon™

www.lectlaw.com/ref.html

'Lectric law library's dictionary offers explanations for thousands of law-related words, terms, and phrases that are alphabetically arranged.

Duhaime's Law Dictionary

www.wwlia.org/diction.htm

Another alphabetically arranged "plain English" legal dictionary, this one posted by The Worldwide Legal Information Association.

Court TV Glossary of Legal Terms

www.courttv.com/legalterms/glossary.html

Court TV's alphabetically arranged "plain English" legal dictionary.

Shark Talk: EveryBody's Legal Dictionary

www.nolo.com/dictionary/wordindex.cfm

Yet another "plain English" dictionary, this one from Nolo Press.

Jurist: The Law Professors' Network

jurist.law.pitt.edu/

A really interesting legal-resource site maintained by the University of Pittsburgh. Among other features, it links to homepages and e-mail addresses of law professors around the country, law school syllabi, and other useful resources for legal research.

A Smattering of General References

WWWebster Dictionary

www.m-w.com/dictionary.htm

Online, searchable Merriam-Webster dictionary.

A Web of On-Line Dictionaries

www.yourdictionary.com/

Allows you to look up definitions based on *Merriam-Webster's Collegiate Dictionary*, 10th edition. Also includes links to more than 500 dictionaries of over 140 different languages.

Roget's Internet Thesaurus

www.thesaurus.com

As the name implies, this is the online, searchable version of *Roget's Thesaurus*.

WWWebster Thesaurus

www.m-w.com/thesaurus.htm

The online, searchable Webster's thesaurus.

Bartlett's Familiar Quotations On-Line

www.columbia.edu/acis/bartleby/bartlett

From Columbia University's Project Bartleby, a word-searchable, online version of Bartlett's.

ILC Glossary of Internet Terms

www.matisse.net/files/glossary.html

A glossary of Internet terms provided by Internet Literacy Consultants™.

3 A Government of Laws and Not of Men: The Ubiquitous Nature and Ambiguous Position of Law in American Culture

> Scarcely any political question arises in the United States that is not resolved, sooner or later, into a judicial question. Hence all parties are obliged to borrow, in their daily controversies, the ideas, and even the language, peculiar to judicial proceedings.
> —Alexis de Tocqueville, 1835[1]

Law is as American as apple pie. From John Adams' famous adage commending government grounded in the firmness of law rather than the volatility of the people, through Alexis de Tocqueville's observation on our civilization's propensity toward the legalistic, through such familiar idioms as "I'm gonna take this case all the way to the Supreme Court!" and "There oughta be a law!," American culture is—and always has been—saturated with legal rhetoric, legal consideration, *and* legal action. Law in American culture is ubiquitous—it is everywhere and it is everywhere all of the time. And so is our use of it. Indeed, the resort to formal law—to the courtroom—has even touched such "other" cultural icons as motherhood,[2] the flag,[3] baseball,[4] and, yes, even apple pie.[5]

At the same time, not every American loves apple pie and not everyone loves the law. Indeed, while America is no doubt the most legalized culture in history, it is a culture that simultaneously despises the very laws and lawmakers to which it so frequently resorts. There exists within our cultural selves not only John Adams, but Henry David Thoreau. Thus, alongside the American psyche that reveres "[a] government of laws, and not of men,"[6] there is the American self that shouts:

I heartily accept the motto, "That government is best which governs least;" and I should like to see it acted up to more rapidly and systematically. Carried out, it finally amounts to this, which also I believe, —"That government is best which governs not at all;" and when men are prepared for it, that will be the kind of government which they will have (Thoreau [1849] 1975, 789).

The two sides of the American self are occasionally played out and most easily seen publicly in the extremes. On the one hand, our most legalistic selves are represented by the juristic saga of eleven-year-old Katie Rose Sawyer. "Only in America," after all, could a fifth-grade "marriage" end in court and a judicial restraining order.

But when young Ms. Sawyer "divorced" ten-year-old Cody Finch after just four months, the estranged Mr. Finch punched her on the playground, and Katie's parents, rather than contacting Cody's folks, "took 'em to court."[7] On the other hand, "only in America" (or, as they would put it, "Ameri*k*a") could we find a Posse Comitatus, a group so hostile to law that it rejects even the Constitution and "accept[s] no *higher authority* above the level of the Sheriff in the county in which [members] reside" (emphasis in original).[8]

But those are surely the extremes. Most of us are not hyperlitigious—we are mostly able to settle childish or simple disputes without resort to judicial intervention.[9] Nor are most of us so antagonistic toward law that we reject the foundations of law itself. We are neither Sawyers nor Posse Comitatus.[10] And yet within us, as a culture, both are engaged in a continual struggle. Indeed, American culture is, at once, the most highly individualistic and, thus, the most hostile to formal structures (law) *and* the most prone to resolve problems by resorting to formal structures (law). The struggle between the two American selves is as old as—in fact, older than—America itself. In the end, it is a cultural struggle between individual liberty on the one hand, and social order on the other—a struggle that has defined and shaped the whole of our legal history and structure.

This chapter presents a framework for considering the role of law specifically in American culture. It begins with a brief discussion of the ideological foundation of American society, a foundation that inevitably set the stage both for the ubiquity of law in America *and* for our cultural equivocation on matters legal. We then consider how this ideological framework reproduced itself in the formal structures of American law and politics. Finally, as a prelude to subsequent chapters, we briefly address this cultural/philosophical replication in the practice of American law and society today.

Individual Liberty versus Social Order: Foundations of the American Legal Paradox

Over the course of most of the twentieth century, from the Bolshevik Revolution in 1917 until the fall of the Berlin Wall in 1989, America fought a relentless battle against the evils of ideology. To many Americans, the very term "ideology" produces the twin specters of Hitler in Munich and Stalin in Red Square—tyrants spewing forth rigid dogma to mindless, impoverished masses. Whether fomenting fascism or communism, America suffered the unremitting threat of these two ideologues and their predecessors and successors for over seven decades. The association made "ideology" a dirty word, something to which no "pragmatic," "free-thinking" American would ever subscribe.

Yet, in many respects, the United States is the most ideologically bound nation on earth. For all our economic, ethnic, racial, and religious diversity, we do (at least loosely) subscribe to a common system of thought that has had an amazing persistence and influence over us—and, more importantly, for our purposes, over our approach to law. This system of thought—American ideology—began over three hundred years ago in the English liberal revolution of the seventeenth century, and particularly its views of human nature, legal authority, and the place of legal authority in both liberating the best aspects and restraining the worst aspects of that nature.

Law and the Classical View of Human Nature: Political Culture

To point to a single foundation of an American system of thinking about law and nature is risky business. Certainly, this nation's great intellects, including and especially, the Founders, were among the most eclectic of legal/political scholars. American thinking prior to 1776 was heavily influenced by the ancients and the moderns—by Aristotle *and* Voltaire, by Cicero *and* Rousseau, by Tacitus *and* Montesquieu (see, e.g., Bailyn 1967, 26–29). Thus, short of performing a successful seance and, even then, getting such politically disparate individuals as Jefferson, Adams, Madison, and Hamilton, to agree on a single intellectual wellspring, we can probably only guess (in the rigorous language of the highly skilled social scientist, this is called "going out on a very brittle limb") at relative levels of influence. A good guess, however, would give the English classical liberals, particularly the seventeenth-century philosopher John Locke, pride of place. According to Locke, the natural state of human beings is one of perfect freedom, equality, and independence (Locke 1960, 287).

Each of us, in the "State of Nature" is a free agent, free to "order [our] actions, and dispose of [our] possessions and persons as [we] think fit," subject only to the "Law of Nature" (Locke 1960, 287). So far so good, but whatever the "Law of Nature" is,[11] it is *not* a very good executor of its own rules—indeed, at least in an earthly sense, the "Law of Nature" has no enforcement capability. So each of us free, equal, and independent beings is at the mercy of all the other free, equal, and independent beings. Although, according to Locke, "the Law of Nature be plain and intelligible to all rational Creatures; yet Men being biased by their Interest, as well as ignorant for want of study of it, are not apt to allow of it as a Law binding to them in the application of it to their particular Cases" (Locke 1960, 369). In other words, we're all free, equal, independent, *and* pretty darned selfish. The State of Nature, then, is no paradise, but rather a potentially hellish condition, "full of fears and continual dangers" (Locke 1960, 368). The problem, then, is: How do we keep all the others from killing us, hurting us, and taking our stuff?

The punch line—one that perhaps seems obvious—is that we agree to enter into a political society, regulated by common positive law, and enforced by civil government. The wild and wooly State of Nature, in which individuals, constrained only by the "thou shalt nots" of Natural Law, preyed on others and their property, has been transformed into an orderly community, governed by specific, common legislative prohibitions and commands, implemented by a common executive, and adjudged by a common magistrate. We now have organized, common enforcement:

And thus the commonwealth comes by a power to set down what punishment shall belong to the several transgressions they think worthy of it, committed amongst the members of that society (which is the power of making laws), as well as it has the power to punish any injury done unto any of its members by any one that is not of it (which is the power of war and peace); and all this for the preservation of the property of all the members of that society, as far as is possible. But though every man entered into society has quitted his power to punish offences against the law of Nature in prosecution of his own private judgment, yet with the judgment of offences which he has given up to the legislative, in all cases where he can appeal to the magistrate, he has given up a right to the commonwealth to employ his force for the execution of the judgments of the commonwealth whenever he shall be called to it, which, indeed, are his own judgments, they being made by himself or his representative. And herein we have the original of the legislative and executive power of civil society, which is to judge by standing laws how far offences are to be punished when committed within the commonwealth; and also by occasional judgments founded on the present circumstances of the fact, how far injuries from without are to be vindicated, and in both these to employ all the force of all the members when there shall be need (Locke 1960, 342–43).

The natural state of men without law is recast into "[a] government of laws, and not of men."

Okay, this is an obvious and desirable solution. But it begins to set up one of the great and enduring dilemmas of classical liberalism, and thus, of American culture. For in instituting this new orderly community, we individuals pay a price in liberty, equality, and independence. We agree to cede some of our natural liberty, equality, and independence to the commonwealth. We give up some of that which is intrinsic and essential to us as human beings—a serious business, indeed.

Thus, the problem becomes: How do we keep the forces of government—of law—from "extend[ing] farther than the common good" (Locke 1960, 371)? How do we keep the power that is now vested in the law from overwhelming what is left of our natural liberty, equality, and independence? Clearly, Locke believed that "Wherever Law ends, Tyranny begins" (Locke 1960, 418). But, as history has amply demonstrated, law itself, and the makers of law, have a propensity toward tyranny as well. This is an issue that very much concerned our original lawmakers, the framers of the U.S. Constitution.[12]

Balancing Individual Liberty and Social Order: The Madisonian Solution

The lineage from Locke to the Founders is at its clearest in the Declaration of Independence. Indeed, Jefferson borrowed quite liberally from *The Second Treatise* by Locke, not only in thought, but in actual word.[13] Rhetorical flourishes aside, however, the liberal framework established by the likes of Mr. Locke—including all its problems and paradoxes—figured very prominently in the conceptual structure of the Constitution itself, or in other words, our basic law.

In fact, the Founders could easily fit their own experiences into the extreme possibilities. Whether one accepts a "civics course" view of the Founders as selfless political saints, concerned only for the welfare of all future Americans, or the far more cynical image of them as rapacious, self-serving landowners and wealthy merchants concerned only with locking into permanent place their own material advantages, or more likely, as something in between, to their minds, they had seen just about the worst of both worlds—both the tyranny of law and the tyranny of lawlessness. After all, from their point of view, they had long suffered under the "absolute Tyranny" of a system of British law, so onerous and unfair that it threatened to destroy their "unalienable Rights" (Declaration of Independence). On the other hand, their initial attempt at self-government under the Articles of Confederation posed the opposite problems, that is, of the lack or impotency of law. Likening the Confederation to the ancient Grecian republics, the *Federalist Papers* characterized the situation under the Articles as one of "weakness," "disorder," and, potentially, "destruction." Under such circumstances, a kind of *real* "State of Nature" plays itself out with "[t]he more powerful members, instead of being kept in awe and subordination, tyranniz[ing] successively over all the rest"

(*Federalist* #18, para. 4 [Madison]). Thus, these men, empiricists in the Age of Empiricism,[14] could point to real experience—their own and historical others—as proof of the liberal thesis—as proof that somewhere between complete liberty and complete order there lay a balance and the key to that balance was law.

We come now to our own preeminent liberal philosopher, empirical thinker, and legal artisan, James Madison. In many ways, it is Madison's particular spin on human nature and his particular legal approach to alleviating the problems and enhancing the possibilities of that nature, that forms the basis of American legal culture—at least that side of the legal, cultural American self that sees law as the great counterbalance to the excesses of liberty and order.

Like Locke, Madison was convinced that man was naturally free and independent. At the same time, like Locke, he was convinced of man's natural propensity to savage others. "If men were angels," Madison asserted, "no government would be necessary" (*Federalist* #51, para. 4). Obviously, we very unangelic mortals need laws to control us or impose order on our nonbeatific selves. Having made that observation, however, Madison had to confront the flip side of the problem: If men are not angels, neither do angels govern men.[15] Clearly, history had (and has since) shown that those who make and enforce laws are fully as fallible and corruptible as the rest of us. Sounds a lot like John Locke, right? The big difference is that, unlike John Locke who spent his life largely as a theoretician,[16] Madison had the rare and exhilarating opportunity to take his insights on human nature and his opinions on how to exploit and control human nature, and fashion out of those views the fundamental law of a nation—a law that revolves around the Madisonian theory of factions.

That we as individuals are fallible—that we are likely to act in the most unangelic of ways if left completely to our own devices—is bad enough. But we human beings are terribly complex animals, for although born independent, we are also social creatures, which means that we inevitably are led to band together. Were we naturally to affiliate as various components of the heavenly choir, the world would be paradise with or without the maze of rules and regulations that permeate our existence. However, given the very imperfect nature of individual humans, it is highly likely that our tendency toward socialization will also be imperfect. So, harken back to that State of Nature with all us avaricious individuals preying on each other's ideas, properties, and beings; only this time, imagine whole groups of individuals victimizing weaker groups and individuals. This is the State of Nature as Madison sees it.

According to Madison, humans are, by nature, "factious" creatures. "The latent causes of faction," he tells us, "are . . . sown in the nature of man. . . ." (*Federalist* #10, para. 6). Consequently, humans will always seek out those who share their interests. This is fine in the context of an angelic chorus, but, of course, Madison doesn't see the situation in such celestial terms. Rather, he defines a faction as "a number of citizens, whether amounting to a majority or a minority of the whole, who are united and actuated by some common impulse of passion, or of interest, *adverse* to the rights of other citizens, or to the permanent and aggregate interests of the community" (*Federalist* #10, para. 2; emphasis added). Thus, factions, while inevitable, can be—indeed, unchecked, will be—pretty dangerous entities:

A zeal for different opinions concerning religion, concerning government, and many other points, as well of speculation as of practice; an attachment to different leaders ambitiously contending for pre-eminence and power; or to persons of other descriptions whose fortunes have been interesting to the human passions, have, in turn, divided mankind into parties, inflamed them with mutual animosity, and rendered them much more disposed to vex and oppress each other than to co-operate for their common good. So strong is this propensity of mankind to fall into mutual animosities, that where no substantial occasion presents itself, the most frivolous and fanciful distinctions have been sufficient to kindle their unfriendly passions and excite their most violent conflicts (*Federalist* #10, para. 6).

Factions, according to Madison, have thus been the downfall of humankind from the beginning of time. The question is: What do you do about them?

For Madison, the answer to that question starts in the very structure of law. If factions are so destructive, clearly one solution to their catastrophic impacts would be cutting them off at the knees, so to speak, or, as Madison put it, "removing the causes of faction." This would seem to be the most direct resolution and could be accomplished simply "by destroying the liberty which is essential to [the] existence [of factions, or] . . . by giving to every citizen the same opinions, the same passions, and the same interests" (*Federalist* #10, para. 3). Except, of course, this resolution is neither simple nor very desirable. For in effect, Madison is saying that to eliminate the causes of faction, liberty itself would have to be extinguished and the entire human race turned into a bunch of unfeeling, unthinking robotrons. Thus, on "removing the causes of faction," Madison himself says:

It could never be more truly said than of the first remedy [destroying liberty], that it was worse than the disease. Liberty is to faction what air is to fire, an aliment without which it instantly expires. But it could not be less folly to abolish liberty, which is essential to political life, because it nourishes faction, than it would be to wish the annihilation of air, which is essential to animal life, because it imparts to fire its destructive agency.

The second expedient [giving everybody the same opinions] is as impracticable as the first would be unwise. As long as the reason of man continues fallible, and he is at liberty to exercise it, different opinions will be formed. As long as the connection

subsists between his reason and his self-love, his opinions and his passions will have a reciprocal influence on each other; and the former will be objects to which the latter will attach themselves (*Federalist* #10, para. 4, 5, 6).

Under the classical understanding of human nature, the causes of faction cannot be removed. Now what? Well, according to Mr. Madison, this means taking a very different path. Rather than creating regulations that would seek to eliminate the causes of faction, the law itself, he says, should be organized in such a way that it controls the deleterious *effects* of factions (*Federalist* #10, para. 8). Enter the constitutional framework.

Madison reasoned that the best way to control the effects of factions within the basic legal structure was to work *with* human nature rather than against it, for "what is government itself," he asks, "but the greatest of all reflections on human nature" (*Federalist* #51, para. 4)? Thus, if human nature is inevitably free, if it is inevitably competitive, and if it inevitably is prone to sectarianism, the law should be structured in such a way that those inevitable forces are marshaled or controlled to the greater good. In essence, the intent is to use the ability—the natural tendency—of human beings to freely and competitively associate toward the goal of self-interest as the very means by which that ability—that tendency—is kept in check so that it neither destroys individual liberty nor tears the fabric of a well-ordered social system. In a nutshell, "Ambition must be made to counteract ambition" (*Federalist* #51, para. 4), and all this must be accomplished within the framework of law. Thus, Madison says, "In framing a government which is to be administered by men over men, the great difficulty lies in this: you must first enable the government to control the governed; and in the next place oblige it to control itself. A dependence on the people is, no doubt, the primary control on the government; but experience has taught mankind the necessity of auxiliary precautions"(*Federalist* #51, para. 4).

What all this means is spelled out for us constitutionally in a system designed to control the effects of faction both within the population at large and within government itself. Let us begin, then, where Madison begins, with the people themselves. Note above that he says that the government must be both dependent on the people *and* able to control the people. In effect, he is saying that the law used to police the citizenry should ultimately come from the citizenry itself. As we all learn in first grade, this is called democracy, a form of citizen-based lawmaking for which we have the ancient Greeks to thank. But, Madison, a student of those same democracy-loving ancient Greeks, believed strongly that their undoing was none other than faction: "[S]uch democracies," he warned, "have ever been spectacles of turbulence and contention; have ever been found incompatible with personal security or the rights of property;

and have in general been as short in their lives as they have been violent in their deaths" (*Federalist* #10, para. 11). Under a pure democracy, a permanent majority faction might form, dictating thought, religion, and property distribution for all—in other words, undermining liberty. Or, under a pure democracy, multiple, uncontrolled factions might arise, each seeking to establish political and economic dominance, as we humans traditionally have, through war—in other words, undermining order. Pure democracy, then, cannot control the effects of faction.

Rather, our basic law is structured in the form of a republic, "a government in which the scheme of representation takes place" (*Federalist* #10, para. 12).[17] We govern ourselves, but only indirectly through the selection of specified lawmakers, including members of Congress, the president, and, even more indirectly, federal judges. This indirect form of lawmaking—this republic—works to control the ruinous effects of factions in two ways. In the first place, by dividing us up into electoral districts—by actually fostering more competition—the plan supposedly ensures that no single, permanent crushing majority can ever snuff out a single, permanent weakened minority. Thus, the third congressional district of Maryland has interests different from those of the second congressional district in Georgia, which differ from those of the fifth district in Massachusetts, which deviate from those of New York's eighth, and so on. Factional ambition within the electorate—the people—itself is theoretically countered by hundreds (currently 435) of other geographically defined factions, making it "less probable that a majority of the whole will have a common motive to invade the rights of other citizens; or if such a common motive exists, it will be more difficult for all who feel it to discover their own strength, and to act in unison with each other" (*Federalist* #10, para. 18). A republic, then, preserves liberty by making it hard for enduring majorities to take root.

A republic, in addition, is ostensibly less likely to devolve into the sort of factional warfare that can plunge a society into chaos. Madison thus imagines a representative lawmaking establishment capable of "refin[ing] and enlarg[ing] the public views, by passing them through the medium of a chosen body of citizens, whose wisdom may best discern the true interest of their country, and whose patriotism and love of justice will be least likely to sacrifice it to temporary or partial considerations" (*Federalist* #10, para. 14). Presumably, we citizens, armed with the ability to choose our leaders, will select from among us the "best and brightest." They, in turn, will perfect and temper our legal demands through the art of debate and compromise.

If all this sounds oddly idealistic—if the notion that we will choose from among us the few who are better than the whole rings somewhat naive—Madison, stu-

dent of human nature, is ahead of us. He admits that "the effect may be inverted. Men of factious tempers, of local prejudices, or of sinister designs, may, by intrigue, by corruption, or by other means, first obtain the suffrages, and then betray the interests, of the people" (*Federalist* #10, para. 14). In other words, human nature being what it is (fallible, avaricious, and so on), the best and the brightest may turn out to be a bunch of charlatans! The possibility calls for "auxiliary precautions."

Thus, under the complete Madisonian legal design, the republican strategy of dispersing and dividing power among the electorate is applied as well to the governing framework itself through such familiar devices as separation of powers, checks and balances, and federalism.

Ambition is made to counteract ambition not only among the electorate, but among their elected officials, so that government is obliged "to control itself" (*Federalist* #51, para. 4). Madison explains:

In the compound republic of America, the power surrendered by the people is first divided between two distinct governments, and then the portion allotted to each subdivided among distinct and separate departments. Hence a double security arises to the rights of the people. The different governments will control each other, at the same time that each will be controlled by itself. . . . It is of great importance in a republic not only to guard the society against the oppression of its rulers, but to guard one part of the society against the injustice of the other part. Different interests necessarily exist in different classes of citizens. If a majority be united by a common interest, the rights of the minority will be insecure. [The best] . . . method . . . of providing against this evil . . . [is] by comprehending in the society so many separate descriptions of citizens as will render an unjust combination of a majority of the whole very improbable, if not impracticable. . . . [This] method will be exemplified in the federal republic of the United States. Whilst all authority in it will be derived from and dependent on the society, the society itself will be broken into so many parts, interests, and classes of citizens, that the rights of individuals, or of the minority, will be in little danger from interested combinations of the majority. . . . Justice is the end of government. It is the end of civil society. It ever has been and ever will be pursued until it be obtained, or until liberty be lost in the pursuit. In a society under the forms of which the stronger faction can readily unite and oppress the weaker, anarchy may as truly be said to reign as in a state of nature, where the weaker individual is not secured against the violence of the stronger; and as, in the latter state, even the stronger individuals are prompted, by the uncertainty of their condition, to submit to a government which may protect the weak as well as themselves; so, in the former state, will the more powerful factions or parties be gradually induced, by a like motive, to wish for a government which will protect all parties, the weaker as well as the more powerful. . . . In the extended republic of the United States, and among the great variety of interests, parties, and sects which it embraces, a coalition of a majority of the whole society could seldom take place on any other principles than those of justice and the general good; whilst there being thus less danger to a minor from the will of a major party, there must be less pretext, also, to provide for the security of the former, by introducing into the government a will not dependent on the latter, or, in other words, a will independent of the society itself. It is no less certain than it is important, notwithstanding the contrary opinions which have been entertained, that the larger the society, provided it lie within a practical sphere, the more duly capable it will be of self-government. And happily for the REPUBLICAN CAUSE, the practicable sphere may be carried to a very great extent, by a judicious modification and mixture of the FEDERAL PRINCIPLE (*Federalist* #51, para. 9, 10).

Viewed in this way through the eyes of the Father of the Constitution, America's legal foundation—its basic constitutional framework—is nothing less than an holistic attempt to manipulate human nature itself as a means of balancing the two conflicting human needs for individual liberty, on the one hand, and social control, on the other. The stage was thus set long ago (indeed, at the beginning) for the American self that celebrates and indulges in a "government of laws. . . ."

Fighting Law with Law: The Anti-Federalist Response

But what of the other "self," the one personified by Thoreau, the one that eschews the legal saturation of the culture, or the legalization of human nature? It, too, at least in a form, was there from the beginning. Note, for example, Patrick Henry's observation on the "disposition in the people of this country to revolt against the *dominion of laws*" (Henry 1788; emphasis added). Clearly, Henry and many of his fellow Anti-Federalists, were unconvinced that the sort of strong republic that Madison felt essential to maintaining a healthy balance between liberty and order would maintain an adequate equilibrium—order, perhaps, but at the expense of liberty:

I need not take much pains to show that the principles of [the proposed constitutional] system are extremely pernicious, impolitic, and dangerous. . . . It is not a democracy wherein the people retain all their rights securely. . . . [I]t does not leave us the means of defending our rights. . . . [W]e are told that we need not fear; because those in power, being our representatives, will not abuse the powers we put in their hands. I am not well versed in history, but I will submit to your recollection, whether liberty has been destroyed most often by the licentiousness of the people, or by the tyranny of rulers. I imagine, sir, you will find the balance on the side of tyranny . . . (Henry 1788).

Of course, in true American fashion—true even of the Thoreau-like self—the antidote offered by the Anti-Federalists to the poison of too much law was the Bill of Rights, that is, more law![18] If the body of the Constitution was designed to suppress the worst symptoms of the "disease of factions," the Bill of Rights was designed to sustain the "contagion of liberty" (Bailyn 1967, 230) that gripped the old colonies before independence, and the new nation for years thereafter. In any event, law was seen as the answer to both epidemics—both the bad and the good.

Law and the Classical View of Human Nature: Economic Culture

In many respects, then, the legal solution to the tension between liberty and order represents the core of American political culture. Thus, as we have said, law and politics are inextricably intertwined, and they were from the very beginning. Our legal/political culture, however, does not exist in a vacuum. Rather, law and politics are further entwined with—they are both part and parcel of—our economic culture. This culture, too, was formed from the classical understanding of human nature, responding likewise to the felt tension between the need for liberty, on the one hand, and order on the other.

The Theory of Property Rights

Recall that Locke justified the need for civil law in terms of the "preservation of the property of all the members of that society, as far as is possible" (Locke 1960, 342). This, it should be noted, was no throwaway phrase. Indeed, according to Locke, "The great and *chief end* . . . , of Men uniting into Commonwealths, and putting themselves under Government, *is the Preservation of their Property*" (Locke 1960, 368–69; emphasis in original). It is axiomatic, from a classical liberal perspective, that each of us, being free, equal, and independent, has "a 'property' [interest] in [our] own 'person.' [And t]his nobody has any right to but himself" (Locke 1960, 305). It is a crucial notion, from a classical liberal perspective, therefore, that property is intrinsic to the individual.

Certainly we all feel ownership over ourselves, if not, perhaps in terms of property. Indeed, as we discuss in chapter 8, such legal fundamentals as slander and libel law grew out of these notions of property in self—we are, after all, our reputation, and if that reputation is damaged, so are we. Moreover, the notion of property in ourselves provided the basis for early conceptions of privacy rights.[20] The question is, though, how does this "'property' in [our] own 'person'" translate to a right to property in *things*. According to classical economics a la John Locke, the right to property in things flows directly from the inherent right to "'property' in [our] own 'person'":

The "labour" of [a person's] body and the "work" of his hands, we may say, are properly his. Whatsoever, then, he removes out of the state that Nature hath provided and left it in, he hath mixed his labour with it, and joined to it something that is his own, and thereby makes it his property. It being by him removed from the common state Nature placed it in, it hath by this labour something annexed to it that excludes the common right of other men. For this "labour" being the unquestionable property of the labourer, no man but he can have a right to what that is once joined to, at least where there is enough, and as good left in common for others (Locke 1960, 305–306).

The work we put into extracting something from the earth gives value and meaning to that something that wasn't there before. Because we give it value and meaning, it becomes ours. So, for example, a stalk of wheat growing in a meadow really has no worth until some enterprising individual comes along, picks it, mills it, mixes it with water, and bakes it. By virtue of the labor invested in it, the worthless stalk of wheat has become a useful food product and it has become a useful food product *only* because of the individual's effort; therefore, it belongs to her—in Locke's words, it becomes her "private right" (Locke 1960, 306).

Of course, this "free range" wheat is available to any hardworking person who wants to make it her own—after all, we are born free and independent. But we are leaving something important out of the equation. In addition to being born free and independent, we are born equal. In a nutshell, to Enlightenment thinkers such as Locke steeped in natural law theory, this meant that "God gave [the earth] to mankind in common" (Locke 1960, 304). It belongs to all of us. Does this throw a monkey wrench into property rights? Well yes, but not right away. In the mythical state of nature, all things being equal, there really is no scarcity. Our wheat-enhancing friend can only use so much of the earth's bounty—in reality, only what she and her kin need. There's plenty more for everybody else. Because her labor has given the wheat value, it is unquestionably hers. But, the mythical state of nature has (and had since Locke's time) long since given way to a state of large and concentrated populations, cities, machinery, and, most important, money, and thus the inevitable monkey wrench.

And thus came in the use of money; some lasting thing that men might keep without spoiling, and that, by mutual consent, men would take in exchange for the truly useful but perishable supports of life. And as different degrees of industry were apt to give men possessions in different proportions, so this invention of money gave them the opportunity to continue and enlarge them (Locke 1960, 318–19).

No longer would people simply take what they *needed* to subsist. Some might, and would, take what they *wanted* to live better than everyone else—the property is no less theirs, but it has become very problematic indeed. Thus, the need for law.

Property Rights and the Constitution

As in our earlier discussion, all of this has a direct relevance to the American legal experience. It is relevant in several respects. First, it is relevant to the constitutional structure—that elemental legal manipulation of human nature, particularly human nature as it manifests itself in group form or faction. Of course, we already know what factions are and the damage they can do. We also know

that, according to Madison, "the most frivolous and fanciful distinctions have been sufficient to kindle their unfriendly passions and excite their most violent conflicts." However, although anything may incite factional warfare, one thing far outweighs all the others in bringing out the worst in human nature. Thus, Madison tells us:

But the most common and durable source of factions has been the various and unequal distribution of property. Those who hold and those who are without property have ever formed distinct interests in society. Those who are creditors, and those who are debtors, fall under a like discrimination. A landed interest, a manufacturing interest, a mercantile interest, a moneyed interest, with many lesser interests, grow up of necessity in civilized nations, and divide them into different classes, actuated by different sentiments and views. The regulation of these various and interfering interests forms the principal task of modern legislation, and involves the spirit of party and faction in the necessary and ordinary operations of the government (*Federalist* #10, para 6).

The major task of the legal edifice, then, is to add stability to the system of property through the structured interplay of all those claiming various property rights.

But, property as right is more than an element of constitutional construction. It enters into the substance of the document as well. Because liberty was so inextricably entwined in the minds of eighteenth-century men with property ownership, the Bill of Rights placed it front and center. Thus, government was prevented, not only from locking you up or, in the worst-case scenario, from stringing you up without jumping through due procedural hoops, but also from taking your property without a similar amount of jumping. So, in its litany of essentials, the Fifth Amendment clearly states that no person shall "be deprived of life, liberty, or *property*, without due process of law; nor shall private property be taken for public use, without just compensation"[21] (emphasis added).

At least two other early legal offshoots of the classical theory of property rights are worth mentioning for their impact on American legal culture.

Property Rights and Land Policy

Hence, as a second outgrowth, as we have seen, Locke himself was well aware that the state of nature days where "property" was widely and freely available to one-and-all had long since passed. *Except*, according to Locke, that there remained on earth a *kind of* state of nature even as late as the eighteenth century. And that *kind of* state of nature was America. "Thus," according to Locke (1960, 319), "in the beginning, all the world was America. . . ." America was a place of vast territory, stretching (endlessly, it must have seemed to an urbanized Englishman) from one ocean to another. In America, property, the essence of individual liberty, was there for the taking. But, of course, America wasn't really the state of nature, so the taking of the essence of individual liberty would proceed, by law, in an orderly fashion. According to Lawrence Friedman, "Public land law [of the late eighteenth century] flowed from one basic choice":

The government did not choose to manage its land as a capital asset, but to get rid of it in an orderly, fruitful way. A whole continent was sold or given away—to veterans, settlers, squatters, railroads, states, colleges, speculators, and land companies. On the surface, one sees in this policy the powerful influence of free enterprise and laissez-faire. The government possessed a resource of incalculable value; but it was determined to denationalize it as soon as possible. True, the land was sold for cash, but money was not used to aggrandize the government. Yet divestment was never the whole policy, nor even the sole reason for policy. The professed social goal was never to make government weaker or smaller; but to create a country of free citizens, living independently on their land (Friedman 1973, 203).

The result has been a persistent cultural mind-set in which property is not some mere theoretical right, but an actual prerogative—certainly, one worth fighting endless legal battles over.[22]

Property Rights and Contract Law

American law and legal culture have also been shaped by liberal notions of contract. Voluntary contract is the foundation of civilized social relationships, and it permeates every aspect of life under liberal theory. Hence, for example, "Conjugal society is made by a voluntary compact between man and woman" (Locke 1960, 337); employers maintain powers over workers "no greater than what is contained in the contract between 'em" (Locke 1960, 340); and civil society is born when some people enter into a covenant with other people "for their comfortable, safe, and peaceable living one amongst another. . . ." (Locke 1960, 349). Private or public, contractual relationships are ubiquitous and, in Western culture, viewed as primal. As one of Locke's liberal progeny (and a name far more familiar to modern Americans), Adam Smith, explains:

Whether this propensity [toward contractual relationship] be one of those original principles in human nature of which no further account can be given; or whether, as seems more probable, it be the necessary consequence of the faculties of reason and speech, it belongs not to our present subject to inquire. It is common to all men, and to be found in no other race of animals, which seem to know neither this nor any other species of contracts. Two greyhounds, in running down the same hare, have sometimes the appearance of acting in some sort of concert. Each turns her towards his companion, or endeavours to intercept her when his companion turns her towards himself. This, however, is not the effect of any contract, but of the accidental concurrence of their passions in the same object at that particular time. Nobody ever saw a dog make a fair and deliberate exchange of one bone for another with another dog. Nobody ever saw one animal by its gestures and natural cries signify to another, this is mine, that yours; I am willing to give this for that. When an animal wants to obtain something either of a man or of another animal, it has no other means of persuasion but to gain the favour of those whose service it requires. A puppy fawns upon its dam, and a spaniel endeavours by a thousand attractions to engage the attention of its master who is at dinner, when it wants to be fed by him. Man sometimes uses the same arts with his brethren, and when he has no other means of engaging them to act according to his inclinations, endeavours by every servile and fawning attention to obtain their good will. He has not time, however, to do this upon every occasion. In civilised society he stands at all times in need of the cooperation and assistance of great multitudes, while his whole life is scarce sufficient to gain the friendship of a few persons. In almost every other race of animals each individual, when it is grown up to maturity, is entirely independent, and in its natural state has occasion for the assistance of no other living creature. But man has almost constant occasion for the help of his brethren, and it is in vain for him to expect it from their benevolence only. He will be more likely to prevail if he can interest their self-love in his favour, and show them that it is for their own advantage to do for him what he requires of them. Whoever offers to another a bargain of any kind, proposes to do this. Give me that which I want, and you shall have this which you want, is the meaning of every such offer; and it is in this manner that we obtain from one another the far greater part of those good offices which we stand in need of. It is not from the benevolence of the butcher, the brewer, or the baker that we expect our dinner, but from their regard to their own interest. We address ourselves, not to their humanity but to their self-love, and never talk to them of our own necessities but of their advantages. Nobody but a beggar chooses to depend chiefly upon the benevolence of his fellow-citizens. Even a beggar does not depend upon it entirely. The charity of well-disposed people, indeed, supplies him with the whole fund of his subsistence. But though this principle ultimately provides him with all the necessaries of life which he has occasion for, it neither does nor can provide him with them as he has occasion for them. The greater part of his occasional wants are supplied in the same manner as those of other people, by treaty, by barter, and by purchase. With the money which one man gives him he purchases food. The old clothes which another bestows upon him he exchanges for other old clothes which suit him better, or for lodging, or for food, or for money, with which he can buy either food, clothes, or lodging, as he has occasion (Smith 1776, Book I, chapter 2).

Sounding the Lockean and Madisonian (i.e., classic seventeenth- and eighteenth-century liberal) themes of intrinsic human selfishness and self-interest, Smith placed the notion of contract squarely among the basic needs of humankind. Of course, there are needs and there are needs. In an age where, at least on European soil, some needers were kings and aristocrats and others were peasants and townsfolk, needs were not equitably distributed, nor were contractual relationships necessarily equitable arrangements. However, with the rise of liberal theory and its emphasis on equality in a nation specifically founded on that equality—one with no manifest aristocracy or inherited status—contract could assume the shape and form of the "true bargain" (Friedman 1973, 245), with significant implications for American law. Thus, "Modern [American] contract law was ... born staunchly proclaiming that all men are equal because all measures of inequality are illusory" (Horwitz 1977, 161). This notion of legal equality under contract, in turn, had four major interrelated consequences for American legal culture.

First, as the "law of contract" became more and more dominant throughout the nineteenth century, it gave a particular cast to the American legal persona. In a very real sense, the rise of contract law was a manifestation of the split American psyche—that which wants law to stand out of the way so that individual initiative can flourish, on the one hand, and that which wants the law to clean up all those individual messes, on the other. Contracts, of course, are primarily private agreements. They are not dominated by government (i.e., legislative or executive) fiat. Rather, government's role in the area of contracts is to enforce, mediate, or resolve disputes arising from these private bargains. As we know, the branch of government charged with mediating and resolving private disputes is the judiciary. Thus, the dominance of contract law assured that Americans would be spending plenty of time in court.

Second, as Smith might have predicted, the dominance of private contract law eased the way for the entrenched place of the competitive market (capitalism) as the driving economic force in America. With the nineteenth-century role of law as mediator rather than dictator, a private market economy could rather easily take hold; hence, his "invisible hand" theory.

Third, while "[c]ontract as a branch of law can best be called residual, [dealing] with those areas of business life not otherwise regulated" (Friedman 1973, 245), it ultimately gave rise to much of twentieth-century positive law, including commercial law, bankruptcy law, consumer law, and insurance law (Friedman 1984a, 143–44).

Finally, contract law fixed in the American psyche, for many decades to come, the notion that we are all legal equals, no matter what the social and economic reality. Under the "will theory [of contractual obligation] with which American [legal] writers expressed the ideology of a market economy in the early nineteenth century" (Horwitz 1977, 185), everybody was on equal negotiating footing—masters with servants, employers with employees, landholders with tenant farmers, and capitalists with laborers. The notion was expressed as late as 1915 by the U.S. Supreme Court:

The principle is fundamental and vital. Included in the right of personal liberty and in the right of private property—partaking of the nature of each—is the right to make contracts. This right is as essential to the laborer as to the capitalist, to the poor as to the rich. . . . (*Coppage v. Kansas*, 236 U.S. 1, at 44 (1915)).[23]

Of course, in reality nothing could have been further from the truth—in real life, absent any leveling of the playing field, masters, employers, landholders, and capitalists can trump servants, employees, tenant farmers, and laborers every time. Thus, throughout the nineteenth century, as courts vigorously enforced the terms of contractual obligations, guess who won almost every time? But, then, the law said all were equal and so be it (more on that, however, later).

*   *   *

From the Founders' liberal intellectual wellspring, then, was born a political economic arrangement in which law played the role of balance beam, a mechanism designed to maintain the delicate equilibrium between individual freedom and independence, on the one hand, and social order, on the other. It was a tall order—one that law attempted to fill by pervading American culture like no other.

Scarcely Any Problem . . . The Dominion of Laws in America

It is now worth repeating, in part, the quote with which we began this chapter: "Scarcely any political question arises in the United States that is not resolved, sooner or later, into a judicial question."[24] Published by a young French visitor in the 1830s as part of a massive cultural/political critique of America, the sentence speaks volumes about the very early legalization of this country. To those who complain so vigorously today about the "hyperlitigiousness" of modern America,[25] one need only point to de Tocqueville's *Democracy in America* as indication that the "good old days" were just as lawsuit crazed, relatively speaking, as the bad old here-and-now. What, after all, are many of the great legal decisions of the nineteenth century but lofty opinions conveniently appended to what might seem like rather petty arguments? We know *Marbury v. Madison*, 5 U.S. 137 (1803), as the great landmark case in which Chief Justice John Marshall established the principle of judicial review, but in its inception it was just some guy claiming he *deserved* a judgeship and *deserved* to have no less than the Supreme Court hand it to him. Would his suit today be called frivolous? Would he be accused of tying up the courts (indeed, *the* Court) with self-indulgent demands? Perhaps.

The point is that the stage was set with law, it was set for Americans to use, and use it Americans did in multiple arenas. After all, the legal structure set down by the framers included federalism, which meant that law would not only (or even mostly) issue from the national government, but from state governments as well, each with its own peculiar constitution, statutes, and regulations. Each state also had its own set of courts to which law-savvy and, more important, *legally enfranchised* citizens could resort to with individual problems and vexing "political question[s]."

Thus, Americans, even in the nineteenth century, were prone to approach the legal bench—the balance beam of law—with all manner of private and public disputes. Indeed, to those, noted above, who complain about the increasing litigiousness of American society *today*, the statistical evidence indicates that our supposedly self-reliant, morally upright forebears were just as, if not more, litigious. For example, a study of litigation even before the Revolution found in Virginia a

litigation rate of 240 per thousand[,] more than four times that in any contemporary American county for which we have data. In a seven-year period, 20% of the adult population appeared in court five or more times as parties or witnesses. In Salem County, Massachusetts, about 11% of the adult males were involved in court conflicts during the year 1683. . . . "[M]ost men living there had some involvement with the court system and many of them appeared repeatedly" (Curtis 1977, 287, cited in Galanter 1983b, 41).

Once independence was achieved, Americans continued to go to court. Thus, Roland Rotunda (1988, 14) notes that "[a] careful study of the statistics shows that the litigation rate in recent years in the United States is about half of what it was during the early nineteenth century. In the federal courts the length of civil cases has also shortened, from about 3.5 years in 1900 to 1.16 years in 1980." An exhaustive study of litigation in St. Louis found "that individual plaintiffs initiated [lawsuits] at a generally higher rate before the Civil War than since" (McIntosh 1990, 79).

True, the claims being pressed by individual litigants in decades and centuries past were different, reflecting respective social and economic pressures and mores. Not surprisingly, in the early nineteenth century, for example, contract and property claims crowded court dockets. At present, family disputes and such tort-based controversies as personal injury and product liability do (McIntosh 1990, 47–76). But, the fact remains there really never was the "golden, prelitigious era" (Galanter 1983b, 11) that some would harken back to.

Moreover, then, as now, law was much more than a sterile and segregated governmental exercise. Then, as now, it suffused American culture—so much so, that de Tocqueville could speak of "all parties [being] obliged to borrow, in their daily controversies, the ideas, and even the language, peculiar to judicial proceedings" (de Tocqueville 1835). Thus, trials of celebrities and interesting or (more likely) tawdry trials involving just plain folk have long been mainstays of the American entertainment milieu—rivaling, in the pre–mass media days, the O. J. Simpson and Louise Woodward spectacles.[26] For example, during the nineteenth century,

Breach-of-promise cases became a genuine social phenomenon. Many people attended trials dealing with broken hearts and broken promises for purposes of entertainment. Presaging modern tabloid journalism, the media of that earlier generation often covered breach-of-promise suits in a manner that veered toward sensationalism. . . . [T]he parties who brought these suits, almost always women, became favorite targets of commentators (Williams 1995, 1025).

Throughout the twentieth century, the media have treated us to (and we have devoured) dozens of "trials of the century." The first *two*, according to *Washington Post* writer Peter Carlson, burst into the headlines in 1907 when a wealthy playboy murdered a famous architect in a tawdry love triangle, and a union leader allegedly tried to hire an assassin to kill a former governor. These two seminal "trials of the century" were followed in breathtaking succession by the 1921 rape trial of actor Fatty Arbuckle; the 1925 Scopes "Monkey Trial"; the 1934 Gloria Vanderbilt custody trial; the 1935 trial of Bruno Richard Hauptmann for kidnapping and murdering Charles Lindbergh's baby; the 1945 Nuremberg trial, in which twenty-two Nazi leaders, including Hermann Goering and Albert Speer, were tried for crimes against humanity; the 1961 trial of Adolf Eichmann, the Nazi concentration camp commandant; the 1969 trial of the Chicago 8, antiwar activists accused of conspiracy to incite riots at the 1968 Democratic National Convention; the 1970 Los Angeles trial of Charles Manson and his hippie "family" for murdering actress Sharon Tate and six other people; the court-martial of Lt. William Calley for murdering scores of Vietnamese civilians at My Lai; the trial of Angela Davis; the trial of Patty Hearst; the Lee Marvin palimony trial; the Pulitzer divorce trial; the trial of subway vigilante Bernhard Goetz; the trial of Claus von Bulow; and the trial of televangelist Jim Bakker. More recent "trials of the century" have included those of Mafia don John Gotti, Mike Tyson, the policemen who assaulted Rodney King, William Kennedy Smith, Mayor Marion Barry, and, of course, O. J. Simpson (Carlson 1999, C1). Oh, and let's not forget the Clinton "trial of the century" by the U.S. Senate.

Like us, our ancestors were not merely content with genuine law, but whiled away the hours between sensational real trials with legal fiction. Hence as law librarian Marlyn Robinson reports,

Modern readers most likely think this explosion [in legal fiction] a recent phenomenon, but before there was [Scott] Turow, there were Voelker and Gardner, Post and Collins, and a host of lesser known lawyer/authors. . . . [For example, in America, Edgar Allen] Poe's influence was immediate and widespread. Sensational mystery stories appeared in newspapers, were serialized in magazines and published in books. Abraham Lincoln was a great admirer of Poe, even writing a story for the Quincy, Illinois Whig on April 15, 1846, titled "The Trailor Murder Mystery." It was based on a peculiar murder/disappearance case he defended, and which is detailed in several biographies (Robinson 1998, 21, 24).

Of course, there was always the other side of the coin as well. As we do now, our progenitors may have loved their law, but they could hate it just as much as we. Yes, they even told nasty lawyer jokes. Thus, for example,

The nineteenth-century readers and spellers of American schoolchildren often contained a game called "the Colonists," which ranked various occupations. Farming, of course, always stood at the head of the list. The attitude toward lawyers was contained in the following quatrain:

To fit up a village with tackle for tillage Jack Carter he took to the saw.

To pluck and to pillage, the same little village Tim Gordon he took to the law (Post 1987, 379).

Probably no one, before or since, could pillory the legal profession quite as well as turn-of-the-century humorist Will Rogers, who said of lawyers, among other things, that

a lawyer writes the way he does "so that endless others of his craft can make a living out of trying to figure out what he said" (Rogers, cited in Vinson 1996);."The minute you read something and you can't understand it, you can be sure it was written by a lawyer" (Rogers, quoted in Emswiler 1994).

"I don't think you can make a lawyer honest by an act of legislature. You've got to work on his conscience. And his lack of conscience is what makes him a lawyer" (Rogers, quoted in Silver 1994, 869).

On observing the Scopes Monkey Trial: "We had that 'monkey trial' down in Tennessee to prove that man descended from the apes but I never believed that. Because I never yet met an ape who was devious, heartless or greedy, I always figured man was descended from lawyers" (Rogers, quoted in Strossen 1993, 2137).[27]

So, even in our romanticized past, law was ubiquitous, everywhere, and all of the time.

Needless to say, the trend, begun by the Founders, toward ever increasing cultural legalization has continued apace. Absolutely speaking, cultural critics can point to more law, in more legal forums, used by more people. But, the *more* being complained about is really just more of the same—more of the American tendency to love, and thus, use the law; more the American tendency to hate, and thus, complain about the law. Several factors have contributed to these tendencies, such as democratization, the growth of the legal profession, the complexity and speed of modern life, more causes of legal action, more and stricter criminal law, a recent shortage in judges, and the pervasiveness of the mass media.

More Democracy = More Law

First, many more people today are legally enfranchised and politically viable than they were during the eighteenth and nineteenth centuries. Then, for the most part, only white men were fully participating members of the polity. Until as late as 1828, even many white men were

denied full participation due to state property requirements on the vote. While nonvoters and the poor were not necessarily barred from using the law to stake personal claims and air political questions, their disenfranchisement severely narrowed the possibilities for success. When the law said all were equal, it also contained a rather odd theoretical notion of equality. Thus, as we know, legal claims revolved largely around property and contracts during the 1800s. This emphasis had enormous implications for the legal empowerment of nonvoters and the nonelite. Recall, for example, the "will theory" of contract mentioned earlier in which the law abstracted every contractual relationship into an equal meeting of minds, determination, and capacity. In fact, this supposedly "neutral" way of applying law "permitted judges to apply the same set of rules that were applicable between sophisticated businessmen of relatively equal information and bargaining power to labor and consumer contracts between vastly unequal parties" (Horwitz 1992, 15). In short, until the late nineteenth century, labor could be expected to lose in court almost every time. An illustration of the problem was the common employment practice of signing up laborers for an extended period of time. Under these contracts, the worker agreed to toil for as long as a year, only *after* which he would receive any wages.

If he left his employment before the end of the term, jurists reasoned, the employee could receive nothing for the labor he had already expended. The contract, they maintained, was an "entire" one, and therefore could not be conceived of as a series of smaller agreements. Since the breach of any part was therefore a breach of the whole, there was no basis for the employee to recover on the contract (Horwitz 1992, 186).

After all, the desperate, uneducated laborer had agreed to the contract and was viewed as the *legal* equal of his employer.[28]

Of course, others were even more disadvantaged. Because married women were largely considered the legal chattel of their husbands, prevented from owning property in their own names or entering into individual business contracts, a trip to the courthouse over such matters would be a meaningless adventure at best. One need only look at the century's most notorious case, that of *Dred Scott v. Sanford*, 60 U.S. 393 (1856),[29] to realize the discouraging legal horizons confronting the nation's largest minority population.

Of course, between 1865 and 1870, the Thirteenth Amendment freed the slaves, the Fifteenth enfranchised men of color, and the Fourteenth specifically invalidated the Supreme Court's *Dred Scott* decision. Roughly five decades later, the Nineteenth Amendment opened the doors of active citizenship to women. An exceedingly hard-fought and bloody labor movement, combined with the growth and growing political power of the middle class, succeeded finally in affording workers *some* measure of bargaining power with employers and *some* measure of legislative protection. Eventually, in true American fashion, all these and successive new political participants would take advantage of the truest of American mainstays, the law. More democracy meant more law.

More Lawyers = More Law

Second, as seen in chapter 5, the profession of law in America has been a real growth industry. Today, lawyers number approximately 900,000, meaning that in the United States, for every thirty people, there is a lawyer.[30] That number is expected to rise substantially by the year 2005.[31] Such was not always the case. As Lawrence Friedman reports:

There was a time, long ago—a golden age, if you will—when there were very few lawyers in what is now the United States. In some colonies, especially those dominated by the clergy, there was a good deal of hostility to lawyers. It may or may not be significant that Plymouth Colony, in the seventeenth century, expelled its first lawyer, Thomas Morton, for various "misdemeanors," including trading with the Indians, drinking to excess, and other "beastly practices" (Friedman 1984a, 231).

"Beastly practices," indeed. And we thought lawyers were unpopular today!

From such beastly beginnings, however, the profession blossomed, experiencing a major growth spurt after the Revolution. After all, a government of "laws" would always need some "men" knowledgeable in its ways, particularly where there were land deals to be fought and won, contracts to be signed and disputed, and debts to be accrued and collected. Nineteenth-century America was ripe for the flowering of the legal profession, with "lawyers increas[ing] far faster than the population" (Friedman 1984a, 268–79). The profession kept flowering and flowering. Thus, the number of lawyers more than doubled during the two decades between 1880 and the turn of the century; even as courtroom work decreased, "lawyers prospered," proving themselves "exceedingly nimble at finding new kinds of work and new functions" in an increasingly complex economy with all its increasingly complex laws (Friedman 1984a, 549–50).

Yet, all that was a mere budding compared to the real blossoming that burst forth during the latter half of the twentieth century. Hence, in 1950, there were roughly 250,000 lawyers nationwide. There are more than three and one-half times that many today (Wice 1991, 35).

Why such constant, colossal growth in the profession? One explanation lies in the increasing democratization of society as a whole, a process reflected as well in the bar. Although the profession of law had always been relatively friendly to the sons of the middle class, the middle class itself was fairly small and very white throughout the nineteenth century, and the profession's congeniality toward sons was literal—daughters need not apply. As the middle class expanded over the course of the twentieth century to include many more white sons and a goodly number of nonwhite sons and daughters of all colors, so too did the American bar.[32]

But, of course, there was more to the growth in lawyering than mere democratization of the ranks. The move from a simple agrarian society to a complex industrial society requiring, eventually, an ever more elaborate regulatory state, to the tangled technology-based society of today, has meant ever more legal work. In complex societies, people and human entities such as corporations increasingly need mediators to negotiate their relationships, represent their interests, mediate their disputes, and challenge their grievances—all the things that lawyers do, and all the things that lawyers do in the confounding language and conduct of the law.

Increasing Complexity = More Law

Apart from the role of lawyers, the sheer complexity of modern life has added to the depth and breadth of the law. Save perhaps a few self-styled "survivalists," we are no longer even marginally self-sufficient. We literally depend upon others for everything—from the radio that wakes us in our bank-mortgaged or landlord-owned home, to our morning toilet and breakfast, to the schools at which we deposit our children early in the day, to the computer networks on which we work, to the car that carries us home on publicly maintained roads, to our evening entertainment. Because we are today so thoroughly dependent, when accidents occur or problems develop, we can almost always blame it on someone else. The more grievous problems and the more irreconcilable blames become fodder for legal action.

As numerous social observers have pointed out over the course of the twentieth century, the sheer complexity of modern living has tended to increase feelings of alienation, anomie, and anxiety. Social institutions that may once have worked to address individual problems now seem distant and removed, focusing on the global rather than the personal. In these respects, the labyrinthine bureaucratic state may act to increase the overall attractiveness of courts:

Unlike our other institutions . . . , courts are theoretically open to the idiosyncratic problems of ordinary people. Executive agencies and legislatures are more in the business of promulgating rules with general scope. . . . Indeed, courts are better equipped than other agencies of government to respond to individual claimants, and to address individual problems expediently (if not expeditiously) and with greater freedom of option (judges still retain a great deal of discretion) (McIntosh 1990).

Or, as former Chief Judge Rose Bird of the California Supreme Court once said in an opinion: "In almost no other context within our governmental system does an individual have the opportunity to take a problem straight to the decision makers who represent the full force and power of that particular branch of government."[33]

Finally, the pace of modern society—so much faster than that of our forebears—increases the possibilities for legal action. Quite simply, the margin for error has become increasingly smaller. Our ability to inflict harm quickly and on a large scale has been considerably enhanced by interdependency and technology. Thus, a satellite suddenly spins out of control, disrupting communications for millions, including emergency hospital personnel[34]; an overworked shipmate falls asleep at the wheel of an enormous oil tanker causing massive wildlife and coastline damage[35]; a nuclear facility rapidly melts down, contaminating a huge geophysical region for decades, perhaps centuries, to come[36]; and lethal gases escape from a factory and kill thousands within just a few weeks.[37] Such is the stuff of modern life, of modern litigation.

More Causes of Action = More Law

More democratic demands by more democratic participants coupled with more lawyers to articulate those demands in an increasingly complicated society meant, over the course of the twentieth century, an escalation in the legal causes over which people could sue and expect to recover damages. Thus, the nation's extensive history of discrimination began a long overdue era of redress after mid-century, marked, particularly, by all manner of civil rights legislation that allowed the victims of discrimination (racial,[38] followed by age,[39] gender,[40] and then disability[41]) to take their grievances to court. In addition, such modern concerns as the perceived continuing degradation of the environment,[42] threats to safe working conditions,[43] and the increasing number of Americans receiving governmental entitlements,[44] to name just three broad categories, increased the opportunities for legal action, especially in the federal court system.

Fear of Crime = More Law

Particularly during the 1980s and 1990s, the public's perception of rising and more heinous criminal activity and politicians' reactions to and willingness to capitalize on such perceptions, spurred a great deal of legislative activity—more actions were criminalized, were criminalized federally,[45] and were criminalized with more severe sanctions. This activity increased the caseload of the nation's courts, causing backlogs in civil cases, which in turn, heightens feelings that there's too much court activity going on.[46]

Fewer Judges = Slower Law

At the same time that lawmakers (especially federal lawmakers) have been filling the nation's court dockets with criminal cases, they have been slow to fill judicial vacancies. This problem was particularly acute in the late 1990s, due in large part to partisan logjams between President Clinton and the Republican Senate. The administration itself was slow to name replacements for retired district court and appellate judges, and the Senate was slow to act on or refused to begin consideration of nominees. Thus, in mid-1998, eighty-five federal judgeships were vacant, and forty-seven judicial nominations were pending in the Senate.[47] Again, the result is backlog and attendant public perceptions of too much litigation.

More Media = (The Perception of) More Law

Finally, the mass media have probably greatly exaggerated our perceptions of the law—not so much in terms of its ubiquity (for so it is and ever was) as in terms of its use, or, in the view of many, its misuse. Where our nineteenth-century forebears had actually to walk down the street to see a lawyer, ride into town to buy the latest legal thriller, or buggy to the county seat to catch a juicy trial, today the law is in our living rooms, just a click away by remote control. Court TV, after all, is there to amuse twenty-four hours a day, and the most scintillating legal dramas (remember O. J.?) may even get full network coverage. Then, there are *The Peoples' Court*, *Judge Judy*, and the full array of daytime soaps and nighttime dramas populated by a breed of fictional trial attorneys who never met a case that could be settled outside of court. Of course, for connoisseurs of such morning and afternoon fare as Jerry Springer and Monteil Williams, there's the almost unending parade of advertisements by personal injury lawyers begging for your business. If all that's not enough, for those with the resources to subscribe to premium channels or the initiative to drive to Blockbuster, there's the John Grisham movie of the month.

Moreover, the media tends to play up legal "atrocity stories—that is, citation of cases that seem grotesque, petty, or extravagant" (Galanter 1983b, 10). Recall, for example, the tale of Katie Rose Sawyer and Cody Finch with which we began this chapter—obviously *not* legal business as usual, but legal business well documented, nonetheless, by the nation's press. Then, of course, what American hasn't rolled his eyeballs at the story of the "McDonald's Coffee Lady," now a virtual household term? Add to that such media favorites as the ex-Mouseketeer who took Disneyland to court because her grandchildren saw Mickey take his head off,[48] or the California parents who sued when their daughter lost a spelling bee,[49] or the high school student who filed suit over a broken prom date.[50] Surely, we could all agree that this is the stuff of litigation run amok! The problem with such an understandable reaction is that it is based, at best, on a distortion of reality.

The media broadcast such tales precisely *because* they are unusual—unusually capricious, unusually stupid, or unusually cute. In addition, the media usually only tell part of the tale. The fact is that sometimes such cases sound ridiculous when reduced to two paragraphs in a newspaper "style" section, but are really serious, legitimate claims.[51] On the other hand and not infrequently, the truly frivolous case is actually dismissed by the court in which it is filed as—guess what?—frivolous! The fact that the case is dismissed, however, never garners as prominent a place or as much newsprint or anywhere near the commentary as its filing, leaving the public to believe that such cases are the chief culprits clogging our courts and destroying our culture.[52]

Not infrequently, then, such "atrocity stories" have a way of permutating into legal "war stories" (Galanter 1983b, 10), used by politicians (many of whom are themselves lawyers[53]) and corporate leaders to demonstrate "that *excessive* litigation places [burdens] on society" (emphasis added).[54] Or, more boldly, as in the words of House Majority Whip John Kasich (R-OH), to make the point that "Everybody in America is fed up with being sued by everybody for everything."[55]

Ubiquity and Ambiguity in the New Millennium

So, law continues to fill every nook and cranny of American life, causing us—as it ever has—to simultaneously exploit it and excoriate it. But does it still, in the twenty-first century, function (or try to function) as society's balance beam, perched precariously as the counterweight between our conflicting appetites for liberty, on the one hand, and order, on the other?

In 1937, against a backdrop of increasing demands for social justice and individual rights, Justice Benjamin Cardozo coined the phrase "ordered liberty" (*Palko v. Connecticut*, 302 U.S. 319, at 325 (1937)). Some rights, he reasoned, were so fundamental, so intrinsic, that "neither liberty nor justice would exist if they were sacrificed" (*Palko*, 326). Not surprisingly, he placed the law, over which he and his eight colleagues on the Supreme Court were given final say, front and center in the task of ordering liberty. In ways great and small, this has remained the task of law in the new millennium.

In great ways, it is easiest to see and most difficult to achieve. In small ways, it is more obscure, but more mundane in its accomplishments and errors. The great ways still make their passage to the nation's highest court, although now involving nuances undreamed of by Cardozo. Clearly, for example, it was Cardozo's belief that "neither liberty nor justice would exist if . . . free-

dom of thought, and speech . . . were sacrificed." "Of that freedom," he opined, "one may say that it is the matrix, the indispensable condition, of nearly every other form of freedom" (*Palko*, 326–27). Doubtless, Justice Cardozo had in mind what today might seem the rather quaint practices of political pamphleteering and town square oration, along with more standard contemporary fare as radio broadcast commentary and the mass-distributed printed press. Just as doubtless, however, he did not have in mind the Internet. Yet, his successors, inevitably, are being asked to sort through the ancient dilemma of liberty versus order in that most modern of venues.

Thus, in *Reno v. ACLU*, 521 U.S. 844 (1997), for the first time, the Supreme Court confronted the clash between free speech and public morality on the World Wide Web. In an attempt to address public concerns over the easy accessibility of pornography on the Internet, Congress passed the *Communications Decency Act of 1996* (CDA), prohibiting the knowing transmission to minors of "indecent" or certain "patently offensive" communications. Although the Court acknowledged that the community has a "legitima[te] and importan[t] . . . goal [in] protecting children from harmful materials," it nonetheless found the CDA to be a patent violation of "'the freedom of speech' protected by the First Amendment" (*Reno*, at LEXIS p*10). In other words, in cases such as these, society's order interest has to be both compelling and narrowly tailored to overcome the individual's liberty interest. Whether immersed in issues of communication, criminal justice, property ownership, civil rights, or any of the myriad of weighty concerns that make up the docket of the high court, in one way or another, law continues, more than two centuries after Madison penned the *Federalist Papers*, to play the balance beam in the inexorable struggle between freedom and social control.

In small ways, the law's attempt to balance individual liberty interests against society's need for order is the everyday stuff of litigation. For instance, I freely enter into an arrangement with a local contractor who agrees to renovate my kitchen for a specified amount within a specified period of time. When, one year later, I am still barbequing in the freezing cold, drinking tap water from the bathroom sink, and keeping milk in my now-leaking cooler, I take the bum to court. I am seeking to preserve my interests, but within the orderly framework of the judicial system. That very afternoon, the police arrest my neighbor, John Q. Public, for holding up a nearby 7-Eleven. Although they are clearly law's frontline agents of order, the police presumably must make some effort to preserve John's liberty interests, informing him in some manner of his basic rights even as he is held in custody. Meanwhile, two blocks down, my town's most notorious eccentric begins painting his house day-glow pink and installing a front-yard still, all toward realizing his dream of running a successful brew pub and exotic dance theatre. It is *his* property, after all, the essence, he claims as a good classical liberal, of his liberty. But we, his neighbors, worry about the stability of our environs—that is, about the value of *our* property. So, armed with a variety of local ordinances and zoning laws, we take him to court. Late that night, my best friend decides she can no longer tolerate living with her husband of twenty years. She could just steal away in the dark, reveling in her newfound independence. But, over the course of two decades and under the weight of a state-issued marriage license, she has accumulated, with her now estranged mate, a house full of furniture, a sizable joint mutual fund, six "gold cards" worth of debt, and, oh yes, three kids. Of course, she begins combing the yellow pages for a good divorce attorney. And, so it goes.

Needless to say, all of this activity (great and small) in which we turn to the law to solve the primal American conflict between liberty and order further exacerbates our countervailing tendency to turn away from law—to condemn its "dominion" over our existence. Inevitably, when my rich contractor manages to win a favorable judgment after a long, exhausting adjudication, I grouse about the "unfairness" of the system. Likewise, a miserable John Q. Public, while privately maintaining his innocence, nonetheless feels himself forced into a plea bargain, which includes a year in jail. My neighbor, compelled by a court order to rip out his beer-making paraphernalia, joins a local militia bent on subverting formal law. My friend, several years later, is disheartened by the court's inability to extract any of the legally required child support payments from her ex-husband. Groups supporting censorial controls on Internet content are dismayed by the ability of nine unelected justices to stymie such controls in the name of abstract concepts such as free speech. The split American legal psyche is alive and well.

*   *   *

In this, and the previous chapter, we have explored the general terrain of law, both law in its broadest senses and law in the American context. Now that we have reviewed the basic principles and themes of law, we turn to the institutions, processes, and actors that give life and meaning to the law in society in chapter 4.

Law on the Web

Helpful Hints

This chapter has concentrated heavily on historical documents, and the Web contains many excellent sites for easily accessing such items. But, in our own searches for such websites, we have run across many that are questionable for the purposes of scholarly research and reliance. Therefore, this might be a good place to talk about discriminating among websites on the Internet.

A good rule of thumb is to always be aware of the site's domain. Currently, the Internet assigns addresses according to the field of endeavor (or domain) of the user. For example, if you see *.gov* in an address it means the site is maintained by a government agency, and *.edu* indicates the website of an educational institution, such as your university or college. The designation *.org* means the page sponsor is a nongovernmental organization, such as the American Civil Liberties Union or the Christian Coalition. When you see *.com*, it means the site was put there by a commercial concern, a business of some type. Next, *.mil* would indicate a military site, and *.net* refers to network resources or to sites of those who maintain the network. In addition, sites maintained or created by individuals abroad may indicate their origin. For example, British sites generally contain *.uk* as an indicator; Canadian sites, *.ca*, and Australian sites, *.au*.

When doing academic research, it is generally (although by no means always) best to look first to websites containing *.gov* or *.edu* if such sites are available and useful to your area of interest. Given their mission, we expect government agencies and academic institutions to offer us complete and relatively unbiased information. Of course, there are enormous exceptions to this rule. Your member of Congress by now probably has his or her own web page. That page will have a *.gov* designation. Your member of Congress also probably has lots of opinions on lots of subjects and given the natural partisanship of legislative bodies, his or her opinions on subjects may be pretty biased. Similarly, you may find yourself smack in the middle of a page set up by some professor, with a duly assigned *.edu*. Well, professors very often harbor and disseminate distinct ideological preferences. The point here is to be careful.

Now, having said that in general (if not in particular cases) *.gov* and *.edu* are the preferable ways to go in the world of scholarly web research, this is not to say that all other domains must be avoided. On the contrary, there are many excellent and wonderfully informative commercial and organizational websites on the net. For example, if you want to do research on freedom of speech, by all means visit the American Civil Liberties Union (ACLU) site (www.aclu.org/); it's very extensive. But during your visit, remember that the ACLU has a perspective and that colors what it offers you. Similarly, if you are doing research on church–state relations, you may well find the Christian Coalition's site very useful (www.cc.org/). As good as its information may be, the Coalition's site will be biased. Let's say you want to do research on abortion, and specifically, statistics on public support for choice. Logically, you might want to visit the sites of some of the organizations aligned on either side of the issue. You might, for instance visit the site of the National Abortion Rights Action League (NARAL) (www.naral.org/), a mainstream pro-choice group, and then visit the site of the National Right to Life Committee (NRLC) (www.nrlc.org/), a mainstream pro-life group. Notably, both groups use statistics from the same source, the Alan Guttmacher Institute (www.agi-usa.org/). But, just as notably, NARAL spins those statistics to demonstrate widespread support for rights a la *Roe v. Wade*, while NRLC spins them to show declining public approval for abortion.

Commercial (*.com*) sites may contain terrific and terrifically useful information as well. After all, many of the best general-purpose, law-related sites are commercially maintained. Again, always proceed with caution. Commercial sites may contain some bias and they may be trying to sell you something. In any event, when you are utilizing a site that may contain biased or otherwise questionable information, always try to check that information elsewhere, if possible. Whether or not you can double check, you should always be aware of the site's bias and you should always let the reader of your work know that you are aware of the bias and what the bias is.

Of course, you know (and no doubt so would your audience) all about the biases of such organizations as the ACLU, the Christian Coalition, NARAL, and NRLC. However, sometimes you'll be surfing the web, find a page that has what seems like great information, but other than an indecipherable address, seemingly no other identification. Be extra wary here. You may be able to find out who put the site up through the "page source" and "page information" viewers. Or, you may be able to follow an embedded link back to its homepage. A colleague tells a story of an otherwise very diligent student who turned in a wonderful report on smoking hazards. The very scientific, detailed data came from the web. But when the professor and the student followed the page back to its source, they discovered (much to the embarrassment of the student), that it was collected and posted by an eighth-grade kid! We have nothing against eighth graders and we're sure you don't either, but we're also certain that you wouldn't want to base a graduate dissertation, senior thesis, or even a freshman term paper on one of their research efforts.

You'll also find lots of very slick-looking political pages on the web that are chock-full of opinion and data, but not identifying an organization with which you're familiar. Be very careful of these, too. Sometimes they're simply the random thoughts of Joe Schmoe, individual webster, and thus, not useful at all. Sometimes, you'll find such pages linked to various Klan, Nazi, or militia groups. Clearly, the web should be available to a huge range of political ideas, including those we don't agree with, find distasteful, or find repulsive, but most likely you wouldn't want to use information posted by the Ku Klux Klan as the basis of your research efforts.

Which brings us specifically to the wealth of historical data and documents now posted on the web. As seen be-low, all of the great historical figures mentioned in this chapter, including Locke, Madison, and de Tocqueville, are well represented on the Internet. But, as you may discover, many of these writings have been posted by groups with a distinct political perspective. Normally, these groups—even the most extreme—simply upload documents intact, and then provide commentary. But sometimes, they very selectively edit the documents to give them the correct spin. Very occasionally, they will actually change wording to fit their purposes. Thus, one more true cautionary tale, this one, from firsthand experience.

A couple of years ago, one of our students was writing a paper on the separation of church and state. A pioneering soul (a mere four years ago when this occurred!), he decided to do much of his research on the net. In order to make the point that the "wall of separation" was never so very high or solid as some would suggest, he quoted at length from a nineteenth-century judicial opinion. Now, nineteenth-century jurists often referred to God, and even Christianity, as the foundation of the United States, but this particular opinion seemed, very suspiciously even for the nineteenth century, to be suggesting no "wall" at all! As it turns out, the student's version of the opinion had been posted by a far right-wing fundamentalist group, which not only had selectively edited the real opinion to suit its purposes, but had actually added whole phony phrases. The point, again: Be careful and always double check.

Indeed, when using the web to access historical documents we strongly suggest that you *always* check the net document against a library hard copy. In terms of historical manuscripts, the Internet is most useful in allowing you to copy and paste passages to your own word-processed paper. (That is what we did, for example, with *The Federalist Papers* and passages from de Tocqueville.) But those passages should carefully be checked against real library hard copy. (Again, that is what we did.)

If it seems that we used a lot of probablies, maybes, sometimes, and other weasel words in this section, you're right. The fact of the matter is that when using the World Wide Web to do research, you have to use your own good judgment as a scholar. At this point in your careers, we assume that you don't simply accept something because it appears in a library book. The same principle applies to Internet research, only more so. Be critical, do *not* accept words, phrases, and statistics just because they are there in hypertext.

Appearing below are some good sources for historical data.

A Smattering of Early Classical Liberals

John Locke, Second Treatise on Government

www.swan.ac.uk/poli/texts/locke/lockcont.htm

The entire *Second Treatise* by Locke, viewable and downloadable in a convenient chapter-by-chapter format. The site is maintained by the University of Wales at Swansea.

John Locke, Additional Works

weber.ucsd.edu/~dmckiern/locke.htm

This site, maintained through the Division of Social Sciences, University of California, Santa Barbara, contains links to many of Locke's works.

Adam Smith, *An Inquiry into the Nature and Causes of the Wealth of Nations*

www.bibliomania.com/NonFiction/Smith/Wealth/

This site, maintained by Bibliomania, contains *The Wealth of Nations*, conveniently divided into chapters.

Modern History Sourcebook, Montesquieu: *The Spirit of the Laws*, 1748

www.fordham.edu/halsall/mod/montesquieu-spirit.html

Edited version of Montesquieu's views on separation of powers, which were so influential with the American Founders. This is contained in a nicely done "History Sourcebook," edited by Paul Halsall at Fordham University.

Thomas Hobbes, *Leviathan*

www.vt.edu/vt98/academics/books/hobbes/leviathan

Maintained through Virginia Tech University.

A Smattering of American Historical Documents

Great Political Documents Page

www.hn.psu.edu/faculty/jmanis/document.htm

This site, maintained through Penn State, Hazleton, allows you to download important historical political documents in Adobe portable document format (PDF).

Constitutional Documents for Downloading

www.law.uiuc.edu/fac/rrotunda/www/const.htm

Just as the name suggests. Site is maintained through the College of Law, University of Illinois at Urbana-Champaign.

Search All Historical Documents

lcweb2.loc.gov/const/mdbquery.html

Library of Congress service allows you to do word searches of early congressional documents (including the Declaration of Independence, the Federalist Papers, and the Constitution).

Milestone Historical Documents

www.earlyamerica.com/earlyamerica/milestones/

Includes The Newburgh Address, The Whiskey Rebellion, Proclamation of Neutrality, The Treaty of Greenville, Thomas Paine's "Common Sense," The Non-Importation Agreement, The Articles of Confederation,

George Washington's Journal, The Declaration of Arms, The Paris Peace Treaty of 1783, Letter of Transmittal of the U.S. Constitution, Declaration of Rights, Jay's Treaty, The Northwest Ordinance, the *Alien and Sedition Act*, and Washington's Farewell Address.

The Declaration of Independence

lcweb2.loc.gov/const/declar.html

Search Documents from the Continental Congress and Constitutional Convention

lcweb2.loc.gov/const/ccongquery.html

Includes 273 documents from the Continental Congress and the Constitutional Convention, 1774–89, in searchable form. Also links to documents in browsable form.

The Articles of Confederation

www.earlyamerica.com/earlyamerica/milestones/articles/text.html

Federalist Papers Search

www.law.emory.edu/pub-cgi/usfedwais

An excellent searchable version of the *Federalist Papers*, provided by Emory University's Law School.

Federalist Papers Search

lcweb2.loc.gov/const/fedquery.html

Another excellent searchable site for the *Federalist Papers*.

The Papers of James Madison

www.virginia.edu/pjm/

As the title suggests, this University of Virginia site allows you to access Madisonian documents. Includes a biography and history.

Thomas Jefferson, the Film by Ken Burns, Public Broadcasting System

www.pbs.org/jefferson/

Very good site created in conjunction with the PBS television presentation of *Jefferson*, by Ken Burns. Among other features, you can explore Jefferson's most important and controversial writings, and transcripts of twenty-four interviews conducted for the film, many featuring scholars' interpretations of Jefferson's elusive phrase, "pursuit of happiness."

Thomas Jefferson on Politics & Government: Quotations from the Writings of Thomas Jefferson

etext.virginia.edu/jefferson/quotations/

As the name suggests.

Constitution Search

lcweb2.loc.gov/const/constquery.html

A searchable version of the Constitution.

The U.S. Constitution

www.law.cornell.edu/constitution/constitution.overview.html

The Constitution annotated and in section-by-section format, from Cornell University Law School.

The U.S. Constitution

lcweb2.loc.gov/const/const.html

The Bill of Rights

lcweb2.loc.gov/const/bor.html

Constitutional Amendments, XI–XXVII

lcweb2.loc.gov/const/bor.html

About the Constitution of the United States

lcweb2.loc.gov/const/abt_const.html

Brief history and explanation of the Constitution with links to appropriate provisions.

The Alexis de Tocqueville Tour Exploring Democracy in America

www.c-span.org/alexis/

An excellent site maintained by C-SPAN. Includes biographical information on Alexis de Tocqueville, modern references to de Tocqueville and his writings, information on de Tocqueville's visit to America, the text of *Democracy in America*, and other resources.

Henry David Thoreau

history.hanover.edu/19th/thoreau.htm

Provided by Hanover College, contains "Civil Disobedience," among other works.

4   In and Around the Web: The Structures and Processes of Law

The Structure of the Web: State and Federal Court Systems

The next time you are outdoors—in a garden, on a deck, in the woods—or the next time you find yourselves in the throes of writer's block, fixating on a long-neglected ceiling corner, take note of the spider's handiwork. What, at first glance, may appear to be a mess of tangled strings is actually a purposefully designed edifice. The spider's web has structure. True, to those nonentomologists among us, the web may appear disorderly, dumbfounding, and difficult to comprehend, but toward the spider's purpose (and, presumably, to the entomologist's eye), the thing has a certain deliberate order. This is true of the law as well—it too has structure. Like the spider's web, the web of law is very complex and, except to insiders, may seem entirely bewildering, but it has structure.

The structure of the American legal web, and thus its complexity, is driven by the principles of separation of powers, checks and balances, and federalism. So, theoretically, the task of law is divided among lawmakers (the legislative branch), law enforcers (the executive branch), and law interpreters (the judicial branch). Of course, even theoretically, the edifice began to teeter right from the beginning because the Founders, in attempting to make "ambition . . . counteract ambition," added checks and balances to the mix, giving the lawmakers power over the enforcers and interpreters, the law enforcers power over the makers and interpreters, and the law interpreters power over the makers and enforcers. Moreover, they threw federalism into the mix, resulting in the whole system replicating itself over (today) fifty additional systems. Thus, even in its most pristine, original form, the structure of American law is very complicated.

Because of the complexity and vastness of the legal web, in the rest of this chapter we concentrate on that portion of the structure most closely identified with the day-to-day functioning and delivery of the law, the American court system, which in turn, creates a complex web within the web of law. We begin with a very brief and general discussion of court organizing principles. From there, we move on to that point in the web where most of us having direct contact with the law would meet it, the state court system. Finally, we examine the federal court system, a somewhat more rarefied, though certainly intermeshed, portion of the legal web.

Court Organization and Structure: General Principles

In many ways, although courts tend to be the most mysterious of our governmental institutions, they tend to be the most familiar part of the legal system. When we think about the law, we usually have courts in mind. This tends to be the case even though most of us do not have much experience with courts. You may serve on a jury or go to traffic court or go through a divorce, but very few laypeople, except, of course, for jurors and a few litigants, have ever experienced a real live trial. Moreover, when we move beyond the trial courts up to the level of appeals courts, generally only lawyers and judges are directly involved.

On the other hand, almost everybody has watched a TV or movie trial. As suggested in chapter 3, litigation has been a staple of American entertainment since the time of the Founders. Whether it comes packaged as the real thing (in the forms of gavel-to-gavel O. J. Simpson coverage, or the endless leaks and rumors that made up the news of President Clinton's legal/political woes, or the full platter of murders and romantic misadventures that constitute the daily fare offered by Court TV), as the semi-real thing (in the ever stern but fair judgments of Judges Joe Brown and Judy), or as pure fiction (in such forms as Scott Turow novels, John Grisham movies, or any one of the many lawyer-centered dramas that have been a mainstay of television since the 1950s), the media is where most of us get our impressions of the system and structure of our courts.

Now there is certainly nothing wrong with court-based entertainment—indeed, it can be absolutely riveting, sometimes a lot of fun, and occasionally even educational. It is riveting and fun because court-based entertainment tends to focus on the unusually dramatic, the unusually glamorous, and the unusually horrific. It is occasionally educational because it offers us a slice of law, usually in easily digestible form. At the same time, however, these entertainment-oriented attributes can be very misleading. As unusual as the entertainment bill of fare is, the real work of courts, more often than not, is the stuff of everyday life, and as simple as TV makes it all seem, the American court system is incredibly complex—a huge web of detailed yet overlapping jurisdictional boundaries.

Indeed, let us begin with the term *jurisdiction* for it is key to the organization and work of the courts. Jurisdiction has to do with the legal limitations on the types of cases a court may hear and decide. Jurisdiction may be set by a constitution, or, in the case of supreme courts, largely by the court itself, but the most common source of court jurisdiction is the legislature. Thus, as much as we may like to think of the law as being above politics, in fact, even on this most basic point—the kinds of cases courts can hear and decide—legislative politics is the starting point.

How do legislatures, or constitutions, or sometimes courts, classify jurisdiction? Generally, according to three kinds of considerations: geography, subject, and function.

First, courts are authorized to hear and decide conflicts that arise within specific *geographical jurisdictions.* For instance, a Maryland court has no jurisdiction to try a person accused of committing a crime in Oregon. Further, a court's political boundaries (i.e., its geographical jurisdiction) are typically drawn along the lines of other governmental bodies such as cities, counties, or states. Hence, the trial court for Baltimore County, Maryland, would generally not have jurisdiction over a crime or civil suit arising in Prince George's County, Maryland.

Jurisdiction is also determined by *subject* matter. For example, state trial courts of limited jurisdiction (which we shall discuss subsequently) are restricted to hearing a circumscribed category of cases, typically misdemeanor crimes and civil suits involving small amounts of money. In contrast, trial courts of general jurisdiction are empowered to hear all other types of cases (generally speaking, cases the legislature deems more serious such as criminal felonies and civil claims with no dollar limitations). In addition, certain types of cases are not allowed to be brought to court. For instance, courts have no jurisdiction to decide church disputes over doctrinal matters. Or, for another example, the U.S. Supreme Court will not hear cases involving so-called "political questions," although, as we discuss below, what constitutes a political question changes from Court to Court and era to era.

Finally a court's jurisdiction is set by *functional* considerations. Functionally, a court may have either *original jurisdiction* or *appellate jurisdiction,* and some courts have both. Most courts in this country are courts of original jurisdiction, which means they have the authority to hear and decide a case in the first instance—in other words, if there is to be a trial, here is where it occurs. Appellate jurisdiction, on the other hand, means that a court has the authority to review cases that have already been decided by a court of original jurisdiction or a trial court.

The principal difference between a trial and an appeal is that a trial focuses on determining facts, whereas an appeal focuses on correctly interpreting the law. Obviously, both sets of courts are dealing with facts and law, but the principal focus is different. So, for example, if a person is charged with committing murder, the trial court's primary job is going to be to consider and weigh evidence and witnesses about the alleged facts of that murder—whether the defendant could be placed at the scene of the crime, whether the weapon used was hers, whether she had a motive, and so on.

Now, let's say that our ill-begotten friend is convicted of the abovementioned crime. A criminal defendant who loses at trial can appeal her case. She would appeal alleged legal errors. She might claim, for example, that the police seized the weapon from her home illegally and then, further, that the court compounded the error by allowing the weapon to be introduced at trial. Or she might claim that the judge gave biased instructions to the jury, or that the judge allowed the prosecutor to proceed in a prejudicial manner. These are all questions of law and these are the kinds of questions an appellate court would consider. To take some well-known real life examples, had Mr. Simpson been convicted, he would have appealed, for instance, the judge's allowing his friend to relate the content of a dream in court. He would have contended that as a matter of legal procedure—of law—Judge Ito should not have allowed a witness to talk about what he claims the defendant related to him about a dream.[1] Similarly, Timothy McVeigh appealed his Oklahoma bombing conviction on grounds of "juror misconduct, unfair exclusion of evidence that 'someone else may have committed the bombing,' prejudicial pretrial publicity and inflammatory testimony by victims' relatives" ("McVeigh Conviction, Sentence Upheld," 1998).[2] Appeals courts consider these kinds of questions, and only rarely do they go over the facts again.

Because of this difference in function, trial and appeals courts operate very differently. In appellate courts, no witnesses are heard, no trials are conducted, and juries are never used. Indeed, the appeals process is often entirely conducted on the basis of paper records and briefs, although in some cases the lawyers representing both sides will present their arguments orally. In addition, instead of a single judge deciding, which is the norm in trial courts, groups of judges generally make appellate decisions. Most appeals courts most of the time assign three judges to hear cases, although some courts, such as the U.S. Supreme Court, utilize all of their judges almost all of the time, and others will, in rare, extremely controversial cases, vote to hear a case *en banc,* bringing all of the court's judges together.[3] Finally, where appellate judges often will provide written reasons justifying their decisions, trial court judges hardly ever do.

Our system of federalism, too, has jurisdictional implications. We are blessed (or cursed, depending on your perspective) with a dual court system in this country: one national system and fifty state systems—in other words, fifty-one court systems. To put it in overly simplistic terms, federal courts have exclusive jurisdiction over federal laws and state courts have exclusive jurisdiction over state laws, but this is indeed an oversimplification.

The basis for federal court jurisdiction is the U.S. Constitution. Over the years, this vague jurisdictional outline has been fleshed out by Congress in numerous detailed statutes. While these rules are very complicated, according to Lawrence Baum (1998, 23), it is possible to boil federal jurisdiction down into three broad categories:

1. *Federal question jurisdiction* is based on the subject matter of cases. Federal courts are entitled to hear all civil and criminal cases that are based on the U.S. Constitution, on treaties with other nations, and on federal statutes.
2. *Federal party jurisdiction* consists of cases in which the federal government is a party. Nearly all cases brought by or against the federal government, a federal agency, or a federal officer can be heard in federal court.
3. *Diversity jurisdiction* is based on geography. Federal courts can hear cases in which there is a diversity of citizenship between the parties (if they are citizens of different states or if one is a citizen of a foreign nation), as long as the suit is for $75,000 or more.

Some disputes involve both state and federal law. For instance, narcotics possession or transporting kidnap victims across state lines violate both federal and state laws, which means the accused could be tried twice. Or, a particular act may violate one set of state laws and an entirely different set of federal laws. An obvious example of this would be the police officers involved in the infamous Rodney King beating. They were accused of violating a variety of state assault laws; they were also accused of violating the federal civil rights law—same act, but two different sets of laws were at issue and two different jurisdictions involved. Indeed, dual jurisdictional crimes have been increasing at an enormous rate over the past decade, as Congress has moved to federalize more and more criminal activity,[4] involving a substantial number of crimes that previously were the sole domain of state justice systems—everything from narcotics possession to carjackings to failure to pay child support. This congressional tendency to nationalize sanctions for bad behavior contributes mightily to the federal courts' caseload,[5] encourages jurisdiction shopping by aggressive prosecutors, and the blurs lines of sovereign authority and accountability, "threaten[ing]," according to Chief Justice William Rehnquist, "to change entirely the nature of our federal system . . ." (Rehnquist quoted in Suro 1999, A2).

Still, although (literally) millions of cases move through the federal courts every year and the number of these cases is increasing, the fact of the matter is that for most of us who find ourselves in court because of an unhappy marriage, an altercation with a neighbor, or an unlucky highway encounter with a state trooper, our legal adventures will begin and end in a state court system. In fact, of all the cases in the litigation universe, state courts will hear about 98 percent of them. Let us begin, then, with a brief overview of state courts.

The State Court System

State court systems—and the federal system, for that matter—are organized hierarchically. Thus, most state systems feature a series of minor trial courts, major trial courts, a smaller number of intermediate appeals courts, and a single supreme court. To all four of these court prototypes there are exceptions and a great deal of variation, but this four-level pyramid is the general rule.

LOWER TRIAL COURTS

At the bottom of the pyramid, generally, are courts of limited subject jurisdiction or so-called petty grievance courts. Such courts will be located all over a state with a bit more concentration in urban areas. They handle the least serious crimes (e.g., traffic offenses, public drunkenness, and simple trespass) and they handle the least serious civil claims (lawsuits in which, relatively speaking, only a small amount of money is in dispute).[6] These courts go by a lot of different names depending on the jurisdiction and they may be fairly specialized, such as a traffic court, police court, or small claims court. Over the past thirty years, numerous states have moved to consolidate most of these small courts under a single system of limited jurisdiction courts, which handle a variety of matters including traffic offenses, most misdemeanors, landlord-tenant cases, and other small civil suits.[7]

Such courts were originally designed to move justice along a little more quickly and with a bit less formality than a litigant would encounter in the more formal major trial court situation. For example, a typical minor court criminal scenario would involve an arrested individual being brought before a judge or magistrate where the charges against him would be read and where a decision would be made about whether or not the individual is entitled to a state-appointed attorney based on his income. If the defendant is charged with a felony, typically bail will be set at this point and his case referred to the major trial court. However, if he is charged with a misdemeanor the defendant's case may well be disposed of right then and there, usually with the defendant pleading guilty and the judge, magistrate, or, in some cases, a justice of the peace, setting a fine or jail term (Abadinsky 1995, 148–49).

UPPER TRIAL COURTS

As suggested, more serious crimes and weighty financial claims fall under the purview of the major trial courts. These, too, go by a confusing variety of names depending upon the state in which they are located. For example, in Maryland, the major trial courts are called the state circuit courts (not to be confused with the federal circuit courts of appeal); in New York, they are referred to as supreme courts (not to be confused with the U.S. Supreme Court); and in California, they are known as superior courts. Generally speaking, upper-division state courts are drawn around geographical locations, such as a county or very large city. Occasionally, upper-division courts are functionally divided. This is the case in New York's famously byzantine system.[8]

Theoretically, the more formal (and, for aficionados of legal fiction, the more familiar) court procedures click in at the upper-court level. In truth, however, as we discussed in subsequent sections, only a very small percentage of the cases that get filed in the major courts of original jurisdiction ever go to a full trial. The vast majority are settled out of court, dropped, or compromised.

Of course, in cases that do go to trial, there will be a winning side and a losing side. Losers can do one of two things—they can either accept judgment and call it quits (which, at least in civil cases, most do) or, unless they are a losing prosecutor in a criminal case, they can appeal. In other words, losers can take their case to a higher court, which will check for errors made at trial. In most states, this is the job of the intermediate courts of appeal.

INTERMEDIATE APPEALS COURTS

Like trial courts, these appeals courts go by different names depending on the state. In Maryland, they are called courts of special appeals. In Illinois, they are simply the appellate courts. In Texas, the appellate role is itself functionally divided into two sets of courts, a court of criminal appeals, which, as the name implies, handles criminal cases, and a court of appeals that tackles civil disputes. Regardless of name or division, these courts are usually given mandatory jurisdiction by the legislature, meaning they have to consider all legal appeals. Because they are appeals courts, judges work in groups when deciding cases, typically in groups of three.

SUPREME COURTS

If a losing litigant remains dissatisfied with the outcome of her case after appeal, she *may* be able to appeal further to a state supreme court. In a very few states which do not have intermediate appeals courts—such as Rhode Island—the state supreme court has to consider the appeal. However, in the majority of states, the supreme court has a good bit of discretion over its caseload. For example, a large state supreme court

would have to consider death-penalty appeals and it may have to consider constitutional questions, but would decide for itself among the remainder of appeals those that warrant additional consideration.

Fortunately, most states have appropriately designated their supreme courts as "supreme court." Of course, there are exceptions. In Maryland and New York, for example, the highest court is simply the state court of appeals. In Texas, the supreme court hears only civil cases, while the court of criminal appeals serves as the court of last resort for criminal cases (Abadinsky 1995, 152–53).

Whatever their name, whatever their level, and whatever the final disposition, state courts are real workhorses. In 1994, according to the National Center for State Courts, nearly 13.2 million criminal cases were filed in the nation's state courts, and over 14 million civil filings were recorded. Nearly 200,000 juvenile and almost half a million domestic cases were filed. Traffic filings topped 52 million. In most of these areas (see Figure 4.1), there have been dramatic increases over the past decade.

The Federal Court System

The federal court system shares with the state court systems a hierarchical structure. At the same time, however, the federal system is at once a good deal simpler and a bit more complex than the typical state system. It is simpler in the sense that within the national constitutional court structure there is no analogous layer of lower courts; instead, there is a single layer of trial courts. It is also descriptively simpler, for while there are fifty state systems—most a bit different and some very different from the others—there is only one federal system. It is more complex than some state systems because of functional divisions within the courts, the result of a set of ad hoc or "as needed" courts, and what amounts to two general layers of federal court, a set of constitutional courts and a set of special or statutory courts (see Figure 4.2).

FEDERAL CONSTITUTIONAL COURTS

The largest and most familiar group of courts within the federal system are the constitutional courts. They are known as constitutional courts because they have been established (directly in the case of the Supreme Court and indirectly by Congress in the case of the trial and appeals courts) under authority of Article III of the Constitution.[9] These courts follow the general trial-to-intermediate-appeal-to-supreme-court pattern of state courts.

U.S. District Courts. Within the federal constitutional court system, the primary layer consists of ninety-four

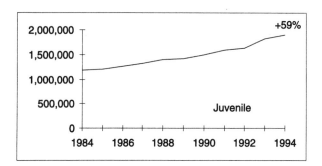

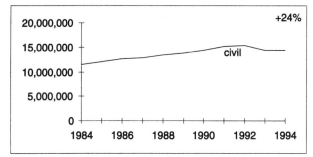

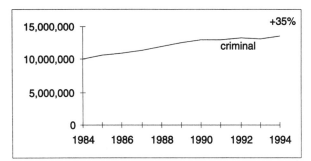

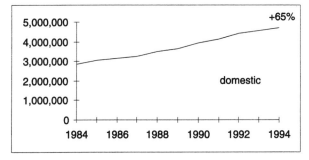

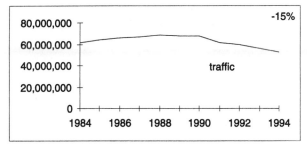

Figure 4.1. State Court Filings, 1984–94

Source: The National Center for State Courts, "National State Court Caseload Trends, 1984–1994 Caseload Highlights," available at www.ncsc.dni.us/research/csp/csphigh1.htm (accessed 2 June 2000).

U.S. District Courts. These are the trial or original jurisdiction courts. U.S. District Courts are scattered throughout the country, each state and territory and the District of Columbia having at least one within its borders, and bigger states having more than one. There are 649 district court judgeships, and how many judges a district gets depends on its population and workload (Baum 1998, 29). For example, the district court for Idaho has only two judges.[10] But the district court for the southern district of New York assigns twenty-eight judges to its Manhattan courthouse alone.[11] These judges are technically appointed by the president with the advice and consent of the Senate and they serve for life terms. (See chapter 5 for more on the judges.)

In general, the district courts mark the point of entry for all federal cases, criminal and civil. Thus, they are "do-everything" or general jurisdiction courts. However, in order to alleviate some of the work of these courts, Congress has authorized what amounts to two subsystems within the districts. First, district courts may employ magistrates to conduct the preliminary stages of criminal cases, the sentencing of misdemeanor offenders, the review of Social Security disputes, the supervision of court orders, and, in some cases if the litigants agree, the conducting of full trials.

Bankruptcy judges also do a lot of the district court work. About 1.5 million bankruptcy claims are filed annually in federal district courts,[12] and these claims are handled mostly by the special judges, thus relieving the district court judges of a huge burden. Each of the 326 bankruptcy judges is appointed by the court of appeals in which the district court is located and each serves a fourteen-year term.[13]

Three-Judge District Courts. To further complicate matters, Congress has authorized, as part of the federal trial system, three-judge district courts. These courts are created on an ad hoc (which is to say, as they are needed) basis, and they are disbanded after the particular case has been decided.

Around the turn of the century, Congress decided that certain types of high-profile cases should be heard first by a group of judges, rather than by a single trial judge. For instance, if a state law were being challenged as violating the federal Constitution, Congress felt that there would be less resentment of the federal courts if the findings were made by a group of judges and, further, if these findings could be directly appealed to the U.S. Supreme Court. Although the courts were rarely convened during the first half of the twentieth century, the entire landscape changed in the 1950s with the advent of widespread civil-rights litigation pressing claims against state governments. Indeed, by the 1970s, over three hundred of these panels were being convened every year. This explosion in the use of the three-judge courts led to considerable criticism. For instance, former Chief Justice

Supreme Court
of the United States

U.S. Circuit Courts of Appeal		U.S. Court of Appeals for the Federal Circuit			U.S. Court of Military Appeals	
U.S. District Courts and Territorial Courts	U.S. Tax Court	U.S. Court of International Trade	U.S. Claims Court		U.S. Court of Veterans Appeals	Army, Navy, Marine, and Coast Guard Courts of Military Review
[3-Judge District Courts]						

Figure 4.2. The U.S. Court System

Source: "Understanding the Federal Courts," The Federal Judicial Homepage, available at www.uscourts.gov/understanding_courts/gifs/figure1.gif.

Warren Burger argued that the constant creation of these panels seriously threatened the other work of the courts, because the judges chosen had to put aside all of their other casework. He also was irked by the fact that the Supreme Court was forced to review all of their decisions, adding tremendously to the workload of the Court. As a result, in 1976, Congress heavily restricted the use of three-judge district courts. Today, they are mostly limited to cases involving legislative reapportionment and a small number of cases involving the *Civil Rights Act* and the *Voting Rights Act*.[14] The number of cases heard annually by these courts averages about twenty.[15]

Three-judge district courts are convened when a party files suit in district court involving one of the limited sets of issues allowed by law. The district judge immediately notifies the chief judge of the appeals court for that district; whereupon the chief judge appoints two other judges to sit with the district court judge. One of those judges has to be an appeals court judge and all three judges have to put aside any other cases they have been working on and devote full attention to the case at hand. Appeals from a three-judge district court bypass the intermediate appeals process, instead going directly to the Supreme Court (Baum 1998, 32).

U.S. Circuit Courts of Appeal. Like litigants in state court, most losing federal litigants have the right to one appeal. If exercised, that right will generally land the parties in one of twelve U.S. Circuit Courts of Appeal. As shown in Figure 4.3, the circuits cover different regions of the country, with all but one blanketing at least three states or territories. Eleven circuits are identified by their number. For example, the Fourth Circuit Court of Appeals has jurisdiction over federal appeals in Maryland, West Virginia, Virginia, and North and South Carolina. The largest circuit, the Ninth, has jurisdiction over California, Oregon, Washington State, Idaho, Nevada, Montana, Arizona, Alaska, and Hawaii. The Twelfth Circuit Court, located in the District of Colum-

bia, has been designated the U.S. Court of Appeals for the D.C. Circuit.

There are currently 167 circuit court judgeships (Baum 1998, 34). Like the district judges, they are appointed by the president, confirmed by the Senate, and they serve for life. Also like districts, circuits are staffed according to caseload. Thus, the First Circuit serving Maine, Massachusetts, and Rhode Island, has only six judicial slots, while the Ninth Circuit, covering most of the far western states including California, has twenty-eight judgeships.

Cases are usually decided by three-judge panels within the circuit, although in rare, very controversial cases, a majority of the judges may vote to have a full hearing of a case before all judges in the circuit.

The circuit courts have no original jurisdiction—they are strictly appeals courts. Congress has given them jurisdiction over two broad categories of cases. First, and perhaps obviously, they are authorized to review the decisions of the district courts and this mandate accounts for about 90 percent of their caseload. They may also hear appeals from some administrative agencies—for example, the Securities and Exchange Commission, the Federal Communications Commission, and the National Labor Relations Board. These kinds of appeals make up only a small part of what most of the circuits do, although, as you might imagine, they make up a much greater part of the D.C. Circuit's workload because the headquarters of most of the administrative agencies are located in Washington.

U.S. Supreme Court. In almost all cases, a decision by a circuit court will end a litigant's adventures in the federal court system, because in most cases, it exhausts the right to one appeal. Litigants may request a hearing before the Supreme Court, but since that Court now has almost complete discretion over its caseload and because the high court has in recent years limited itself to only around 155 cases a year, of which only a little over

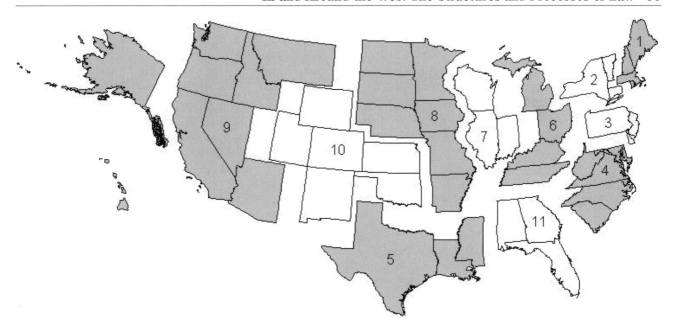

Figure 4.3. Map of U.S. Circuit Courts of Appeal

Source: The Georgetown University Law Library, available at www.ll.georgetown.edu:80/Fed-Ct/ (accessed 6 June 2000).

one-half are announced in full published opinions, litigants' chances of a hearing before the Supreme Court are infinitesimally small.[16] In other words, the all-American notion often expressed in the defiant phrase, "I'm gonna take my case all the way to the Supreme Court," is a fanciful one to say the least.

In jurisdictional terms, the Supreme Court is unique among the nation's courts. Its very importance—the reason so many would like to take their cases "all the way to the Supreme Court"—derives from the fact that it is the only court with nationwide jurisdiction. When a state supreme court speaks, it speaks to and for the citizens of its state; when a federal appeals court rules, it rules to and for the residents of its circuit. But, when the U.S. Supreme Court decides an issue, the decision affects all of us, regardless of specific geographic location.

Jurisdictionally, a Supreme Court review is rare in other respects as well. Technically, there are five ways that a litigant's case can get to the Supreme Court: through (1) original jurisdiction, (2) appeals, (3) certiorari, (4) certification, and (5) extraordinary writs.

Article III of the Constitution actually gives the Court some *original or trial jurisdiction*: "In all Cases affecting Ambassadors, other public Ministers and Consuls, and those in which a State shall be party" (*U.S. Constitution*, Article III, Section 2), the Constitution authorizes the Court to conduct trials. In truth, however, the trial power of the Supreme Court has been very broadly construed to give it almost complete discretion over whether it will or will not accept such cases and Congress has authorized the lower federal courts to hear these kinds of disputes in the first instance. The result is that the high

court seldom accepts such cases and it seldom accepts them for two reasons. First, these cases generally do not present issues of significance to anyone beyond the actual parties. Two recent such cases are illustrative. For example, in 1995, the Supreme Court considered a boundary dispute between Illinois and Kentucky, which boiled down to how the low water mark of the Ohio River should be measured (*Illinois v. Kentucky*, 513 U.S. 177 (1995)). More recently, New Jersey and New York went mano-a-mano over the ownership of Ellis Island (*New York v. New Jersey*, 118 S.Ct. 1726 (1998)). During its 2000–01 term, the Court will consider a fight between Maryland and Virginia involving plans to build a drinking water pipe in the Potomac River (Masters and Shear 2000, B1). Although such cases may be great matters of pride to the parties involved and may even imply the loss or gain of significant revenue, they are not of great legal importance to the rest of the nation. As a result, generally speaking, the Court does not like to spend its scarce resources on them.

Second, the Court tends to shy away from original jurisdiction cases because it is not set up to function like a trial court. The Court was designed to be an appellate tribunal—not a trial court. Thus, even when the justices do accept cases under the Court's original jurisdiction, they usually appoint a special master to conduct the trial.[17]

Primarily, then, the Supreme Court *reviews cases* already decided by lower courts. This, after all, is what it was actually set up to do. In reviewing cases, the Court has almost complete discretion—mostly it decides for itself which cases it wishes to consider. There are, however, some cases where review is mandatory and these are called *appeals*, that is, cases in which a party dissatisfied with a lower court ruling requests a review and reversal by the Supreme Court. Traditionally, the Court's mandatory appellate jurisdiction included cases in which a lower court—either state or federal—declared a law unconstitutional, or cases in which a state court upheld a state statute that was alleged to be in violation of the U.S. Constitution. In 1988, however, Congress changed the law to virtually eliminate mandatory appeals. In fact, today the Court is legally obliged to decide only those few cases appealed from the special three-judge district courts mentioned above.

Another rarely employed method of review is *certification*. Under the Court's appellate jurisdiction, lower courts can file "writs of certification," asking the justices to respond to questions aimed at "clarifying" federal law. Only judges can do this. Parties to the case cannot make such requests, nor may legislators or executives. Certification is very seldom requested, and even less frequently granted.

The Court may also occasionally grant so-called *extraordinary writs*, including writs of *mandamus*, *prohibition*, and *habeas*. A writ of mandamus is an order to a lower court to do something, prohibition is an order to a lower court not to do something, and habeas is the right of a person convicted in one court to challenge that conviction in another (O'Brien 1996, 195). Again, the Court has enormous discretion over the issuance of such writs.

When the Supreme Court does give full hearing to a case, it is generally done via a *writ of certiorari* (or, simply, a writ of cert, or, even more simply, cert). In a petition for a writ of certiorari, litigants ask the Court, literally, to become informed about their cases by requesting the relevant lower court to send up the record of the case. The majority of the roughly seven thousand cases that arrive at the Court every year come as cert requests. The Court has complete discretion over which it grants and which it rejects. The vast majority of these requests are denied. When the Court does grant cert, it means that the justices have decided to give the case a full review; if the petition is denied, the decision of the lower court remains in force. The procedure for determining which petitions will be granted is a long and complex one, involving initial winnowing by the clerks of the Court, the chief justice, and, finally, a vote of all nine justices themselves. The Court will not issue a writ of certiorari unless four of the nine justices agree. In the tradition of the Court, this is known as the "rule of four" (O'Brien 1996, 236–45).[18]

In determining its caseload, the high court acts under a number of largely self-imposed procedural constraints. Thus, for example, a case must be *justiciable* in order for the court to hear it. In other words, it has

to be appropriate for courts. The Constitution itself tells us that justiciability is limited to "Cases" and "Controversies," meaning that questions have to be presented in an adversarial contest (the form of a lawsuit) and they must be capable of being resolved through the judicial process. If all of this sounds rather indistinct, it is. The Court itself has said that justiciability is "a concept of uncertain meaning and scope" (*Flast v. Cohen*, 392 U.S. 83, at 95 (1968)).[19] But, while the Court hasn't said exactly what justiciability *is*, it has said there are certain characteristics that make suits *nonjusticiable* (O'Brien 1996).

For instance, the Supreme Court will not issue advisory opinions, nor will it offer advice on hypothetical issues where no real lawsuit is involved. For example, however much it might expedite the policymaking process, Congress cannot request judicial review in the middle of drafting a bill. The Court will not offer its opinion until the legislation is signed, sealed, delivered, and contested by someone in the form of a bona fide lawsuit. The Constitution does not necessarily prohibit advisory opinions, and, in fact, some state courts do issue such judgments upon request from their legislators and governors, but the Supreme Court has always declined to do so.

Collusion is also considered nonjusticiable. The Court will not decide cases where the litigants both want the same outcome—cases where there is no real adversity between the litigants or where similarly inclined parties simply want to "test" the law. Theoretically, there has to be a genuine fight between the litigants.[20]

Mootness is also a characteristic of nonjusticiability. A moot case is one where the controversy has ended by the time the case gets to the Supreme Court. A related concept is that of *ripeness*—a case is not ripe if it is premature—if it has not yet resulted in a full-blown controversy.

Like all questions of justiciability, the Court has, at times, played fast and loose with both mootness and ripeness. For example, Norma McCorvey (a.k.a. "Jane Roe") had long since delivered her baby and given it up for adoption by the time the Court decided *Roe v. Wade*. In that case, the Court waived normal rules of justiciability, reasoning that in fact her case was a class action and that "Roe" could become pregnant again (410 U.S. 113 (1973)).

Perhaps the trickiest and most malleable of nonjusticiable characteristics is Court consideration of so-called *political questions*. As early as 1803 in the landmark case of *Marbury v. Madison*, Chief Justice Marshall determined that "questions in their nature *political* can never be made in this court" (5 U.S. 137, 170 (1803)). What Marshall meant was that some questions—even some constitutional questions—are better addressed by the other branches of government. For example, as Americans discovered in 1998 and 1999, there is no more momentous a political/constitutional procedure than the impeachment process. Yet, the Court has strongly suggested that despite the constitutional crisis that is impeachment, it would be loathe to enter this political fray (See *Nixon v. United States*, 506 U.S. 224 (1992)).[21]

Again, however, the Court is far from consistent in this area of justiciability. It has left itself considerable wiggle room, for while it may not rule on such issues, the Court itself "must, in the first instance, interpret the text in question and determine whether and to what extent the issue is [political]" (*Clinton v. Jones*, 520 U.S. 681 (1997) at LEXIS p*36, fn. 34; citations omitted). For instance, at one time, the Court firmly stood for the proposition that legislative redistricting and political gerrymandering were political questions (*Colegrove v. Green*, 328 U.S. 549, at 552 (1946)). In the 1960s, however, the Court changed course, becoming forever involved in this highly charged political arena (see, e.g., *Baker v. Carr*, 369 U.S. 186 (1962)).[22]

Work Volume of the Federal Constitutional Courts.
Like their state counterparts, federal courts do a lot of business. Although most of this business is settled without trial (discussed below), the filings alone are staggering. Hence, over 49,000 criminal cases were filed in federal district courts in 1997, marking an increase of about 1,500 cases over the previous year. Over the long haul, civil filings have also increased, 19 percent from 1993 to 1996, then dipped a bit in 1997 when they numbered about 265,000. The circuit courts have also seen their work expand. Even with pretrial settlements as the norm, enough trials are conducted to ensure numerous appeals—in 1997, over 52,000 (Administrative Office of the U.S. Courts 1999, 16).

Of course, unlike the district and circuit courts, the Supreme Court can control its caseload. In fact, the number of cases actually accepted by the high court has declined over the past several decades: During the mid- to late 1980s, the Court accepted, on average, 180 cases per term; by the mid-1990s, the average was about 100. Still, the Supreme Court has seen considerable growth in requests for certiorari, averaging around 7,000 a year by 2000. Screening the growing number of petitions adds substantially to the judicial workload (Baum 1998, 36–37).

SPECIALIZED FEDERAL COURTS

In addition to the familiar "constitutional" court system, the federal judicial process features a number of special purpose courts. Some of these courts were created by Congress under authority of Article III of the Constitution (much like the general-purpose constitutional courts) and some under Article I.

Article I Courts.   The most extensive group of Article I courts are the *U.S. Territorial Courts*. Established by Congress to function much like the U.S. District Courts, the territorial courts are located in the districts of Guam, the U.S. Virgin Islands, and the Northern Mariana Islands. Unlike the district courts, however, the territorial courts, in addition to their federal functions, have jurisdiction over local cases. These courts are also sometimes given duties that are not strictly judicial in nature. The judges of these courts are appointed for ten-year terms.

In 1924, under Article I of the Constitution, Congress established a special *U.S. Tax Court*. This court decides controversies between taxpayers and the Internal Revenue Service involving underpayment of federal income, gift, and estate taxes. Its decisions may be appealed to the federal courts of appeals and are subject to the review of the U.S. Supreme Court on writs of certiorari. The tax court is comprised of nineteen judges who are appointed by the president for fifteen-year terms. In addition, there are currently seventeen special tax-trial judges appointed by the chief judge, who serve under the rules and regulations of the court. Although its offices are located in Washington, D.C., the tax court hears cases in about eighty cities (U.S. Courts 1997b, 89922).

The *U.S. Court of Federal Claims* has jurisdiction over cases involving "tax refunds, federal taking of private property for public use, constitutional and statutory rights of military personnel and their dependents, backpay demands from civil servants claiming unjust dismissal, persons injured by childhood vaccines, and federal government contractors suing for breach of contract" (U.S. Courts 1998b, 89921). Moreover, most suits against the government for claims in excess of $10,000 are tried by these courts.[23] There are sixteen U.S. Claims Court judgeships and judges are appointed by the president with the advice and consent of the Senate for terms of fifteen years. The court is located in Washington, D.C., but will hear cases in locations convenient to the parties.

In order to expedite claims of military veterans, in 1988, Congress created the *U.S. Court of Veterans Appeals*, which exercises exclusive jurisdiction over the decisions of the Board of Veterans' Appeals. Cases heard by the court include disputes over veterans' and survivors' benefits, and loan eligibility and educational benefits. Decisions of the court are subject to limited review by the U.S. Court of Appeals for the Federal Circuit (U.S. Courts 1997b, 89920). Seven judges, nominated by the president and confirmed by the Senate, sit on the court, which is located in Washington, D.C. Like the other Article I courts, the veterans court will travel to the location of the dispute.

The U.S. Court of Appeals for the Armed Forces (formerly, the U.S. Court of Military Appeals) was created in 1951. The court considers "questions of law arising from trials by court-martial in the United States Army, Navy, Air Force, Marine Corps, and Coast Guard in cases where a death sentence is imposed, where a case is certified for review by the Judge Advocate General of the accused's service, or where the accused, who faces a severe sentence, petitions and shows good cause for further review" (U.S. Courts 1998b, 89919). Decisions are appealable to the Supreme Court. Located in Washington, the court employs five civilian judges, appointed by the president with the advice and consent of the Senate, for fifteen-year terms.

Article III Courts. Two of the special-purpose courts created by Congress are established under Article III of the Constitution. The *U.S. Court of Appeals for the Federal Circuit* was created in 1982, by merging of the old U.S. Court of Claims and the Court of Customs and Patent Appeals. The court has appellate jurisdiction over cases arising in "the U.S. Court of Federal Claims, the U.S. Court of International Trade, the U.S. Court of Veterans Appeals, the International Trade Commission, the Board of Contract Appeals, the Patent and Trademark Office, and the Merit Systems Protection Board. The Federal Circuit also hears appeals from certain decisions of the secretaries of the Department of Agriculture and the Department of Commerce, and cases from district courts involving patents and minor claims against the federal government" (U.S. Courts 1997b, 8997). Twelve judges sit on the federal circuit. They are appointed for life by the president with the advice and consent of the Senate.

The U.S. Court of International Trade was established in 1980 with trial powers similar to those of the U.S. District Courts, but limited to disputes involving international trade and customs. The nine judges are nominated by the president, confirmed by the Senate, and serve life terms. Their decisions are subject to review by the U.S. Court of Appeals for the Federal Circuit (U.S. Courts 1998b, 89912). (See Table 4.1.)

Work in the Web: The Criminal and Civil Processes

Depending upon one's perspective, numerous adjectives could be attached to spiders. Many find them fascinating, beautiful, and intelligent. Others look at the eight-legged creatures and conjure up such descriptions as annoying, unpleasant, and scary. Regardless of whether you like spiders or are sympathetic to arachnophobia, one characterization no one attaches to spiders is "lazy." Spiders are busy creatures—busy building their webs; busy ambushing, wrapping, and ingesting their prey; and busy having and tending to future generations of spiders. The law, too, is a very busy thing. Indeed, the business of law makes the spider, by comparison, seem something of a piker. For one thing, despite its intricacy, the spider's web generally has but a single function: the capture of prey.[24] On the other hand, as we suggested in chapter 3, American law tries to achieve multiple—and sometimes conflicting—functions. Moreover, whereas, in the event of damage or ruin, the spider spins her web anew, law's spinnerets tend to add to the existing web, layering complexity upon complexity.

In general, we can break the business of the law down into two very broad processes: that which deals with civil issues, and that which is concerned with criminal problems. In the following sections, we examine both.

One of the first cuts one needs to make in talking about work in the legal web is the distinction between *substantive* law and *procedural* law.

Substantive law is concerned with actual content—the real meat of the law. For example, the substance of a criminal law would tell us, as it did when Timothy McVeigh bombed the Murrah Federal Building in Oklahoma City, killing 168 people, that use of weapons of mass destruction and first-degree murder are punishable offenses and that the punishment for those offenses is

Table 4.1. Specialized (Article I or Statutory) Federal Courts

COURT	AUTHORITY	TYPE	JURISDICTION
Territorial Courts	Article I	Trial	Local and federal general jurisdiction Over Guam, the U.S. Virgin Islands, Northern Mariana Islands
Tax Court	Article I	Trial	Disputes between taxpayers and the IRS
Court of Federal Claims	Article I	Trial	Claims against federal government
Court of Veterans Appeals	Article I	Appellate	Veterans' benefits
Court of Appeals for the Armed Forces	Article I	Appellate	Uniform Code of Military Justice
Court of Appeals Federal Circuit	Article III	Appellate	Appeals from the Claims, International Trade, and Veterans Appeals Courts, and various boards and departments
Court of International Trade	Article III	Trial	International trade and customs

Source: U.S. Courts. 1997b. "Understanding the Federal Courts," Federal Judiciary Homepage. Available at: www.uscourts.gov/ understanding_ courts/89922.htm (accessed 1 October 1998).

imprisonment or death. Or the substance of a civil law-suit might say that if one person causes the death of another he is monetarily liable to the survivors of the victim. Thus, in the most famous such suit in recent memory, the survivors of Nicole Simpson and Ronald Goldman sued O. J. Simpson for so-called wrongful death and were awarded millions of dollars. Those kinds of things make up the substance of law or the content of law and they are generally defined by legislatures, although you will also find lots of substantive law in constitutions, in executive orders, and coming out of judicial opinions.

Procedural law has to do with the operation of law, that is, with the manner in which law is applied. It is the rules of law itself. In a sense, law *is* rules, but these rules themselves are bound by other rules—rules of process. These rules of process make the law manageable by ensuring its efficient administration. Even more important, they supposedly ensure that the law itself will be applied evenly, consistently, and fairly to everybody. Thus, when Timothy McVeigh unsuccessfully appealed his conviction, he claimed that he had been denied *due process* of law by such procedural errors as jury misconduct and the exclusion of mitigating evidence at trial (*U.S. v. McVeigh*, 153 F.3d 1166; 1998 U.S. App. LEXIS 21877 (10th Circuit Court of Appeals, 1998)).

All law has elements of both substance and procedure. If, for instance, you look at the Constitution you can clearly see both the substance and procedure of law. As a matter of substance, the president has to be thirty-five years old or older, he has to be a natural-born citizen, he is the chief executive officer, he is the commander-in-chief, and he is to be elected. As a matter of procedure, the Constitution tells us the manner in which he is to be elected, how he might be removed, and, in important respects, it tells *him* the manner in which he is to carry out some of his duties.

A second obvious cut we can make in talking about kinds of law is that between *criminal* and *civil*. Simply stated, criminal law deals with activities that have been *forbidden by government*—this can mean anything from a parking violation to murder. In the American judicial process, the violation of a criminal law is a violation not simply against another individual or group, but against government itself. Government acts as a proxy for the individual victim. This is why in criminal litigation you always see cases referred to as *State v. Smith* (or, in some states, as *People v. Simpson* or *Commonwealth v. Woodward*), or *U.S. v. McVeigh*. Thus, legally, Timothy McVeigh committed a crime against all of us, not just against the unfortunate victims in the Murrah Federal Building. In order to convict someone of a criminal act, the government needs to convince a judge or jury that the defendant is guilty *beyond a reasonable doubt.*[25]

Civil law, on the other hand, generally governs relationships between individuals in the course of their *private* affairs. Hence, civil law deals with matters such as contracts, property, wills, divorces, and personal relationships. Unlike criminal prosecutions where the government is always an active participant, the government's main interest in civil cases is to provide a forum (the courthouse) and process (the rules) for the peaceable resolution of disputes. Thus, theoretically, in civil cases the government does not care who wins a dispute as long as the dispute is settled peacefully. The government cares a lot in a criminal case because it is always a party to the case. But, unless the government is a party to a civil case (which it sometimes is), it theoretically it does not care about the outcome. In order to find a person liable in a civil case, the plaintiff or plaintiffs (the person or group bringing the complaint) need only convince a judge or jury that the defendant's wrongdoing has been demonstrated by a *preponderance of evidence.*[26]

It is possible for a single action or set of facts to give rise to both a criminal and a civil action—and this is becoming increasingly prevalent. For just about every criminal action, there is also a civil remedy. For example, if you were to run a red light and go crashing into another's car, the police, presumably, would issue a ticket based upon the criminal act of ignoring a traffic signal. Of course, there would still be the matter of your victim's damaged car, and damage to property comes under the civil law of tort—on top of having to pay a hefty fine to the state, you could find yourself paying out-of-pocket or insurance expenses to the person whose car you totaled.

Or, take the more famous case of O. J. Simpson. Of course, he was prosecuted by the people of California for the criminal act of murder—an act of which he was acquitted. Subsequently, however, Mr. Simpson was sued by the survivors of his ex-wife and her friend for the civil act of wrongful death and for this act he was found liable. Clearly, the act of murder and the act of wrongful death are analogous—in nonlegal terms, they are the same thing. However, the former is a crime, prosecutable by the state, subject to proof beyond a reasonable doubt, and, if proven, punishable by imprisonment or death. The latter is a civil wrong, argued by individuals, subject to proof by a preponderance of evidence, and, if proven, punishable by compensation to the victims. At times, the criminal and civil processes may even be launched simultaneously. For example, four New York City police officers charged in 1997 with brutalizing a Haitian immigrant were tried under federal criminal statutes in U.S. District Court early in 1999. The victim, Abner Louima, also filed a civil suit against the city, the indicted officers, and other parties seeking unspecified damages.[27] In the following sections, we review the criminal and civil processes.

The Criminal Process

GUILTY PLEAS

Whether we are discussing criminal or civil proceedings, the single most important thing to know about the legal process is that because of scarce resources, the system strongly encourages parties "to forego bringing cases and to 'settle' cases—that is, to bargain to a mutually acceptable outcome" (Galanter 1994, 357–58). The system, in other words, seeks to avoid full-blown trials. On the criminal side of the fence, this means that the vast majority of cases are *plea bargained*. Indeed, although plea bargaining as a method of adjudication has declined somewhat in recent years, it continues to account for 89 percent of felony convictions in state courts, with trials accounting for the remaining 11 percent (Brown and Langan 1998).[28] Plea bargains accounted for almost 93 percent of all convictions in the U.S. District Courts during the twelve-month period ending in September 1997 (U.S. Courts 1998a, Table D-4).

Plea bargaining is popular in the judicial process generally because it saves considerable time and resources over the alternative trial route—and time is money. Hence, while the average time from date of arrest to felony conviction is about nine months when a full-blown jury trial is employed and eight months under a bench (judge only) trial scenario, plea-bargained cases take only about five and a half months to run their course (U.S. Courts 1998a, Table D-4).

Court savings in time and money, however, are not the only variables explaining the widespread use of plea bargaining. Plea bargaining is popular because individual participants in the criminal process believe that they will gain something from a guilty plea. First, in addition to reducing time and financial strains on the court generally, plea bargaining reduces time and financial strains on individual court players. For example, judges, full-time prosecutors, and public defenders are always faced with a crushing load of cases and plea bargaining allows them to process more of these in a shorter period of time. Moreover, private defense attorneys benefit from plea bargaining in the most literal sense of time being money. For them, "quick turnover of cases is the most profitable mode of practice [since their fees] will not increase enough to pay for the extra time required to try a case . . ." (Baum 1998, 183).

Time of a different sort can play into a defendant's calculations. According to the Bureau of Justice Statistics, "Prison sentences were much longer for felons convicted by a jury trial (12 years) than for felons who pleaded guilty (5 years) or were convicted at trial by a judge (7 years)" (Brown and Langan 1998). Nor is this simply a statistical anomaly. Several studies have convincingly demonstrated that harsher sentences for those

who refuse to play the plea bargain game are frequently meted out in a kind of "He takes some of my time, I take some of his" prosecutorial mentality (see, e.g., Uhlman and Walker 1980, cited in Neubauer 1997, 260).

Second, the plea bargain allows the participants to achieve desirable results. Trials—particularly jury trials—can be risky business for all involved. Despite the proliferation of jury consultants, jury selection and, even more so, jury outcomes, are far from scientific certainties. Plea bargaining, on the other hand, offers a kind of certitude of outcome—perhaps not the best possible outcome, but clearly not the worst. Thus, the prosecutor is assured of a conviction and the defendant and his attorney can generally be satisfied that they received a lighter sentence than would have been the case had a conviction resulted from trial (Baum 1998, 184). Statistically, the differences in outcome are quite dramatic: "[a]n estimated 58% of felons convicted by a jury received a prison sentence, compared to 58% of those convicted by a judge and 44% of those who pleaded guilty" (Brown and Langan 1998).

Finally, plea bargaining is promoted by the close working relationships of those "who make up the core of the courtroom work group—attorneys and judges . . ." (Baum 1998, 185). According to Baum (1998, 185),

Plea bargaining is facilitated by these relationships, which foster the development of regular bargaining procedures and tacit understandings about feasible terms under particular circumstances. The interdependence of work group members also strengthens the pressures for plea bargaining. Not all lawyers and judges like plea bargaining, and many come to their jobs expecting to bring cases to trial. But they generally adapt to a system that is dominated by such bargaining, primarily because they learn its advantages from veteran lawyers and judges.

Despite its pervasiveness and despite all of the obvious advantages, plea bargaining has long been, and continues to be, very controversial. After all, theoretically, the American criminal justice system is founded on two principles. One of those principles is that certain basic rights and liberties should not be violated in bringing the guilty to justice; the second is that only individuals who are clearly guilty of certain specified wrongdoing deserve officially administered punishment and that punishment should be proportional to the wrongdoing. In other words, one should clearly deserve punishment, and the punishment should fit the crime. As a result, plea bargaining tends to be controversial both among civil libertarians *and* among those who support stronger and tougher law and order.

Civil libertarians have long maintained that the plea bargain deprives defendants of full constitutional rights to due process. The Constitution, after all, clearly favors "public trials" by "impartial juries" (*U.S. Constitution*, Amendment VI). Plea bargains, of course, are neither public nor conducted in front of juries. Moreover, those concerned with the constitutional rights of criminal defendants maintain that plea bargains are often coercive in nature: The defendant knows that if he doesn't plead, the court is likely to treat him much more harshly. For example, in the most common type of explicit bargaining arrangement, the prosecutor's charge bargain, a defendant may be told that the number of charges against him will be reduced in exchange for a guilty plea. The Bureau of Justice Statistics reports that in 1994, 39 percent of felony jury trials nationwide resulted in convictions on multiple offenses while only 18 percent of guilty pleas involved more than one offense (Brown and Langan 1998). Of course, these outcomes make a tremendous difference in the severity of the sentence ultimately meted out. As a result, many worry that innocent people may agree to plead guilty rather than risk an adverse jury decision based on more and more serious charges. It is generally assumed that this kind of pressure impacts some groups more than others—an indigent defendant, unable to make bail, would be more inclined to bargain as a means of hastening the end of his ordeal, while a mentally retarded individual may find it very difficult to resist the pressure to bargain. Because there is generally no appeal from a guilty plea, it is impossible to know how many innocent defendants may be railroaded into confessing guilt.

On the other hand, law-and-order advocates maintain that the second principle of justice is regularly violated by plea bargaining. Truly guilty defendants very often do get a considerable break under the system. They do not pay the full price of the crime as determined by the legislature. Police, in particular, may "view the bargaining process as giving criminals the impression that the law is easily manipulated. [They] much prefer a conviction on the crime the defendant actually committed rather than a plea to a lesser one" (Neubauer 1997, 262).

THE TRIAL PROCESS

Although plea bargaining is (far and away) the norm, trials get the notice in the criminal justice system. They get the notice for several reasons. First, trials, not plea bargains, are the *constitutional* prescription for bringing the accused to justice—that is, trials, not plea bargains, are the concern of the Sixth Amendment.[29]

Second, trials are great entertainment. And, as we noted in chapter 3, the entertainment value of a "good trial" has long been an American recreational mainstay. Depending on the circumstances, trials offer us great drama, mystery, and oratory. Today, of course, the mass media have brought all of these elements even closer to us through occasional network coverage of high-interest prosecutions and daily trial broadcasts on Court TV.[30]

Finally, although trials are rare occurrences when compared to plea bargains, prosecutions in America are so pervasive that even the paltry 11 percent that eventually result in trial make for huge numbers. In 1994, according to the Bureau of Justice Statistics, an estimated 872,217 felons were convicted in state courts alone. Thus, almost 96,000 of these were the result of trials before a judge or jury—by any measure, a whole bunch of trials (Brown and Langan 1998).

Trials, as opposed to plea bargains, may occur for any number of reasons. For example, a prosecutor—often, an elected official—may feel that offering a reduced charge in exchange for a plea would result in political outrage. This would especially tend to be the case in high-profile murder prosecutions. On the other hand, a defendant may feel that the uncertainties of trial are more attractive than the certainties of an offered plea. A recent legal development, with several variations, has exacerbated this tendency. Over the past decade, as part of the "get-tough-on-crime" political atmosphere, every state and the federal government have altered sentencing legislation in order to reduce the discretion of judges (Baum 1998, 199). One variation is so-called sentencing guidelines that direct judges to take specific actions in individual cases (Neubauer 1997, 278). Historically, judges in the United States have had enormous discretion in applying sentences to individual convicts. Sentencing guidelines, which may, according to the jurisdiction, be *voluntary* or *mandatory*, take much of this discretion away (see Figure 4.4).

A well-publicized variation on sentencing guidelines is the so-called "three strikes and you're out" laws. Such laws mandate sentence "enhancements" for repeat offenders. For example, California's seminal "three-strikes" law prescribes twice the normal sentence for a person previously convicted of a violent or serious felony and dictates a life sentence for anyone convicted of two previous violent or serious felony convictions.[31] The law is having a profound impact on the California criminal justice system. First, in only the first six months after the law's enactment, there were more than 7,400 second- and third-strike cases filed in California courts. More important for present purposes, however, the law is having a significant impact on the plea-bargaining system. According to the California Legislative Analyst's Office,

Public defenders and criminal defense attorneys appear to be advising their clients that there is little to lose by refusing to plea bargain and taking their cases to jury trial, given the much longer prison sentences defendants face if convicted of a second- or third-strike offense. Available data indicate that only about 14 percent of all second-strike cases and only about 6 percent of all third-strike cases have been disposed of through plea bargaining. In addition, there is some evidence that persons charged with a violent or serious offense for the first time (a first-strike) are also less likely to plead guilty because a conviction would result in any subsequent offenses being charged under the "Three Strikes" law.[32]

Excerpts from Federal Sentencing Table

The federal sentencing guidelines take into account both the *seriousness of the offense* and the *offender's criminal history*. The guidelines currently provide for forty-three levels of offense seriousness, with more serious crimes receiving higher numbers. Thus, the most serious offense is rated 43, and the least serious 1. The guidelines also assign each offender to one of six criminal history categories based on the extent of the offender's past misconduct and how recently past crimes took place. For example, Category 1 would be assigned to those with the least serious records and to many first-time offenders. Category 6, on the other hand, would include those with lengthy records. Appearing below is an excerpt from the Federal Sentencing Table. The excerpt illustrates the various sentences that a mid-range offender would expect to receive depending on his or her past criminal record.

Sentencing Table (excerpt)
(in months of imprisonment)

OFFENSE LEVEL	CRIMINAL HISTORY CATEGORY					
	I	II	III	IV	V	VI
19	30–37	33–41	37–46	46–57	57–71	63–78

Figure 4.4. Sentencing Guidelines: The Federal Example
Source: United States Sentencing Commission, "An Overview of Federal Sentencing Guidelines," available at www.ussc.gov (accessed 6 June 2000).

If a defendant does choose the trial route, he or she will be part of a process that moves along according to a series of well-established steps (see Figure 4.5). A trial begins with opening statements to the judge or jury, almost always (except in very rare cases where a defendant chooses and is allowed to represent himself) presented by representing attorneys. In criminal cases, the prosecutor (the state's attorney) always opens first. The prosecutor is allowed to proceed first on the legal theory that he or she has initiated the case and that he or she has the more difficult job to do. The prosecutor, after all, is charged with the *burden of proof*: "the obligation . . . to prove his allegations."[33] And, in criminal trials, of course, this means proving "beyond a reasonable doubt." The defense attorney, who gives her or his statement second, need prove nothing, but only seek to rebut the prosecutor's theory.

Following opening statements, the prosecution will present its *case in chief,* including its major evidence. Generally speaking, evidence is provided in two forms: physical and testimonial. *Physical evidence* includes real objects, which, in criminal cases, are typically weapons, fingerprints, confiscated illicit goods, or documents. *Testimonial evidence* is provided by witnesses. In a typical criminal trial, testimonial evidence provided by witnesses is largely related to facts of which they have personal knowledge. For example, a bystander may recount her observation of a shooting, a friend may de-

scribe his conversation with a defendant, or a police officer may relate her role in a drug bust. Occasionally, expert witnesses may be asked to testify. Expert witnesses are people "having special training or experience in [a] technical field," who are "permitted to state [their] opinions concerning those technical matters even though [they were not] present at the event."[34] For example, a psychiatrist or psychologist may be called to discuss the mental health of a defendant, a forensic pathologist may be asked to describe wounds, or, increasingly, an expert in DNA may be required to explain to jurors the meaning of genetic evidence.[35]

Following the prosecution's case, the defense may present its case. The defense is not required to present a case since it has no burden of proof, but generally will make some presentation. Like the prosecution, the defense may wish to present evidence, although defense evidence would be *exculpatory*—that is, evidence intended to clear or excuse the defendant. The defense, of course, may also wish to present witnesses of its own. These may or may not include the defendant who, because of the Fifth Amendment,[36] need not testify at all.

In some cases, following the defendant's presentation, the prosecutor may wish to present a *rebuttal*. A prosecutor's rebuttal might include, for example, challenging the testimony or character of a witness for the defense.

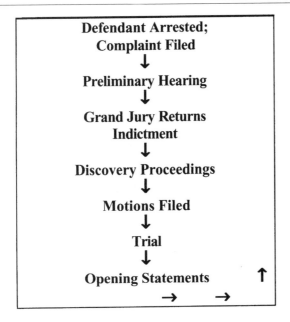
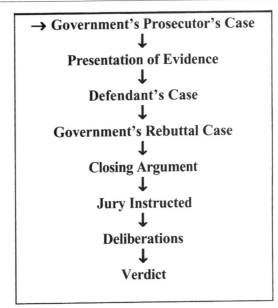

Figure 4.5. Trial Progression of Criminal Actions
Source: U.S. Courts, "Understanding the Federal Courts," The Federal Judiciary Homepage, "Trial Progression of Criminal Actions," available at www.uscourts.gov/understanding_courts/gifs/figure4.gif.

After both sides have completed their cases, attorneys will present *closing arguments*. Again, the prosecution goes first, followed by the defense. Attorneys are not allowed to present new evidence to the judge or jury, but merely to summarize their arguments and appeal to their version of truth and justice.

If the trial utilizes a jury, the jury will now be given *instructions*. This process involves the judge, usually after consultation with opposing attorneys, providing the jury with lengthy directions explaining how the law applies to the case at hand and advising the jurors to find the facts in accordance with certain legal definitions and instructions. This is no mean feat. Judges, fearful of having trials overturned on appeal because of faulty instructions, tend to gravitate toward the highly legalistic and technical in their instructions. Jurors, on the other hand, are laypeople, and studies have repeatedly found that while they generally try to adhere to judicial instructions, they frequently fail to understand them (see, e.g., Steele and Thornburg 1988).

The jury *deliberates* in secret after the instructions are given, whether they understand those instructions or not. The results of these discussions, in criminal cases, may be a *verdict* of guilt or innocence. In cases where the jury is unable to reach a verdict, it is said to be a *hung jury* and the trial ends with no decision.[37] Where a verdict of guilt is handed down, the result of most criminal trials, a *sentence* must next be determined. If the conviction was for a misdemeanor, this will generally occur immediately after the verdict. If the conviction was for a felony, the judge will usually set a date for a separate *sentencing hearing* where both sides may present cases

for relatively harsh (prosecutor) or lenient (defense) penalties. After the presentations, the judge hands down the sentence.[38]

APPEALS AND POST-CONVICTION REMEDIES

Criminal defendants found guilty at trial will most likely want to *appeal* their convictions. Historically, this is a relatively new phenomenon. Because convicts tend not to be wealthy and because appeals are expensive, throughout most of our history, most convicted individuals were effectively denied the right to appeal. However, a series of Supreme Court rulings during the 1950s and 1960s dramatically changed the landscape.[39] Today, many criminal convicts do appeal, adding tremendously over the past three decades to the workload of the nation's appellate courts. Moreover, implementation of sentencing guidelines throughout the nation has added significantly to the appellate caseload. For example, before the federal *Sentencing Reform Act of 1984* was passed, convicted offenders could only appeal their convictions. The act, however, provides for appellate review of sentences from which both the defendant and the government may appeal (Bureau of Justice Statistics 1995, 61). A number of states have implemented similar appellate rights under their sentencing guidelines.

Although its work constitutes only a small part of the total criminal justice appellate landscape—most criminal appeals take place in state court systems—the workload of the federal circuit courts is illustrative. In 1995, for example, the U.S. Courts of Appeals received 11,000 criminal appeals. In most cases by far, the ruling of the trial court was affirmed; in other words, the convicted defendant lost his or her appeal.[40]

In addition to regular appeals, *prisoners* may challenge their convictions in federal courts on certain limited grounds. These post-conviction attempts to seek remedies are called *collateral attacks*—and they are simply attempts to avoid the effects of one court decision by bringing a different court proceeding. Collectively, such "attacks" challenging the constitutionality of imprisonment are known by the more familiar term, *habeas corpus*. These kinds of collateral attacks are different from appeals in several respects. First, the convict actually has to be in prison to file. Second, they generally can only raise constitutional questions. For example, petitions might "allege that the police, prosecutor, defense counsel, or trial court deprived the prisoners of their Federal constitutional rights, such as the right to refuse to answer questions when placed in police custody, the right to a speedy and fair trial, and the right to effective assistance of counsel" (Hanson and Daley 1995).[41] Third, unlike appeals, which are generally limited to issues raised at trial, habeas petitions may raise issues not brought out at trial. Fourth, such petitions are heard, in the first instance, not by appeals courts, but rather, by other trial courts. When state prisoners file habeas petitions, their requests are considered by the U.S. District Courts.

Although the *writ of habeas corpus* is as old as the Constitution itself,[42] and its extension to state prisoners seeking relief in federal court dates from a congressional act of 1867, a series of Supreme Court rulings during the 1960s greatly expanded the scope (see *Sanders v. United States*, 373 U.S. 1 (1963)); *Fay v. Noia*, 372 U.S. 391 (1963); and *Townsend v. Sain*, 372 U.S. 745 (1963)) and, thus not surprisingly, the number of prisoners filing. Over most of the 1990s, roughly 10,000 habeas petitions were filed annually in the federal district courts, constituting about 4 percent of the civil caseload of the national trial courts.[43]

Habeas petitions tend to be filed by those convicted of the most serious crimes, with about 62 percent involving violent crimes (Hanson and Daley 1995, 13). These prisoners are more likely to file because they have received longer sentences that generally exceed the state appellate process. Notably, however, prisoners petitioning from death sentences make up only 1 percent of the habeas caseload. Notably, also, despite public and political perceptions to the contrary, the vast majority of habeas petitions fail. Because habeas petitions are technically civil requests (see fn. 43), and because there is no right to counsel in civil cases, the majority of filings (93 percent) are undertaken without attorney assistance, are disposed of fairly perfunctorily by the reviewing court, and are generally unfavorable to the prisoner. Thus, Hanson and Daley found in a sample of habeas petitions that "[a] large majority of the petitions were dismissed. Sixty-three percent of the issues were dismissed either

by the court or by the petitioner. Virtually all other issues were denied on their merits. The court granted 1% of the issues and remanded another 1% to the State courts for further proceedings" (Hanson and Daley 1995, 18).

Notwithstanding the fact that most habeas petitions are denied, since the 1970s there has been an ongoing assault on the writ. The assault has proceeded on two fronts: the judicial and the political. Judicially, both the Burger and Rehnquist Courts have placed restrictions on habeas appeals, attempting to cut back Warren Court enhancements of the writ (see especially *Stone v. Powell*, 428 U.S. 465 (1976)); *Wainwright v. Sykes*, 433 U.S. 72 (1977); *Engle v. Issac*, 456 U.S. 107 (1982); *Marshall v. Longberger*, 259 U.S. 422 (1983); *Teague v. Lane*, 489 U.S. 288 (1990); and *McCleskey v. Zant*, 499 U.S. 467 (1991)).

More important, political *perceptions*—often very much at odds with the actual data—that habeas appeals result in the release of many dangerous criminals, in delays in the implementation of the death penalty, and in tremendously backlogged courts have resulted in dramatic legislative changes to the writ. Thus, in 1997, Congress passed *The Antiterrorism and Effective Death Penalty Act*, which drastically limits habeas on several fronts (Pub. L. No. 104-132, 110 Stat. 1218; codified as amended in various sections of 28 U.S.C.). First, until passage of the act, there were no time limits on the filing of habeas petitions. Under the act, however, death-row inmates now have only six months from their final state court proceeding to file a habeas corpus petition. Other prisoners have only a year, provided the state makes counsel available to the prisoner. Second, the new law bars state prisoners from beginning a second round of habeas proceedings without getting authorization from a three-judge appellate panel. Moreover, if the panel denies the request, the filing prisoner cannot appeal the denial of the request to the Supreme Court (upheld in *Felker v. Turpin*, 518 U.S. 651 (1996)). The law does allow for exceptions when new facts about the case are discovered, but only if those facts could not have been discovered earlier "through the exercise of due diligence"—a difficult hurdle to overcome in light of the fact that convicted inmates tend to have no counsel and prisons are drastically cutting back on the resources available to prisoners.

Third, under the new law, prisoners cannot receive relief simply because their convictions or sentences were wrongful as a matter of federal law. Prior to enactment of the anti-terrorism law, a federal court could order a new trial or sentencing if the federal judge concluded that a prisoner was being held in custody in violation of the Constitution or laws or treaties of the United States. Under the new law, however, prisoners have to show that the conviction or sentence violated "clearly established Federal law, as determined by the Supreme Court of the United States." This creates a real roadblock for habeas-seeking convicts because the Supreme Court hears very few cases, and its decisions, though important, provide only a few of the threads that make up the fabric of federal law. Under the new law, even if a federal judge concludes that a prisoner's conviction or sentence was in error, the prisoner cannot secure a new trial unless there already happens to be a Supreme Court decision addressing a very similar situation.

The Civil Process

If the criminal process is largely distinguished by plea bargaining, the civil process is mostly characterized by *settlements*. As is the case on the criminal side of the ledger, few civil claims ever go to trial. Indeed, few potential claims ever even get filed in court, much less go to full trial. For example, Miller and Sarat (1980, cited in Baum 1998, 227) found among people who consider themselves to be victims of discrimination, "fewer than three in five complained about the matter, fewer than one in thirty hired a lawyer, and fewer than one in a hundred filed a lawsuit." Similarly, the number of actual filings where personal injury is involved is surprisingly low. Thus, the Sarat and Miller study found that in injury torts involving $1000 or more only about 3.8 percent "resulted in court filings" (p. 228). A 1991 study reported by the *New England Journal of Medicine* found that only about one in eight patients injured by medical negligence files a malpractice claim and only one in sixteen receives compensation from a court or through settlement. These figures strongly suggest that most individuals who perceive themselves to be harmed either find alternatives to litigating or swallow hard and assume the "stiff upper lip." In any event, they would seem to belie Congressman Kasich's (R-OH) hyperbolic reference in the previous chapter to the effect that everybody is suing "everybody for everything" (*Congressional Record*, 103d Cong., 2d sess., 1994, 140).

This is not to suggest, however, that civil filings are insubstantial. After all, Americans always have been, and remain, a very litigious people. Thus, despite the fact that most of us most of the time either choose to ignore our grievances or settle our disputes through nonlegal channels, the overall incidence of civil litigation is huge. Thus, the National Center for State Courts reported over 14 million civil case *filings* (excluding domestic and juvenile) in state courts in 1994 (NCSC 1994b).

PURSUING LITIGATION

People pursue civil litigation for a variety of reasons. For example, a few individuals "come to use the law as an arena for manipulation and play, a place to toy with enemies and to gain strategic successes by pummeling one's opponents with legal charges and summonses. . . . [This type] come[s] to regard the court as entertainment, as a place to try out dominance games with others to see what will happen" (Merry 1990, cited in Baum 1998, 232–33). No doubt illustrative of this kind of individual is Larry Klayman, trade lawyer and founder of the conservative "watchdog" group Judicial Watch. Klayman, described by an acquaintance "as the sort of guy who'd 'sue you for criticizing his tie,'" launched at least eighteen lawsuits against the Clinton administration alone. Nor does this intrepid litigator merely confine himself to avowed political enemies. Klayman's legal targets include not only the Clintons, but his own mother whom he has sued to redeem expenses he incurred taking care of his grandmother. According to Klayman, "I wish we could have settled it in the family, but we couldn't. So what do you do?" (Segal 1998, A1) Well, what indeed?

Of course, the Klaymans of the world are relatively few and far between.[44] Most individuals who initiate lawsuits do so only very infrequently and for more material reasons. For instance, launching a legal action may be particularly attractive where the financial costs of doing so are relatively low (Baum 1998, 232). Personal injury cases worked by lawyers on contingency fee[45] would be a good example, since research shows that virtually all [personal injury] plaintiffs pay their lawyers on a contingency basis" (Kritzer 1998, 268). Similarly, small claims brought in lower state trial courts can be relatively cheap to litigate.

Litigation may also be pursued under conditions where a party sees no other recourse to an injurious situation. Such would generally be the case in divorce filings and bankruptcy proceedings (Baum 1998, 233).

Lawsuits may be filed because litigants assume the potential gains will outweigh the costs of litigation. For some, no doubt, these perceptions are fueled by headline media accounts of rare multimillion-dollar jury awards (see below). For others, most often business concerns, the gains need not necessarily be direct monetary awards. For instance, so-called SLAPP suits, instituted by businesses against citizens protesting development plans, are designed literally to harass, that is, to make it too expensive for the citizen activists to demonstrate (Baum 1998, 233).

Businesses may launch strategic suits to slow or crush their competition. For example, the field of patent infringement lawsuits is now burgeoning (in federal courts, growing from 1,500 in 1992 to more than 2,100 in 1997) as "[c]ompanies in fiercely competitive technology industries from communications and software to drugs and biotechnology are giving the 12-gauge lawsuit a prominent place in the corporate gun cabinet." Defending against such suits can be incredibly expensive and those targeted charge that they constitute little more than legal harassment (Korman 1998).

TYPES AND INCIDENCE OF CIVIL LITIGATION

Why people and organizations litigate is related to the types of litigation pursued in the nation's courts. In general, civil law may be said to encompass a number of broad legal categories, including *domestic* or *family law* (which, in turn, includes a number of subcategories, the most prominent of which are divorce, custody disputes, and adoption agreements); *juvenile law* (a unique hybrid of civil and criminal, dealing in delinquent youthful offenders and cases of child neglect); *contract law*, involving legally recognized promises; *property law* (including real property and estates, titles and liens, and inheritance); and *tort*, involving the redress of private wrongs. Often, because of the issues involved and their unique legal stature, domestic and juvenile law are considered to be analytically and categorically distinct from the rest of civil law, so that when researchers discuss civil filing trends or politicians complain about the so-called litigation explosion, they are really usually referring to contract, property, and tort. Indeed, in the case of political complaints about caseload growth, the boogeyman is generally torts alone.

According to a 1993 survey of civil filings in twenty-nine states, including domestic but excluding juvenile filings, domestic cases by far outweighed other classes of civil suits, comprising 41 percent of total filings. By contrast, property claims (including real property and estates) made up about 17 percent of filings, contract disputes were involved in 11 percent, and torts in 10 percent. (See Table 4.2.) When only contract, property, and tort are included, property claims lead the pack at 46 percent of the total, followed by contract disagreements at 28 percent, and tort claims at 25 percent (Smith et al. 1995).

A Tort Crisis?   Despite findings such as these, the clear perception among many is that torts are to blame for the nation's clogged civil dockets. When politicians such as Congressman Kasich complain that "Everybody in America is fed up with being sued by everybody for everything,"[46] they generally have tort filings in mind. Indeed, the so-called tort "crisis" has become a political hot potato of rather grand proportions. Whether or not there is a genuine tort crisis, however, is debatable.

For example, special interests such as the U.S. Chamber of Commerce, the National Association of Manufacturers, and the American Tort Reform Association describe the current tort system as "out of control"[47] and characterized by "excessive litigation" that "burdens" American society and hampers "U.S. competitiveness abroad."[48] On the other hand, groups such as Ralph Nader's Public Citizen and the Association of Trial Lawyers of America refer to the current tort system as the public's best line of attack against "reckless corporations, polluters, doctors, insurance companies, and other

Table 4.2. Civil Case Filings in General Jurisdiction Courts in 29 States, 1993

CASE TYPE	TOTAL	PERCENT
Total number	5,929,537	100
Domestic relations	2,448,150	41
Small claims	732,977	12
Contracts	639,783	11
Estates	606,722	10
Torts	572,041	10
Real property rights	439,947	7
Mental health	90,608	2
Civil appeals	93,339	2
Other	305,970	5

Note: States include AK, AZ, CA, CO, CT, FL, HI, ID, IN, KS, ME, MD, MA, MI, MN, MO, NV, NJ, NM, NY, ND, OH, OR, TN, TX, UT, WA, WI, and WY.

Source: Steven K. Smith, Carol J. DeFrances, Patrick A. Langan, and John Goerdt, *Tort Cases in Large Counties*. Bulletin NCJ-153177 (Washington, D.C.: Bureau of Justice Statistics, U.S. Department of Justice, 1995).

wrongdoers...."[49] The former advocate substantial reforms, limiting the liability of businesses and medical professionals and capping monetary awards to winning plaintiffs. The latter view such reforms as "threats to America's civil justice system."[50] In general, the warring parties come down to businesses, the insurance industry, and doctors (those who perceive themselves to be hurt by tort litigation) on the one side, and consumer groups and trial lawyers (those who perceive themselves to be helped) on the other.

Statistically, the data paint a rather mixed picture. In a study of tort filings in sixteen states, the National Center for State Courts reports that between 1975 and 1983, filings remained relatively constant at around the 200,000 mark. Between 1983 and 1986, filings increased substantially to about 350,000. Since about 1990, however, tort filings have been declining (NCSC 1994a). Thus, the data paint a picture of significant increases during the decade of the 1980s, moderated by a slow decline during the 1990s.

Although raw numbers of claims make up a part of the debate over the so-called tort crisis, such statistics appear to be less important to the opposing sides than two additional aspects of the current tort landscape: the amount and type of jury awards to successful plaintiffs and the relative merits of the claims themselves. Clearly, a large part of the debate over tort centers squarely on damages awarded to winning plaintiffs. Businesses regularly complain about the extent of product liability awards, while doctors echo the refrain in the field of malpractice, mostly pointing to so-called "runaway-jury" awards of multimillion-dollar punitive damages.[51] Again, the actual data, though spotty, paint a more complex picture.

In a study of 378,000 tort cases disposed from 1 July 1991 to 30 June 1992 in state general jurisdiction courts, analysts from the Bureau of Justice Statistics (BJS) and the Center for State Courts found that the vast majority (77 percent) of tort dispositions involved automobile accidents and "premises liability cases alleging harm from inadequately maintained or dangerous property (17%). . . ."[52] In fact, most tort cases (47 percent) involved individuals suing individuals, while suits against institutions (e.g., businesses, the government, and hospitals) accounted for roughly 42 percent of the cases. The two most frequently cited types of cases by businesses and medical professionals seeking tort reform—product liability and medical malpractice cases—accounted for only 8 percent of total dispositions (Smith et al. 1995).

Moreover, the large majority of cases were disposed of not by jury verdicts, but by settlement. Indeed, jury verdicts accounted for only 2 percent and bench verdicts for only 1 percent of dispositions overall, although "[m]edical malpractice claims (7%) were more likely than product or premises liability, auto, or toxic substance cases to be disposed by a jury or bench trial" (Smith et al. 1995). Unfortunately, very little systematic data are available on the terms or costs of settlement to the contending parties. As a result, the rare trial verdicts—particularly jury trial decisions—tend to get the lion's share of both analytical and political attention.

So, who wins these relatively rare cases? The BJS data indicate that plaintiffs do fare better than defendants when they take their chances at trial—plaintiffs won 53 percent of all cases sampled, and defendants, 45 percent. In specific types of cases, however, the numbers tell a different story. Thus, while plaintiffs won 60 percent of car accident cases, defendants (doctors and hospitals) won 74 percent of jury verdicts in medical malpractice suits (Smith et al. 1995).

It is important to note that while all of us are struck from time to time by the kinds of eye-popping, multimillion-dollar awards that make the news headlines, these are very rare. Thus, for example, the Center for State Courts reports that the percent of awards over $1 million in tort cases disposed by juries was only 8 percent, although that number jumps to 25 percent in medical malpractice and 15 percent in product liability cases (NCSC 1994a). Whatever one concludes from these data, it is important to keep in mind that torts constitute a relatively small percentage of civil claims overall; that tort filings have been decreasing, not increasing, over the past decade; that among tort claims alone, very few ever go to trial before juries; that even before juries, many times (and particularly in medical malpractice cases), the defendant, and not the plaintiff, wins; that in cases where the plaintiff does win before a jury, relatively few million dollar–plus awards are made; and that many of these awards are reduced on appeal. Thus, the mega-awards touted in headlines are very atypical indeed.

Still another issue raised in the tort debate is over the relative merits of tort actions. As discussed in chapter 3, stories about lawsuits brought on seemingly ridiculous grounds abound and have clearly been used to fuel the debate over tort reform. The American Tort Reform Association (ATRA), for instance, links to its web page an entire online menu of tort "horror stories," designed to demonstrate "a legal system that's out of control."[53] While some of these lawsuits are indeed goofy on the face of things,[54] others are made to look nutty when, in fact, serious issues are at stake,[55] and still others have been deemed "frivolous" by courts.[56]

Regardless of whether the data support a tort crisis, tort reform gained considerable political momentum during the 1990s. As of 1997, legislatures in forty-six states had enacted statutes either prohibiting punitive damages or "reducing their frequency and size" (Pace 1997, 1589). Moreover, in 1996, Congress passed *The Common Sense Product Liability Legal Reform Act* (H.R. 956, 104th Cong. [1996]). The law, vetoed by President Clinton, sought to preempt state law in several key areas, including raising plaintiffs' burden of proof and placing caps on punitive damages awards. Unquestionably, Congress will revisit the issue in the not-too-distant future. Notably, however, a number of state courts have begun striking down state legislative efforts, primarily on grounds that they represent legislative usurpations of judicial power (see e.g., *State ex Rel. Ohio Academy of Trial Lawyers v. Sheward*, 1999 Ohio LEXIS 2580 (Supreme Court of Ohio, 1999)), striking down the Ohio tort reform statute in its entirety as a violation of constitutional separation of powers).

THE CIVIL TRIAL PROCESS

When litigants do take their cases the full nine yards, the civil trial process looks, in many respects, like the criminal process—that is, the case may be brought before a jury or the bench (a judge sitting alone); the plaintiff presents her case first, followed by the defendant; and judgments are rendered after the case is concluded. There are, however, some important distinctions, a few of which are worth noting here. For example, those bringing civil suits—the plaintiffs—do not seek verdicts of guilty as the prosecutor would in a criminal case. Rather, civil plaintiffs urge the courts to find defendants *liable* for their wrongdoing. In turn, civil proceedings do not result in sentences, but rather, where the plaintiff is successful and the defendant is found liable, in *remedies*, usually assessed in the form of monetary *damages*. Where juries in criminal trials usually number twelve, a civil jury frequently is smaller and may be composed of as few as six members without running afoul of constitutional requirements. Finally, for our purposes, civil juries and judges are not held to the "beyond a reasonable doubt" standard of criminal trials, but rather to a less rigid "preponderance of evidence" criterion, where one side's set of facts is simply "more *convincing* to the trier than the opposing evidence."[57]

CIVIL APPEALS

As is the case in criminal cases, losing civil litigants have the right to appeal. Again, it is important to note that most potential civil grievances are probably never filed in court and of those that are, relatively few go to trial. Thus, we would expect appeals from trial judgments to represent a very small slice of total civil complaints. While our expectation would be correct, it is also the case that civil appeals abound.

Thus, in 1997, the federal circuit courts of appeal handled more than 19,000 nonprisoner-related[58] civil filings.[59] Notably, while the number of civil appellate filings has increased over the past decade, as a proportion of all federal appellate filings, civil filings have decreased.[60] The litigation crunch in the federal circuits is a result of increasing criminal, not civil, cases.

The decision to launch a civil appeal is a complex one, related closely to money. Thus, the decision to appeal is often driven by the size of the financial judgment against the losing party—the bigger the judgment, the more likely an appeal. As a result, "appellate court cases are unrepresentative of trial court filings because large dollar amounts are more likely to be involved" (Neubauer 1997, 392).

The decision to appeal is also related to the financial wherewithal of litigants. Appeals are quite expensive: generally speaking, lawyers must be paid, trial transcripts prepared, briefs printed, and filing fees paid. Unlike criminal appeals, where indigents are afforded these necessities free of charge, the burden of civil appellate costs is borne solely by the appellant, except in rare cases of legal pro bono work or the ever decreasing assistance of legal aid. Thus, we would expect civil appellants generally to be relatively more wealthy than the trial court population. Finally, and not surprisingly, the decision to appeal is related to the chances for success (Neubauer 1997, 392). Lawyers are thus crucial to the business of appellate courts since their experience in given case permutations determines whether they recommend appeal to their clients.

Conclusion

Like law itself, the structures and processes of law are everywhere—in trial and appellate courts, in state and federal jurisdictions, in civil claims and criminal prosecutions. Moreover, these structures and processes are daily faced with the conflicting demands of law. The courtroom itself, and the procedures employed therein, are designed to bring *orderly* resolution to conflict,

while presumably safeguarding the *liberty* interests of the combatants. The dual function itself can—and does—produce its own friction. This is often most apparent in the realm of criminal procedure. The law sets up venues and procedures whereby the people, through their surrogate, the state, may exact justice—even revenge—against those who break the rules of society. The prosecution is thus the people's agent of order. At the same time, the law has in place processes—nontrivial rules such as the Fourth, Fifth, and Sixth Amendments to the Constitution—designed to protect the liberty of those captured by the forces of order. This, in turn, has fostered, in recent years, further conflict in society at large, often between civil libertarians who fear the erosion of constitutional defendants' rights[61] and those who claim that crime victims are short-changed in a system that pays too much heed to the legal needs of "criminals."[62]

Of course, lawyers are first among a number of actors crucial to the process and substance of law in general. In the next chapter, we explore the players involved in the web of law.

Law on the Web

In this chapter we cover a vast terrain, including the structures and processes of the legal web. Appearing below are some general-purpose websites for exploring courts and court organizations.

A Smattering of Court and Court-Related Sites

The United States Supreme Court

www.supremecourtus.gov/

In addition to opinions and orders, includes the Court's calendar, docket, and rules.

The Federal Judiciary Homepage

www.uscourts.gov/

Website of the Administrative Office of the (Federal) Courts with sections about the U.S. Courts, publications and directories, and links to other relevant sites.

Federal Judicial Center

www.fjc.gov/

Website of the Federal Judicial Center, the federal courts' agency for research and continuing education. Includes lots of online publications and links to other court-related sites.

United States Senate, Committee on the Judiciary

www.senate.gov/~judiciary/

Among other information, provides data on federal judicial nominations, including nomination hearings, statistics, executive sessions, and the current appointment status of, among others, U.S. District Court judges, U.S. Court of Appeals judges, U.S. Court of Federal Claims judges, U.S. attorneys, and U.S. marshals.

U.S. Department of Justice
www.usdoj.gov/

Homepage for Department of Justice with links to various agencies and publications.

United States Sentencing Commission
www.ussc.gov/

Homepage of the Sentencing Commission, including mission and some reports.

The Federal Court Locator
vls.law.vill.edu/Locator/fedcourt.html

Villanova's Center for Information Law and Policy locator includes a map of the U.S. Circuits, "clickable" to court homepages and links to a searchable Supreme Court database.

Law Research
www.lawresearch.com/cfjudic.htm

Another good page with links to courts and other law-related sites.

U.S. Court of Appeals for the Federal Circuit
www.fedcir.gov/

First Circuit Court of Appeals, Recent Decisions
www.law.emory.edu/1circuit/

Sponsored by Emory University.

www.ljextra.com/public/daily/XD1ca.html

Sponsored by "Law Journal Extra," a service of American Lawyer Media, Inc.

Second Circuit Court of Appeals, Recent Decisions
www.tourolaw.edu/2ndCircuit/

Sponsored by Touro College Jacob D. Fuchsberg Law Center and Pace University School of Law.

Third Circuit Court of Appeals, Recent Decisions
vls.law.vill.edu/Locator/3/index.htm

Sponsored by Villanova University.

Fourth Circuit Court of Appeals, Recent Decisions
www.law.emory.edu/4circuit/index.html

Sponsored by Emory University.

Fifth Circuit Court of Appeals
www.law.utexas.edu/us5th/us5th.html

Links to Fifth Circuit homepage and opinions sponsored by the University of Texas Law School.

Sixth Circuit Court of Appeals, Recent Decisions
www.law.emory.edu/6circuit/index.html

Sponsored by Emory University.

Seventh Circuit Court of Appeals
www.kentlaw.edu/7circuit/

Seventh Circuit: Searchable Database
www.kentlaw.edu/cgi-bin/fx?DB'7circuit

Sponsored by Kent University School of Law.

Eighth Circuit Court of Appeals, Recent Decisions
www.wulaw.wustl.edu/8th.cir/

Sponsored by Washington University School of Law; includes circuit opinions, docket sheets, circuit calendar, and circuit rules and publications.

Ninth Circuit Court of Appeals, Recent Decisions
www.ca9.uscourts.gov/

The circuit's homepage.

Tenth Circuit Court of Appeals, Recent Decisions
www.kscourts.org/ca10/

Sponsored by Washburn University School of Law Library; keyword searching is available.

Eleventh Circuit Court of Appeals, Recent Decisions
www.law.emory.edu/11circuit/

Sponsored by Emory University.

D.C. Circuit Court of Appeals, Recent Decisions
www.ll.georgetown.edu/Fed-Ct/cadc.html

Sponsored by Georgetown University's School of Law.

National Center for State Courts
ncsc.dni.us/

Publications and research on state courts.

State Court Websites
ncsc.dni.us/COURT/SITES/Courts.htm#state

An extensive array of links to state court websites, alphabetically listed by state; provided by the National Center for State Courts.

State Justice Institute
www.statejustice.org/

Homepage of the State Justice Institute, established by federal law in 1984 to award grants to improve the quality of justice in the state courts, facilitate better coordination and information sharing between state and federal courts, and foster innovative, efficient solutions to common problems faced by all courts. Site includes publication downloads and other resources.

International Court of Justice
www.icj-cij.org/

Homepage for the Court of International Law under the auspices of the United Nations.

A Smattering of Process-Related Sites

Federal Rules of Evidence

www.law.cornell.edu/rules/fre/overview.html

The full set of rules and comments, provided by Cornell University's Legal Information Institute.

Rules of the U.S. Supreme Court

www.supremecourtus.gov/ctrules/ctrules.html

Rules of the Supreme Court available in PDF format.

Bureau of Justice Statistics, U.S. Department of Justice

www.ojp.usdog.gov/bjs/

Great statistics and statistical studies on crimes and victims, criminal offenders, law enforcement, prosecution, courts and sentencing, corrections, and justice-related expenditures and employment. Also, links to crime and justice data from other sources.

5 Denizens of the Web: Lawyers, Judges, Juries, and Interest Groups

Webs are centers of activity only because they are home to creatures able to engage in active enterprise. So, the spider's web at various times is a hospitable (and oftentimes inhospitable) residence to a variety of baby spiders, mosquitoes, flies, wasps, and the spider herself.

Of course, this is the point at which we could well take the analogy too far, specifically naming human mosquitoes, flies, wasps, and spiders. The possibilities for comparison are endless, and some are obvious, but we decline to make them. Suffice it to say that, in one way or another, as we illustrate in subsequent chapters, we are all a part of the larger web of law and society and we are all, in one way or another, caught up by events spun out in the smaller segment of the web that is the judicial system.

Still, some beings get caught in webs by sheer happenstance, while others are there by design. No doubt, most of us are in the legal web by chance—by simply living in this society, we are caught in this web. But some of us are in the web by specific intent, if not our own, then that of others close by. This chapter focuses on the regulars or "insiders" to the web. We begin with a discussion, then, of lawyers, followed by brief reviews of the roles and functions of judges, juries, and interest groups.

Lawyers

Of all the denizens of the web of law, the most obvious, crucial, *and* controversial are the lawyers themselves. Americans, as discussed in chapter 3, love lawyers *and* love to hate them. Thus, lawyers have been among our great heroes: Abraham Lincoln and Thomas Jefferson were, of course, lawyers. Popular culture has given us lawyers to love as well: the fictional Atticus Finch of *To Kill a Mockingbird* and the ubiquitous Johnny Cochran and Gerry Spence of the 1990s talk-show circuit are obvious examples. At the same time, lawyers have been among our greatest villains: Clearly, to many Americans, lawyer Kenneth W. Starr is the scoundrel du jour.[1] Of course, the popular imagination, whether expressed in literature, jokes, or office banter, is replete with facsimiles of the greedy, mercenary attorney. About lawyers, in short, we are ambivalent. As novelist, screen writer, and lawyer, John Grisham has said: "Though Americans distrust the profession as a whole, we have an insatiable appetite for stories about crimes, criminals, trials and all sorts of juicy lawyer stuff" (Grisham 1992, 33).

One is tempted to say that we'd better love "lawyer stuff," for just as the law is part of us and all around us, so lawyers are part of us and all around us—and their numbers are growing. In 1997, according to the Census Bureau, individuals listing "lawyer" (including judges) as their primary occupation totaled 925,000, marking an extraordinary increase of 274,000 over 1983 numbers. Although such ratios are very imperfect, that works out to roughly one lawyer for every 272 people in the United States (U.S. Census Bureau 1998).[2] Moreover, these numbers are expected to keep growing, although more moderately, with increases of between 10 and 20 percent projected through the year 2006 (Bureau of Labor Statistics 1998).

Legal Education

In order to practice law, a person needs to be licensed or admitted to a bar under rules established by the high court in the state in which he or she wishes to practice. The first step in this admission process is education. Most states require bar applicants to complete a four-year college education and a full course of study at a law school accredited by the American Bar Association (ABA). Currently, the ABA accredits 179 law schools. With few exceptions, graduates of schools not approved by the ABA may only take the bar examination and practice in the state where the unaccredited school is located.[3] In 1997, seven states accepted some form of "reading the law"—studying law in a law office solely or in combination with study in a law school (Baum 1998, 60).[4] The bottom line, however, is that most prospective lawyers should expect to receive a bachelor's degree followed by a law school education.

For most, that law school education will involve a three-year course of study.[5] Admittance to law school generally requires that students take and perform well on the Law School Admission Test (LSAT), a standardized exam that heavily emphasizes logical skills, which tends to strike terror in the hearts of even the best college undergraduates. Generally speaking, law school administrators feel that a student's LSAT score is the single best predictor of how she or he will perform in law school. Also important in the application process are the prospective student's grade point average, the quality of his or her undergraduate school, letters of recommendation from professors, previous work and extracurricular experience, and occasionally a personal interview.

Competition for available seats in law schools is brisk, but the level of competition varies over time. For example, during the 1970s and 1980s applications to law schools far outnumbered available seats. With the coming of age of the "baby bust" in the 1990s, applications, and thus, rivalry for seats, "decreased markedly." Demographers, however, anticipate that the new "baby boom echo," now making its way through the nation's elementary and secondary schools, will mean fierce renewed competition among applicants in the very near future (U.S. Census Bureau 1998).

In many respects, law school education is the same regardless of where one goes. As a general rule, first-year students take a required set of courses including contracts, torts, and constitutional law. Thereafter, while some requirements persist, students are freer to pursue specialized electives of interest. More and more law schools also offer clinics, internships, and moot courts to give students some practical experience during their legal education. All law schools offer opportunities to edit or write for one or several journals.

Although there is a certain sameness to the law school curriculum and although students may usually expect to get a quality education regardless of the school attended, to paraphrase George Orwell, "All law schools are equal, but some are more equal than others." In short, law schools get ranked and these rankings lend much to the prestige of the schools and to the employment prospects of their graduates. Undoubtedly, the most influential (and most controversial) of these rankings is the one published annually by *U.S. News and World Report*. Inevitably, Yale tops the list of so-called Tier 1 (the best of the best) schools. Nor are the remaining "anointed" a huge surprise. Following Yale, in its "1998 Annual Guide," *U.S. News* ranked Harvard, Stanford, Columbia, Chicago, New York (NYU), Berkeley (Boalt Hall), Duke, the University of Michigan (Ann Arbor), the University of Pennsylvania, the University of Virginia, Cornell, Georgetown, and Northwestern as stellar institutions. The rankings are based, in descending order of importance, on reputation,[6] selectivity,[7] placement success,[8] and faculty resources.[9] Thus, prestige and exclusivity beget prestige and exclusivity.

While rankings such as those published by *U.S. News* are extremely controversial,[10] they are not the only aspects of legal education in contention. The very content and methods of legal education are sometimes cited as producing future lawyers with corporate or "hierarchical" mentalities who disdain postgraduate work aimed at less-advantaged populations, such that fields like poverty and public interest law are deemed the bottom of the professional barrel (e.g., Kennedy 1990, 38–58;

Turow 1977). In particular, critics point to the form and substance of training at the nation's most prestigious law schools, which themselves are mimicked by less prominent institutions. Thus, for example, Harvard law professor Duncan Kennedy calls law school education "ideological training for willing service in the hierarchies of the corporate welfare state" (Kennedy 1990, 38).[11]

In addition, law schools have been criticized for favoring some demographic groups over others, in the past through overt discrimination, and now, through more subtle kinds of biases. Because law traditionally has been a white man's profession, certain groups continue to be underrepresented in law school, compared to their numbers in the general population, although there has been substantial progress. For example, African Americans were only 7.6 percent of the total first-year law students in 1997. Asian American first-year students totaled 6.5 percent, Hispanics 5.8 percent, and Native Americans 0.8 percent (Klein 1997, A6). Some experts worry that these percentages will actually begin declining as schools increasingly dismantle affirmative action programs in the wake of unfavorable court decisions and popular referenda.[12]

Underrepresentation applies to women as well as minorities, although the number of women in law school is beginning to catch up to their proportion of the general population. Hence, in 1997, according to the American Bar Association, law school enrollment for women reached 44.4 percent (Goldhaber 1998, 7).

Traditionally, too, the economically disadvantaged have found law school to be forbidding terrain. Obtaining a legal education is a tremendously expensive endeavor. For example, an in-state student attending the University of Maryland Law School could expect, conservatively, to have to cough up about $16,400 in expenses during his first year alone.[13] Not surprisingly, costs tend to skyrocket as one moves into the private "Tier 1" schools. Thus, a Yale student could anticipate forking over a virtual fortune in excess of $35,000—again, during her first year![14] For all but the most wealthy, these kinds of expenditures mean that the graduating law student will find herself in substantial debt by the end of her three-year educational stint—a Yalie, well in excess of $100,000, not counting any outstanding undergraduate loans.

Legal Work and Money

Of course, one very significant result of this kind of cost crunch is a tendency for law school graduates to look for the best-paying jobs. It probably goes without saying that such jobs are not found in government or in the public-interest sector of law, but rather in private practice, and particularly in private *corporate* practice.

At the very top of the heap, in 1997, the New York firm of Cleary, Gottlieb, Steen & Hamilton paid as much as

$102,000 to a first-year associate and Dewey Ballantine paid $98,000 in salary, along with a $3,000 bonus (Fisk 1998). In 2000, the California firms Gunderson Dettmer and Brobeck Phleger set first-year salaries at a staggering $125,000 plus bonuses (McClintock 2000). More seasoned attorneys in the elite corporate sector, including big firm partners and Fortune 500 in-house counsel, could expect financial packages in the high hundreds of thousands—even millions—of dollars. For example, in 1997, Philippe P. Dauman, deputy chairman, executive vice president, general counsel and chief administrative officer of New York's Viacom Inc., raked in a $ 1.1 million salary, with a $ 2.75 million bonus to sweeten the already pretty sweet pot (McClintock 2000).

Of course, overall, attorneys like Dauman are few and far between. Still, where one works can make a huge difference in pay even for the non-Daumans of the world. Thus, in 1998, as the salaries above suggest, corporate counsel and large-firm attorneys—the lawyers for big capital—could anticipate the highest salaries. At the other end of the spectrum are public interest and legal aid lawyers. For example, the starting salary for an attorney at the Public Citizen Litigation Group in Washington, D.C., was just $27,000 (*National Law Journal* 1 June 1998, 15). Her counterpart in the same city choosing (and chosen) to work at the prestigious private firm of Patton Boggs L.L.P. could expect to out-earn her by $53,000 during the first year of employment alone (p. 11). Indeed, the law offers a wide variety of remuneration: a first-year legal aid (aid to the poor) attorney could expect to make in the mid-$20,000 range (p. 13); a public defender, in the mid-$30,000 range (p. 14); an attorney for a federal agency in the high $30,000 range (p. 8); a city attorney in the $40,000 range (p. 13); and an assistant professor of law in the mid-$60,000 range (p. 15). A seasoned solo practitioner could expect to earn in the mid- to upper $30,000 range (Nelson 1994, 394, table 7).

How much an aspiring lawyer can hope to earn is related not only to the type of work he or she chooses, but to where he or she has gone to school. In turn, these figures are related to the relative prestige of the graduating institution and to the vagaries of regional economics—law school graduates, particularly those graduating from public institutions, tend to practice law in the region and state where their law school was located. So, for example, and not surprisingly, at one end of the spectrum, the median salary of Yale's class of '97 who entered private practice was $80,000; the median salary of their counterparts from the University of Montana was $31,000 (*National Law Journal* 1 June 1998, 15).

Although white men continue to be disproportionately represented among practicing attorneys—and very heavily so among the most elite corporate counsel (Goldhaber 1998, 7)—they actually are making lower starting salaries than women and minorities. Thus, the median starting salary for men in the law school gradu-

ating classes of 1996 was $50,000; for women, it was $51,500. In the same year, the median starting salary for minorities was $60,000; for nonminorities, it was $50,000 (*National Law Journal* 1 June 1998, 15).

The vast majority of lawyers—about seven out of every ten—make their living in private practice, either in law firms or in solo practices. Of the remainder, most hold positions in government. Others are employed as house counsel by a wide variety of institutions including utilities, banks, insurance companies, real estate agencies, manufacturing firms, welfare and religious organizations, and other business firms and nonprofit organizations. Some lawyers work only part-time in the law, maintaining other occupations as full-time avocations (Bureau of Labor Statistics 1998).

Lawyers and Clients

The special information that lawyers derive from their studies ensures them a separate rank in society, and they constitute a sort of privileged body in the scale of intellect. This notion of their superiority perpetually recurs to them in the practice of their profession: they are the masters of a science which is necessary, but which is not very generally known; they serve as arbiters between the citizens; and the habit of directing to their purpose the blind passions of parties in litigation inspires them with a certain contempt for the judgment of the multitude. Add to this that they naturally constitute a body; not by any previous understanding, or by an agreement that directs them to a common end; but the analogy of their studies and the uniformity of their methods connect their minds as a common interest might unite their endeavors. Some of the tastes and the habits of the aristocracy may consequently be discovered in the characters of lawyers. They participate in the same instinctive love of order and formalities; and they entertain the same repugnance to the actions of the multitude, and the same secret contempt of the government of the people. I do not mean to say that the natural propensities of lawyers are sufficiently strong to sway them irresistibly; for they, like most other men, are governed by their private interests, and especially by the interests of the moment (de Tocqueville 1835).

Many would say that not much has changed since Alexis de Tocqueville made the observation noted above. Because of the costs of law school training; because of the lure of big money[15]; because, some (such as de Tocqueville and Kennedy) would say, of their training and the conservative nature of law itself; and because of the structure of the bar, the legal profession continues to demonstrate a certain "contempt for . . . the multitude." Certainly, for most lawyers, this "contempt" is neither overt nor even consciously felt. But if the practice of law itself, especially in the service of, and accessibility to, various kinds of clients is any indication, the subtle forces at work in M. de Tocqueville's time continue to have force today.

Some of this may be seen in differential client service—the wealthy, and particularly wealthy institutions, get the best legal assistance. Thus, since the very beginnings of the so-called corporate bar—large law firms and in-house counsel servicing business interests—in the late 1800s, the tendency has been for the top graduates of the top schools to gravitate toward it. Note, for example, the following observation made in 1933 by Karl Llewellyn, one of the foremost legal scholars of the early to mid-twentieth century:

Most of [the bar's] best brains . . . [are] in the service of large corporations. They are the ablest of legal technicians. I doubt if the world has ever known abler. But their main work is in essence the doing of business. . . . The practice of corporation law not only works for business men toward business ends, but develops within itself a business point of view. . . .[16]

In effect, Llewellyn was saying that corporations get the best legal service available. This fact has been noted repeatedly over the years. For instance, John Heinz and Edward Laumann, in a study of "the social structure of the bar," recognized two distinct "hemispheres" within the practice of law. One "hemisphere" consists of attorneys in large firms dispensing a very specialized, well-resourced lawyering to large organizations, such as corporations, unions, and governments. The other "hemisphere" includes lawyers in small practices serving individual clients. Generally speaking, lawyers in the latter "hemisphere" are less able to specialize and have fewer resources to offer their clients (Heinz and Laumann 1982, 319).

Marc Galanter has noted a similar phenomenon, although from a different perspective. Looking at the law from the angle of clients, he divides the litigation world into "Repeat Players (RPs)"—those who engage in "many similar litigations over time"—and "One Shotters (OSs)"—those "who have only occasional recourse to the courts" (Galanter 1994, 358). In general, RPs tend to be large, wealthy, institutional concerns, while OSs tend to have much less wealth and to be individual litigants. For a variety of reasons, RPs tend to do better in the judicial process than OSs. Add lawyers to the mix and the advantages of RPs are further magnified. For example, even accounting for the fact that an OS client may be able to avail herself of a legal specialist (i.e., a personal injury lawyer or a public defender), she may still be disadvantaged by some "distinctive features" of lawyers who tend to cater to the OS population. According to Galanter (1994, 363–64),

First, they tend to make up the "lower echelons" of the legal profession. Compared to the lawyers who provide services to RPs, lawyers in these specialties tend to be drawn from lower socio-economic origins, to have attended local, proprietary or part-time law schools, to practice alone rather than in large firms, and to possess low prestige within the profession. . . .

Second, specialists who service OSs tend to have problems of mobilizing a clientele (because of the low state of information among OSs) and encounter "ethical" barriers imposed by the profession which forbids solicitation, . . . referral fees, advances to clients, and so forth.

Third, the episodic and isolated nature of the relationship with particular OS clients tends to elicit a stereotyped and uncreative brand of legal services. . . .

Fourth, while they are themselves RPs, these specialists have problems in developing optimizing strategies. What might be good strategy for an insurance company lawyer or a prosecutor—trading off some cases for gains on others—is branded unethical when done by a criminal defense or personal injury plaintiff lawyer. It is not permissible for him to play his series of OSs as if they constituted a single RP.

Conversely, the demands of routine and orderly handling of a whole series of OSs may constrain the lawyer from maximizing advantage for any individual OS. . . . "[F]or all but the largest [personal injury] claims an attorney loses money by thoroughly preparing a case and not settling it early."

The fact of the matter is that the majority of the "best" (top graduates) of the "upper echelon" (those graduating from the *U.S. News* "Tier 1" schools) of the law work, in Lawrence Friedman's (1998, 289) words, "for the status quo." In de Tocqueville's words, almost two hundred years earlier, they exhibit an "instinctive love of order and formalities" that makes them "the most powerful, if not the only, counterpoise to the democratic element" (de Tocqueville 1835). The legal profession, then, both reflects existing social hierarchies and adds to the relative advantages and disadvantages of the classes within.

This is not to say that only the rich get law and justice—only that they get *better* and *more* law and justice. There are—and always have been—lawyers willing to work for dissident voices and economic outsiders. For example, the late William Kunstler was a tireless advocate for, mostly, left-wing defendants. The American Civil Liberties Union has defended every despised group from Communist revolutionaries to Nazi racists. The "Dream Team's" extraordinary leader, Johnny Cochran, regularly represents poor litigants in police brutality and racism cases. The truth is, however, that few of the poor or politically outcast could ever hope for the kind of legal representation afforded by a Cochran or a Kunstler. True, poor criminal defendants, the bulk of those accused of serious crimes, receive free legal representation from public defenders or court-appointed lawyers (Friedman 1998). But such lawyers, as good and caring as they may try to be, have enormous caseloads and are often unable to give their clients anything but the most perfunctory representation. Moreover, as we discuss in chapter 9, there is growing realization that lawyers selected in court-appointed systems may actually be substandard from a number of perspectives.

Civil representation of the poor is even more problematic. The Constitution does *not* guarantee anyone a lawyer for a civil case. Some lawyers do occasionally take on such cases free of charge, touching a very few poor individuals. Sometimes the poor do receive government assistance in civil cases, but this has been declining. Note, for example, Friedman's (1998, 290) description of the short, unhappy life span of the Legal Services Corporation, begun in the 1960s as part of President Johnson's War on Poverty initiative:

From the start, there was controversy over the program. Landlords were annoyed when poverty lawyers helped tenants fight eviction. Conservatives thought it was absurd to pay one agency of government to bring lawsuits against the rest of government. They considered poverty lawyers radicals, whose main aim was to drum up "activist" lawsuits, not to help the poor with ordinary legal problems. Many political leaders agreed. [Office of Economic Opportunity] lawyers had the annoying habit of fighting city hall. Some governors, too, tried to get rid of the program in their states. One of these was the governor of California, Ronald Reagan. Later he became president, and as president he proposed cutting off all federal money, leaving the states in charge of legal aid if they chose to support this kind of program. Congress balked, and the program continued. But the opposition made its mark. The program, in the 1990s, is a muted version of what began so boldly in a prior generation. Its vital fuel—money—has been reduced. And recent law has reined in some of its more visible—and effective—tactics. Since 1995, staff lawyers, for example, can no longer bring class actions.

As de Tocqueville predicted, we should not expect radical change from the legal profession.

Judges

If, within the legal profession itself, corporate partners and Fortune 500 counsel such as Philippe Dauman represent the pinnacle of the professional hierarchy, within the public's mind, judges represent that pinnacle. Of course, even within the legal profession, certain judges—the justices of the U.S. Supreme Court, some intermediate federal appeals judges, and some state supreme court judges are considered the summit of law.

Judicial Selection

Elite or not, judging is a rare occupation. According to the Census Bureau, judges nationwide number about 40,000 (U.S. Census Bureau 1998). Of course, the vast majority of these judges are—and are required to be—lawyers. However, after obtaining that (almost always) necessary law degree, how one gets to be a judge varies by jurisdiction. Some judges are appointed to their positions, usually by the chief executive officer with some input from a legislative body.[17] This is true of at least some judgeships in seven states (Baum 1998, 115). At its most familiar, this is the method employed by the federal government, where the president nominates individuals to fill judicial openings and the Senate must approve. Typically, an appointed judge is appointed for life.

A good many states allow the public to elect at least some of its judges. Such elections may be on partisan ballots (twelve states) or, more frequently, on nonparti-

san ballots (nineteen) where party labels are not displayed. Twenty states employ a hybrid system for at least some of their judicial offices, known variously as the "Missouri" or merit plan system (Baum 1998, 115). Merit plan systems vary considerably by state, but a fairly general pattern involves the governor appointing a judge after a nominating commission presents her with a list of candidates. Generally, these commissions are made up of lawyers who are elected by other lawyers, laypeople appointed by the governor herself, and the chief judge of the supreme court in the state. Thereafter, in order to keep some measure of electoral accountability, after a certain number of years or at the next general election, the judge has to run for retention on the popular ballot, usually to be voted up or down on a yes or no vote. In sum, then, judges may be appointed, elected, or both, and considerable variation of method exists both across and within jurisdictions.

The choice of method for selecting judges reflects some very basic differences in legal-political philosophy—and these differences date all the way back to the founding of the United States. Judicial appointment with lifetime tenure reflects a belief that law is (or should be) above politics and those who interpret the law should be both better than the public at large and shielded from the passionate impulses of the public at large. This philosophy—the basis for federal judicial selection—was well articulated by Alexander Hamilton during the public debate surrounding ratification of the Constitution. Thus, on the subject of judicial competency, Hamilton (*Federalist* #78) defended appointment and life tenure because

there can be but few men in the society who will have sufficient skill in the laws to qualify them for the stations of judges. And making the proper deductions for the ordinary depravity of human nature, the number must be still smaller of those who unite the requisite integrity with the requisite knowledge. These considerations apprise us, that the government can have no great option between fit character; and that a temporary duration in office, which would naturally discourage such characters from quitting a lucrative line of practice to accept a seat on the bench, would have a tendency to throw the administration of justice into hands less able, and less well qualified, to conduct it with utility and dignity.

Even more important to Hamilton was the notion that the judiciary should be free of electoral politics—that it should be free of any need to consider the passionate impulses of the majority, either directly or through its elected representatives, over the neutral constancy of the law:

If, then, the courts of justice are to be considered as the bulwarks of a limited Constitution against legislative encroachments, this consideration will afford a strong argument for the permanent tenure of judicial offices, since nothing will contribute so much as this to that independent spirit in the judges which must be essential to the faithful performance of so arduous a duty. This independence of the judges is equally requisite to guard the Constitution and the rights of individuals from the effects of those ill humors, which the arts of designing men, or the influence of particular conjunctures, sometimes disseminate among the people themselves, and which, though they speedily give place to better information, and more deliberate reflection, have a tendency, in the meantime, to occasion dangerous innovations in the government, and serious oppressions of the minor party in the community....

But it is not with a view to infractions of the Constitution only, that the independence of the judges may be an essential safeguard against the effects of occasional ill humors in the society. These sometimes extend no farther than to the injury of the private rights of particular classes of citizens, by unjust and partial laws. Here also the firmness of the judicial magistracy is of vast importance in mitigating the severity and confining the operation of such laws. It not only serves to moderate the immediate mischiefs of those which may have been passed, but it operates as a check upon the legislative body in passing them; who, perceiving that obstacles to the success of iniquitous intention are to be expected from the scruples of the courts, are in a manner compelled, by the very motives of the injustice they meditate, to qualify their attempts.

In other words, as Justice Anthony Kennedy recently put it, "The law makes a promise. The promise is neutrality. If that promise is broken, the law ceases to exist. All that's left is the dictate of a tyrant, or a mob."[18]

Of course, while Hamilton's strong argument won the day for the appointment and life tenure of federal judges, the fact that so many state jurists are elected by popular vote suggests a very different line of thought—a line of thought that argues strongly that in a democratic republic all officials, including judges, should be directly accountable to the popular will for their actions. On the understanding that judges make policy just as surely as legislators and executives, they too should answer to the majority. Hence, no less than Thomas Jefferson ([1820] 1905, 297–98) himself wrote:

A judiciary independent of a king or executive alone, is a good thing; but independent of the will of the nation is a solecism, at least in a republican government.... To consider the unelected judges as the ultimate arbiters of all constitutional questions would place us under the despotism of an oligarchy.[19]

Of course, how well either method actually serves its underlying premises is itself a subject of great debate. For example, Hamilton argued that appointment with life tenure is the best way to identify and retain those "few men in the society who will have sufficient skill in the laws." However, studies have indicated that, at least at the state level, individuals of similar training and experience end up being judges regardless of the selection system.[20]

The issue of judicial independence—of judicial neutrality toward parties and issues and fidelity to law above politics—is a much more difficult one. Ask any judge—appointed or elected, state or federal, trial or ap-

pellate, Democrat or Republican—and she will claim (and, no doubt, usually believe) that partisanship, ideology, and political considerations play absolutely no part in her legal decision making. Any judge, if asked, would proclaim (and, no doubt, usually believe) himself to be a thoroughly impartial servant of the law (see, e.g., McIntosh and Cates 1998, chapter 1). Regardless of mode of selection, this is what we expect from judges and, no doubt, this is what most judges try to achieve. At the same time, however, there is little doubt that political ideology and partisan leaning—the outcome, generally, of years of socialization before coming to the bench—play some part in judicial decision making. After all, even in the most fully and familiar of appointive systems, Republican presidents tend to nominate Republicans to judicial slots because they expect them to rule like, well, Republicans. So, too, and for the same reason, Democratic presidents try to award judgeships to Democrats.

This is not to suggest that judges subconsciously vote on party lines. It is to say, however, that judicial ideological predisposition does make a difference, particularly on some kinds of issues. For example, partisan differences tend especially to play themselves out in the area of criminal case law. Thus, during the mid-1960s at the height of the so-called "due process revolution,"[21] the Supreme Court consisted of six Democrats and three Republicans, the appointees of four Democratic presidents (Franklin D. Roosevelt, Truman, Kennedy, and Johnson) and one moderate Republican (Eisenhower).[22] By contrast, the 1990s saw considerable whittling away of the "revolution"[23] under a Court dominated by seven Republicans and two Democrats, appointees of four Republican presidents (Nixon, Ford, Reagan, and Bush) and one Democrat (Clinton).[24] Candidates for state elective positions may be quite outspoken on the criminal law front, sometimes openly campaigning as "law-and-order" aficionados and "get-tough-on-crime" types, all the while, of course, touting their judicial objectivity and impartiality.

At the same time, identifying clearly partisan or ideological decisions is much more difficult in the judiciary than it is in the legislative or executive branches—at least, the identification takes on different dimensions. Thus, while few if any judges would admit that their decisions are liberal or conservative, or Democratic or Republican, if pressed, a judge will sometimes willingly identify himself as being restrained or activist in his judicial decision making. Generally speaking, regardless of whether a judge is *really* restrained or activist, the politically correct public response for a judge to take is one of restraint. These terms are themselves both murky and politically charged, particularly the term judicial "activism."[25] The point is made by excerpting the definitions of a variety of political scientists, law professors, legislators, and judges. Thus, for example, Holland (1991, vii) defines judicial activism as the belief "that it is legitimate for [judges] to formulate social policy. . . ." For Wolfe (1991, 32), it is, more boldly, "the exercise of 'legislative' power by courts." DeLay (1998) deems it the "unilateral . . . impos[ition by a judge] of legislative remedies." Baum (1998, 317) prefers to put it in terms of indicators, such that frequent use of judicial review is good evidence of court activism. Horowitz (1977, 19) would call it the difference between "saying no" to the other branches and "commanding" or "requiring" action. Bork (1990, 17) apparently demarcates it as any court action that fails to offer an "adequate [constitutional] reason for frustrating the democratic outcome." To Berger (1986, 8–12), it is simply making, rather than interpreting, laws. Schubert (1972, 17) defines it as "decisions [that] conflict with those of other policymakers." Maltz (1983, 825) tells us that it is the judicial defining of "courses of action that other branches of government may not pursue." Merrill (1987, 622) says it is "the lack of fidelity to constitutional text." Mullenix (1986, 156) asserts it is "a cynical disregard for clearly expressed congressional intent. . . ." Putting on a happier face, Barber (1988, 836) maintains that it is "the practice of judges forming their best understanding of general constitutional ideas. . . ." Well, you get the idea.

No less cloudy is the politically more acceptable term, "restraint." It, too, has various meanings and can be quite fungible. For example, House Majority Whip Tom DeLay (R-TX) who made a practice of referring to the federal judiciary in terms such as "despotic" and "dictatorial" (DeLay 1998), viewed "restrained" judges as ones who simply "apply the law." Of course, application means interpretation—presumably to Rep. DeLay's satisfaction.

Judges themselves, at various times and with a variety of implications, have undertaken to define judicial restraint. Most commonly, it is judicially defined, in one way or another, as "the practice of deferring to rationally based legislative judgments" (U.S. v. Lopez, 514 U.S. 549, at 604 (1995) (Souter, J., dissenting)). But, of course, judges frequently disagree over principles such as "rational basis." Not infrequently, even the most avowedly deferential judges are more or less deferential to the will of political majorities depending on the issue at hand. For example, Chief Justice Rehnquist, beginning with his notable dissent to Roe v. Wade over a quarter of a century ago, has maintained often that judges should almost always yield to the will of political majorities. However, as numerous commentators have noted:

Rehnquist's commitment to a kind of judicial abstinence has not been unwavering. He is less inclined to defer to the political branches in cases involving states' rights, property rights, and race. During the past two decades, maintaining that the Constitution is color-blind, he has lent his support to a series of decisions striking down affirmative-action programs and voting districts constructed [by legislative majorities] for the benefit of racial minorities (Rosen 1999, 31).

Equally as dicey is the issue of accountability. For appointed jurists, accountability is necessarily removed from direct public control. If there's a bad apple in the judicial barrel, it can only be discarded through the legislative impeachment process. Elective judicial positions, however, are premised on public accountability. Yet, that accountability itself is further premised on public awareness. Here, the record is pretty bleak. Voters typically know little or nothing about candidates for judicial office or for retention (Baum 1998, 127). When we bother to vote for judges at all it is usually as an ignorant afterthought to the "real" presidential, congressional, gubernatorial, or mayoral contest that heads the ballot. Where possible, judges mostly get selected on party identification alone. Of course, in nonpartisan elections (the majority of judicial elections), most voters do not even have this minimal information. Unless the judgeship in question happens to have hit the front pages for some unlikely[26] or highly politically charged reason,[27] the typical voter must rely on vague name recollection, a wild guess, or, in retention elections, a generalized desire to maintain or rock the status quo—in any event, not on any of the criteria generally thought of as enhancing democratic accountability.

Judicial Work

Regardless of how one gets there, being a judge is a pretty darned good job—though not as good, some would say, as it used to be. A judge can expect to make in the high five- to six-figure range depending on jurisdiction and rank. For example, topping the judicial heap, in 1997 Chief Justice Rehnquist earned $171,500; the eight associate justices, $164,100. During the same year, federal district court judges had salaries of $133,600, and circuit court judges earned $141,700. Annual salaries of associate justices on state supreme courts averaged $101,800 in 1997, and ranged from about $68,900 to $133,600, while state intermediate appellate court judges earned on average $91,000, and ranged from $79,400 to $124,200 (Bureau of Labor Statistics 1998). Such salaries are hardly chicken feed, though compared to what a really seasoned top-notch attorney could earn in the private sector, they are relatively low. The tradeoffs are prestige and power.

Clearly, the judicial office carries with it tremendous prestige. Generally speaking, public opinion ranks judges near the top of the occupational heap in terms of status. Thus, for example, one study of occupational prestige ranked judges generally at about the high position of doctors, with college professors, "regular" lawyers, airline pilots, and nurses trailing behind. Supreme Court justices outranked even doctors (Bureau of Labor Statistics 1998).

Power, too, is an occupational bonus. Judges decidedly reign over their courtrooms. As one commentator put it:

No one has yet invented a protractor fine enough to measure the angle to which even the most respectable lawyers bow and scrape before judges. No matter what their personality, when approaching the bench they tend to sound like Eddie Haskell of "Leave It to Beaver" talking to June Cleaver. They compliment the judge's appearance, lavish him with honorifics, pore over his decisions, praise his erudition, double over with laughter at even his lamest jokes (Margolick 1989, B9).

Judicial power, of course, is more than just the feigned sycophancy of courtroom supplicants. Although much of judicial work is routine, judges do make life-and-death decisions (sometimes, literally) and even a "routine" judicial decision on a technical question involving evidence introduction, permissible questioning of witnesses, or jury instructions may have a profound effect on the outcome of any individual case. Some judicial decisions have much broader sweep. For example, U.S. District Court Judge Thomas Penfield Jackson, overseeing the antitrust trial of Microsoft, may ultimately determine the configuration of the powerful software market in America (see, e.g., *U.S. v. Microsoft*, 65 F. Supp. 2d 1; 1999 U.S. Dist. LEXIS 17110 (U.S. District Court for the District of Columbia, 1999)). And, of course, many feel that the Supreme Court determined the outcome of the presidential election of 2000 (*Bush v. Gore*, 121 S.Ct. 525 (2000)).

Some appellate court decisions may have even more profound consequences for the state of law and society. Thus, for example, although implementation was slow and shaky to say the least, the Supreme Court's 1954 decision in *Brown v. Board of Education* ultimately resulted in changing the entire social fabric of the South, if not the entire nation. Brown is only the most obvious example.

Despite the extent of potential power, judges increasingly complain about loss of necessary authority, particularly over sentencing decisions. Congressional and state legislative imposition of sentencing guidelines and mandatory minimum sentences over the past decade have left many judges feeling like "little more than calculators."[28] The effect, many judges complain, has been to transfer power from the judicial bench to the executive prosecutor's office.

Juries

While lawyers and judges make up what might be called the professional regular denizens of the web, others—nonprofessionals—are crucial to its functioning. One such group of players is juries. Because, as we discussed above, most lawsuits get settled or plea bargained, juries do not play nearly as large a role in the real world of law as a steady diet of legal fiction or Court TV watching would lead us to believe. Only 4.3 percent of federal criminal cases now end in jury verdicts and only 1.5 percent of civil cases are resolved by juries (Glaberson 2001). Still, the majority of actual trials are jury trials

and so these lay denizens of the legal web are important, though, many would argue, not nearly as important as they once were.

Certainly, our founding fathers considered them essential—essential not only to the administration of justice, but to the entire fabric of our liberal democratic republic. Thus, Thomas Jefferson ([1789] 1924, 83–84) wrote of juries,

Were I called upon to decide whether the people had best be omitted in the Legislative or judiciary department, I would say it is better to leave them out of the legislature. The execution of the laws is more important than the making of them.

John Adams ([1766] in Bailyn 1992, 74) said that the jury placed inside the "executive branch of the constitution . . . a mixture of popular power." Because of this popular power, "the subject is guarded in the execution of the laws." Finally, Alexander Hamilton (*Federalist* #83) observed:

The friends and adversaries of the plan of the [constitutional] convention, if they agree in nothing else, concur at least in the value they set upon the trial by jury; or if there is any difference between them it consists in this: the former regard it as a valuable safeguard to liberty; the latter represent it as the very palladium of free government. For my own part, the more the operation of the institution has fallen under my observation, the more reason I have discovered for holding it in high estimation; and it would be altogether superfluous to examine to what extent it deserves to be esteemed useful or essential in a representative republic, or how much more merit it may be entitled to, as a defense against the oppressions of an hereditary monarch, than as a barrier to the tyranny of popular magistrates in a popular government.

Juries, then, were considered crucial to the maintenance of liberty.[29]

Nor did this notion of juries as the cornerstone of the republic end with the ratification of the Constitution. According to de Tocqueville (1835), observing our political institutions in the 1820s,

The institution of the jury may be aristocratic or democratic, according to the class from which the jurors are taken; but it always preserves its republican character, in that it places the real direction of society in the hands of the governed, or of a portion of the governed, and not in that of the government. Force is never more than a transient element of success, and after force comes the notion of right. A government able to reach its enemies only upon a field of battle would soon be destroyed. The true sanction of political laws is to be found in penal legislation; and if that sanction is wanting, the law will sooner or later lose its cogency. He who punishes the criminal is therefore the real master of society. Now, the institution of the jury raises the people itself, or at least a class of citizens, to the bench of judges. . . . The jury is pre-eminently a political institution; it should be regarded as one form of the sovereignty of the people: when that sovereignty is repudiated, it must be rejected, or it must be adapted to the laws by which that sovereignty is established. The jury is that portion of the nation to which the execution of the laws is entrusted, as the legislature is that part of the nation which makes the laws; and in order that society may be governed in a fixed and uniform manner, the list of citizens qualified to serve on juries must increase and diminish with the list of electors. This I hold to be the point of view most worthy of the attention of the legislator; all that remains is merely accessory.

From the vantage point of the late twentieth century and early twenty-first centuries, statements like those of Jefferson, Adams, Hamilton, and de Tocqueville seem absolutely extraordinary. Far from feeling that "the real direction of society" has been placed in her hands, the typical potential juror today is likely to greet a jury summons with all the enthusiasm of being told by her dentist that she needs several root canals. Once (and probably unhappily) on the jury, far from being buoyed by the knowledge that he stands as a "barrier to . . . tyranny," the typical juror is likely to feel oppressed by judicial instructions, mostly telling him what he may *not* do. And far from feeling like the "guardian" of all her fellow citizens, a juror today is just as likely to be criticized for having come to an ignorant decision.[30] What happened, then, to bring us from a time two hundred years ago, when juries were "the real master of society," to the present time marked by increasing calls for the abolition of the institution? A number of forces have contributed to the demise of the American jury.

First, according to legal historian Morton Horwitz, the answer lies in rapid economic changes, aided and abetted by America's growing professional bar. Thus, writing on the "transformation of American law" between 1790 and 1860, Horwitz (1977, 141) observed:

It should . . . come as no surprise . . . that in most cases "merchants were not fond of juries." For one of the leading measures of the growing alliance between bench and bar on the one hand and commercial interests on the other is the swiftness with which the power of the jury is curtailed after 1790.

Juries, armed with the power not only to judge the facts of a case, but to judge law itself, were widely viewed among the emergent capitalist class and its increasing number of attorney allies as destabilizing elements. In order to expand and take firm root, capital needed reliability in law—legal power in the hands of lay jurors was, well, just too damned democratic to provide that stability. As a result, the bench and bar developed "three parallel devices . . . used to restrict the scope of juries":

First, during the last years of the eighteenth century American lawyers vastly expanded the "special case" or "case reserved," a device designed to submit points of law to judges while avoiding the effective intervention of a jury. . . . A second crucial procedural change—the award of a new trial for verdicts "contrary to the weight of evidence"—triumphed with spectacular rapidity in some American courts at the turn of the century. The ward of new trials for any reason had been regarded with profound suspicion by the revolutionary generation. . . . Yet not only had the new trial become a standard weapon in the judicial arsenal by the first decade of the nine-

teenth century; it was also expanded to allow reversal of jury verdicts contrary to the weight of evidence, despite the protest that "not one instance . . . is to be met with" where courts had previously reevaluated a jury's assessment of conflicting testimony." [Finally, and more fundamentally, d]uring the first decade of the nineteenth century . . . the Bar rapidly promoted the view that there existed a sharp distinction between law and fact and a correspondingly clear separation of function between judge and jury (Horwitz 1977, 141–43).

These changes in procedure ultimately transformed the jury from a law-interpreting, and thus, a legally eminent, body, to one largely subjected to judicial manipulation and control. They were ultimately transformed from independent triers of law to dependent triers of fact, a transformation completed by 1895 with the Supreme Court's rejection of a jury's right to judge the law (*Sparf and Hansen v. United States*, 156 U.S. 51, at 64–106 (1895)). John Adams' poignant assertion that "It is not only [the] right [of the juror], but his duty . . . to find the verdict according to his own best understanding, judgment, and conscience, though in direct opposition to the Court" (*Sparf and Hansen*, 143–44 (Gray, J., dissenting); emphasis added) was ultimately reduced to a quaint, but meaningless, historical shibboleth.[31]

Other related forces—social, political, demographic, and technological in nature—contributed as well to the decline in the importance of the jury. Note, for example, de Tocqueville's observation above that "the list of citizens qualified to serve on juries must increase and diminish with the list of electors." We are mostly chosen to be jurors on the basis of voter registration records. During the late eighteenth and early nineteenth centuries, the chosen were indeed the "chosen"—that small, white, male, and relatively prosperous group of fully invested citizens. The jury, designed to safeguard the citizenry from the corrupt vagaries and designs of officialdom run amok, was largely extracted from the same elite pool as those potentially capricious and calculating officials. However, as the franchise became increasingly "common," beginning with the Jacksonian Revolution through the ratification of the Fifteenth and Nineteenth Amendments and ending with the *Voting Rights Act of 1965*, so, too, the pool of potential jurors was decreasingly reflective of the upper class. The jury was looking more and more like the mob, so feared and so restrained in the original constitutional design.

Nor, to be honest, did the jury of commoners always do itself proud. Before Supreme Court rulings had fully institutionalized the right of people of color and women to sit on juries, it was not uncommon for all white male juries, contrary to any evidence, to find African Americans guilty of crimes against whites, or later, to acquit white killers of blacks and civil rights workers, in spite of overwhelming evidence (Abramson 1994, 61–62).

In addition, as we have noted above, the seemingly inexorable tendency over the course of this century to more and more settlements before trial, both in criminal and civil cases, has made the jury something of a juridical anomaly—a kind of tool of crisis that only kicks in when no other peaceful solution can be reached.

Finally, many critics of the modern jury believe that far from representing "the very palladium of free government," it increasingly represents an obstacle to true justice. The argument goes that the trend in civil cases toward more and more complex controversies and in criminal cases toward more and more sophisticated methods of fingerprinting, including, notably, DNA "fingerprinting," means that the evidence and arguments are incomprehensible to the average lay juror. As trial attorney Clay S. Conrad (1998, 44) has noted:

Any first-year law student has probably grown accustomed to hearing law professors condescendingly criticize the jury. "And do you think the jury pays attention to instructions or merely disregards them?" "Can a jury possibly understand DNA evidence?" "Could a jury of laymen conceivably comprehend this contract?" Given the nature of the jury system, neither professors nor practicing lawyers find it necessary to substantiate such criticisms. Some law students may even find that to put themselves above the jury sounds witty and superior.

Nor is this simply a conceit of law professors and their more puffed-up progeny. Many judges have expressed similar misgivings about the intellectual abilities of jurors in light of increasingly complex forms of evidence.[32] As one observer has put it, "There is growing . . . impatience with the very institution of the jury trial" (Gildea 1994, 456).

This sort of impatience has led to renewed calls for reform, most of which would ultimately result in the further legal-political diminution of the jury. The most radical of these view the jury as "an inefficient anachronism, a luxury of democratic illusion which we can no longer afford" (Brodin 1990, 17), and thus call for outright abolition of the institution. Others, generally aimed at civil juries, would simply modify the function of the jury, for example, from broad-based delivery of general verdicts to more narrow transmission of special verdicts.[33] Whatever the ultimate resolution, the jury—the only institution that places the law directly "in the hands of the governed"—is an institution in deep trouble.

Interest Groups

Of course, juries are not the only "civilians" with their hands *in* the law. Needless to say, litigants are crucial to the process of law. As we have already discussed, litigants come in a variety of shapes and sizes, harboring a variety of motives and agendas. Thus, we concentrate here on a particularly important configuration of litigants, namely, interest groups, for the number of groups seeking influence in the judicial process has mush-

roomed in modern times, with considerable impact on the web of law and society.

Of course, group politics, broadly construed, have always been integral to the web—indeed, in important respects, group politics are the very *foundation* of the American web. Recall, then, the discussion in chapter 3 of Madison's theory of faction, a theory which forms the basis of our entire constitutional scheme—the Constitution is one giant legal attempt to mitigate and balance factional (or group) impulses.

As even the most casual observer of American politics over the years would attest, group politics has remained the lynchpin of society.[34] Thus, interest groups have long pressed the political establishment in attempting to get what they want—that is, the *laws* that they want. Since the founding, interest groups have lobbied the legislative and executive branches (the term "lobby" actually comes from the tendency of early congressional supplicants to hang around hotel lobbies in attempts to buttonhole members) and have financed the electoral campaigns of those seeking office.

Such time-honored and recognized means of influence peddling, however, are mostly considered unethical—even illegal—when applied to the judiciary. The rules of the judicial process simply prohibit such direct encounters between lobbyists and judges. Thus, if interest groups want to influence the outcomes of legal disputes, they have to find alternative routes of "lobbying"—routes that correspond to the norms of the judiciary.

Strategies and Tactics of Group Litigation

In order to avoid direct encounters with judges, yet still influence judicial decisions, interest groups rely primarily on two legal strategies: (1) they sponsor test cases, and (2) they file amicus curiae briefs.

TEST CASES

In general, groups sponsor test cases—that is, cases designed to test specific legal arguments and doctrines—by supplying the attorneys and funds necessary to carry a case to the appellate level. For example, the American Civil Liberties Union—a frequent, traditional group participant in the judicial process—regularly provides attorneys, research support, and other court-related expenditures to litigants interested in testing principles primarily emanating from the Bill of Rights (see, e.g., *Reno v. ACLU*, 521 U.S. 844 (1997)). The NAACP Legal Defense Fund—a longtime group participant—provides attorneys and resources to litigants interested in pursuing racial equity principles (see, e.g., *U.S. v. Georgia*, 171 F.3d 1333; 1999 U.S. App. LEXIS 6306 (11th Cir. 1999)). While this kind of liberal interest group participation has been a mainstay of court business for a long time, conservative interest groups, such as a variety of "right-to-life" interests, have also gotten into the test case business in a big way (see, e.g., *Pastors for Life v. Gynecology Clinic, Inc.*, 1999 S.C. LEXIS 1999 (South Carolina Supreme Court, 1999), cert. denied, 120 S. Ct. 862 (2000)). Quite often, this kind of test case activity—whether liberal or conservative—goes further than just providing attorneys and funds for appellate argument. For example, it is not uncommon for groups, prior to litigating a case, to very literally inundate law reviews with articles presenting constitutional or other legal justifications for their causes, later citing those very articles as authority in their legal briefs.

Thus, launching a test case is expensive, time consuming, and an extremely complex game. Despite this, many groups believe it to be a worthwhile venture. Certainly this has been true over the course of this century for political "outs," organizations that historically have not had the political muscle necessary to influence the elected branches of government.[35] The most obvious example of this was the NAACP's quest to attain equal constitutional status for African Americans. When that organization formed in 1909, southern state legislatures literally denied blacks access to their floors—they literally could not lobby the legislature. On top of that, most blacks were prevented from voting, so they had no representation in legislatures. Under those circumstances, it was virtually impossible for that group to affect policy in the traditional arenas—the majoritarian arenas—of government. As a result, they, and other groups,[36] strategically turned to the courts—the antimajoritarian branch of government—where they could be, and were, more successful.

Not do only historically disadvantaged groups use litigation as a strategic tool. Increasingly, more conservative groups—business organizations and trade associations, for example—use the litigation strategy. They do so for several reasons.

First, powerful or not, occasionally just about everyone suffers losses in the legislature. A good line of defense against a legislative loss may be to launch a legal challenge against whatever undesired bit of legislative business upended the group's preferred agenda. In this respect, litigation may be a good, if expensive and very uncertain, way of shaking up or maintaining the political status quo.

Second, and related to the above, many groups now perceive the appellate courts—and particularly, the U.S. Supreme Court—to be the final arbiter of the law. Although court opinions are seldom as definitive or as final as the popular mythology would suggest,[37] many groups have the perception that while legislation is always in flux—or subject to change—court decisions have a much greater degree of permanency—particularly if you're lucky enough to get a hearing before the Supreme Court.[38]

THE AMICUS CURIAE BRIEF

If a group does win a test case, direct sponsorship can have substantial benefits, but direct sponsorship also carries significant costs. Again, it is a very expensive activity; and a group may end up looking very bad if it loses a few significant cases. For these reasons, many groups, instead of, or in addition to, directly supporting cases, will simply file so-called *amicus curiae* briefs. Literally, "friend-of-the-court" briefs, amicus briefs actually involve befriending one of the parties to a lawsuit, such that nonparties (groups not directly involved in a lawsuit) will file briefs in support of one of the litigants in a case. Filing an amicus brief is far less expensive than direct sponsorship, but still may influence the outcome of a case and demonstrate support for a particular legal position.

Aside from sponsorship and brief filing, groups may seek to influence judicial outcomes in less direct, though no doubt riskier, ways. Of course, individuals running for elective state judgeships may, like legislators and executives, accept campaign finance contributions. How much influence such campaign contributions have on subsequent judicial decisions, however, is really unknown. Moreover, interest groups do seek to influence even the supposedly pristine environment of federal judicial selection. One need look no further than the parade of groups testifying before the Senate Judiciary Committee whenever a Supreme Court nomination is at stake.

In addition, some groups do seek to influence judicial decision making in ways that their influence is almost impossible to gauge. For example, when the Supreme Court announced its intention to consider the abortion-related case of *Webster v. Reproductive Health Services* (492 U.S. 490 (1989)), in addition to an enormous number of brief filings (seventy-eight), groups on both sides of the abortion issue held vigils outside the Court, marched and protested, and waged major media campaigns (O'Connor 1998). In short, pro-life and pro-choice forces seemed to be treating the Supreme Court as if it were Congress considering a piece of legislation and not a judicial body deliberating points of law.

FREQUENCY OF ORGANIZED PARTICIPATION

In recent years, between 60 and 70 percent of all cases decided by the Supreme Court with a full opinion were directly sponsored, on at least one side of the issue, by a group. Roughly 80 percent of all cases garnered at least one group amicus brief and most cases attract several amici. On these traditional litigation measures, a considerable amount of court-centered group activity abounds.

Moreover, the level of interest-group participation before the courts has mushroomed in recent years. Thus, in the 1930s, fewer than 2 percent of Supreme Court cases attracted amici briefs. In the following decade, the number jumped substantially to a little over 18 percent.

During the mid-1950s to mid-1960s, there was another increase to almost 24 percent, followed, during the 1970s, by a huge leap to 54 percent. Finally, the 1980s and into the 1990s witnessed yet another tremendous leap to roughly 80 percent (Epstein 1991, 351).

Why these dramatic increases in group participation before the Court? A number of factors may be at work.

First, across all areas of government there has been an explosion of pressure group activity since the late 1980s. Interest groups have been moving into every arena of government at record levels. Court activity is just one—albeit a rather unique—aspect of the general trend.

Second, within this general trend, the number of organizations dedicated to using litigation as a policy strategy has skyrocketed over recent years. Thus, a 1976 survey of public-interest law included ninety-two groups that used litigation as their primary or one of their primary policy stratagems. An identical survey, published a little over a decade later in 1989, included more than 250 (Epstein 1991, 354ff). Stated simply, more organizations are inevitably going to generate more group-backed litigation.

Third, the Supreme Court itself has probably encouraged group activity in several ways. For example, in 1963 the Court asserted that "groups which find themselves unable to achieve their objectives through the ballot frequently turn to the courts.... Under the conditions of modern government, litigation may be the sole practicable avenue open to a minority to petition for redress of grievances" (*NAACP v. Button*, 371 U.S. 415 (1963)).

Moreover, the Court has upheld legislation awarding attorneys fees to groups defending the public interest in certain areas of law. Even though the Court, under its own rules, may reject motions to file amicus briefs, it seldom does. The bottom line is that the Supreme Court has itself encouraged the incredible proliferation of group activity in the judicial process over the past few decades.

GROUP PARTICIPANTS

As most observers of the American political process would readily point out, lobbying in the legislative and executive branches is very much dominated by commercial interests. As E. E. Schattschneider (1960, 34–35) pointed out in his critique of pluralism some four decades ago, "The flaw in the pluralist heaven is that the heavenly chorus sings with a strong upper-class accent." Thus, part of the damning critique of the so-called pressure system is characterized by the old saw that "money talks."

Be that as it may, for a number of reasons many Americans have come to believe that group influence on the Courts is very different. Hence, the mid-century litigation successes of African-American interests and War-

ren Court–era decisions favoring defendants and other disadvantaged groups have fed the notion that courts are particularly amenable to minority interests and unpopular groups. Moreover, the media, which devotes few resources to covering appellate decision making, when it does cover such tends to focus on the occasional high-profile, constitutional case. Such cases frequently involve facially noneconomic interests such as those involving race, censorship, and abortion.

Court statistics, however, tell a very different story. If we look overall at groups that sponsor litigation—excluding government—we find that commercial interests dominate pressure group activity at least in the Supreme Court. In fact, commercial interests sponsor more litigation than all other interests combined. Statistical examinations of amicus participants—again, excluding government—similarly suggest commercial domination (Epstein 1991, 354). Thus, the same interests that dominate the pressure system in the legislative and executive branches dominate the system in the judicial.

GROUP EFFICACY

Of course, "judicial lobbying," for all its growth, need not be particularly effective. After all, judges are our most insulated public officials. They are insulated precisely so they will not be swayed by the usual "down-and-dirty" of pressure politics. Thus, determining group efficacy in the courts is hardly a straightforward exercise, but one that may be gleaned in a couple of ways.

One way is to ask whether groups influence a court's decision to hear a case in the first place. Do group-backed cases stand a better chance of receiving a full hearing by the judiciary? The answer here is unequivocally, "yes." Researchers looking at all cases filed with the Supreme Court have found that the addition of just one amicus curiae brief in support of the Court giving a case a full hearing increases the likelihood of full review by 40 to 50 percent (Epstein 1991, 359–63). The fact that a group backs a petition for a case to be heard, thus, would seem to make a big difference.

Whether or not groups actually influence judicial opinions, however, is a much more complicated question. Here, social scientists are even more reliant on indicators. Thus, for example, some studies have suggested that group-backed litigation is more successful than cases that are not supported by groups. In the area of discrimination, studies have shown that cases sponsored by groups have a considerably larger likelihood of winning than those that are not sponsored by groups (Epstein 1991, 360–61). Yet another indicator is the fact that appellate judges quite often use the arguments presented in amici briefs in their own opinions.

Statistical indicators aside, however, social scientists and experts on jurisprudence have engaged in a long-running debate over the real, long-term impact of group action, particularly in the area of civil rights. As early as 1974 in a groundbreaking study, Stuart Scheingold (1974, 5) referred to a "myth of rights," tending to "tunnel the vision of both activists and analysts leading to an oversimplified approach to a complex social process—an approach that grossly exaggerates the role that lawyers and litigation can play in a strategy for change." Over the years, Scheingold's has been joined by numerous critiques of litigation as an effective strategy for change. Notable among these was Gerald Rosenberg's exhaustive 1991 study of several high-profile reform efforts. Rosenberg (1991, 336) concluded that "attempts to use courts to produce significant social reform in civil rights, abortion, women's rights, the environment, reapportionment, and criminal rights . . ." have had "mostly disappointing results. . . ." Hampered by a lack of implementation power and political hostility, courts, according to Rosenberg, are particularly ineffectual venues for reform (see, e.g., Dolbeare and Hammond 1971; Horowitz 1977).

Other analysts, however, disagree with these negative critiques. Significantly, Michael McCann's 1994 study of pay equity reform suggests that Rosenberg, Scheingold, and other critics have taken a far too narrow view of legal strategies. According to McCann, even where other, nonlitigation-based strategies were more effective on the face, activists effectively employed legal language and litigation threats to strengthen movements, to teach and rally new members, and to put pressure on other institutions and political players. Thus, litigation and law-based strategies may be essential elements of reform, with social movements gaining more from the legal process than simply winning cases (McCann 1994).

GOVERNMENT AS PARTICIPANT

If commercial interests dominate the private pressure system that "lobbies" the courts, government itself dwarfs even monied interests. Hence, if we think of the government as a group, then clearly government predominates in the litigation process. Of course, governments are the plaintiffs in all criminal actions and that fact alone makes them litigators-in-chief. In addition, governments get sued a lot and so spend a great deal of time in court defending themselves. It is worth noting, too, that governments are wildly successful in court. Prosecutors win most of their cases and judges, in administrative cases, tend to give the benefit of the doubt to government's side of things.

One very special indication of the government's strength as a litigant is found in the U.S. Solicitor General, the legal representative of the U.S. government, and a position so well regarded and successful that it is often referred to as the "tenth justice." The office has complete control over Justice Department appeals to the Supreme Court. Moreover, the solicitor general fre-

quently files amicus briefs in cases that interest the federal government. It is, in other words, a very powerful position.

That power is borne out in a couple of respects. For example, recent studies have shown that in deciding to hear a case, the Supreme Court will grant review about 70 percent of the time the solicitor general requests it; for all other groups, the rate is about 10 percent (see, e.g., Segal 1991, 376–82). Thus, the solicitor general is much more successful in getting the Court to hear cases than other groups.

Moreover, when it comes to amicus briefs, the solicitor is also incredibly effective. One study found that over a fifty-year period, the party supported by the solicitor general won 74 percent of the time before the Court (Segal 1991, 230). Other studies have confirmed these findings.

Conclusion

In this and the previous chapter, we have painted, with a very broad brush, a general picture of the structures, processes, and denizens of our legal-social web. On even the most cursory viewing, it is clearly a vast, deep, and complex edifice.[39]

In the section and chapters that follow we explore the web of law and society from the perspective of the individual and social life cycle. Regardless of whether we are ever judges, lawyers, jurors, or even litigants, and regardless of whether we know it or not, we are all regular, and regularly, participants in the web. We will begin with a brief section overview, followed by considerations of law and relationships, law and the beginning of life, law and personal identity, law and the end of life, and law in the larger political economy.

Law on the Web

A Smattering Legal Actors (Lawyers and Judges)

LAWYER ASSOCIATIONS

The American Bar Association
www.abanet.org/

The National Lawyers' Association
www.nla.org/

The National Lawyers' Guild
www.nlg.org/

American Bar Association, Commission on Women in the Profession
www.abanet.org/women/home.html

The National Bar Association
www.nationalbar.org/

Hispanic National Bar Association
www.hnba.com/

National Asian Pacific American Bar Association
www.napaba.org/index.html

Lesbian and Gay Law Association
www.le-gal.org/

The Association of Trial Lawyers of America
www.atlanet.org/

The Corporate Bar
www.corporatebar.org/

National Association of Attorneys General
www.naag.org/

National Association of Criminal Lawyers
www.criminaljustice.org/

National District Attorneys Association
www.ndaa.org/

National Association for Public Interest Law
www.napil.org/

National Association of Counsel for Children
naccchildlaw.org/

National Legal Aid and Defenders Association
www.nlada.org/

LAW SCHOOLS

Law Schools: USA
www.findlaw.com/02lawschools/fulllist.html
Alphabetically listed links to the nation's law schools.

JUDGE-RELATED SITES

The Judicial Conference of the United States
www.hyperlaw.com/jcjudges.htm

The Judiciary Leadership Development Council, Inc.
www.primenet.com/~jldc/
Sponsors seminars and conferences for judges.

National Judicial College
www.judges.org/
Offers a variety of programs to judges and other court personnel.

American Judges Association
aja.ncsc.dni.us/

A membership organization of which the goals are to improve the effective and impartial administration of justice, to enhance the independence and status of the judiciary, to provide for continuing education of its members, and to promote the interchange of ideas of a judicial nature among judges, court organizations, and the public.

Judicial Watch
www.judicialwatch.org/

Conservative foundation established to monitor judges and judicial opinions for ideological purposes.

Part II

Law and the Web of Life

Introduction

Now that we have traversed the surface of the web, it is time to enter. As we suggested in chapter 1, we are all—whether or not we want to be and whether or not we know it—part of the web of law and society. We are part of it before we are born and after we are laid to rest. Law affects all that we do all of the time. In this part of the book, we examine the breadth and meaning of that influence.

Our examination of the web in this section is based on the individual life cycle, key aspects of our lives that we all share in common. Of course, we are all born, we all assume identities, most of us manage to traverse the difficult terrain from childhood to adulthood, and we all die. The vast majority of us also form relationships—a few are close and loving, many more are simply casual or utilitarian. In all of this, law is implicated.

Thus, law and life, in the nature of webbed relations, are enmeshed. Unfortunately, webs are not neat linear affairs. They bend, they curve, they are sinuous and messy. Where does a web begin and where does it end? These are difficult, perhaps impossible, questions to answer. Taken in part, it is all confounding enough. As we suggested in chapters 2 and 3, there is no single starting point for law. Although on superficial examination an individual life seems to be traveled along a straight line from birth to death, a more thorough examination suggests that not even life is so straightforward. Hence, law and life in toto are truly dumbfounding.

The problem, from an organizational perspective, is where to begin and, of course, where to end. In attempting to solve or at least to mitigate this problem, we ask the two unanswerable questions, "Where does life begin?" and "Where does law begin?" These are the chicken-or-egg kinds of questions in a more abstract form. Needless to say, either one could keep a good philosopher going for all of her professional life, a luxury that neither we nor you have. For these limited purposes, we instead seek thoughtful and functional answers.

Marking the beginning of life, of course, can be a very morally, politically, and legally charged exercise. Where some place the marker at birth, others place it at quickening,[1] fetal viability,[2] or conception, and still others in the "potential" existence of an unfertilized egg. We decline to involve ourselves in this debate. Instead, for purposes of this book, we place the marker at the point of relationship. For regardless of whether one's moral, political, or legal opinion places the beginning of life at birth, fetal

movement, viability, conception, or in its potential, we can all agree that none of us would be here absent the relationship between our mother and our father.[3]

Very broadly defined, law also begins in relationships. Indeed, there would be no need for law if each of us occupied our own little islands, living isolated and solitary lives. We could do whatever we wanted. It is only when we come in contact with others that we and they need protection, assurances, and rules. Law orders relationships, both between and among familiars and between and among strangers.

Thus, law and life have a common and complex impetus—relationships. It is with intimate relationships, the particular kind of relationship that exists, for example, between husbands and wives or parents and children, that we begin this part of the book. Chapter 6 examines law and relationships, from the law's involvement in our romantic lives to its interest in our family lives.

In chapter 7, we look at law and the beginning of life, apart from the immediate family environment. The law intervenes even before we are born, calling for legal intervention in procreative decisions. Outcomes have escalated as technology increasingly has changed reproduction. Once we are born, the law is there as well, demanding that we be licensed, vaccinated, and educated. It also prohibits us from a variety of activities that, as adults, we could otherwise enjoy.

A large part of the psychological task of growing up involves forming identities. Here, too, the law enters. The law recognizes, in all its ambivalent and complex wonder, rights we have to our individual identities and reputations. Thus, in chapter 8, we analyze the law's role in our identities. Having been born and spent a lifetime forming relationships and identities, we all face the end of life. Again, the law looms large. This is the subject of chapter 9. While the first four chapters of Part II examine law mostly from the perspective of the individual life, we take the opportunity in chapter 10 to think about law in the context of the broader sociopolitical structure.

So, the law is ubiquitous from the beginning to the end of our lives. Throughout our lives, it attempts to perform the dual purposes of imposing order and preserving liberty. Thus, for example, law, through the granting of marriage licenses, authenticates intimate relationships so that property and responsibility may be shared and transferred in an orderly manner. Law demands a certain level of educational attainment so that the young may become productive members of the social system. Law prevents children from seeing and doing things that adults may be able to see and do as a means of fostering moral development in future civic participants. Law sees to it that society's elderly—those on the way out of the web—are not pushed out before their natural time. All these and many more are common illustrations of law's pull toward order.

At the same time, law assures us that most of us may choose the mate of our heart's desire. It affords considerable individual parental latitude in choosing the manner, mode, and setting of the educational experience. It leaves open to adult discretion any number of "vices" that are put out of legal reach of youngsters. Law allows the dying to refuse technologically heroic methods aimed at forestalling death's inevitable call. All of these and many more are common illustrations of law's tug toward liberty. In addition, all of these placed side by side with their order-enhancing cousins have caused conflict. Much of this conflict is played out in subsequent chapters.

6 Law and Relationships

> Marriage, while from its very nature a sacred obligation, is nevertheless, in most civilized nations, a civil contract, and usually regulated by law. Upon it society may be said to be built, and out of its fruits spring social relations and social obligations and duties, with which government is necessarily required to deal.
>
> —*Reynolds v. U.S.* 98 U.S. 145, at 166 (1878)

Love and Family

This statement by Chief Justice Waite, writing in 1878 for a unanimous Supreme Court upholding a statutory prohibition against polygamy, speaks volumes about the role of law in personal relationships. Even "in respect to this most important feature of social life," the law intervenes; it is "usually regulated by law."[1] This means that individuals are free to engage in personal relationships so long as they do not contradict a valid social policy. Otherwise, as the *Reynolds* Court noted, "every citizen [would] become a law unto himself. Government could exist only in name under such circumstances" (98 U.S. 145, 167). Thus, once again, we see the classic conflict between individual freedom and social order.

In such cases we face a crucial variation on the liberty/order model: conflict among individual freedom, religious tenets, and the state. As Justice Waite noted, the institution of marriage has a religious base, "from its very nature [it is] a sacred obligation." Indeed, religious leaders are among a very small number of nongovernmental officials empowered by state governments to issue valid marriage licenses. Religious marriage ceremonies are ancient rituals; however, the modern state has assumed legal responsibility for overseeing the relationship in which the parties agree to the terms of a binding contract. Usually religion-sanctioned unions are recognized by the state, but this is not necessarily true. The *Reynolds* case, after all, eventuated from a situation where wedding vows exchanged under the auspices of the Morman church were contested by the state and ultimately invalidated in the courts.[2] Similarly, and much more recently, homosexual marriages have been sanctioned in some religious ceremonies at various locations around the country; however, none are currently recognized as valid under state law.[3] On 26 April 2000, Vermont Governor Dean signed into law the nation's first and thus far only "civil union" statute, intended to grant rights to homosexual couples parallel to those generally recognized in marriage.[4]

Even this legislation, however, does not sanction same-sex *marriage*.

Finally, Justice Waite also correctly observes that private marital relationships involve and produce serious public policy issues: "[O]ut of its [marriage's] fruits spring social relations and social obligations and duties, with which government is necessarily required to deal." For example, when a husband and father dies owing a debt, does the debt die with him, or is the obligation to repay it passed to his heirs within the family? When a poverty-stricken couple have children, does the state have any obligation to ensure that their children receive a minimal level of medical care? Moreover, constitutional litigation—Reynolds argued that his First Amendment freedom of religion was being denied—also holds potential for conflict concerning federalism, the division of authority between states and the federal government. State laws have traditionally provided most of the basic rules affecting everyday life, especially those rules most directly concerning families and personal relationships, and state courts represent the typical arena for the overwhelming majority of such controversies.[5] By contrast, the jurisdiction of federal courts is limited to cases that involve either a claim under a federal statute or the U.S. Constitution, or a dispute arising between citizens of different states. Federal courts are generally not available for controversies involving family and personal relationships (covering both domestic relations and torts),[6] unless one or both parties raises a substantial federal or constitutional question.

Although authority remains very decentralized, the importance of and demand for national rules have increased over the twentieth century. Indeed, the protection of the family has been considered central to survival of the nation. Again, the brief passage from Justice Waite's *Reynolds* opinion is instructive: "Upon it society may be said to be built." A full century later, Justice Powell echoed that view in *Moore v. City of East Cleveland, Ohio* (431 U.S. 494, at 503–504 (1977)), stating:

"Our decisions establish that the Constitution protects the sanctity of the family precisely because the institution of the family is deeply rooted in this Nation's history and tradition. It is through the family that we inculcate and pass down many of our most cherished values, moral and cultural."[7] Thus, the family is a critical social, political, ideological (see, e.g., Rubin 1986), and *legal* entity of nationwide importance.

Judicial opinions are but a mild reflection of the positions articulated in political debate, social commentary, religious dogma, and public policy. It is of no small wonder then that the U.S. Congress has addressed family issues in major pieces of legislation such as the *Full Faith and Credit for Child Support Orders Act of* 1994[8] and the 1997 *Protection of Marriage Act*,[9] candidates for political office at all levels campaign on a "traditional family values" platform, and public policy at all levels of government is enacted ostensibly in the name of the family. However, such policy forays are inherently contradictory. Legislating family issues pierces the most private of all spheres by favoring or encouraging some decisions over others, and labeling some private choices good, stigmatizing others, and rendering still others criminal acts (see, e.g., Burt 1979). Indeed, as of 1997, 1,049 federal statutes grant benefits to persons based on their marital status (see Robb 1997, 263), including bankruptcy protection, burial rights, medical benefits, pension benefits, welfare benefits, government education loans, surviving spouse rights relating to veterans benefits, copyright protection, and Social Security benefits.[10] Unmarried individuals, even those living as husband and wife, are usually not so favored. Clearly, government penalizes some fundamentally private decisions and rewards others.

Just how far the government can go to intervene in the private affairs of its citizens is clearly an important question. This means that whenever public policy is enacted in this realm, legal challenge is a certainty. As we have become more rights conscious, particularly during the course of the twentieth century, the tendency is to argue that there are some intrusions into private affairs that *no* government should make, a position that necessitates "making a federal case" out of the challenge and pursuing it as far as possible in the federal court system.

Making a federal, or a constitutional, case out of family issues has at least two important consequences. First, it goes directly to the heart of the relationship between the family unit and the state. It either challenges the traditional autonomy of family life, which viewed families as small governmental entities that ought to be left free to choose their own individual courses with regard to the whole range of life events. Or, it challenges the obligation and authority of the state to enact social policies intended to enhance the common welfare. Second, constitutionalizing family issues also leads to legalization of relationships among and between members, thus deconstructing the unit into autonomous individuals and destroying the traditional rule-making authority (e.g., husbands cannot abuse their wives because women have independent rights). In the following sections we address these issues.

Family v. the State

Generally, we do not consider the state to be in an antagonistic relationship with the institution of the family. Quite the contrary. Despite rhetorical harangues that wax poetically (and not so poetically) about the virtues and glory of a past steeped in "family values," government policy has consistently supported the "nuclear family" concept (man, woman, and their biologically linked children), fully embracing the "building block of society" image.[11] The tensions observable today result from the attempt to sustain the mythical model of the nuclear family as a government unto itself, impenetrable by the state, hierarchically structured in which the man of the house exercised unchallenged authority and was the primary provider and guardian, in which the wife played the role of homemaker and emotional anchor, and in which children obeyed their parents and respected their elders, within a real-world political economic context dominated by classical liberal ideology.

The sources of today's conflict were noted by Alexis de Tocqueville in the 1830s during his observational journey across our newly developing nation. He found it particularly striking that Americans had incorporated the spirit of democracy into the family concept, rejecting the European aristocratic model in which marriages were arranged and families emphasized lineage over all else. Under the European model, girls became wives well before they were women, and through no choice of their own; relationships between parents (especially fathers) and children were emphatically cold and distant; and the eldest son held superior status, accruing all benefits of lineage, with any siblings usually receiving little or none. "Among aristocratic nations," de Tocqueville stated,[12] "social institutions recognize, in truth, no one in the family but the father; children are received by society at his hands; society governs him, he governs them. Thus the parent not only has a natural right but acquires a political right to command them; he is the author and the support of his family, but he is also its constituted ruler." The United States, however, operated on a fundamentally different model, in which "the family, in the Roman and aristocratic signification of the word, does not exist. . . . In democracies, where the government picks out every individual singly from the mass to make him subservient to the general laws of the community, no such intermediate person is required; a father is there, in the eye of the law, only a member of the community, older and richer than his sons." Moreover, the decision to marry—that is, to form a family—was entirely a matter of free choice among both men and women.

That it took as long as it did before the underlying tensions between family and state were played out in the legal arena is rather surprising. As seen in the 1878 *Reynolds* example discussed earlier, there are times when the government can intervene in the decision to form a family. In that instance, the issue was polygamy, and the Supreme Court approved restrictions on individual free choice.[13] The Court subsequently recognized that the Constitution guarantees a right to marry (*Maynard v. Hill*, 125 U.S. 190 (1888)) and deemed it to be "essential to the orderly pursuit of happiness by free men" (*Meyer v. Nebraska*, 262 U.S. 390, at 399 (1923)). Thus, the position that the Court has assumed with regard to this question is that the state must make an extraordinarily strong showing that its restriction represents a minimal intrusion in order to accomplish an essential policy objective. In other words, the state must demonstrate a "compelling" rationale in order for the rule to survive judicial scrutiny. Few restrictions have survived this test, laws criminalizing polygamy being one. Moreover, in 1967 a married couple successfully challenged a Virginia statute that outlawed interracial marriage (*Loving v. Virginia*, 388 U.S. 1 (1967)). Others include limitations depending upon the closeness of blood relationship (e.g., biological siblings cannot marry, nor in most jurisdictions, may first cousins), and states may impose requirements such as a minimum age, blood tests, and a marriage license.

In a growing number of jurisdictions, gay and lesbian couples are filing litigation challenging state laws disallowing their legal right to marry. In Hawaii, for example, Judge Chang's finding, after trial, that the state had not met its burden of showing a compelling interest in restricting legal marriage only to the heterosexual community has proven to be quite controversial (*Baehr v. Miike*, 910 P.2d 112, 1st Cir. Ct. HI, 1996).[14] The state supreme court added to the controversy by accepting the possibility that recognition of same-sex unions may be required under Hawaii's equal rights amendment, remanding the issue to the trial court for further consideration *(Baehr v. Miike*, 910 P.2d 112 (HI 1996)).[15] In addition, the Vermont Supreme Court heard oral arguments in a case challenging its marriage laws in November 1999, and delivered a landmark opinion on 20 December. The trial court had "recognized the link between marriage, sexual intercourse, and procreation" in holding against the three same-sex couples who filed the challenge.[16] The state supreme court reversed, holding "that the State is constitutionally required to extend to same-sex couples the common benefits and protections that flow from marriage under Vermont law. Whether this ultimately takes the form of inclusion within the marriage laws themselves or a parallel 'domestic partnership' system or some equivalent statutory alternative, rests with the

Legislature. Whatever system is chosen, however, must conform with the constitutional imperative to afford all Vermonters the common benefit, protection, and security of the law" (*Baker v. Vermont*, 744 A.2d 864, at 867 (S Ct VT 1999)). In so doing, the Court noted that "our opinion provides greater recognition of—and protection for—same-sex relationships than has been recognized by any court of final jurisdiction in this country" (at 42–43). The state house and senate immediately set to work on legislation extending parallel marriage rights to all same-sex couples obtaining a "civil union" license, and Governor Dean signed it into law on 26 April 2000.[17]

In the November 2000 election, we witnessed a backlash from Vermont voters, however, with a number of opponents being swept in the lower house of the state legislature. On 16 March 2001, the state house of representatives overwhelmingly voted in support of a bill outlawing same-sex marriage. Although it was not expected to pass the senate, the Vermont action was not the only response to *Baker* "civil union" decision. Indeed, thirty-five states enacted some variation of a defense of marriage statute limiting marriage to heterosexual couples, two had outlawed civil unions, and legislation was pending in several others (Ferdinand 2001).

Cases and controversies such as those discussed above indicate that the decision to create a family by the act of marriage, although a highly private one, must comply with the state's notion of acceptability—so long as the restrictions behind that notion are based in sound rationale. With only a few notable exceptions, individuals then are free to choose with whom they wish to tie the matrimonial knot. This establishes a basic definition for the "nuclear" family under the law. However, we know that most families have more than two members[18] and that families come in many varieties other than the nuclear one. Because the law is so deeply entangled in our lives, such issues have significant legal implications. Chambers (1985, 805) has argued "that as government frees people to live their family lives as they choose, people feel no more free, in part because much government involvement is required to facilitate the new freedom."

What Is a Family?

As we shall see, a number of rights are directly connected to and accrue from recognition of family status, like the right to marry as already discussed, the right to procreate, and so on. But do we have a right to live in a family? If so, can the government determine, through its lawmaking processes, what is and is not a valid family? This was precisely the issue that was presented in *Moore v. City of East Cleveland*, Ohio (431 U.S. 494 (1977)). Like most towns and cities across the country, East

Cleveland was empowered with zoning authority that it could employ in order to manage and control population and economic growth. Again, like many other jurisdictions, "as a means of preventing overcrowding, minimizing traffic and parking congestion, and avoiding an undue financial burden on [its] school system" (at 499–500), the city designated some areas as restricted to single-family residences. So far, so good. However, hoping to limit the number of people who might cram themselves into a single house, East Cleveland took the additional step to define what it meant by "single family." Under the zoning ordinance, a permissible family could include a head of household and spouse, any of their parents, and any unmarried children without children of their own. If there were children with kids, only one such cluster could reside in the house. In effect, the ordinance limited the family to one set of grandchildren, and it threatened violators with fines and jail terms, leading to the following case:

Moore v. East Cleveland, 431 U.S. 494 (1977)

Mrs. Inez Moore, lives in her East Cleveland home together with her son, Dale Moore, Sr., and her two grandsons, Dale, Jr., and John Moore, Jr. The two boys are first cousins rather than brothers; . . . John came to live with his grandmother and with the elder and younger Dale Moores after his mother's death. In early 1973, Mrs. Moore received a notice of violation from the city, stating that John was an "illegal occupant" and directing her to comply with the ordinance. When she failed to remove him from her home, the city filed a criminal charge. Mrs. Moore moved to dismiss, claiming that the ordinance was constitutionally invalid on its face. Her motion was overruled, and upon conviction she was sentenced to five days in jail and a $25 fine (at 495–96).

Mr. JUSTICE POWELL delivered the judgment of the Court and the Plurality Opinion (at 496ff):

East Cleveland . . . has chosen to regulate the occupancy of its housing by slicing deeply into the family itself. . . . In particular, it makes a crime of a grandmother's choice to live with her grandson in circumstances like those presented here.

When a city undertakes such intrusive regulation of the family, . . . the usual judicial deference to the legislature is inappropriate. This Court has long recognized that freedom of personal choice in matters of marriage and family life is one of the liberties protected by the Due Process Clause of the Fourteenth Amendment. . . . A host of cases . . . have consistently acknowledged a "private realm of family life which the state cannot enter."

. . . There are risks when the judicial branch gives enhanced protection to certain substantive liberties without the guidance of the more specific provisions of the Bill of Rights. As the history of the *Lochner* era demonstrates, there is reason for concern lest the only limits to such judicial intervention become the predilections of those who happen at the time to be Members of this Court. That history counsels caution and restraint. But it does not counsel abandonment, nor does it require what the city urges here: cutting off any protection of family rights at the first convenient, if arbitrary boundary—the boundary of the nuclear family. . . .

Ours is by no means a tradition limited to respect for the bonds uniting the members of the nuclear family. The tradition of uncles, aunts, cousins, and especially grandparents sharing a household along with parents and children has roots equally venerable and equally deserving of constitutional recognition. Over the years millions of our citizens have grown up in just such an environment, and most, surely, have profited from it. Even if conditions of modern society have brought about a decline in extended family households, they have not erased the accumulated wisdom of civilization, gained over the centuries and honored throughout our history, that supports a larger conception of the family. Out of choice, necessity, or a sense of family responsibility, it has been common for close relatives to draw together and participate in the duties and the satisfactions of a common home. Decisions concerning child rearing, which *Yoder, Meyer, Pierce* and other cases have recognized as entitled to constitutional protection, long have been shared with grandparents or other relatives who occupy the same household—indeed who may take on major responsibility for the rearing of the children. Especially in times of adversity, such as the death of a spouse or economic need, the broader family has tended to come together for mutual sustenance and to maintain or rebuild a secure home life. This is apparently what happened here. . . .

[T]he Constitution prevents East Cleveland from standardizing its children—and its adults—by forcing all to live in certain narrowly defined family patterns.

MR. JUSTICE BRENNAN, with whom MR. JUSTICE MARSHALL joins, concurring (at 507ff).

[T]he zoning power is not a license for local communities to enact senseless and arbitrary restrictions which cut deeply into private areas of protected family life. East Cleveland may not constitutionally define "family" as essentially confined to parents and the parents' own children. The plurality's opinion conclusively demonstrates that classifying family patterns in this eccentric way is not a rational means of achieving the ends East Cleveland claims for its ordinance, and further that the ordinance unconstitutionally abridges the "freedom of personal choice in matters of . . . family life [that] is one of the liberties protected by the Due Process Clause of the Fourteenth Amendment." I write only to underscore the cultural myopia of the arbitrary boundary drawn by the East Cleveland ordinance in the light of the tradition of the American home that has been a feature of our society since our beginning as a Nation—the "tradition" in the plurality's words, "of uncles, aunts, cousins, and especially grandparents sharing a household along with parents and children. . . ." The line drawn by this ordinance displays a depressing insensitivity toward the economic and emotional needs of a very large part of our society.

MR. JUSTICE STEVENS, concurring in the judgment (at 513ff).

There appears to be no precedent for an ordinance which excludes any of an owner's relatives from the group of persons who may occupy his residence on a permanent basis. Nor does there appear to be any justification for such a restriction on an owner's use of his property. The city has failed totally to explain the need for a rule which would allow a homeowner to have two grandchildren live with her if they are brothers, but not if they are cousins. Since this ordinance has not been shown to have any "substantial relation to the public health, safety, morals, or general welfare" of the city of East Cleveland, and since it cuts so deeply into a fundamental right normally associated with the ownership of residential property—that of an owner to decide who may reside on his or her property—it must fall under the limited standard of review of zoning decisions. . . . Under that standard, East Cleveland's unprecedented ordinance constitutes a taking of property without due process and without just compensation.

MR. CHIEF JUSTICE BURGER, dissenting (at 521ff).

It is unnecessary for me to reach the difficult constitutional issue this case presents. Appellant's deliberate refusal to use a plainly adequate administrative remedy provided by the city should foreclose her from pressing in this Court any constitutional objections to the city's zoning ordinance. Considerations of federalism and comity, as well as the finite capacity of federal courts, support this position. In courts, as in hospitals, two bodies cannot occupy the same space at the same time; when any case comes here which could have been disposed of long ago at the local level, it takes the place that might well have been given to some other case in which there was no alternative remedy.

Clearly this was a difficult issue. There seems to have been some consensus on the Court that the family is extraordinarily important and that government attempts to fashion a definition that criminalizes people whose own concept of family differs from the official one are highly suspect. Beyond this, however, no line of argument could muster even a simple majority among the justices. The plurality (represented by Justice Powell) waxed eloquently about the role of families in our history and determined that the right to live in a family is protected by a "substantive" understanding of constitutional due process. East Cleveland's goal, although a lofty one, does not justify its means (imposing a restrictive definition of a permissible family unit). Justices Brennan and Marshall agreed but would go further to find that the concept of family is so highly personal and private a matter that government has no business attempting to prescribe a definition. Justice Stevens took a different route to reach the same conclusion that the ordinance must be voided, finding that it represented an unnecessary interference with citizens' property rights. The dissenting view (represented by Chief Justice Burger) was to avoid the issue altogether, suggesting that Mrs. Moore's complaint should have been directed to the appropriate administrative unit at the local level rather than channeled into the already overburdened court system.

This was an important legal development, but it did not mean that "family" is entirely a matter of individual choice, particularly among the lower economic classes. Indeed, the lifestyles of people receiving welfare benefits and other forms of public assistance have come under intense regulatory scrutiny. As Rubin (1986, 147) observes, "Whereas one set of rules governs such matters as husband-wife relationships, marriage and divorce, the ownership of property, custody of children, parental rights and family-child relationships for non-dependent families, another set of regulations, enacted by legislatures and administered by welfare agencies, governs the same kind of relationships in families receiving public assistance."

An extreme example comes from the state of Wisconsin. In an attempt to deal with the chronic problem of nonpayment of court-ordered support by absent parents (often referred to as "deadbeat dads"), the state legislature enacted a ban on the issuance of marriage licenses to individuals with such personal histories. The state hoped thereby to encourage parents to support their children (so that the state would not have to do so), and to minimize the opportunities for procreation among people likely to produce more welfare recipients, thus simply adding to the state's burden. The marriage ban would be removed if the "deadbeat" could persuade a judge that his support obligations to current children were now being met and would likely continue. If convinced, the judge must formally grant permission allowing the petitioner to obtain a marriage license. Upon challenge, the U.S. Supreme Court struck this scheme down as a violation of equal protection (*Zablocki v. Redhail* 434 U.S. 374 (1978)), declaring the right to marriage to be among our fundamental liberties. A state may not block the poor from marrying but allow everyone else to do so freely; a state may not condition access to a constitutional right on the basis of income. Justice Powell concurred (at 397) on this one but worried about the majority's conclusion that marriage is a fundamental right, warning that this would undermine all state regulations of marriage (including blood tests and bans against bigamy, incest, as well as homosexual pairings).

Justice Powell's forecast has proven to be correct. Contemporary disputes over the nature and character of marriage and family have produced a number of recent controversies that call the traditionally accepted meanings into question. A series of federal and state cases raise important questions concerning the right to marry, particularly among individuals of the same gender.[19] Moreover, as we discuss a bit later, technological developments have forced the courts to grapple with the dimensions of our "right to procreate," placing further stress upon the concept of family and the legal relationships within it.

The Decision to Dissolve a Family

Given the great social and political value placed upon the institution of marriage and the ideological rhetoric employed to characterize the family, as indicated by the above discussion, it is no small wonder that laws have been enacted throughout our history not only in the interest of preserving the integrity of marriage and family, but also to make it difficult to dissolve. Indeed, through most of the nineteenth century, because divorce was viewed as a threat to marriage, family stability, and by extension to national survival, most states required their legislative bodies to approve each disengagement request individually (see, e.g., Friedman 1985; Riley 1991). Authorization of divorce by judicial decree did make the process a bit more accessible, but until the idea of "no-fault" divorce began to catch on in the 1970s,[20] the law generally required a trial in which one party proved to a court's satisfaction that the defendant's actions had irretrievably shattered the marriage, with acceptable grounds for dissolution, such as adultery, chronic drunkenness, cruelty, and the like, specified by statute. This, because of the costs and the public spectacle involved, had the desired effect, from the state's perspective, of discouraging divorce. But it also probably enhanced the prospect of desertion, and it meant that many people continued to live together under very unhappy circumstances. Moreover, the trial requirement actually produced an informal system of outright collusion among parties, where one of them would simply agree to be found at fault and help the other to "prove" it (see, e.g., Jacob 1988; Friedman 1984b; Rheinstein 1972; Blake 1962; Riley 1991).

Beginning in the 1960s, advocates of divorce reform called for the legal recognition of no-fault divorce. Under this concept, a divorce may be granted on grounds such as incompatibility, irreconcilable differences, or an irretrievable breakdown of the marriage relationship. The court examines the condition of the marriage rather than the question of whether either party is at fault. This type of proceeding eliminates the need for one party to accuse the other of a traditional ground for divorce.

Table 6.1 reports marriage and divorce statistics in the United States since 1940, and indicates that, while the rate of marriages (number per 1,000 population) has remained fairly consistent over the years, although it has trended slightly downward, divorces surged after 1970.[21]

By 1987, all fifty states had adopted no-fault divorce, exclusively or as an option to traditional fault-grounded divorce. No-fault divorce has become a quick and inexpensive means of ending a marriage, especially when a couple has no children and relatively few property assets. In fact, the ability to end a marriage using no-fault procedures has led to criticism that divorce has become too easy to obtain, allowing couples to abandon a marriage at the first sign of marital discord.[22] At least one state legislature has responded by allowing couples to

set their own terms for divorce at the time of their marriage. Louisiana's "covenant marriage" statute leaves the no-fault system in place for those choosing a standard arrangement, but allows individual couples to set the bar much higher if they wish.[23]

In 1971, the Supreme Court came very close to declaring a right to divorce (*Boddie v. Connecticut*, 401 U.S. 371), striking down Connecticut's inflexible fee structure as an impermissible denial of access to the poor to state proceedings required for obtaining a decree of dissolution. When a state provides no alternative but to utilize its forums, it cannot restrict admission on the basis of income.[24] Note also that only the state can grant a divorce, which releases the parties from the contract that binds them legally together. The divorce decree is another contract of sorts that also often comes with strings attached, such as alimony distributions, division of property and assets, child custody arrangements, and the like, which are enforceable by state power. Churches have no such authority, although some, like the Roman Catholic Church, refuse to recognize divorce.

Moreover, most states now recognize an implied contract of marriage in instances where two individuals have cohabited for an extended period of time, albeit without benefit of a state-issued license, but now find themselves in conflict over disengagement. This probably originates from the famous Lee Marvin palimony litigation (*Marvin v. Marvin*, 18 Cal.3d 660, 134 Cal. Rptr. 815, 557 P.2d 106 (Cal.) (1976)). In this case, Michelle Triola, the woman with whom actor Lee Marvin had lived for more than a decade, sued for financial support after their break-up. Although they never married, she claimed that they had reached an explicit agreement and implicit understandings regarding their respective roles in the relationship and her future dependency upon his income. California's supreme court overturned several precedents to find that agreements between unmarried cohabitants should be enforced. While the court did not recognize their relationship as a marriage, it did say that contracts, both those explicitly entered into (written and signed by both parties for future reference) as well as those that are reached im-

Table 6.1.   Marriage and Divorce in the United States, 1940–96

	MARRIAGE RATE			DIVORCE RATE	
YEAR	RAW NUMBER	PER 1000 POPULATION	YEAR	RAW NUMBER	PER 1000 POPULATION
1996	2,344,000	8.8	1996	1,150,000	4.3
1990	2,443,489	9.8	1990	1,182,000	4.7
1980	2,390,252	10.6	1980	1,189,000	5.2
1970	2,158,802	10.6	1970	708,000	3.5
1960	1,523,000	8.5	1960	393,000	2.2
1950	1,667,231	11.1	1950	385,000	2.6
1940	1,595,879	12.1	1940	264,000	2.0

Source: National Center of Health Statistics, available at www.cdc.gov/nchswww/fastats (accessed 20 January 1999).

plicitly (implied by the couple's behavior), are legally binding. Although judges of other states have been slow to follow California's lead (some have adopted variations on the *Marvin* model; others have rejected it), one clear result is a growing legalization of our most private love relationships. Indeed, *Marvin* genre cases are not at all uncommon, and prenuptial contracts, unheard of until fairly recently, are now rather routinely deployed among the wealthy to shield property assets from poor judgment in their personal love life.

Breach of Promise to Marry

Because so many rights and benefits accrue from the marriage relationship, and because it is such a private decision that we have come to understand as our own individual prerogative, it is not surprising that individuals have sued both for the right to marry whom they choose and to disengage from an undesirable marriage relationship. Historically, the marriage status was particularly important for women, whose rights of citizenship were limited and whose property rights derived only indirectly through their husbands. Their marriageability would be significantly diminished if they could not present themselves as "pure" virgins to potential husbands. A woman, then, suffered incalculable damages if, during the interim between a marriage proposal and the wedding date, the lovers engaged in sexual intercourse, only to have her fiancé break the engagement. Given the gravity of the consequences, state courts provided legal recourse to jilted women allowing them to sue under common law for damages, including the actual expenses incurred preparing for the wedding, in addition to embarrassment, humiliation, and loss of subsequent marriage opportunities.[25] Trials associated with such claims, involving testimony and evidence about the parties' most intimate and private activities, were public spectacles, drawing crowds of people from miles around who saw them as a form of entertainment.

The breach of promise to marry as a cause of action began in Europe more than three hundred years ago, arising from the historical tradition of arranged marriages in which property and status were primary considerations. Litigation allowed families, rather than individuals, to recover damages as a consequence of broken promises. The first suits in the United States were allowed by state judges under common law principles and were based primarily in tort, but the action gradually became more grounded in contract law. By 1930, breach of promise to marry litigation had come under heavy criticism and had become increasingly unpopular among lawmakers, however, because of vague rules of evidence, cries of excessive jury damage awards, and the potential use as leverage to obtain large out-of-court settlements. Moreover, the number of such claims ap-

parently reached rather alarming proportions across the states.[26] State legislatures began to take action to restrict perceived abuses in the 1930s, and as of 1995, about half the states had enacted preventive legislation, some banning it as a cause of action altogether (Williams 1995). The legal shift also corresponds roughly with the blossoming legal focus on the individual (as opposed to the communal family), with a general loosening of divorce law across the states and spreading acceptance of divorce among the population. The consequences to women suffering a broken promise of marriage were simply not so severe as they once were. Indeed, such changes could be construed as a reflection of the gradual acknowledgment of the individual rights of women and a drift toward recognition of equal gender rights under the law. This does not mean that women have achieved full equal rights. Nor does it mean that broken matrimonial promises vanished from the court dockets. They did not, with many focusing upon the engagement ring. Once a ring was offered and accepted, it became more than mere symbolism; it raised the stakes to the man who wished to reconsider his future. As courts heard the inevitable conflicts arising over ownership of a ring, judges generally considered the problem to be within the same conceptual realm as marriage itself and applied a fault-based reasoning to find a resolution. In the words of one such court:

On principle, an engagement ring is given, not alone as a symbol of the status of the two persons as engaged, the one to the other, but as a symbol or token of their pledge and agreement to marry. As such pledge or gift, the condition is implied that if both parties abandon the projected marriage, the sole cause of the gift, it should be returned. Similarly, if the woman, who has received the ring in token of her promise, unjustifiably breaks her promise, it should be returned.

When the converse situation occurs, and the giver of the ring, betokening his promise, violates his word, it would seem that a similar result should follow, i.e., he should lose, not gain, rights to the ring. In addition, had he not broken his promise, the marriage would follow, and the ring would become the wife's absolutely. The man could not then recover the ring. The only difference between that situation, and the facts at bar, is that the man has broken his promise. How, on principle, can the courts aid him, under such circumstances, to regain a ring which he could not regain, had he kept his promise? "No man should take advantage of his own wrong." Of course, were the breaking of the engagement to be justifiable, there would be no violation of the agreement legally, and a different result might follow (*Mate v. Abraham*, 62 A.2d 754, at 754–55 (N.J. 1948)).[27]

By the 1980s, the tide was shifting toward a no-fault approach to conflicts between former lovers, again following the trend in divorce case reasoning. In 1987, New Jersey Superior Court Judge Haines, responding to one such case, obviously felt that the movement away from the fault-based rule, followed by a majority of states, toward a no-fault rationale represented sound public policy:

In ancient Rome the rule was fault. When the woman broke the engagement, however, she was required not only to return the ring, but also its value, as a penalty. No penalty attached when the breach was the man's. In England, women were oppressed by the rigidly stratified social order of the day. They worked as servants or, if not of the servant class, were dependent on their relatives. The fact that men were in short supply, marriage above one's station rare and travel difficult abbreviated betrothal prospects for women. Marriages were arranged. Women's lifetime choices were limited to a marriage or a nunnery. Spinsterhood was a centuries-long personal tragedy. Men, because it was a man's world, were much more likely than women to break engagements. When one did, he left behind a woman of tainted reputation and ruined prospects. The law, in a *de minimis* gesture, gave her the engagement ring, as a consolation prize. When the man was jilted, a seldom thing, justice required the ring's return to him. Thus, the rule of life was the rule of law—both saw women as inferiors....

The majority rule, even without its constitutional infirmity, will not stand elementary scrutiny. Its foundation is fault, and fault, in an engagement setting, cannot be ascertained. What fact justifies the breaking of an engagement? The absence of a sense of humor? Differing musical tastes? Differing political views? The painfully-learned fact is that marriages are made on earth, not in heaven. They must be approached with intelligent care and should not happen without a decent assurance of success. When either party lacks that assurance, for whatever reason, the engagement should be broken. No justification is needed. Either party may act. Fault, impossible to fix, does not count (*Aronow v. Silver*, 223 N.J. Super. 344, at 348–49 (1987)).[28]

Intrafamily Litigation

As we have noted, the law historically attempted to sustain the mythical model of the nuclear family as a government unto itself, impenetrable by the state, and hierarchically controlled by the husband/father. This policy essentially ruled out most intrafamily litigation and diminished the criminal exposure to individual family members in their treatment of one another.[29] We have discussed the general difficulty people faced in trying to untie the matrimonial knot, but generally speaking, the posture of the law created especially high hurdles for women.[30] The widespread and dominant opinion throughout the nineteenth and early twentieth centuries was that it was the man's responsibility to control the actions of his family; after all, it was he who paid the penalty for any wrongdoing or malfeasance by any of his wards. The general expectation was that a wayward, lazy, unruly, or ill-tempered wife or child should be dealt with by the man of the house, and the state would not second-guess his tactics. Some women and children, then, could expect to be beaten (or worse) and generally treated in ways that would not be acceptable by today's standards. For example, responding to a petition for divorce in 1862, the North Carolina Supreme Court voiced the opinion of the time. The petitioner, Mrs. Joyner,

claimed that her husband had beat her with a horsewhip and a switch, but the court dismissed her petition:

The wife must be subject to the husband. Every man must govern his household, and if by reason of an unruly temper, or an unbridled tongue, the wife persistently treats her husband with disrespect, and he submits to it, he not only loses all sense of self-respect, but loses the respect of the other members of his family, without which he cannot expect to govern them, and forfeits the respect of his neighbors. Such have been the incidents of the marriage relation from the beginning of the human race.... [I]n our opinion, the circumstances attending the act, and giving rise to it, so far justify the conduct of the husband as to take from the wife any ground of divorce for that cause, and authorize the court to dismiss her petition, with the admonition, "If you will amend your manners, you may expect better treatment" (*Joyner v. Joyner*, 59 N.C. 322 (1862)).

This kind of position was not at all unusual and reflected the general policy of treating intrafamily conflict as a purely private problem, best left to the family itself to resolve. Clearly, the courts put more emphasis on the family as a unit rather than on the rights of individuals. Indeed, once established, preservation of a family became a high priority of the state, notwithstanding the claims of its inferior members.

This also sheltered parents from being sued, primarily for claimed personal injuries, by their children. The first judicial pronouncement of the parental immunity rule was articulated by the supreme court of Mississippi in *Hewlette v. George* (68 Miss. 703 (1891)). In *Hewlette*, a minor daughter sued her mother for false imprisonment, alleging that she was wrongfully committed to an insane asylum. Basing its decision entirely on policy grounds, the court held that a child cannot sue for personal injuries resulting from a parent's wrongdoing, because such causes of action would undermine the "peace of society, and of the families composing society, and a sound public policy, designed to subserve the repose of families and the best interests of society...." Following *Hewlette*, state judges in a number of localities adopted the common-law parental immunity rule to promote their understanding of the state's responsibility and public policy of preserving "family harmony and tranquility." Some states even disallowed minor children from recovering from their parent for injuries resulting from rape (e.g., *Roller v. Roller*, 79 P. 788 (Wash. 1905)) and brutal beatings (e.g., *Cook v. Cook*, 124 S.W. 2d 675 (Mo. Ct. App. 1939); *McKelvey v. McKelvey*, 77 S.W. 664 (Tenn. 1903)).

Eventually, however, a number of judges and legal practitioners began to question the rationale underlying the policy. Indeed, does it really promote family harmony to allow a tyrant to go unchallenged? By the same token, how far can the state go in second-guessing the private decisions of parents in the thorny project of raising children?[31] Should minor children be allowed to use the legal system to challenge the discretion and authority of their parents? These are not easy questions. The courts have opted against providing blanket immunity and attempted to steer a reasonable middle course. The Wisconsin Supreme Court was the first to repudiate its common-law policy providing complete parental immunity (*Goller v. White*, 122 N.W.2d 193 (Wis. 1963)) and narrowed the field of unchallengeable actions to those involving "an exercise of parental authority . . . or ordinary parental discretion with respect to the provision of food, clothing, housing, medical and dental services, and other care" (at 198). Other state courts have followed this course,[32] thus recognizing a zone of privacy within a family that may not be abrogated without a clear and compelling interest. For example, children cannot sue to recover damages for psychological distress caused by divorce (see, e.g., *Mroczynski v. McGrath*, 216 N.E.2d 137 (Ill. 1966)), and they cannot pursue a claim for "inadequate parenting" (e.g., *Burnette v. Wahl*, 588 P.2d 1105 (Or. 1978)).

These developments run parallel to opinions from the U.S. Supreme Court, which has tried to find a delicate balance between protecting parental discretion and recognizing the obligation of the state to promote the general welfare and well-being of its citizens. For example, in 1925 the Court stated that requiring all children to attend public schools "is an unreasonable interference with the liberty of parents and guardians to direct the upbringing of their children,"[33] a position reiterated in 1972 in a case where an Amish community successfully defended parental rights to make educational decisions: "The history and culture of Western civilization reflect a strong tradition of parental concern for the nurture and upbringing of their children. The primary role of the parents in the upbringing of their children is now established beyond debate as an enduring American tradition. . . . The child is not the mere creature of the state; those who nurture him and direct his destiny have the right, coupled with the high duty, to recognize and prepare him for additional obligations."[34]

However, the rationale utilized by the courts on such matters is not a clear one. In some cases, parents are given unquestioned authority over the upbringing of their children; whereas in others, the state has been allowed to intervene in the parent-child relationship. For example, the U.S. Supreme Court has upheld state law compelling vaccination against infectious disease over the objections of parents. In *Jacobson v. Massachusetts*, 197 U.S. 11, at 30 (1905), the Court affirmed a state's authority, acting pursuant to its police power, to require vaccination of adults and children regardless of their wishes, reasoning that one family's autonomy interests cannot trump the state's obligation to protect the entire community.[35] Moreover, the state may intervene to protect a child from physical harm likely to result from the religious motivations of the parents. A parental decision to withhold a blood transfusion necessary to save a mi-

nor child's life, for instance, can be overridden by the state (*Jehovah's Witnesses v. King County Hospital*, 390 U.S. 598 (1968)).[36]

Justice Rutledge, in 1944, recognized the intractable dilemma the courts face in such situations:

To make accommodation between these [religious and parental] freedoms and an exercise of state authority always is delicate. It hardly could be more so than in such a clash as this case presents. On one side is the obviously earnest claim for freedom of conscience and religious practice. With it is allied the parent's claim to authority in her own household and in the rearing of her children. The parent's conflict with the state over control of the child and his training is serious enough when only secular matters are concerned. It becomes the more so when an element of religious conviction enters. Against these sacred private interests, basic in a democracy, stand the interests of society to protect the welfare of children, and the state's assertion of authority to that end, made here in a manner conceded valid if only secular things were involved. The last is no mere corporate concern of official authority. It is the interest of youth itself, and of the whole community, that children be both safeguarded from abuses and given opportunities for growth into free and independent well-developed men and citizens. Between contrary pulls of such weight, the safest and most objective recourse is to the lines already marked out, not precisely but for guides, in narrowing the no man's land where this battle has gone on (*Prince v. Massachusetts*, 321 U.S. 158, at 165 (1944)).

The Court was addressing a situation in which a mother, who was a Jehovah's Witness, was found in violation of the Massachusetts child labor laws for directing her minor children to sell (they were actually soliciting donations) religious literature on street corners. Finding in favor of the state, Justice Rutledge noted that "[p]arents may be free to become martyrs themselves. But it does not follow they are free, in identical circumstances, to make martyrs of their children before they have reached the age of full and legal discretion when they can make that choice for themselves" (321 U.S. 158, at 170).

The upshot of all of this is that the law contains conflicting biases, one reflecting general public policy, in favor of insulating the family from state intrusion (which would include allowing some private litigation to go forward), providing wide latitude to decisions made within a family unit. The second bias again reflects general policy aimed at fulfilling the state obligation to safeguard the public's safety and well-being, particularly that of minor children. The conflict between these two policies is further complicated by a gradual drift toward the legalization of relationships as courts have recognized rights of individuals as distinct from those that flow from their kinship.

At least one jurisdiction (Florida) has granted a minor child standing to sue in the attempt to terminate the parental relationship.[37] Kimberly Mays, a teenager at the time of this filing, was apparently switched at birth with another child and raised by Robert Mays. When the mistake was uncovered some years later, her biological parents attempted to insert themselves into her life. Both Robert and Kimberly objected, and the state courts allowed the young Mays to assert her own individual rights. Such actions remain rather unusual, but, as the sociopolitical definition of "family" continues to evolve and technology challenges the meaning of biological connectedness, we are likely to witness an increasing array of circumstances in the nation's courtrooms. We address a number of these issues in chapter 7 (see also, e.g., Melton 1993).

A number of changes have added complexity to family relations, particularly in light of increasing legalization of relationships. Life expectancy increased substantially across the span of the twentieth century at the same time that divorce became far easier to obtain. In addition, development of artificial insemination techniques and surrogate motherhood have successfully decoupled the heretofore essential biological connections among family members. These parallel trends have produced a huge pool of middle-aged and older adults whose access to grandchildren is placed in immediate jeopardy or is lost altogether, and, given the increasing difficulty of defining family connections, a secondary pool of people whose close emotional bonds with children are suddenly broken. Some have filed suit seeking full or partial custody,[38] but a more common action is a claim demanding court-ordered visitation rights. Such litigation has been fostered by legislation. Indeed, the American Association of Retired Persons (AARP) and other organizations have engaged in an intense lobbying effort over the past decade, resulting in enactment of some form of grandparents' rights statute in all fifty states. In many cases, the statute extends to biologically unrelated third parties. Generally, the rationale underlying such legislation is the argument that there is more to a family than simply parents and children, and that the most important issue to weigh is the "best interest of the child" (see, e.g., Greenhouse 2000). When claims are filed, it places the parent(s) in the position of defending his/her prerogative and authority to make important decisions about how children will be raised. Often, state statute requires that the child be represented by separate court-appointed counsel, thus undermining the long-standing assumption that parents act in the best interest of their children.

The U.S. Supreme Court heard oral arguments on 12 January 2000 in one such case originating in the State of Washington. The background of the lead case (consolidated with two other similar appeals) is summarized in the court records as follows:

Natalie and Isabelle Troxel are the daughters of Brad Troxel and Tommie Granville, who never married. After their separation, Brad lived with his parents, Jenifer and Gary Troxel, and the girls visited their father at their grandparents' home on occasion. Brad committed suicide in May 1993. At first the girls continued to visit the Troxels regularly, but their mother

soon decided to limit visitation. In December 1993, the Troxels filed a petition . . . to obtain visitation rights with their grandchildren. In 1995, the trial court entered a visitation decree ordering visitation one weekend per month, one week during the summer, and four hours on each of the Troxels' birthdays. Granville appealed, during which time she married Kelly Wynn, who adopted the girls in February 1996 (*In re Custody of Sarah Smith*, 137 Wn.2d 1, 969 P.2d 21 (1998)).

In 1998 the Washington Supreme Court upheld a reversal of the trial court and invalidated the state visitation statutes, finding it to be an unconstitutional deprivation of parents' fundamental rights concerning the upbringing of their children. In part the Court stated:

"Short of preventing harm to the child, the standard of "best interest of the child" is insufficient to serve as a compelling state interest overruling a parent's fundamental rights. State intervention to better a child's quality of life through third party visitation is not justified where the child's circumstances are otherwise satisfactory. To suggest otherwise would be the logical equivalent to asserting that the state has the authority to break up stable families and redistribute its infant population to provide each child with the "best family." It is not within the province of the state to make significant decisions concerning the custody of children merely because it could make a "better" decision (*In re Custody of Sarah Smith*, 137 Wn.2d 1, 969 P.2d 21 (1998), available at law.about.com/newsissues/law/library/docs/bl-troxel-wa.htm).

The case attracted broad attention, with a range of advocacy groups inserting their particular take on the questions as *amicus curiae* participants. The AARP, with a number of other organizations representing older citizens, argued in favor of the law, while the ACLU and a variety of religious organizations touted the importance of parental autonomy. Gay and lesbian groups highlighted their position that all child-custodial parent relations be treated equally under the law. The U.S. Supreme Court heard the case in fall 1999 and upheld the Washington court (*Troxel v. Granville*, No. 99-138 (2000)). Writing for a 6–3 majority, Justice O'Connor reasoned that

it cannot now be doubted that the Due Process Clause of the Fourteenth Amendment protects the fundamental right of parents to make decisions concerning the care, custody, and control of their children. . . . The Washington nonparental visitation statute is breathtakingly broad. According to the statute's text, "*[a]ny person* may petition the court for visitation rights *at any time*," and the court may grant such visitation rights whenever "visitation may serve *the best interest of the child*." §§26.10.160(3) That language effectively permits any third party seeking visitation to subject any decision by a parent concerning visitation of the parent's children to state-court review. Once the visitation petition has been filed in court and the matter is placed before a judge, a parent's decision that visitation would not be in the child's best interest is accorded no deference (*Troxel*, at 7–8; emphases added).

Moreover, attempts to preserve and enhance cultural diversity also create some problematic issues within this legal domain. For example, Coleman (1996) recounts the 1989 case of a recent Chinese immigrant, Dong Lu Chen, tried in New York for second-degree murder of his wife, whose unfaithfulness he had discovered just prior to killing her with a hammer. Although the evidence was fairly overwhelming, the trial judge found Chen guilty of manslaughter in the second degree and imposed a sentence of probation, on the logic that the defendant's daughters would have a better chance of marriage (for cultural reasons) if they were not further stigmatized by their father's being imprisoned (see *People v. Chen*, No. 7774/87 (N.Y. Super. Ct. 1989)). Honor has been raised as a justification for murder of a spouse (usually in such cases a husband has killed his wife), and it has also been advanced as a rationale for killing children. *People v. Wu* (186 Cal. Rptr. 868, Ct. App. 4th Dist. 1991) involved a Chinese woman who had been rejected by her lover after the birth of their child. She wanted to return home but felt that she could not take her illegitimate child with her because of the likely treatment they would receive in China. She murdered her child but failed in her own suicide attempt, and she was convicted of second-degree murder. A California Court of Appeals reversed the conviction holding that the jury should have been allowed to consider her cultural background (see also, e.g., *People v. Kimura*, No. A-091133 (Santa Monica Super. Ct. 1985)). In a case involving child care, a Danish couple was arrested in 1997 in New York City when they left their fourteen-month-old child in a stroller outside a Manhattan restaurant. They sued the city for malicious prosecution, seeking $20 million, arguing that their behavior is routine in Denmark (Hamblett 1999; see also, e.g., *State v. Chong Sun France*, 379 S.E.2d 701 (N.C. Ct. App. 1989)).[39]

To address questions regarding when and under what circumstances to intervene or to allow full, unfettered family privacy rights and discretion does, indeed, take the courts and other lawmakers into a "no man's land," and the law in this area continues to evolve, often in different directions. Aside from the difficult issue of determining the contours of family autonomy, some concepts have proven to be quite thorny. What conditions are "harmful" to a child that allow the state to intervene or that give the child (or a representative) the right to sue the family? When do children attain "the age of full and legal discretion when they can make that choice for themselves"? Some of these questions have arisen in the area of procreation rights, to which we now turn.

Stanley v. Illinois (405 U.S. 645 (1972)) offers a legal bridge between the section above regarding intrafamily relations and the set of issues that cluster around the right to procreate. The *Stanley* court confronted a situation where a father was denied custody of his two children upon the death of their mother, because the children had been born out of wedlock. Under Illinois law, minor children of a single mother were to become wards of the state in the event that she died. Because he was an unwed father, Peter Stanley was prohibited access to his natural children and even denied a hearing to determine his fitness to retain custody. Had he been married, custody would not have been an issue. Similarly, had he been an unwed mother, the legal presumption would have worked in his favor. Stanley filed suit, arguing that the statute violated both his rights to equal protection and to due process. The Illinois courts ruled against him, but the U.S. Supreme Court found differently: "The Court has frequently emphasized the importance of the family. The rights to conceive and to raise one's own children have been deemed 'essential,' 'basic civil rights of man,' and 'rights far more precious than property rights.' 'It is cardinal with us that the custody, care and nurture of the child reside first in the parents, whose primary function and freedom include preparation for obligations the state can neither supply nor hinder.'"[40]

Chief Justice Burger, joined by Justice Blackmun, disagreed, choosing to view the family and family relationships in strictly legal terms:

I agree with the State's argument that the Equal Protection Clause is not violated when Illinois gives full recognition only to those father-child relationships that arise in the context of family units bound together by legal obligations arising from marriage or from adoption proceedings. Quite apart from the religious or quasi-religious connotations that marriage has—and has historically enjoyed—for a large proportion of this Nation's citizens, it is in law an essentially contractual relationship, the parties to which have legally enforceable rights and duties, with respect both to each other and to any children born to them. Stanley and the mother of these children never entered such a relationship (405 U.S. 645, at 663 (Burger, C. J., dissenting)).

We see several tensions at work in this case. One set of issues involved sorting through and distinguishing the parent-child relationship under varying circumstances and the role of the state in such matters. Second, there is clearly a strong inclination to convert the most private of relationships into legal ones. The act of procreation has legal consequences, which are further complicated by the conflict generated by changing perspectives. Procreation was once considered essentially as a family project, the right to conceive accruing to duly licensed married couples; whereas the *Stanley* majority seems to accept it as an individual right.

To Procreate or Not to Procreate

Having affirmed the right to marry in 1923 (*Meyer v. Nebraska*), it was only a matter of time before the issue of procreation would come before the U.S. Supreme Court. *Meyer* was decided during a period of intense public debate regarding the genetic correlates of human behavior, and a number of state legislatures enacted statutes in the general welfare that restricted private individual choices. As discussed earlier, one of the products of the eugenics movement was a legislative ban (in some states) against interracial marriages, a measure that was ultimately voided by the Supreme Court. Another policy instrument that became increasingly popular during the first quarter of the twentieth century was forced sterilization, particularly of convicted criminals and the "feebleminded," rationalized as a way of reducing the number of people who were a "burden or threat to the social body" (Luker 1996, 33).[41] In 1927, the U.S. Supreme Court addressed the question in a case arising from the Commonwealth of Virginia. Carrie Buck, an eighteen-year-old inmate in the State Colony for Epileptics and Feeble Minded (where her mother and illegitimate daughter were also housed), was scheduled for a sterilization procedure that had become routine for others in her situation. The state provided an elaborate, multiphase hearing process; thus the Court addressed the substantive issues squarely. Justice Holmes, writing for an 8–1 majority, upheld the policy. Stated in part:

We have seen more than once that the public welfare may call upon the best citizens for their lives. It would be strange if it could not call upon those who already sap the strength of the State for these lesser sacrifices, often not felt to be such by those concerned, in order to prevent our being swamped with incompetence. It is better for all the world, if instead of waiting to execute degenerate offspring for crime, or to let them starve for their imbecility, society can prevent those who are manifestly unfit from continuing their kind. . . . Three generations of imbeciles are enough (*Buck v. Bell*, 274 U.S. 200, at 207 (1927)).[42]

Fifteen years later in 1942, the Court took a very different approach in invalidating a forced sterilization law of Oklahoma. This time, the challenge was directed against state policy mandating sterilization of habitual criminals (*Skinner v. Oklahoma*, 316 U.S. 535 (1942)). The Court overturned the statute, suggesting that the right to procreate, which follows from the right to marry (confirmed in *Meyer*), is so basic that it cannot be negated. "We are dealing here with legislation which involves one of the basic civil rights of man. Marriage and procreation are fundamental to the very existence and survival of the race. He is forever [if sterilized] deprived of a basic liberty" (316 U.S. 535, at 541).

The right to procreate has a number of implications, especially in light of recent scientific and technological developments, and we consider some of these in chapter 7. But the right to procreate also implies its opposite, the right not to do so, and the courts have addressed this issue as well. The first sense of direction from the U.S. Supreme Court in this venue came in 1965 with *Griswold v. Connecticut* (381 U.S. 479), nullifying a Connecticut statute that prohibited the use of contraceptive birth control devices. Although the U.S. Constitution fails to address the subject directly, the Court interpreted the

various liberty guarantees expressed in the first ten amendments to include a number of unspecified rights, among them being the right to marital privacy: "Would we allow the police to search the sacred precincts of marital bedrooms for telltale signs of the use of contraceptives? The very idea is repulsive to the notions of privacy surrounding the marriage relationship" (381 U.S. 479, at 485–86). The right to decide not to procreate is thus a matter of privacy, accruing to married couples, upon which no state should be allowed to intrude. The Court wanted to make itself very clear on this point:

We deal with a right of privacy older than the Bill of Rights—older than our political parties, older than our school system. Marriage is a coming together for better or for worse, hopefully enduring, and intimate to the degree of being sacred. It is an association that promotes a way of life, not causes; a harmony in living, not political faiths; a bilateral loyalty, not commercial or social projects. Yet it is an association for as noble a purpose as any involved in our prior decisions (381 U.S. 479, at 486).

Griswold is clearly a significant legal landmark, even if the opinion has come under heavy criticism from those who argue that the Court engaged in unprincipled policymaking and selective interpretation. Moreover, it begs an equally important question. If the Constitution creates a zone of privacy and the ancillary right to make decisions regarding whether to conceive and "bear a child" free from any state interference, does this privacy right apply only to married couples? Or, does it extend to all individuals regardless of marital status?[43] Seven years later the Court answered that question in a challenge to a Massachusetts law that criminalized the distribution of contraceptives to unmarried individuals:

It is true that in *Griswold* the right of privacy in question inhered in the marital relationship. Yet the marital couple is not an independent entity with a mind and heart of its own, but an association of two individuals each with a separate intellectual and emotional makeup. If the right of privacy means anything, it is the right of the individual, married or single, to be free from unwarranted governmental intrusion into matters so fundamentally affecting a person as the decision whether to bear or beget a child (*Eisenstadt v. Baird*, 405 U.S. 438, at 453 (1972)).

The contrast in focus between *Griswold* and *Eisenstadt* is a stark one, even if it represents a logical progression in the understanding of constitutional rights. At the core of *Griswold*, and the line of precedents that led to it, was the family project—promotion, enhancement, and protection of the family and decisions made within the family unit. The primary thrust of legal language describes the family as sacrosanct, the building block of society, essential to the "survival of the race," and as such it held a higher-order status in our system of rights and privileges than those that might be claimed by individuals. Indeed, individuals held a particular constellation of rights explicitly because of their membership in a legally recognized marriage/family. *Eisenstadt* chucks all of those distinctions, stating that rights are rights, not dependent upon any designated set of relationships and associations, to be enjoyed by all individuals (adults) as a matter of citizenship.

Finally, the Court reaffirmed this understanding of individual rights and extended its application to minors in *Carey v. Population Services International* (431 U.S. 678 (1977)), striking down a New York law that prohibited the sale of contraceptives to nonadults.

Although "[t]he Constitution does not explicitly mention any right of privacy," the Court has recognized that one aspect of the "liberty" protected by the Due Process Clause of the Fourteenth Amendment is "a right of personal privacy, or a guarantee of certain areas or zones of privacy." This right of personal privacy includes "the interest in independence in making certain kinds of important decisions".... The decision whether or not to beget or bear a child is at the very heart of this cluster of constitutionally protected choices. . . . This is understandable, for in a field that by definition concerns the most intimate of human activities and relationships, decisions whether to accomplish or to prevent conception are among the most private and sensitive (431 U.S. 678, at 684–85; citations omitted).

Taken together, the above series of cases establishes a basic civil right under the due process clause to decide "whether or not to beget or bear a child." Thus, the Court's decisions stand firmly for the proposition that the right to procreate, and the right not to procreate, are fundamental constitutional guarantees regardless of age and marital status. The basis for this legal development is controversial, entailing an understanding of privacy not stated explicitly in the Constitution, an understanding that in turn cries out for further development. First, the reasoning de-links marriage from procreation, accepting the notion that the decision whether to have a child is a private option reserved to each individual, protected from government interference. Second, it says that the sexual activity of an individual who has attained sufficient age falls within a private domain and must be shielded from government intrusion. Age of consent is an important demarcation, and the state legislatures and courts have struggled with creating a definition that is reasonable and defendable. As a result, the law varies on this score from one state to another, producing a patchwork of minimum ages regarding independence and privacy on such matters as marriage and contraception, and differing definitions for statutory rape. Moreover, a focus on individual rights in this domain has produced inevitable questions regarding homosexuality and abortion.

Same-Sex Relationships

Until fairly recently, all states outlawed sodomy, generally defined as any form of oral or anal copulation. Although rarely applied to heterosexual couples in practice, most legislation made no distinctions based upon sexual orientation. The U.S. Supreme Court was presented with such a case in 1986 (*Bowers v. Hardwick*, 478 U.S. 186). A Georgia police officer pursuing an unrelated matter was allowed into Michael Hardwick's home by a roommate. Upon entrance into Hardwick's bedroom, the officer observed a homosexual act in progress and made an arrest under Georgia law criminalizing sodomy. Hardwick filed suit in federal district court, claiming that the state law violated his right to privacy under the U.S. Constitution. By a 5–4 majority, the Supreme Court found that the individual privacy protected by the Constitution did not "extend a fundamental right to homosexuals to engage in acts of consensual sodomy" (478 U.S. 186, at 191–92). Indeed, the opinion focuses exclusively upon this issue, despite the fact that the law in question made no distinction on the basis of sexual orientation. The majority was clearly reticent about expanding the right to privacy in this context, and worried about the precedential implications:

The Court is most vulnerable and comes nearest to illegitimacy when it deals with judge-made constitutional law having little or no cognizable roots in the language or design of the Constitution. . . . There should be great resistance to expand the reach of the Due Process Clauses to cover new fundamental rights. Otherwise, the Judiciary necessarily would take upon itself further authority to govern the country without constitutional authority (at 194).

In a passionate dissent, Justice Blackmun, joined by Justices Brennan, Marshall, and Stevens, countered:

This case is [not] about "a fundamental right to engage in homosexual sodomy," as the Court purports to declare, ... Rather, this case is about "the most comprehensive of rights and the right most valued by civilized men," namely, "the right to be let alone." *Olmstead v. United States*, 277 U.S. 438, 478 (1928) (Brandeis, J., dissenting). The statute at issue, Ga. Code Ann. 16-6-2 (1984), denies individuals the right to decide for themselves whether to engage in particular forms of private, consensual sexual activity. The Court concludes that 16-6-2 is valid essentially because "the laws of . . . many States . . . still make such conduct illegal and have done so for a very long time". . . . The sex or status of the persons who engage in the act is irrelevant as a matter of state law. In fact, to the extent I can discern a legislative purpose . . . , that purpose seems to have been to broaden the coverage of the law to reach heterosexual as well as homosexual activity. I therefore see no basis for the Court's decision to treat this case . . . solely on the grounds that it prohibits homosexual activity (478 U.S. 186, at 199–201, Blackmun, J., dissenting).

The majority opinion relies heavily upon historical legal tradition of criminalizing sodomy; however, they did not note that by 1986 nearly half (twenty-three) the state legislatures had repealed their antisodomy statutes, a movement that began in the early 1970s.[44] Moreover, most of the remaining statutes have since been challenged under their respective state constitutions, and by 1999 the laws of seven states had been invalidated.[45] Indeed, on 23 November 1998, the Supreme Court of Georgia, in *Powell v. State* (510 S.E.2d 18), overturned the statute that Michael Hardwick had violated, stating, "We cannot think of any other activity that reasonable persons would rank as more private and more deserving of protection from governmental interference than unforced, private, adult sexual activity. We conclude that such activity is at the heart of the Georgia Constitution's protection of the right of privacy" (510 S.E.2d 18, at 24). According to the American Civil Liberties Union, five states still prohibit consensual homosexual sodomy,[46] and thirteen others criminalize such activity without distinction.[47] The ACLU and other advocacy organizations have litigation pending in several of these jurisdictions and plan to launch legal challenges and to lobby the legislatures in the remaining states.[48] On the other side of the ledger, a number of rival organizations have worked equally diligently to defend existing law in legislative and judicial arenas as challenges arise.[49]

Abortion

The emergence and magnification of privacy as an individual right, and contraception as a personal prerogative, inevitably led to issues concerning abortion. Historically, the act of aborting the fetus of a pregnant woman was firmly a matter of state law, because it falls under the broad rubric of health and welfare, and the federal government really had no jurisdiction. In the early years of the republic, state judges followed (with state-to-state variations) British common law that criminalized abortion. Generally, a line was drawn at "quickening," or the point at which fetal movement is detectable by the mother. Prior to this stage the procedure was, in most jurisdictions, permitted, particularly to save the life of the mother; whereas post-quickening abortions were considered a serious criminal offense. In 1821, the Connecticut state legislature became the first to enact a statute that specifically defined post–fetal movement abortions as a felony, and by 1860 the legislatures of all the states had done so. Religious beliefs and the tendency to legislate public morality were obvious motivating forces, but medical practitioners also provided a strong case for prohibiting abortion unless the mother's life was at risk. After all, surgical procedures were extremely clumsy, especially compared to today's standards, anesthetics and other medicines were rudimentary at best, and sterilization and risk of infection were significant problems (see, e.g., Rubin 1982, 1986; Luker 1984; Frohock 1983; Mohr 1978).

By 1970, the world was a very different place. The women's movement was in full flower. Medical science had made tremendous strides, and abortion, particularly

in the early stages, could be completed quite safely. State laws were in many cases more than one hundred years old, written in response to conditions that no longer existed, and often carried penalties that seemed extraordinarily harsh. Moreover, thousands of women underwent illegal abortions each year, despite dreadful conditions[50] (e.g., Luker 1984), and public opinion was in favor of easing restrictions (e.g., Blake 1971). In this context, a few state legislatures rewrote their abortion statutes during the 1970 session to make the practice legal during the early stages of pregnancy.[51] New York, for example, allowed licensed physicians to perform abortions as an elective procedure through the first twenty-four weeks, and the state's highest court, the New York Court of Appeals, upheld the statute in 1972 (*Byrn v. New York City Health & Hospitals Corp.,* 286 N.E.2d 887).

Although we have oversimplified matters, suffice it to say that the stage was set for *Roe v. Wade* (410 U.S. 113, 1973),[52] a constitutional challenge to a Texas statute that banned all abortions unless performed to save the mother's life. Here, the appellants asserted that the freedom to choose whether to have a child should be the mother's, not the state's, and grounded their argument in the Court's line of opinions establishing the right to privacy, particularly in the area of contraception. The state countered that it has an obligation to protect the health and safety of all its citizens. Abortion is an entirely different matter from contraception, the Texas Attorney General (and a number of supportive amici) reasoned. Once conceived, a fetus represents potential life, deserving the status of personhood and thus the state's protection. Life begins at conception, and this is sufficient basis to demonstrate compelling interest in protecting that life, in addition to ensuring the health and welfare of the mother.

The Court, with Justice Blackmun writing the lead opinion for a seven-member majority, addressed the competing claims by dividing pregnancy into three stages, or trimesters. First, the Court could find no constitutional basis for finding that life begins at conception. Rather, life begins at birth. The justices did concede, however, that the potential for life is enhanced as a pregnancy progresses toward full term and fetal development reaches a stage of "viability" outside the mother's womb. During the first three months, individual liberty and privacy interests are paramount, and the Constitution protects the mother's right to make an abortion decision, with consultation from her physician and without state interference. Because the procedure becomes more complex and risky during the second trimester, and the state has a clear interest in protecting the woman's well-being, regulations to ensure safety are permissible. By the end of the sixth month, a fetus has typically developed to a point where life outside the womb is sustainable, strengthening the state's interest in protecting fetal life and allowing for greater regulatory involvement.

Thus, the *Roe* Court struck down all existing anti-abortion statutes. No state could restrict abortion during the first trimester of pregnancy, but regulations concerning maternal health would be permitted during the second trimester. At viability (assumed to occur at the end of the sixth month), state interest is much enhanced, and post-viability abortions could be more heavily stipulated, a set of issues the Court addressed specifically in the companion case from Georgia, *Doe v. Bolton*, 410 U.S. 179 (1973). In *Doe*, the same majority concluded that a woman has a constitutional right to a third-trimester abortion, if it is her physician's "best clinical judgment," considering her age, "physical, emotional, psychological [and] familial" circumstances, that such a procedure is "necessary for her physical or mental health."

The *Roe* opinion irretrievably changed the legal landscape, substantially expanding the constitutionally protected zone of individual privacy, further unlinking issues of conception and childbearing from a family-centered nexus and connecting them to an individual-focused understanding of legal rights, and converting the issue of abortion from the exclusive realm of state law into a constitutional question, thus rendering all state legislative actions subject to review by federal courts. Not surprisingly, *Roe* triggered a political firestorm, and since 1973 interest groups on both sides have marshaled their forces to apply pressure in every conceivable lawmaking arena. The Supreme Court's constitutional interpretation cannot be overturned by legislation, but necessitates either an amendment to the Constitution or a change in direction by the Court itself. The amendment process is daunting, requiring an overwhelming majority (two-thirds vote in favor by both the U.S. Senate and the House of Representatives, and approval by three-fourths of the fifty state legislatures). Needless to say, several efforts to mount an amendment campaign have fallen far short of the necessary marks. However, the direction of the Court can be influenced via the appointment process, and Republican presidents have used their appointment opportunities to replace retiring *Roe* majority members with new justices likely to agree with the dissenters.[53] In addition, the pressure placed upon state legislatures to enact an array of restrictions on the abortion procedure has been unrelenting, and many have done so. Virtually all state legislation written since 1973 has been challenged by litigation from *Roe* defenders, with some being upheld under judicial scrutiny and others found to be invalid.

In 1976, the Court, by a vote of 7–2, struck down Missouri law that required written spousal consent for elective abortions, parental consent for minors, and that attempted to prohibit second-trimester abortions as a danger to maternal health (*Planned Parenthood of Central Missouri v. Danforth*, 428 U.S. 52 (1976)). In 1980, the Court (divided 5–4) upheld the Hyde Amendment,

passed by the U.S. Congress in 1976, which severely limited the use of any federal funds to reimburse the cost of abortions under the Medicaid program, finding that although abortion is a constitutional right, the states are not obliged to pay for the procedures. In other words, while states cannot interfere with a woman's first-trimester abortion decision, they are not required to ensure availability of the procedure (*Harris v. McRae*, 448 U.S. 297 (1980)). In 1986 (again the split was 5–4), the Court voided provisions of a Pennsylvania state law that required women seeking abortions to receive information on the possible health dangers of abortion, a list and explanation of alternatives, and details about fetal development during pregnancy, that mandated meticulous records of abortions performed in the state, that required third-trimester abortions to be conducted in a way that would maximize fetal survival, unless this would significantly increase risk to the woman, and that prescribed that a second doctor attend all third-trimester abortions to care for a child who survives the procedure (*Thornburg v. American College of Obstetricians and Gynecologists*, 476 U.S. 747 (1986)). "The States are not free, under the guise of protecting maternal health or potential life, to intimidate women into continuing pregnancies" (at 759).

By 1989, Justices Burger, Powell, Stewart, and Douglas, all members of the *Roe* majority, had been replaced by more conservative justices (Scalia, O'Connor, Stevens, and Kennedy), and Justice Rehnquist (one of the two dissenters) had been elevated to chief justice. The Court seemed ready to reverse its direction. Missouri had rewritten its abortion statute once again, this time declaring that life begins at conception and mandating viability tests as early as the second trimester. A badly divided Court upheld the law, with a plurality agreeing that the state has a compelling interest in fetal life from the beginning stages of pregnancy and suggesting that the *Roe* tripartite rationale should be abandoned (*Webster v. Reproductive Health Services*, 492 U.S. 490 (1989)). Justice Scalia, in his concurrence, asserted that *Roe* should simply be overturned.[54] Justice O'Connor, in another concurring opinion, argued that technological advances were pushing the point of viability increasingly earlier, thus heightening the state's interest to determine viability and threatening to render the trimester scheme arbitrary and rigid. Although she voted to uphold the Missouri statute, she saw no reason to use this case as a vehicle to overturn *Roe*'s central premise. Justice Blackmun, joined by Justices Brennan and Marshall, worried about the future:

Today, *Roe v. Wade*, 410 U.S. 113 (1973), and the fundamental constitutional right of women to decide whether to terminate a pregnancy, survive but are not secure. Although the Court extricates itself from this case without making a single, even incremental, change in the law of abortion, the plurality and JUSTICE SCALIA would overrule *Roe* (the first silently, the other explicitly) and would return to the States virtually unfettered authority to control the quintessentially intimate, personal, and life-directing decision whether to carry a fetus to term. Although today, no less than yesterday, the Constitution and the decisions of this Court prohibit a State from enacting laws that inhibit women from the meaningful exercise of that right, a plurality of this Court implicitly invites every state legislature to enact more and more restrictive abortion regulations in order to provoke more and more test cases, in the hope that sometime down the line the Court will return the law of procreative freedom to the severe limitations that generally prevailed in this country before January 22, 1973 (492 U.S. 490, at 537–38 (Blackmun, J., concurring in part and dissenting in part)).

In fact, many states did take *Webster* as an invitation to enact an increasing array of abortion restrictions, thus "provok[ing] more and more test cases." For example, the following year, the Court (6–3) upheld an Ohio statute that required parental notification before an abortion can be performed on a minor, unless the young woman is able to obtain a judicial decree to bypass the requirement (*Ohio v. Akron Ctr for Reproductive Health*, 497 U.S. 502 (1990)). During the same term, the Court (5–4) struck down a similar Minnesota law because it required notification of both parents, but upheld (5–4) a mandatory forty-eight–hour, post-notification waiting period, to allow parents time to discuss the situation with an underage daughter (*Hodgson v. Minnesota*, 497 U.S. 417 (1990)).

In 1992, with only three members of the *Roe* Court remaining (the two dissenters, Justice White and now Chief Justice Rehnquist, and Justice Blackmun, the primary *Roe* author), the Court produced new coordinates for the abortion law matrix (*Planned Parenthood v. Casey*, 505 U.S. 833 (1992)).[55] Although the *Casey* majority (5–4) did not explicitly overturn *Roe*, they jettisoned the trimester framework, rejected "strict scrutiny" as the standard for judicial review in favor of a new and less rigorous "undue burden" standard, and allowed fetal "viability," the point at which the state's interest becomes "compelling," to become adjustable. In addition, the Court upheld a twenty-four–hour waiting period, to provide time for counseling and last-minute reflection and reconsideration, an informed consent requirement to ensure that all women seeking an abortion are given extensive information about the procedure, and a parental consent provision for minors. The Court did, however, invalidate that portion of the Pennsylvania statute that required spousal consent.

Casey has replaced *Roe* as the central precedent in the controversial area of abortion law, and, although *Roe* was not explicitly overturned, its framework was clearly and substantially altered. State legislatures are the primary law providers, and the Court has allowed them much wider latitude to develop regulations than was possible under *Roe*. For example, a number of states require fetal viability tests and ban elective abortions

after viability, mandate a twenty-four– to forty-eight–hour waiting period during which women must be provided with state-authorized information and counseling, compel parental notification, and sometimes consent, in the case of minors (although a judicial "bypass" or waiver is available), and require extensive record keeping.

Moreover, several states have enacted prohibitions on late-term, "partial-birth" abortions, a procedure in which the fetus is delivered feet first and then the skull is crushed and drained.[56] Legal challenges have followed swiftly, and several courts have blocked enforcement of the laws[57]; however, legislators have also moved quickly to rewrite the statutes. During the 1999 term, the Supreme Court heard a challenge to Nebraska's statute, and in late June 2000, a solid 6–3 majority struck it down under the Casey "undue burden" reasoning (*Stenberg v. Carhart*, No. 99-830 (2000)), primarily because the legislation provided no exception to protect the health of the mother. By implication, similar statutes enacted by twenty-eight other states were also rendered constitutionally suspect. The U.S. Congress has also made several attempts to enact a federal ban on partial-birth abortions, but the effort met two presidential vetoes, including one in September 1998.[58]

Conclusions

Familiarity breeds contempt—and children.[59]

Family law was historically heavily value laden and highly moralistic, strongly favoring order over individual liberties. Traditionally falling within the province of the states under their police power and obligation to promote public health and well-being, the law of families was precisely that. In general terms, legislative policy promoted and enhanced a hierarchical family structure and discouraged any challenges to it, such as divorce. The courts, for their part, adopted a parallel policy as inevitable conflicts were litigated, developing a set of common law principles that shielded husbands from liability in the treatment of their wives, insulated parents from children's tort claims, and gave parents wide latitude to make decisions about how to raise their children. State interference in any of these private decisions, such as with compulsory education laws, and bans on the use of contraceptive devices, were considered highly suspect. Only those laws that could withstand the most exacting judicial scrutiny, where the state could justify its intrusion with a compelling argument, were allowed to stand (e.g., laws prohibiting polygamy, and laws requiring mandatory vaccination of children against infectious diseases). Moreover, the family unit was considered more important under the law than any particular individual member, with the possible exception of the husband/father. A number of rights accrued to individuals (especially women) only when they were members of a legally recognized family unit.

To say the least, the law regarding family and love relationships has changed dramatically, particularly during the second half of the twentieth century. As seen in the previous discussion, the legal nucleus of the family atom has been split, with the focus shifting to concentrate upon individual particles. "Families of course continue to consist of individuals linked together in special ways, and the law frequently takes these connections into account. . . . [However,] the tendency for law and social programs to break the family down into its component parts and to treat family members as separate and independent [is pervasive]. This shift of legal emphasis from 'the' family, or even 'families' in all their various forms, to the individual family member seems to have come about more by accident that by design" (Glendon 1989, 295).

The rights movement of the twentieth century mobilized a variety of interest groups whose primary agenda was the promotion of the rights of individuals regardless of social standing, income, race, religion, age, gender, and sexual orientation, just to name a few. To the extent that such organizations have been successful, legal rights have been disconnected from many of the traditional forms of status, including family status, and attached to personhood.

These trends also correspond to other changes in the law. For example, we have also seen the rise of the notion

that courts and legislatures should not attempt to impose "values" (except for equality, individual liberty, and tolerance); and that "values" (except for equality, individual liberty, and tolerance) are a matter of subjective taste or preference. . . . [T]he posture of legal neutrality has been welcomed by judges and legislators, who are otherwise hard put to justify preferring the values of one sector of the population to those of another.

By relinquishing most of its overt attempt to promote any particular set of ideas about family life, modern family law is thus tracking certain well-established trends in modern law. In its pragmatism, its antiformalism, its aspiration towards neutrality with respect to diverse life-styles and opinions, and its bureaucratic character, family law has been swept along by the strong currents that presently predominate in Western legal systems (Glendon 1989, 297).

Similar issues have come into play when individuals resolve to end a spousal relationship. Again, this is a highly personal decision, but it is one in which the state has always held an active interest. Indeed, as Justice Waite's opinion cited above suggests, a marriage license is a legally binding contract issued by the state. Until well into the twentieth century, most of the state legislatures, in the interest of preserving the family unit, made it very difficult to break a marriage contract and obtain a divorce. That traditional model, however, was based upon status, male-dominated hierarchy, and gender-

based role assumptions. Although public pressure has yielded statutory changes across the nation to make the process less onerous, and the number of divorces has skyrocketed as a consequence, there are considerable differences among the states on this score. As women have secured more rights (e.g., to own property, to enter workforce sectors of their own choosing, to be paid equal wages, and so on), most of the legal assumptions underlying the old model that governed family law have given way to a focus on gender equality and individual rights and an application of contract law to even our most personal relationships.[60] Divorce has obviously become a more accessible process. In 1940, the divorce rate was one-sixth the rate of marriage; whereas today it is about one-half. Even children can sue to divorce their parents.[61]

Moreover, the courts have recognized an implied contract in situations where couples were never legally married. Relationships, even highly personal ones, are governed by contract law that must conform to duly enacted public policy. Historically, a range of marriage-related issues have been litigated, and each time the courts must balance the rights of individuals to make such decisions for themselves against the power of the state to act in the interest of promoting order. Generally speaking, we are free to make choices in our family and love relationships, so long as we do not contradict a public policy enacted by the government for legally sound reasons. In other words, the state reserves the right to intervene. Similarly, the relationships between parents and children are of keen interest to the state. One need look no further than laws regulating child custody, abortion, school attendance requirements, and child abuse, to find that a place is set for the state at the family dinner table. These and related issues of the law of childhood are the subject of chapter 7.

Law on the Web

This chapter has been about relationships. As we have seen, the law is very much involved in these most essential elements of human existence. After all, as individuals and as a body politic, relationships are our chief concern in life. Because of this concern, news organizations highlight relationships—whether between nations, between citizens and states, between (usually) estranged families members, between hostile strangers, and even, of course, between presidents and White House interns. Indeed, the news media are our prime source of information about relationships other than our own. The news media are very definitely a large and growing segment of the web.

Just as you would in accessing other sources of information, you must be discriminating in accessing the news. Individuals and organizations often post "news items," which can be accurate, but they can also be completely fabricated. In any case, information provided will be slanted toward the objectives of the host, and thus, is not reliable. As a result, you should never cite a news article from an individual or organization's web page. Rather, you should always go to an established, respected press for such information—and all those presses, as the sites below demonstrate, are well represented on the Internet.

Even when accessing the well-established press, however, a couple of caveats are in order. First, although most of the presses represented on the web allow you to read and download recent stories for free, most charge you for accessing data from their archives (usually items more than two weeks old). In these cases, you might do just as well to research library hardcopy or microfiche. Second, even the established press can make mistakes. Indeed, the rush to be first to post items on the web has recently caused considerable embarrassment to several venerable press institutions. The bottom line: Always double check.

With those caveats in mind, the following are some of the more reliable media represented on the web.

General News Links/Indices

American Journalism Review Newslinks
ajr.newslink.org/news.html

Newspapers Online
www.newspapers.com/

The Internet Public Library, Online Newspapers
www.ipl.org/reading/news/

Newspaper Links
www.newspaperlinks.com/

Newsrack
www.newsrack.com/

Online Newspapers
nw3.nai.net/~virtual/sot/papers.html

Kidon Media-Link
www.dds.nl/~kidon/media-link/papers.shtml

The Drudge Report, Front Page Listing
www.drudgereport.com/

A Smattering of Major American Newspapers

The Los Angeles Times
www.latimes.com/

The Chicago Tribune
chicagotribune.com/

Wall Street Journal Interactive Edition
update.wsj.com/

The New York Times on the Web
www.nytimes.com/

The Washington Post
www.washingtonpost.com/

The Baltimore Sun
www.sunspot.net/

A Smattering of News Magazines

U.S. News Online
www.usnews.com

The entire issue of the weekly, plus news updates and RealAudio interviews.

Time Magazine
pathfinder.com/time/

The current edition of the weekly news magazine, including full-text articles and special reports.

PBS Online NewsHour
www.pbs.org/newshour/

Web version of the television news broadcast.

American Spectator Online
www.spectator.org/

Excerpts from this conservative investigative reporting and commentary magazine.

Major Broadcast Media

CBS
www.cbs.com/

NBC
www.nbc.com/

ABC
www.abcnews.com/

CNN
www.cnn.com/

C-SPAN
www.cspan.org/

National Public Radio
www.npr.org/

Political Journals

National Journal
www.nationaljournal.com

Congressional Quarterly
www.cq.com

*   *   *

Of course, relationships do not simply manifest themselves on the pages of newspapers and magazines. The Internet is full of relationships! Indeed, wisely or not, people form relationships over the web through such now familiar vehicles as chat rooms. Relationships of various kinds are also the subject of thousands of web pages. We list a few of the thousands that might prove useful toward doing further research into some of the subjects broached in this chapter.

Families in Law and Society

Federal Interagency Forum on Child and Family Statistics
www.childstats.gov/

Office of Family Assistance, DHHS
www.acf.gov/programs/ofa/

The Administration for Children and Families, DHHS
www.acf.dhhs.gov/

Findlaw Family Law Library
library.findlaw.com/Family.html

Court TV Family Law Forum
www.courttv.com/legalhelp/asklaw/family/

Findlaw Family Law: State Forms and Information
www.findlaw.com/01topics/15family/statefam.html

Marriage in Law and Society

Cornell Legal Information Institute, Marriage: An Overview
www.law.cornell.edu/topics/marriage.html

Cornell Legal Information Institute, Divorce: An Overview
www.law.cornell.edu/topics/divorce.html

Rutgers School of Law, Pathfinder Series, Same-Sex Marriage
www.rci.rutgers.edu/~axellute/ssm.htm

Lambda Legal Defense and Education Fund
www.lambdalegal.org/

Gay and Lesbian Politics: WWW and Internet Resources
www.indiana.edu/~glbtpol/

Reproduction and Abortion in Law and Society

The Alan Guttmacher Institute for Reproductive Research
www.agi-usa.org/

Abortion Laws of the World
cyber.law.harvard.edu/population/abortion/abortionlaws.htm
Links to the abortion laws of seventy countries, from Afghanistan to Zimbabwe.

Abortion and Reproductive Rights Database
gopher://gopher.well.sf.ca.us:70/11s/Politics/Abortion

National Abortion Rights Action League
www.naral.org/
Pro-choice special interest.

National Right to Life Committee
www.nrlc.org/
Pro-life special interest.

7 Law and the Beginning of Life: Birth, Infancy, and Childhood

When we think about law casually, we generally think about it either in very abstract ways or as something that happens to someone else. Law is either those murky constitutional precepts that tend to confound even trained law professors or it is the latest headlined murder trial involving a defendant so odious as to be almost unrecognizable as a fellow human being. But make no mistake, law is not simply the purview of the lofty and the loathsome. The web of law envelops all of us, it envelops us on a daily basis, and it envelops us from the very beginning of life—indeed, in some respects, it envelops us before our lives even begin.

Thus, in the last chapter, we discussed relationship, that which is the progenitor of both life and law. In this chapter, we will investigate the role of law at the beginning of life. Here, as much as any area we will explore, are some of the sharpest pangs of controversy felt as we enter the new millennium and law is either right in the middle of these controversies or struggling mightily to find its place. In this chapter, we examine such issues as law and the technology of procreation, law and birth, and law and childhood outside of the family.

Law and the Beginning of Life: General Considerations

The natural right of the father (parent) to the custody of his child is not an absolute property right, but rather a trust reposed in the father (parent) by the state as *parens patriae* (*Gardner v. Hall*, Court of Chancery of New Jersey, 26 A.2d 799 at LEXIS p*33 (1943)).

Since ancient times, the law has been concerned with the beginning of life and its reach here, as the court above suggests, is potentially very long. Indeed, the concept of *parens patriae* (Latin for "parent of his country") grew out of early English common law "prerogatives of the King, who was charged with the duty to 'take care of such of his subjects, as are legally unable . . . to take proper care of themselves and their property'" (W. Blackstone, *Commentaries*, 239, cited in Baddeley 1983, 444). In modern times, it has come to stand for the proposition that while children "are assumed to be subject to the control of their parents, if parental control falters, the State must play its part as *parens patriae*" (*Schall v. Martin*, 467 U.S. 253, at 265 (1984)).

Traditionally, the state's role as *parens patriae* has been associated with such child welfare issues as orphaning, abandonment, abuse, and juvenile delinquency—if parents die, leave their children, or *very* badly abuse them *and* the authorities learn of the abuse, or if the child herself engages in criminal behavior, the state takes over as caretaker.[1] These are all concerns of that vast American legal labyrinth known as the juvenile justice system. In the interests of protecting children, promoting health, and bettering society, however, the law reaches well beyond the truly dysfunctional or destructive childhood experience. Indeed, the law touches even the most idyllic childhood from birth to the many legal benchmarks of adulthood. Moreover, contemporary social concerns and modern technological developments have broadened the reach of the law and, perhaps more importantly, promise to broaden that reach even further in the not-too-distant future.

Law and the Beginning of Life: Technology, Social Change, and the Question of Parentage

In 1978 Baby Louise Brown was born in Great Britain. Her birth made headlines around the world and was deemed amazing, astounding, something out of a science fiction future. To many readers of this book, the world reaction to the birth of Baby Louise will probably seem quaint, rather silly or elicit "ho-hums" in hindsight, rather like the huge commotion that attended Lindbergh's trans-Atlantic flight in a twin-engine plane or Gutenberg's invention of a very simple printing press. For Louise Brown was the world's first "test-tube" baby, and while in vitro fertilization (IVF) remains the conception exception, it is now rather commonplace. We no longer bat an eye when a single, twinned, or even triple birth results from IVF; now, we only think about the implications when the procedure results in six or more babies at once.[2] But, those multiple births, gaining in frequency, have very real implications for law and society, as do the plethora of ever-increasing technologies, everything from the (now) old stand-bys, such as artificial insemination and IVF, to more controversial techniques like embryo transfer and surrogate motherhood, and all the way to the likely not-too-distant occurrence of human cloning. Reproductive technology is advancing at breakneck speed. Today, familiarity isn't the only thing that breeds children.

As the preceding chapter demonstrates, the Supreme Court has long since acknowledged a right to reproductive autonomy (see, e.g., *Skinner v. Oklahoma*, 316 U.S. 535 (1942); *Griswold v. Connecticut*, 381 U.S. 479 (1965); *Eisenstadt v. Baird*, 405 U.S. 438 (1972); *Roe v. Wade*, 410 U.S. 113 (1973); and *Carey v. Population Services International*, 431 U.S. 678 (1977)). In truth, however, the landmark reproductive cases are largely about who does *not* become a parent. Just as difficult are questions of who *is* a parent? Of course, traditionally, law has often had to settle disputes over parentage. After all, no less than King Solomon himself came up with an effective (if, by modern standards, somewhat disturbing) method for assigning parental rights. Solomon notwithstanding, divorce and support disputes have long placed judges smack in the middle of parentage questions.

But modernity has added layer upon layer of nuance and ambiguity to questions of genealogy. Some of these questions stem primarily from changing social mores. No longer, for example, do Mom and Dad necessarily feel compelled to marry each other before or even after the little bundle of joy comes along. Some potential moms and dads (same-sex couples) can't legally marry even if they want to.

Some of the questions are technologically driven, and courts and legislatures are scrambling to catch up. Surrogacy, pregnancies that result from the genetic materials of only one member of a couple, and, indeed, pregnancies that result from genetic materials wholly outside the couple, are becoming more and more frequent. The law has spoken to these issues only interstitially to date, but increasingly it is being asked to provide Solomon-like answers. Then, of course, there's the looming prospect of human "Dollys," sure to confront and shake the legal web in the not too distant future. These and other questions of birth and parentage are the subjects of this section.

Technology, Birth, and Law

The wealthy suitor advertising in the Harvard Crimson seeks a woman who is tall, athletic, and smart. This, thought freshman Kate Naessen as she read it, could be describing her. She's 5 feet 11. She swims. Her college board scores topped 1400. For a week she struggled to decide whether to answer the stranger. Finally, she replied with a feeler via e-mail.

This suitor is no love-starved man seeking someone to share caviar by candlelight. This is a childless couple offering $50,000 to an "intelligent, athletic egg donor" who "must be at least 5'10", have a 1400+ SAT score [and] possess no major family medical issues." Naessen is among about 200 women who have responded to the half-page ads that appeared in the Crimson and student papers in six other top universities (Sege 1999, A1).

While the item reported above may well be an example of gross excess, it is a grossly excessive example of the growing trend toward reproductive technologies. Egg "donation," among of the newest of the new reproductive technologies, is growing by leaps and bounds, driven by increased numbers of infertile and aging couples anxious to have children of their "own." According to the Centers for Disease Control and Prevention, in 1996, egg donation was employed more than 5,000 times, marking a 50 percent increase in just a single year. Moreover, the number of clinics offering the technique has grown from one a decade ago to roughly 230 in 1996 (Vobejda 1999, A1).

In general, reproductive technologies are mushrooming and so are their offshoots. Thus, for example, in 1999, it is estimated that "some 75,000 infants will be born as a result of reproductive technologies—more than twice as many as will be available through traditional adoption" (Vobejda 1999, A1). In addition, labs across the United States currently house more than 150,000 embryos suspended in liquid nitrogen tanks (with 19,000 more added each year). Such statistics have prompted Lori B. Andrews, director of the Institute for Science, Law, and Technology at Chicago-Kent College of Law, to ask:

What next? Will the couple who paid $50,000 for an egg from an Ivy League student sue if the child isn't doing algebra by kindergarten? If a couple seeking a baby boy undergo sex selection at the Genetics and IVF Institute in Fairfax (one of the few places in the country that offers the service) and get a girl instead, can they sue for the lifetime difference in earnings between a female and a male? (Andrews 1999)

Nor need this brave new world merely be the stuff of hypothetical query. Take, for example, the recent case of Donna and Richard Fasano, a white couple from Staten Island, New York, and Deborah Perry-Rogers and Robert Rogers, a black couple from New Jersey. Both sets of potential parents were clients of the same Manhattan fertility specialist. The good news: in December 1998, the Fasanos hit natal pay dirt, becoming the proud parents of twin baby boys. The story, however, involves a turn-of-the century twist: One twin was white, the other black. Thus, the bad news. It seems that the couples' shared fertility guru, Dr. Lillian Nash, accidentally implanted some of the Rogerses' embryos into Donna Fasano. As a result of this multi-cultural birthing, the Fasanos are unhappily ceding custody of the black baby to the Rogerses, the Rogerses have launched litigation against Dr. Nash, and the Fasanos are expected soon to follow suit—malpractice, that is (Grunwald 1999, A1).

Indeed, it is in the courtroom that what law there is to be found in the world of reproductive technology—and there is surprisingly little—is being fashioned. Legislatures have been painfully slow, even loathe, to act. After all, since 1973, reproduction has been the great social minefield of American politics, and like any minefield, a place to be avoided if at all possible.[3] The result is a little bit of confusing legal patchwork within what is otherwise a huge legal void.

The problem with this courtroom-based approach, as Andrews points out, "rests in some stark differences between medicine and law":

If a lawyer from 100 years ago were set down in a modern courtroom, he—and, of course, it would be a he—would soon feel completely at home. But if a doctor from the late 1800s were to find himself among the liquid nitrogen tanks, laparoscopy equipment and ultrasound machines of a modern in vitro fertilization (IVF) clinic, he wouldn't have the foggiest idea what to do. While medicine looks ahead, law turns back to precedent. When cases about cars first reached the courts, judges applied the rules governing horses and buggies. When computer software was introduced, judges looked to doctrines covering printed books. But where should we turn for precedents to cover entirely new medical questions, involving the handling of human embryos, for example, or the sale and bartering of genetic material? What should I tell the doctor who asked me recently whether a woman has a right to her dead husband's sperm? And now that a child can have three mothers (genetic, gestational and rearing), who is responsible when all—or perhaps none—want the child? While much attention has been focused on the special problems involving the multiple births created by fertility clinics—septuplets, octuplets—less attention is given to the question of multiple parents, and the disputes that can arise when something goes wrong (Andrews 1999).

As the Fasano-Rogers tale suggests, things *can* be expected to go wrong. And, they've been going wrong for a surprisingly long time.

Take, for example, the 1968 case (from California, where else?) of *People v. Sorenson* (68 Cal. 2d 280; 437 P.2d 495; 1968 Cal. LEXIS 162; 66 Cal.Rptr.7; 25 A.L.R.3d 1093 (1968)). There, a court determined that the husband of a woman, who with his consent was artificially inseminated with semen of a third-party donor, was indeed the legal father of the child and thus liable for child support (at 283–84). But, sperm donation is one thing—low-tech and old hat, by today's standards. The legal story gets more complicated as newer and more complex procedures are added to the mix. Consider, for instance, the seminal (no pun intended) case of *Davis v. Davis* (842 S.W. 2d 588 (Tenn. Sp Ct., 1992)), the result of a divorce and custody dispute between Mary Sue and Junior Davis that began back in February 1989.

The Davises' fractured marriage was standard fare, and the terms of divorce agreeable to both, but for one issue. Earlier in their union, as a result of Mary Sue's dysfunctional fallopian tubes, the couple was unable to conceive naturally. The Davises thus turned to in vitro fertilization. After several unsuccessful attempts at IVF, the Davises opted to delay subsequent procedures in favor of cryogenic preservation, freezing fertilized ova in nitrogen and storing them at sub-zero temperatures for later transfer. Unfortunately, for all their excitement at the prospects of this amazing (then) new technology, they apparently never "considered the implications of

storage beyond the few months it would take to transfer the remaining 'frozen embryos,' if necessary. There was no discussion, let alone an agreement, concerning disposition in the event of a contingency such as divorce" (at 592).

Well, divorce does happen—a lot—and the pesky settlement "issue" mentioned above was, of course, the disposition of the "frozen embryos," a task laid in the lap of Tennessee Judge W. Dale Young, who, with the nation's entire legal establishment looking over his shoulder, valiantly fought his way through the tangle of technology using, for lack of precedent, a good bit of "horse sense . . ." (*Davis v. Davis v. King*, 1989 Tenn. App. LEXIS 641 (1989)). Judge Young's "horse sense" informed him that "human life begins at conception," that "Mr. and Mrs. Davis [had] produced human beings, in vitro," and thus that "the best interests of the child or children, in vitro, [was] for their Mother, Mrs. Davis, to be permitted the opportunity to bring them to term through implantation" (at 641).

An appeals court, demurring at the implications of Judge Young's determination of the beginning of life—a determination at odds not only with federal constitutional law (see *Roe v. Wade*, 410 U.S. 113 (1973)), but with that of the state,[4] "swung . . . far [indeed] in the opposite direction" (842 S.W. 2d 588, at 595), preferring to imbue the embryos with characteristics more akin to property than to personhood, and so ruling that both "parties share[d] an interest in the seven fertilized ova" (at 589).

Needless to say, the case next found its way to the Tennessee Supreme Court which, although affirming the appellate court's judgment giving Junior an interest in the embryos, ruled that

preembryos are not, strictly speaking, either "persons" or "property," but occupy an interim category that entitles them to special respect because of their potential for human life. It follows that any interest that [parties] . . . have in the preembryos . . . is not a true property interest. However, they do have an interest in the nature of ownership, to the extent that they have decision-making authority concerning disposition of the preembryos, within the scope of policy set by law (at 597).

Now, this was difficult terrain, and by any measure the Tennessee courts attempted to traverse it artfully. But, discounting the role of the fertility clinic, the Davis case involved only a mother and a father, both genetically linked to the frozen embryos in question. The already rocky road gets a good deal more treacherous—scientifically, economically, emotionally, *and* legally—when individual third parties enter the scene. Two recent California cases illustrate the problems increasingly faced by courts, guided by only scant legislative or case directive.

The first case involves so-called "traditional surrogacy," an arrangement where a woman is impregnated with the sperm of a married man with the prior understanding that the resulting child is to be legally the child of the married man and his infertile wife. Under such conditions, the surrogate is both the birth mother and the genetic mother of the child. But should plans go awry, is she the legal mother?

Like many couples, Robert and Cynthia Moschetta had difficulty conceiving a child—in their case, because Cynthia was sterile. In 1989, the Moschettas agreed to pay Elvira Jordan $10,000 to be artificially inseminated with Robert's semen and to bear his "biological off-spring." Jordan promised that Robert "could obtain sole custody and control of any child born. She also promised to sign all necessary papers to terminate her parental rights and 'aid' Cynthia . . . in adopting the child" (*In re the Marriage of Cynthia J. and Robert P. Moschetta*, 25 Cal. App. 4th 1218, at 1223; 1994 Cal. App. LEXIS 616; 30 Cal. Rptr. 2d 893 (Court of Appeal of California, Fourth Appellate District, Division Three, 1994)). Happily, in November 1989, Elvira became pregnant with Robert's child. However, within months of the joyous news, the Moschettas began having marital problems, and in April 1990, Robert asked Cynthia for a divorce. In May, in the midst of her birth labor, Elvira learned of the divorce action. The following day, she gave birth to a baby girl, Marissa. And, that is when the legal fun-and-games began:

Jordan [immediately] began to reconsider the surrogacy agreement, and for two days she refused to allow Robert to see the baby. On May 31 she relented, and allowed Robert and Cynthia to take the child home after they told her they would stay together. However, the marriage deteriorated; and within seven months, on November 30, 1990, Robert left the family residence, taking Marissa with him. Less than a month later, on December 21, Cynthia filed a petition for legal separation, and a petition to establish custody of Marissa; less than a month after that, on January 11, 1991, she filed a petition to establish parental relationship, alleging she was the "de facto mother" of Marissa. In February Jordan sought to join the dissolution action (granted in March), while Robert filed responsive pleadings requesting a judgment of dissolution rather than legal separation (at 1223).[5]

In 1992, a trial court held that both Robert Moschetta and Elvira Jordan were the legal parents of Marissa, ceding joint legal and physical custody of the child to the father and the surrogate. An appeal followed in which Robert challenged the trial court's determination of parentage, contending that he and his estranged wife, Cynthia, and *not* Elvira, were Marissa's legal parents. Interestingly, for her part, Cynthia supported the judgment at trial.

The appeals court, giving lengthy and thoughtful consideration to what little—and only tangentially related—law it had to go on, affirmed the trial court's judgment that Robert and Elvira were the baby's true and legal parents, but strongly suggested in remanding the case that Marissa's best interests lay in Robert being

afforded sole custody rights. More important, the court spoke eloquently to some of the "disquieting" realities of this brave new world of technology-driven, but legally ill-defined, reproduction:

Infertile couples who can afford the high-tech solution of in vitro fertilization and embryo implantation in another woman's womb can be reasonably assured of being judged the legal parents of the child, even if the surrogate reneges on her agreement. Couples who cannot afford in-vitro fertilization and embryo implantation, or who resort to traditional surrogacy because the female does not have eggs suitable for in vitro fertilization, have no assurance their intentions will be honored in a court of law. For them and the child, biology is destiny. The result is disquieting. Much has been written in the surrogacy area of the pain visited on the birth mother who contemplates giving up her child. Not so much appears to have been written about the disruption to the intended parents, who have—to put the matter in classic estoppel language—relied to their detriment in deciding to bring a child into the world. Let us be blunt here: Marissa would never have been born if Robert and Cynthia Moschetta had known Elvira Jordan would change her mind. On this point Robert Moschetta is certainly correct that surrogacy is fundamentally different than adoption, which contemplates a child already conceived.

On the other hand, there is also no doubt that enforcement of a surrogacy contract prior to a child's birth presents a host of thorny legal problems, particularly if such contracts were specifically enforced. Any result is disquieting (at 1235).

In its opinion above, the *Moschetta* court spoke of the greater legal assuredness in more "high-tech solution[s]" than the sort of "traditional surrogacy" available to Robert and Cynthia. Yet, high technology of the sort the court had in mind, specifically, "gestational surrogacy," where the sperm of a married man is artificially united with the egg of his wife, and the resulting embryo implanted in another woman's womb, has presented courts with its own "host of thorny legal problems," particularly where "gestational surrogacy" itself has undergone further technological leaps and bounds. Consider the case of John and Luanne Buzzanca, Pamela Snell, and Baby Jaycee.

In 1994, John and Luanne hired Snell to be their gestational surrogate. But theirs was not to be a "normal" gestational surrogacy arrangement. Rather, John and Luanne employed Pamela to bear them a child using egg and sperm not their own, but from *anonymous* donors. Oh, modernity! As you've no doubt guessed—this being the common thread among all these uncommon stories—shortly before the baby's birth, John filed for divorce. However, unlike Robert Moschetta, John Buzzanca wanted nothing to do—particularly, nothing *financial* to do—with the baby-to-be. But, wait, you "ain't heard nothin' yet."

In an (understandably) headline-grabbing decision, Orange County Superior Court Judge Robert Monarch declared that the child, by then two years old and named Jaycee, had no biological ties either to the Buzzancas or to the surrogate mother, Snell. Jaycee, according to the trial court, effectively had no parents at all! Notably, in its initial consideration of *Buzzanca*,[6] and with a clear nod to the difficulties encountered in *Moschetta*, California's Fourth District Court of Appeal issued a very unambiguous plea for help: "Once again, the need for legislation in the surrogacy area is apparent. We reiterate our previous call for legislative action" (*In re the Marriage of John A. and Luanne H. Buzzanca*, 61 Cal. App. 4th 1410; 72 Cal. Rptr. 2d 280 (Court of Appeal of California, Fourth Appellate District, Division Three, 1998)). However, in the absence of such "assistance," the court was forced to strike out on its own.

Thus, getting "right to the point ...," the appeals court reversed the trial court judgment, asserting that "Jaycee never would have been born had not Luanne and John both agreed to have a fertilized egg implanted in a surrogate" (at 1412). That being the case, the law "makes a husband the lawful father of a child born because of his consent to artificial insemination . . . [and] the same parity of reasoning [demands] . . . [j]ust as a husband is deemed to be the lawful father of a child unrelated to him when his wife gives birth after artificial insemination, so should a husband and wife be deemed the lawful parents of a child after a surrogate bears a biologically unrelated child on their behalf" (at 1412–13). (Sorry, John, Luanne's the mom and you're the dad, "every bit as much as if things had been done the old-fashioned way" (at 1426).) In other words, the court ruled that in establishing legal parenthood, intent to become parents is more important than any genetic relationship. Still, again though, the court acknowledged the confusing legal jumble created by the patchwork case approach characteristic of reproductive technology, no doubt speaking for many judges in "[a]gain . . . call[ing] on the Legislature"

to sort out the parental rights and responsibilities of those involved in artificial reproduction. No matter what one thinks of artificial insemination, traditional and gestational surrogacy (in all its permutations), and—as now appears in the not-too-distant future, cloning and even gene splicing—courts are still going to be faced with the problem of determining lawful parentage. A child cannot be ignored. Even if all means of artificial reproduction were outlawed with draconian criminal penalties visited on the doctors and parties involved, courts will still be called upon to decide who the lawful parents really are and who—other than the taxpayers—is obligated to provide maintenance and support for the child. These cases will not go away.

Courts can continue to make decisions on an ad hoc basis without necessarily imposing some grand scheme, looking to the imperfectly designed Uniform Parentage Act and a growing body of case law for guidance in the light of applicable family law principles. Or the Legislature can act to impose a broader order which, even though it might not be perfect on a case-by-case basis, would bring some predictability to those who seek to make use of artificial reproductive techniques. As jurists, we recognize the traditional role of the common (i.e., judge-formulated) law in applying old legal principles to new technology. . . . However, we still believe it is the Legislature,

with its ability to formulate general rules based on input from all its constituencies, which is the more desirable forum for lawmaking (at 1428).[7]

Yet, legislative ordering remains the clear exception. For, "while there are pages of adoption laws on the books in each state, [as of 1999] only three states—Florida, Virginia and New Hampshire—[had] enacted legislation to address reproductive technology in any comprehensive fashion" (Andrews 1999).

LAW AND CLONING

So, what about the possibility that worldwide amazement over "Dolly the Sheep" turns to even greater astonishment over "Dolly the Person"? The prospect, according to most experts, is inevitable—and inevitable sooner rather than later. Already,

[a] team of American researchers has quietly begun trying to create the world's first batches of cloned human embryos, and another team has resumed its controversial cloning of embryos that are part human and part cow, according to scientists involved in the work (Weiss 1999, A1).

Regardless of how queasy, outraged, or doubtful we may be about the possibility of human or near–human cloning, it is on the technological horizon. But, what of the role of law in this the most far-flung of human reproductive endeavor?

In a nutshell: There is little. To date, the most far-reaching legal effort in the area of cloning was undertaken by President Clinton. On 4 March 1997, the president, expressing his view "that human cloning would have to raise deep concerns, given our most cherished concepts of faith and humanity," banned "the use of any Federal funds for any cloning of human beings" (Clinton 1997). In addition, he made examination of the subject a top priority of the National Bioethics Advisory Commission.[8]

Congress has been slower to act. Despite a series of efforts in the House of Representatives early in 1998, cloning legislation has stalled: "Caught between the desire not to support anything resembling abortion and an equally strong desire not to interfere with medical research, Congress has repeatedly failed to muster the votes necessary to pass legislation relating to cloning in the private sector" (Weiss 1999). Congress-watchers do expect a battle to erupt in the near future over the extent to which federal monies can be used to study human embryonic stem cells.[9] Because legislation generally lags behind technology, it is likely that cloning law awaits the arrival of the first clone, followed, no doubt, by the first clone litigation.

Law and the Beginning of Life in a Changing Society

As technology has presented courts with challenging questions of parentage, so have changing social mores and lifestyles. Clearly, where once children born and raised outside the traditional framework of a female mother wedded to a male father were relegated to the legal sub-status of "bastard," they now have all the legal rights to care as their "legitimate" contemporaries (*Levy v. Louisiana*, 391 U.S. 68 (1968)).[10] Occasionally, the two challenges—the technical and the social—merge, representing true judicial headaches. Consider, for example, the case of *Karin T. v. Michael T.* (127 Misc. 2d 14; 484 N.Y.S.2d 780 (Family Court of New York, Monroe County, 1985)), thrown in the lap of a New York Family Court judge in 1985. Of course, the case involved our now usual scenario of a relationship on the rocks, and it involved the no longer too unusual fact of children produced by artificial insemination. Nevertheless, this was a case with a real difference. In 1977, Karin and "Michael" were wed by a minister. "Michael," however, was born "Marlene" and only by dressing and "liv[ing] like a man," had she/he obtained a valid marriage license (at 15). Things changed, however, after the relationship floundered, shortly before the birth of the second child. Then, conveniently, did Michael/Marlene publicly fess up to the ruse, declaring the 1977 marriage null and void, and seeking to avoid the kind of court-ordered child support normally mandated following divorce. Because their wedding was fraudulent, argued Michael/Marlene, there was no real divorce to be had. Moreover, she asserted, since she was not a biological parent, nor had she signed adoption papers, the children were not hers. Thus, she could not be liable for their support.

The judge, on the other hand, saw the situation quite differently. Acknowledging that while "[a]s a general rule only biological or adoptive parents are liable for the support of children, [nevertheless, w]here extraordinary circumstances require, courts have held nonparents responsible for the support of children" (at 16). The court continued in its ruling against Michael T. to assert that

certainly the document which was signed by the respondent and by which these children were brought into the world gives rise to a situation which must provide these two children with remedies. To hold otherwise would allow this respondent to completely abrogate her responsibilities for the support of the children involved and would allow her to benefit from her own fraudulent acts which induced their birth no more so than if she were indeed the natural father of these children. Of course, the respondent was free to engage and live in any lifestyle which she felt appropriate. However, by her course of conduct in this case which brought into the world two innocent children she should not be allowed to benefit from those acts to the detriment of these children and of the public generally.... The term "parent" is not defined in [New York's Domestic Relations Law] except in biological terms and the court has found no authority to the contrary. Ballantine's Law Dictionary 911 (3d ed) defines "parent" as "[the] father or mother". In Black's Law Dictionary 1003 (5th ed 1979) "parent" is defined as "[one] who procreates, begets, or brings forth offspring." The actions of this respondent in executing the agreement above-referred to certainly brought forth these offspring as if done biologically. The contract and the equitable estoppel

which prevail in this case prevent the respondent from asserting her lack of responsibility by reason of lack of parenthood. This court finds that under the unique facts in this case, respondent is indeed a "parent" to whom such responsibility attaches (at 18–19).

While the obligation to support children financially "brought forth" in one way or another seems relatively clear, questions of physical custody sometimes place courts and "parents" in legally murkier waters.

For example, in custody and visitation cases, courts have tended to rule that there is "no difference between a parent living with someone of the opposite sex without the benefit of marriage and a parent living in a committed relationship with someone of the same sex" (*J.B.F. v. J.M.F.*, 730 So. 2d 1186, at 1189 (Court of Civil Appeals of Alabama, 1997)).[11] Thus, in a 1999 ruling by the Massachusetts Supreme Court, upholding the visitation rights of a lesbian estranged from her longtime partner, Justice Ruth Abrams noted: "It is to be expected that children of nontraditional families, like other children, form parent relationships with both parents, whether those parents are legal or de facto" (*E.N.O. v. L.M.M.*, 429 Mass. 824, at 829; 711 N.E.2d 886 (Supreme Judicial Court of Massachusetts, 1999)).

There are, however, exceptions (see, e.g., *S.E.G. v. R.A.G.*, 735 S.W. 2d 164 (Mo. Ct. App. 1987); *Dailey v. Dailey*, 635 S.W. 2d 391 (Tenn. Ct. App. 1982); and *Bottoms v. Bottoms*, 249 Va. 410, 457 S.E.2d 102 (Va. 1995)). For instance, in 1995, the Virginia Supreme Court sided with a grandmother seeking to take custody of her young grandson from her own lesbian daughter (*Bottoms v. Bottoms*, 249 Va. 410; 457 S.E.2d 102 (Va. 1995)). Although the mother's lesbianism was hardly the only issue of fitness in *Bottoms v. Bottoms* and although the Virginia high court noted that "a lesbian mother is not per se an unfit parent . . . ," it nevertheless ruled that it could

not overlook the mother's [lesbian] relationship . . . , and the environment in which the child would be raised if custody is awarded the mother. We have previously said that living daily under conditions stemming from active lesbianism practiced in the home may impose a burden upon a child by reason of the "social condemnation" attached to such an arrangement, which will inevitably afflict the child's relationships with its "peers" and with the community at large (at 420).

Adoption

Beyond issues of support and custody where parents, through one means or another, have had an active part in bringing forth a human life, lies the more traditional means of caring for and parenting children "brought forth" by others: adoption. In important respects, adoption lies opposite technology-driven childbirth on the regulatory spectrum. Where there is little law governing technological reproduction, there is a vast, vast labyrinth of state, federal, and even international law governing couples' or individuals' decisions to adopt.

WHO MAY ADOPT

Domestic adoptions—that is, those in which American children are adopted by American parents—are largely governed by individual state laws.[12] Those wishing to adopt must meet certain eligibility thresholds that vary by state. At a minimum, most agencies—both public and private—require so-called "home studies" as a means of assessing parental fitness. In addition, most states mandate "background checks and probationary placement periods as well … [and], both public and private agencies may require parents to meet certain age and health requirements" (Kleiman 1997, 330).

Although most state law does not technically disqualify any particular classification of potential parent,[13] most agencies employ ranking systems that put

young, happily married couples at the top of the waiting list; single, older, and disabled people in the middle; and homosexuals and severely disabled people at the bottom. In short, agencies look for parents who fit traditional notions of family: "The standards an adoptive parent must meet in order to provide for the best interests of a particular child have historically reflected preference for marital, age, income, and religious participation requirements modeled after the ideal majoritarian family." Thus, people who are single, older, gay, or disabled are not always "acceptable" (Kleiman 1997, 344).

Over the past thirty years, a particularly contentious issue in the area of adoption law has been transracial adoptions. The subject reached public consciousness in 1972 when the National Association of Black Social Workers (NABSW), reacting to an increase in white adoptions of black children, denounced the practice as racial "genocide." NABSW's criticism resulted not only in "a 30% decrease in the practice over the course of one year" (Perez 1998, 209), but in a considerable legal sea change as well, for "[a]fter the release of [NABSW's] statement, many agencies 'either established same race placements or used the NABSW report to justify existing race-matching policies'" (p. 209). State law, in many areas, followed suit, with jurisdictions instituting "matching or holding policies authorizing the delay of transracial placements for periods ranging from three months to several years" (p. 210). For example, California mandated a waiting period of ninety days after a child was put up for adoption during which time an agency had to make a search for same-race parents. Only after such period could the child be considered for transracial adoption (p. 210).

State and private agency regulations discouraging transracial adoptions were abetted by federal law. For instance, although Title VI of the *Civil Rights Act* generally forbids the use of race, color, or national origin in the delivery of benefits, an exception was made in the case of adoption, making it "appropriate to consider race, color, or national origin as one of several factors."[14] More recently, however, as a result of a changing political climate, Congress has acted to change that interpretation of Title VI. Thus, in 1994, it passed the *Multiethnic Placement Act* (MEPA) (42 U.S.C. 5115(a) (1994)), designed "to promote the best interests of children by—(1) decreasing the length of time that children wait to be adopted; (2) preventing discrimination in the placement of children on the basis of race, color, or national origin" (Perez 1998, 218). To accomplish this, Congress used a familiar "carrot-and-stick" approach, prohibiting agencies receiving federal grant funds from using race in adoption placements. MEPA was followed in 1996 by the *Adoption Promotion and Stability Act*, forbidding agencies from hampering or rejecting adoptions made "on the basis of race, color, or national origin of the adoptive or foster parent, or the child involved" (Pub. L. No. 104-188, 1808(c)(1)(A)-(B), 110 Stat. 1755, 1904). As a result, "Today, only Arkansas and Minnesota maintain matching or preference policies that require preference for adoptions within the same racial group" (Perez 1998, 211).[15] Nevertheless, despite official legal changes, evidence suggests that many adoption agencies remain resistant to transracial placements, treating them "at best as a last-resort option to be considered only after minority families have been recruited and appropriate waiting periods exhausted" (Bartholet 1991, 1204; see also Bartholet 1998.)

Not only is adoption governed by private agency regulation, state law, and federal mandate, but increasingly by the laws of other nations. As international adoptions have increased, "from 8,102 children in 1989 to 13,620 children in 1997" (Gold 1998, 110),[16] so have legal entanglements. Indeed, the growing number of Americans wishing to adopt foreign-born children,[17] "must satisfy three governmental entities in order to successfully complete the process … —the federal government, the foreign government, and finally the individual state government" (Gold 1998, 111).

ADOPTIONS GONE WRONG

If the practice of adoption—unlike IVF—is nearly as old as mankind itself, so too are problems within adoptive relationships. Clearly, a central theme of many fairy and folk tales is the horrific adoptive situation in which the adoptive parent (usually in the form of a cruel and conniving step*mother*) sadistically abuses *her* adoptive child for the purpose of aggrandizing herself or her biological children. Witness poor Ella forced to sleep among the cinders or little Hansel and Gretel cast out alone into the frightening forest. Less common, though nevertheless told, are stories of cunning, sometimes downright depraved, adoptees who, to gain throne or fortune, manipulate doting adoptive parents at the expense of their own biological offspring. Whatever the nightmarish twist, such grim (and in many cases, Grimm) tales point to an ancient lineage of adoption pitfalls.

Modern case law suggests that such pitfalls are not just the stuff of ancient fairytales. For the adoptive child, as chapter 6 points out, there may be relief in "divorcing" her abusive adoptive parents. Or, as we outline below, under the most extreme scenario, she, like any child, may be taken into state care.

More recently, however, a new breed of litigation, brought by exasperated adoptive parents has been gaining attention. Consider, for example, the story of Bill and Tracy McClellan and their fourteen-year-old adopted son, Billy. In 1994, the McClellans adopted then ten-year-old Billy after a year as his foster parents. Although the McClellans knew that their son had had a difficult early childhood, their attempts to gain complete information on his past from Erie County, Ohio, social welfare agents were generally ignored, resulting in only scant data.

As the McClellans were later to discover, Billy had a huge file indeed, one indicating that he had been raped at age four, that he had engaged in extreme cruelty to animals, and that, at a very young age, he had become aggressively promiscuous—in short, that Billy was "a very troubled child" (Vobejda 1998, A1). Well, there are troubled children and there are troubled children—in Billy's case, the designation "very troubled" may have been a gross understatement. Adopted into the McClellan family, as he reached puberty, Billy began to manifest his difficulties in a variety of just plain awful ways, the worst of which included apparent attempts to murder his mother and siblings. As a result, Billy was eventually placed in a very costly residential treatment center for which the McClellans were being billed. Now, in danger of losing their home and with few financial resources left to care for their other adopted children, Tracy and Bill are considering asking a judge to overturn the adoption on the grounds that they were deceived about Billy's early childhood. The authorities' failure to provide them with full information on Billy's background, they claim, makes theirs a case of "wrongful adoption."

While adoption is an ancient practice—and, no doubt, problem adoptions, nearly as ancient—the wrongful adoption tort is, relatively speaking, brand new, born only as recently as 1986 when the Ohio Supreme Court declared a county adoption agency liable for fraudulent misrepresentation of an adopted child's background (*Burr v. Board of Stark County Commissioners*, 23 Ohio St. 3d 69; 491 N.E.2d 1101 (Supreme Court of Ohio, 1986)). The Ohio decision was followed by a succession of court rulings finding public and private agencies liable for fraud in intentionally misrepresenting or failing to provide full background information on adoptees.[18] Generally speaking, in such cases, the adoptive parents do not wish to "return" their child, but rather to recover

the often very considerable costs of caring for children with extreme emotional, mental, or physical disabilities. In some cases, as a last resort, parents may seek to have a judge "overturn the adoption"—in effect, giving the child back.[19] Although such cases are fairly rare, they have been increasing in frequency.[20] More important, these cases are expected to rise even further in large part due to recent federal efforts to increase substantially the number of foster children placed in adoptive homes by making it easier to terminate biological parental rights and through providing generous subsidies to states.[21]

Law and the Beginning of Life: Infancy

The fact that the law reaches us even before we are born or parented is now well established. Not surprisingly, then, it touches us the second we emerge from the womb. To begin with, the law wants to know who we are and considering that we seemingly have very little to tell about our newly emerged selves, the law wants to know quite a bit—and it wants to tell quite a few people about it. Thus, all states require that newborns be registered in some detail. Maryland's requirements are illustrative:

(a) Birth in institution. —

(1) Within 72 hours after a birth occurs in an institution, or en route to the institution, the administrative head of the institution or a designee of the administrative head shall:

(i) Prepare, on the form that the Secretary provides, a certificate of birth;
(ii) Secure each signature that is required on the certificate; and
(iii) File the certificate.

(2) The attending physician shall provide the date of birth and medical information that are required on the certificate within 72 hours after the birth.

(3) Upon the birth of a child to an unmarried woman in an institution, the administrative head of the institution or the designee of the administrative head shall:

(i) Provide an opportunity for the child's mother and the father to complete a standardized affidavit of parentage recognizing parentage of the child on the standardized form provided by the Department of Human Resources under § 5-1028 of the Family Law Article;
(ii) Furnish to the mother written information prepared by the Child Support Enforcement Administration concerning the benefits of having the paternity of her child established, including the availability of child support enforcement services; and
(iii) Forward the completed affidavit to the Department of Health and Mental Hygiene, Division of Vital Records. The Department of Health and Mental Hygiene, Division of Vital Records shall make the affidavits available to the parents, guardian of the child, or a child support enforcement agency upon request.

(4) An institution, the administrative head of the institution, the designee of the administrative head of an institution, and

an employee of an institution may not be held liable in any cause of action arising out of the establishment of paternity.

(5) If the child's mother was not married at the time of either conception or birth or between conception and birth, the name of the father may not be entered on the certificate without an affidavit of paternity as authorized by § 5-1028 of the Family Law Article signed by the mother and the person to be named on the certificate as the father.

(6) In any case in which paternity of a child is determined by a court of competent jurisdiction, the name of the father and surname of the child shall be entered on the certificate of birth in accordance with the finding and order of the court.

(7) If the father is not named on the certificate of birth, no other information about the father shall be entered on the certificate.

(b) Birth outside institution. —

Within 72 hours after a birth occurs outside an institution, the birth shall be verified by the Secretary and a certificate of birth shall be prepared, on the form that the Secretary provides, and filed by one of the following, in the indicated order of priority:

(1) The attending individual.

(2) In the absence of an attending individual, the father or mother.

(3) In the absence of the father and the inability of the mother, the individual in charge of the premises where the birth occurred (Md. Code Ann. § 4-208 (1998)).

Nor are our newborn selves simply required to convey all of this information to state agencies. Today, we are required to obtain Social Security numbers from the federal government. Moreover, our parents—at least those fortunate enough to receive job-related benefits—will have to navigate corporate law and bureaucracy, as they negotiate family-leave policy,[22] and health and life insurance benefits.

Law and Childhood Health

Public health is typically regarded as a scientific pursuit, and, undoubtedly, our understanding of the etiology and response to disease is heavily influenced by scientific inquiry. Less well understood is the role of law in public health. Law is an essential part of public health practice. Law defines the jurisdiction of public health officials and specifies the manner in which they may exercise their authority. The law is a tool in public health work, which is used to establish norms for healthy behavior and to help create the social conditions in which people can be healthy. The most important social debates about public health take place in legal fora—legislatures, courts, and administrative agencies—and in the law's language of rights, duties, and justice. It is no exaggeration to say that "the field of public health … could not long exist in the manner in which we know it today except for its sound legal basis" (Gostin, Burris, and Lazzarini 1999, 61; citations omitted).

There it is again: law.

As a society—and as individuals—our concerns about health tend to be greatest at the beginning and at the end of life. We worry most about the health of those just

coming into the world and those about to leave it. For the college student pulling a week of "all-nighters" during finals or the twenty-, thirty-, forty-, or fifty-something juggling the demands of work and family on a steady diet of caffeine (thinking only occasionally, guiltily, maybe wistfully, about that never-used health club membership), health is seldom a priority. We are urged (sometimes even through legally constructed incentives and disincentives) to get regular check-ups, eat well, quit smoking, and exercise a lot, but the extent to which we do (or do not do) these things is up to us.

During early childhood, the law and health are most clearly intertwined under two circumstances. The one, discussed in chapter 6, involves the occasional refusal of parents to seek medical treatment for their seriously ill children. The other, however, is far more universal, touching (literally) most of us from just after birth until our teenage years. That other is the general requirement that we be vaccinated against infectious diseases.

Childhood immunization requirements are the legal purview of state governments. Although no state mandates vaccinations directly, all fifty require children to undergo a series of immunizations[23] prior to attending school—no shots, no schooling (Aspinwall 1997, 109). Over time, as a society, such requirements have been generally accepted. However, they have not been *universally* accepted. As a result, forty-eight states allow religious exemptions (p. 110). Again, the Maryland code is instructive:

Unless the Secretary of Health and Mental Hygiene declares an emergency or an epidemic of disease, a child whose parent or guardian objects to immunization on the ground that it conflicts with the parent's or guardian's bona fide religious beliefs and practices may not be required to present a physician's certification of immunization in order to be admitted to school (Maryland EDUCATION Code Ann. § 7-403 (1998)).

Recently, resistance to legally mandated immunizations has been growing, not just among religious groups, but among some self-styled political conservatives, libertarians, and alternative medicine advocates who believe the risks of vaccinations outweigh the benefits[24] or who believe that government-mandated shots are a frightening example of Big Brother run amok. The new resistance has been abetted by three factors. First, the very success of vaccines has fostered opposition. Because, for example, people no longer see polio or its victims, some tend to question the necessity of polio vaccinations. According to former secretary of health and human services, Dr. Louis Sullivan, "Many of our citizens cannot remember seeing a child with measles or polio, but they are constantly reading and hearing about the adverse reactions linked to the vaccines that have nearly vanquished these threats in the United States" (cited in Pollak 1999, F7). Second, recent increased governmental initiatives have raised suspicions among anti- or smaller-government ideologues. Particularly disturbing to such factions have been Clinton administration efforts to increase aid for research into and disbursement of vaccines, along with the creation of immunization registries, central data banks designed to remind parents and physicians about when the next shot is needed (p. F7). Thus, for example, Dawn Richardson, president of Parents Requesting Open Vaccine Education (PROVE), testified at a Centers for Disease Control and Prevention hearing on registries in 1998 that "[t]hese U.S. government agencies and officials are ostensibly using public health to create a massive networked computer database . . . to monitor, intimidate, harass and punish loving, conscientious parents, their children and their health-care providers if they do not conform with every government-recommended vaccination" (cited in Lowy 1999, A25). Finally, and not surprisingly, the new resistance to vaccinations has been abetted by the ever-increasing ease with which advocacy may be propagated over such media as talk radio and television and, of course, the Internet.[25]

From whatever quarter, the complaints are beginning to have legal impact. For example:

In Idaho, a proposal by Gov. Dirk Kempthorne, a Republican, to create a statewide immunization registry drew sharp opposition from the Christian Coalition. A bill authorizing the program was passed in March [1999] after changes were made to mollify critics, but legislators refused to provide any money for it.

In Ohio and Texas, state lawmakers are considering proposals that would exempt virtually any child from vaccine requirements if the child's parents are philosophically opposed to vaccines.

In Illinois, the state Senate approved a broad philosophical exemption to vaccine requirements. [As of mid-1999 t]he bill is pending in the House where it has drawn opposition from doctors' groups, health officials and drug companies.

Sixteen other states already provide some type of philosophical exemption. . . .

[In 1998], public health officials in Texas purged the state's immunization registry of the files of nearly 700,000 children following complaints from PROVE and other critics that the registry violated the children's privacy and the parents' rights because vaccination information was entered without first obtaining parents' permission.

A bill under consideration in Ohio would suspend a year-old state law that requires the hepatitis-vaccination for all children entering kindergarten. In New Jersey, Gov. Christine Todd Whitman, a Republican, refused to sign a bill that would have required all schoolchildren to receive the hepatitis-vaccination (Lowy 1999, A25).

While immunization remains the most widespread law-based approach to childhood health, other, more generalized public health issues often center on their youthful impact. In recent years, legal battles over cigarettes and guns have tended to gain support because of the products' adverse effects on children. For example,

as part of the $206-billion legal settlement reached in 1998 between cigarette companies and the states, companies agreed to replace billboard advertisements featuring such kid-friendly mainstays as Joe Camel with antismoking messages, largely aimed at young people. A number of states plan to use a significant share of their settlement monies to implement enhanced antitobacco education programs.[26]

Similarly, following 1999's Columbine High School massacre, numerous legislators nationwide moved, in the face of considerable resistance from the gun lobby, to mandate child-safety devices on handguns. To date, the most successful effort has culminated in Maryland where Democrat Governor Parris Glendenning signed so-called "smart gun" legislation mandating built-in locks on all new guns sold within the state beginning in 2003 (LeDuc 2000, B4).

Moreover, primarily in response to the toll of gun violence on children and teenagers, a number of jurisdictions have initiated tobacco-style lawsuits against gun manufacturers. Beginning with New Orleans in 1998, by mid-2000, twenty-eight local governments had lawsuits pending against components of the industry. One major effect has been that in response to the federal government threatening to join the localities, the nation's largest handgun manufacturer, Smith & Wesson Corporation, agreed to begin providing trigger-locking devices and speed up development of "smart gun" technology (Walsh and Vise 2000, A1).

Over the course of the 1990s, a particularly controversial legal effort designed to enhance the physical well-being of children has been aimed at prenatal health. Specifically, a number of states have begun prosecuting drug-addicted and alcoholic pregnant women on grounds of fetal endangerment and murder. As of 1997, over two hundred women in twenty states—pregnant or new mothers—had been arrested (Paltrow 1999, 1002). The prosecutions that have profound legal implications have mustered mixed reactions from state appellate tribunals. Two recent cases are illustrative.

In 1992, Cornelia Whitner pled guilty to criminal child neglect under South Carolina's *Child Abuse and Endangerment Act* (S.C. Code Ann. 20-7-50 (1985)). Ms. Whitner's case was particularly provocative because hers did not involve child abuse in the typical understanding of the term. Rather, Whitner was accused of criminal neglect "for causing her baby to be born with cocaine metabolites in its system by reason of [her] ingestion of crack cocaine during the third trimester of . . . pregnancy" (*Whitner v. South Carolina*, 328 S.C. 1; 492 S.E.2d 777, at 779 (1997)). For that offense, she was sentenced to an eight-year prison term, a punishment from which she sought post-conviction relief on grounds that the use of the word "person" in the state's Children's Code should not include fetuses. She advanced two important arguments.

First, she claimed that the law violated her constitutional right to privacy, contending "that the Constitution protects women from measures penalizing them for choosing to carry their pregnancies to term" (at 785). In rejecting this claim, the South Carolina Supreme Court held that "the State's interest in protecting the life and health of the viable fetus is not merely legitimate. It is compelling" (at 385). Moreover, and to its mind more important, the court asserted that

we do not think any fundamental right of Whitner's—or any right at all, for that matter—is implicated under the present scenario. It strains belief for Whitner to argue that using crack cocaine during pregnancy is encompassed within the constitutionally recognized right of privacy. Use of crack cocaine is illegal, period. No one here argues that laws criminalizing the use of crack cocaine are themselves unconstitutional. If the State wishes to impose additional criminal penalties on pregnant women who engage in this already illegal conduct because of the effect the conduct has on the viable fetus, it may do so. We do not see how the fact of pregnancy elevates the use of crack cocaine to the lofty status of a fundamental right (at 785–86).

Failing the constitutional privacy issue, Whitner argued that her prosecution could lead to statutorily "absurd results." Were the court to interpret "child" to include viable fetuses, she claimed, "every action by a pregnant woman that endangers or is likely to endanger a fetus, whether otherwise legal or illegal, would constitute unlawful neglect under the statute. For example, a woman might be prosecuted . . . for smoking or drinking during pregnancy" (at 781). Again, the court rejected her claim, reasoning that "the same arguments against the statute [could] be made whether or not the child has been born" (at 781–82). After all, a parent of a born child could be "guilty of child neglect or endangerment even though the underlying act—consuming alcoholic beverages—is itself legal" (at 782). Perhaps significantly, in 1998, the U.S. Supreme Court refused to review the decision (*Whitner v. South Carolina*, 328 S.C. 1; 492 S.E.2d 777; rehearing denied November 19, 1997, cert. denied, May 26, 1998, Reported at 523 U.S. 1145 (1998)).

What Whitner might have considered one of the "absurd results" was at issue recently in the Wisconsin courts. On the night of her baby's birth, Deborah J. Z. achieved another, more dubious, denouement: a blood alcohol concentration that exceeded 0.30 percent. Apparently not the result of early celebrations, Deborah allegedly told a hospital nurse, "if you don't keep me here, I'm just going to go home and keep drinking and drink myself to death and I'm going to kill this thing because I don't want it anyways [sic]" (*State v. Deborah J.Z.*, 1999 Wisc. App. LEXIS 581 *2 (Court of Appeals of Wisconsin, District Two, 1999)). Presumably as a result of Deborah's behavior, her baby girl was born "extremely small, [with] no significant subcutaneous fat, [with] physical features . . . [indicating] fetal alcohol effects. . . ,

[and with a] blood alcohol level [of] 0.199% . . . " (at *2). Deborah was subsequently slapped with a criminal complaint charging her with attempted first-degree intentional homicide and first-degree reckless injury.

Deborah's appeal centered on a single argument: "[T]he plain language of the statutes under which she was charged does not apply to the conduct in question because both statutes require that the conduct must be directed toward a 'human being'" (at *4). Because the homicide and reckless injury statutes in question define "human being" as "one who has been born alive," Deborah argued that her unborn child was not covered by either.

Sidestepping the constitutional quagmire, a state appeals court agreed with Deborah, ruling that "according to the plain language of the first-degree intentional homicide and first-degree reckless injury statutes, the legislature did not intend for these statutes to apply to actions directed against an unborn child. [On the contrary,] the legislature clearly intended to exclude an unborn child when it limited the definition of a 'human being' to include only 'one who has been born alive'" (at *8–*9).

To date, most courts have tended, like that in Wisconsin, to repudiate prosecutions based on maternal conduct before birth.[27] "Nevertheless, attempted prosecutions have not vanished and may in fact be on the upswing" (Mills 1998, 989).

On a related front, information about the unborn fetus is increasingly easier to obtain and could have important legal implications. For example, does a physician expose himself to tort liability for failing to test effectively for birth defects? In closely watched litigation presented to the Georgia Supreme Court in July 1999, Jennifer and Andrew Etkind argued that if they had known that their now four-year-old son would be born with Down's Syndrome, they would have sought an abortion. According to their "wrongful birth" claim, Dr. Ramon Suarez should have tested more thoroughly and warned them. Such malfeasance is inexcusable in today's world, they argued, and sought monetary damages from the doctor to help defray the substantial costs that will be required to address their son's medical conditions for his entire life. The state high court ruled against the Etkinds, thus preventing their case from going to trial. The state legislature had not provided for such a cause of action, and the court was not prepared to break new ground (*Etkind v. Suarez*, 271 Ga. 352 (1999)).[28] But the New Jersey Supreme Court decided in the opposite direction, allowing plaintiffs to proceed with their claim (*Canesi v. Wilson*, 730 A.2d 805 (N.J. 1999)). The issues have also been presented before at least one U.S. District Court (*Provenzano v. Integrated Genetics*, 22 F. Supp. 2d 406 (D.N.J. 1998)). There, parents of a child born with birth defects sued the lab that negligently analyzed amniocentesis samples. The parents testified that even if they had received proper information from the test, they would not have aborted the fetus. A wrongful birth claim may be maintained on these facts, because the real harm is the deprivation of the parents' "right to decide whether to abort." The issue of whether plaintiffs would have actually decided to abort is a question for the jury to assess when considering proximate cause and damages. With the availability of an expanded array of prenatal genetic testing, we are likely to see related litigation increase.

Law and Education

Law and Compulsory Education

No doubt the law's greatest impact on childhood writ large consists of state requirements that children be educated. All fifty states have compulsory education laws, the major difference among them being the age range for which schooling is mandatory.[29] Hence, by law, the vast majority of us *must* be schooled for anywhere from nine to thirteen years of our lives. There are exceptions to the universal compulsory attendance requirement. For example, the Supreme Court has held that:

[A] State's interest in universal education, however highly we rank it, is not totally free from a balancing process when it impinges on fundamental rights and interests, such as those specifically protected by the Free Exercise Clause of the First Amendment, and the traditional interest of parents with respect to the religious upbringing of their children so long as they ... "prepare [them] for additional obligations" (*Wisconsin v. Yoder*, 406 U.S. 205, at 214 (1972)).

Aside from strictly religious exemptions, states may provide additional school exceptions. A small, but rapidly growing number of families, apparently dissatisfied with the schools for academic, social, religious, or moral reasons, are choosing to school their children at home.[30] Home schooling, however, is hardly free from the states' legal reach. Although the Supreme Court has said that states may not "unreasonably interfere ... with the liberty of parents and guardians to direct the upbringing and education of children under their control" (*Pierce v. Society of Sisters*, 268 U.S. 510, at 534–35 (1925)), it has also recognized the states' strong interest in "reasonably ... regulat[ing] all schools ... and ... requir[ing] that all children of proper age attend some school ..." (at 534).

The extent to which states regulate home schooling varies dramatically. For example, some require that parent-teachers be well educated themselves,[31] while others mandate no particular education, experience, or certification for home-based educators.[32] Some states attempt to keep a fairly careful eye on curriculum and student progress[33]; others apparently are more trusting.[34]

Of course, most of us do go to school in institutional settings during childhood,[35] and we go for a long time,

from kindergarten, beginning at age four, five, or six through the twelfth grade, generally ending somewhere between our sixteenth and nineteenth birthdays. There, we are normally taught by professionals, certified by state law. We take a long course of curricula, mandated by lawmaking bodies such as state legislatures, county councils, and school boards. Increasingly, we spend our days preparing for and taking a series of legally required exams to test our achievement and compare us to other students across our counties, states, and nation.[36] Statutes and administrative orders governing these basic educational mainstays are legion and vary greatly by jurisdiction.

As with all aspects of law and society, modernity has added tremendously to the legal complexity of education. While even the most current twists and turns of law and education are far too numerous to thoroughly cover in a single section of a single chapter of a single book,[37] a few contemporary twists are worth mentioning.

Law, Religion, and Education

Although hardly new among issues facing childhood education, the question of religion in public schools continues to spark intense debate. Notably, the problem begins in constitutional interpretation. What comprises "an establishment of religion" in public schools? What constitutes a "prohibit[ion of] ... free excercise"?[38]

Legally, one could say the debate began roughly a half-century ago when the Supreme Court held that the establishment clause, forbidding state-sponsored religion, applied to the states just as it does to federal actions and institutions (*Everson v. Board of Education*, 330 U.S. 1 (1947)). Having so ruled, the Court entered a tangled web indeed—public schools, after all, are run by state governments. Thus, the Court found itself faced with a difficult series of "religion-in-schools" questions at mid-century (see, e.g., *Illinois ex rel. McCollum v. Board of Education*, 333 U.S. 203 (1948)[39] and *Zorach v. Clauson*, 343 U.S. 306 (1952)),[40] which culminated in its celebrated decisions outlawing state-sponsored prayer in public schools (see, e.g., *Engel v. Vitale*, 370 U.S. 421 (1962)[41] and *School District v. Schempp*, 374 U.S. 203 (1963)).[42]

Of course, those rulings were really only the beginning—the beginning of resistance, counter-resistance and, naturally, lots of litigation. In the late 1990s, a series of school shootings[43] prompted yet another round of legal argument, pitting one against the other, diametrically opposed views about the role of religion in secular education. A few of many recent actions are worth noting.

In 1993, the Alabama legislature enacted a "school prayer" statute permitting

[o]n public school, other public, or other property, non-sectarian, non-proselytizing student-initiated voluntary prayer, invo-

cation and/or benedictions . . . during compulsory or non-compulsory school-related student assemblies, school-related student sporting events, school-related graduation or commencement ceremonies, and other school-related student events (Ala. Code § 16-1-20.3(b) (1995)).

The act was challenged as a violation of the establishment clause in 1996 by Americans United for Separation of Church and State and the Alabama ACLU on behalf of local students, parents, and teachers. The state maintained that the law simply permitted students' free exercise of their religious beliefs. In 1997, U.S. District Judge Ira DeMent ruled

§ 16-1-20.3 . . . unconstitutional because it (1) unreasonably restricts the private speech and religion rights of public school students; (2) was not enacted for a secular purpose; (3) has the primary effect of endorsing religion; (4) has the further effect of coercing public school students to participate in religious activity; and (5) creates excessive entanglement between religion and the state by forcing school officials to continually monitor both the content of prayer and the conduct of dissenting students (*Chandler v. James*, 958 F. Supp. 1550, at 1567; 1997 U.S. Dist. LEXIS 4603 (1997)).

On appeal, the Eleventh Circuit upheld Judge DeMent's basic ruling, but remanded the case for further consideration of subsidiary issues (*Chandler v. James*, 180 F.3d 1254 (U.S. Court of Appeals for the 11th Circuit, 1999)).

In 1995, Mary Pat Peck and other affected residents of Upshur County, West Virginia, brought suit in federal court against the Upshur County School Board. The suit sought relief against a board policy allowing Bibles to be made available during school hours so that students who wanted to might take one for their personal use. U.S. District Court Judge Irene M. Keeley ruled that "[t]he distribution of Bibles and other religious materials by private citizens constitutes protected expression under the First Amendment" (*Peck v. Upshur County School Board*, 941 F. Supp. 1465, at 1469 (U.S. Dist. Ct. for the Northern District, WV, 1996)). The Fourth Circuit upheld the Bible distribution policy in secondary schools, but not in elementary schools (*Peck v. Upshur County School Board*, 155 F.3d 274 (U.S. Court of Appeals for the 4th Circuit, 1998)).

In 1995, Rachel Bauchman, a high school student in Salt Lake City, filed a complaint against her music teacher, her school, the Salt Lake City School District, and school and district administrators, claiming they violated the Establishment, Free Exercise, and Free Speech clauses of the U.S. and Utah Constitutions, her statutory civil rights (42 U.S.C. at 1983 (1994)), and her rights under the *Religious Freedom and Restoration Act* (42 U.S.C. at 2000bb (1994)). Among other things, Ms. Bauchman complained that her music teacher required students "to perform a preponderance of Christian devotional music"; that he "selected songs for the religious messages they conveyed"; that the student choral

group "was required to perform Christian devotional songs at religious sites dominated by crucifixes and other religious symbols"; that he "selected religious sites for Choir performances with the purpose and effect of publicly identifying the Choir with religious institutions"; that he "berated and ostracized students, like herself, who dissented against his religious advocacy"; and that he "deliberately scheduled the Choir to sing two explicitly Christian devotional songs during West High School's 1995 graduation." She further complained that the remaining defendants knew of but refused to take any effective measures to prevent the teacher from promoting religion in music classes (*Bauchman v. West High School*, 132 F.3d 542, at 546 (U.S. Court of Appeals for the 10th Circuit, 1997) (June 26, cert. denied, 1998)). Ms. Bauchman's complaints were dismissed as failing to demonstrate real constitutional threat by a U.S. District Court and the Tenth Circuit Court of Appeals. In 1998, the U.S. Supreme Court declined to hear her appeal.

A group of students sued the Beaumont, Texas, School District when its superintendent instituted a "clergy-in-schools" program, permitting clergy to serve as counselors and mentors to students. Students were chosen at random without parental permission. A U.S. District Court judge dismissed the complaint for reasons of standing, but went on to imply that the Beaumont program passed constitutional muster. On appeal to the Fifth Circuit, however, the program was judged to have the purpose and effect of promoting religion and representing excessive entanglement between church and state in violation of the establishment clause (*Doe v. Beaumont Independent School District*, 173 F.3d 274, at 286ff (U.S. Court of Appeals for the 5th Circuit, 1999)).

On 18 June 1999, the U.S. House of Representatives passed, as part of a larger juvenile crime measure, a provision providing that "[t]he power to display the Ten Commandments on or within property owned or administered by the several States or political subdivisions thereof is hereby declared to be among the powers reserved to the States respectively" (H. R. 1501, §1202 (106th Cong., 1st sess., 1999)). The provision, which has yet to be acted upon by the Senate, is specifically geared toward display of the Commandments on schoolhouse walls. As of 2000, eight state legislatures were considering similar legislation (Brumas 2000, A12).

Since its policy of allowing chaplain-delivered prayers before varsity football games was challenged in 1995, Santa Fe High School in Texas permitted students, elected by fellow students, to deliver pregame prayers or "invocations." The case was considered by the Supreme Court in 2000, which held the practice unconstitutional in violation of the establishment clause (*Santa Fe Independent School District v. Doe*, U.S. Supreme Court, No. 99C62 (2000)).[44]

Law and the Voucher Debate

While the decade of the 1990s saw increasing alarm among some over the moral atmosphere in the nation's public schools, it also witnessed increasing complaints about the quality of education in those institutions. Naturally, attempts to manipulate the law were front and center amid the arsenal of those seeking improvement. Much of the movement toward legal improvement of elementary and secondary education took the form of an onslaught of legislatively mandated performance testing.[45] Legally, however, the most controversial endeavors focused on the creation of so-called voucher plans, under which

the state issues a document called a voucher to each parent for each child eligible to attend public schools. The parent then delivers that voucher to the school of his or her own choice. The number of vouchers received by a school determines the amount of tax funds available to the school to finance the education at that school (Bruno 1989, 10 quoted in Cirelli 1997, 483).

School voucher programs tend to be legally tricky because they frequently involve state funds going to parochial schools, which represent the largest percentage of private schools in the United States. Although the Supreme Court has ruled that public funding of private schools is acceptable if it has a secular purpose, does not promote or restrict religion, and avoids creating "excessive government entanglement with religion" (*Tilton v. Richardson*, 403 U.S. 672 (1971)), the line-drawing here can be very fine and very complex indeed. For example:

- In 1995, the Wisconsin legislature expanded a Milwaukee voucher program to include parochial and sectarian schools. In 1997, a trial court held that the expanded voucher plan violated the church-state provisions of the Wisconsin Constitution. While the decision was affirmed by the Wisconsin Court of Appeals, the Wisconsin Supreme Court reversed the decisions, upholding the program's constitutionality (*Jackson v. Benson*, 218 Wis. 2d 835; 578 N.W.2d 602 (Wisconsin Supreme Court, 1998)).
- In 1995, the Ohio legislature passed a pilot scholarship program for the City of Cleveland designed to enable students to attend nonpublic schools. Scholarship recipients, chosen by lot, receive a fixed percentage of the tuition charged by the alternative school of their choice, up to a maximum of $2,500. Approximately 80 percent of the schools that registered to take part in the program were sectarian.

  Because of the heavy preponderance of religious schools, the program was challenged as a violation of the First Amendment. Although the Ohio Supreme Court struck down the program for running afoul of a state constitutional provision limiting bills to one subject, it ruled that the program did not breach the establishment clause (*Simmons-Harris v. Goff*, 86 Ohio St. 3d 1; 711 N.E.2d 203 (Supreme Court of Ohio 1999)). In 1999, however, when the legislature reenacted the voucher system, federal District Court Judge Oliver Solomon permanently enjoined the state from administering the program ruling that it had the "impermissible effect of advancing religion by resulting in government indoctrination of religious beliefs [and] creating an incentive to attend religious schools" (*Simmons-Harris v. Zelman*, 72 F. Supp. 2d 834, at 864 (U.S. District Court for the Northern District of Ohio, Eastern Division, 1999)).

- Because Chittenden Town School District in rural Vermont has only ninety-five students in grades nine through twelve, it does not maintain a high school. Rather, it pays tuition to other public high schools or approved independent schools for the purpose of educating its small population. Until recently, these payments went only to nonsectarian schools, but in 1996, the board approved tuition payment to Mount Saint Joseph Academy, a Catholic school stressing specifically Catholic theology and spiritual development. Following the board's decision, the Vermont State Commissioner of Education terminated state education aid to the district. The local school district then sued the state, asserting, among other things, that tuition reimbursement to the parochial school was constitutional and seeking an order to restore state funding. The state counterclaimed that the Chittenden decision to make tuition payments to Mount Saint Joseph Academy violated the establishment clause of the First Amendment to the United States Constitution and Chapter I, Article 3 of the Vermont Constitution.[46]

  In 1999, the case was reviewed by the Vermont Supreme Court which noted, in a mood probably not unlike that felt by many other courts dealing with such issues in the current political/moral atmosphere,

  that the subject under consideration is one which is liable to be viewed too much on either side through the medium of feeling; and any judicial investigation of it may be regarded as treading upon forbidden ground. A decision one way may be regarded as promoting irreligion, licentiousness and immorality; and a decision the other way be considered as encroaching upon religious freedom (*Chittenden Town School District v. Vermont Department of Education*, 1999 Vt. LEXIS 98, at LEXIS *11 (Supreme Court of Vermont, 1999)).

But, then, judges are there to make those tough decisions at the interstices of law and morality, liberty and order. In a unanimous decision, the Court held the Chittenden district policy was in violation of the Vermont constitutional prohibition against religious establishments.

- In June 1999, Florida Governor Jeb Bush signed into law the nation's first statewide school voucher program, permitting students at the state's worst schools to get a private or parochial education at taxpayer expense.[47] Still being litigated on 7 March 2000, a Tallahassee trial judge ruled the law unconstitutional (Hallifax 2000, 4).

Law, Education, and Civic Socialization

One of the long established purposes of public education is the socialization of good citizens. In its most obvious manifestation, millions of school children across the nation engage daily in a ritualistic recital of the Pledge of Allegiance.[48] Most public *and* sectarian schools choose students whose proud duty it is every day to raise and lower the flag. Although the majority of schools are closed for the summer when the nation celebrates its birthday, most elementary schools use the occasion of less weighty national and state holidays to discuss, at least implicitly, the values and proud heritage of being an American.

However, to a far greater extent than today, in the not-too-distant past, the teaching of citizenship was fused with a particular academic curriculum. For example, to baby boomers, like generations before, Christopher Columbus was the courageous seafarer who discovered America, not the ruthless conqueror who brought devastating disease to a thriving native population. Thomas Jefferson was the virtually sanctified author of the Declaration of Independence, not a morally enigmatic slaveholder. Any number of settlers and pioneers, from the sixteenth-century Pilgrims to the nineteenth-century covered-wagon brigades, were brave souls who civilized the wilderness, not unwitting tools for a scheme of indigenous genocide. In short, children growing up through roughly the 1960s were part of an almost universally accepted curricular endeavor designed to produce proud civic participants.

Of course, for a variety of profound social and economic reasons, the consensus that made positive civic education possible began to erode during the 1960s and 1970s. Two particularly contentious issues—traditionally white, Euro-centered curricula and English-language instruction—continued to reverberate into the legal educational environment of the 1980s, 1990s, and beyond.

BILINGUALISM

In the early 1970s, a group of non–English-speaking Chinese students brought suit against the San Francisco Unified School District claiming that its failure to provide any form of special instruction violated their civil rights. The Supreme Court agreed. Basing its decision on the *Civil Rights Act of 1964*, which bans discrimination based "on the ground of race, color, or national origin," in "any program or activity receiving Federal financial assistance" (42 U.S.C. § 2000d), and departmental regulations promulgated in response to the act,[49] the Court held it "obvious that the Chinese-speaking minority receive fewer benefits than the English-speaking majority from respondents' school system which denies them a meaningful opportunity to participate in the educational program—all earmarks of the discrimination banned by the regulations" (*Lau v. Nichols*, 414 U.S. 563, at 568 (1974)). "Simple justice," noted Justice Douglas for the majority, "requires that public funds, to which all taxpayers of all races contribute, not be spent in any fashion which encourages, entrenches, subsidizes, or results in racial discrimination" (at 569).

Although the high court did not mandate any particular remedy to the problem of the Chinese students, it did mention, as a possibility, "[g]iving instructions to this group in Chinese . . ." (at 565). In other words, the Court suggested offering a system of bilingual education. The Court's judgment was followed by congressional action in the form of the *Equal Educational Opportunity Act of 1974*, requiring recipients of federal funds to take "appropriate action to overcome language barriers that impede equal participation by its students in its instructional programs" (20 U.S.C. § 1703(f) (1974)). In response to federal judicial and legislative actions, and facing increased immigrant populations particularly during the 1980s and 1990s, many states and local school districts acted to implement bilingual programs.

Resistance to bilingual education,[50] which was controversial from the beginning, grew during the 1980s and 1990s among those who perceived it as a clear example of heavy-handed federal intrusion into local educational decision making, as an unfairly expensive mode of education foisted on native taxpayers largely for the benefit of immigrant children, as an assault on the nationally unifying effects of a single English language, and as a future economic and social hindrance to non–English-speaking youngsters. The most significant assault to date, not surprisingly, occurred in California.

In 1998, California voters approved, by a wide margin (61 percent to 39 percent), Proposition 227, a ballot initiative entitled "English Language in Public Schools" and intended to dismantle the state's many bilingual education programs. The statute amends the California Education Code to change the system under which students who are limited in English proficiency are educated in California's public schools. Under the Prop 227 scheme, children are to "be taught English by being taught in English":

Children who are English learners shall be educated through sheltered English immersion during a temporary transition period not normally intended to exceed one year. Once English learners have acquired a good working knowledge of English, they shall be transferred to English language mainstream classrooms (Initiative, § 305).

In order to broaden its appeal, sponsors of the initiative added several waiver provisions, including release for older students and students who, having tried English immersion, appear to be failing.

Opponents of Prop 227 brought suit in federal district court the day following its enactment, requesting an injunction against implementation of the law (*Valeria G. v. Wilson*, 12 F. Supp. 2d 1007 (U.S. District Court for the Northern District of California, 1998)). They claimed that the act violated the *Equal Educational Opportunities Act*, the supremacy clause of the U.S. Constitution, Title VI of the *Civil Rights Act*, and the equal protection clause of the U.S. Constitution. Finding the plaintiffs' arguments weak on all counts, Judge Charles A. Legge refused to issue the injunction.

The effects of Proposition 227 on the future of bilingual education are, to date, uncertain. On the one hand, following the popular and judicial success of the initiative, other states are attempting similar measures.[51] On the other hand, in California itself, enough waivers have been granted and enough resistance manifested by teachers and school administrators that bilingual education continues to thrive despite its apparent defeat at the polls (Anderson and Sahagun 1998, A1).

CURRICULUM BATTLES

Regardless of the language with which students learn their ABCs (or analogous letters and characters), beginning in the late 1960s, some educators and leaders of minority groups began questioning the very basis of the elementary and secondary curriculum, claiming that its "Eurocentric" thrust resulted in a misreading of history, presenting at the same time a falsely benevolent picture of the European conquest of the Americas and of the intentions of the constitutional framers, while downplaying or disguising such atrocities as slavery, Jim Crow, the displacement and genocide of the American Indian, and the exclusion of women from early public life. Moreover, they charged that the heavy concentration on literature, history, and even science from the perspective of white men of European extraction resulted in lowered self-esteem and a lack of identifiable role models among minority and female students, inhibiting learning, academic success, and core rights. Thus, according to one commentator:

Socialization is an academic function in which the values, politics, and economics of the dominant group are transferred through curriculum, much of which is culturally biased. If a state imposed curriculum is culturally biased or racially homogeneous, the academic function of socialization is a vestige of de jure segregation. It imposes stereotypical conceptions of African-Americans on all children and denies them their First Amendment right to receive accurate information about the historical development of values, knowledge, and commodities (Neely 1994, 132).

As early as the 1960s, the Black Panther Party, dissatisfied with the progress—indeed, the very premise of legal desegregation—instituted its own Afrocentric schools, designed to instill Black pride and power among African American children. Thirty years later, in the 1990s, the apparent failure of desegregation,[52] nearly a half-century after the Supreme Court declared state-run segregated schools unconstitutional (*Brown v. Board of Education*, 347 U.S. 483 (1954)), has prompted additional efforts to diversify curriculum. While many schools and school districts across the nation have acted to implement (at least in name) a so-called multicultural curriculum designed to integrate African, Asian, and Latin history and literature into the entire course of study, some have attempted a wholesale rejection of European-based cultural modes. Among the most controversial of these have been efforts to promulgate Afrocentric curricular designs.

At least one such effort resulted in a federal court case. In 1993, Sanford and Janelle Grimes brought suit in district court alleging that the New York City public school curriculum injured African Americans through systematic bias. The curriculum, they asserted,

distorts and demeans the role of African Americans and excludes the existence, contributions, and participation of African Americans in the various aspects of world and American culture, sciences, history, arts and other areas of human endeavor, resulting in emotional and psychological harm denying [African American students] the full and equal benefits of public education and subjecting [them] to discrimination under a program receiving federal financial assistance (*Grimes v. Sobol*, 832 F. Supp. 704, at 706 (U.S. District Court for the Southern District of New York, 1993)).

Claiming rights under federal civil rights statutes and the Fourteenth Amendment, the Grimes children sought relief in the form of a declaration that the curriculum was discriminatory, an injunction barring the school system from perpetuating the allegedly racially discriminatory aspects of the curriculum, and an order directing the New York State Education Department to submit a revised curriculum, including "the existence, true participation and contributions of African Americans and other non-whites . . . and which would eliminate the discriminatory aspects of the existing public school curriculum . . ." (at 707).

Judge Kimba Wood dismissed the complaint citing two deficiencies. First, according to Judge Wood, the plaintiffs failed "to come forward with the specific allegations of fact necessary to sustain [a] claim of" intentional constitutional discrimination (at 708). Second, according to the judge, nothing in the history of the federal civil rights legislation, nor its implementing regulations, indicated that they were meant to "encompass the regulation of curricular content" (at 713).

Other, more recent, Afrocentric endeavors and controversies include:

- In the mid-1990s, in an effort to improve the educational environment for inner-city African American boys, the Detroit public school system approved nine African-centered all-male schools. Following a court challenge, girls were admitted to the academies. As of 1996, at least twenty-one of the city's public schools used an Afrocentric curriculum (Butty 1996).
- In 1996, the Milwaukee School Board became the storm center of a fight between ardent proponents of Afrocentric education and their equally ardent opponents (Lawrence 1996). The battle became so heated that during the school board's discussion, the home of board member Leon Todd, who proposed a failed ban on the curriculum, was fire bombed.
- A similar battle occurred in Kansas City in 1997 when civil rights attorney Arthur A. Benson announced plans to challenge expansion of an existing Afrocentric elementary program into one of the city's high schools (Horsley 1997).
- In a move combining bilingualism and multiculturalism, Oakland, California attracted nationwide attention in 1997, when the school board there endorsed a system of teaching Ebonics or Black English. So intense was the ensuing furor that the board subsequently retreated from some of its more ambitious proposals including training teachers to speak the language and applying for federal bilingual education funds.[53]

LAW AND COURTESY?

Certainly a mainstay of intergenerational friction is the older generation's belief that the younger generation lacks the basic elements of respect and courtesy that they (the older generation) so clearly possessed. Generally speaking, the older generation has conveniently forgotten that their own elders voiced very similar complaints about them. But, so it goes.

In very large ways, the law, as a vehicle for order, has always mandated a kind of civic politeness—traffic laws, after all, force (or attempt to force) us to be courteous to our fellow drivers, antivandalism statutes force (or attempt to force) us to be respectful of others' property, nuisance laws force (or attempt to force) us to be mindful of others' peace and quiet, and so forth. But, surely, you might say, simple day-to-day words of politeness are beyond the reach of law. Well, mostly, they are—but, only *mostly*.

In 1999, the Louisiana legislature became the first in the nation to pass a *Student Respect Law*. In relevant part, the law provides that "each city and parish school board shall require each student in each public school ... to exhibit appropriate conduct. ..." The legislature defines "appropriate conduct" in the following way:

When any public school student is speaking with any public school system employee while on school property or at a school sponsored event, such student shall address and respond to such public school system employee by using the respectful terms "Yes, Ma'am" and "No, Ma'am" or " Yes, Sir" and "No, Sir", as appropriate, or "Yes, Miss, Mrs., or Ms. (Surname)" and "No, Miss, Mrs., or Ms. (Surname)" or "Yes, Mr. (Surname)" and "No, Mr. (Surname)," as appropriate, each such title to be followed by the appropriate surname (1999 *La. ALS* 917; 1999 La. ACT 917; 1999 La. SB 1098).

Law, Education, and Sexual Harassment

One of the most profound changes to occur in the legal atmosphere of primary and secondary education has been the application of sexual harassment laws and the threat of sexual harassment lawsuits to schools. Cynthia Gorney tells a "small story" to illustrate:

The setting for the very small story, which we will refer to as the Milk-Bag Incident ... is a public middle-school cafeteria in Duluth, Minn. The time of year is mid-February. Because it is lunchtime, numerous schoolchildren are crowded together at the tables with their food and their milk, which in Duluth is doled out not in cartons but in single-serving plastic bags with straws.

At one cafeteria table, set together in close quarters amid the commotion: several boys, two girls, a milk bag. One of the boys picks up the milk bag. No violence is about to erupt; this is a story about schoolchildren that contains no guns or homicidal rages. All the boy does next is shape the milk bag into a recognizable replica of manly genitalia, including scrotum. The boy announces his achievement to everyone within earshot, which includes the girls at his table, and points out that the genitalia he has sculptured is fully tumescent. (The boy's exact choice of words will not be printed here, but fits into what would probably qualify as "age appropriate" disgusting language for a modern American sixth grader, which is to say: really disgusting language.) The boy and his friends, brandishing the tumescent milk bag, fall about in general hilarity. The bell rings. Lunch period comes to a close.

Sometime in the course of the next few days, the girls—like the boys, these are sixth graders, 12 years old—appear at the office of the school vice principal to report that they wish to make a complaint. Do the girls use the term "sexual harassment"? Possibly, for they have encountered these words in a middle-school assembly and one or two contemporary novels assigned at their grade level, but probably not. Maybe they use the word "harassment." Maybe they use the word "gross." In any case they understand that there is a Procedure, and the vice principal, having paid close attention to the training that instructed her to do so, now sets the Procedure into motion: she pulls out a harassment complaint form. (Sexual harassment, sexual advances or other forms of religious, racial or sexual harassment by any pupil, teacher, administrator or other school personnel, which create an intimidating, hostile or offensive environment, will not be tolerated under any circumstances.) She asks the girls whether they want to fill out the form and sign it. They do. She calls up the Duluth school system harassment specialist (Gorney 1999, 43).

It would certainly be a long and hyperbolic stretch to say that the traditional schoolhouse attitude that "boys will be boys"—smiling or looking the other way when six-year-old Jimmy acts out his passionate feelings by chasing and hitting the girl of his dreams, when sixteen-year-old Harry graphically portrays the alleged sexual prowess of a classmate on a bathroom wall, when twelve-year-old Johnny fashions a milk-bag scrotum—has gone away. It is no stretch, however, to say that school administrators who today get caught looking the other way may be in for big, big trouble. So says the Supreme Court.

During the school year 1993–94, fifth-grader La-Shonda Davis was repeatedly subjected to harassment by a fellow classmate. Among other things, the boy, known as G. F., attempted to touch LaShonda's breasts and genitals, made numerous vulgar statements, and engaged in other physically obscene activities. Despite LaShonda's ongoing complaints to her teacher and her attempts to discuss the matter with the school principal, nothing was done to end G. F.'s behavior—not even the simple act of separating him from his victim in the classroom. As a result, LaShonda filed suit in federal district court against the board of education, the school district's superintendent, and the school principal, alleging that because the defendants were recipients of federal funding, they were liable for "the deliberate indifference . . . to the unwelcome sexual advances [which] . . . created an intimidating, hostile, offensive and abusive school environment in violation of Title IX [of the Civil Rights Act]" (*Davis v. Monroe County Board of Education*, 526 U.S. 629, at 636 (1999)). The district court dismissed LaShonda's claim, concluding that because the defendants themselves had no part in the harassment they could not be sued. An Eleventh Circuit panel reversed the district court, but on an en banc rehearing ruled that the defendants had not been given sufficient notice under the law that they could be sued for their inactions, thus again railroading LaShonda's lawsuit. Ms. Davis appealed to the Supreme Court, which took up her case in 1999.

In a 5–4 decision, with Justice O'Connor delivering the opinion, the Court ruled, with potentially vast implications for the administration of schools, that deliberate indifference on the part of school authorities to "harassment . . . so severe, pervasive, and objectively offensive that it can be said to deprive the victims of access to the educational opportunities or benefits provided by the school" (at 629) may trigger a cause of action for damages against those officials under Title IX. Although the threshold set by the Court is indeed a high one (authorities must have demonstrated deliberate indifference and the acts complained of must be very "severe, pervasive, and objectively offensive") the message sent is that "schools must protect their students from sexual harassment by other students" or face the threat of expensive, time-consuming, and embarrassing litigation (Ely 1999, 5). For the present, experts believe that while such lawsuits will undoubtedly increase substantially,[54] the likeli-

hood of plaintiffs succeeding under the Court's present standard is low (see, e.g., Fisk 1999, B19). The greatest impact of the decision, however, is likely to be regulatory, giving administrators "an extra incentive to push principals, teachers and others to be even more vigilant against harassment than they would be otherwise" (Taylor 1999).

Law and the Problem Kid: Juvenile Justice in America

Regardless of the setting (home, school, or the neighborhood playground), and regardless of the law governing that setting, "kids will be kids" and sometimes "kids being kids" can involve some pretty disturbing behavior. Some of that behavior, like America's most beloved bad boy, Tom Sawyer's tendency to pull Becky Thatcher's pigtails, we (though perhaps not Becky) chalk up to the normal vagaries of childhood—what clearly would be wrong if perpetrated by one adult on another or by an adult on a child is often ignored or met with a very mild rebuke if inflicted on one child by another, even under the new harassment rules. But, there is behavior and there is behavior. While most of us, no doubt, would view a stern lecture as sufficient to chastise Minnesota's "milk-bag" boys, most of us, no doubt, would recommend a more severe course of action when it comes to behavior like that of G. F. toward LaShonda.[55] Of course, children have been known to do much worse than G. F.

Until the turn of the twentieth century, wayward children could be arrested, charged, tried, and jailed like adults. In 1899, Cook County, Illinois, became the first jurisdiction to establish a separate juvenile court charged with the dual functions of meting out justice to delinquents under the age of sixteen and with processing neglected or abused children. Following Cook County's lead, by mid-century, all the states, the District of Columbia, and Puerto Rico had instituted special juvenile courts (*In re Gault*, 387 U.S. 1, at 14 (1967)). Such courts were designed with the benevolent purpose of "aid[ing]—not punish[ing]—children, [and so] the due process guarantees of the adult criminal court were absent" (Abadinsky 1991, 282). Proceeding under the compassionate principle of *parens patriae*, juvenile courts were able

to deny to the child procedural rights available to his elders . . . by . . . asserti[ng] that a child, unlike an adult, has a right "not to liberty but to custody." He can be made to attorn to his parents, to go to school, etc. If his parents default in effectively performing their custodial functions—that is, if the child is "delinquent"—the state may intervene. In doing so, it does not deprive the child of any rights, because he has none. It merely provides the "custody" to which the child is entitled. On this basis, proceedings involving juveniles were described as "civil" not "criminal" and therefore not subject to the requirements which restrict the state when it seeks to deprive a person of his liberty (387 U.S. 1, at 17; footnotes omitted).

Then, in 1964, young Gerald Francis Gault was taken into custody by Gila County, Arizona, authorities. Gerald was accused of making a lewd phone call to a neighbor while still on probation for an earlier juvenile offense. At the time of Gerald's arrest, his parents were at work and no notice was left for them about their son's detention. Moreover, they were not served notice of the hearing conducted the following day before a judge of the juvenile court. The hearing itself lacked any of the traditional hallmarks of due process—no one was sworn, nor were any transcripts or recordings made. Following the hearing, Gerald was taken to a detention home for several days, after which he was released with no explanation. In a court order filed after his release, Gerald was judged "delinquent." No appeal was permitted by Arizona law in juvenile cases (at 4–6).

On a writ of habeas corpus, Gerald charged that the Arizona Juvenile Code was unconstitutional because it lacked any requirement that parents and children be apprised of the specific charges, did not require proper notice of a hearing, and did not provide for an appeal. Moreover, he charged that the judicial proceedings and order "constituted a denial of due process of law because of the absence of adequate notice of the charge and the hearing; failure to notify appellants of certain constitutional rights including the rights to counsel and to confrontation, and the privilege against self-incrimination; the use of unsworn hearsay testimony; and the failure to make a record of the proceedings" (at 9–10). The Supreme Court agreed.

"Under our Constitution," wrote Justice Fortas for the majority, "the condition of being a boy does not justify a kangaroo court" (at 28). Even, perhaps especially, where children are concerned:

Failure to observe the fundamental requirements of due process has resulted in instances, which might have been avoided, of unfairness to individuals and inadequate or inaccurate findings of fact and unfortunate prescriptions of remedy. Due process of law is the primary and indispensable foundation of individual freedom. It is the basic and essential term in the social compact which defines the rights of the individual and delimits the powers which the state may exercise (at 20).

As a result, the Court ordered substantial procedural changes to the adjudicatory stages of state juvenile justice systems, including the following requirements: (1) that adequate and timely written notice be afforded the child and his parents or guardian, informing them "of the specific issues that they must meet"; (2) that the child and his parents be advised of their right to counsel and, if they are unable to afford counsel, that an attorney will be appointed; (3) that the constitutional privilege against self-incrimination is applicable in such proceedings; and (4) that "a juvenile in such proceedings must

be afforded the rights of confrontation and sworn testimony of witnesses available for cross-examination" (at 31–57).

In the years following the *Gault* decision, the Court was asked several times to review juvenile justice procedures. In toto, the resulting patchwork of rulings retains some aspects of the older justice system based in civil law and the concept of *parens patriae*, while adding some of the more familiar due process guarantees of the adult criminal system. For instance, the Court applied the "beyond a reasonable doubt" standard of proof to juvenile adjudications (*In re Winship*, 397 U.S. 358 (1970)). On the other hand, reasoning "that juveniles, unlike adults, are always in some form of custody . . . [and] are not assumed to have the capacity to take care of themselves . . . " (*Schall v. Martin*, 467 U.S. 253, at 265 (1984)), it deemed constitutionally permissible the "pretrial detention of an accused juvenile delinquent based on a finding that there is a 'serious risk' that the juvenile 'may before the return date commit an act which if committed by an adult would constitute a crime'" (at 254).

As it stands today, the juvenile justice system is a vast labyrinth, varying in specific procedures and institutions from state to state. In general, juvenile court systems are charged with carrying out a near-crushing array of judicial and welfare functions. As Howard Abadinsky explains, the typical juvenile court has jurisdiction over the following categories of cases:

1. *Delinquency*, or behavior that if engaged in by an adult, would constitute a crime. In the case of certain very serious criminal behavior, for example, murder, the law may require a transfer of the case for prosecution in adult criminal court.
2. *Status Offense*, or behavior that would not constitute a crime if committed by an adult, but that (based on *parens patriae*) provides the basis for governmental intervention in the life of a child, for example, truancy, being beyond the control of parents, addiction to drugs or alcohol, running away from home, sexual promiscuity (almost invariably referring to the behavior of girls).
3. *Neglect or Abuse*, or the cases of children who are neglected or abused by their parents or guardians.
4. *Dependency*, or the cases of children who do not have parents or guardians available to provide proper care (Abadinsky 1995, 285).

Most of the cases that flow through the juvenile justice system are delinquencies, and the numbers here are substantial. Thus, in 1997, law enforcement agencies made an estimated 2.8 million arrests of juveniles (Snyder 1997). A substantial number of these cases—approximately 1.7 million—are processed in juvenile courts (Sickmund 1997a), where probation is the most common disposition (National Center for Juvenile Justice 2000).

Once within the juvenile system, an accused delinquent will go through a process that mimics, in fundamental respects, the adult criminal court experience. A *preliminary hearing* will be held, informing the parties of their rights and determining whether the youth should remain in custody. In cases of child abuse and neglect, a guardian-advocate may be appointed for the child and she may be placed temporarily into foster or shelter care (Abadinsky 1995, 287–88).

Juvenile *adjudicatory hearings*, the purpose of which are to allow a judicial decision on whether or not a youthful offender or neglected child should be made a ward of the court, simulate criminal trials. Thus, to begin, a plea, admitting or denying the charges, is entered. If the plaintiff denies, evidence is presented to prove beyond a reasonable doubt that a delinquent offense was committed. The court needs only the civil preponderance of evidence in cases of status offense, neglect, or abuse. Finally, if the charges are proven, the judge will enter a finding of delinquency, status offense, abuse, neglect, or dependency (Abadinsky 1995, 287–88).

During the final stage of the process, the *dispositional hearing*, the judge determines which resolution "will best serve the interests of the child, his or her family, and the community." As Abadinsky (1995, 289–90) explains, in cases of delinquency, disposition may include:

1. *Commitment to a state youth authority* or the juvenile division of the department of corrections. . . . 2. *Probation* . . . for a period not beyond the age of twenty-one. . . . 3. *Conditional discharge* and release to parents on the condition that no further delinquent acts will take place. 4. *Out-of-home placement*, often in the form of a commitment to the child welfare agency, which will arrange for a foster or residential treatment setting that can provide counseling and education. . . . 5. *Referral* to a public or private agency with specialized services. . . . 6. *Detention*, usually for no more than thirty days, in a juvenile facility and then release to probation supervision. . . .

Law and Maturity: The Sundry Legal Benchmarks of Adulthood

Over the course of the 1990s and into the early twenty-first century, America's near-obsession mentality with the subject of crime prompted its politicians to respond with a flood of new criminal initiatives (see chapter 4). Because the public perceived the amount of juvenile crime in particular to be rising precipitously,[56] front and center among those initiatives has been a raft of state and federal laws making it much easier to try juveniles as adults. Thus, from 1992 through 1995, forty states and the District of Columbia passed laws that have the effect of conferring legal adulthood on often very young people for purposes of criminal prosecution (Sickmund 1997b). As a result of these changes, "juvenile courts

nationwide waived 12,300 delinquency cases to adult court in 1994," for a whopping increase of 71 percent in waived cases between 1985 and 1994 (Butts 1997).

The chances of one remaining a delinquent child, rather than "growing up" to become a full-fledged adult criminal, became, over the course of the 1990s, far less likely and far more confusing than at any time since the turn of the last century. While most states continue to cede original jurisdiction to juvenile courts for persons seventeen years of age and younger (Sickmund 1998), as the figures above suggest, the numbers of acceptable exclusions have grown tremendously.[57]

Historically, the age of the offender and the current offense have been the criteria State legislatures established for determining eligibility for criminal prosecution. In the past 20 years, State legislatures have increased the population of juveniles eligible for criminal prosecution by expanding these criteria across each of the three mechanisms described in the previous section. In response to the perceived increase of violent juvenile crime, legislatures have, since 1992, added significantly to the list of offenses now considered serious and/or lowered the age for which certain juveniles could be tried in criminal court (Torbet 1996).

Thus, becoming a responsible, legal adult, in the most unsavory meaning of that term, is happening earlier and more often to greater numbers of young people.[58]

Hopefully, most of us will not have our entry into adulthood marked by being waived into the criminal justice process. Hopefully, most of us will achieve legal adulthood less painfully. But, what is adulthood? When you think about it, there are many differing landmarks that denote our passage from kid to grown-up. Many, if not most, of these markers are legally defined. Moreover, many of these markers differ depending on where you live, what you've done, and even what gender you are. Of course, as the preceding suggests, one of those legal markers is being tried and convicted as an adult and this varies considerably by state and the gravity of the prosecuted offense—the worse the crime, the more likely is the perpetrator to be considered an adult.

A more common and less tragic benchmark is the age at which compulsory schooling ends—when the state decides you've learned as much as you really have to squeak by. As a preceding section noted, depending on where you reside, this may be as young as fifteen or as old as eighteen.

For many young people, the freedom that (young people *imagine*) comes with adulthood is marked by that most American rite of passage, acquisition of a driver's license. Here, again, state law determines maturity. In most states, motorized adulthood is achieved in some form at age sixteen. However, the age varies. For example, in New York, the standard licensing age is eighteen (N.Y. CLS Veh & Tr § 502 (1999)), while in South Dakota, a legal driver can be as young as fourteen (National Highway Traffic Safety Administration [NHTSA]

1999). Increasingly, states are gradually phasing in this marker of adulthood, placing restrictions on newly licensed drivers for up to eighteen months (NHTSA 1999).

For many, adulthood means marriage, and here, too, the individual states decide when a person is grown up enough to engage in this supposedly mature institution. Today, most states follow the pattern of the *Uniform Marriage and Divorce Act*, which sets the age of legal union at sixteen with parental consent and eighteen without such acquiescence (Glendon 1989, 48). *Most* states, however, are not *all* states and some set other limits. For example, New Hampshire allows boys as young as fourteen and girls as young as thirteen to wed with the blessing of their parents (Jimenez 1998, 7).

Some signs of the passage from youth to adult maturity are more uniform across the nation. For example, one legal marker of manhood (literally, *man*hood) is set directly by the federal government. Almost all male U.S. citizens and resident aliens must register for the draft on attaining the age of eighteen.[59] Despite the fact that the United States converted to an all-volunteer military in 1973,[60] men aged eighteen to twenty-five must register in the event that a national crisis prompts a resumption of the draft.

Of course, adults are expected to work. Most of us view at least our first real job as an indicator of maturity and freedom. Here, too, federal rules and regulations are the primary laws governing our transition to adulthood. The Department of Labor under authority of the *Fair Labor Standards Act* (see generally, 29 C.F.R. 570) sets a minimum age of sixteen for most full-time nonagricultural[61] employment, allowing certain part-time exceptions for those between the ages of fourteen and sixteen.[62] In order to engage in occupations deemed particularly hazardous—specifically manufacturing and mining—an individual must be at least eighteen years of age.[63]

For better or worse, some important maturity benchmarks are closely associated with the legal ability to engage in adult vices. Certainly, one of the more dubious rites of passage performed by generations of American youth is the practice of *legally* getting drunk on attaining that magic birthday when the *real* ID can be boldly presented to any bartender. (This birthday manifestation of legal maturity is generally followed by the massive—but legally acquired—morning-after hangover.)

Like most benchmarks of maturity, the legal drinking age is governed by state law; however, in the case of drinking, state law has been heavily influenced (some would say coerced) by federal mandate. Thus, as of 1984, twenty-seven states and the District of Columbia had set their legal drinking age below twenty-one, some going as low as eighteen. However, in that year, President Reagan signed into law an amendment to federal highway transportation funding that threatened to punish states with minimum drinking ages below twenty-one by withholding up to 10 percent of their federal highway funds. Although a number of states tried to resist what was seen as intrusive legislation (see especially, *South Dakota v. Dole*, 483 U.S. 203 (1987)),[64] eventually all buckled under the peril of losing substantial highway money. Consequently, drinking as a legal mark of adulthood is effectively set nationwide at twenty-one years of age.

For many, too, no journey into the realm of adulthood would be complete absent the ability to view large quantities of sex and violence on the big screen. Traditionally, the regulation of movie viewing has been a private endeavor, marked by the familiar Hollywood rating system.[65] Here, the industry-set standard for adult fare has been the "R" rating, which allows theaters to turn away anyone under seventeen years of age unaccompanied by an adult. Of course, as any American teenager could tell any American adult, the chance of an unaccompanied kid under seventeen actually being turned away from an R-rated film is roughly equal to the likelihood of snow falling in Atlanta in July. Even here, however, lawmakers, if not the law itself, are beginning to make their presence felt. Thus, in reaction to the school shooting incidents of the late 1990s, particularly the massacre at Littleton, policymakers have begun putting increasing pressure on the movie industry to actually enforce the rating system.[66] Of special note, in 1999, President Clinton brokered an agreement by theater owners to begin carding teens for all R-rated films. Although many doubt that the new industry self-policing effort will result in any long-term change in underage viewing habits,[67] the president's involvement does mark law's movement into yet another pathway to adulthood.

When does one shed the trappings of youth in exchange for the armor of adulthood? The answer, of course, is when the law says you do. The law says you do at a wide variety of points at which you could be as young as twelve and as old as twenty-one, with a bewildering array of legal benchmarks in between.

Conclusion

Normally, we look at law as something of, by, and for adults. Adults, after all, do make the law. That which we think of as typically legal—the bringing of a lawsuit, for example—is generally instituted by grown-ups. But, as the preceding discussion makes clear, the law is ubiquitous throughout our childhood as well.

In addition, the central tension of American law—the constant pull-and-tug between liberty and order—is evident in its youthful reach. We seek—indeed, demand—the freedom to procreate by any means. Yet when procreative technologies go wrong or when procreative relationships run aground, we expect law to step in and set things right—to bring order to breakdown through divorce and custody law.

In rearing our procreative products, we expect—even demand—autonomy. At the same time, however, as a social unit, we seek law's ordering influence to educate, strengthen, and even punish the progeny that represent our collective future.

We grow naturally from children into presumably independent adults, and yet we accept—even depend on—law's markers of adulthood as a means of ordering our transition into the grown-up world. In the law's long reach into childhood, reality and its metaphor achieve a truly stunning coherence. For just as a child fiercely seeks independence from her parents, while simultaneously craving parental order, so we all, as individuals, ferociously demand autonomy, while collectively insisting on social order. The law—even through childhood—is expected to provide the balance.

This chapter has focused on many of the obvious concerns and benchmarks of childhood. One crucial component of growing up, however, deserves a discussion all its own. As children, and long into adulthood, we develop and assume identities. We develop as persons on our own *and* as collective entities. While this may seem, at first blush, to be truly a realm of individual psychology—surely, law has no presence here!—law has been and is utterly crucial to individual and group identity. This is the subject of the next chapter.

Law on the Web

This chapter has been about birth and childhood, and nowhere, perhaps, have technological advances created so many ethically and legally disturbing questions, or so much social unease. Nowhere is the law in such flux as legislators slowly attempt to grapple with or avoid these "brave new world" questions, and judges are forced to piece together rules (often out of whole cloth) on a case-by-case basis.

As legislators have dropped or refused to catch the ball and judges have grabbed it only when thrown in their laps, the burgeoning field of bioethics has increasingly taken the lead in trying to frame the issues and fashion potential legal solutions to these and other technology-driven questions. Presented below are a few such groups maintaining sites on the Internet.

A Smattering of Governmental Bioethics Sites

National Bioethics Advisory Commission, National Institutes of Health

bioethics.gov/cgi-bin/bioeth_counter.pl

The National Human Genome Research Institute, Ethical, Legal and Social Implications (ELSI)

www.nhgri.nih.gov/ELSI/

U.S. Food and Drug Administration

www.fda.gov/

A Smattering of University-Sponsored Sites

University of Pennsylvania, Center for Bioethics, Bioethics Internet Project

www.med.upenn.edu/bioethics/

National Reference Center for Bioethics Literature

guweb.georgetown.edu/nrcbl/

Center for Biomedical Ethics, University of Virginia

hsc.Virginia.EDU/medicine/inter-dis/bio-ethics/

The Kennedy Institute of Ethics, Georgetown University

guweb.georgetown.edu/kennedy/

A Smattering of Religious Sites

National Catholic Bioethics Center

www.ncbcenter.org/home.html

Center for Bioethics and Human Dignity

www.bioethix.org/

A Christian site.

The Union of American Hebrew Congregations, Committee on Bio-Ethics

uahcweb.org/bioethic.html

A Jewish site.

General Education Research Site

Schooling is a huge part of nearly every childhood experience. Of course, education is largely defined and mandated by law. Moreover, this law is largely the product of state legislators, county councils, and local school boards. State education policies may be accessed by searching for individual state departments of education, too numerous (by fifty) to cite here. However, for some good general research on education, consider the following website:

The U.S. Department of Education, Research and Statistics

www.ed.gov/stats.html

A Smattering of General Juvenile Justice Sites

Unfortunately, when things go wrong in childhood, the justice system must step in. Here, too, the main points of access are the individual state juvenile justice systems. Many good general juvenile justice sites, however, are available on the Web. Appearing below are a just few of many.

U.S. Department of Justice, Office of Juvenile Justice and Delinquency Prevention
ojjdp.ncjrs.org/

The National Center for Juvenile Justice, A Research Division of the National Council of Juvenile and Family Court Judges
www.ncjj.org/

The American Bar Association, Juvenile Justice Center
www.abanet.org/crimjust/juvjus/home.html

The Center for Juvenile and Criminal Justice
www.cjcj.org/

The Children's Defense Fund, Youth Violence and Crime
www.childrensdefense.org/juvenilejustice/index.html

Cornell University, Legal Information Institute, Juvenile Justice Law Materials
wwwsecure.law.cornell.edu/topics/juvenile.html

A Smattering of Federal Websites on Legal Age Transitions

While waiver from juvenile justice to adult criminal court marks one very tragic transition from childhood to adulthood, as the preceding discussion demonstrates, there are many other legal markers. Some, of course, are governed by individual state laws. However, for a few federal websites discussing particular legal age transitions, please see the following:

U.S. Department of Labor
www.dol.gov/

U.S. Department of Transportation, National Highway Traffic Safety Administration
www.nhtsa.dot.gov/

U.S. Selective Service System
www.sss.gov/

8 Law and Identity

Law and Identity: General Considerations

This morning I alarmed myself. While shaving, without thinking, I began to shave my chin and the area below my lower lip before I did my upper lip. It was as if I had forgotten for a second how to be me. My shaving procedure is invariable: soften whiskers with hot washcloth, lather bar in soap dish, shave right cheek and jaw first, then left, then upper lip, and lastly the tricky, knobby region of the chin, with its need to hold fast the lower lip with the upper teeth. I have cut myself more often in this region than any other, and save it for last. Suddenly, I was tackling it out of sequence. My identity had been usurped by an alien who had not been briefed upon just this trifling detail; another hand than mine had taken over (Updike 1997, 215).

Our identities—who we are, how we think of ourselves, and how others think of us—are the sum total of a huge array of great and small genetic legacies, environmental influences, personal relationships, and individual habits. So, the protagonist of John Updike's postapocalyptic novel, *Toward the End of Time*, discovers how dependent his sense of self is on as mundane an act as shaving. All of us at times "don't feel like ourselves" when some small incident (perhaps a viral infection, a sleepless night, a missed routine) interrupts the usual flow of our being.

Some of who we are is learned and over time adapted to our individual quirks—from how we shave, brush our teeth, cook our meals, and make our beds, to how we study, how we work, and how we care for our families. Of course, such facets of our personalities, treasured as they may be, are generally changeable. If a life-long habit of perfunctory dental care suddenly results in a raft of cavities and gum disease, we can begin, with only a little trouble, to take better and different care of our teeth. Although it takes more effort and resolve, we can respond to a semester's worth of Fs by rethinking and redoing our study habits.

Some of who we are, however, cannot be changed at all, or can only be changed as the result of monumental effort against truly astounding odds. Thus, generally speaking, and with few exceptions (in other words, for all practical purposes), we cannot change our gender or our race. For many among us, physical and mental disability is either unalterable or merely ameliorable. Although the proposition is certainly a contentious one, more and more experts and advocates are coming to the conclusion that sexual orientation is genetically given rather than chosen. While America is still sustained by the

Horatio Alger narrative, if one is born rich, she will no doubt remain rich; if one is born to the middle class, he will likely remain in the middle class; and if one is born poor, the odds are fairly good that she will live out her life below, on, or around the poverty level. How the law responds to and deals with both the alterable and inalterable or nearly inalterable facets of human identity is the subject of this chapter.

Law and Identity: Property in Ourselves

In two very broad philosophical and structural senses, American law was actually set up to deal with the problem of identity writ large. Thus, to begin, recall our discussion of property rights in chapter 3. From a classical liberal perspective, property is intrinsic to the individual—at its most basic level, we all possess ownership over ourselves. Hence, Locke's contention:

From all which it is evident, that though the things of nature are given in common, yet man, by being master of himself, and proprietor of his own person, and the actions or labour of it, had still in himself the great foundation of property. . . (Locke [1690] 1960, ch. 5).

Clearly, we possess ourselves and this possession of self is the great wellspring of individual freedoms acknowledged and codified by the framers of our own Constitution.

Tragically, as we all know, this did not prevent many of those great liberal thinkers from owning other people and thus dispossessing them of any proprietorship in their own selves. Indeed, not until "the 1st day of January, A.D. 1863" were even some persons declared "forever free" (*The Emancipation Proclamation* 1862).[1] And, not until 1865 did the Constitution acknowledge that:

Neither slavery nor involuntary servitude, except as a punishment for crime whereof the party shall have been duly convicted, shall exist within the United States, or any place subject to their jurisdiction (*U.S. Constitution*, Amendment XIII, § 1).

Now, property in self may mean many things. For one, the notion of ownership over ourselves gives rise to the idea of individual privacy. Such constitutional principles as those explicitly stated in the Fourth Amendment and implied in constitutional interpretations such as *Roe v. Wade* are grounded in the notion that we, not the government and not others, are our own proprietors. This means, in the words of one of the nation's greatest lawyers and judges, Louis Brandeis, that we have a "right to be let alone."[2] Thus, as discussed in chapter 6, we possess substantial autonomy over, and the "right to be let alone" in, our reproductive capacities. In many respects, this was the great self-ownership issue of the latter part of the twentieth century. But our self-ownership has other important—and very important *legal*—implications beyond the physical and procreative. It has equally important psychological and reputational ramifications as well. For example, you are, in effect, your reputation, and if that reputation is damaged so are you. Should another besmirch your reputation, that person, for all practical purposes, besmirches your identity. Such is the basis for the law of slander and libel. Because we own ourselves to a significant degree, it means that just as we may seek to recover legal damages when someone vandalizes or destroys our home, car, or other real property, so we may seek to recover legal damages when someone injures or devastates us.

Of course, you are also your physical identity—property or ownership over self accrues to your body as well as your character. Hence, should another cause you bodily injury, you may sue, in effect, placing monetary value on your lost or damaged physical property.

Rectifying Damage to Self

Thus, in the most simplistic terms, as individuals, we inherit and build two forms of identity over our lifetimes. One is physical—when we view our mirror image we see a self who is big or small, strong or weak, blonde or brunette, black or white, and so forth. The other, however, is more complex. It is the sum of our personality and personal accomplishments. For this there is no true mirror image, only a psychological representation that we project to ourselves and seek to project to others. Either of these forms of identity may be injured, and even destroyed. The potential for injury to both forms is well recognized by the law.

PHYSICAL DAMAGE

The most easily recognized and measurable damage to self is physical. If I lose a leg or arm it alters me tremendously—it changes my ability to conduct my daily affairs, to earn a living, even the way I perceive myself. Moreover, such a catastrophe is readily and obviously apparent to others.

Physical injury is at the heart of tort law, the law of civil wrongs. According to Lawrence Friedman, "[p]robably 95 percent of all tort claims are for personal injury" (Friedman 1998, 169). Thus, to offer an all-too-common example, if some jerk rear-ends me at a traffic light causing a painful back injury, I may sue her at tort in an effort to recover damages. Indeed, as Friedman notes, personal injury law "deals above all with the wrenching, grinding effects of machines on human bodies."[3] Not surprisingly, then, given the all-American love affair with the car, the vast majority of tort claims today are automobile related.

Two offshoots of personal injury tort—product liability and medical malpractice—were particularly prominent and controversial during the latter part of the twentieth century. Product liability law involves injuries caused by defective products. For example, Stella Liebech, the now very famous "McDonald's Coffee Lady," sued the giant burger chain over injuries sustained from its defectively hot beverage. Medical malpractice involves harms caused by medical personnel or institutions. For example, if my surgeon removes the wrong organ, I may sue him for malpractice. Both of these categories and other personal injury torts are discussed more fully in other chapters and little more than passing mention need be made here. However, it is worth noting, as we did in chapter 4, that despite the swell in journalistic and political interest and despite all the debate engendered by product liability and medical malpractice, the two categories account for only a very small proportion of personal injury claims. Nevertheless, groups that get stuck with the bill when plaintiffs do win such suits—corporations that produce and deliver products, the insurance industry, and doctors—are among the most powerful in the nation. Thus, we tend to hear their legal complaints perhaps a bit more clearly than those of the less powerful.

REPUTATIONAL DAMAGE

Certainly a major physical injury can have a huge impact on an individual's self-identity. In some cases, the law even acknowledges this in the form of compensation for "mental anguish." If an injury leaves a person fearful, anxious, or depressed, for example, she may be able to recover compensatory damages for those largely intangible qualities that so alter self. But, our bodies, no matter how important they are to the total "us," are only a part of who we are. Our self-ownership—our identity—goes to more than legs or arms. Indeed, it is that which hopefully goes deep within and presumably is projected far without—our good names, our fine characters, our reputations, our "inviolate personality" (Warren and Brandeis 1890, 205).

The law has long recognized the importance of reputation and personal characteristics. At English common law, reputation was treated "as an interest existing *outside* the individual persona, an intangible 'asset' of social or professional life that may be inventoried like any other stock-in-trade" (Smolla 1992, 118). Not surprisingly, then, for a great deal of legal history reputation, like real property, was really something possessed only by the wealthy and powerful—the very few considered substantial enough to have a good name that might be defamed. Defamation of character or libel might carry either criminal sanction or the potential for civil damages depending upon who was the subject of the invective—seditious libel being a criminal offense against the crown or government and civil libel being a tort against a private citizen. The British monarchy, showing great sensitivity to its good name, was big on issuing seditious libel edicts. Thus, for example, in 1275, the monarchy handed down *De Scandalis Magnatum*, a law penalizing false or critical speech against the king (O'Brien 1995, 366). This was followed by subsequent such dicta over the years including, notably, *Scandalum Magnatum*, which gave rise to the notorious Star Chamber during the sixteenth and seventeenth centuries. In any event, it was considered serious business indeed to impugn the royal character![4]

As it crossed the Atlantic Ocean, weathered a revolution, and was squeezed through the American constitutional framework, the law of libel found itself faced with a rather formidable bar in the First Amendment. A neighbor or coworker's malicious gossip is a small thing and relatively easily countered compared to printed (or, today, broadcast) material that might circulate much more widely, for much longer periods of time. Yet, the legitimate interests of the press might easily run afoul of a person's (or government's) good name, with very serious consequences for financial and personal relationships.[5] The relationship between libel and the First Amendment has thus provided considerable fodder for the courts.

In 1960, the *New York Times* ran a full-page advertisement entitled, "Heed Their Rising Voices." The ad charged that southern black students, engaging in nonviolent protest to gain civil rights and liberties "were being met by an unprecedented wave of terror by those who would deny and negate that document [U.S. Constitution] which the whole world looks upon as setting the pattern for modern freedom. . . ." In relevant part, the page went on to say,

In Montgomery, Alabama, after students sang "My Country, 'Tis of Thee" on the State Capitol steps, their leaders were expelled from school, and truckloads of police armed with shotguns and tear-gas ringed the Alabama State College Campus. When the entire student body protested to state authorities by refusing to re-register, their dining hall was padlocked in an attempt to starve them into submission. . . .

Again and again the Southern violators have answered Dr. King's peaceful protests with intimidation and violence. They have bombed his home almost killing his wife and child. They have assaulted his person. They have arrested him seven times—for "speeding," "loitering" and similar "offenses." And now they have charged him with "perjury"—a felony under which they could imprison him for ten years . . . (*New York Times v. Sullivan*, 376 U.S. 254, at 257–58 (1964)).

Although the advertisement accused no one by name, L. B. Sullivan, the police commissioner of Montgomery, Alabama, sued the *New York Times* in a civil libel action, claiming that the ad implicitly defamed his character as police chief. Moreover, Sullivan demonstrated that the advertisement contained false information. As a result, a Montgomery County jury awarded him damages of $500,000, the full amount claimed. On appeal, the supreme court of Alabama affirmed the jury's judgment. Thereafter, the case became the subject of the U.S. Supreme Court's most far-reaching and important statement to date on the law of libel.

Overturning the judgment against the *New York Times*, the Court held that because of the countervailing importance of the First Amendment, "[a] State cannot . . . award damages to a public official for defamatory falsehood relating to his official conduct unless he proves 'actual malice'—that the statement was made with knowledge of its falsity or with reckless disregard of whether it was true or false" (at 255). In short, although the Court has continuously maintained that proven libel is accorded no First Amendment protection (see, e.g., *Beauharnais v. Illinois*, 343 U.S. 250 (1952)), the ruling set an exceedingly high hurdle for public officials wishing to claim libelous action.

Still, in spite of the fact that the United States probably has more public officials than any other nation on earth, most of us are not among that anointed many. Nevertheless, we may be "public figures," people of "general fame or notoriety in the community, and pervasive involvement in the affairs of society" (*Gertz v. Welch*, 418 U.S. 323, at 352 (1974)). In such cases, the difficult "actual malice" standard applies, particularly if the story is so-called "hot news," the immediacy of which might make really thorough investigation impossible before publishing (*Curtis Publishing Co. v. Butts*, 388 U.S. 130, at 157 (1967)).

Deciding exactly who *is* a public figure is often a difficult legal call, and increasingly so in a world of lightning-fast media and self-confessional fare from Jerry Springer to Jenny Jones. Andy Warhol's prediction that we would each achieve "fifteen minutes of fame" seems less and less futuristic all the time. A case in point is that of Richard Jewell, the hapless Centennial Olympic Park security guard, who, for several days following the 1996 bombing that killed one and injured 111 others, did indeed *revel* as a hero, granting dozens of self-promotional interviews. The tide turned very badly indeed for Jewell, however, when the *Atlanta Journal-Constitution*, acting on an FBI tip, published a report naming him not as the heroic figure previously assumed, but as the chief suspect. Jewell, whose name was later cleared, was subjected for weeks to a humiliating media onslaught and, as of this writing, was in the process of suing the newspaper. Before his case goes to trial, however, Georgia courts must decide whether Jewell is a public figure who has to prove "actual malice" or a mere private citizen who need only demonstrate "negligence" (see below). Not surprisingly, lawyers for both sides cite differing precedent. The *Journal-Constitution* claims that "Jewell 'freely assumed a position very close to center stage in the public discussion of the Olympic Park bombing controversy . . . ,' [making him] a 'limited-purpose public figure in connection with the controversies that surrounded the bombing. . . .'" (Peter C. Canfield, attorney for the *Atlanta Journal-Constitution*, quoted in Schmitt 1999a). Jewell's attorneys, on the other hand, argue that "'[a]bsent clear evidence of general fame or notoriety in the community and pervasive involvement in the affairs of the society, an individual should not be deemed a public personality for all aspects of his life'" (L. Lin Wood Jr., attorney for Richard Jewell, citing *Gertz* and quoted in Schmitt). Trial Judge John R. Mather chose to take a middle-ground approach, declaring Jewell a "*limited* public figure," who must prove "actual malice." Judge Mather's decision was being appealed at the time of this writing (Schmitt 1999b).

What, however, if one is neither a "public official" nor a "public figure"? After all, public officials and most public figures are people who intentionally "thrust themselves to the forefront . . . , invit[ing] attention and comment." In a very real sense, they "voluntarily expose . . . themselves to increased risk of injury from defamatory falsehood concerning them" (*Gertz v. Welch*, 418 U.S. 323, at 343 (1974)). Despite all of their disingenuous complaints about paparazzi and nettlesome fans, the Leonardo DiCaprios of the world are front and center because they sought to be so situated. Moreover, such individuals "usually enjoy significant . . . access to the channels of effective communication . . . hence hav[ing] a . . . realistic opportunity to counteract false statements. . . " (at 343).

Typically, however, all of us "just plain folk" out there—be we professors, students, lawyers, construction workers, or sales clerks—do not purposely thrust ourselves into the public limelight. For us, an unpleasant, character-defaming story would probably come as a complete blind side. Thus, for us, the possibility of accessing "channels of effective communication" to rebut false stories is pretty low. Most of us do not retain full-time publicists and press agents. Hence, for us, the Court has set a somewhat lower bar for collecting on a libelous action.

"Private individuals," according to the Court, are "more vulnerable to injury, and the state interest in protecting them is correspondingly greater" (*Gertz*, at 345) than, for example, it would be in the case of a "public" individual. Therefore, "negligence, as contrasted with a showing of willful or reckless disregard" (at 353 (Blackmun, J., concurring)), is all a private libel plaintiff need demonstrate.

PRIVACY DAMAGE

Closely related to libel is invasion of privacy. Here, too, American law acknowledges the importance of self-ownership—of identity—but, here, too, the self faces formidable barriers. Rodney Smolla offers a fourfold characterization of legal invasions of privacy: invasion of privacy by appropriation, by intrusion, by false light, and by causing emotional distress (Smolla 1992, 141–50). Each of the four has generated its own considerable case law.

Invasion of privacy by *appropriation* is more familiarly known as the "right of publicity." Described by the originator of the concept, Judge Jerome Frank, as "a right in the publicity value" (*Haelan Laboratories, Inc. v. Topps Chewing Gum, Inc.*, 202 F.2d 866, at 868 (1953); cert. denied, 346 U.S. 816 (1953)) in a person's name or likeness, the doctrine prevents mostly commercial enterprises from making a profit off of the unauthorized use of another's image. In essence, it protects one's "pecuniary interest in the commercial exploitation of his [own] identity" (*Carson v. Here's Johnny Portable Toilets, Inc.*, 698 F.2d 831, at 835 (6th Cir., 1982)).

Take for example, the weighty case of Johnny Carson and the unauthorized toilet. Carson, the longtime (pre-Leno) host of television's *Tonight Show*, was introduced nightly throughout a nearly three-decade period by sidekick, Ed McMahon, with the phrase, "Here's Johnny!" The problem arose in the 1980s when a Michigan-based porta-potty company began marketing its convenience stations as "Here's Johnny Portable Toilets, The World's Foremost Commodian." Thoroughly unamused by the play on words, the comedian sued, claiming, among other things, that the toilet company had violated his right to publicity. The Sixth Circuit agreed, allowing it to flesh out a fairly broad reading of the concept, including not just the appropriation of precise name or likeness, but of closely identified inferences, as well (*Carson*, at 835).

Although public officials, figures, and even us lowly nobodies, if caught in a newsworthy story, may anticipate and have to put up with a good deal of unwanted press coverage, the courts have distinguished between legitimate news gathering and illegitimate *intrusion* or "psychic trespass" (Smolla 1992, 145). For example, even in pursuit of good copy on so very public a figure as the late Jacqueline Kennedy Onassis, a journalist may not block the movement of or endanger his subject's life and limb (*Galella v. Onassis*, 533 F. Supp. 1076 (SDNY, 1982)). Thus,

under certain circumstances, surveillance may be so "overzealous" as to render it actionable. . . . It does not strain credulity or imagination to conceive of the systematic "public" surveillance of another as being the implementation of a plan to intrude on the privacy of another. Although acts performed in "public", especially if taken singly or in small numbers, may not be confidential, at least arguably a right to privacy may nevertheless be invaded through extensive or exhaustive monitoring and cataloguing of acts normally disconnected and anonymous (*Nader v. GMC*, 25 N.Y.2d 560, at 570, 572; 255 N.E.2d 765 (Court of Appeals of New York, 1970)).

Hence, while notoriety may indeed reduce "the 'space' in which a public [or newsworthy] person may enforce the laws of psychic trespass . . . , diminish[ing her] capacity legally to insist . . ." that she be left alone, "the press enjoys no freestanding First Amendment exemption from the rules of intrusion . . . " (Smolla 1992, 145–46).

An individual's privacy may be violated by presenting him in a "*false light*," even if that "false light" does not result in the kind of reputational damage characteristic of libel. A case in point was that of Margaret Cantrell, the widow of one of forty-three victims of a catastrophic bridge collapse in West Virginia in the late 1960s. As part of a human interest follow-up to the disaster, a reporter for the *Cleveland Plain Dealer* chose to focus on Cantrell and her children. Among other inaccuracies in the story, it portrayed the Cantrells as living in abject poverty. According to Cantrell, the article caused her and her children "to suffer outrage, mental distress, shame, and humiliation" (*Cantrell v. Forest City Publishing*, 419 U.S. 245, at 248 (1974)). Under the common-law standard of malice, sustainable by proving that falsehoods were knowingly or recklessly published, the Supreme Court upheld a jury verdict in favor of Cantrell's "false light" invasion claim.[6]

Courts have also recognized the tort of *emotional distress* caused by "the intentional or reckless infliction of 'severe' emotional distress on another through conduct that is 'outrageous'" (Smolla 1992, 148). For a public official or figure beset by a media onslaught, however, this one is particularly difficult to win. The legal principle, made uncharacteristically famous—uncharacteristically famous for a legal principle, that is—in both book[7] and film,[8] was articulated by the Supreme Court in *Hustler Magazine v. Falwell* (485 U.S. 46 (1988)).

In 1983, America's foremost smut peddler, Larry Flynt, ran an ad parody in *Hustler Magazine* depicting the Reverend Jerry Falwell having sex with his mother in an outhouse. Needless to say, Falwell did not find the caricature funny and sued Flynt and his magazine for, among things, emotional distress. A jury ruled for the minister, awarding him compensatory and punitive damages in recovery for his distress, and the Fourth Circuit upheld the verdict. A unanimous Supreme Court, however, reversed, mandating far-reaching First Amendment protection of satire, no matter how offensively depicted or how stressful to the public figure lampooned:

[I]n the world of debate about public affairs, many things done with motives that are less than admirable are protected by the First Amendment.... "Outrageousness" in the area of political

and social discourse has an inherent subjectiveness about it which would allow a jury to impose liability on the basis of the jurors' tastes or views, or perhaps on the basis of their dislike of a particular expression. An "outrageousness" standard thus runs afoul of our longstanding refusal to allow damages to be awarded because the speech in question may have an adverse emotional impact on the audience. . . . [Thus,] public figures and public officials may not recover for the tort of intentional infliction of emotional distress by reason of publications such as the one here at issue without showing in addition that the publication contains a false statement of *fact* which was made with "actual malice," i.e., with knowledge that the statement was false or with reckless disregard as to whether or not it was true (*Hustler*, at 53–57).

The First Amendment's ability to trump perceived invasions of privacy causing deep emotional distress is not limited to lampoons on famous personalities. Publication of newsworthy items, lawfully obtained, about the ordeals suffered by the most ordinary among us are protected no matter how insufferable the emotional impact. Take, for example, the case of B. J. F., a sexual assault victim, whose name the *Florida Star* printed in full after obtaining it from a police report. The paper itself had an internal policy of *not* publishing the names of sexual offense victims and Florida law made "it unlawful to 'print, publish, or broadcast . . . in any instrument of mass communication' the name of the victim of a sexual offense" (*Florida Star v. B. J. F.*, 491 U.S. 524, at 526 (1989)). According to B. J. F., the impact of the publication coming on top of the rape itself was emotionally devastating and she instituted a civil suit under the Florida statute seeking to recover damages. A trial and appeals court sided with B. J. F., awarding her $75,000 in compensatory damages and $25,000 in punitive damages. The U.S. Supreme Court, however, reversed, holding that "'if a newspaper lawfully obtains truthful information about a matter of public significance then state officials may not constitutionally punish publication of the information, absent a need to further a state interest of the highest order'" (at 534, citing *Smith v. Daily Mail Publishing Co.*, 443 U.S. 97, at 103).

If the First Amendment stands as an imposing hurdle to overcome in preserving one's privacy—one's "inviolate personality"—so, too, do other legal and market forces. Multiple examples flow from the presidential sex–financial-file-travel scandals of the 1990s. Jeffrey Rosen, legal analyst for the *New Yorker* magazine, relates the following disturbing legal scenario swirling around White House aide, Paul Begala:

[In 1998], Begala received a notice ordering him to testify; and at first he thought that it was a joke. . . . Issued by Larry Klayman, a conservative lawyer who has filed suit on behalf of the Reagan and Bush employees whose F.B.I. files turned up in the Clinton White House, the notice demanded that Begala produce any records, notes, correspondence, or diaries that might cast light on the Clinton Administration's mishandling of the confidential information in those files. "I was living in Texas when Filegate broke," Begala told [Rosen]. "I tried to explain over and over that I don't know anything about the use of the F.B.I. files.

Nevertheless, Klayman subjected the White House aide to a six-hour deposition. "He was going through the list of every person I ever had lunch with," Begala recalled. "He asked the most personal stuff." As Klayman combed through Begala's appointment calendar, Begala explained that he was scheduled to meet with a friend of his priest in Texas, whereupon Klayman exclaimed, "Name your priest; I will name my rabbi!" Begala said afterward, "If you had told me that in America I'd be sitting, under oath, arguing about the name of my priest—it was a surreal experience. And then he turned over the videotape of the deposition to Geraldo."

As [Rosen and Begala] talked in Begala's office, his twenty-three-year-old secretary, Stacy Parker, typed quietly at a desk next to his. Begala explained that he and Parker aren't allowed to discuss the Klayman suit, because after she sifted through Begala's papers and E-mail in an attempt to respond to Klayman's demands, Klayman deposed her, too. In the course of her deposition, Parker told Klayman that she had been a White House intern at the same time as Monica Lewinsky, and that she had dined on occasion, with [presidential friend] Vernon Jordan. This prompted Klayman to ask if Jordan had offered Parker counsel about whether she could tell the truth in her deposition; he also asked if she had discussed her testimony with her boyfriend, whose name Klayman was eager to know ... (Rosen 1998, 36).

As Rosen puts it, "It may seem ironic that a lawsuit filed to protect privacy [Klayman's theorizes that the Clinton Administration used government files to defame adversaries such as Linda Tripp] could produce so many privacy violations of its own. But this has been the recurring dynamic of the Clinton scandals" (p. 36). Hence, the conservative *American Spectator* magazine could be said to have set all the ignominy in motion when, in 1994, it hinted at Paula Jones's humiliating Little Rock hotel encounter with then Governor Clinton, thus invading her privacy and resulting not only in the sexual fishing expeditions of Jones' attorneys, but, eventually, those of prosecutor writ large, Kenneth Starr (p. 36).

Indeed, perhaps increasingly, privacy may be transgressed by the legal process itself. Recall Justice Brandeis's assertion, noted above, that we have a "right to be let alone." Originally made by *lawyer* Brandeis in an 1890 *Harvard Law Review* article excoriating the intrusive press of the time, *Justice* Brandeis applied it to prosecutorial power in 1928:

The protection guaranteed by the [Fourth and Fifth] Amendments is much broader in scope. The makers of our Constitution undertook to secure conditions favorable to the pursuit of happiness. They recognized the significance of man's spiritual nature, of his feelings and of his intellect. They knew that only a part of the pain, pleasure and satisfactions of life are to be found in material things. They sought to protect Americans in their beliefs, their thoughts, their emotions and their sensations. They conferred, as against the Government, the right to be let alone—the most comprehensive of rights and the right most valued by civilized men. To protect that right, every unjustifiable intrusion by the Government upon the privacy of the individual, whatever the means employed, must be deemed a violation of the Fourth Amendment. And the use, as evidence in a criminal proceeding, of facts ascertained by such intrusion must be deemed a violation of the Fifth (*Olmstead v. United States*, 277 U.S. 438, at 478–79 (Brandeis, J., dissenting)).

Written by Brandeis in dissent, the concept, as it applies to criminal investigations, gained brief ascendancy with a Court majority in the 1960s (see especially, *Katz v. United States*, 389 U.S. 347 (1967)), but has since undergone considerable erosion in the face of increasing deference to police and prosecutorial powers. Thus, for example, today it is no breach of one's privacy if police rummage through your garbage without a search warrant (*California v. Greenwood*, 486 U.S. 35 (1988)), nor snatch an unwarranted aerial eye view of your fenced-in backyard (*California v. Ciraolo*, 476 U.S. 207 (1986)).

Nor are barriers to assertions of privacy limited to mundane criminal investigations, as Paul Begala's encounters with Larry Klayman's civil suit demonstrate, and as former Senator Bob Packwood (R-OR) could tell you. Packwood, a four-term member, was publicly accused by a number of women staffers and lobbyists of making inappropriate sexual advances over his length of service in the Senate. The charges led to an investigation of his conduct by the Senate Ethics Committee, which subpoenaed numerous items, including the Senator's personal diaries "in which he record[ed] his observations of public events, but also include[ed] highly personal reflections and information about his private life" (*Senate Select Committee on Ethics v. Packwood*, 845 F. Supp. 17, at 18 (U.S. District Court for the District of Columbia, 1994)). No matter. The Committee wanted to look at it all and when Senator Packwood objected that "the subpoena violate[d] his right to privacy under the Fourth Amendment to the U.S. Constitution . . . [by] authorizing] the Ethics Committee to 'rummage' through his most private thoughts and reflections and intimate details of his personal life" (at 21), Judge Thomas Penfield Jackson of the U.S. District Court for the District of Columbia countered that the Senate's need to "maintain public confidence in [itself] as an institution" (at 22) trumped Senator Packwood's "private thoughts and reflections and intimate . . . personal life." Of course, President Clinton would know a thing or two about revealing the intimacies of personal life both for civil and criminal legal action!

PRIVACY IN THE INFORMATION AGE

Diaries, such as those kept by Senator Packwood, are traditional, ageless means of maintaining "private thoughts and reflections." But, really, few of us keep ongoing personal diaries or journals much beyond that nifty little book with the lock received Christmases ago, and abandoned when our seven-year-old self became bored with personal reflection somewhere following the third or fourth entry. Where many more of us increasingly (and pretty thoughtlessly) reveal our "inviolate" selves is in our electronic communication, and e-mail sure as heck isn't safe from prying eyes.

Thus, it is now fairly clear that if you are one of the many millions who employ e-mail for communications at your job, your employer is pretty free to monitor your "talk" and take action based on what he "hears" (see, e.g., *Bourke v. Nissan Motor Corporation in U.S.A.*, California Court of Appeals, Second Appellate District, Case No. B068705 (July 26, 1993)). Michael Smyth, an employee of the Pillsbury Company in Pennsylvania, discovered this in 1996. Although Pillsbury "repeatedly assured its employees, including [Smyth], that all e-mail communications would remain confidential and privileged ... [and] that e-mail communications could not be intercepted and used by [the company] against its employees as grounds for termination or reprimand" (*Smyth v. Pillsbury Company*, 914 F. Supp. 97, at 98 (U.S. District Court for the Eastern District of Pennsylvania, 1996)), it did precisely those things to Smyth when it intercepted some of his more frank comments to a supervisor. When Smyth sued, in part over privacy, the U.S. District Court informed him that there are "no privacy interests" in company e-mail communications. According to Judge Weiner, "the company's interest in preventing inappropriate and unprofessional comments or even illegal activity over its e-mail system outweighs any privacy interest the employee may have in those comments" (at 101).

It can all get *much* more personal. Indeed, "electronic discovery" and "electronic evidence" are being used increasingly in civil and criminal lawsuits across the nation (Withers 1999, 6). Although federal law offers some protection against unwarranted intrusions into and adversarial use of electronic discourse, the protection is limited and the intrusion and use appear to be expanding.[9] In criminal cases, the expanding (first) resort to cyber-generated evidence is illustrated by the ever-larger workload of Loudon County, Virginia, Sheriff Ron Horac whose full-time job it is to serve warrants on America Online (AOL), the giant Internet provider headquartered in Loudon:

As soon as word of the deadly shootings at Columbine High School in Colorado got to Investigator Ron Horac . . . , he knew it was going to be a bad week. . . . In the Columbine case, FBI agents went directly to the company within hours, seeking material Eric Harris was believed to have posted or stored on AOL's service about music, video games and bomb-making. But Horac knew a deluge of legal requests was coming. He generally handles about 20 warrants a month, a number that's been steadily rising over the past few years. After the Columbine attack, things went right through the roof, and the pace continues. "Just about every high school in the country had some form of copycat. We were getting a lot of emergency requests," he says. Each of those requests came in the form of

a search warrant, issued by a judge, that requires AOL to turn over any and all information about a user who has allegedly done something illegal, usually using AOL as a conduit to the Internet (Weise 1999, A10).

According to Deborah Schepers, attorney for the Minneapolis-based data retrieval firm Ontrack, "[a]s much as 30% of the evidence used in legal cases is now electronic" (Schepers paraphrased in Weise 1999, A10). As lawyer Michael Leventhal of Wolf, Rifkin & Shapiro in Los Angeles puts it, "In trial, e-mail is the gift that keeps on giving" (Leventhal quoted in Weise, A10). Nor is this limited to the legal system's attempts to sort out the sordid mental states of the Eric Harrises or Ted Kaczynskis of the world.

Indeed, the most law-abiding among us may have our personal thoughts and deeds exposed to public trial thanks to the many "gifts" offered in cyberspace. Hence, e-mail messages to and about lovers and steamy chat room exchanges are increasingly moving front and center in contentious divorces (Glod 1999, A1). For several years, Internet and legal experts have noted the tendency of otherwise very cautious individuals to leave messages that would have been torn to shreds and burned in hardcopy, on disks or thoughtlessly stored on the hard drive, for angry spouses to retrieve. But, say you are among the very careful few, having double and triple deleted your online passions and smashed your computer, to boot. You still may not be out of the woods. Thus, according to AOL spokesman, Rich D'Amato, the service provider "receives a steady stream of civil subpoenas requesting subscriber information, often for divorce cases. . . . [And while] AOL usually is only able to produce records showing how much time a customer spent online, . . . the company occasionally can recover the text of a message or a chat room exchange . . . " (D'Amato quoted in Glod 1999, A1).[10]

PRIVACY AND SELF AT THE MILLENNIUM

"Privacy is a necessary element of quality life in modern society" (Cate 1997, 101). Indeed it is! Or, at least, we like to talk about and claim it a lot. At the same time, as we stand on the precipice of the new millennium, multiple countervailing forces seem destined to challenge our private selves.

Of course, there have long been constitutional trumps to privacy—the First Amendment and the legitimate police power of the state standing in the historical forefront. But, as the foregoing suggests, much of the modern challenge is market and technology driven, and here we may be our own worst enemies. In significant ways, we always have been, and technology has merely exacerbated the tension. Much of this is inherent in the conflict between liberty and order. We want the police to easily catch the "bad guy" and the rejected, faithful spouse to quickly get his due. Such is essential to a well-ordered society. Of course, we never, ever imagine that *we* might be one of the "bad guys"; on the contrary, when we wind up on the wrong end of a police investigation (or speed trap), liberty concerns—including our "right to be let alone"—suddenly rise up. Similarly, the vast bulk of unfaithful husbands and wives are cads who deserve the humiliation and financial devastation of being exposed by their victimized spouses. Of course, when *we* are unfaithful there's always a good reason and *we* should be "let alone." As James Gleick aptly puts it:

Certainly where other people's privacy is concerned, we seem willing to lower our standards. We have become a society with a cavernous appetite for news and gossip. Our era has replaced the tacit, eyes-averted civility of an earlier time with exhibitionism and prying. Even borderline public figures must get used to the nation's eyes in their bedrooms and pocketbooks. That's not Big Brother watching. It's us (Gleick 1996, 130).

In such traditional conflicts involving police heat and passionate heart, technology—from e-mail to radar guns, from chat rooms to cell phones—makes the social task of "ordering" a bit easier. The disorder is more public and more readily gathered.

But, as Gleick suggests above, it is not simply in new twists on old turns that technology and market forces have presented Y2K and beyond challenges to self. Whole new questions are emerging as we enter the twenty-first century. It may no longer be government—against whom are offered protections in one federal and fifty state constitutions and countless statutes—that we need most fear as the great potential intruder, but rather, corporations. Here, in the name of convenience and efficiency, is a partial list of what government, but mostly, corporations know about you:

- Your health history, your credit history, your marital history, your educational history, your employment history.
- The times and telephone numbers of every call you make and receive.
- The magazines you subscribe to and the books you borrow from the library.
- Your travel history: you can no longer travel by air without presenting photographic identification; in a world of electronic fare cards tracking frequent-traveler data, computers could list even your bus and subway rides.
- The trail of your cash withdrawals.
- All your purchases by credit card or check. In a not-so-distant future, when electronic cash becomes the rule, even the purchases you still make by bills and coins could be logged.
- What you eat. No sooner had supermarket scanners gone online—to speed check-out efficiency—than data began to be tracked for marketing purposes. Large chains now invite customers to link personal

identifying information with the records of what they buy, in exchange for discount cards or other promotions.
- Your electronic mail and your telephone messages. If you use a computer at work, your employer has the legal right to look over your shoulder while you type. More and more companies are quietly spot checking workers' e-mail and even voice mail. In theory—though rarely in practice—even an online service or private Internet service provider could monitor you. "Anyway," advises a website at, naturally, paranoia.com, "you should assume that everything you do on line is monitored by your service provider."
- Where you go and what you see on the World Wide Web. Ordinarily, net exploring is an anonymous activity, but many information services ask users to identify themselves and even to provide telephone numbers and other personal information. Once a user does that, his or her activity can be traced in surprising detail. Do you like country music? Were you thinking about taking a vacation in New Zealand? Were you perusing the erotic-books section of the online bookstore? Someone—some computer, anyway—probably already knows (Gleick 1996, 130).

Again, Gleick (1996, 130) frames the issue very well:

In public opinion surveys, Americans always favor privacy. Then they turn around and sell it cheaply. Most vehemently oppose any suggestion of a national identification system yet volunteer their telephone numbers and mothers' maiden names and even—grudgingly or not—Social Security numbers to merchants bearing discounts or Web services offering "membership" privileges. For most, the abstract notion of privacy suggests a mystical, romantic, cowboy-era set of freedoms. Yet in the real world it boils down to matters of small convenience. Is privacy about Government security agents decrypting your E-mail and then kicking down the front door with their jackboots? Or is it about telemarketers interrupting your supper with cold calls?[11]

Some technologies with specifically self-invasive applications are either here or just over the horizon. In the near future, no doubt, we will be convinced, in the names of efficiency and security, to allow banks and other financial concerns to maintain retinal, iris, facial, hand, and voice records on us so that our relevant body parts may be scanned at ATMs and check-out counters.[12]

Advancing medical technologies, too, impose real risks to privacy and threats to the self. For example, as beneficial as it may well be, the growing field of genetic diagnostics that allows clinicians to detect genes that may cause disease and early death carries with it a substantial potential price tag:

Many social risks of genetic testing have been identified and can occur even if the test was negative or indicated that an individual was an asymptomatic carrier. The risks include stigmatization, loss of health or life insurance, loss of employment or educational opportunities, and inability to adopt a child. . . . Privacy and confidentiality may also be threatened if a family member gets a genetic test, and the results imply that untested relatives also have the disease or are at increased risk of having the disease, or being a carrier. In addition, it is sometimes necessary to take samples from several family members in order to determine the genotype of one individual. Some family members may not wish to submit themselves to the physical discomforts and risks of giving samples. They may not wish to know their genotype, or may not wish others to know. Here, the autonomy of individuals is in conflict (Cho 1999).[13]

The promises and the problems of genetic testing likely will increase significantly in the near future now that the U.S. Human Genome Project and Celera Genomics Corporation[14] have initially identified "all the estimated 80,000 genes in human DNA, determin[ing] the sequences of the 3 billion chemical bases that make up human DNA, [and] stor[ing] this information in databases. . . ."[15]

Congress has acted in a limited way to address the potential for abuse here. In 1996, it passed the *Health Insurance Portability and Accountability Act* (HIPAA) (Pub. L. 104-191; 110 Stat. 1936). Among factors that may not be used to deny or limit insurance coverage in group plans, the act includes genetic information. Moreover, the law specifically excludes genetic data from being considered a preexisting condition under such plans. The congressional plan, however, leaves a number of significant issues and problems uncovered by law. According to Francis Collins, director of the National Human Genome Research Institute,

Americans are still largely unprotected by federal law against insurance rate hikes based on genetic information and against unauthorized people or institutions having access to the genetic information contained in their medical records. . . . [Moreover, t]he protections in HIPAA do not extend to the individual health insurance market. Thus, individuals seeking coverage outside of the group market may still be denied access to coverage and may be charged exorbitant premiums based on genetic information. While only approximately 5 percent of Americans obtain health insurance outside the group market today, many of us will, at some point in our lifetime, purchase individual health insurance coverage. Because genetic information persists for a lifetime and may be transmitted through generations, people who are now in group plans are concerned about whether information about their genes may, at some point later in their life, disallow them from being able to purchase health insurance outside of the group market. Second, while HIPAA prohibits insurers from treating individuals within a group differently from one another, it leaves open the possibility that all individuals within a group could be charged a higher premium based on the genetic information of one or more members of the group. Finally, HIPAA does nothing to limit an insurer's access to or release of genetic information. No federal law prohibits an insurer from demanding access to genetic information contained in medical records or family history or requiring that an individual submit to a genetic test. In fact, an insurer can demand that an individual undergo genetic testing as a condition of coverage.

Further, there are no restrictions on an insurer's release of genetic information to others. For example, at present, an insurer may release genetic information, and other health related information, to the Medical Information Bureau which makes information available to other insurers who can then use it to discriminate. Because genetic information is personal, powerful, and potentially predictive, it can be used to stigmatize and discriminate against people (Collins 1997).

To date, at least twenty-three states have enacted laws that prohibit genetic discrimination by insurers (Yesley 1998, 656).

Insurance aside, current law does little to stop employers from discovering the presumably private genetic histories of potential and current employees. According to a recent survey of over 1,000 companies undertaken by the American Management Association (AMA), nearly 51 percent subject new hires to a series of medical tests and many do not inform applicants or employees about the nature of tests being preformed. Moreover, after making a job offer, the new boss may insist on "medical record disclosure, require a pre-employment physical or even review insurance records for genetic information." According to the AMA survey, "some employers ask applicants directly about their genetic health and family medical history. . . . [M]ore than 200 firms surveyed, or 21.7%, obtain such information from potential employees, and 6% use the information 'to make such decisions as whom to hire or promote'" ("Genetic Discrimination" 1999).

As of 1998, eleven states had enacted laws prohibiting genetic discrimination in employment, though the strength of these laws varies considerably (Yesley 1998, 656). Among the more potentially far-reaching have been those enacted by Wisconsin, Iowa, and New Hampshire (Kaufmann 1999, 434). For example, New Hampshire law provides that:

I. No employer, labor organization, employment agency, or licensing agency shall directly or indirectly: (a) Solicit, require or administer genetic testing relating to any individual as a condition of employment, labor organization membership, or licensure. (b) Affect the terms, conditions, or privileges of employment, labor organization membership, or licensure or terminate the employment, labor organization membership, or licensure of any individual based on genetic testing.

II. . . . [N]o person shall sell or otherwise provide to an employer, labor organization, employment agency or licensing agency any genetic testing relating to an employee, labor organization member or licensee or to a prospective employee, labor organization member or licensee.

III. Any agreement between an employer, labor organization, employment agency, or licensing agency and an individual offering employment, labor organization membership, licensure, or any pay or benefit to that individual in return for taking a genetic test is prohibited.[16]

Unlike some states, Congress has yet to specifically confront genetic testing for and in employment. Although the *Americans with Disabilities Act of 1990* (ADA) (104 Stat. 337, 42 U.S.C. § 12132) prohibits employment discrimination based on disability, none of its provisions addresses precisely whether it is unlawful to discriminate based on an "unexpressed genetic condition" (Rothstein, Gelb, and Craig 1998, 404).

Courts have arguably long been in the business of assessing genetic tests, given that paternity testing has been a mainstay of family law litigation for some time. But, they are only now beginning to clarify the law as it applies to privacy and discrimination in employment. A case in point was provided recently by the Ninth Circuit (*Norman-Bloodsaw v. Lawrence Berkeley Laboratory*, 135 F.3d 1260 (U.S. Circuit Court of Appeals for the Ninth Circuit, 1998)).

Lawrence Berkeley Laboratory, a research institution jointly operated by California and federal agencies, has long conditioned employment on mandatory pre-placement medical examinations. Among other things, the examinations require prospective job holders to provide blood and urine samples. According to a group of past and present administrative and clerical employees who have sued Lawrence, unbeknownst to them and without their consent, the lab tested all of their samples for syphilis, while testing black applicants for sickle cell anemia and women applicants for pregnancy.[17] On the basis of these allegations, the plaintiffs maintain that Lawrence violated the ADA by requiring a medical examination "that was neither job-related nor consistent with business necessity"; that it violated the federal and state constitutional right to privacy "by conducting the testing at issue, collecting and maintaining the results of the testing, and failing to provide adequate safeguards against disclosure of the results"; and that, by targeting African Americans for sickle-cell trait testing and women for pregnancy testing, it violated Title VII of the *Civil Rights Act* (*Norman-Bloodsaw*, at 1265–66).

Although a district court dismissed the suit on each of the grounds, the circuit court reinstated all but the ADA claim (at 1273–74).[18] Hence, on the issue of constitutional privacy, Judge Reinhardt asserted that

One can think of few subject areas more personal and more likely to implicate privacy interests than that of one's health or genetic make-up. . . . The constitutionally protected privacy interest in avoiding disclosure of personal matters clearly encompasses medical information and its confidentiality. . . . Although cases defining the privacy interest in medical information have typically involved its disclosure to "third" parties, rather than the collection of information by illicit means, it goes without saying that the *most basic* violation possible involves the performance of unauthorized tests—that is, the non-consensual retrieval of previously unrevealed medical information that may be unknown even to plaintiffs. These tests may also be viewed as searches in violation of Fourth Amendment rights that require Fourth Amendment scrutiny. The tests at issue in this case thus implicate rights protected under both the Fourth Amendment and the Due Process Clause of the Fifth or Fourteenth Amendments (at 1269; citations omitted).

Moreover, Judge Reinhardt noted that Title VII might well be implicated "if the employment of women and blacks at Lawrence was conditioned in part on allegedly unconstitutional invasions of privacy to which white and/or male employees were not subjected" (at 1272). Although the case has yet to culminate in trial, the appeals court ruling does suggest that undisclosed testing of workers' bodily fluids might violate their rights and that employers may need specific consent for invasive genetic testing.

A QUARTER OF LAND, A CACHE OF CASH, AND HUMAN SPLEEN: LAW AND THE SALE OF SELF

In some respects, what I do with my "inviolable" self is my business as long as it does not hurt anyone else and as long as I know I'm doing it. If I choose to be part of a Jenny Jones panel on "People Who Secretly Love Their Sisters' Husbands' Best Friends' Stepmothers," well, presumably, that's my business.[19] More likely, and on a more sober note, if, as a condition of employment, I "voluntarily" submit to genetic testing that, too, is my decision. So, the question becomes, are there any limits to what I can do with myself?

There are, perhaps, obvious "yeses" to the question, though because this is the law with which we are dealing, even the seemingly obvious may have edges of ambiguity. Most apparent, we may not, by virtue of the Thirteenth Amendment, sell ourselves into slavery.[20] Nor, except in parts of Nevada,[21] may we sell our bodies for sex,[22] although thanks to the miracles of modern communications technologies, presumably we may sell our disembodied selves for the purposes of titillating anonymous others (see, e.g., *Sable Communications v. FCC*, 492 U.S. 115 (1989)).[23] Nor, according to the laws of most states, may we commit suicide, although here, as we shall see in the next chapter, the law is in considerable flux and may be at its most equivocal.[24]

If I may not sell myself (nor, presumably, mutilate myself to the point of extinction), may I, in the alternative, sell parts of myself? As the law stands now, the answer is—as it often is in law—yes and no. Some parts of myself I may sell in some jurisdictions; others I may not.

Recall in chapter 7, the couple advertising for the tall, intelligent, athletic, genetically unblemished egg donor in, among other "ivy" papers, the *Harvard Crimson*. Put another way, the couple was attempting to buy, for a cool $50,000, some human eggs, the product of a human body. No doubt, most readers will find this excessive and not a little distasteful and disquieting. Some may even find it morally and ethically repugnant. Legally, however, it is perfectly okay. Hence, at present, none of the states or the federal government prevent the buying and selling of sperm and eggs. Typically done through the brokerage of fertility clinics, a sperm "donor" can expect to receive roughly $50.00 for his service and product, while an egg "donor" would generally be compensated in the neighborhood of $2,000 for hers[25]—because of the time, pain, and uncertain future health risks involved, a good deal more compensation than her male counterpart, but a far cry from the $50,000 mentioned above. Although clinics and providers alike refer to these transactions as "donations," in reality, the sperm and eggs are treated, at least economically, as commodities for sale on an open market. Indeed, in some instances, brokers do not even bother with the pretense of "donation," as "Ron's Angels" clearly demonstrates. New to the world of web commerce, "Ron's Angels" is dedicated to auctioning the eggs of "beautiful, healthy and intelligent" models at starting bids of "$15,000–$150,000 in $1,000.00 increments."[26]

The law may kick in where sperm and egg have already come together creating a human embryo. Presently, eleven states and the District of Columbia forbid or limit the sale of embryos.[27] The state of Florida, for example, makes it a crime to "knowingly advertise or offer to purchase or sell, or purchase, sell, or otherwise transfer, any human embryo for valuable consideration" (Fla. Stat. § 873.05 (1998)).

Perhaps, obviously, a major reason underlying state regulation of embryos, as opposed to sperm or eggs, has to do with the larger national divide over abortion and the beginning of life. However, legally, there is another crucial distinction to be made between sperm and eggs, on the one hand, and embryos, on the other. The former fall under the category of biologically regenerative tissue, while the latter, the product of a particular coupling, may be considered nonregenerative. In a larger sense—a sense that goes well beyond reproductive technologies—this is the critical legal differentiation in the permissible sale of body parts. Indeed, almost all states permit the sale of "human by-products such as blood, blood products, hair, in vitro preparations of human cells, sperm, ovum and other bodily tissues that are readily renewable by the human body." Such body parts are considered "regenerative," and, moreover, their transfer for pay "is viewed by state law [if not by the individual and the marketplace] as the provision of a service instead of the sale of a good . . . " (Banks 1995, 73–74).

Thus, while one may sell away any number of bodily bits and pieces, the law does draw a line. But, that line may be bright or rather blurry depending upon jurisdiction. Hence, while all states strictly limit the sale of nonregenerative organs (livers, kidneys, lungs, and the like), some allow exceptions while others do not. For example, Maryland is one of several states that expressly forbids the "[b]uying, selling, or transporting" of organs from human bodies "alive or dead," with the exception of blood or plasma (Md. HEALTH-GENERAL Code Ann. § 5-408 (1998)). Georgia, on the other hand, while prohibiting the "buy[ing] or sell[ing] . . . , [the] offer[ing]

to buy or sell, or . . . [the] . . . assist[ing of] another in buying or selling or offering to buy or sell a human body or any part of a human body or . . . human fetus . . . ," excepting "self-replicating body fluids, or hair," nonetheless, allows the sale and purchase of organs for the express purpose of "health sciences education" (O.C.G.A. § 16-12-160 (1999)). In all states, a legitimate "donor" may be compensated, as in Georgia, "for actual expenses, including medical costs, lost income, and travel expenses" (O.C.G.A.), but though the terms are not always crystal clear and though exceptions are made, in general we can say that organ selling is legally taboo.[28]

Given the acute shortage of organs nationwide,[29] numerous commentators have questioned general policies prohibiting the sale of organs, attributing our apparent collective abhorrence over selling body parts to such factors as a "widely felt repugnance to the notion of trafficking in human flesh" (Cohen 1995, 24, quoted in Robinson 1999, 1020, n. 8) and the nation's "long and unhappy historical experience with slave markets" (Crespi 1994, 21, quoted in Robinson 1999, 1020, n. 8). But, if I possess proprietorship over myself, why should the law so widely prevent the marketing of *parts* of myself? The answer may lie in one of only a small handful of cases addressing the issue of body part ownership.

In 1976, John Moore was hospitalized at the UCLA Medical Center for blood work related to a diagnosis of hairy-cell leukemia. During his stay, hospital personnel withdrew "extensive amounts of blood, bone marrow aspirate, and other bodily substances" (*Moore v. Regents of the University of California*, 51 Cal. 3d 120, at 125; 793 P.2d 479 (Supreme Court of California, 1990)). Several days later, Moore's attending physician, Dr. David W. Golde, recommended, as a life-saving measure, a splenectomy, the removal of Moore's spleen.

Before the operation, Golde and a university researcher, Shirley G. Quan, "'formed the intent and made arrangements to obtain portions of [Moore's] spleen following its removal' and to take them to a separate research unit. . . . These research activities 'were not intended to have . . . any relation to [Moore's] medical . . . care.' However, neither Golde nor Quan informed Moore of their plans to conduct this research or requested his permission" (*Moore*, at 126). At this time, "Golde [was] aware that 'certain blood products and blood components were of great value in a number of commercial and scientific efforts' and that access to a patient whose blood contained these substances would provide 'competitive, commercial, and scientific advantages'" (at 126). After the operation, Moore was told that he had to return to the medical center for subsequent blood, blood serum, skin, bone marrow aspirate, and sperm work, which he did, several times, between 1976 and 1983, traveling a great distance from his home in Seattle because he was told that the work could *only* be done at UCLA. On each occasion, unbeknownst to

Moore, his cells were being exploited for further research by Golde, Quan, and others.

In 1979, Golde established a cell-line from Moore's T-lymphocytes and thereafter, university "[r]egents applied for a patent on the cell line, listing Golde and Quan as inventors" (*Moore*, at 127). The venture turned out to be exceedingly profitable for all concerned—all concerned, that is, except Moore!

With the Regents' assistance, Golde negotiated agreements for commercial development of the cell line and products to be derived from it. Under an agreement with Genetics Institute, Golde "became a paid consultant" and "acquired the rights to 75,000 shares of common stock." Genetics Institute also agreed to pay Golde and the Regents "at least $330,000 over three years, including a pro-rata share of [Golde's] salary and fringe benefits, in exchange for . . . exclusive access to the materials and research performed" on the cell line and products derived from it. On June 4, 1982, Sandoz [Pharmaceuticals Corporation] "was added to the agreement," and compensation payable to Golde and the Regents was increased by $110,000. "[T]hroughout this period, . . . Quan spent as much as 70 [percent] of her time working for [the] Regents on research" related to the cell line (at 127–28).

Moore, not surprisingly, sued, claiming that Dr. Golde and others had violated their fiduciary duty to disclose relevant facts requiring his consent *and* claiming that he had been deprived of his own property—his own genetic material—without his authorization. The decision of the California Supreme Court was, frankly, amazing.

Although the court ruled in favor of Moore's first claim, holding that a physician must disclose personal interests, such as research or economic interests unrelated to a patient's health that may affect his medical judgment, it ruled against him on the issue of ownership. Thus, Judge Panelli, writing for the California high court, reasoned that the usual laws of property do not apply to bodily organs or byproducts. Rather, apparently, our bodily interests are regulated by other statutory law:

[T]he laws governing such things as human tissues, transplantable organs, blood, fetuses, pituitary glands, corneal tissue, and dead bodies deal with human biological materials as objects sui generis, regulating their disposition to achieve policy goals rather than abandoning them to the general law of personal property. It is these specialized statutes, not the law of conversion, to which courts ordinarily should and do look for guidance on the disposition of human biological materials (*Moore*, at 137; citations omitted).

The legislature, reasoned the court, has good reason to make this distinction, since, among other things, to lump body parts under the general law of property might relegate biological materials to unsafe hands (at 141) and, more important, would inhibit "socially useful activities, such as researchers who have no reason to believe that their use of a particular cell sample is, or may be, against a donor's wishes" (at 143). The bottom line, at least according to the most extensive legal discussion to date, is that while we may sell some of our body parts and byproducts, they do not, for legal purposes, constitute real property and we do not necessarily own them, at least once they've been removed from us! Put another way, by another court, "A man's sperm or a woman's ova or a couple's embryos are . . . unique form[s] of 'property,' not the same as a quarter of land, a cache of cash, or a favorite limousine" (*Hecht v. Superior Court of Los Angeles*, 50 Cal. App. 4th 1289, at 1295 (Court of Appeal of California, 1997)).

IF I CAN'T OWN MY SPLEEN, CAN I OWN MY THOUGHTS ABOUT SPLEENS? LAW AND INTELLECTUAL PROPERTY

Just as injury to self may be physical or nonphysical, principles of sale may involve physical or nonphysical "property." This is very much a part of one's identity or concept of self. In recent years, a considerable body of law has developed around the concept of "intellectual property," "[p]roperty that can be protected under . . . law, including copyrightable works, ideas, discoveries, and inventions. Such property would include novels, sound recordings, a new type of mousetrap, or a cure for a disease."[30] Hence, Moore may not have owned the byproducts of his body, but Dr. Golde, under the law of intellectual property, could own the byproduct of the byproducts of Moore's body. Go figure.

Of course, notwithstanding the particular jurisprudence of the *Moore* case, under different circumstances—circumstances in which Dr. Golde had honestly and in a timely fashion informed Moore of his research agenda—we would probably all want the good doctor to receive something for the cell line he developed. The cell line was, after all, the result of *his* many years of intellectual training, *his* intellectual creativity, *his* considerable intellectual skill, and *his* hard intellectual work—in other words, something that the law might well view as *his* intellectual property.

Generally speaking, what we today refer to as "intellectual property" is an amalgam of three longstanding areas of law: copyright, patent, and trademark. Copyright is governed primarily by the U.S. Copyright Law (17 U.S.C. §§ 101–810), which, in turn, is derived directly from the U.S. Constitution, Article I, section 8, giving Congress the power to "promote the progress of science and useful arts, by securing for limited times to authors and inventors the exclusive right to their respective writings and discoveries." The U.S. Copyright Office, a division of the Library of Congress, implements the law (see generally, lcweb.loc.gov/copyright/). Copyright protects the works of writers and artists giving them exclusive rights of publication or exclusive rights to determine who shall publish their works.[31] The law applies to "any tangible medium of expression, now known or later developed," and encompasses works of literature, music, drama, pantomimes, choreography, pictures, graphics, sculptures, motion pictures and other audiovisual works, recordings, software, and architecture (17 U.S.C. at § 102). Currently, an author's work is "protected from the moment of its creation and is ordinarily given a term enduring for the author's life plus an additional seventy years after the author's death" (U.S. Copyright Office 1999, 5).

Patents and trademarks, too, are under the auspices of the federal government, specifically, the U.S. Patent and Trademark Office (PTO), an agency of the Department of Commerce (see generally, www.uspto.gov/). A patent for an invention is the grant of a property right to the inventor, issued by the PTO. The term of a new patent is twenty years from the date on which the application for the patent was filed in the United States or, in special cases, from the date an earlier related application was filed, subject to the payment of maintenance fees. U.S. patent grants are effective only within the United States, U.S. territories, and U.S. possessions (U.S. Patent and Trademark Office 1995). Like copyright, patent law is constitutionally derived.[32] Under current law, any person who "invents or discovers any new and useful process, machine, manufacture, or composition of matter, or any new and useful improvement thereof, may obtain a patent" (35 U.S.C.S. § 101 (1999)).[33]

A trademark is a "word, phrase, symbol or design, or combination of words, phrases, symbols or designs, which identifies and distinguishes the source of the goods or services of one party from those of others" (USPTO 1995). Unlike copyrights, which are currently granted for life plus seventy years, or patents for twenty, "trademark rights can last indefinitely if the owner continues to use the mark to identify its goods or services. . . ."[34] For example, as long as McDonald's continues to use its Scottish prefix to identify everything from its recipe for cooking chicken flesh to its particular configuration of playground equipment, the "Mc" belongs to it.[35] "Federal registration is not required to establish rights in a mark, nor is it required to begin use of a mark. However, federal registration can secure benefits beyond the rights acquired by merely using a mark" (USPTO 1995).

As you might imagine, given the ancient constitutional lineage, a vast body of case law has developed around intellectual property—far too vast to cover in these pages.[36] However, some principles and problems—particularly, of modern vintage—are worth mention.

For instance, one of the most important limitations to copyright is found in the doctrine of *fair use*. Although you are accorded ownership of your original work, others may reproduce it, free of charge, under limited circumstances and for a series of limited purposes (17 U.S.C.S. §§ 107–118), including "criticism, comment, news reporting, teaching, scholarship, and research" (U.S. Copyright Office 1998). The limits of fair use are very unclear, are constantly evolving, and have been the

subject of numerous lawsuits over the years. Take for example, the case of the "Pretty Woman."

Certainly to members of the baby-boom generation, one of the more familiar rock ballads was Roy Orbison's 1964 recording of "Oh, Pretty Woman," a song in which the male singer innocently fantasizes about meeting an attractive woman he has just seen "walkin' down the street." Orbison and coauthor, William Dees, assigned their rights to Acuff-Rose Music which, in turn, registered the song for copyright protection.

We now fast-forward to 1989. In that year, Luther Campbell (a.k.a. "Luke Skyywalker"), leader of the then-popular rap group, 2 Live Crew, wrote and produced a song entitled "Pretty Woman." Where Orbison's version was an innocent romantic paean to the ideal woman of the author's dreams, Campbell's version conveyed an utterly repulsive prostitute, the object of crude and misogynistic sexual suggestion.[37] Sung to a dissonant version of Orbison's original tune, Campbell clearly meant his "Pretty Woman" to be a parody of the earlier work. Indeed, 2 Live Crew informed Acuff-Rose about the parody offering to give full credit for ownership and authorship of the original song to Acuff-Rose, Dees, and Orbison, and offering to pay a fee for the use they wished to make of it. When Acuff-Rose refused to give the rap group permission, it went ahead regardless and released CDs, cassettes, and records of "Pretty Woman" on the album "As Clean As They Wanna Be."

Within a year, the album had sold almost a quarter of a million copies and Acuff-Rose sued for copyright infringement. At trial, the U.S. District Court judge found in favor of defendant, Campbell, citing fair use doctrine, but the Sixth Circuit reversed, reasoning that the "blatantly commercial purpose [of the Campbell song] . . . prevents this parody from being a fair use" (*Campbell v. Acuff-Rose Music*, 510 U.S. 569, at 574 (1994), citing 972 F.2d 1429, at 1439). The U.S. Supreme Court disagreed.

According to Justice Souter, writing for the Court, "From the infancy of copyright protection, some opportunity for fair use of copyrighted materials has been thought necessary to fulfill copyright's very purpose, 'to promote the Progress of Science and useful Arts . . .'" (at 575). Parody, according to Souter, does fit this niche:

[P]arody has an obvious claim to transformative value. . . . Like less ostensibly humorous forms of criticism, it can provide social benefit, by shedding light on an earlier work, and, in the process, creating a new one (at 579).

Although the Court stopped short of enunciating a truly sweeping rule—"fair use," it noted, must necessarily be judged on a case-by-case basis—it did articulate a general, if hardly a "bright line," rule for fair use in parody: "[T]he more transformative the new work, the less will be the significance of other factors, like commercialism, that may weigh against a finding of fair use" (at 579).[38]

Parody or no, music has been at the heart of a great deal of modern intellectual property litigation. A good bit of the battle here has revolved around an issue near and dear to the hearts of many college students, downloading music off the Internet—a practice put in the less flattering terms of "online *piracy*" by the music industry and many artists (see Recording Industry Association of America 1999). In general, from the point of view of the industry and its recording artists, the problem arises when unauthorized sites using compression technology provide recordings online. Personal computer users are then able to download and play the music without permission from, or compensation to, the artists or record labels. The music industry believes that the practice is costing it a fortune. Artists believe that they are being robbed of their individual accomplishments. In any event, we have here a classic conflict pitting individual liberty against individual attainment.

Responding to industry concerns, in 1997 Congress specifically made such practices illegal (*No Electronic Theft (NET) Act*, Pub. L. 105-147), but, of course, policing the law is another problem altogether—sites can go up and down easily and identifying and confiscating illegal hard copy is difficult at best. Hence, as one alternative strategy, the industry has gone after so-called MP3 recording devices, digital audio compression algorithms that make audio files "smaller" by a factor of twelve to one without significantly reducing sound quality. The industry has been keen to regulate, reduce, or eliminate the use of MP3s because

[b]y most accounts, the predominant use of MP3 is the trafficking in illicit audio recordings, presumably because MP3 files do not contain codes identifying whether the compressed audio material is copyright protected. Various pirate websites offer free downloads of copyrighted material, and a single pirate site on the Internet may contain thousands of pirated audio computer files (*Recording Industry of America v. Diamond Multimedia Systems*, 1999 U.S. App. LEXIS 13131, at LEXIS *4 (United States Court of Appeals for the Ninth Circuit, 1999)).

Hence, in the late 1990s, the Record Industry Association of America (RIAA) decided to wage a litigation assault against MP3s. Its chosen target, Diamond Multimedia Systems, develops and manufactures the Rio, a portable MP3 device, along with the Rio Manager, software that allows users to download files to the Rio itself via a parallel port cable that plugs the Rio into the computer. Claiming that Rio failed to meet the copyright requirements for digital audio recording devices under the *Audio Home Recording Act of 1992* (AHRA) (17 U.S.C.S. at 1001 et seq. (1999)),[39] RIAA sought to enjoin the manufacture and distribution of Rio.

In a highly technical decision, but one which represented a huge blow to the industry, a unanimous Ninth Circuit panel ruled that Rio was not a "digital audio recording device" subject to the rules and limitations of AHRA. "[T]o be a digital audio recording device," the court ruled, "the Rio must be able to reproduce, either 'directly' or 'from a transmission,' a 'digital music recording'" (*Recording Industry of America v. Diamond Multimedia Systems*, 1999 U.S. App. LEXIS 13131, at LEXIS *10–11 (United States Court of Appeals for the Ninth Circuit, 1999)). Because the Rio does not *directly* reproduce digital music, it does not fall within the ambit of AHRA.[40] On the contrary, the court continued, "Rio's operation is entirely consistent with the act's main purpose—the facilitation of personal use. . . . The Rio merely makes copies in order to render portable, or 'space shift,' those files that already reside on a user's hard drive. . . . Such copying is paradigmatic non-commercial personal use entirely consistent with the purposes of the act" (at *20–21).[41]

Music makers, however, have far from given up the legal battle. Lately, the industry and artists have targeted song swap software companies trading in MP3 files, along with networks that abet their use. One such suit was filed in federal court in 2000 by the heavy metal rock band, Metallica, against Napster, Inc., the University of Southern California, Yale University, and Indiana University. Metallica claims that Napster and the universities encourage users to trade songs and recordings without the band's permission. While, by spring 2000, Napster had become wildly popular with students, according to Metallica drummer, Lars Ulrich, "It is . . . sickening to know that our art is being traded like a commodity rather than the art that it is. The trading of such information—whether it's music, videos, photos, or whatever—is, in effect, trafficking in stolen goods" (Reuters News Service 4 April 2000).[42]

The industry and artists scored a substantial victory against Napster in 2001 when a number of record companies and entertainment conglomerates charged the swap site with "contributory and vicarious copyright infringe[ment]" (*A&M Records v. Napster, Inc.*, No. 00-16401, U.S. Court of Appeals for the 9th Circuit (2001)). As a result of this lawsuit, Napster is now required to prevent customers from exchanging files within three days after record labels ask the site to remove them from its search index. Whether this signals the death knell for Napster and other swap sites is, at this writing, uncertain.

Online challenges to intellectual property are hardly limited to audio appropriations. Indeed, the Internet has not only added new twists to such old problems as music piracy, but has created whole new categories of its own. Take, for example, the wholly web-based phenomenon of domain names. Names, of course, are crucial to establishing and retaining identity. Domain names are integral parts of Internet identity, each name consisting of at least two parts: the "top level," which constitutes the far-right part of the address and indicates the type of organization, and the "second level" which usually identifies the entity maintaining the website (Brown 1999, 248; see also, Chase 1998, 3). Thus, a top-level domain might read ".edu," indicating an educational organization,[43] while the second level would indicate the organization itself—say, "towson" (for Towson University) or "umd" (for the University of Maryland, College Park). For organizations that maintain websites, the second-level domain is the crucial one, the one that allows easy, identifiable, and memorable access by potential students, clients, or consumers. It is, for example, greatly to the advantage of Towson University that current and potential students need only type in www.towson.edu, just as Pizza Hut benefits from www.pizzahut.com/ and the president from www.whitehouse.gov/. Domain names must be registered for use at a small annual fee and no two names may be alike,[44] and here is where the problems have arisen.

"Cybersquatting," for instance, is the practice of buying up domain names for the $70 annual fee, knowing that the "second level" is trademarked by or strongly associated with some other entity and then selling the domains back to the associated organizations, often at exorbitant prices. For example, imagine that the authors, in addition to their academic day jobs, manufactured and sold a particularly successful line of widgets under the trade name, Catoshgets (obviously, McWidget would be a catchier name, but that's another story, right?). Imagine further that we had been slow (professors generally are) in getting our product up on the web. For a little more than pocket change, a forward-thinking cyber squatter could register catoshgets.com. The upshot: When we finally get around to putting up a page, we find our obvious and desirable address has been taken and if we want it, it's gonna cost us a whole lot more than $70.[45]

In order to address the problem, aggrieved entities have relied on the *Federal Trademark Dilution Act of 1995* (FTDA) (15 U.S.C.S. § 1125 (1999)). Where, under previous trademark infringement legislation, a litigant had to prove "consumer confusion," under FTDA, "The owner of a famous mark [is] . . . entitled . . . to an injunction against another person's commercial use in commerce of a mark or trade name, if such use begins after the mark has become famous and causes dilution of the distinctive quality of the mark . . . " (at (c) (1)). In other words, the law makes it easier to stop trademark encroachments. Although FTDA does not specifically mention domain names, "supporters felt the Dilution Act would function as a weapon to prevent trademark infringement on the Internet" (Brown 1999, 247). Indeed, overall those claiming trademark infringement seem to be winning the litigation wars.

One such case began in 1995 when Panavision, a supplier of motion picture equipment, attempted to register a website as Panavision.com. Much to the corporation's chagrin, however, it was unable to do so because Dennis Toeppen had already registered such a site, using it to display his photographs of the city of Pana, Illinois. When Panavision contacted Toeppen about the matter, he "offered to 'settle the matter' if Panavision would pay him $13,000 in exchange for the domain name" (*Panavision v. Toeppen*, 141 F.3d 1316, at 1319 (U.S. Court of Appeals for the Ninth Circuit, 1998)). After Panavision refused Toeppen's demand, he registered Panavision's other trademark, Panaflex, as a domain name, and employed that site simply to display the word "Hello."[46]

Although Toeppen argued that his use of the trademarked name in his domain name did not constitute a commercial use under the meaning of FTDA, the Ninth Circuit disagreed. Noting that "Toeppen's argument misstates his use of the Panavision mark," the court used the occasion to make a potentially broader statement about cybersquatting. Toeppen's use, the court asserted, "is not as benign as he suggests":

[His] "business" is to register trademarks as domain names and then sell them to the rightful trademark owners. He "acts as a 'spoiler,' preventing Panavision and others from doing business on the Internet under their trademarked names unless they pay his fee." . . . Toeppen traded on the value of Panavision's marks. So long as he held the Internet registrations, he curtailed Panavision's exploitation of the value of its trademarks on the Internet, a value which Toeppen then used when he attempted to sell the Panavision.com domain name to Panavision (at 1375 (citations omitted)).

In short, Toeppen was in violation of FTDA (see also, *Avery Dennison Corporation v. Sumpton*, 999 F. Supp. 1337 (United States District Court for the Central District of California, 1998)).[47]

Although litigation has tended to favor those claiming infringement, the cost of winning can still be very expensive. As a result, Congress is now in the process of amending trademark protection once again, this time, specifically aimed at domain names. Hence, the *Intellectual Property and High Technology Technical Amendments Act of 2001* (S. 320, 107th Cong., 1st sess. (2001)), as the Senate bill is currently called, would make civil action involving the registration, trafficking, or use of a domain name easier to win. Moreover, toward further discouraging cybersquatting in the first place, the bill increases the statutory damages available.[48]

Although domain name disputes tend mostly to involve aggrieved corporations, these corporations are, for many *legal* purposes, just like us, individual entities (see *Santa Clara County v. Southern Pacific Railroad*, 118 U.S. 394 (1886)). Critical to the identity of any individual entity is its—her, his—name. This is true whether we take "name" in its most literal sense to mean the tag "Sue Smith" or "John Johnson" or "General Motors."[49] Or, if we take "name" in the less tangible sense of *good* name or reputation. In either case, the law is there and in either case, as the foregoing suggests, our identities may be caught up in the pull-and-tug between the forces of liberty and order.

FALSE IDENTITY AND IDENTITY THEFT: THE PROBLEM
OF PHONY IDS AND CREDENTIALS ON THE INTERNET

While we tend to think of identity as a long developmental process, beginning at birth and progressing in a slow, deliberate linear fashion through old age, clearly, a part of the American experience is built on the notion that identity can be reinvented—sometimes abruptly, and even radically. Our greatest of all literary protagonists, Huckleberry Finn, was continually conjuring up creative identities for himself as he traveled the Mississippi and as necessity dictated. Our Horatio Alger tradition tells us that the poor self can be refashioned into the rich self. Today, increasingly, we turn to chemicals and surgeries that we hope will remake our depressed selves into happy selves, our fat selves into skinny selves, our sagging selves into firm selves, our bald selves into hairy selves, and our impotent selves into virile selves. Whether such reinventions are good or bad, they are quintessentially American, they presumably do no harm to others, and they are lawful.

Not all self-reinventions, however, are so socially harmless. When an individual reinvents himself or even steals another's identity for the purpose of defrauding others, we clearly draw the line. Hence, unlike Huck Finn, whose multiple identities arose from the need for self-preservation, boyish adventure, and even, at turns, heroism, his antagonists, the villainous King and Duke, employed self-invention for fraudulent purposes, ultimately paying the price in a good dose of tar and feathers. While we no longer exact that particular price for fraud, imprisonment and fines await those so caught today. The problem, however, is in the catching and it is a problem growing by leaps and bounds thanks largely to the Internet.

Thus, the Internet has made obtaining false identification and identity theft a relatively easy enterprise. According to Senator Susan Collins (R-ME), chair of the Permanent Subcommittee on Investigations,

The high quality of the counterfeit identification documents that can be obtained through the Internet is astounding. With little difficulty, my staff was able to use Internet materials to manufacture convincing IDs that would allow me to pass as a member of our armed forces, a reporter, a student at Boston University, or as a licensed driver in Florida, Michigan, and Wyoming, to name just a few of the identities I could assume. . . . Web sites . . . offer a vast and varied product line, ranging from driver's licenses to military identification cards to federal agency credentials, including those of the Federal Bureau of Investigation and the Central Intelligence Agency. Other sites offer to produce Social Security cards, birth certificates, diplomas. . . . Some Web sites sell fake IDs complete with state seals, holograms, and bar codes to replicate a license virtually indistinguishable from the real thing. Thus, technology now allows Internet site operators to copy authentic identification documents with an extraordinary level of sophistication and then mass produce those fraudulent documents for their customers. These counterfeit identification documents are relatively easy to manufacture. With only a

modest understanding of the Internet and $50.00 worth of supplies purchased from an arts and crafts store, one can design authentic-looking identification documents within a few hours, or even minutes (Collins 2000).

At first blush, all this would seem rather easy to resolve. Law enforcement, presumably, could simply prosecute the purveyors of such documents. Prosecution, however, is far from easy. In the first place, fake ID sites attempt to insulate themselves from the law by claiming that the documents they produce (or allow their users to produce) are merely available for fun and entertainment, not for fraud. Take, for example, "Best Fake Ids.com," which purports to sell templates for "fun novelty IDs" (www.bestfakeids.com/ [accessed 23 May 2000]). These "fun" identifications include, among many others, drivers licenses, gun licenses, back stage passes, journalist credentials, and educational certificates and diplomas. While the enterprise emphasizes the aspects of "novelty" and "fun" (presumably, there's nothing quite so "fun" as a fake gun license!), with a wink and a nod, it simultaneously promises a product "so realistic that you could fool your own mother." Indeed, the site includes the following bold guarantee:

Get a job as a Resident Activity Coordinator GUARANTEED—good jobs are so hard to find and the system doesn't make it any easier. For those of you who don't have a clue what a Activity Coordinator is, it's a person who plans all of the activities for individuals in nursing homes, or pre-school children. To receive a certificate you must take a course that runs about a thousand plus dollars. The price on the course varies depending on your area. Click on the link above to view our certification certificates.

Why, after all, pay "a thousand plus" and the drudgery of classroom hours when a few minutes and $39.97 will turn the trick?

In addition to the fun and novelty subterfuge, such Internet activity is particularly impervious to capture. Site operators who fear the law may be on their trails simply shut down, reappearing in a new guise elsewhere on the web. Or, as the subcommittee staff found, "In one case, . . . a fake-ID website [with an] American operator listed his address and phone number in one Asian country and made it appear that his e-mail address originated from a country in the South Pacific" (Mayer 2000). Thus, forces of order face substantial jurisdictional hurdles in dealing with this growing problem.

Law and Identity: Group Identity

American law fundamentally deals with identity in another crucial sense as well. After all, the identity game may, and usually does, involve multiple players. We tend to identify with those who share certain essential aspects of our identities, certainly not our shaving habits and probably not our precise names, but very often our gender, racial heritage, economic class, sexual orientation, and disability status, to name but a few group classifications. This transference of individual identity to group identity is nothing less than the factional impulse that Madison tells us is "sown in the nature of man." Moreover, as discussed in chapter 3, it was toward controlling the deleterious effects of factions—the tendency for factions to fight, to try to crush other weaker factions—that our system of law was structured. It was, as we have seen, a sweeping attempt to manipulate human nature toward its betterment.

As we all know, however, as broad as the sweep was, at the beginning, its beneficial aspects were narrowly confined to a small proportion of the populace. America's largest minority populations were either enslaved or removed to small, inhospitable "homelands." Political rights and liberties were confined to a single gender and, for several decades, to a relatively small economic strata. Political rights and liberties, in other words, were based on status and wealth identity. In time, though, the law had to respond to those factions left out of the original plan.

Because the role of law in recognizing, facilitating, and mediating modern group identity is largely the realm of civil rights politics and policy, a thorough discussion is better left to any one of the hundreds of casebooks, political analyses, and historical accounts that cover this vast landscape either in its entirety or in its discrete parts. Ours, then, will be but a brief and very particularized exploration and overview. We begin with a summary of law's recognition of group identity generally, briefly reiterating the Madisonian principle and subsequent group-directed legal developments. We then briefly review the role of law in one of the many groups with which individual Americans might identify: racial groupings. Although law has had crucial implications for other group identities (to note only the most obvious, gender,[50] class,[51] disability status,[52] and sexual orientation[53]), race has been chosen here because in many important respects law actually *created* this identity.

Groups in Law: An Overview

Of course, as Madison saw it, group formation was (and is) inevitable. Put in terms of identity, we all have "sown" in our very "nature" the impulse to associate with—to characterize ourselves in terms of—one or several groups. But, while the urge to group identity is natural, all of the consequences of that urge are not necessarily good. Indeed, according to Madison, my tendency to identify with one group may well set me in opposition to other groups, and oppositional groupings are the stuff of conflict, repression, warfare, and chaos.

Thus, recall that at its most primal (in the American context, primal being the constitutional structure set up in 1787), American law—with all its separation, checks, and balances—attempts to reconcile incipient group conflict. It attempts to bring order to what, unregulated, would otherwise be the bedlam of faction. The system, needless to say, has not been perfect. One need only point to that greatest of national rendings, the Civil War. For what, after all, was that war but a coalition of Northern, industrial, abolitionist factions opposing, on blood-drenched battlefields, a coalition of Southern, agricultural, slaveholding factions?

After the Civil War ended, the law stepped in again. The charter law that made order—through union, checks, and federalism—hadn't been strong enough. More glue—glue in the form of a constitutional amendment, the Fourteenth—was needed to bring uniformity to factious impulses across states. And it was this legal adjunct, with its promise of *state*-provided due process and *state*-afforded equal protection that ultimately permitted many factions, previously without voice, the chance to partake of the law itself.[54] It did not happen overnight, nor without considerable struggle, nor without a great deal more law—law, frequently, judicially rendered. Our system—the Madisonian system—favors, in the first instance, legislative activity. Groups (a.k.a. factions) place demands on legislators who, in turn, create statutory law, the product of compromise and conciliation. Presumably, the structure and process of the legislature are such that the group with "the most"—hopefully, the most popular backing or the most socially beneficial claim, but, often, the most organization or the most money—will get most of what it wants, but not to the extent that other groups get nothing at all. The structure and process ostensibly are designed to give the majority ("the most") what it wants, while protecting minorities from political obliteration. This is the essence of a democratic republic.

But, of course, in order to place demands on the legislature, you need to get in the front door—you need to be able to access the structure and process through which your demands can be heard and acted upon. Historically, some groups have been met with a well-sealed legislative front door. What then? Well, the "what then" was also suggested, if not always utilized, in the structure of our "limited Constitution . . . which contains certain specified exceptions to the legislative authority. . . . " (Hamilton, *Federalist* #78). One such exception, according to no less than Alexander Hamilton, is an independent judiciary, without which "all the reservations of particular rights or privileges would amount to nothing." Legislatures *can* do wrong things: they *can* "occasion dangerous innovations in the government," they *can* enact "unjust and partial laws," and they *can* bring about "serious oppressions of the minor party in the community." Against such "infractions of the Constitution . . . and the occasional ill humors in the society . . . the independence of the judges may be an essential safeguard. . . . "

Some would certainly argue—and many could attest—that for certain "minor parties" solicitude from, much less access to, even the judiciary historically did little to "stem serious oppressions." Just ask Dred Scott (*Dred Scott v. Sanford*, 60 U.S. 393 (1857))[55] or Homer Plessy (*Plessy v. Ferguson*, 163 U.S. 537 (1896))![56] But, clearly, the possibility existed and eventually, one might say, the courts recognized their special constitutional "duty," as Hamilton put it (Hamilton, *Federalist* #78). They recognized it, for instance, in the unlikely venue of a footnote to a case examining *The Filled Milk Act of 1923*, noting that "prejudice against discrete and insular minorities may be a special condition, which tends seriously to curtail the operation of those political processes ordinarily to be relied upon to protect minorities, and which may call for a correspondingly more searching judicial inquiry" (*U.S. v. Carolene Products*, 304 U.S. 144, at 153, fn. 4 (1938)). In other words, bias against some groups may be so great that they cannot get in that legislative front door short of judicial interference. As Justice Brennan put it twenty-five years later:

[Group] litigation is not [merely] a technique of resolving private differences; it is a means for achieving the lawful objectives of equality of treatment.... [Litigation] is thus a form of political expression. Groups which find themselves unable to achieve their objectives through the ballot frequently turn to the courts. And under the conditions of modern government, litigation may well be the sole practicable avenue open to a minority to petition for redress of grievances (*NAACP v. Button*, 371 U.S. 415, at 429–30 (1963)).

These were judicial invitations to another door. And, modern groups have RSVP-ed accordingly, sponsoring test cases, filing supportive amicus briefs, and working to change rules of standing to apply actual personal injury criteria to large, legally amorphous parties.[57] The result has been a sea change over the course of the twentieth century in the way that the law views group identity and the way that group identifiers view the law.

Law and Race

Three races, naturally distinct, and, I might almost say, hostile to each other, are discoverable among them at the first glance. *Almost insurmountable barriers had been raised between them by education and law*, as well as by their origin and outward characteristics, but fortune has brought them together on the same soil, where, although they are mixed, they do not amalgamate, and each race fulfills its destiny apart (de Tocqueville 1835: chapter XVIII).

Nowhere has this been more true than in the relationship between race and law. Note above, de Tocqueville's early nineteenth-century observations on the "three races"—as he described them, the "white European," the "Negro," and the "Indian." Note further, and very significantly, his assertion that law was the edifice upon which "almost insurmountable barriers" had been

raised. Law and race—indeed, "race law"—has been part and parcel of our nation's history. W. Haywood Burns offers one particularly egregious example from our mid-history: "In 1855 white men sitting in the Kansas legislature, duly elected by other white men, passed a law that sentenced white men convicted of a rape of a white woman to up to five years in prison, while the penalty for a black man convicted of the same offense was castration, the cost of the procedure to be rendered by the desexed" (Burns 1998).

LAW AND AFRICAN AMERICANS

Of course, in one way or another, the law recognized race much earlier. Even the Constitution, in apportioning representatives and taxes, explicitly recognized one race (Indians were excluded) and euphemistically acknowledged another as "three fifths of all other Persons" (African slaves included for these purposes) (*U.S. Constitution*, Article 1, Section 2). Indeed, much of seventeenth-, eighteenth-, and nineteenth-century law was about stripping the very human identity from the enslaved Africans and African Americans. At best, much of law and many lawmakers sought to categorize—to identify—blacks as "distinct." Thus, did the author of the nation's very loftiest "truth"—"that all men are created equal"—reason that

blacks, whether originally a distinct race, or made distinct by time and circumstances, are inferior to the whites in the endowments both of body and mind. It is not against experience to suppose, that different species of the same genus, or varieties of the same species, may possess different qualifications (Jefferson 1787, query XIV).

In the case of the enslaved African people, these "different qualifications" resulted in a kind of hybridized status, with the law viewing them, according to Madison,

in the mixed character of persons and of property. This is in fact their true character. It is the character bestowed on them by the laws under which they live; and it will not be denied, that these are the proper criterion; because it is only under the pretext that the laws have transformed the negroes into subjects of property, that a place is disputed them in the computation of numbers; and it is admitted, that if the laws were to restore the rights which have been taken away, the negroes could no longer be refused an equal share of representation with the other inhabitants (Madison, *Federalist* #54).[58]

Although the post–Civil War Amendments (the Thirteenth, Fourteenth, and Fifteenth) were supposed to remedy the legal divide, the law continued to differentiate according to racial identity. After Reconstruction, statutes, ordinances, and party bylaws in the South (Jim Crow) relegated blacks to less than full citizenship status. In the north, zoning laws, legislative distribution of educational resources, military segregation, and lending practices had many of the same results. That these laws might ultimately have an insidious effect on the very character—the very identity—of the group differentiated was acknowledged by the Supreme Court when it asserted, in 1954, that "[t]o separate [black children] from others of similar age and qualifications solely because of their race generates a feeling of inferiority as to their status in the community that may affect their hearts and minds in a way unlikely ever to be undone" (*Brown v. Board of Education*, 347 U.S. 483, at 494 (1954)). Such was the very intimate and complex (and, in this case, devastating) relationship between legal status and identity.

If the law "taketh away," it may also "giveth"—or, at least, it may be used as an instrument for remediating that which was taken in the first place. With the raft of civil rights judicial decrees, legislation, and executive orders following only too slowly the Court's 1954 desegregation ruling, the law attempted to undo the identity damage it had wreaked for hundreds of years. The solution to the legally reinforced "feeling of inferiority," ultimately accepted by all three law-giving branches during the second half of the twentieth century, was integration of the races. In identity terms, not only was legal integration seen as a way of diminishing one group's "feeling of inferiority," but

[t]his integrationalist vision seems to reflect, at the ideological level, the occasional glimpses we attain in personal relations of a deep shared identity as fellow human beings in what are often the very best moments of social life. The aspiration for racial integration confirms our sense of the possibility of true and authentic relations that transcend racial status and other forms of cultural distance and difference. And integrationism appeals to the utopian ideal that those moments could be translated into organized institutional practices because, at the core, we are all the same, "regardless of race" (Peller 1990, 775).

Throughout the 1960s, 1970s, and 1980s, in particular, the push to legally integrate the races moved well beyond the Court's mid-century pronouncement that "[s]eparate educational facilities are inherently unequal" (*Brown v. Board of Education*, at 495). The following year, the Court ordered desegregation to take place "with all deliberate speed" and deployed its own small "army" of southern district court judges to make sure it happened (*Brown v. Board of Education (Brown II)*, 349 U.S. 294, at 301 (1955)).[59] It did not happen speedily. After all, judges, as Hamilton assured us, have "no influence over either the sword or the purse; no direction either of the strength or of the wealth of the society; and can take no active resolution whatever" (*Federalist* #78). At the very least, they need some support—support which did not begin to crystallize until the executive sword holders sent military troops into the South[60] and the legislative purse keepers began tightening the money strings against recalcitrant segregationists.[61]

Thereafter, toward the legal goal of integration, courts ordered and approved public school–based plans from busing (see *Swann v. Charlotte-Mecklenburg Board of Education*, 402 U.S. 1 (1971))[62] to magnet programs (see for one of many examples, *Vaughns v. Board of Education of Prince George's County*, 574 F. Supp. 1280 (U.S. District Court for the District of Maryland, 1983)).[63] Congress outlawed discrimination in public accommodations,[64] employment,[65] housing,[66] and voting.[67] Executive pronouncements and orders mandated affirmative action in hiring and promotion.[68]

THE LAW OF "WHO'S WHO": DISCRIMINATION, ANTI-DISCRIMINATION, AND LEGAL DEFINITIONS OF RACE

The legal gains, hard fought and won by the African American community, while widely accepted in broad principle, have often been contentious in particular detail. Clearly, this has been the case with affirmative action and busing.[69]

In part, as Christopher A. Ford puts it, the controversies may have to do with the way that law "administer[s] identity" (Ford 1994, 1231). Take for example, the modern case of the "Mixed-Up Malones," an affirmative action controversy that landed in the lap of a Massachusetts state judge in 1989 (*Malone v. Haley*, No. 88-339 (Sup. Jud. Ct. Suffolk County, Mass., July 25, 1989)).[70] The dispute had its origins in 1975 when Paul and Philip Malone, twin brothers, tested for jobs with the Boston Fire Department. Having scored poorly, they were rejected. Undaunted, two years later, the twins tried again. This time, however, the "fair-haired and light-skinned" brothers self-identified as black, and the department, under a court-ordered affirmative action program designed to remedy past discrimination, hired the Malones based on this identification. Thereafter, the brothers spent ten presumably happy years as Boston firefighters.

Legal problems began brewing in 1987 when the brothers applied for promotion to lieutenant. On physical appearance, a hearing officer declared that the Malones were not black and had, in fact, falsified their earlier applications in violation of state personnel rules. Not only were the twins not promoted, they were fired. They appealed the decision, noting that in 1977, the department relied on racial self-identification and claiming that they should continue to be considered black for hiring and promotion purposes.

Judge Herbert Wilkins relied on a "three-part test for adjudicating claims to racial identity" (Ford 1994, 1233). The Malones, he asserted,

might have supported their claim to be Black[:] (1) by visual observation of their features; (2) by appropriate documentary evidence, such as birth certificates, establishing Black ancestry; or (3) by evidence that they or their families hold themselves out to be Black and are considered to be Black in the community (quoted in Ford 1994, 1233).

The Malones, the judge held, met none of these criteria.

The judicial rendering here is important, not because most, or even many, people are wont to purposely fake a racial identity, but, rather, because, as the Fifth Circuit put it, "figures speak and when they do, Courts listen" (*Brooks v. Beto*, 366 F.2d 1, at 9 (U.S. Court of Appeals for the Fifth Circuit, 1966)). The fact of the matter is that much of "[m]odern anti-discrimination law depends fundamentally upon statistical showings of minority group under-representation" (Ford 1994, 1234). Discrimination and its remediation in employment, education, and voting, for example, is "often only provable through statistics" (p. 1235). Racial identification is thus very important.

While such legal-statistical identifications may be relatively clear and easy in some cases, they can be murky indeed in other areas—areas such as race. As Ford (p. 1239) puts it:

While sex is (arguably) a dichotomous variable, race is nothing of the sort. "Biologically it is a continuous variable, or, to be precise, a series of variables, most of which are continuous. A person's racial identity is largely a social phenomenon, rather than a biological one."

And, Ford might have a noted, a *legal* phenomenon.

For not only do we identify racially, but the law identifies us racially. Indeed, this has been the case for a long, long time—so long, in fact, that it is difficult to tell whether our self-identifications today are the result of our factious natures or are mere artifacts of centuries-old legal classifications. Consider the case of Homer Plessy in 1896.

In shorthand form, Plessy's case is best known by students today as generating the Supreme Court's infamous "separate but equal" doctrine, a legal tenet finally discarded by the Court in 1954. Plessy was denied a "white" seat on a Louisiana train because, as we all know, he was "black." Or, was he black? Plessy himself said, "no." Indeed, his argument, in the first instance, was "that [his small] mixture of colored blood was not discernible . . . , and that he was entitled to every right, privilege and immunity secured to citizens of the United States of the white race . . ." (*Plessy v. Ferguson*, 163 U.S. 537, at 541 (1896)). Louisiana law, however, said otherwise. Under that state's complex statutory schema, simplified in terms of the "one drop" rule, Plessy's genetic legacy—he contained "seven eighths Caucasian and one eighth African blood" (at 541)—made him legally black.

Nor was Louisiana the only American state to pass racial identification laws. They were pervasive. In some states, "any visible admixture of black blood stamp[ed] the person as belonging to the colored race."[71] In others, the law "depend[ed] upon the preponderance of blood."[72] In still others, "the predominance of white blood [needed] only be in the proportion of three fourths."[73] Unquestionably, legislatures and courts spent a lot of time and a long time legally classifying white

against black. As the poet Langston Hughes put it as late as 1953,

[J]ust one drop of negro blood makes a man colored. One drop you are a negro. Now why is that? Why is Negro blood so much more powerful than any other kind of blood in the world? If a man has Irish blood in him people will say "He's part Irish." If he has a little Jewish blood they'll say "He's half-Jewish." But if he has just a small bit of colored blood in him—bam! He's a negro! Not just part negro. No, be it ever so little if that blood is black, he's a negro (Hughes 1953, 85).

Here, Hughes was speaking not in the language of poetry, but in the language of law! Thus, in important respects, we keep racial identification statistics today as a means of ameliorating the legally based racial identifications of yesterday.

LAW AND NATIVE AMERICANS

In the observation cited at the beginning of this section, de Tocqueville referred to the existence in early America of three races. As discussed above, one of the racial identifications made by the young French aristocrat was "the Negro." De Tocqueville himself, of course, belonged to that race which, in *his* words, was "pre-eminently so called . . . the MAN . . . , the white or European. . . ." The third was "the Indian."

The nexus between American law and the nation's indigenous people is a complex labyrinth of treaty obligations, congressional statutes, and tribal rule (for a good general summary, see Canby 1987). Native American tribes are considered "sovereign entities with inherent powers of self-government, [but] subject to exceptionally great powers of Congress to regulate and modify the status of tribes" (p. 3).

Identity is a central feature of this legal web. Thus, in order to be federally recognized, tribes must construct identity rules and Native Americans wishing to affiliate with a tribe must conform to the rules (Padget 1997, 391). Over time, these identity rules have become increasingly racial. According to Cindy Padget, "The concept of 'Indian,' especially tribal identity, has evolved in American history from one of self-identity, including cultural, community, and political communalities . . ." (p. 393). Such "self-identity" was characteristic before the coming of Europeans. According to Mark Neath, however, "In contrast to Indian self-identity before contact with the Europeans, most tribes now accept an explicitly racial conception of tribal identity for purposes of tribal membership" (Neath 1995, 691). Hence, tribal membership today is generally premised on "blood quantum" (p. 699), requiring tribal participants to have flowing in their veins a certain proportion of tribal blood or to have been born on the reservation. For example, the Jicarilla Apache Constitution limits tribal membership to "persons of three-eighths or more Jicarilla Apache Indian blood . . . whose mother or father is a member of the

Jicarilla Apache Tribe" (p. 699).[74] Significantly, where "in the past two hundred years . . . race-based conception[s] of tribal identity [were] often imposed on Indians by the federal government, today tribes voluntarily invoke race-based definitions of 'Indian' because they narrow the pool of tribal members . . . " (p. 699). The reason, not surprisingly, has its basis in law—law with profound economic implications.

Thus, identification is crucial to tribes in gaining certain federal benefits. More significant, though, tribalization along racial lines has been abetted by the *Indian Gaming Regulatory Act* (IGRA), which provides for the operation of gaming by Indian tribes as a means of promoting tribal economic development (25 U.S.C. §§ 2701–21). Indeed, gaming on reservations, free of most federal and state taxes, has been an economic boom for some tribes and a powerful economic lure for others. Because, under IGRA, tribes must use revenues either for public purposes or for distribution to members on a per capita basis (e.g., members of California's Agua Caliente tribe each receive "a monthly check for about $2,000—a figure that could rise dramatically in the future" [Booth 2000, 18]), the strong incentive is for tribes to define themselves racially more and more narrowly (Neath 1995, 697). Thus, with passage of IGRA, claims of tribal identity became "suddenly popular, not just with ersatz members but with pedigreed Native Americans who had left their communities years ago in search of better opportunities" (Annin 1994, 44). Ultimately, then, "'Indianness' [has become] not a self-actualizing concept of tradition and history, but rather a rigid legal term of art . . . " (Padget 1997, 394). Currently, the Bureau of Indians Affairs (BIA) recognizes 556 tribal entities eligible for funding and services (BIA 2000). Of these, 160 tribes in twenty-four states have entered into gaming compacts (BIA 1999).

While this tendency toward narrow racial categories has an immediate economic upside, many Indians worry about the longer-range downsides:

What the National Congress of American Indians recognized in 1986 is just as true today: strict blood quantum definitions of "tribe" and "Indian" have pernicious effects and pose a fundamental dilemma. On the one hand, tribes need to sustain economic growth and protect their limited gaming resources from Indian "wannabes." A strict blood quantum requirement serves this purpose by excluding many potential tribal members. On the other hand, if tribes maintain blood quantum requirements for tribal membership, they face two likely consequences: population decline and increased federal encroachment on tribal sovereignty (Neath 1995, 698).

LAW, STATISTICS, AND RACIAL IDENTITY: CENSUS POLITICS AT THE TURN OF THE CENTURY

The issue of race classifications is once again, at the turn of the century, at the center of political debate and legal consequence. Because of America's growing mixed-race and -ethnic population, a movement has taken shape to eliminate racial classifications or, at the very least, to allow multiple classifications in legal paperwork.[75] Although the campaign has met with some legislative success,[76] it has met with considerable resistance as well, because "[m]ost civil rights and advocacy groups . . . oppose . . . multiracial classification[s] out of concern that [they will] dilute the numbers of people who identify with a particular race" (Fiore 1997, A1). Thus, according to opponents of multiracial classifications:

If you're lobbying [for multiracial classifications], that's all well and good, but put it in some kind of historical and contemporary context. We still collect statistics on race because racism still exists and all the statistics that we collect on race serve to monitor that, to protect against housing discrimination, employment discrimination (Lisa Jones quoted in Sconiers 1994, 15A).

The legal identity stakes have been at their highest recently over changes to the U.S. Census Bureau's method of collecting race data, data that ultimately are pivotal to federal and state program administration, benefit allocations, and civil rights compliance surveillance. For the past several decades, Census respondents have been confined to identifying themselves with a single racial/ethnic category: for example, American Indian or Alaska Native; Asian; Black or African American; Hispanic or Latino; Native Hawaiian or Other Pacific Islander; or White. Multirace activists, along with their congressional proponents, pushed to have a separate "multiracial" variable included in the 2000 Census. Civil rights groups argued for maintenance of distinct racial classifications. As a compromise, but one that has left many still dissatisfied, the Bureau began, with the 2000 Census, allowing respondents to choose more than one racial/ethnic category (Office of Management and Budget 1999).

From the obviously insidious "one-drop" rules to the presumably beneficial ethnicity categories found on countless late-century forms, the law has fostered, if not created, racial identity. Here, we can clearly see law's tendency toward order. Nineteenth-century and early-to mid-twentieth–century racial classifications were designed to segregate, to pigeonhole, to stereotype. But, if the law's role is to perform the dual functions of preserving order while maintaining liberty, here the law failed miserably—preserving a truly pernicious order at a terrible cost to liberty. Law's continuing efforts at racial identification are latter-day attempts to redress the imbalance, but they remain controversial.

Conclusion

In this chapter, we have explored the role of law and identity. Our identities—that which we feel as our inner selves and that which we project to the outside world—are developed over a lifetime—in part by our own wills, in part by outer forces, including law. Regardless of impetus, however, we expect law to protect these identities from assault or, at the very least, to aid us, if need be, in rectifying damage done, whether that damage be physical or reputational. We expect it to liberate our individual selves from harms that go to the core of our beings by placing limits on (by ordering) what others may do to us or take from us.

Hopefully, most of us will live out our identities without major harm, free to develop ourselves over many decades, for, in important respects, our identities live on long after we are gone. Thus, we work on our identities until the end of life. It is to the role of law at the end of life that we turn in the next chapter.

Law on the Web

Identity, both individual and group, is an intrinsic part of the web of law and society. It is also, in its many legal manifestations, a huge part of the World Wide Web. In this chapter, we have addressed a number of issues involving the "individual" self, including the need for self ownership, privacy, and reputational good name. Below is a small sample of websites dealing with these issues.

A Smattering of Privacy Sites

The Electronic Privacy Information Center
www.epic.org/privacy/

The Privacy Rights Clearinghouse
www.privacyrights.org/

American Civil Liberties Union, Privacy Rights Page
www.aclu.org/privacy/

A Smattering of Intellectual Property Sites

U.S. Patent and Trademark Office
www.uspto.gov/

U.S. Copyright Office
lcweb.loc.gov/copyright/

Stanford University Libraries, Copyright and Fair Use, A Searchable Data Base
fairuse.stanford.edu/

*   *   *

As part of his course offerings, Professor James Boyle of Washington College of Law, American University, maintains an excellent site, much of which is devoted to intellectual property. Professor Boyle is the author of *Sha-*

mans, Software and Spleens: Law and Construction of the Information Society (1996).
james-boyle.com/

ONLINE INTELLECTUAL PROPERTY JOURNALS

Intellectual Property and Technology Forum
www.bc.edu/bc_org/avp/law/st_org/iptf/

Journal of Intellectual Property
www.kentlaw.edu/student_orgs/ipls/jip/jip.html

Intellectual Property Law Review
www.mu.edu/law/ipwebpage/iplawrev.html

Intellectual Property Law Journal
ubmail.ubalt.edu/~ubiplj/

Journal of Intellectual Property Law
www.lawsch.uga.edu/~jipl/

Intellectual Property Magazine
www.ipmag.com/

Intellectual Property Today
www.lawworks-iptoday.com/

*   *   *

Not surprisingly, the factional impulse has proliferated on the web. Below are some interest group websites. The list is not meant to be exhaustive, but merely exemplary (literally thousands of groups maintain sites on the web). Note that because these sites are maintained by advocacy groups, much of the information contained within them is partisan in nature. Note also that for a variety of reasons we have tended to concentrate on what might be termed the more "mainstream" of these groups (i.e., those which, no matter how much you may disagree with their politics, work within the framework of the legal system).

A Smattering of Racial Identity Organizations

National Association for the Advancement of Colored People (NAACP)
www.naacp.org/

The National Urban League
www.nul.org/

The American Indian Movement (AIM)
www.aimovement.org/

National Congress of American Indians
www.ncai.org/

League of United Latino American Citizens (LULAC)
www.lulac.org/

National Council of La Raza
www.nclr.org/

Committee of 100
www.committee100.org/

Addresses issues concerning the Chinese American community.

Japanese American Network
www.janet.org/

A Smattering of Women's Organizations

National Organization for Women (NOW)
www.now.org/

American Association of University Women
www.aauw.org/index.html

National Women's Political Caucus
www.nwpc.org/

Independent Women's Forum
www.iwf.org/

An anti-feminist group.

A Smattering of Class-Based Organizations

LABOR

AFL-CIO
www.aflcio.org/

United Auto Workers
www.uaw.org/

International Brotherhood of Teamsters
www.teamster.org/

United Mine Workers of America
www.access.digex.net/~miner/

American Federation of State, County, and Municipal Employees
www.afscme.org/

Communications Workers of America
www.cwa-union.org/

United Farm Workers
www.ufw.org/

American Federation of Teachers
www.aft.org//index.htm

LaborNet
www.labornet.org/

BUSINESS

The Business Roundtable
www.brtable.org/

U.S. Chamber of Commerce
www.uschamber.org/

POVERTY

Association of Community Organizations for Reform Now (ACORN)
www.igc.org/community/

National Association of Community Action Agencies
www.nacaa.org/

National Law Center on Homelessness & Poverty
www.nlchp.org/

A Smattering of Gay Organizations

The Human Rights Campaign
www.hrcusa.org/

National Gay and Lesbian Task Force
www.ngltf.org/

A Smattering of Disability Rights Organizations

American Association of People with Disabilities
www.aapd.com/

American Disability Association
www.adanet.org/

A Smattering of Animal Rights Organizations

Animal Legal Defense Fund
www.aldf.org/

Animal Rights Resource Site
www.animalconcerns.org/

People for the Ethical Treatment of Animals
www.peta-online.org/

American Society for the Prevention of Cruelty to Animals
www.aspca.org/

9 Law and the End of Life

We come at last to that part of life about which few of us like to think. Although the therapist may encourage us to "face up to it," and the financial analyst may warn us to "plan for it," most of us prefer to push it to the deep recesses of our consciousness. After all, to "face up to" or to "plan for" death is to acknowledge its inevitability, something few of us are willing to dwell on—and the younger we are the less apt we are to do so.

Not so the web of law; indeed, as we shall see, issues surrounding the very inevitable end of life make up a large and, with the graying of the baby boom generation, a growing segment of the web.[1] Like Shelley's "traveler," the law moves with us from "cradle to grave" (Shelley 1820).

In this chapter, we explore law at the end of life. We begin by reviewing law's modern role in making the last days, months, and years of life's journey more comfortable. Next, we contemplate the nexus between law and life's physical end, including technologies that try to keep life going longer and longer and the legal ability (or inability) we have to end life when pain or despair make continuation unbearable. Finally, we briefly describe law's very ancient concern with the end in questions surrounding the distribution of property, debts, and taxes.

Law in the Golden Years: Modern Concerns of Old Age

While the treatment of the aged in this Nation has not been wholly free of discrimination, such persons, unlike, say, those who have been discriminated against on the basis of race or national origin, have not experienced a "history of purposeful unequal treatment" or been subjected to unique disabilities on the basis of stereotyped characteristics not truly indicative of their abilities. [O]ld age does not define a "discrete and insular" group in need of "extraordinary protection from the majoritarian political process." Instead, it marks a stage that each of us will reach if we live out our normal span (*Massachusetts Board of Retirement v. Murgia*, 427 U.S. 307, at 313–14, 1976 (*per curiam*); citations deleted from original).

The *Murgia* Court came about as close to defining "old age" as one will find in American case law. It is simply the inevitable endgame of life that "each of us will reach if we live out our normal span." As discussed in chapter 6 within the context of early life and childhood, age demarcations are inherently subjective and arbitrary. This is equally true with regard to the other end of life's continuum. For legal purposes, age is both quite deter-

minate (one can calculate in years, months, days, even seconds) and indeterminate. It is not clear when a child is no longer appropriately considered a child; nor is it any more clear when a person crosses the threshold to become elderly. In *Murgia*, the Court addressed a Fourteenth Amendment equal protection challenge to a Massachusetts law that set that threshold for uniformed police offers at age fifty, mandating retirement from the force for all who reached that milestone. Significantly, the justices determined that age, unlike race, is not a "suspect classification," and that the state need only demonstrate a rational basis for making age-related distinctions. The Court reasoned: "Through mandatory retirement at age 50, the legislature seeks to protect the public by assuring physical preparedness of its uniformed police. Since physical ability generally declines with age, mandatory retirement at 50 serves to remove from police service those whose fitness for uniformed work presumptively has diminished with age. This clearly is rationally related to the State's objective" (*Murgia*, at 314–15). (Only Justice Marshall dissented from this view, finding instead that the state's argument was entirely irrational.)

Some fifteen years later, the Court considered a similar challenge to a Missouri constitutional provision mandating retirement of all judges at age seventy.[2] Although a bit more divided, a majority reached a similar conclusion: "The Missouri mandatory retirement provision, like all legal classifications, is founded on a generalization. It is far from true that all judges suffer significant deterioration in performance at age 70. It is probably not true that most do. It may not be true at all. But a State 'does not violate the Equal Protection Clause merely because the classifications made by its laws are imperfect'. . . . The people of Missouri rationally could conclude that the threat of deterioration at age 70 is sufficiently great, and the alternatives for removal sufficiently inadequate, that they will require all judges to step aside at age 70. This classification does not violate the Equal Protection Clause" (*Gregory v. Ashcroft*, 501 U.S. 452, at 473 (1991), quoting *Murgia*, at 316).

The Court reiterated this logic in one of the set of opinions delivered at the turn of the twenty-first century. In *Kimel v. Florida Board of Regents*, Justice O'Connor, writing for a 5–4 majority, stated: "Our Constitution permits States to draw lines on the basis of age when they have a rational basis for doing so at a class-based level, even if it 'is probably not true that those reasons are valid in the majority of cases" (120 S. Ct. 631, 647 (2000)).[3]

What Is Old Age?

While age is generally measured in years, it is more than objective chronological fact. To be classified as young or old is in part an individualized subjective perception, a set of expectations about the collective future, and a function of the contemporary socioeconomic milieu. Thus, what is understood as old age is a changing phenomenon and social reality. For example, upon his visit in the 1830s, de Tocqueville observed, among many other things, that the short average life expectancy of the period, about thirty-five years, produced a population that was restless, full of bravado, and willing to take high risks for the thrill of the moment.

Their taste for physical gratifications must be regarded as the original source of that secret disquietude which the actions of the Americans betray and of that inconstancy of which they daily ford fresh examples. He who has set his heart exclusively upon the pursuit of worldly welfare is always in a hurry, for he has but a limited time at his disposal to reach, to grasp, and to enjoy it.

The recollection of the shortness of life is a constant spur to him. Besides the good things that he possesses, he every instant fancies a thousand others that death will prevent him from trying if he does not try them soon. This thought fills him with anxiety, fear, and regret and keeps his mind in ceaseless trepidation, which leads him perpetually to change his plans and his abode (de Tocqueville 1835, Book II, Chapter 13).

Indeed, there was no reason to delay gratification, because death was a constant threat to all who survived birth. The threat of death, of course, haunts us all, but the time horizon for those who lived in the early 1800s was short by today's standard, and most people had little reason to conjure up a long-term life strategy. No doubt, it was precisely that kind of perspective and expectation that led Alexander Hamilton and Vice President Aaron Burr to a fateful dueling field in 1804. Left dead at the ripe old age of forty-nine, Hamilton had long surpassed the expected life-span of his birth cohort. In fact, he outlived his own son who had also been killed in a duel three years earlier.

By the turn of the twentieth century, the average American citizen could expect to live about forty-seven years. This was a statistically significant improvement, but socially not a profound one for the vast majority of the population. Life was hard. Childbirth was risky, childhood was short, and adolescence was nonexistent. Tuberculosis, scarlet fever, smallpox, polio, influenza, and other infectious diseases swept through the population in waves, and only the very strong, the very lucky, and the very wealthy survived into what today we would consider old age. The census of 1900 indicates that a rather small minority, 4 percent (or about 3.1 million people), of the American population was sixty-five or older.

The first half of the twentieth century saw general conditions improve with advances in sanitation, housing, and overall economic well-being. Moreover, treatment of infectious diseases became much more effective. As a result, people were living longer. In 1940, the ranks of the sixty-five and older population had swelled to 9 million, and by 1950 average life expectancy had increased to sixty-eight years.

Quality of life continued to improve during the latter half of the twentieth century, with growing economic prosperity, great strides in nutritional and medical research, more successful treatment of chronic diseases (such as cancer and heart disease), and the like. As a consequence, average life expectancy has risen steadily to about seventy-seven years in 2000. On the other end of the spectrum, the infant mortality rate has decreased dramatically. Indeed, since 1950, the infant mortality rate has dropped from 29.2 (per 1,000 live births) to just over seven. This means that more people survive the first year of life, and a higher percentage of each birth cohort live to middle age and beyond. By the year 2000, the sixty-five and older contingent of the population had climbed to 34.7 million and is projected to bulge to 53.2 million by 2020 as the baby boomers of the 1950s reach that milestone. Considering the issue from a slightly different perspective, during the twentieth century, the number of persons in the United States under age sixty-five tripled; while the number aged sixty-five or over increased by a magnitude of eleven, from 4 percent to about 16 percent of the total population. Meanwhile, the grayest of the gray, those eighty-five years old or more, now represent the fastest-growing group among the nation's elderly.

Suffice it to say that old age was not the issue in the nineteenth century that it has become—socially, economically, politically, and legally. As the *Murgia* Court noted, "physical ability generally declines with age," and later in *Gregory*, the Court observed that we can expect to "suffer significant deterioration in performance" as we advance towards life's end. Thus, the twentieth-century Court, unlike its predecessors, could work from the assumption that "if we live out our normal span," we can all expect to experience significant deterioration in abilities and performance.

As we recounted above, the number of people for whom that assumption became a reality was increasing considerably by the 1920s, and as that happened, the elderly and their unique problems began to appear on the radar screens of policymakers. The social and economic convulsions produced by the Great Depression of the 1930s brought the elderly clearly into focus. Until then, people who lived into their sixties and beyond, and who had left the workforce and hence were no longer earning an income, relied upon a patchwork support system that included their friends and families, voluntary pension programs by some employers (for a select number of employees), and private charities, to provide a sufficient level of sustenance until their ultimate death. During the Depression, private pension systems were wiped out by the stock market crash, massive unemployment placed most families under extreme economic stress and unable to care for their elders, and charities were completely swamped. With no cash reserve and no reliable source of support, older workers fortunate enough to have jobs had no incentive to quit. Franklin Roosevelt was elected in a landslide in the presidential election of 1932 with a promise to address the mounting economic morass with quick and decisive action. On 8 January 1934, President Roosevelt announced his intention to provide for Social Security. The first step was to create, by executive order, a Committee on Economic Security, empowered to study the problems and devise a concrete set of legislative proposals. The Committee's recommendations were presented to Congress in January 1935, and the *Social Security Act of 1935* (SSA) was signed into law on August 14.[4]

The SSA created a trust from which disbursements would be made to older citizens (sixty-five years and over), funded by a payroll tax and employer contributions. The act was a major piece of the New Deal package, guaranteeing a security benefit to the nation's oldest citizens. It was designed also to produce an economic stimulus. Older workers would retire from their jobs, making room for younger, presumably more productive ones who desperately needed employment, and they would spend their Social Security checks, thus injecting new cash into the struggling economy.

Roosevelt's plan was not without its detractors, however, and the legislative enactment immediately triggered litigation. The act's opponents argued, among many other points, that Congress had violated its constitutional authority to create policy that would enhance the "general welfare" by extending benefits only to one segment of the population, old people, and that it had breached the Tenth Amendment power of the states to address social policy of this kind (see, e.g., Wolfskill 1962).[5]

Justice Cardozo, writing for the majority upholding the act's constitutionality, stated:

The purge of nation-wide calamity that began in 1929 has taught us many lessons. Not the least is the solidarity of interests that may once have seemed to be divided. . . . Spreading from State to State, unemployment is an ill not particular but general, which may be checked, if Congress so determines, by the resources of the Nation. . . . The hope behind this statute is to save men and women from the rigors of the poor house as well as from the haunting fear that such a lot awaits them when journey's end is near.

Congress did not improvise a judgment when it found that the award of old age benefits would be conducive to the general welfare. . . . Among the relevant facts are these: The number of persons in the United States 65 years of age or over is increas-

ing proportionately as well as absolutely. What is even more important the number of such persons unable to take care of themselves is growing at a threatening pace. More and more our population is becoming urban and industrial instead of rural and agricultural. The evidence is impressive that among industrial workers the younger men and women are preferred over the older. In times of retrenchment the older are commonly the first to go, and even if retained, their wages are likely to be lowered. . . . With the loss of savings inevitable in periods of idleness, the fate of workers over 65, when thrown out of work, is little less than desperate. . . .

The problem is plainly national in area and dimensions. Moreover, laws of the separate states cannot deal with it effectively. Congress, at least, had a basis for that belief. States and local governments are often lacking in the resources that are necessary to finance an adequate program of security for the aged. . . (*Helvering v. Davis*, 301 U.S. 619, at 641–44 (1937); notes deleted from original).

Thus, the SSA passed constitutional muster, and in 1940 the first benefits were paid to workers, sixty-five and older, who had retired. Although it has been amended a number of times since, usually to expand benefits, the legislation proved to be among the most politically popular and resilient policies of the twentieth century. By mid-century, the sixty-five–plus segment of the population, whose ranks had swelled to about 15 million, began to organize for the first time to promote their interests through the legislative process and through the courts.[6] In 1958, for example, the American Association of Retired Persons (AARP) was founded, and by the end of 1999, the organization could boast a membership of over 30 million.[7]

The SSA of 1935 is a significant landmark. First, it legally defined old age as beginning at sixty-five years. Thus, we were given a fixed legal definition of old age at a time when length of life has substantially increased, and when, from a range of other perspectives, the threshold marking senior status is clearly not fixed. Moreover, as Friedman (1984c, 9) has argued, by mandating retirement from the active workforce at age sixty-five in order to receive benefits, it was "an act of age discrimination," a matter that has been debated since the SSA was enacted and become increasingly heated as life expectancy has grown longer and people wish to keep working longer.

Thus, one of the primary targets of the AARP and affiliated organizations was age discrimination in employment, and their lobbying efforts soon began to bear fruit. By 1961, New York and California had added age discrimination to civil rights legislation prohibiting discriminatory hiring and firing practices with regard to race.[8] In 1964, the U.S. Congress enacted the *Older Americans Act* (OAA) as part of President Lyndon Johnson's Great Society program, and one of its stated objectives was to promote "opportunity for employment with no discriminatory personnel practices because of age."[9] The *Age Discrimination in Employment Act of*

1967 (ADEA) made it illegal for private-sector employers (with twenty-five or more employees) to refuse to hire, or to fire, a worker because of age.[10] In 1994, Congress amended the ADEA, extending coverage to all state and local governments (29 U.S.C. §§ 621 et seq. (1994 ed. and Supp. III)), which, as we observed above, the Supreme Court invalidated in *Kimel*, finding that state agencies need only demonstrate a rational basis for discriminating according to age.

Litigation claiming workplace age discrimination has been robust under ADEA; however, providing convincing evidence and demonstrating clear animus is inherently difficult (see, e.g., Crawshaw-Lewis 1996). For example, a company might legitimately choose not to promote or refuse to hire an older employee for salary reasons. To the employee, the result is discriminatory and the cost-saving rationale a mere pretext. Under the law it is not, unless there is evidence that the decision was predicated by intentional discrimination. The Supreme Court held salary and discrimination to be analytically distinct in *Hazen Paper Co. v. Biggins* (507 U.S. 604 (1993)), with the result being that executive employment decisions have been easier to defend. The Court also held that decisions based upon stereotyped characterization and expectation that disparage older workers are invalid under ADEA provisions. Again, however, clear evidence that employment decisions hinged upon discriminatory stereotypes is necessary. Age-related comments by a supervisor, referring to an employee as an "old fart," for example, are not of themselves sufficient to prove age discrimination.[11]

A second issue targeted by the AARP and other gray lobby organizations is medical care. As people live longer, the likelihood that they will require extended medical care and hospitalization increases substantially. Indeed, the growing ranks of the elderly translates into a considerable increase in the number of potentially infirm citizens with significant medical needs (see, e.g., Crimmins and Ingegneri 1993). In addition, the second half of the twentieth century witnessed a boom in the nursing home and hospice care industries. As the Supreme Court aptly noted in *Murgia*, "physical ability generally declines with age" (427 U.S. 307, at 315), and in *Gregory*, "the threat of deterioration at age 70 is ... great" (501 U.S. 452, at 473). Congress responded in 1965 with legislation establishing the Medicare (42 U.S.C. 1395 et seq.) and the Medicaid (42 U.S.C. 1396 et seq.) programs as Title XVIII and Title XIX, respectively, of the *Social Security Act*.[12]

The Medicare program (Title XVIII) was established with two parts, each with its own trust fund. One part was the Hospital Insurance (HI) program to cover hospital costs, and the Supplementary Medical Insurance (SMI) program covers expenses not covered by HI. Benefits under each program are extended to all who have participated in the Social Security system. Medicaid (Title XIX) was established as a federal–state matching entitlement program in response to the widely perceived inadequacy of "welfare medical care" under public assistance.

Medicaid was designed to ensure that low-income individuals and families would be provided with adequate care, and the program immediately became the largest source of funding for medical and health-related services for the nation's "have nots," many of whom are elderly. In 1996, for example, more than 36 million people received Medicaid benefits, at a cost of $160 billion dollars.[13]

Because each state sets its own standards and contingencies in order to administer the program under broad federal guidelines, the system has become a complex web of varying eligibility and benefit regulations.[14] Needless to say, the legislative extensions to the *Social Security Act*, intended to address the special health and medical needs that accompany advancing age, have made "eldercare" advocacy (both political and legal) a growth industry. Indeed, since 1965, a plethora of new lobbying organizations has become active across the state legislatures to promote expansion of the programs' coverage.

Moreover, the federal and state courts have been kept busy addressing a wide range of issues that have been produced by the programs' administration. Once the state has decided to institute a policy extending benefits, questions of eligibility quickly become nontrivial, and the state may not arbitrarily reduce or terminate benefits to those receiving them. These have been heavily litigated issues.[15] In addition, the government assumes some responsibility for guaranteeing an acceptable quality of medical and health care services and facilities, and each state has implemented an elaborate system of regulations. Finally, criminal law has come into play in response to serious incidents of fraud, false claims, reports, and the like. In short, the decision to extend medical benefits to the nation's elderly through the Medicare and Medicaid programs gave rise to a virtual cottage industry of lawmaking, litigation, and enforcement.

Law and the End of Life: Death and Dying

Just as the present technological revolution is jumbling our way of thinking about birth and life's inception, it is confusing our ideas about death. Where, as we suggested above, an average American in 1915 could expect to die at around age fifty, he may now expect to live until he is seventy-six.[16] These impressive gains in life expectancy result from a number of factors including better and more plentiful foodstuffs,[17] increased knowledge in the areas of nutrition,[18] health,[19] and exercise,[20] and much less dangerous living[21] and working[22] conditions than our forebears faced—all the result of law. They also result, of course, from stunning advances in medical technologies—technologies that can truly be double-edged swords. For while many are kept alive longer, many of those are not necessarily kept alive better. Just as the law is struggling to catch up with technologies that are redefining the beginning of life, it is scrambling to keep pace with technologies that are redefining the end of life. This section explores law's attempt to stake out territory in the "brave new world" of death. Here, we see very clearly, as much as, if not more than in any area we have investigated, the difficult role of law in maintaining the delicate balance between individual liberty and social order. For here, the question becomes does the individual or does society define the end of a person's life?

What Is Death?

As the law records your birth, so does it define your death—and has, for a long time. For over two hundred years, the common law definition of death was the "cessation of life, [the] permanent [irreversible] cessation of all vital signs."[23] Generally referred to as the cardiopulmonary definition of death, one's demise was legalized upon "the absence of pulse, heartbeat, and breathing" (Kibble-Smith 1985).

By the 1980s, medical developments had raced ahead of law sufficiently to make the mere lack of breath, pulse, and beating heart inadequate as a legal definition and prompting widespread adoption of a "whole brain death" delineation. Today, every state but New Jersey and New York employs some variation on the so-called "whole brain death" standard. Thus, for example, in addition to the "cessation of circulatory and respiratory functions," Maryland law adds the "[i]rreversible cessation of all functions of the entire brain, including the brain stem" (Md. Health-General Code Ann. § 5-202 (1999)).

But, who makes the "cessation" call? Under what circumstances is it made? Clearly, medical technology can keep the heart beating, the lungs respiring, the body feeding long after the person has ceased being able to do so on her own. Moreover, and notwithstanding the natural termination of life-sustaining functions, is life lived in excruciating pain or progressive loss of control life worth living? To whom does this decision fall? Over the past several decades, judges have often had to make these difficult calls.

Law and the Individual's Decision to Die

In many ways, law's modern brush with such quality of death issues began "[o]n the night of April 15, 1975, [when,] for reasons still unclear, Karen Quinlan ceased breathing for at least two 15 minute periods" (*In the Matter of Karen Quinlan*, 70 N.J. 10, at 23 (Supreme Court of New Jersey, 1976)). The lapses were critical and tragic, leaving Karen comatose and "in a chronic and persistent 'vegetative' state, having no awareness of any-

thing or anyone around her and existing at a primitive reflex level" (at 23). According to expert medical witnesses, she had lost the "more highly developed [part of the] brain which is uniquely human which controls our relation to the outside world, our capacity to talk, to see, to feel, to sing, to think" (at 24). Moreover, throughout a long hospital stay in intensive care, Karen was fed by way of a nasogastric tube and her breathing was assisted by way of a respirator, without which experts agreed she probably would not live long. Despite her condition and despite the fact that no form of treatment could cure or even improve her status, Karen's physicians and numerous medical experts contended that "removal from the respirator would not conform to medical practices, standards and traditions" (at 25). In purely biological terms, Karen was *not* "brain dead."

What experts, whether legal or medical, divine based on complex statutory criteria or scientific standards may be quite different from the layperson's simple emotional or sensory reaction. To Joseph Quinlan, the perpetually vegetative being whose life hung on the function of a respirator was no longer the daughter he had loved so much. His daughter was dead, and he wanted the wasted body that once housed her spirit and higher brain dead, too. Thus, Quinlan asked to be appointed his daughter's guardian. In addition, he requested that the grant of guardianship give him an express power to authorize the discontinuance of all extraordinary medical procedures that sustained Karen's vital processes. Quinlan argued that his daughter had a right, grounded in privacy interests, to refuse bodily intrusions such as the supposedly life-sustaining respirator. Further, he contended that in the absence of her own competency, her guardian, carrying out her pre-coma wishes, should be able to assert the right on her behalf.

A unanimous New Jersey Supreme Court agreed with Karen's father. "We have no hesitancy," the Court asserted, "in deciding . . . that no external compelling interest of the State could compel Karen to endure the unendurable, only to vegetate a few measurable months with no realistic possibility of returning to any semblance of cognitive or sapient life" (*Quinlan*, at 39). Relying particularly on *Griswold v. Connecticut*[24] and *Roe v. Wade*,[25] the New Jersey Court asserted an "unwritten constitutional right of privacy" in the U.S. Constitution, "[p]resumably . . . broad enough to encompass a patient's decision to decline medical treatment under certain circumstances, in much the same way as it is broad enough to encompass a woman's decision to terminate pregnancy under certain conditions" (*Quinlan*, at 40). The state's interest in "the preservation and sanctity of human life," according to the Court, "weakens and the individual's right to privacy grows as the degree of bodily invasion increases and the prognosis dims. Ultimately there comes a point at which the individual's rights overcome the State interest" (*Quinlan*, at 40–41). Karen's case, in the opinion of the Court, had clearly passed that point. Indeed, so clearly had it passed the point that Karen herself could no longer assert her interests. Thus,

If a putative decision by Karen to permit this non-cognitive, vegetative existence to terminate by natural forces is regarded as a valuable incident of her right of privacy, as we believe it to be, then it should not be discarded solely on the basis that her condition prevents her conscious exercise of the choice. The only practical way to prevent destruction of the right is to permit the guardian and family of Karen to render their best judgment, subject to the qualifications hereinafter stated, as to whether she would exercise it in these circumstances. If their conclusion is in the affirmative this decision should be accepted by a society the overwhelming majority of whose members would, we think, in similar circumstances, exercise such a choice in the same way for themselves or for those closest to them. It is for this reason that we determine that Karen's right of privacy may be asserted in her behalf, in this respect, by her guardian and family under the particular circumstances presented by this record (at 40–41).[26]

In spite of an increasing number of so-called "right-to-die" cases arising in the years following the *Quinlan* decision,[27] the U.S. Supreme Court avoided the issue for more than a decade until confronted in its 1989–90 term with the case of a young Missouri woman, Nancy Cruzan. Although the circumstances of her incompetency were less mysterious than those of Karen Quinlan's, Nancy Cruzan faced a very similar situation.

In 1983, Cruzan lost control of her car, the ultimate result being a "persistent vegetative state" of life (*Cruzan v. Director, Missouri Department of Health*, 497 U.S. 261, at 266 (1990)). Thereafter, Cruzan was kept alive by means of artificial nutrition and hydration. After concluding that their daughter would never regain her mental faculties, Nancy's parents sought court authorization for termination of the artificial procedures. Their request was granted by a Missouri State trial court, which found that Nancy "had a fundamental right under the State and Federal Constitutions to refuse or direct the withdrawal of 'death prolonging procedures.'"[28] Moreover, the trial court concluded that Nancy's conversations with a housemate some years earlier established her wish to terminate the procedures. The Missouri Supreme Court, however, disagreed, refusing to read a substantial right to privacy into either the federal or Missouri Constitutions, finding a strong state policy in favor of preservation of life embodied in the Missouri living will statute, and dismissing as "unreliable" Nancy's wishes as expressed to her former roommate (*Cruzan*, at 268). The U.S. Supreme Court granted *cert* to consider the question whether an individual, suffering circumstances such as those of Cruzan, has a right under the U.S. Constitution that would require hospitals to withdraw life-sustaining treatment.

Writing for a bare majority,[29] Chief Justice Rehnquist upheld the Missouri Supreme Court decision, reasoning that the state has a general interest in "the protection and preservation of human life," as well as more particular interests in safeguarding incompetents from potential abuses by surrogates. The "United States Constitution [does not] forbid . . . the establishment of [such] procedural requirement[s] by . . . State[s]"(*Cruzan*, at 280). In short, the Court deferred to states' determinations about the appropriateness of terminating treatment for incompetent patients. Moreover, it indirectly encouraged the use of "living will" documents as more determinative of patients' ultimate wishes than the sort of thoughtless conversations Cruzan had had with her housemate before the accident.

Nevertheless, the Court did recognize a longstanding common law right to refuse medical treatment (*Cruzan*, at 270). The Court, in addition, explicitly recognized a constitutionally protected "liberty interest" to refuse life-saving procedures. Indeed, according to the chief justice, had the case involved a competent individual, "we assume that the United States Constitution would grant [her] a constitutionally protected right to refuse lifesaving hydration and nutrition" (*Cruzan*, at 229). The question remained, however, does the right to refuse infer a right to die?

Just twenty-one days before the Supreme Court issued its *Cruzan* decision, in Michigan, fifty-four-year-old Janet Adkins "died of an injection of potassium chloride in the back of a 1968 Volkswagen camper van."[30] Adkins had been diagnosed with Alzheimer's disease and, according to her husband, wanted to die. She was assisted in her efforts by then little-known medical pathologist, Dr. Jack Kevorkian.

Of course, Dr. Kevorkian would become *very* well-known—indeed, a full-blown national celebrity—during the 1990s, as the country's foremost crusader and activist for legalizing assisted suicide. Through public appearances, writings (see especially, Kevorkian 1991), and, most especially, through often openly assisting in or presiding at more than one hundred deaths,[31] Kevorkian, to a large degree, single-handedly framed the "right-to-die" debate during the last decade of the twentieth century.

Despite his crucial public role, however, Kevorkian's actual legal influence was locally limited to Michigan, where he kept state prosecutors, judges, juries, and legislators extremely busy throughout the decade arresting, trying, and aiming legislation at him until finally managing to convict him of second-degree murder in 1999.[32]

While Kevorkian's exploits grabbed the public limelight, the campaign for a legal "right to die" proceeded on several fronts, leading, in 1997, to the U.S. Supreme Court. Two fact scenarios, two separate constitutional claims, and two circuit court opinions a continent apart led to the Court's first—and to date, only—set of rulings on physician-assisted suicide.

In Washington, four doctors and their gravely ill patients filed suit against the state, claiming that its ban on assisted suicide violated the due process clause by inhibiting the personal choices of mentally competent, terminally ill adults to commit physician-assisted suicide. The Washington plaintiffs won favorable rulings from a U.S. District Court (*Compassion in Dying v. Washington*, 850 F. Supp. 1454 (WD Wash. 1994)) and the Ninth Circuit (*Compassion in Dying v. Washington*, 79 F.3d 790, at 798 (1996), *en banc*)).

Meanwhile, in New York, a group of physicians and their patients challenged that state's ban on equal protection–clause grounds, claiming that New York's practice allowing one class of patients to hasten their deaths by directing the removal of life-support systems, while disallowing others wishing to hasten their deaths by self-administering prescribed drugs, accorded different treatment not rationally related to any legitimate state interests. There, a trial court ruled against the plaintiffs (*Quill v. Koppell*, 870 F. Supp. 78 (SDNY 1994)), but the Second U.S. Circuit agreed with their claim (*Quill v. Koppell*, 80 F.3d 716 (1996)).

The Supreme Court reversed both circuits. Thus, in the Washington case—arguably, the more important of the two—Chief Justice Rehnquist, writing for the Court, emphatically asserted:

The history of the law's treatment of assisted suicide in this country has been and continues to be one of the rejection of nearly all efforts to permit it. That being the case, our decisions lead us to conclude that the asserted "right" to assistance in committing suicide is not a fundamental liberty interest protected by the Due Process Clause (*Washington v. Glucksberg*, 521 U.S. 702, at 728 (1997)).

The high court having found no fundamental liberty interest, the state needed to demonstrate only that its ban was rationally related to legitimate government interests. According to the chief justice, the state had numerous such stakes, including:

an "unqualified interest in the preservation of human life.". . . [A]n interest in preventing suicide, and in studying, identifying, and treating its causes. . . . [A]n interest in protecting the integrity and ethics of the medical profession. . . . [A]n interest in protecting vulnerable groups—including the poor, the elderly, and disabled persons—from abuse, neglect, and mistakes. . . . [And, an interest in avoiding] the path to voluntary and perhaps even involuntary euthanasia (*Washington*, at 728–31).

In the New York case, too, the Court upheld the state bar on physician-assisted suicide, easily dismissing the equal protection claim. Again, the chief justice:

On their faces, neither New York's ban on assisting suicide nor its statutes permitting patients to refuse medical treatment treat anyone differently than anyone else or draw any distinctions between persons. Everyone, regardless of physical condition, is entitled, if competent, to refuse unwanted lifesaving medical treatment; no one is permitted to assist a suicide. . . . [W]e think the distinction between assisting suicide and withdrawing life-sustaining treatment, a distinction widely recognized and endorsed in the medical profession and in our legal traditions, is both important and logical; it is certainly rational (*Vacco v. Quill*, 521 U.S. 793, at 800 (1997)).

The effect of the Court's 1997 rulings was to leave in the hands of the individual states the decision to allow or ban assisted suicide. To date, states overwhelmingly have chosen to err on the conservative side of banning the practice. Hence, thirty-eight states explicitly criminalize assisted suicide by means of statute. Six other states and the District of Columbia may prosecute assisted suicides as common-law crimes. In five states, the law is unclear (Pratt 1999).

Only in Oregon is physician-assisted suicide a clearly legal option. The Oregon *Death with Dignity Act*[33] began in 1994 as a citizen initiative, passed by voters on a slim 51-percent majority. Implementation was delayed by court injunction until 1997 when a legislative referendum asking voters to repeal the act was rejected by Oregonians. The act allows terminally ill Oregon residents to use prescriptions obtained from their physicians for self-administered, lethal medications. Ending one's life in accordance with the law does not constitute illegal suicide. While legalizing physician assistance, the act specifically prohibits euthanasia, where a physician or other person directly administers a medication to end another's life.[34] In the first full year of its operation, twenty-three people received legal prescriptions for lethal medications, of which fifteen died after taking their lethal medications, six died from their underlying illness, and two remained alive.[35]

In reaction specifically to the Oregon legislation, in 1999, the U.S. House of Representatives passed *The Pain Relief Promotion Act of 1999* (H. R. 2260, 106th Cong., 1st sess.). The bill, on which the Senate has not acted as of this writing, would effectively overturn the Oregon death with dignity law by barring "doctors from using federally controlled drugs such as morphine to cause death" (Koch 1999).

Law and the State's Decision to End Life

Overwhelmingly, then, governments in the United States have constructed high legal barriers to willful death. At the same time, however, governments across the country have not been adverse to imposing death on the unwilling through capital punishment. Indeed, the vast majority of jurisdictions—thirty-eight states and the federal government—currently authorize the death penalty as punishment for certain crimes (see Tables 9.1 and 9.2).

Although a widespread statutory option throughout the nation, actual imposition of the death penalty is highly concentrated in five, primarily southern, states (see Table 9.3). Thus, throughout the twenty-one-year period from 1 January 1977—the year following the Supreme Court's reimposition of the death penalty (*Gregg v. Georgia*, 428 U.S. 153 (1976)) after a four-year hiatus (*Furman v. Georgia*, 408 U.S. 238 (1972))—to 31 December 1998, five hundred convicts in eighteen states were put to death. However, as seen in Table 9.4, nearly two-thirds of those executions occurred in Texas, Virginia, Florida, Missouri, and Louisiana (Snell 1999). (Both *Gregg* and *Furman* are discussed later in this chapter.)

American law's contemporary entanglement with state-sponsored death began in 1972 when the Supreme Court considered the cases of three indigent African American convicts sentenced to death in the states of Georgia and Texas (*Furman*). Two of the men had been convicted of rape; one was a murderer. At issue before the Court was whether the imposition and execution of the death penalty constituted "cruel and unusual punishment" within the meaning of the Eighth and Four-

---

Table 9.1. Capital Offenses by State

Alabama. Capital murder with a finding of at least 1 of 9 aggravating circumstances (Ala. Code §13A-5-40 and §13A-5-49).

Arizona. First-degree murder accompanied by at least 1 of 10 aggravating factors.

Arkansas. Capital murder (Ark. Code Ann. 5-10-101) with a finding of at least 1 of 10 aggravating circumstances; treason.

California. First-degree murder with special circumstances; train wrecking; treason; perjury causing execution.

Colorado. First-degree murder with at least 1 of 13 aggravating factors; treason. Capital sentencing excludes persons determined to be mentally retarded.

Connecticut. Capital felony with 9 categories of aggravated homicide (C.G.S. 53a-54b).

Delaware. First-degree murder with aggravating circumstances.

Florida. First-degree murder; felony murder; capital drug trafficking.

Georgia. Murder; kidnapping with bodily injury or ransom where the victim dies; aircraft hijacking; treason.

Idaho. First-degree murder; aggravated kidnapping.

Illinois. First-degree murder with 1 of 15 aggravating circumstances.

Indiana. Murder with 16 aggravating circumstances (IC 35-50-2-9). Capital sentencing excludes persons determined to be mentally retarded.

Kansas. Capital murder with 7 aggravating circumstances (KSA 21-3439). Capital sentencing excludes persons determined to be mentally retarded.

Kentucky. Murder with aggravating factors; kidnapping with aggravating factors.

Louisiana. First-degree murder; aggravated rape of victim under age 12; treason (La. R.S. 14:30, 14:42, and 14:113).

Maryland. First-degree murder, either premeditated or during the commission of a felony, provided that certain death eligibility requirements are satisfied.

Mississippi. Capital murder (97-3-19(2) MCA); aircraft piracy (97-25-55(1) MCA).

Missouri. First-degree murder (565.020 RSMO).

Montana. Capital murder with 1 of 9 aggravating circumstances (46-18-303 MCA); capital sexual assault (45-5-503 MCA).

Nebraska. First-degree murder with a finding of at least 1 statutorily defined aggravating circumstance.

Nevada. First-degree murder with 13 aggravating circumstances.

New Hampshire. Six categories of capital murder (RSA 630:1 and RSA 630:5).

New Jersey. Purposeful or knowing murder by one's own conduct; contract murder; solicitation by command or threat in furtherance of a narcotics conspiracy (NJSA 2C:11-3C).

New Mexico. First-degree murder in conjunction with a finding of at least 1 of 7 aggravating circumstances (Section 30-2-1A, NMSA).

New York. First-degree murder with 1 of 12 aggravating factors. Capital sentencing excludes persons determined to be mentally retarded.

North Carolina. First-degree murder (N.C.G.S. 14-17).

Ohio. Aggravated murder with at least 1 of 8 aggravating circumstances. (O.R.C. §§ 2903.01, 2929.01, and 2929.04).

Oklahoma. First-degree murder in conjunction with a finding of at least 1 of 8 statutorily defined aggravating circumstances.

Oregon. Aggravated murder (ORS 163.095).

Pennsylvania. First-degree murder with 18 aggravating circumstances.

South Carolina. Murder with 1 of 10 aggravating circumstances (§ 16-3-20(C)(a)). Mental retardation is a mitigating factor.

South Dakota. First-degree murder with 1 of 10 aggravating circumstances; aggravated kidnapping.

Tennessee. First-degree murder.

Texas. Criminal homicide with 1 of 8 aggravating circumstances (TX Penal Code 19.03).

Utah. Aggravated murder (76-5-202, Utah Code annotated).

Virginia. First-degree murder with 1 of 12 aggravating circumstances (VA Code § 18.2-31).

Washington. Aggravated first-degree murder.

Wyoming. First-degree murder.

Source: Tracy L. Snell, *Capital Punishment 1998*, Bulletin NCJ 179012 (Bureau of Justice Statistics, U.S. Department of Justice, December 1999). Available at www.ojp.usdoj.gov/bjs/pubalp2.htm#Capital Punishment (accessed 6 January 2000).

Table 9.2. Federal Laws Providing for the Death Penalty

8 U.S.C. 1342 — Murder related to the smuggling of aliens.

18 U.S.C. 32-34 — Destruction of aircraft, motor vehicles, or related facilities resulting in death.

18 U.S.C. 36 — Murder committed during a drug-related drive-by shooting.

18 U.S.C. 37 — Murder committed at an airport serving international civil aviation.

18 U.S.C. 115(b)(3) [by cross-reference to 18 U.S.C. 1111] — Retaliatory murder of a member of the immediate family of law enforcement officials.

18 U.S.C. 241, 242, 245, 247 — Civil rights offenses resulting in death.

18 U.S.C. 351 [by cross-reference to 18 U.S.C. 1111] — Murder of a member of Congress, an important executive official, or a Supreme Court Justice.

18 U.S.C. 794 — Espionage.

18 U.S.C. 844(d), (f), (i) — Death resulting from offenses involving transportation of explosives, destruction of government property, or destruction of property related to foreign or interstate commerce.

18 U.S.C. 924(i) — Murder committed by the use of a firearm during a crime of violence or a drug-trafficking crime.

18 U.S.C. 930 — Murder committed in a Federal Government facility.

18 U.S.C. 1091 — Genocide.

18 U.S.C. 1111 — First-degree murder.

18 U.S.C. 1114 — Murder of a Federal judge or law enforcement official.

18 U.S.C. 1116 — Murder of a foreign official.

18 U.S.C. 1118 — Murder by a Federal prisoner.

18 U.S.C. 1119 — Murder of a U.S. national in a foreign country.

18 U.S.C. 1120 — Murder by an escaped Federal prisoner already sentenced to life imprisonment.

18 U.S.C. 1121 — Murder of a State or local law enforcement official or other person aiding in a Federal investigation; murder of a State correctional officer.

18 U.S.C. 1201 — Murder during a kidnapping.

18 U.S.C. 1203 — Murder during a hostage taking.

18 U.S.C. 1503 — Murder of a court officer or juror.

18 U.S.C. 1512 — Murder with the intent of preventing testimony by a witness, victim, or informant.

18 U.S.C. 1513 — Retaliatory murder of a witness, victim, or informant.

18 U.S.C. 1716 — Mailing of injurious articles with intent to kill or resulting in death.

18 U.S.C. 1751 [by cross-reference to 18 U.S.C. 1111] — Assassination or kidnapping resulting in the death of the President or Vice President.

18 U.S.C. 1958 — Murder for hire.

18 U.S.C. 1959 — Murder involved in a racketeering offense.

18 U.S.C. 1992 — Willful wrecking of a train resulting in death.

18 U.S.C. 2113 — Bank-robbery-related murder or kidnapping.

18 U.S.C. 2119 — Murder related to a carjacking.

18 U.S.C. 2245 — Murder related to rape or child molestation.

18 U.S.C. 2251 — Murder related to sexual exploitation of children.

18 U.S.C. 2280 — Murder committed during an offense against maritime navigation.

18 U.S.C. 2281 — Murder committed during an offense against a maritime fixed platform.

18 U.S.C. 2332 — Terrorist murder of a U.S. national in another country.

18 U.S.C. 2332a — Murder by the use of a weapon of mass destruction.

18 U.S.C. 2340 — Murder involving torture.

18 U.S.C. 2381 — Treason.

21 U.S.C. 848(e) — Murder related to a continuing criminal enterprise or related murder of a Federal, State, or local law enforcement officer.

49 U.S.C. 1472-1473 — Death resulting from aircraft hijacking.

Source: Tracy L. Snell, *Capital Punishment 1998*, Bulletin NCJ 179012 (Bureau of Justice Statistics, U.S. Department of Justice, December 1999). Available at www.ojp.usdoj.gov/bjs/pubalp2.htm#Capital Punishment (accessed 6 January 2000).

teenth Amendments. In a decision featuring five concurrences and four dissents, the Court judged that in these cases it did, effectively vacating death sentences nationwide. Although Justices Brennan and Marshall argued that capital punishment was per se unconstitutional, the prevailing view—that of Justices Douglas, White, and Stewart— hinged on the basically standardless manner in which the penalty was imposed. According to Justice Stewart,

These death sentences are cruel and unusual in the same way that being struck by lightning is cruel and unusual. For, of all the people convicted of rapes and murders in 1967 and 1968, many just as reprehensible as these, the petitioners are among a capriciously selected random handful upon whom the sen-

tence of death has in fact been imposed. My concurring Brothers have demonstrated that, if any basis can be discerned for the selection of these few to be sentenced to die, it is the constitutionally impermissible basis of race. But racial discrimination has not been proved, and I put it to one side. I simply conclude that the Eighth and Fourteenth Amendments cannot tolerate the infliction of a sentence of death under legal systems that permit this unique penalty to be so wantonly and so freakishly imposed (*Furman* (Stewart, J., concurring); citations omitted).

Over the course of the next several years, the death penalty came to a halt in the United States, as individual jurisdictions attempted to fashion legislation that would meet constitutional muster. Then, in 1976, five cases, consolidated for review, and covering death penalty stat-

Table 9.3. Prisoners Under Sentence of Death by Region and State, 1997 and 1998

REGION AND STATE	PRISONERS UNDER DEATH SENTENCE, 12/31/97	PRISONERS UNDER DEATH SENTENCE, 12/31/98
U.S. Total	3,328	3,452
Federal	14	19
State	3,314	3,433
Northeast	234	244
Connecticut	5	5
New Hampshire	0	0
New Jersey	14	14
New York	0	1
Pennsylvania	215	224
Midwest	482	497
Illinois	161	157
Indiana	44	45
Kansas	0	1
Missouri	89	90
Nebraska	11	11
Ohio	175	191
South Dakota	2	2
South	1,828	1,895
Alabama	159	178
Arkansas	38	40
Delaware	15	17
Florida	367	372
Georgia	108	109
Kentucky	31	36
Louisiana	70	75
Maryland	17	17
Mississippi	62	65
North Carolina	176	187
Oklahoma	136	144
South Carolina	68	68
Tennessee	99	97
Texas	439	451
Virginia	43	39
West	770	797
Arizona	120	120
California	487	512
Colorado	4	3
Idaho	19	19
Montana	7	6
Nevada	86	84
New Mexico	4	4
Oregon	20	23
Utah	10	10
Washington	12	14
Wyoming	1	2

Source: Tracy L. Snell, *Capital Punishment 1998*, Bulletin NCJ 179012 (Bureau of Justice Statistics, U.S. Department of Justice, December 1999). Available at www.ojp.usdoj.gov/bjs/pubalp2. htm#Capital Punishment (accessed 6 January 2000).

Table 9.4. Number of Persons Executed by Jurisdiction, 1930–98

STATE	SINCE 1930	SINCE 1977
U.S. Total	4,359	500
Texas	461	164
Georgia	389	23
New York	329	
California	297	5
North Carolina	274	11
Florida	213	43
South Carolina	182	20
Ohio	172	
Mississippi	158	4
Louisiana	157	24
Pennsylvania	154	2
Alabama	152	17
Virginia	151	59
Arkansas	135	17
Kentucky	104	1
Illinois	101	11
Missouri	94	32
Tennessee	93	
New Jersey	74	
Oklahoma	73	13
Maryland	71	3
Arizona	50	12
Washington	50	3
Colorado	48	1
Indiana	47	6
District of Columbia	40	
West Virginia	40	
Nevada	36	7
Federal System	33	
Massachusetts	27	
Oregon	21	2
Connecticut	21	
Delaware	20	8
Utah	18	5
Iowa	18	
Kansas	15	
Montana	8	2
New Mexico	8	
Wyoming	8	1
Nebraska	7	3
Idaho	4	1
Vermont	4	
New Hampshire	1	
South Dakota	1	

Source: Tracy L. Snell, *Capital Punishment 1998*, Bulletin NCJ 179012 (Bureau of Justice Statistics, U.S. Department of Justice, December 1999). Available at www.ojp.usdoj.gov/bjs/pubalp2. htm#Capital Punishment (accessed 6 January 2000).

utes in Georgia, Florida, Texas, Louisiana, and North Carolina, were presented to the Court.

At issue in the primary case, *Gregg v. Georgia*, 428 U.S. 153 (1976), was the imposition of the death penalty for murder resulting from an armed robbery. The penalty, sentenced to Troy Gregg, was applied following a set of procedures mandated by the Georgia legislature following *Furman*. The question before the Court was whether the imposition of the sentence of death for the crime of murder under the revised laws of the five states violated the Eighth and Fourteenth Amendments. The Court ruled that in the cases of Georgia, Florida, and Texas it did not, thus effectively reinstituting capital punishment.

Again, the Court was divided both on reasoning and on judgment. However, Justices Stewart, Powell, and Stevens, announcing the judgment of the Court upholding the law in three states, concluded that "[t]he punishment of death for the crime of murder does not, under all circumstances, violate the Eighth and Fourteenth Amendments" (*Gregg*, at 175). According to Justice Stewart, the judiciary has a limited role to play in criminal sentencing:

[I]n assessing a punishment selected by a democratically elected legislature against the constitutional measure, we presume its validity. We may not require the legislature to select the least severe penalty possible so long as the penalty selected is not cruelly inhumane or disproportionate to the crime involved. And a heavy burden rests on those who would attack the judgment of the representatives of the people (*Gregg*, at 175).[36]

Since *Gregg*, the Supreme Court's death penalty docket has largely sought to clarify procedural bounds to capital punishment.[37] Thus, the Court has held that the imposition of the death penalty for rape alone is "grossly disproportionate" and thus unconstitutional (*Coker v. Georgia*, 433 U.S. 584 (1977)). In addition, the Court has ruled that the death penalty is age limited, setting a threshold of sixteen years on executions[38] (see Table 9.5). At the same time, however, it has ruled that death sentences imposed on mentally retarded convicts are not necessarily unconstitutional.[39]

In favor of capital defendants, the Court has ruled that sentencing juries must be informed of mitigating circumstances (*Lockett v. Ohio*, 438 U.S. 586 (1978)), including mental retardation (*Penry v. Lynaugh*, 492 U.S. 302 (1989)). But, to the presumed detriment of those facing the death penalty, it has upheld the use of "victim impact

Table 9.5. Minimum Age Authorized for Capital Punishment, 1998

AGE 16 OR LESS	AGE 17	AGE 18	NONE SPECIFIED
Alabama (16)	Georgia	California	Arizona
Arkansas (14)[a]	New Hampshire	Colorado	Idaho
Delaware (16)	North Carolina[b]	Connecticut[c]	Louisiana
Florida (16)	Texas	Federal system	Montana
Indiana (16)		Illinois	Pennsylvania
Kentucky (16)		Kansas	South Carolina
Mississippi (16)[d]		Maryland	South Dakota[e]
Missouri (16)		Nebraska	Utah
Nevada (16)		New Jersey	
Oklahoma (16)		New Mexico	
Virginia (14)[f]		New York	
Wyoming (16)		Ohio	
		Oregon	
		Tennessee	
		Washington	

Note: Reporting by states reflects interpretations by state attorney general offices and may differ from previously reported ages.

[a]See Ark. Code Ann. 9-27-318(b)(2)(Repl. 1991).

[b]Age required is 17 unless the murderer was incarcerated for murder when a subsequent murder occurred; then the age may be 14.

[c]See Conn. Gen. Stat. 53a-46a(g)(1).

[d]The minimum age defined by statute is 13, but the effective age is 16 based on interpretation of U.S. Supreme Court decisions by the Mississippi Supreme Court.

[e]Juveniles may be transferred to adult court. Age can be a mitigating factor.

[f]The minimum age for transfer to adult court by statute is 14, but the effective age is 16 based on interpretation of U.S. Supreme Court decisions by the State attorney general's office.

Source: Tracy L. Snell, *Capital Punishment 1998*, Bulletin NCJ 179012 (Bureau of Justice Statistics, U.S. Department of Justice, December 1999). Available at www.ojp.usdoj.gov/bjs/pubalp2.htm#Capital Punishment (accessed 13 January 2000).

statements" at the sentencing phase of trial (*Payne v. Tennessee*, 501 U.S. 808 (1991)).

Among death penalty controversies, the most troublesome are those revolving around the disproportionate application of the sanction to certain groups—notably, the poor and minorities.

THE POVERTY CONNECTION

According to the American Civil Liberties Union, "Ninety percent of criminal defendants in this country who are charged with a capital crime are indigent when arrested, and virtually all are penniless by the time their case reaches the appeals stage. In California, the state with the largest death row population, less than 2 percent were represented at trial by retained counsel."[40] For the vast majority of poor capital defendants the problem, more often than not, is one of counsel. Although guaranteed legal representation through the first appeal,[41] by most assessments, indigent capital defendants tend to receive "grossly unqualified" assistance (Coyle, Lavelle, and Strasser 1990).[42] Stephen Bright, director of the Southern Center for Human Rights, provides the following tragic example:

After years in which she and her children were physically abused by her adulterous husband, a woman in Talladega County, Alabama, arranged to have him killed. Tragically, murders of abusive spouses are not rare in our violent society, but seldom are they punished by the death penalty. Yet this woman was sentenced to death. Why?

It may have been in part because one of her court-appointed lawyers was so drunk that the trial had to be delayed for a day after he was held in contempt and sent to jail. The next morning, he and his client were both produced from jail, the trial resumed, and the death penalty was imposed a few days later. It may also have been in part because this lawyer failed to find hospital records documenting injuries received by the woman and her daughter, which would have corroborated their testimony about abuse. And it may also have been because her lawyers did not bring their expert witness on domestic abuse to see the defendant until 8 p.m. on the night before he testified at trial (Bright 1994, 1835–36).[43]

In fact, the majority of high-rate death penalty states do not have public defender systems, relying instead on court-appointed lawyers, underpaid and with no particular experience in the very special realm of capital punishment. According to the American Bar Association (ABA),

Jurisdictions that employ the death penalty have proven unwilling to establish the kind of legal services system that is necessary to ensure that defendants charged with capital offenses receive the defense they require. Many death penalty states have no working public defender programs, relying instead upon scattershot methods for selecting and supporting defense counsel in capital cases. For example, some states simply assign lawyers at random from a general list—a scheme destined to identify attorneys who lack the necessary qualifications and, worse still, regard their assignments as a burden.

Other jurisdictions employ "contract" systems, which typically channel indigent defense business to attorneys who offer the lowest bids. Other states use public defender schemes that appear on the surface to be more promising, but prove in practice to be just as ineffective (ABA 1998, 224)

Nor is the problem limited to the states. Even lawyers appointed in the federal system receive inadequate compensation to ensure competent defense. Indeed, no less than the chief justice has noted the problem, requesting additional monies from Congress and asserting that "[a]dequate pay for appointed counsel is important to ensure that a defendant's constitutional right to counsel is fulfilled" (Rehnquist 2000).

THE RACE CONNECTION

In addition to the poverty problem, race persists as a disturbing and complicating element in capital punishment. Of the 3,404 prisoners under sentence of death nationwide at the end of 1998, 43 percent were black, a figure hugely disproportionate to the percentage of African Americans in the total population (Snell 1999). Indeed, according to one observer, "Race is more likely to affect death sentencing than smoking affects the likelihood of dying from heart disease. [Yet, t]he latter evidence has produced enormous changes in law and societal practice, while racism in the death penalty has been largely ignored" (Dieter 1998).

The problem, of course, is nothing new—nor is its recognition. Atticus Finch, the lawyer-hero of Harper Lee's 1960 novel, *To Kill A Mockingbird*, clearly recognized it in his defense of Tom Robinson, accused, in a capital case, of raping a white girl (Lee 1960). Before that, in 1940, the great novelist Richard Wright provided the tragic portrait of Bigger Thomas, sentenced to death for the accidental killing of a white woman, while his intentional murder of a black woman went largely ignored (Wright [1947] 1993). In real life, the so-called "Scottsboro Boys," seven black youth, were convicted in Alabama in 1931 for the crime of sexually assaulting two white girls. The jury had, within its discretion, the authority to sentence the young men to as few as ten years of imprisonment; it chose, instead, the death penalty (*Powell v. Alabama*, 287 U.S. 45 (1932)). Few doubted that the key element in the jury's decision was the race of the defendants and victims. As Justice Marshall pointed out in his 1972 *Furman* concurrence:

[A] look at the bare statistics regarding executions is enough to betray much of the discrimination. A total of 3,859 persons [were executed between 1930 and 1972]. . . . Of the executions, 3,334 were for murder; 1,664 of the executed murderers were white and 1,630 were Negro; 455 persons, including 48 whites and 405 Negroes, were executed for rape. It is immediately apparent that Negroes were executed far more often than whites in proportion to their percentage of the population (*Furman v. Georgia*, at 364 (Marshall, J., concurring); citations omitted).

In recent years, the statistical analyses have become far more sophisticated and, to many, far more convincing. At the same time, the problem has remained peculiarly intractable. Take, for example, the case of Warren McCleskey. In 1978, McCleskey, a black Georgian, was convicted of killing a white police officer during the course of a robbery, and he was sentenced to death.

As part of his habeas petition, McCleskey claimed that the Georgia capital-sentencing process was administered in a racially discriminatory manner. His case, which reached the Supreme Court in 1987 (*McCleskey v. Kemp*, 481 U.S. 279 (1987)), centered around the "Baldus Study," a statistical examination of the death sentence in Georgia that demonstrated a disparity in the imposition of capital punishment based on the race of the murder victim and, to a lesser extent, the race of the defendant, with black defendants who killed white victims having the greatest likelihood of receiving death.[44] The study, McCleskey claimed, established that application of the death penalty was irrational, arbitrary, capricious, and, thus, unconstitutional, violating the Eighth Amendment and both the equal protection and due process clauses of the Fourteenth. In a 5–4 decision rendered by Justice Powell, the high court rejected his claim on all counts.[45]

Beginning with McCleskey's equal protection argument, Powell maintained that in order to prevail, the defendant "must prove that the decisionmakers in *his* case acted with discriminatory purpose" (*McCleskey*, at 292; emphasis added). This he had not done, relying instead on the generalized findings of the "Baldus Study." Although the Court has accepted statistical patterns as proof of discrimination in other equal protection cases,

the nature of the capital sentencing decision, and the relationship of the statistics to that decision, are fundamentally different from the corresponding elements in the venire-selection or Title VII [of the Civil Rights Act] cases. Most importantly, each particular decision to impose the death penalty is made by a petit jury selected from a properly constituted venire. Each jury is unique in its composition, and the Constitution requires that its decision rest on consideration of innumerable factors that vary according to the characteristics of the individual defendant and the facts of the particular capital offense (*McCleskey*, at 295).

In short, for purposes of applying statistical findings to equal protection analyses, the criminal justice system in general and the death penalty in particular are unique:

McCleskey's statistical proffer must be viewed in the context of his challenge. [He] challenges decisions at the heart of the State's criminal justice system. "One of society's most basic tasks is that of protecting the lives of its citizens and one of the most basic ways in which it achieves the task is through criminal laws against murder." Implementation of these laws necessarily requires discretionary judgments. Because discretion is essential to the criminal justice process, we would demand exceptionally clear proof before we would infer that the discretion has been abused (*McCleskey*, at 297; citations omitted).

Nor was the Court sympathetic to McCleskey's Eighth Amendment due process claim. There is, asserted Powell, "a constitutionally permissible range of discretion in imposing the death penalty"—a range met by the State of Georgia and within which McCleskey's sentence was not disproportionate to his crime by any traditional indicia (*McCleskey*, at 305–306).

Writing in dissent, Justice Brennan admitted that under his view "the death penalty is in all circumstances cruel and unusual punishment forbidden by the Eighth and Fourteenth Amendments" (*McCleskey*, at 320 (Brennan, J., dissenting)).[46] Nevertheless, he took particular umbrage at the circumstances surrounding McCleskey's sentence:

At some point in this case, Warren McCleskey doubtless asked his lawyer whether a jury was likely to sentence him to die. A candid reply to this question would have been disturbing. First, counsel would have to tell McCleskey that few of the details of the crime or of McCleskey's past criminal conduct were more important than the fact that his victim was white. Furthermore, counsel would feel bound to tell McCleskey that defendants charged with killing white victims in Georgia are 4.3 times as likely to be sentenced to death as defendants charged with killing blacks. In addition, frankness would compel the disclosure that it was more likely than not that the race of McCleskey's victim would determine whether he received a death sentence: 6 of every 11 defendants convicted of killing a white person would not have received the death penalty if their victims had been black, while, among defendants with aggravating and mitigating factors comparable to McCleskey's, 20 of every 34 would not have been sentenced to die if their victims had been black. Finally, the assessment would not be complete without the information that cases involving black defendants and white victims are more likely to result in a death sentence than cases featuring any other racial combination of defendant and victim. The story could be told in a variety of ways, but McCleskey could not fail to grasp its essential narrative line: there was a significant chance that race would play a prominent role in determining if he lived or died (*McCleskey*, at 321; citations omitted).

Since *McCleskey*, statistics continue to demonstrate race disparity in capital sentencing. For example, the most recent "Baldus Study," an examination of the death penalty in Philadelphia, found continuing patterns of "arbitrariness and discrimination in the administration of the death penalty . . . [and] not [merely] confined to southern jurisdictions" (Baldus et al. 1998, 1738). At the same time, since the retirements of Justices Brennan, Marshall, and Blackmun, there is no longer a single justice on the Supreme Court who is fundamentally opposed to the principle or current application of the death penalty; while among core death penalty decision makers—district attorneys in capital punishment states—almost 98 percent are white (Pokorak 1998).

AND WHAT OF INNOCENCE?

Finally, regardless of race or economic status, with the growing sophistication of DNA analysis, there has been an increasing trend—one which should give pause to even the most die-hard advocates of the death penalty—toward the exoneration of death row inmates. According to the Death Penalty Information Center, "[S]ince 1973, over 80 people have been released from death row with evidence of their innocence" (Dieter 1997). Indeed, in Illinois, the problem has become so acute—since the death penalty was reinstated there "23 years ago, 13 death row inmates have been cleared of murder charges, compared to 12 who have been put to death" (Claiborne 2000, 4)—that Republican Governor George Ryan imposed a moratorium on executions, pending an extensive study of a system deemed "'fraught with errors' and 'broken'."[47] Throughout most of the nation, however, the increasing possibility of criminal exoneration is being met with stiff resistance toward the goal of ever-quicker executions, as states shorten and streamline death appeals and as Congress limits the scope of habeas (see chapter 4), all sanctioned by the Supreme Court.[48]

The End

In the end (literally), no matter which way we go, something must be done with our remains. Here too, there is the law.

In many ways, the modern legal brush with the postmortem began in the late 1800s when artisans and entrepreneurs specializing in death—undertakers, embalmers, and funeral directors—sought increased status and economic fortune via the state's imprimatur, professional licensing (Friedman 1973, 398–99). At the time,

[t]hey had many rivals. Doctors embalmed the dead. Clergymen controlled funerals. Many undertakers were part-time funeral directors, who sold coffins and caskets as the mainstay of their business. In the late 1800s, Hudson Samson, president of the Funeral Directors National Association of the United States, prepared a model legislative act for licensing embalmers. At the same time, Samson tried to uplift the artifacts of professional funerals. (In 1889, he designed a "special eight poster, oval-decked funeral car"; in 1989, a magnificent wooden drape hearse.) It was all part of one general movement, to give tone and economic strength to the occupation, in short, to "professionalize" these doctors of the dead. Samson wanted a law to regulate "the care and burial of the dead the same as there is for the practice of medicine." In 1894, Virginia passed the first licensing law. . . . Thereafter, only registered embalmers could practice the "science of embalming." By 1900, some twenty-four states had passed similar legislation (Friedman 1973, 398).

Today, the provision of funeral services is governed largely by a tangled web of religious ritual, individual state law, and some federal consumer protection law. At the state level, the disposal of our "remains" is regulated in part by insurance law (overseeing the honest disbursement of death benefits), transportation law (licensing hearses), and a variety of zoning laws and cemetery

oversight rules (regulating burial sites). The heart of most state funeral law, however, remains in occupational licensing oversight. Maryland law is instructive. Thus, in Maryland, a state board of morticians, appointed by the governor with the advice and consent of the senate, sets standards and oversees the licensing, advertising, and inspection of morticians, mortician apprentices, funeral directors, and funeral homes.[49]

Although funeral regulation is traditionally a function of state law, a substantial proportion of the funeral industry traverses the route of interstate commerce and thus implicates federal law as well. Of particular importance here is regulation and consumer protection undertaken by the Federal Trade Commission (FTC).[50] Hence, the FTC monitors and sanctions unfair or deceptive acts or practices in selling or offering to sell funeral goods or funeral services to the public (16 C.F.R. 453.2). The so-called "Funeral Rule," administered by the FTC, requires "funeral providers to provide consumers with information regarding funeral products and services and ensures consumers pay for only the products and services they want and need" (FTC 1998). While violators may be subject to litigation, a recently developed "Funeral Rule Offenders Program"—a venture generated jointly by the FTC and the National Funeral Directors Association (NFDA)—offers funeral homes found to be in violation of the rule an opportunity to make voluntary payments and receive training rather than face possible enforcement action by the FTC and the state attorneys general (FTC 1998).

Law and the Afterlife: Ancient Concerns of Succession

If at the death of a man who holds a lay "fee" of the Crown, a sheriff or royal official produces royal letters patent of summons for a debt due to the Crown, it shall be lawful for them to seize and list movable goods found in the lay "fee" of the dead man to the value of the debt, as assessed by worthy men. Nothing shall be removed until the whole debt is paid, when the residue shall be given over to the executors to carry out the dead man's will. If no debt is due to the Crown, all the movable goods shall be regarded as the property of the dead man, except the reasonable shares of his wife and children.

If a free man dies intestate, his movable goods are to be distributed by his next-of-kin and friends, under the supervision of the Church. The rights of his debtors are to be preserved (*Magna Carta*, 1215[51]).

As the sections of *Magna Carta* quoted above suggest, law has long been concerned with the orderly transfer of that which we can't take with us—our heirs and, more importantly, our creditors should receive their fair shares of our lives' work under a watchful legal eye. This section briefly reviews the ancient lineage of law in the transfer of property after death.

Although the law has ever been involved in *succession*, the process of transferring a dead person's property or rights, its involvement has not always been so legalistic or formal as it is today. According to Adam Hirsch (1996, 1060),

In colonial times, settlers were content to give effect to nuncupative (oral) wills or even to depositions by friends or family concerning the decedent's dispositive preferences as expressed to them casually. The court then ordered distribution "according to the minde [*sic*] of the deceased."

While such informality may have worked in a small-scale agricultural economy, "flexibility and individualized handling of estates," according to Lawrence Friedman (1973, 219), "was a luxury that a mass society, with mass ownership of wealth, could not afford." Thus, began the birth of a complex and sometimes daunting system of probate law.

Wills, individuals' declarations of how they want their property distributed after their deaths, are the basic form of succession. In general, wills are characterized by three customary requirements: they must be written, they must be signed, and they must be attested to—that is, authenticated by witnesses. Of the three, the most formal—some would say, archaically so—and the most likely to act as an impediment, is the *attestation* requirement. All states currently dictate that between two and three witnesses formally attest to the validity of a will in front of a third party, often a lawyer, an accountant, or notary public. At common law, the idea was to have several disinterested parties present to guard "the testator [will maker] against various nefarious acts, such as fraud or undue influence" (Mann 1994, 1042). Today, however, as Bruce Mann (1994, 1042) notes, "witnesses tend to be either family members, who are well-placed to commit the acts they are supposed to prevent, or comparative strangers in a lawyer's office or bank who sign when and where they are told and hardly see themselves as the testator's sentinels."

This complex law of succession may sometimes lead to very absurd results. Thus, in all states, if a will is formally typed, failure to abide by proper attestation will most likely invalidate the will in the eyes of the court. At the same time, a number of states do recognize so-called *holographic wills*, wills that are handwritten and signed with no witnesses. This leads, in many states to a kind of "schizophrenic" outcome in which

either a will must be thoroughly formalized by virtue of witnesses and so on, or it must be thoroughly informalized by virtue of a statement wholly in handwriting. A will that is neither formal nor informal, but rather semi-formal—such as an estate plan typed and signed (but not witnessed) on a pre-printed will form—be it even an official statutory will form published with the state's imprimatur—is of no legal effect whatsoever (Hirsch 1996, 1071).

Regardless of the form of will, or no will at all, when an individual dies, his or her estate is subject to probate. *Probate* is a court proceeding in which debts are settled, taxes paid, and whatever is left transferred to the decedent's legal heirs. Like the rules surrounding wills themselves, probate varies according to individual state law. Thus, in some states, if an estate is relatively small and the will uncontested, the probate procedure may be quickly and fairly easily consummated; other states retain more formalized and complicated probate procedures.

In general, probate involves four basic steps. First, the court will appoint someone to inventory and distribute the estate. Where the departed has left a valid will (in legal terms, where she has died *testate*), this person will be the *executor* named in the will. Where there is no will (where the deceased is *intestate*), the court itself will name an *administrator*.

The executor or administrator is then responsible for collecting, itemizing, and appraising all of the assets that are subject to probate. He or she then must pay outstanding debts and taxes, although most states permit a portion of the estate to be set aside for survivors, out of the long reach of creditors. Finally, what is left over is distributed to the estate's heirs. Where there is no will, state law determines the legal heirs; in most cases, the estate is divided among the surviving spouse and the decedent's closest blood relatives.[52]

Although probate is the most common form of succession, it is not the only form. Property that was placed in a *living trust*[53] prior to death or property held in *joint tenancy*[54] may pass to beneficiaries without court supervision. So too may life insurance and retirement account benefits (Hames and Ekern 1998, 212).

Of course, as the foregoing suggests, not only are death and taxes inevitable, they are inextricably intertwined. Indeed, "[o]ne of the oldest and most common forms of taxation is the taxation of property held by an individual at the time of his death."[55] Unlike the transfer of property to heirs, which is governed by individual state law, the transfer of property to government (in other words, taxes) is a federal concern as well. This was not always the case. Early in American history, death taxes were primarily levied by state governments, with federal death taxes imposed only sporadically in times of war or threatened war. Thus, for example, "[t]he first Federal death tax was imposed from 1797 until 1802 as a stamp tax on inventories of deceased persons, receipts of legacies, shares of personal estate, probates of wills, and letters of administration to pay for the development of strong naval forces felt necessary because of strained trade relations with France" (U.S. Congress 1998). Thereafter, a sixty-year hiatus ensued until a federal inheritance tax was imposed to offset the costs of the Civil War. In 1898, the federal government imposed its first estate tax to finance the Spanish-American War. Estate taxes as a permanent feature of the federal revenue system did not take hold until 1916 with the onset of World War I (U.S. Congress 1998).

The current Federal Estate Tax (26 U.S.C. § 2001) is a levy on decedents' property before transfers to debtors or heirs take place. In addition, many states impose such taxes. Although more sophisticated estates may transfer many assets prior to death in the form of gifts, the Federal Gift Tax law (26 U.S.C. §2501) is "generally designed to prevent complete tax avoidance by this route" (26 U.S.C. §2501, LII, "Estate and Gift Tax"). Since 1976, federal estate and gift tax law has been unified, with a single graduated rate schedule applicable to transfers.[56] Recently, federal death tax law has come under increasing criticism (e.g., Joint Economic Committee 1998). Numerous bills were introduced during the 106th Congress to reduce or eliminate the estate tax,[57] and President Bush, too, has promised to eliminate or substantially scale down the death tax.

Conclusion

In this chapter, we explored law's role at the end of life, from old age to death to burial to succession, the temporal parallel to celestial afterlife. The inevitability of death is well attended by the inevitability of law.

In many ways, law's ordering function is clearest here at the end. We structure law to make our grandparents', parents', and our own last years as neat and carefree as possible. We place law in the role of bulwark against the moral chaos we fear would arise should some (maybe many) of us seek to determine our own ends—or those of our loved ones. At the same time, we let law end the lives of those few whom we have determined most hideously breached society's commandments. And we use law, after all is said and done, to transfer, in an orderly fashion, that which we "can't take with us."

Yet, as the foregoing suggests, it is not without struggle that we give way at the end to the ordering proclivities of law. From age-discrimination litigation to "right-to-die" claims, to the often long struggles of death-row inmates trying to avoid execution, to the ongoing battle aimed at ending inheritance taxes, individuals employ law's liberty motif to fight its ordering devices. The inherent battle, it seems, is inevitable—right down to the bitter end.

Law on the Web

In this chapter we have talked about law as it relates to aging and dying. Much of what we have discussed, particularly in the last section, involves ethical issues with

which the law is only now beginning to grapple. For web-related information on law, bioethics, aging, and death, see the sites listed in chapter 6. A number of sites, however, deal specifically with aging and end-of-life questions. A few of those are listed below.

Aging

U.S. Social Security Administration
www.ssa.gov/

U.S. Administration on Aging, Department of Health and Human Services
www.aoa.dhhs.gov/

National Institute on Aging, National Institutes of Health
www.nih.gov/nia/

American Association of Retired Persons
www.aarp.org/
The nation's most powerful lobby representing the elderly.

GeroWeb Virtual Library on Aging, Wayne State University
www.iog.wayne.edu/GeroWebd/GeroWeb.html
Provides links to many aging-related sites, including legal public policy sites.

The Gerontology Center at Penn State University
geron.psu.edu/
One of many good university-sponsored gerontology centers.

Gerontology Research Group
www.grg.org/

Gerontological Society of America
www.geron.org/

National Senior Citizens Law Center
www.nsclc.org/
Legal advocacy organization and information clearinghouse.

Center for Medicare Advocacy
www.medicareadvocacy.org

The National Academy of Elder Law Attorneys, Inc.
www.naela.com/
Assists lawyers, bar organizations, and others who work with older clients and their families.

Right to Die

The Hemlock Society
www.hemlock.org/

DeathNET
www.rights.org/deathnet

Choice In Dying
www.choices.org/

Death Penalty

Death Penalty Information Center
www.essential.org/dpic/

Amnesty International
www.amnestyusa.org/rightsforall/dp/index.html

American Civil Liberties Union
www.aclu.org/issues/death/hmdp.html

Death Penalty.Net
www.deathpenalty.net/

Focus on the Death Penalty
www.uaa.alaska.edu/just/death/index.html

The Law of Succession

Numerous attorneys have websites (some quite good) that explain succession in the states where they are located. For good, general starting points on this subject, Cornell's Legal Information Institute cannot be beat.

Estate and Gift Tax: An Overview
www.law.cornell.edu/topics/estate_gift_tax.html

Estate Planning: An Overview
www.law.cornell.edu/topics/estate_planning.html

Estates and Trusts: An Overview
www.law.cornell.edu/topics/estates_trusts.html

10 Law and Political Economy

Sadly, Father's Bible failed to warn him that the newly elected President Martin Van Buren would abruptly establish the National Bank and change the lending rules, causing the famous Panic of '37. Thanks to Van Buren's National Bank, soon all the small-monied borrowing men like Father were left holding packets of worthless paper—piles of currency issued by various states and high mountains of mortgaged titles to vast tracts of western land and farms that could be neither sold for one-tenth their cost nor rented for the interest due on the unsecured loans that had purchased them barely a year before. The lucky fellows and the bankers and politicians who understood the system and thus had been able to anticipate the sudden deflation of value that inevitably follows hard upon a speculative boom, those men sold off their properties early and high and walked away counting their profits. Within weeks, they were doing the President's bidding, calling in their neighbors' loans and hiring sheriffs to seize land, houses, livestock, and even the personal property of the stubbornly foolish men who persisted in believing that the decline was only a temporary aberration. For those men, men like John Brown, surveyor, tanner, and small-time stockman, the collapse of the land boom was catastrophic.

—Banks 1998, 82–83

Our discussion thus far has centered upon the role of law in the life cycle of *individuals*. In the pages that remain we move to a higher level of analysis. Much of law's relationship with the individual has been modified in recent years, as we have seen, by technological changes. Technological development restructures every aspect of communal life, cutting across all dimensions, including the sociological (the ways in which people relate to one another and the processes by which they cluster), psychological (the concept of the self and understandings of one's purpose and role), political (the distribution of power) and economic (the value of labor and production, and wealth distribution and market movements).[1] In many ways, such developments help to define the community in which we conduct our daily lives and construct long-range strategies and plans. Moreover, technology, especially in transportation and communications, influences perceptions of quality of life, determines employment opportunities and choices, and, more generally, influences relationship structures and the contours of what we understand to be our primary community. This chapter addresses the relationship between law and the society in aggregate terms, as we collectively experience a revolution in technologies at the turn of a new century. In what capacities does the law serve the community as the larger political economy

transforms? Does law facilitate change? Does it serve to mitigate the effects of such shifts? If so, is the law entirely neutral and passive, available and open to all parties who seek it, easing the way for all alike?

Technology has played a crucial role in political economic development, and technological change presents enormous challenges to the law-making system. In what capacities does the law serve the community as the larger political economy transforms? We argue that developments in technological, political, and economic spheres produce increasingly complex sets of interconnectedness, a tangled web of relationships that is, at the same time, legally based and dependent, yet presents a serious challenge to legal governance. One could argue that the macroeconomic engine acts as a social centrifuge in which individual particles are, in one sense, bound to a common process but are also separated and spun helter-skelter in different directions. Law is a mechanism for imposing order in the face of a growing diversity of purpose and an increasing divergence. Given the high premium placed upon history and experience (precedent) in the U.S. legal system, old law is generally not destroyed in the process of confronting new circumstances. Rather, layers are piled upon layers producing increasingly intricate and complex legal orders as we move from one era to the next.

169

In the following sections we begin by reiterating the foundational premises of law in the American context. Thereafter, we look at the role of law in the early political economy of the nation—an economy marked by the development of the physical transportation infrastructure and the emergence of capitalism. Finally, we examine briefly the relationship of law and economy in the modern landscape, marked by the flowering of communication systems in a context of advanced capitalism.

Community, Relational Politics, and the Founders' Solutions

Arguably, formal law would not be necessary if we all acted with a common purpose and if we all behaved altruistically. However, as Madison observed in *Federalist* #10 in 1787, self-centered purpose, at worst, and competing visions of the collective good, at best, are unchangeable aspects of the human condition. To attempt to instill within "every citizen the same opinions, the same passions, and the same interests" would be an exercise of pure "folly." Thus, if we are to preserve individual liberty, we must be prepared to live with the consequences—in particular, that people will tend to think and act in selfish terms and that they will band together with others who are like-minded (into "factions") in the attempt to dominate rivals. Here, it is worth reiterating Madison's truism:

The latent causes of faction are thus sown in the nature of man; and we see them everywhere brought into different degrees of activity, according to the different circumstances of civil society. . . . But the most common and durable source of factions has been the various and unequal distribution of property. Those who hold and those who are without property have ever formed distinct interests in society. Those who are creditors, and those who are debtors, fall under a like discrimination. A landed interest, a manufacturing interest, a mercantile interest, a moneyed interest, with many lesser interests, grow up of necessity in civilized nations, and divide them into different classes, actuated by different sentiments and views. The regulation of these various and interfering interests forms the principal task of modern legislation, and involves the spirit of party and faction in the necessary and ordinary operations of the government (*Federalist* #10).

As we have seen, Madison's remedy was a structural one, and his imprint on the constitutional design of government is obvious. Only by creating a complex lawmaking system, he reasoned, could we both enhance liberty and force opposing factions to work together to find acceptable solutions in the midst of conflicting purposes and visions.[2]

Hamilton agreed that economic and property distributions produced important political demarcations, but he also thought that the propertied class was most likely (and probably better equipped) to govern: "[F]rom the natural operation of the different interests and views of the various classes of the community, whether the representation of the people be more or less numerous, it will consist almost entirely of proprietors of land, of merchants, and of members of the learned professions, who will truly represent all those different interests and views" (Hamilton, *Federalist* #36). In addition, he argued that commercial development went hand in hand with the political developments that Madison addressed. A robust economy based upon both domestic exchange and foreign trade was essential to survival of the new nation, but that would require guidance (regulation) from the central government at the expense of state autonomy. To tie his arguments to those of Madison's, Hamilton (*Federalist* #53) suggested that "the increased intercourse among those of different States will contribute not a little to diffuse a mutual knowledge of their affairs, as this again will contribute to a general assimilation of their manners and laws." In other words, the federal government's authority to regulate interstate commerce was crucial to producing a nation, although consisting of disparate views and interests, capable of bridging the factional divides.[3] After considerable debate, Hamilton's vision was also written into the Constitution as Section 8 of Article I, granting Congress the power "to regulate commerce with foreign nations and among the several States."

As deliberation over the merits of the proposed Constitution unfolded, it was clear that structural complexity would be insufficient to waylay the fear that government might become oppressive to individual freedom. Indeed, the relational distance between government officials and the people could be widened by their difference in status, and the "ruling class" might use its power as decision makers to oppress the citizenry. To accommodate that concern and to lubricate the ratification process, it was agreed that the constitutional text should be amended to include formal limitations on government power guaranteeing specific individual civil rights and liberties. The Constitution was approved in 1789, and Amendments I through X (the Bill of Rights) were immediately added, all being ratified in 1791. Thus, our formal legal system was born from a distrust of human motivation and structured in a manner that would diminish the likelihood that law would be used as a mechanism of dominance and oppression, but instead serve to intervene in the ongoing and inevitable struggles and conflicts produced by the dynamics of social, economic, and political evolution.

Despite the Founders' construction of a legal system to deal with problems of self-interest and oppression, they did not find a cure for conflict. People fight. They fight individually, and they fight collectively. There has never been a shortage of provocations. The Founders hoped to harness that energy and channel it in a constructive direction, reasoning that debate and argumentation in a public forum was a far more civilized method of combat than exchange of gunfire. (This is despite the fact that a few years later Hamilton himself was killed in a duel with Vice President Aaron Burr.) The legislative process was constructed to allow wholesale, unfettered debate among all competing factions. Assuming that, although people are selfishly motivated, they are also rational, the founders believed that compromise will be preferred over complete stalemate. Thus, legislation, the general law written to apply equally to all, should eventuate from an argumentative but deliberative, contemplative, give-and-take process. This allows competing groups to conduct their warfare in a face-to-face, civilized manner and to produce results that are constructive to general political and economic well-being. One can quibble with the merits of these assumptions, but they are basic to the legislative design.

For those situations involving individualized or smaller-scale conflict where the parties refuse to compromise, and where individuals or minor factions contest the fairness of legislation as it applies to them, a court system was created and given coequal governing branch status. Here, a disinterested third party is assigned the task of considering the merits of all claims and rendering a decision that complies with preexisting principles of right and wrong. Again, the idea was that this is a much more civilized and constructive method of fighting. In this manner, wrongs could be righted, replacing the "eye-for-an-eye" approach with something like "money for an eye."[4]

Law and Political Economy in the Nineteenth and Early Twentieth Centuries

The great bulk of the early legal developments in the United States occurred in the courts, especially the state courts, in response to conflicts produced by economic exchanges. As Madison had noted, the most significant divisions in any society are created by the unequal distribution of property and the economic relationships that flow from it. Courts across the states brimmed with litigation during the first half of the nineteenth century, and the overwhelming majority of the caseload involved economic issues, such as property rights and ownership disputes, and enforcement of debts and commercial contracts (see, e.g., Horwitz 1977; Friedman 1985; Hurst 1950, 1982). Even a preponderance of the tort actions had an economic tinge.[5] Given the fact that our system was established as the world's first experiment in liberal capitalism, this is not surprising. It also complies well with Hamilton's and Madison's observations. Indeed, most rights stemmed from property ownership, and commerce, property, and property rights are mentioned several times in the Constitution. Quite frankly, the vast majority of citizens were far more concerned with economic survival and/or property accumulation than they were with whether they could speak freely in the town square, obtain a divorce, pray in the public school, engage in consensual sodomy, or whether they possessed the right to die. The law and legal system were mobilized to intervene in the most significant conflicts, and, in aggregate terms, this meant economic conflicts, largely determining ownership and enforcing contractual obligations. Horwitz (1977) presents compelling evidence to suggest that in response to their case flow, judges across the states fairly quickly came to view their role as primary architects of law, where the common-law principles they applied and developed in individual cases would serve as guideposts for entire conflict genres. Moreover, laissez faire was a strong one,[6] arguing against any form of legislative regulation of economic matters and emphasizing such principles as individual free will and *caveat emptor*, thus adding to the centrality of judicial decisions (but see Gillman 1993).[7] An important consideration in addressing individual cases, then, was the public interest, even if it was not raised by any of the parties, and economic growth and expansion were undoubtedly considered to be in the public interest. Such an approach saved considerable time and effort for everyone involved (it was not necessary to reinvent the wheel each time a creditor-debtor relationship turned sour), and it served to concretize expectations. Clearly in the economic realm, efficiency is preferred to inefficiency, and it helps to be able to predict who will prevail in a fight (certainty is preferred over uncertainty) in order to calculate the potential costs and benefits of further engagement.

In general, the law of the nineteenth century reflected the political balances of power. Law was generated to facilitate the growth and expansion of commerce, industrial development, and trade. Legislatures did their best to stimulate economic expansion with legislation that, for example, standardized the money currency; granted rights-of-way for road, rail, bridge, and canal development; adopted uniform basic rules of legal procedure and practice across the states; and authorized charters for financial and insurance institutions and a full range of transportation corporations. The issuance of charters was an especially important matter of public policy. These were consigned primarily by state legislatures,[8] allowing individual investors in an entrepreneurial project to incorporate, thus minimizing the financial risk to themselves in the event that the venture failed. Moreover, from the states' perspective, the instrument served a very useful public interest purpose, stimulating the development of badly needed and costly facilities and transportation infrastructures—such as ferry operations, bridge and canal construction, and road and rail development—that made it possible for goods to be transported more quickly to and from population centers.

Ordinarily, the charter provided an implicit (sometimes explicit) local monopoly and allowed the corporation to realize a profit by collecting user fees and tolls.[9] As the nineteenth century progressed, the process of incorporation was routinized and rendered less complicated, but in the early years it was an involved and cumbersome practice, requiring separate legislation for each venture. Clearly, those in command of the decision-making processes were attempting to employ the law as an instrument to engineer a particular economic goal—as much growth as possible as quickly as possible.

Although their responsibilities and roles were different, constrained to respond to specific "cases and controversies," the conflicts arising from charters forced judges to take a broader view and many seem to have adopted a policy perspective similar to that of their legislative contemporaries. During the first few decades, judges upheld contracts because they were considered binding legal instruments, reasoning that to do otherwise would lead to economic chaos, creating a level of uncertainty about the future that would discourage entrepreneurial and investment activities (see, e.g., *Fletcher v. Peck*, 10 U.S. 87 (1810)). In particular, the charters conveyed by the state to corporations were considered contracts (see, e.g., *Dartmouth College v. Woodward*, 4 Wheat. 518 (1819)), and, accordingly, once the state entered into a contractual relationship, it must honor its terms.

To promote the public policy objective of accelerating economic growth, states often conceded a local monopoly, thereby maximizing the likelihood that the project would be profitable to the corporation. In the transportation field, especially, this eventually produced some thorny political economic conflicts and legal problems for judges. A good system of interconnecting roads, for example, or ferry service across a river, clearly promoted the state's objective. However, if successful, growth generated demand for more transit capability, and, as technology improved, better modes of transportation. If the demand were not met, local expansion would surely stall, and economic development would simply occur in a more hospitable location. Did the state violate its earlier contract if it issued a charter for a new project and thus jeopardizing the profitability of the existing one? As Horwitz (1977, 114) observes, "a startling variety of complicated economic changes began to unfold, which further undermined eighteenth century legal assumptions. Common roads were displaced by turnpikes, and ferries were threatened by the erection of bridges. Soon turnpikes were in turn challenged by canals, and canals by railroads, with each new step creating a complex of legal questions for which the past supplied only the dimmest of guidance." Yes, even way back then, technology presented law with enormous challenges.

One such case, *The Proprietors of the Charles River Bridge v. The Proprietors of the Warren Bridge* (36 U.S.

420 (1837)), arose in the 1830s and presented a real test to accepted doctrine of contracts, corporations, and monopolies. In 1785, the Massachusetts legislature had issued a charter creating a corporation to build and maintain a bridge across the Charles River connecting Boston and Charlestown. The ferry operations, dating back to 1650, had become outmoded, and it was clear that a bridge, now technologically feasible, was necessary to stimulate the local economy. The bridge was completed and went into operation in 1786, and it did have the desired effect. The population of the Boston-Charlestown area more than tripled between 1785 and 1827. Moreover, the bridge proprietors were allowed to exact a toll, which, given the robust increases in traffic, had reached $30,000 per year by 1827, a tidy sum for that era. Among the primary recipients of the project was Harvard University, which had owned the original ferry and had entered into a long-term beneficial arrangement within the terms of the Charles River Bridge operation (see, e.g., Kutler 1971). In other words, the project was a grand public policy success for the legislature, an impressive profit-making venture for the corporation, and a dependable income source for Harvard. Nevertheless, the Charles River Bridge could not comfortably accommodate anticipated transit demand if expansion continued at its current pace.

In 1828, the state legislature chartered The Proprietors of the Warren Bridge to erect a second edifice less than one mile from the old one. In addition, the Warren Bridge would convert to government control and offer free passage after a period of six years, a sufficient length of time for the corporation to realize a reasonable profit on its investment. The Charles River Bridge owners, facing financial meltdown, cried foul and filed suit, claiming that the new charter violated their contract with the state. Precedent was on their side. However, the forty-year interim had seen not only a burgeoning population but also a rich array of economic developments, in large part due to the success of their bridge. At the same time, it had produced a clear shift in the balance of political power, as evidenced by the Warren Bridge charter and the corporation's inability to muster sufficient force to block the legislation. Their recourse was to appeal to the judiciary to enjoin the competing project and force the state to honor its longstanding contract. The case was argued before the Supreme Judicial Court of Massachusetts in 1829. The Court was too closely divided on the legal issues to reach a decision, and the resulting opinions indicate that the judges placed the current understanding of the public interest (or that of the current dominant political economic factions) at the forefront of their reasoning.[10] Finally, the controversy met a similar fate before the U.S. Supreme Court. Although the case was not an easy one, the Court ultimately found in favor of the state and against the Charles River Bridge owners in 1837.[11] Writing for the majority, Chief Justice Taney gave considerable weight to the policy implications:

But the object and end of all government is to promote the happiness and prosperity of the community by which it is established; and it can never be assumed, that the government intended to diminish its power of accomplishing the end for which it was created. And in a country like ours, free, active, and enterprising, continually advancing in numbers and wealth; new channels of communication are daily found necessary, both for travel and trade; and are essential to the comfort, convenience, and prosperity of the people. A state ought never to be presumed to surrender this power, because, like the taxing power, the whole community have an interest in preserving it undiminished. And when a corporation alleges, that a state has surrendered for seventy years, its power of improvement and public accommodation, in a great and important line of travel, along which a vast number of its citizens must daily pass; the community have a right to insist . . . "that its abandonment ought not to be presumed, in a case, in which the deliberate purpose of the state to abandon it does not appear." The continued existence of a government would be of no great value, if by implications and presumptions, it was disarmed of the powers necessary to accomplish the ends of its creation; and the functions it was designed to perform, transferred to the hands of privileged corporations. . . . No one will question that the interests of the great body of the people of the state, would, in this instance, be affected by the surrender of this great line of travel to a single corporation, with the right to exact toll, and exclude competition for seventy years. While the rights of private property are sacredly guarded, we must not forget that the community also have rights, and that the happiness and well being of every citizen depends on their faithful preservation (36 U.S. 420, at 547–48).

Justice Story, in dissent (Justice Thompson also dissented), rejected this position, and raised a number of policy concerns of his own. He wondered, for example, why the state should be treated differently from other contractual partners. If the state is allowed to renege on its bargains, would this not jeopardize the legislature's ability to find entrepreneurs willing to undertake costly and risky projects? Moreover, he questioned the logic expressed by the majority:

But with a view to induce the Court to withdraw from all the common rules of reasonable and liberal interpretation in favour of grants, we have been told at the argument, that this very charter is a restriction upon the legislative power; that it is in derogation of the rights and interests of the state, and the people; that it tends to promote monopolies, and exclusive privileges; and that it will interpose an insuperable barrier to the progress of improvement. Now, upon every one of these propositions, which are assumed, and not proved, I entertain a directly opposite opinion; and, if I did not, I am not prepared to admit the conclusion for which they are adduced. If the legislature has made a grant, which involves any or all of these consequences, it is not for courts of justice to overturn the plain sense of the grant, because it has been improvidently or injuriously made. . . .

The erection of a bridge may be of the highest utility to the people. It may essentially promote the public convenience, and aid the public interests, and protect the public property. And if no persons can be found willing to undertake such a work,

unless they receive in return the exclusive privilege of erecting it, and taking toll; surely it cannot be said, as of course, that such a grant, under such circumstances, is, per se, against the interests of the people. Whether the grant of a franchise is, or is not, on the whole, promotive of the public interests; is a question of fact and judgment, upon which different minds may entertain different opinions. It is not to be judicially assumed to be injurious, and then the grant to be reasoned down. It is a matter exclusively confided to the sober consideration of the legislature; which is invested with full discretion, and possesses ample means to decide it. For myself, meaning to speak with all due deference for others, I know of no power or authority confided to the judicial department, to rejudge the decisions of the legislature upon such a subject. It has an exclusive right to make the grant, and to decide whether it be, or be not, for the public interests. It is to be presumed, if the grant is made, that it is made from a high sense of public duty, to promote the public welfare, and to establish the public prosperity. In this very case, the legislature has, upon the very face of the act, made a solemn declaration as to the motive for passing it; that—"The erecting of a bridge over Charles River, &c., will be of great public utility."

What court of justice is invested with authority to gainsay this declaration? To strike it out of the act, and reason upon the other words, as if it were not there? To pronounce that a grant is against the interests of the people, which the legislature has declared to be of great utility to the people? It seems to me to be our duty to interpret laws, and not to wander into speculations upon their policy. And where, I may ask, is the proof that Charles River Bridge has been against the interests of the people? The record contains no such proof; and it is, therefore, a just presumption that it does not exist (36 U.S. 420, at 603–06).

The case had originally been heard by the Marshall Court in 1831, but the justices were so divided that they could not reach a decision. Chief Justice John Marshall had long been a dominating figure, holding the longest tenure of any chief justice in the history of the Court, and he is considered by legal historians to be among the most influential justices ever to have served. Marshall had been an ardent advocate of adhering to contract and private property rights doctrine, as well as a strong proponent of strengthening power of the central government, and his signature is stamped upon a range of important opinions issued during his thirty-four-year engagement. Upon Marshall's death in 1835, President Andrew Jackson, who wished to see states rights preserved, appointed his attorney general, Roger Taney, to the position. Jackson and Marshall were in opposing political camps, and the president was pleased with his opportunity to replace the chief justice with someone more in agreement with him. This was not his only opportunity to shape the judiciary. Indeed, during his two terms, Jackson was able to replace a majority of the seven-member Marshall Court with appointments of his own choosing.[12]

Thus, by the time *Charles River Bridge* was reconsidered in 1837, the Court membership had been overhauled, and the divergent positions articulated by the justices clearly reflected the paramount factions in the larger polity. It is not serendipitous that the dissents by Justices Story and Thompson were so stridently worded, nor that they were issued by two remaining members of the Marshall Court.[13] Chief Justice Taney writes of the opportunities to "partake of the benefit of those improvements which are now adding to the wealth and prosperity, and the convenience and comfort of the civilized world" (36 U.S. 420, at 553). Justice Story, by contrast, prefers to hold onto "the old law . . . , in cases contested with as much ability and learning, as any in the annals of our jurisprudence, in resisting any such encroachments upon the rights and liberties of the citizens, secured by public grants. I will not consent to shake their title deeds, by any speculative niceties or novelties" (at 598). Clearly, they are pursuing different notions of "progress."

These grand themes have been sounded repeatedly throughout our history, particularly during periods of economic transition. There are those whose agenda is to press forward at whatever cost, either because that which is new is always better than the old (terms such as "modern" are nearly always used synonymously with "progress") or because the opening of new markets holds great potential to lift the entire community's "wealth and prosperity, convenience and comfort." On the other hand, another contingent will argue in favor of retaining the old, finding much comfort and security under the current status quo. After all, it is the old technology, the established networks of reliable economic relationships, that have created our current stable and predictable way of life. Beneath the surface of these arguments is a shifting coalitional politics, in which varying factional constellations jockey for advantage and challenge one another for dominance of the policymaking process. This was certainly the context that produced the *Charles River Bridge* controversy. The preeminence of the old political elite was under siege by an emerging one. The cast of characters may change from one era to the next, but this kind of conflict recurs in a repetitive cycle that inextricably links law with economics and politics. The prize might be power for power's sake, but the general presumption is that control of the lawmaking system also creates opportunities to stimulate growth of preferred economic sectors.

These are precisely the kind of factional political problems that Madison and his founding colleagues attempted to address. They constructed a system that would channel conflict in a hopefully productive direction, into official arenas where the most extreme tendencies might be tempered. To a large degree their design has been a supreme success. At both an individual and group level, conflict is generally played on a legitimate field, and participants usually follow the accepted rules of fair play. Law is a critical component of this process, defined both as end product (substance) and as rules of engagement (process). Law is an extension of the market activities of business, and governs literally every aspect of our lives. The United States produces far more lawyers per capita than any other nation, and it is among the most litigious. This does not mean that people do not take the law into their own hands; they have, and they do. Klansmen have engaged in terror and mayhem, while the so-called Army of God, and others of their ilk, have claimed credit for bombed abortion clinics. Moreover, judges and legislators have taken bribes, and laws have been written with clear discriminatory intent. Of course, there was the Civil War. Fortunately, even at their very worst, such activities represent a minority of conflict-resolving incidents. In any event, the Madisonian structure has worked to deflect a huge number of disputes into official forums, even if the structure seems to favor "haves" or the "have nots" (we return to this issue below).

This has been particularly critical as the political economy has lurched from one phase to the next, shifting from one tangle of dominant influences to another, and the cyclical dynamic has a variety of implications. Transition creates a great deal of disjuncture, throwing interaction networks out of sync, outmoding old routines governed by accumulated custom and accepted rules, and creating a high degree of uncertainty. Adapting to the new order, parties—such as those involved in the *Charles River Bridge* controversy—scramble to minimize their exposure to risk and to protect or consolidate their interests. Law and litigation are important components of that adaptation process. Processing claims through the court system is a means for legitimizing the realignment that is happening. Judicial intervention solidifies certain positions, creating benchmarks from which subsequent negotiations and expectations can be calculated. In other words, it seems to have a stabilizing influence.

This understanding of the role of law in the political economy suggests directional causality, the idea being that through the process of mobilization and response, the legal system exerts an influence on subsequent activities in the community. This leads to the notion that law can be used as a tool to plan and manage social and economic growth and development.[14] However, an alternative understanding of the role of law might hypothesize that established law is held in a state of tension by rapidly changing political economic conditions and is realigned in accommodation to the new order (see, e.g., Gordon 1984). Here we would find a dialectical process in which the existing legal model (thesis) is challenged by emerging forces (antithesis), with a series of new questions. Judicial consideration produces a synthesis, a reconciliation of current conflict with inherited legal principles, thus creating a different baseline that is more reflective of the unfolding balance of influences in the community. As the newly minted reasoning penetrates into transaction networks, stability is achieved until the next disturbance. In other words the law is shaped by the confluence of activities external to the legal system.

The *Charles River Bridge* scenario offers evidence to support both arguments. The Massachusetts legislature was attempting to use the law to engineer growth and development by issuing charters to corporations to build two bridges. Although the two acts were four decades apart, the legislative intent was the same in both instances. Moreover, when the second charter was challenged by litigation, the courts used a public interest rationale to reach a conclusion that could be justified in the name of the common good, although it seemed rather clear that the same case would have been decided differently if it had been brought forty years earlier. The fundamental principle did not change (the law's enduring quality), and the act in question was the same (building a transriver bridge). However, the underlying social, economic, and political reality had been transformed dramatically over the forty-year interval. What was at one time considered to be in the public interest (a monopoly service) was, by the end of the period, understood to be its opposite. The legal understanding of the contractual relationship between state and corporation in the conveyance of charters in 1785 was such that much could be left implied. By 1835, given the conspicuous changes in socioeconomic context, that conception no longer held full currency. This example also illustrates an interesting aspect of the legal and economic webs in which we find ourselves. The contours of both law and economics change in an ongoing process. There are no obvious demarcations separating one stage from the next, although one might point to landmark events or cases that suggest a break is occurring. At any given time the primary legal and economic currents trace their roots to an earlier era. In other words, the past is not destroyed to build the present; rather, layers are added to the webs of life as our social system develops, rendering each order more intricate and complex than the last.

Advocacy

One can, thus, approach the relationship between law and society from a range of perspectives. Does law direct the course of economic growth and technological development? Or, do lawmakers find themselves in the position of dealing with the consequences of ebbs and flows in technology and economic markets, simply responding to forces that move in directions largely independent of law? This relationship is a complex one, and generations of scholars have grappled with the question of causality. Law does seem to have an undeniable influence on the course of actions taken by establishing some understanding of rights and obligations among relationship partners and setting boundaries of acceptability with which most decisions comply. The bottom line in understanding these consequences is that law generates and/or reinforces advantages and disadvantages, thus creating impetus for players in any particular field to mobilize their resources in order to protect their preferred position or, on the other hand, to mount a challenge to the current order.

Property and wealth are decisively important resources in this effort, and it is not at all surprising that businesses, corporations, and other organized entities exert significant influences in legislative and judicial lawmaking. This, of course, is nothing new. Indeed, the U.S. Congress and state legislatures have long been the focus of intense lobbying effort by those able to accumulate the necessary resource portfolio; many organize expressly for that purpose. Although a different strategy is required to carry such effort into the judicial branch, resources are an essential ingredient to any attempts in that venue as well (e.g., Bentley 1908; Truman 1951; Schlozman and Tierney 1986; Berry 1989; Herrnson, Shaiko, and Wilcox 1998).

Moreover, successful advocacy in the courts often benefits from the presence of experienced and prominent advocates, whose services require considerable financial compensation, placing them out of reach to most individuals and other parties of limited means. Again, *Charles River Bridge* is illustrative. The upstart Warren Bridge proprietors were represented by Simon Greenleaf, a highly regarded member of the Harvard Law School faculty and one of the best-recognized legal scholars of his day, while the Charles River Bridge corporation retained Daniel Webster as lead counsel. Webster was the preeminent advocate of the era, having argued more cases before the Supreme Court than any other member of the bar (he won most of them). He was widely known for his skills as an orator, and he was a consistent defender of property and business rights under the Constitution (see, e.g., White 1988, 201–92, 664–69; McGuire 1993, 14–15). Again, there is nothing new in this observation. Historically, a relatively small cadre of "mega-lawyers" (Galanter 1983a) are recognized as the most effective advocates in any given era, and given their status and the fees they command, they have tended to represent resource-rich clients, especially corporations (see, e.g., Twiss 1942; Wolfskill 1962; Auerbach 1976; McGuire 1993). Indeed, Galanter (1974) argues that the language of law (especially that emanating from the courts) is usually the consequence of competition among resource-rich parties. These are the only entities who have the financial support and wherewithal to engage the process with the long-range view necessary to take a fight through to the bitter end, where law is made. Parties with fewer resources do not, and they tend to utilize the legal system to achieve concrete outcomes in specific conflicts.

This line of argument has a range of implications for research into the relationship between the legal system and the political economy. It seems rather clear, for example, that "landmark" court cases, such as *Charles River Bridge*, cases where law is unmistakably made, are usually produced by elite conflicts involving competing coalitions of factions. Indeed, the principal parties to such conflicts generally are corporations and other organized entities; where an individual is named, s/he is nearly always underwritten by organized effort. This is equally true whether we are considering litigation of the early nineteenth or the late twentieth century. Indeed, the evidence is more obvious from the record in the latter period, in which each side attracts an increasingly substantial array of third-party support as cases move to successively higher courts with widening jurisdictional reach (e.g., Epstein 1991). The stakes escalate as a case is appealed, not because of the dollar figure attached to the outcome (in fact, damage awards are often reduced on appeal), but because the conflict concerns law, the construction of legal language, and the rationale underlying it. It is for this reason that such cases are so significant. Our focus, for example, has centered on cases of this type.[15] Recognition of the dynamics at play is important to understanding how the law is made.

However, an exclusive focus on elite conflict as represented by disproportionately significant appellate cases misses the great bulk of the workload of courts and important aspects of their role. In fact, examination of ordinary cases would find the majority to involve status unequals whose controversies never move beyond the trial court in which they began. Throughout the nineteenth century, for example, when the courts' agendas were dominated by economic litigation—creditors versus debtors, landowners versus tenants, banks versus individuals and small businesses, sellers versus buyers, and so on (e.g., McIntosh 1990; Friedman and Percival 1976). This reflects the fact that rights of citizenship accrued primarily through property ownership, and, in light of Madison's observations regarding factions, the interlocking of politics, law, and economics seems rather clear.

In the early years of the republic, even the right to vote was attached to property holdings. Slavery was construed under the law as a property rights issue.[16] Although a bloody civil war put an end to slavery, and the adoption of the Thirteenth Amendment in 1865 officially banned the practice forever, lawmakers felt it necessary to amend the Constitution a fourteenth time (1868) in order to require explicitly that state governments recognize rights of citizenship to "all persons."

Although in all likelihood the Fourteenth Amendment was written with the intention of protecting fundamental rights of flesh-and-blood people (see, e.g., Graham 1968), especially the recently freed former slaves, in 1886 the U.S. Supreme Court found in *Santa Clara* that,

for purposes of the amendment's equal protection clause, corporations are persons. Indeed, Chief Justice Waite abruptly closed the door to any debate of the issue, interrupting oral arguments to state flatly: "The court does not wish to hear argument on the question whether the provision in the Fourteenth Amendment to the Constitution, which forbids a State to deny to any person within its jurisdiction the equal protection of the laws, applies to these corporations. We are all of opinion that it does."[17]

Thus endowed with constitutional personhood, the business sector unleashed its attorneys to develop an extensive portfolio of individual rights (see, e.g., Twiss 1942). In fact, corporations, embracing their newfound personhood, paraded before the Court to challenge Progressive era and subsequent New Deal economic reforms and regulations (Twiss 1942; Wolfskill 1962). For their part, the justices were often accommodating, conferring corporate persons with Fourteenth Amendment due-process rights (*Minneapolis & Saint Louis Railway v. Beckwith*, 129 U.S. 26 (1889)), Fifth Amendment due process rights (*Noble v. Union River Logging Railroad*, 147 U.S. 165 (1893)), and search and seizure protections under the Fourth Amendment (*Hale v. Henkel*, 201 U.S. 43 (1906)).[18] In 1905, the Court further insulated businesses from most forms of government interference, particularly with regard to contractual relations (*Lochner v. New York*, 198 U.S. 45 (1905)). The *Lochner* majority, as Justice Holmes noted in dissent, elevated an economic theory (laissez faire) to constitutional status.[19]

A number of commentators have noted that the Court's acceptance of corporations as persons, coupled with its *Lochner*-era substantive due process jurisprudence, was an interpretive silver platter upon which the business sector banqueted for more than a half-century.[20] Much of this development occurred well before the Fourteenth Amendment was construed to apply to individual humans as persons. Indeed, as we have discussed in earlier chapters, the cultivation of individual rights did not take place in earnest until well into the twentieth century. With regard to some issues, such as bargaining over employment contracts, legislatures were forced to acknowledge the unequal position of labor well before the courts, as judges clung to old doctrine until the 1940s.

The U.S. Supreme Court does not dictate an agenda to the nation's trial courts, but its caseload, and that of other appellate tribunals, does reflect major currents of activity in the political economy. Moreover, as we have noted, appellate-level opinions are statements of law that create benchmarks to which members of the public can refer and which take on enhanced significance to those who find themselves in trial-level litigation. The trial courts' agenda continued to be heavily tilted toward economic issues throughout the nineteenth century, although the proportion declined as individuals gained access to courts to sue for divorce in the latter half and as the volume of personal injury claims and criminal prosecutions inched gradually upward.[21] By the 1920s, noneconomic issues accounted for a sizeable percentage of the judicial agenda,[22] and the post–Depression era witnessed a virtual explosion of litigation in which parties sought recognition and protection of their individual rights (see, e.g., Kluger 1976; Manwaring 1962). These movements did not diminish the set of rights held by business and corporate persons. If anything, that legal cache continued to grow. However, they did expand the applicability of law across a wide range of human behaviors and enhanced the analogical linkages among what had been considered quite separable spheres.

The Later Years:
Communication, Community, and Law

Information, consumption, production, markets, and commerce are all highly interconnected concepts in today's world. Recall that Hamilton argued at the founding that economics and commercial intercourse should be harnessed as a means for linking people in distant states and localities together as a nation. Thus the Constitution's commerce clause was born. But birth implies subsequent life, and the law of the commerce clause has grown up and matured with the nation's economic system. There has also been ongoing conflict between the states and the federal government regarding regulation of interstate commerce. As noted above, there was considerable debate about the commerce clause during the ratification process, with some arguing that it was an encroachment on the sovereign power of the states. The language also leaves a number of issues unclear, such as what is to be included within the concept of "commerce," and what measures states can take in the absence of federal action. The first opportunity for the Supreme Court to address the congressional commerce power came in 1824 (*Gibbons v. Ogden*, 22 U.S. 1), in a case challenging New York law that created a steamboat monopoly on the state's waterways. Chief Justice Marshall, for the Court, construed commerce broadly to encompass transportation and all other "intercourse," and struck down the statute as an invalid usurpation of federal authority. The power to regulate interstate commerce, he wrote, is "complete in itself, may be exercised to its utmost extent, and acknowledges no limitations, other than are prescribed in the Constitution." This understanding grants Congress a great deal of latitude in all commercial regulatory matters. Left unclear was the extent of any concurrent state authority, and whether states could act when Congress had not (dormant commerce clause issues).[23]

The question of state power was, of course, a touchy one in the period leading up to the Civil War, and the Supreme Court produced a series of ambiguous opinions, as the justices were no doubt reticent about joining the increasingly bitter conflict. After the war, industrial development took off. Although Congress was slow to act, a number of states did impose regulations within their respective borders, despite considerable pressure from a variety of commercial markets for national standards. Challenges to state regulation of commerce initially found a much more consistent Supreme Court. Indeed, a number of state statutes were invalidated as "dormant" commerce clause violations, on the rationale that congressional failure to act does not cede authority to the states (cf., *Munn v. Illinois*, 94 U.S. 113 (1877); *Wabash, St. Louis & Pacific Ry. Co. v. Illinois*, 118 U.S. 557 (1886)).[24] In matters touching upon interstate commerce, the Constitution grants exclusive authority to the central government. Congress did eventually take significant action, creating the Interstate Commerce Commission in 1887 (Interstate Commerce Act, 24 Stat. 379; see Skorownek 1982). This, of course, set off new rounds of litigation, lobbying, legislation, and further litigation (see, e.g., Ely 1992, 1997), much of it centering on the question of what activities are to be understood as commerce.[25] In 1937, the Court set a modern standard in *NLRB v. Jones & Laughlin Steel Corp.*, 301 U.S. 1 (1937), finding that intrastate activities that "have such a close and substantial relation to interstate commerce that their control is essential or appropriate to protect that commerce from burdens and obstructions" are within Congress's power to regulate (at 37). In *U.S. v. Darby*, 312 U.S. 100 (1941), the Court overturned the distinction it earlier had maintained between "production" and "commerce" (see *Hammer v. Dagenhart*, 247 U.S. 251 (1918)), preferring a practical understanding of commerce to a technical one. Indeed, while production of a good often takes place entirely within a state's borders, those activities can have considerable implications for interstate traffic and exchange.

Although the Court's commerce clause jurisprudence was hard to follow at times,[26] the general thrust through much of the twentieth century was to take an expansive view of congressional authority. Indeed, the commerce clause figured prominently in civil-rights–era case law upholding congressional authority to ban racially discriminatory practices by local commercial establishments (e.g., *Katzenbach v. McClung*, 379 U.S. 294 (1964), prohibiting racial discrimination at local restaurants; and *Heart of Atlanta Motel, Inc. v. United States*, 379 U.S. 241 (1964), prohibiting racial discrimination at local motels).

However, in this area, as in all the others we have explored, the language of the law is inherently ambiguous. Thirty years after *Heart of Atlanta*, a very different Court addressed a set of questions regarding the proper definition of interstate commerce and challenged congressional authority (*U.S. v. Lopez*, 514 U.S. 549 (1995)). In the *Gun Free School Zones Act of 1990* (18 U.S.C. §§ 922), Congress made it a federal offense "for any individual knowingly to possess a firearm at a place that the individual knows, or has reasonable cause to believe, is a school zone." On 10 March 1992, a twelfth-grade student at a Texas high school, Alphonso Lopez, was arrested with a loaded handgun as he arrived at school. He was initially held under a state statute banning possession of firearms on school premises, but the following day, he was charged with violating the federal *Gun Free School Zones Act* and the state charges were dropped. Lopez challenged his prosecution, arguing that firearm possession at a public school has only tangential relation to interstate commerce and that Congress, therefore, had exceeded its constitutional authority. Chief Justice Rehnquist, writing for a five-member majority, agreed, finding that "even these modern-era precedents which have expanded congressional power under the Commerce Clause confirm that this power is subject to outer limits. . . . [To be valid,] *a general regulatory statute* [must] *bear a substantial relation to commerce*" (*Lopez*, at 8–10; emphasis in original).

The government had based its case on the contention that possession of a firearm in a school zone can affect the national economy in at least two ways. First, violent crime produces substantial costs that are broadly distributed by insurance practices. Second, violent crime deters people from traveling to places they believe to be unsafe. Moreover, the presence of guns in schools significantly affects the learning environment and jeopardizes the ability of our schools to produce a productive citizenry, which, "in turn, would have an adverse effect on the Nation's economic well-being" (*Lopez*, at 16).

The *Lopez* majority rejected all those arguments: "Under the theories that the Government presents in support of §§ 922(q), it is difficult to perceive any limitation on federal power, even in areas such as criminal law enforcement or education where States historically have been sovereign. Thus, if we were to accept the Government's arguments, we are hard pressed to posit any activity by an individual that Congress is without power to regulate" (*Lopez*, at 17). Justice Breyer, writing for the four dissenters, reached a completely opposite conclusion, reasoning that isolated acts may seem trivial when considered individually but can clearly accumulate to substantial proportions, and that the courts should grant Congress considerable leeway, as they had done for most of the twentieth century, at least since the New Deal era, to determine linkages between designated activities (such as firearm possession in school zones) and interstate commerce. Citing a number of statistical reports and the series of recent incidents involving guns at middle and high schools around the country, Breyer found

the situation sufficiently serious to draw attention from Congress. Moreover, the dissent noted direct links among the educational process, general occupational prospects, job performance and work productivity, demand for better-educated citizens, competition in the global marketplace and the growing information-technology sector, performance by local school districts, and location decisions by major employers. In short, Congress could easily demonstrate a rational basis for its action in this instance. Finally, and "[m]ore importantly," the dissent argued that

if a distinction between commercial and noncommercial activities is to be made, this is not the case in which to make it. The majority clearly cannot intend such a distinction to focus narrowly on an act of gun possession standing by itself, for such a reading could not be reconciled with . . . the civil rights cases . . . —in each of those cases the specific transaction (the race based exclusion . . .) was not itself "commercial." And, if the majority instead means to distinguish generally among broad categories of activities, differentiating what is educational from what is commercial, then, as a practical matter, the line becomes almost impossible to draw. Schools that teach reading, writing, mathematics, and related basic skills serve *both* social and commercial purposes, and one cannot easily separate the one from the other. American industry itself has been, and is again, involved in teaching. When, and to what extent, does its involvement make education commercial? Does the number of vocational classes that train students directly for jobs make a difference? Does it matter if the school is public or private, nonprofit or profit-seeking? Does it matter if a city or State adopts a voucher plan that pays private firms to run a school? Even if one were to ignore these practical questions, why should there be a theoretical distinction between education, when it significantly benefits commerce, and environmental pollution, when it causes economic harm? (*Lopez*, at 16 (Breyer, J., dissenting); references deleted from original).

The chief justice took serious issue with these positions:

Justice Breyer rejects our reading of precedent and argues that "Congress . . . could rationally conclude that schools fall on the commercial side of the line." Again, Justice Breyer's rationale lacks any real limits because, depending on the level of generality, any activity can be looked upon as commercial. Under the dissent's rationale, Congress could just as easily look at child rearing as "fall[ing] on the commercial side of the line" because it provides a "valuable service—namely, to equip [children] with the skills they need to survive in life and, more specifically, in the workplace". . . . There is a view of causation that would obliterate the distinction of what is national and what is local in the activities of commerce. . . . These are not precise formulations, and in the nature of things they cannot be. But we think they point the way to a correct decision of this case. The possession of a gun in a local school zone is in no sense an economic activity that might, through repetition elsewhere, substantially affect any sort of interstate commerce. Respondent was a local student at a local school; there is no indication that he had recently moved in interstate commerce, and there is no requirement that his possession of the firearm have any concrete tie to interstate commerce (*Lopez*, at 18–19; references deleted from original).

The issues involved in *Lopez* and the competing views of the commerce clause articulated by the justices are important for several reasons. Indeed, the case attracted no fewer than forty-four *amici curiae* participants of various types, including a range of advocacy groups and state, county, and local government organizations, as well as sixteen U.S. Senators and thirty-four members of the House of Representatives. Is the simple act of possessing a firearm within a public school zone a purely individual incident, or is it indelibly connected to a host of other activities, national in scope? Those who are responsible for authoritative interpretation of our laws—in this instance, a most significant phrase of the U.S. Constitution—offer very different perspectives on the identical action. Chief Justice Rehnquist sees the armed Alphonso Lopez as a singular silhouette, linked to nothing beyond himself, perhaps caught in the light cast by state or local criminal law. Justice Breyer, on the other hand, finds Lopez trapped in an intractable web of life in which nearly every conceivable individual action produces waves of reaction among others linked across the entire community landscape by the economic implications of what he has done. Rehnquist argues that some things have no economic impact and are entirely local in scope, such as possessing a gun at a high school. Presumably, there are other activities that fall into a similar category, although it is not altogether clear what they might be (the chief justice did offer a few hints, such as family relations). On the other side of the argument, Justice Breyer seems also to hint that there might be some instances where he and Rehnquist would agree, but he offers little guidance. Indeed, the thrust of his reasoning produces unclear boundaries around that which is purely local. The intersecting webs of law and economics both appear quite ambiguous and, at the same time, thoroughly ubiquitous.

During the 1999 term, the Court revisited the commerce clause in another case of national significance in an application of the *Violence Against Women Act of 1998*. Again, a bare majority found that Congress had overstepped its authority, this time in creating a civil remedy for women alleging that their rights had been violated under the act, thus allowing them to file suit in federal court (*U.S. v. Morrison*, 120 S.Ct. 1740 (2000)). Writing for the five-member majority, Chief Justice Rehnquist noted that "the concern that we expressed in Lopez that Congress might use the Commerce Clause to completely obliterate the Constitution's distinction between national and local authority seems well founded" (at 1753). In short, the *Morrison* Court concluded: "We accordingly reject the argument that Congress may regulate noneconomic, violent criminal conduct based solely on that conduct's aggregate effect on interstate commerce. The Constitution requires a dis-

tinction between what is truly national and what is truly local" (at 1754).

Communications Technology, Politics, and Law

If the nineteenth and early twentieth centuries were marked by law's stimulus of and reaction to the budding of economic capitalism in general and industrialization in particular, the latter part of the twentieth is distinguished by legal catalysts and responses to the overall maturation of capitalism and the so-called "communications revolution." Of course, latter-day "revolution" or no, communication has always been essential to society, economics, and law. Communication is essential to relationships. Indeed, without communication there can be no action to organize social relations, and the process of economic growth and development would lack a critical stimulus. It is indispensable to the formation of cultural consensus, to intellectual exchange, to transfer information and experience both horizontally and across time, and to allow decision makers to exercise informed discretion. Indeed, George Washington had considered it an important responsibility of government to keep people informed of issues pending and actions taken, and he had supported development and maintenance of an extensive, reliable postal system. Madison agreed, but also felt strongly that the people should be able to communicate directly with their representatives, and dependable mail service was necessary to that end.[27]

Among his many observations during his tour of the United States in the 1830s, de Tocqueville noted the importance of communications to the processes of collective action and self-governing[28]:

In order that an association among a democratic people should have any power, it must be a numerous body. The persons of whom it is composed are therefore scattered over a wide extent, and each of them is detained in the place of his domicile by the narrowness of his income or by the small unremitting exertions by which he earns it. Means must then be found to converse every day without seeing one another, and to take steps in common without having met. Thus hardly any democratic association can do without newspapers. . . . If all the inhabitants of the Union had the suffrage, but a suffrage which should extend only to the choice of their legislators in Congress, they would require but few newspapers, because they would have to act together only on very important, but very rare, occasions. But within the great national association lesser associations have been established by law in every county, every city, and indeed in every village, for the purposes of local administration. The laws of the country thus compel every American to co-operate every day of his life with some of his fellow citizens for a common purpose, and each one of them requires a newspaper to inform him what all the others are doing.[29]

In other words, an extensive communications infrastructure allows geographically distant people to engage in meaningful exchange necessary for republican government to be successful, and essential for people scattered across vast territories to establish common bonds and to attach themselves to the union.

Moreover, Katsch (1989, 88) has argued that as print media came more universally into use, they "promoted a model of resolving disputes in which rules could reliably be found in books and then applied. Even among large populations, therefore, print supported the ideal of a law that was public and applied to all, a common law that could overcome barriers of both time and space. During a period of expanding knowledge . . . [t]he production of large numbers of standardized copies enhanced the authority of legal rules. . . . Printed works were also an effective point of reference and served to organize and shape the use of information within the judicial process."

Print distribution and a comprehensive postal system made the world smaller. In addition, they exerted significant democratizing influences and proved to be a core ingredient to economic growth and entrepreneurial development. Both the postal system and print media were extraordinarily important to government officials and politicians in getting their message out to members of the public, wherever they were, and to commercial advertisers in reaching consumers, local or remote. The communications process erupted with the deployment of telegraphy in the nineteenth century. Indeed, newspapers flourished during the late 1800s when they could receive reports from field correspondents across the United States about events as they were unfolding that could be printed in the following day's edition. According to communications historians, "Between 1870 and 1900, the number of daily newspapers in the United States quadrupled, and the number of copies sold each day increased nearly six times" (Douglas 1987, xxiii).

Marconi's introduction of wireless transmission in 1899 created a virtual communications explosion. Distant communication was not only a reality, but the technology for transmission and reception was much cheaper, accessible to government agencies, corporations, and organizations of all types, as well as to enterprising members of the general public, and newspapers could quickly receive updates from around the globe. The economic implications were also quite enormous. For example, orders could be taken and inventory information quickly exchanged from distant locations, thus transforming the entire demand-supply process. These changes also eventuated in a radical transformation in the general understanding of commerce, which in turn, had constitutional implications. As observed in *Lopez* and *Morrison*, it was to become increasingly difficult to distinguish clearly between economic and noneconomic activities, as well as between purely local commerce and interstate commerce.

After the invention of wireless transmission, it did not take long to move from dots and dashes to full audio communication. The airwaves soon brimmed with messages and audio broadcasts from a multitude of sources. As never before, people were connected to news and information sources, and potentially to each other. Anyone able to purchase the necessary hardware could immediately send and receive messages, and by 1920, broadcast from makeshift radio stations. Labor unions, churches, universities, and others quickly set up shop providing direct links to information sources among a vast and expanding receiving audience, and corporations began to develop news and entertainment programming that attracted advertising sponsors.[30] Indeed, by 1930, the newspaper industry was on the decline. Advertising dollars were evaporating as corporate sponsors gravitated to popular radio, where the connection to consumers was more direct, and news broadcasts attracted larger audiences who could hear details of ongoing events immediately rather than wait for tomorrow's newspaper.

The presidential election of 1932 was a watershed for network radio, as people huddled around their receivers listening for the latest returns from across the country. Newspaper sales slumped, rather than boomed as anticipated. The pinnacle of the new era of communications was reached in 1933, when, in the midst of the Great Depression, the newly elected president

gave four momentous "fireside chats." These broadcast talks became not only a Franklin D. Roosevelt specialty but milestones in politics and broadcasting. . . . Roosevelt's "chats" implied a sharing of ideas in a sort of family council. . . . People seemed to feel, according to various observers, that Roosevelt was talking to them directly as individuals, knew their problems, and was interested in them. . . . Such reactions were not universal . . . [b]ut millions found in his calm, measured statements assurance that he was their representative and friend. Their response gave the President—at least for the moment—an incalculable political advantage. The fireside chats and the response they won helped propel through Congress with miraculous speed a broad legislative program (Barnouw 1968, 7).

The political rhetoric of the early twentieth century attending the radio sounded much like that from the founding era regarding the benefits of mail communications. The new technologies promised to connect citizens from across the wide geographic expanse of the United States to each other and to their government. The need for physical proximity is reduced; people can share experiences and communicate without face-to-face interactions. Information is empowering, and mass, immediate access to vast amounts of information potentially has a democratizing influence. By the same token, information, and access to it, has obvious commercial implications for producers, advertisers, and consumers alike, and there are no clear boundaries between the political and the economic.

From a legal perspective, wireless transmission went completely unregulated for more than a decade on the assumption that bandwidth was infinite (see, e.g., Powe 1987). Moreover, property law had been based upon tangible objects, a conception that clearly did not describe either spectrum bandwidth or audio communications.[31] In a 1910 debate in the House of Representatives, one congressman expressed the contemporary understanding rather succinctly: "We have been brought up with the idea that the air was absolutely free to everyone."[32] As historian Susan Douglas (1987, 218) notes, "How could something people thought was absolutely free and impossible to partition actually become property?"

However, it was becoming clear that, although invisible and existing entirely in intangible space, the airwaves contained a finite capacity for transmissions. Interference problems were escalating; frequencies were jammed, especially in the heavily populated areas, by simultaneous use; and there was growing concern that freelancers and anonymous broadcasters were spreading false and misleading information. The call for government regulation was stepped up as indicated by an increasing number of bills introduced in Congress each year. The events surrounding the sinking of the massive ocean liner, *Titanic*, in April 1912, brought the issue home. Distress signals from the ship were picked up immediately from stations and other cruisers too far away to help, while the radio operators on nearby vessels had unfortunately turned off their receivers and gone to bed (they had no emergency provisions or round-the-clock monitor systems). Moreover, central stations were totally jammed by the crush of incoming inquiries, and some anonymous broadcasters signaled that the *Titanic* had been rescued and was in tow, a message that was picked up by newswires and printed in a number of major newspapers the next morning. Congress reacted promptly in July with legislation regulating wireless systems and procedures at sea and on the Great Lakes, followed in August by more general broadcasting regulations in the *Radio Act of 1912* (Douglas 1987, 220–35). The *Radio Act* for the first time recognized the airwaves as finite property, assigned various portions of the spectrum to particular users, required licenses, and mandated that licensees broadcast in the public interest. The legislation was subsequently amended several times, and the Federal Communication Commission (FCC) was formed in 1934 to oversee the nation's airwaves. By 1935, this included the new high-frequency, relatively static-free FM broadcast, and by 1939, television (e.g., Barnouw 1968, 122–30).

Since 1934, the FCC has been an active agency, issuing and reviewing thousands of licenses and promulgating regulations for an expanding industry on the proposition that broadcasters are using a scarce public resource and should, therefore, operate in the public interest. Dramatic developments in the communications industries in the late twentieth and early twenty-first centuries have led some to question the viability of the scarcity rationale. The number of radio and television broadcast stations has dramatically proliferated, the nation's households are rapidly being equipped to receive cable and satellite transmissions,[33] and Internet connections are quickly integrating with telephone, cable, and satellite services.

One can draw clear parallels to the early radio era. The number of information sources has exploded, and the array of choices is impressive. The new technologies are more interactive than the old broadcast, allowing for direct electronic interactions instantaneously point to point around the globe, leading many to argue that they will have dramatic democratizing influences. Indeed, software entrepreneur Bill Gates talks of how the latest desktop utilities empower the individual (Gates 1995), and CNN repeatedly reminds us that "you are what you know." As Judge Betty B. Fletcher, of the 9th U.S. Circuit Court of Appeals, recently noted in a closely watched Internet encryption case, "In this increasingly electronic age, we are all required in our everyday lives to rely on modern technology to communicate with one another" (*Bernstein v. U.S. Department of Justice*, No. 97-16686, 9th Cir. 1999, at 4242; available online at www.ce9.uscourts.gov/).

Moreover, with the convergence of all telecommunications media, probably in Internet cyberspace, individuals are increasingly able to customize their own preferred informational menu. The *Wall Street Journal*, for example, provides an online service called the "Personal Journal," allowing subscribers to receive only individually customized reports on selected topics without the bother of confronting irrelevant information (Putzel 1995; National Public Radio 1995). In fact, the "push" information-delivery model has rapidly become quite popular among the "wired" public. A plethora of services such as The PointCast Network, NETdelivery, Netscape In-Box Direct, and BackWeb (to name a few) deliver specialized news, information, and product announcements on a regular basis to the individual user's desktop. In addition, the much ballyhooed website blocking software, such as NetNanny, CyberSitter, and SurfWatch (among many others), and the television v-chip are additional steps in the same direction.

Sunstein (1995, 1763) suggests that given the forces at work, an unregulated information marketplace will likely lead to "social balkanization in which most people's consumption choices simply reinforce their own prejudices and platitudes, or even worse." Moreover, he argues,

Quite outside of science fiction, it is foreseeable that free markets in communications will be a mixed blessing. They could create a kind of accelerating "race to the bottom," in which many or most people see low-quality programming involving trumped-up scandals or sensationalistic anecdotes calling for little in terms of quality or quantity of attention. It is easily imaginable that well-functioning markets in communications will bring about a situation in which many of those interested in politics merely fortify their own unreflective judgments, and are exposed to little or nothing in the way of competing views. It is easily imaginable that the content of the most widely viewed programming will be affected by the desires of advertisers, in such a way as to produce shows that represent a bland, watered-down version of conventional morality, and that do not engage serious issues in a serious way for fear of offending some group in the audience (Sunstein 1995, 1763–64; notes deleted).

It would be supremely ironic if the telecommunications revolution, which promises to make a nearly unimaginable array of information available to the individual at the click of a mouse, in reality produces a net reduction (perhaps a significant one) in access to and interaction with informational, viewpoint, and communications diversity.

As the enormous growth of e-commerce in the 1990s attests, the economic implications of the information revolution rival those in the political sphere. Indeed, one of the primary reasons people use the Internet is to shop for goods and services. Marketers are able, as never before, to target their advertising to consumer audiences self-identified according to their expressed preferences. Niche marketing does have the potential to be more enriching than a broad-based, blanket communications strategy, where content would by necessity tend toward the bland, noncontroversial denominator. However, the combination of access costs and varying consumer preferences probably means that those who are enriched by differing arrays of information, in effect, segregate themselves from one another and from the less well-connected. In the postindustrial, hyper-information age, then, we see dynamics at work that are similar to those observable during earlier periods of technology-driven transitions. There are forces that pull individuals in opposite directions—one toward social cohesion and solidarity; the other, toward social conflict. Timothy Luke (1991) has argued that "communities today are not much more than an aggregation of atomized individuals organized into discrete geographic-legal units. Community becomes so thin because workplace and residence, production and consumption, identity and interests, administration and allocation are so divided in . . . an advanced industrial society predicated primarily on geographic and social mobility. This division of interests, loss of common historical consciousness, weakening of shared beliefs, and lessening of ecological responsibility is what necessitates alternative approaches to understanding community" (cf. Meyrowitz 1985; Rheingold 1993; Negroponte 1995).³⁴

Community, Relational Distance, and Political Economy

The notion of community is central to understanding social structures and relational distance in human associations, and it is useful in shedding light upon the relationships between law and the larger political economy. Building upon the observations and theories of a number of his contemporaries, nineteenth-century political economist, Ferdinand Tönnies ([1887] 1957) attempted to comprehend the influences of industrialization on those aspects of society that bind people together. Tönnies addressed the question of community by comparing life circumstances in preindustrial and industrial nations, leading to a conceptual distinction between Gemeinschaft and Gesellschaft. Gemeinschaft, most likely observable in preindustrial locations, is marked by a vital, active appreciation of fraternity and family; observance of custom and tradition; and shared values, goals, and language—in short, a sense of bounded community. Industrialization, by contrast, seemed to be accompanied by a form of hyper-individualism in which relationships are instrumental, transitory, and contractually oriented, or Gesellschaft. Tönnies argued that the processes of urbanization and industrialization would lead to the decay of Gemeinschaft and consequently the destruction of traditional community, security, and intimacy (Tönnies [1887] 1957; also see Sennett 1978). Thus, relational distance increases as a social system industrializes and the population gravitates to dense urban centers.

Such observations regarding individuals and their social relations offer useful perspectives into the role of law in the larger political economy. Law is no substitute for intimacy. However, we have tended to deploy law to supplement for the decline in effectiveness of traditional binding agents, to protect ourselves and our assets in a world in which our lives are enmeshed with proportionally fewer trustworthy intimates (Maine 1861, 162ff).

Conflict requires relationships. This statement seems almost trivial; however, it is a crucial starting point. The strategy employed to cope with conflict depends upon the quality and character of the relationship from which the problem developed. Litigation is always an option, but it is an unusually expensive and risky one. Most conflict is resolved without resort to the legal system through some form of negotiation. Indeed, the vast majority of disputes that do get translated into litigation are settled short of trial. A full-course trial requires considerable expenditure of resources and substantial time commitment. It can be a thoroughly humiliating experience, and the outcome is well beyond the control of either party and is fully unpredictable. Most people do not willingly choose such a protracted process, but prefer something less formal that offers a sense of compromise and control. Parties involved in an ongoing, mutually beneficial partnership, and who anticipate continuing their arrangement well beyond today, have every incentive for finding amicable ways for dealing with distress, selecting a strategy that will not jeopardize their future. By contrast, strangers abruptly thrown together in a problem situation have no previous encounters upon which to build trust and no anticipated future. With a relationship based in conflict and no buffering agents, the participants can quickly find themselves in an escalating situation. Finally, parties who are severing ties, or who are perpetual adversaries, have little reason to treat one another gingerly. Strangers and persistent adversaries usually just avoid contact, ignoring small indignities but allowing alienation and estrangement to grow (e.g., Felstiner 1974; Felstiner, Abel, and Sarat 1980–81). When avoidance is not possible, conflict has the potential to accelerate freely.[35] Another way of articulating all of this is that "relational distance" makes a difference in the disputing process. Litigation is most likely where parties are unfamiliar and, as a consequence, relationships tend to be formal where relational distance is greatest.

As we have noted, by the turn of the twentieth century, a comparatively large proportion of people were no longer self-sufficient, but dependent upon the goodwill of a vast web of strangers and faceless corporations. Obviously, the developmental forces did not stall out, and as the economy of our social system continued to develop, the density and complexity of actions and interactions accelerated. The accompanying market diversification requires more definitive divisions of labor, which are, in turn, reinforced in all spheres of community life. When this occurs, a multiplicity of social groupings is created, each with a special identity, but also likely overlapping with others. Hence, there are occupational, professional, recreational, gender-based, age-based, familial, religious, ethnic, ideological, national, and global groups, among many others, each vying for the attention and allegiance of individuals.[36] Group identity allows each individual to situate herself in the larger political economy and it is necessary to the process of collective political action (e.g., Olson 1971). Moreover, it creates a framework for understanding the world, one's role in it, and for discriminating among sources of information (e.g., du Preez 1980). The crosscurrents at work have been observed by a number of social scientists (e.g., Putnam 1995; Coleman 1982b; West and Loomis 1998; cf. Barber 1996).

Indeed, some have argued that an additional concomitant of the growing division of labor in postindustrial societies is decreased importance placed upon the contribution of any given individual. Survival of the larger system depends less upon the actions of any one person than upon the interlocking mutuality of action and performance of groups in the political ecosystem.

This has become particularly exaggerated in the United States, with the proliferation of corporate entities and a host of other organizations, which further devalues the worth of individuals (e.g., Coleman 1974, 1982a).[37] An increasing proportion of the total relations in which a person is engaged, then, involves a collective nonperson on the other side, producing what one commentator has termed an "asymmetric society" (Coleman 1982a). The asymmetry is not only structural, but also entails a growing imbalance in the power and resource center of gravity, which also favors organizations. Further, this also means that, increasingly, individuals' relationships with other people occur within a corporate or organizational milieu, a context that is only marginally or imperfectly controllable by the individual. Compared to a more traditional interaction domain, one-to-one associations occur less by choice and are more random. Moreover, the shared organizational culture is decision driven (from ranks above), distant and diffuse, rather than the result of custom, ritual, and embedded memory.[38] Indeed, as we have observed throughout this book, every aspect of the human life cycle, from birth to youth, to death, and our very identity as well as close personal and family relationships and related decisions, have all become heavily rationalized, laden with law.

Extensive sociopolitical diversification in people's identity has further economic implications, creating opportunity for consumer service and commodity marketers, who view individuals less as citizens of particular states than as consumers of products. Cultural commentator Judith Williamson (1978, 46), summarizes the perspective quite well: "We differentiate ourselves from other people by what we buy. . . . In this process we become identified with the product that differentiates us." Indeed, a perusal of product marketing literature indicates that the major emphasis in that field during the last quarter of the twentieth century has involved segmentation, targeting and penetrating increasingly minute audiences based upon demographic profiles and projected preferences. The magazine industry offers a telling case in point, providing the population with a dazzling array of periodicals with highly specific content and focus. Subscriptions to specialized journals have proliferated in recent years, allowing direct contact by advertisers to their targets. In addition, this phenomenon represents a point of entry for other product marketers and political organizations alike. When combined with public records and other demographic data, specialized magazine subscription lists provide a convenient method for stratifying the population into increasingly smaller identity groups. Indeed, we have witnessed an expanding menu of choices in radio and cable television programming, as industries have perfected the science of niche marketing. The same techniques are now used by advocacy groups and political parties, allowing, for example, political operatives to identify "soccer moms" as an important constituency group, targeted for mobilization in the 1996 election cycle.[39]

Current trends indicate that niche marketing is giving way to household and individual micro-targeting, or "narrowcasting," in which "the primary objects . . . are to (1) increase a given firm's 'share of the customer' rather than simply the share of the market; and (2) to 'collaborate with your customers' through two-way (interactive) communication" (Dawson and Foster 1998, 62).[40] The explosion in information technology has, thus, created new opportunities, and we are often reminded of the "power of information" and the self-empowerment that access to online information sources brings to individuals (e.g., Gates 1995; Negroponte 1995). New technologies allow marketers to deploy an interactive model in which individuals' preferences can be delineated both by direct interaction and by indirect compilations of contacts and purchases.[41] Internet marketers, for example, are intensely interested in profiling as much information as possible about their website visitors so that they can tailor follow-up contacts to the perceived and expressed interests of potential customers.[42] Indeed, when using the communications capabilities of computer networks, most individuals do not realize that their identity can easily be determined,[43] the full record of their activities can be traced and logged,[44] and their messages and files can be opened and read, even if encrypted.[45]

Law is a means of imposing order in the face of growing differences. The greater the degree of differentiation and organization, the less connected individual members of a society are to each other, and, given the multiplicity of competing allegiances, the lower the degree of influence any particular group can exercise over its members. Indeed, the force of inherited custom, tradition, and folkways, as well as informal rules of etiquette and fair play that spontaneously arise in communal situations to enhance integrated group life, are significantly impaired (see, e.g., Ellul 1964, 1973; cf. Grant 1969, 1986). At the same time, individuals have lost their ability to have singular impact both in the collective enterprise and in a growing proportion of their relationships (see, e.g., Dahrendorf 1959; Tajfel 1978). In such a context, it would not be surprising to see expanded use of law as an attempt to compensate for the decay in the mediating influence often attributed to groups and their associated structures. Legislatures are likely to produce an excessive volume of rules and regulations. We might see a tendency to exaggerate isolated instances of disorder, to elevate unrelated episodes of social pathology to the status of crisis indicators, and thus an obligation to create additional law in the name of public order and domestic tranquility (e.g., Glassner 1999). Such has been the reaction to the "missing-children crisis" of the 1980s, and the "road-rage" phenomenon and public school shooting incidents of the 1990s. Indeed, a legal response has a more civilized feel to it than outright repression.

For their part, individuals, as well as organized entities, might make greater use of the law as partial strategy for seeking insulation from what is perceived to be an increasingly risk-filled, unscrupulous world in which traditional ties and connections provide a diminished buffer. Obviously, individual parties can neither legislate nor issue regulations. Their ability to deploy law is attached to litigation in the judicial system. To file suit is more civilized than to engage in acts of violence.

On the other hand, the fact that the 1990s were so marked by isolated and (probably) disconnected horrific events like school massacres indicates that the very forces pulling most of us toward more and more law (John Adams in extremis) are legal repellants to the more alienated among us (Henry David Thoreau in extremis). Hence, one of the more palpable consequences of late twentieth-century anomie is that some individuals have attempted to reinvigorate a particular aspect of their identity and express hostility toward an outside world that threatens to water it down. Indeed, we have seen increases in recent years in the number of reported hate crimes and in the incidence of violence against women. Of course, this being the split legal psyche that is America, the answer has been more law.

Use of law as a compensation device to impose order or seek redress serves a similar function at both the aggregate (legislative) and individual (litigation) level. It allows the raw emotions of outrage and contempt that accompany conflict to be expressed in dispassionate, rational form. Indeed, the dry, composed language of legislation and court filings often masks real intensity and the human emotions that motivated them.[46] The legal process, in this way, can serve as a psychological outlet for society, a particularly important function during times of severe stress and dislocation.

Conclusions

Throughout our history law has been employed by individuals to protect or enhance their interests, and more recently, to develop specific sets of legally recognized rights. At the aggregate level, factional blocs have utilized the system to offset political and economic challenge, to protect their advantages, to create leverage for future opportunities, and to promote competing visions of the public interest. Moreover, conflict between individual liberty, on the one hand, and social order and stability, on the other, has often been woven into mobilization efforts, particularly during periods of intense political economic transformation. In attempting to accommodate both, we have produced a system where our lives and activities are saturated with law.

Our legal system was born out of distrust of the motivations of factions, collections of individuals who would pursue their own interests at the expense of everyone else. That distrust has not likely dissipated. If anything, it has been enhanced as we have attempted to compensate for deterioration in traditional community network and associational infrastructures by legalizing virtually all of our relationships. Throughout this book we have discussed the role of law across the human life cycle and in our most personal decisions and relations. The bulk of these developments has occurred in the postindustrial era. Clearly, the most dramatic ones have taken place in the latter half of the twentieth century. Our interactions with strangers and the legal complications produced by that aspect of our lives have only been touched upon briefly, despite the fact that we have also argued that this encompasses an increasing proportion of our total relationships.

Our social community is based in part upon the assumption of an implied contract that not only binds us all together and gives each of us rights that accrue to members, but also imposes obligations. This, in effect, means that limits can be placed upon our actions in the interest of enhancing the larger social community, a classic conflict between individual liberty and social order. It also means either that we do not trust ourselves, or we do not trust strangers in our midst to "do the right thing."

The state is a metaphor representing the collective interest. It promulgates rules and regulations to protect the public welfare. Law, for example, regulates the marketing of food products in the name of the common good, which in turn protects the health and well-being of each of us individually. Law governing criminal acts, health care delivery, the production and marketing of virtually all products, and the money lending industry, all share a similar characteristic. In other words, the focus of a great deal of law is to protect us from each other, to restrain our relationships with complete strangers, holding each of us to something like a "good faith" standard.

But such law also contradicts the "free will" principle, which, if followed, would assume that each of us should determine for ourselves the best course of action. Free will is based upon the notion that one is able to calculate the risks associated with each available alternative. This is where the caveat emptor axiom came from. Accordingly, the law should not protect you from yourself. If you bought a faulty product, you should suffer the consequences of having made a bad choice, and the larger community would also benefit by your example. In a simple economy where people are largely self-sufficient, such calculations might be possible. In a complex one like ours, where an elaborate division of labor results in a vast web of mutual dependency, the ability to evaluate risk is greatly diminished. Hence, the "free will" principle has given way to the expectation that we will all act

in "good faith" in our dealings with others. Our obligation, then, is not restricted to looking out for what is best for ourselves, but it extends to others with whom we interact as well. Indeed, in order to navigate successfully through a single day's activities, we must rely upon the good faith and rationality of a host of utter strangers, just as they rely upon ours. We must bank upon the assumption that manufacturers design products that are safe to consume. In short, we assume that they take our interests into account as well as their own, and we hold them accountable under the law if they do not.

Arguably the transformations that have occurred as a result of a surge in telecommunications technologies during the last quarter of the twentieth century rival those produced in the preceding century by the processes of industrialization. Over the last twenty-five years there has been massive rearrangement in our basic market infrastructure, as we have moved to an information economy. Some say that we have entered the "information age," that we have become an "information society." The hallmark of the new order, of course, is the Internet, cyberspace,[47] and the World Wide Web,[48] toward which everything seems to be converging. Technological development is important in its own right as a broad social phenomenon (see, e.g., Barber 1996; Gilder 1989). It has significant implications and consequences for our understanding of community, our concept of self and self-value, and for law. Indeed, there is a burgeoning literature that focuses upon the influences of current communications technologies on our legal system (see, e.g., Boyle 1996; Katsch 1989; Tribe 1991; Sunstein 1995). Information technology developments have not only restructured markets and altered the character of our relationships with each other, with groups, and with government, but, as discussion throughout this book has illustrated, they have also changed our fundamental conceptions of life, liberty, and property (in addition to many others, such as death, privacy, equality, and the like). It is not at all clear whether law is used to anticipate change and steer developments in a collectively preferred direction, or whether law is simply used to mitigate the worst consequences of uncontrollable forces. There is evidence to support either case. However, it is clear that law is not a neutral device.

However, it is clear that the process of mobilizing law to reconcile our relationships in light of changing political economic conditions is repeated over and over again. Indeed, one generation produces *Charles River Bridge*; another, *Dagenhart*; and yet another, *Morrison*. These currents produce a series of legal strands that appear quite stable and predictable yet elastic, adaptable to situations as they arise—all of which are virtues. But together they can run in contradictory directions, not only yielding ambiguity but also shedding faint light on an evermore elaborate nexus of social and economic relationships. More often than not, the previous law and the basic understandings that made it comprehensible are not discarded, but appended, producing an increasingly dense and intricate legal web.

Law on the Web

This chapter has addressed the dynamic relationship between law and the larger political economy. As we have seen, technological development is a major driving force that changes essential elements of human existence and correlated law. These are issues of critical interest to a wide range of think tanks and policy institutes of all ideological persuasions. Many of them publish position papers and original research that are available for downloading on their websites. But remember, all of these organizations have a decidedly biased perspective, and one of their primary objectives is to influence opinion leaders and lawmakers in their favor. Among those maintaining extensive websites are the following:

American Enterprise Institute
www.aei.org/

Brookings Institution
www.brook.edu/

Cato Institute
www.cato.org/

Center for Democracy and Technology
www.cdt.org/

Cyberspace Law Institute
www.cli.org/

The Heritage Foundation
www.heritage.org/

The Joint Center for Political and Economic Studies
www.jointcenter.org/

The Potomac Institute for Policy Studies
www.potomacinstitute.com/

RAND
www.rand.org/

Urban Institute
www.urban.org/

11 Epilogue: The Dominion of Laws in America

On Monday, December 12, 1988, the Kleins of Long Island, New York were presumably an ordinary, reasonably happy, American family. Martin was a 34-year-old Manhattan accountant, Nancy, a 32-year-old textile designer, and Arielle, a healthy two-year-old girl. No doubt, the small family was focused on a day, roughly six months in the future, when its ranks would increase by one, for Nancy was then about 10 weeks pregnant. It is probably more than safe to assume that the Kleins, as typical Americans, did *not* spend a great deal of time contemplating the ubiquity of law—its reach into every facet of their lives—nor think much at all about the multiple, often conflicting, aims of law. Indeed, but for the legal side of Martin's clients' financial accounts, the Klein family, in all likelihood, thought little about law at all. But, that was on Monday.

On Tuesday, December 13, 1988, Nancy Klein suffered extensive brain damage as the result of a car accident. The Kleins, previously oblivious to the web of law around them, were suddenly and violently made aware of the legal labyrinth, as the filaments of law met them head-on at the intersections of life, relationships, identity, and, potentially, death.

Although there was some disagreement among medical experts over the best course of treatment for Mrs. Klein, most agreed she would never recover, and Mr. Klein was persuaded by those doctors who recommended that she have an abortion. Whatever slim chance Nancy had for recuperation, they argued, would be strengthened were she not carrying a fetus. Martin, thus, unremarkably (unremarkably because the spouse of a married incompetent is almost always viewed by law as the closest, responsible relative) and with the full backing of Nancy's parents, applied to be his wife's guardian toward the goal of supervising her medical treatment, including an abortion. In what turned out to be a rather remarkable case, however, Mr. Klein was not the only person who petitioned for supervision.

While Martin's application was pending, John Short petitioned the New York court involved in the case to be made Nancy's guardian and John Broderick asked to be named guardian of her fetus. Neither Short nor Broderick had any relationship to Nancy, Martin, or Nancy's family. Indeed, they had never even met the relevant parties. But, Short and Broderick were anti-abortion activists bent on saving the Kleins' unborn fetus.

Given the urgency of the case, legal proceedings moved relatively rapidly. Mineola, New York, trial Judge

Bernard F. McCaffrey ruled that although an abortion was unnecessary, Mrs. Klein had the same right to an abortion as a competent woman. He then named Mr. Klein as her guardian (Schmitt 1989: 26). Undaunted, Short and Broderick appealed. The appeals court also sided with Klein, ruling that "these absolute strangers to the Klein family, whatever their motivation, have no place in the midst of this family tragedy" (*In the Matter of Nancy Klein*, 145 A.D.2d 145, 148–49 (Supreme Court of New York, Appellate Division, Second Department, 1989)). Thereafter, the New York Court of Appeals (the state supreme court) refused to hear a further appeal (*In the Matter of Nancy Klein*, 73 N.Y.2d 705 (New York Court of Appeals, 1989)). And, the anti-abortion activists' attempts to have stays issued by U.S. Supreme Court Justices Marshall and Scalia were unsuccessful. On 11 February 1989, in the seventeenth week of Nancy's pregnancy, the abortion was completed.

The Kleins' story did not end on that day. As before February 11, it was succeeded by considerable media attention, including a made-for-TV movie, notable less for artistic merit (the critics hated it) than for the protests and counterprotests it generated and for marking the television comeback of Henry Winkler (a.k.a., "the Fonz").[1] Moreover, the Kleins were involved in four subsequent litigations—Martin's unsuccessful claim against Short, Broderick, and the hospital; his successful divorce from Nancy; his unsuccessful attempt to retain guardianship after the divorce; and Nancy's personal injury suit.

The Ubiquitous Web

Although little in the way of formal, written law was produced over the course of the Kleins' ordeal (the litigations generated only one judicial opinion and that amounted to just over four pages in length), what courts ruled and wrote is really much less important than the fact that law governed every aspect of the tragic situation *and* of the Kleins' lives.

In a coma, and presumed near death,[2] Nancy's very identity and that of her fetus were subject to the legal process. Nancy herself had to be declared legally incompetent—unable, under law, to think or do for herself as an individual. The courts, moreover, determined the legal status of the fetus, concluding that, at less than twenty-four weeks old, it was "not a legally recognized 'person'"... (*In the Matter of Nancy Klein*, 145 A.D.2d 145, 147 (Supreme Court of New York, Appellate Division, Second Department, 1989)).

Throughout the six-year period in which the accident enveloped the lives of the Klein family, the law was front and center in defining and determining relationships. Under New York law, "[any] person may commence a special proceeding to declare a person incompetent and to appoint a committee of an incompetent" (145 A.D.2d 145, at 147–48, citing *NY Mental Hygiene Law* 78.03 (a)). In other words, anyone may seek to establish a rather deep legal relationship with another under such circumstances. In the Kleins' case, the court determined that the "right of relational privacy" trumped any statutory prerogatives of "absolute strangers" (Rao 1998, 1117). But, the court itself noted that "there is no statutory provision which grants a preference to the incompetent's next of kin, blood relatives or their nominees for such appointments . . ." (145 A.D.2d 145, at 148).

The Kleins' own relationship under stress was the subject of more law. In 1992, the Kleins' marriage was dissolved via a legal proceeding that granted custody of the couple's daughter to Martin. Two years later, in 1994, Martin was forced by court order to relinquish guardianship over his ex-wife and her affairs when a judge shifted legal supervision to Nancy's parents (Alexander 1994, 24).

The boundless quality of law was evident as well during the Kleins' trauma in the almost seamless way that it melded with politics. Certainly, Short and Broderick, affiliates of the advocacy group Operation Rescue, used the forum of the courts less to win a legal battle than to make a political point and to garner media exposure. At the same time, Martin Klein was supported by and received advice from abortion rights activists.

Once Nancy had received the abortion and the initial political-legal battles had ended, a made-for-TV movie, which not only chronicled the legal history of the case but actually took its title from the appeals court opinion, generated more group-based political activity. The Reverend Donald Wildmon, head of the American Family Association and widely known during the 1980s and 1990s for his organized boycotts of television programming, hinted that he might be planning such a protest over the airing of "Absolute Strangers." Wildmon's intimations, in turn, prompted a huge letter-writing campaign in support of the movie, sponsored by such traditionally liberal groups as the Jewish Congress, the Religious Coalition for Abortion Rights, Planned Parenthood, and the National Council of Jewish Women (Sloan 1991).

The Ambiguous Web

The Kleins' tragedy is also illustrative of the ambiguity and difficulty marking the role of law in our lives. The abortion issue alone tends to thrust law into the realm of equivocation. At seventeen weeks, the Klein fetus fell into the second trimester category where it was not yet "a legally recognized 'person'" (*In the Matter of Nancy Klein*, 145 A.D.2d 145, at 147 (Supreme Court of New York, Appellate Division, Second Department, 1989)). The court itself, however, implied that things *might* have been different. In a mere seven weeks, the fetus would have crossed the pregnancy threshold into the third trimester where its potential for life and presumed viability might very well have cast the case in an entirely different light.

Nor were questions of legal relationships simple cut-and-dried ones. New York statutory law, it will be recalled, granted no "preference to the incompetent's next of kin, blood relatives or their nominees" in the appointment of a guardian committee. On the other hand, state case law "established that 'strangers will not be appointed as committee of the person or property of the incompetent, unless it is impossible to find within the family circle, or their nominees, one who is qualified to serve'" (145 A.D.2d 145, at 148, citations omitted). And, even then, a relative may be subordinate to a stranger if the court, acting in "the best interests and welfare of the incompetent," determines "the existence of an adverse interest between the incompetent and his or her next of kin, relative or their nominee" (at 148).

*   *   *

Of course, the Kleins' particular case was unusual in some respects. It was unusual to the extent that each and every human event, no matter how "common," is marked by a unique set of players and circumstances. And, clearly, it was unusual for the extent of media glare—after all, few of us have our major life events made into TV shows, even in this age of media pervasiveness. What was not unusual to the Kleins, however, was the presence of law at each and every turn. And, had the Kleins been previously aware of law, they would have noticed its omnipresence long before the accident in every facet of their lives.

Tragedy, crisis, and problems tend to bring the law into sharp focus. When we are in automobile accidents, when we are mugged, when a neighbor's nightly orgies become unbearable, when an expensive product malfunctions and the manufacturer refuses to compensate, when we are caught going 90 on a 60-mph stretch of road—these are the instances that make us aware of law. But, it is there with or without the difficulties. As we have seen throughout this book, it is there before we are born, after we die, and everywhere in between. It is there at the microlevel of the individual, governing even our most private and intimate decisions. And, it is there at the macrolevel of the political economy that produces structures in which we make those decisions.

Can there be too much law? Well, certainly, that Thoreau-like American self would say, "Yes!" Like Patrick Henry, this self might wish to "revolt against the *dominion of laws.*" Indeed, it is worth noting here that Madison himself warned that "[i]t will be of little avail to the people that the laws are made by men of their own choice if the laws be so voluminous that they cannot be read, or so incoherent that they cannot be understood; if they be repealed or revised before they are promulgated, or undergo such incessant changes that no man, who knows what the law is today, can guess what it will be tomorrow" (*Federalist* #62, para. 15). There will always be—and always has been—that part of the American self that believes we have already passed the point beyond which "laws be so voluminous." Martin Klein may have felt just that way when he discovered that two "absolute strangers," even if ultimately unsuccessful, could petition, under law, to be guardians of his wife and her unborn fetus—in effect, attempting to preempt the most painful and intimate decision of his life. Under far less tragic circumstances, it is, no doubt, the way many of us have felt when "pulled over" for not wearing a seatbelt or exceeding the speed limit by 5 mph.

On the other hand, there will always be—and always has been—that part of the American self that rejoices at being governed by law, which, in fact, always sees the need for more law in an increasingly complex society. Martin Klein may have felt just that way when an appeals court, looking to case law on family relationships and fetal viability, refused the two "absolute strangers" their request. Under far less tragic circumstances, it is, no doubt, the way many of us have felt when, after being dogged by a highway tailgater, we scream out for new law aimed especially at aggressive drivers.

Law truly is as American as the flag, baseball, apple pie, *and* the Constitution. But, so is our propensity to complain about law's ubiquity and ambiguity—its "dominion." Today, as it was over two centuries ago, law is a webbed embodiment—indeed, *the* webbed embodiment—of our long cultural struggle between *individual liberty*, on the one hand, and *social order*, on the other. And, so, through all the changes we would anticipate in this new century, it will very likely remain.

Notes

Chapter 1

1. Holmes, "Speech to the Suffolk Bar Association," *The Speeches of Oliver Wendell Holmes* (1891), cited in Hall (1989, 3).

2. "We the People of the United States, in Order to form a more perfect Union, establish Justice, insure domestic Tranquility, provide for the common defence, promote the general Welfare, and secure the Blessings of Liberty to ourselves and our Posterity, do ordain and establish this Constitution for the United States of America" (*Preamble*, U.S. Constitution).

3. That convention, ratified in response to Nazi war atrocities, is today the basis for the International Court of Justice's prosecution in *Bosnia and Herzegovina v. Yugoslavia*. See the International Court of Justice docket at www.icj-cij.org/idocket/ibhy/ibhyframe.htm (accessed 2 September 1999).

4. We are not the first to use the word "web" in relation to the law, although we use it very broadly while others, far more eloquent than we, have tended to utilize it narrowly in criticism. For example, Solon, the ancient Athenian lawgiver said, "Laws are like spiders' webs, which stand firm when any light, yielding object falls upon them, while a larger thing breaks through them and escapes" (from Plutarch, *The Banquet of the Seven Wise Men* in *Bartlett's* [1968: 68b–69a]). In a similar vein, albeit 2000 years later, the English satirist Jonathan Swift maintained that "Laws are like cobwebs, which may catch small flies, but let wasps and hornets break through" ("A Critical Essay Upon the Faculties of the Mind," 1707, in *Bartlett's* [1968, 388b]). Unlike Swift, we would maintain that the law envelops both flies and wasps, although like Swift, we would admit that it generally swaddles the wasp more gently than it does the fly.

5. Over the past two and a half decades, the Supreme Court has handed down a number of key decisions on the subject of abortion, most notably, its seminal holding in *Roe v. Wade*, 410 U.S. 133 (1973). *Roe* and other abortion-related law are discussed more fully in chapter 6. Throughout this brief chapter, only a very few of many legal examples are cited in footnotes. For more complete discussions, please refer to relevant subsequent chapters.

6. Depending on her state, John's mother, in deciding whether to terminate her pregnancy, may have to receive counseling, wait for some period of time, or abide by additional rules and regulations.

7. For example, during its 1997–98 term, the Supreme Court refused to review a case challenging South Carolina's law allowing the prosecution of pregnant women who use illegal drugs. Lower courts have upheld the law. See footnote 26 below.

8. Although both international labor laws and American law supposedly prohibit the importation of goods manufactured using unfair labor practices, such laws tend to be easily evaded.

9. A variety of laws govern the conditions under which food is prepared. Recently, in light of a number of high-profile bacterial infections, legislatures have been busy amending required cooking temperatures. For example, the New York State assembly recently established 158 degrees as the temperature at which restaurant meat must be cooked, up eighteen degrees from previous standards ("Serving Up Safety," *Times Union* (Albany), 21 October 1997, p. D1).

10. Throughout the past decade, state legislatures and school boards throughout the country have increasingly mandated many competency tests, both for students and teachers. Not to be outdone, even national lawmakers have gotten into the act. Recent proposals being considered in Congress include making federal categorical aid contingent on states instituting competency tests at every grade level and submitting their content and performance standards and assessments to the Department of Education, and giving federal money to states that pay teachers based on merit and test teachers for competency.

11. As of March 2000, the minimum wage set by Congress is $5.15 per hour.

12. Labor-employer relations are governed by a raft of state and federal laws, notably the so-called *Taft-Hartley Act*.

13. See for example, *The Occupational Health and Safety Act of 1970*.

14. See notably, *The Civil Rights Act of 1964*.

15. Title VII of the *Civil Rights Act* prohibits discrimination in employment, including harassment. The law on the subject of sexual harassment, however, has always been vague and confusing. During its 1997–98 Term, the Supreme Court issued a series of rulings seeking to clarify the law. See *Burlington Industries v. Ellerth*, 524 U.S. 742 (1998); *Faragher v. City of Boca Raton*, 524 U.S. 775 (1998); *Gebser v. Lago Vista Indep. Sch. Dist.*, 524 U.S. 274 (1998); and *Oncale v. Sundowner Offshore Services, Inc.*, 523 U.S. 75 (1998).

16. Notably, Title IX of the *Civil Rights Act* mandates equal school athletic opportunities for women.

17. In 1996 Congress passed, and President Clinton signed, *The Defense of Marriage Act*, defining marriage as a union between a man and a woman and allowing states to refuse to recognize same-sex marriages performed in other states. Most states specifically forbid marital union between people of the same gender. Legal actions in Vermont, however, suggest that this might change. In *Baker v. Vermont* 744 A.2d 864 (S Ct VT 1999), several gay couples challenged the constitutionality of the state's "exclusion of same-sex couples from the secular benefits and protections offered married couples." The Vermont Supreme Court employed a balancing test "premised on an appropriate and overriding public interest." The court held that same-sex couples' right to the statutory benefits of marriage outweighs the state's interest in restricting the institution of marriage.

18. A patchwork of state and federal regulatory law currently governs nursing home care. In 1998, President Clinton announced a series of new federal regulations intended to upgrade such care, and requested Congress to take additional action (Goldstein 1998, A3).

19. Although the Supreme Court has said that all Americans have a right not to have their lives prolonged by artificial means (*Cruzan v. Director, Missouri Department of Health*, 497 U.S. 261 (1990)), it has established no such rights for ending life prematurely, leaving the legality of physician-assisted suicide up to the individual states (*Washington v. Glucksberg*, 521 U.S. 702 (1997) and *Vacco v. Quill*, 521 U.S. 793 (1997)).

20. The law here is very ambiguous and a virtual minefield for the consumer. Most body-cleansing products are really synthetic detergent products that come under the jurisdiction of the federal Food and Drug Administration (FDA). Such "detergents" are regulated by the FDA and require ingredient labels. Moreover, "true soaps" that make cosmetic claims (e.g., they claim to moisturize or cure acne) also require FDA labeling. However, "true soaps" that make no such claims, fall under the jurisdiction of the Consumer Product Safety Commission (CPSC), which does not require product labeling. To find out everything you ever wanted to know about the status of soap, visit: vm.cfsan.fda.gov/~dms/cos-215.html, U.S. Food and Drug Administration, Center for Food Safety and Applied Nutrition, Office of Cosmetics Fact Sheet (accessed 21 March 2000).

21. All states have laws requiring the use of seatbelts; most require all passengers to buckle up and require children under the age of four to be in safety seats.

22. In May 1998, Congress passed, and President Clinton signed, the *Transportation Equity Act of 1998*. Over the following six years, the law triggers roughly $200 billion in federal spending on transportation-related items nationwide, including road and bridge repair and mass transit upgrades (Dao 1998, A1).

23. In response to a published report in 1993, finding environmental smoke to be hazardous, many states and localities banned smoking in public and private buildings, including offices, stadiums, and restaurants (Biskupic 1998a, A4). Moreover, Congress has banned smoking in most of the nation's schools, except in designated areas closed to children, and President Clinton has banned it in all federal workplaces (*USA Today*, 22 July 1998).

24. See footnote 27 below.

25. It is illegal in all states for a person under the age of twenty-one to purchase alcoholic beverages. Moreover, in 1995, President Clinton signed into law so-called "zero-tolerance" legislation making it illegal for a person under twenty-one to drive in any state after drinking a measurable amount of alcohol no matter what the state's legal limit is.

26. In 1998, the U.S. Supreme Court refused to review a decision of the South Carolina Supreme Court upholding the conviction of a woman under just such a statute. See *Whitner v. South Carolina*, 328 S.C. 1; 492 S.E.2d 777; rehearing denied November 19, 1997, cert. denied, May 26, 1998, reported at 523 U.S. 1145 (1998). However, as more and more states begin considering or implementing such statutes, it is almost certain that the nation's high court will have to make some determination. Critics of such laws claim that they directly jeopardize (indeed, are aimed at subverting) the fundamental rights of women to reproductive freedom outlined in *Roe v. Wade*, by, in effect, treating fetuses as "persons" under the law. Indeed, in 2001, the Court did address this issue, in part, when it decided in *Ferguson v. Charleston* (No. 99-936 (2001)) that hospitals may not test pregnant women for drugs and subsequently report the results to law enforcement officials.

27. *Texas v. Johnson*, 491 U.S. 397 (1989) and *U.S. v. Eichman*, 496 U.S. 310 (1990).

28. As discussed in several chapters, law is not only *on* the Internet, but it is increasingly concerned *with* the Internet. Our access to and use of the Internet has become an issue of intense legislative activity, as Congress and the state legislatures are forced to deal with such problems as online fraud, junk mail or SPAM, pornography, encryption, funding, and many others. In 1997, for the first time, the Supreme Court got into the Internet act with its decision in *Reno v. ACLU*, 117 S. Ct. 2329 (1997), ruling that the *Communications Decency Act of 1996* (CDA) was unconstitutional.

Chapter 2

1. See, for example, *Regents of the University of California v. Bakke*, 438 U.S. 265 (1978); *American College of Obstetricians v. Thornburgh*, 699 F.2d 644 (3d Cir. 1983).

2. Much has been written about this case. It was frequently cited by judges and justices in the period following Mansfield's decision, and it continued to be a source of legal reference well into the twentieth century. See, for example, Higginbotham (1978); Davis (1975).

3. Indeed, Madison, in *Federalist #54* (see Fairfield 1966), reasoned that slaves were best understood as neither completely property nor completely persons, but a combination of the two. Although not one of the founders, John Locke, a British contemporary, was quite influential in developing a natural law theory in general and a rationalization for slavery in particular. See his *The Second Treatise*, chapter 4, online at www.swan.ac.uk/poli/texts/locke/locke03.html.

4. Alexander Hamilton, *Federalist #1*, in Fairfield (1966, 2).

5. "It is not enough for the knight of romance that you agree that his lady is a very nice girl—if you do not admit that she is the best that God ever made or will make, you must fight. There is in all men a demand for the superlative, so much so that the poor devil who has no other way of reaching it attains it by getting drunk. It seems to me that this demand is at the bottom of the philosopher's effort to prove that truth is absolute and of the jurist's search for criteria of universal validity which he collects under the head of natural law" (Holmes 1918, 40–41).

6. For example, at the U.S. Supreme Court level, the proportion of decisions with at least one dissenting justice has hovered around the 60 percent mark since the mid-1940s (Epstein and Knight 1998, 24). Natural law aside, this degree of nonunanimity is strongly suggestive that justices are motivated by something other than law in making their decisions.

7. See, for example, McIntosh and Cates (1997), for a full discussion of judicial concurrences.

8. See, for example, *EEOC v. Mitsubishi Motor Mfg.*, 102 F.3d 869 (7th Cir. 1996); 960 F. Supp. 164 (C.D. Ill. 1997).

9. For a thorough treatment of such issues, see Herrnson, Shaiko, and Wilcox (1998) and cf. Dahl (1961); Polsby (1963); Lowi (1969); Schattschneider (1960).

10. In addition, the consequences for violating them can be quite severe. Banishment is a common form of punishment among all sorts of groups, ranging from high school cliques, adult social organizations, organized religions, even to families. Street gangs might condemn an offending member to death. An Internet discussion group member who violates the rules of "etiquette" might be "flamed." Whistleblowers face intense ostracism.

11. "A second concept of law is that of bureaucratic or regulatory law. It is distinguished from custom by its public and positive character. Bureaucratic law consists of explicit rules established and enforced by an identifiable government" (Unger 1976, 50).

12. This is much like the problems that Madison addresses in his discussion of factions in *Federalist #10*. Among his remedies is inclusiveness, that is, allowing input of as many perspectives as possible in hopes that reasonable people will accommodate one another and compromise for the betterment of all. If his rationale works at all, it probably works best in legislatures where there are larger numbers (but cf. Dahl 1961; Lowi 1969; Schattschneider 1960).

13. Informal rules have a way of becoming formal ones. This is the case, for example, with regard to university hate speech codes, local restrictions on lawn height, outdoor clothes lines,

and the *Miller* community standard rule in the field of obscenity (*Miller v. California*, 413 U.S. 15 (1973)).

14. Brief for Petitioner, 20–21.

15. Justice White went on to explain: "Striving to assure itself and the public that announcing rights not readily identifiable in the Constitution's text involves much more than the imposition of the justices' own choice of values on the States and the Federal Government, the Court has sought to identify the nature of the rights qualifying for heightened judicial protection. In *Palko v. Connecticut* it was said that this category includes those fundamental liberties that are 'implicit in the concept of ordered liberty,' such that 'neither liberty nor justice would exist if [they] were sacrificed.' A different description of fundamental liberties appeared in *Moore v. East Cleveland*, where they are characterized as those liberties that are 'deeply rooted in this Nation's history and tradition.' It is obvious to us that neither of these formulations would extend a fundamental right to homosexuals to engage in acts of consensual sodomy. Proscriptions against that conduct have ancient roots. Sodomy was a criminal offense at common law and was forbidden by the laws of the original 13 States when they ratified the Bill of Rights. In 1868, when the Fourteenth Amendment was ratified, all but 5 of the 37 States in the Union had criminal sodomy laws. In fact, until 1961, all 50 States outlawed sodomy, and today, 24 States and the District of Columbia continue to provide criminal penalties for sodomy performed in private and between consenting adults. Against this background, to claim that a right to engage in such conduct is 'deeply rooted in this Nation's history and tradition' or 'implicit in the concept of ordered liberty' is, at best, facetious" (478 U.S. 186, 191–94; footnotes and citations deleted).

16. This was true across the states. The only real exception is Louisiana, whose legal system was heavily influenced by the French civil law model, thus producing something of a hybrid system.

17. The Preamble to the Constitution acknowledges a division between that which is public and that which is private: "We the People of the United States, in Order to form a more perfect Union, establish Justice, insure domestic Tranquility, provide for the common defence, promote the general Welfare, and secure the Blessings of Liberty to ourselves and our Posterity, do ordain and establish this Constitution for the United States of America." The Preamble sets up a conflict between two spheres—the private by guaranteeing individual liberty, and the public by guaranteeing the provision of domestic tranquility.

18. "Defeat of Bilingual Education Is Challenged in Federal Court," *New York Times*, 4 June 1998, final edition, sec. A, p. 25. Acting very quickly to decide the matter, U.S. District Judge Charles A. Legge upheld the voter-approved proposition on 15 July (*Valeria G. v. Wilson*, 1998 U.S. Dist. LEXIS 10675 (N.D.CA 1998)).

19. *Osborne v. Power*, 318 Ark. 858; 890 S.W. 2d 570 (SCt. Ark,1994); 515 U.S. 1143 (1995) cert. denied.

20. Conflict implies at least two parties. In fact our entire legal system is constructed upon this premise. Article III of the U.S. Constitution, which establishes the judicial branch of government, states that "the judicial power shall extend to . . . cases . . . [and] controversies" (§ 2, para. 1), requiring a claimant and a respondent. Moreover, all of our courts are constructed on the adversarial model, which assumes disagreement between antagonists.

21. See table—Methods of Execution by State—next page.

22. In *Planned Parenthood v. Casey*, 505 U.S. 833 (1992), the U.S. Supreme Court abandoned the *Roe* "strict scrutiny" rule and adopted a standard that permits states to impose restrictions on abortion procedures as long as they do not "unduly burden" a woman's right to choose. (See discussion later in this chapter.) According to information posted on the National Abortion Rights Action League (NARAL) website, the number of states enforcing mandatory waiting period laws increased from zero before *Casey* to twelve afterward (ID, IN, KS, LA, MS, NE, ND, OH, PA, SC, SD, and UT). Since *Casey*, the number of states enforcing mandatory parental notice or consent laws for minors has risen from thirteen to thirty (AL, AR, DE, GA, ID, IN, IA, KS, KY, LA, ME, MD, MA, MI, MN, MS, MO, NE, NC, ND, OH, PA, RI, SC, SD, UT, VA, WV, WI, and WY). The number of states partially or fully enforcing bans on "partial-birth" abortion and other abortion procedures is nine (AL, GA, IN, MS, NE, SC, SD, TN, and UT). See NARAL, "Who Decides? A State-by-State Review of Abortion and Reproductive Rights," 14 January 1998, available at: www.naral.org/publications/whod98 keyfindings.html (accessed 5 August 1998).

23. Hamilton, *Federalist* #78, 231.

24. U.S. District Judge Harold Baer, Jr. held in an opinion announced in March 1996, that a motion to suppress by a criminal defendant accused of drug trafficking would be upheld because the police in New York City had made a warrantless search of her automobile, in violation of the Constitution. Large amounts of drugs found in the trunk of her car were thus inadmissable in evidence. See *U.S. v. Bayless*, 913 F. Supp. 232 (S.D.N.Y. 1996).

25. Judge Harold Baer, Jr. ultimately reversed himself for reasons that were unrelated to the withering attack he had suffered for his earlier finding. Chief Justice William Rehnquist took the opportunity to address the issue, without specific reference to Judge Baer's plight, in a speech at American University Law School, stating: "There are a very few essentials that are vital to the functioning of the federal court system as we know it. Surely one of these essentials is the independence of the judges who sit on these courts" (Biskupic 1996, A17).

26. The judge stated that the corroborating testimony of another police officer, a written police report, and the inconsistency of the defendant's testimony warranted the reversal.

27. Nina Totenberg, "Judicial Intimidation," *Morning Edition* (National Public Radio), 26 September 1997 (transcript # 97092615-210). On the following morning, President Clinton devoted his weekly radio address to Republican efforts to stall his judicial nominations and to intimidate sitting judges with impeachment threats. "Clinton Castigates GOP Over Judges," United Press International, 27 September 1997.

28. Usually judicial elections are noncompetitive, and it is extremely rare for an incumbent judge, seeking another term, to lose (e.g., Dubois 1980; Wold and Culver 1987).

29. This is not strictly true, because there are several specialized courts, such as the U.S. Court of Claims and the U.S. Court of Military Appeals, that also have national jurisdiction. See chapter 4 for a more complete discussion of the court system structure.

30. The state courts of final appeals are supreme in those cases where their decisions are based entirely upon their own state's constitution. Indeed, states can grant more rights, such as an explicit right to privacy, than those found in the U.S. Constitution. Thus, state courts can insulate themselves from review by the U.S. Supreme Court, as long as they do not restrict language of the national charter.

31. This is a Latin phrase, of which there are many in the law, which literally means, "the decision stands."

32. At one point during his testimony before the Senate Judiciary Committee, Senator Alan Simpson (R-WY) asked Judge Bork why he wanted to be a Supreme Court Justice. "Senator," Bork replied, "I guess the answer is I spent my life

Methods of Execution by State

LETHAL INJECTION	LETHAL INJECTION (cont'd)	ELECTROCUTION	HANGING	FIRING SQUAD	LETHAL GAS
Arizona 1,2	New Hampshire 8	Alabama	Delaware 1,3	Idaho 1	Arizona 1,2
Arkansas 1,4	New Jersey	Arkansas 1,4	New Hampshire 8	Oklahoma 6	California 1,5
California 1,5	New Mexico	Florida 12	Washington 1	Utah 1	Maryland 7
Colorado	New York	Georgia			Mississippi 1,9
Connecticut	North Carolina 1	Kentucky 1,11			Missouri 1
Delaware 1,3	Ohio 1	Nebraska			North Carolina 1
Idaho 1	Oklahoma 6	Ohio 1			Wyoming 10
Illinois	Oregon	Oklahoma 6			
Indiana	Pennsylvania	South Carolina 1			
Kansas	South Carolina 1	Tennessee 13			
Kentucky 1,11	South Dakota	Virginia 1			
Louisiana	Texas				
Maryland 7	Utah 1				
Mississippi 1,9	Virginia 1				
Missouri 1	Washington 1				
Montana	Wyoming 10				
Nevada					
Tennessee 13					

Note: The method of execution of federal prisoners is lethal injection, pursuant to 28 CRR, Part 26. For offenses under the Violent Crime Control and *Law Enforcement Act of 1994*, the method is that of the state in which the conviction took place, pursuant to 18 U.S.C. 3596. If the state has no death penalty, the inmate will be transferred to another state.

1. Authorizes two methods of execution.

2. Arizona authorizes lethal injection for persons sentenced after 15 November 1992; those sentenced before that date may select lethal injection or lethal gas.

3. Delaware authorizes lethal injection for those whose capital offense occurred after 13 June 1986; those who committed the offense before that date may select lethal injection or hanging.

4. Arkansas authorizes lethal injection for persons committing a capital offense after 4 July 1983; those who committed the offense before that date may select lethal injection or electrocution.

5. The Ninth Circuit overturned a lower court ruling that the state's use of the gas chamber is cruel and unusual punishment.

6. Oklahoma authorizes electrocution if lethal injection is ever held to be unconstitutional, and firing squad if both lethal injection and electrocution are held unconstitutional.

7. Maryland authorizes lethal injection for those whose capital offenses occurred on or after 25 March 1994; those who committed the offense before that date may select lethal injection or lethal gas.

8. New Hampshire authorizes hanging only if lethal injection cannot be given.

9. Mississippi authorizes lethal injection for those convicted after 1 July 1984 and lethal gas for those convicted earlier.

10. Wyoming authorizes lethal gas if lethal injection is ever held to be unconstitutional.

11. Kentucky authorizes lethal injection for those convicted after 31 March 1998; those who committed the offense before that date may select lethal injection or electrocution.

12. Florida has endorsed the use of lethal injection if the electric chair is found unconstitutional.

13. Tennessee authorizes lethal injection for those sentenced after 1 January 1999, and those currently on death row will choose between the electric chair and lethal injection.

Source: Bureau of Justice Statistics, *Capital Punishment 1996 Bulletin*, Table 2 (December 1997); updated by Death Penalty Information Center, 27 July 1998, available at www.essential.org/dpic/methods.html (accessed 5 August 1998).

in intellectual pursuit of the law . . . and I think it would be an intellectual feast to be there" (Cawley 1987, 3).

33. 505 U.S. 833, 865ff.

34. Concurring in part and dissenting in part (505 U.S. 833, 912ff).

35. Concurring in part, concurring in the judgment in part, and dissenting in part (505 U.S. 833, 923ff).

36. Concurring in the judgment in part and dissenting in part (505 U.S. 833, 944ff).

37. *American Trucking Association v. Smith*, 496 U.S. 167, at 201 (1990) (Scalia, J., concurring).

38. These notions can be traced back to the arguments of the Founders, who were more natural law oriented. See especially Hamilton's discussion in *Federalist* #78.

39. Friedman (1989, 1582) states the case quite strongly against the legal autonomy perspective, arguing instead for the development of a social theory of law. "It is precisely in the sense of a methodology, a strategy, that the case for (some version of) a social theory is strongest. It seems to me that

there is more explanatory power, more richness, more bite, in exploring the manifold connections between the legal system and its surrounding society, than in treating law as an isolated domain."

Chapter 3

1. Alexis de Tocqueville, "Causes Which Mitigate the Tyranny of the Majority in the United States," Book 1, chapter 16, *Democracy in America*, 1835, C-SPAN, in The Alexis de Tocqueville Tour Exploring Democracy in America, 9 May 1997–20 February 1998, available at xroads.virginia.edu/~HYPER/DETOC/1_ch16.htm (accessed 3 June 1998).

2. See, for example, *In re Baby M*, 109 N.J. 396; 537 A.2d 1227 (1988) in which the New Jersey Supreme Court had to contemplate the nature of motherhood.

3. See *Texas v. Johnson*, 491 U.S. 397 (1989), and *U.S. v. Eichman*, 496 U.S. 310 (1990), the flag-burning cases.

4. See, for example, *Flood v. Kuhn*, 407 U.S. 258 (1979), upholding baseball's exemption from antitrust laws.

5. Indeed, the issue of apple-pie price fixing made it all the way to the Supreme Court in *Utah Pie Co. v. Continental Baking Co.*, 386 U.S. 685 (1967).

6. Original draft of the Massachusetts Constitution (1779).

7. The two families eventually settled the dispute, signing an agreement requiring the children to stay away from each other (*Denver Post*, 6 May 1997, B1).

8. So adverse is the group to the formal law that, according to a member's website, members are offended by the militias "fighting to uphold the standards of the Constitution." "Posse Comitatus," available at www.webexpert.net/posse/p1.html (accessed 24 January 1998).

9. As we suggest in chapter 4, most potentially litigible disputes never get to court, and, of those relatively few that do, most are settled before full-blown trials. Synthesizing much of the literature on disputes, law professor Marc Galanter offers us an interesting way of thinking about all this. First, according to Galanter, many injuries go unnoticed. Violations of product warranties and professional malpractice, for example, "may be difficult to recognize and go undiscovered. Even if the injury is discovered, the injured may not perceive." Second, even when wrongs are discerned, "a common response is resignation, that is, 'lumping it.' [T]he most comprehensive study available . . . report[s] that over one-quarter of those with . . . 'middle range' (i.e., involving the equivalent of $1,000 or more) grievances did not pursue the matter by making a claim." Third, "exit and avoidance—withdrawal from a situation or relationship by moving, resigning, severing relations, etc.—are common responses to many kinds of troubles." Fourth, outside legal adjudication, "disputes are also pursued by various kinds of self-help such as physical retaliation, seizure of property, or removal of offending objects. The amount of self-help in contemporary industrial societies has not been mapped, but it evidently occurs very frequently." Finally, in the case of large grievances, a typical response is to make a claim directly to the other party. Such claims are usually ended either through negotiation—sometimes mediated by an administrator, school principal, or other third party—or by the claimant simply becoming discouraged and abandoning her contention. Only after all this enormous universe of grievances has been settled outside formal legal structures do those relatively few cases go on to the litigation stage. Even then, most of these few do *not* result in full trials—rather, most leave the system via the routes of "attrition, routine processing, bargaining and settlement" (Galanter 1983b, 13–26; internal citations omitted).

10. While it is very difficult to discern actual support for or psychological commitment to law among the American population, a number of very imperfect indicators, largely revolving around support for courts as institutions, point to a mixed conclusion. For example, at the highest level of generality and remove, confidence in the U.S. Supreme Court appears to outweigh that in many other institutions and it appears to be growing. Thus, the Harris Poll (14–18 January 1998) found the Court ranked third among fourteen public and private institutions in levels of public support, far outranking the various media, the White House, and Congress, and that confidence had grown considerably over the previous two years. See, for example, *PollingReport.com*, available at pollingreport.com/ (accessed 21 March 2000). On the other hand, studies seem to demonstrate that the public is less satisfied with local courts, particularly local criminal courts. Notably, however, dissatisfaction appears to be much greater among those who have had personal experience with the courts than among those who have not. This makes a certain amount of sense, according to legal psychologist Tom Tyler, because (and see footnote 9 above) "[m]ost disputes are resolved by the parties themselves and only those cases involving anger, intractable problems, or both end up before judges and mediators. Hence, authorities are constantly faced with the most difficult cases." Because full-blown trials result in a winner and a loser, we would expect half of those who go that route to think legal outcomes stink (Tyler 1997). Also, as the fallout from the O. J. Simpson trial demonstrated, perceptions of the legal process differ according to race. These differences preceded Mr. Simpson's ordeal. Thus, for example, "A national survey commissioned in 1977 by the National Center for State Courts reported that 49% of blacks, 34% of Hispanics and 15% of whites agree with the statement 'courts do not treat blacks as well as they treat whites' and thought it described a 'serious problem that occurs often.' A 1988 *New York Times*/WCBS-TV News poll conducted in New York City found that 45% of whites, but only 28% of blacks, believed that judges and courts in New York City generally treat both races fairly. In the same year, a *Newsday* poll of black New Yorkers found that 40% believed the courts 'mistreat' blacks 'all or most of the time.' A national poll, conducted in 1988 by Media General and the Associated Press, found that 40% of whites and 61% of blacks believe that minorities do not receive equal treatment in the criminal justice system. In a *New York Law Journal* poll, also conducted in 1988, 44% of *all* respondents, including 71% of blacks and 31% of whites, believed that if 'two people—one white, one black—are convicted of identical crimes' the white defendant would get the lighter sentence" (Davis 1989; internal citations omitted).

11. For a discussion of "natural law," see chapter 2. As we have said, natural law or the "law of nature" is an ambiguous concept, and no less so in the context of Locke. At times, Locke appears to take one or another very biblical approach to the concept, variously tying it closely to a form of the Ten Commandments or to Jesus' exhortation to "love thy neighbor as thyself." At other times, he explicitly refers to the law of nature as "reason." This is not necessarily inconsistent with a religious view, for as a rationalist of the Enlightenment period, Locke could well approach the subject of God as reason.

12. For far more thoroughgoing treatments of John Locke, see, for example, Laslett (1960, 3–152). Locke is, in addition, the subject of many websites. Some are particularly valuable for accessing his original works. See, for example, daemon.ilt. columbia.edu/academic/digitexts/ Locke/bio_JL.html (ac-

cessed 27 January 1998) and history.hanover.edu/early/locke/j-l2-001. htm (accessed 27 January 1998).

13. As a scholar well versed in the ideas and ideals of the French and English Enlightenments, Jefferson found his greatest inspiration in the language and arguments of English philosopher John Locke, who had justified England's "Glorious Revolution" of 1688 on the basis of man's "natural rights." See Library of Congress, available at rs6.loc.gov/const/abt_declar.htm (accessed 27 January 1998). So, for example, where Locke (1960, 341) spoke of the rights to "Life, Liberty, and Estate," Jefferson, of course, spoke of "Life, liberty, and the pursuit of Happiness." Nor was this the only obvious example of Jefferson's resort to Locke in framing the Declaration. In fact, according to Donald Doernberg, so extensive was Jefferson's use of Locke that "Richard Henry Lee of Virginia complained that Jefferson had *copied* the Declaration from Locke. Locke's influence on Jefferson is certainly not surprising, since Jefferson spoke of Locke as one of the three greatest men of all time and regarded Locke's work as one of the 'elementary books of public right'" (Doernberg 1985, 65; internal citations omitted, emphasis added). See also Bailyn (1992); Becker (1922); Friedenwald (1974); Maier (1997); Malone (1975); and Wills (1979).

14. Indeed, Locke is often counted as the father of Empiricism. "Empiricism [is] the philosophical doctrine holding that all knowledge is derived from experience, whether of the mind or of the senses. . . . A doctrine basic to the scientific method, empiricism is associated with the rise of experimental science after the seventeenth century. It has been a dominant tradition in British philosophy, as in the works of John Locke, David Hume, and George Berkeley" (*Concise Columbia Encyclopedia* 1991).

15. "If angels were to govern men, neither external nor internal controls on government would be necessary" (*Federalist* #51, para. 4).

16. Locke was an influential and often controversial theoretician. As physician and philosopher to Lord Ashley, the Earl of Shaftesbury, Locke placed himself in opposition to the Stuart monarchy and was forced into exile for five years. Later, he even held political office when, in 1696, he was appointed commissioner of the Board of Trade where he served as a powerful member until 1700 (Laslett 1960, 16–44).

17. Historian Bernard Bailyn (1992, 292) notes that while "'[r]epublic' and 'democracy' were words closely associated in the colonists' minds[,] . . . they evoked a mixed response of enthusiasm and foreboding. For if 'republic' conjured up for many the positive feelings of the Commonwealth era and marked the triumph of virtue and reason, 'democracy'—a word that denoted the lowest order of society as well as the form of government in which the commons ruled—was generally associated with the threat of civil disorder and the early assumption of power by a dictator."

18. In *Federalist* #84 (para. 9), Alexander Hamilton has some fun with this very bit of irony: "[The] bills of rights . . . are not only unnecessary in the proposed Constitution, but would even be dangerous. They would contain various exceptions to powers not granted; and, on this very account, would afford a colorable pretext to claim more than were granted. For why declare that things shall not be done which there is no power to do?"

19. Madison frequently refers to faction as a "disease" in *Federalist* #10.

20. In 1890, a young lawyer, Louis Brandeis (later to become one of the great justices of the U.S. Supreme Court) published, in the *Harvard Law Review*, a tract titled "On the Right to Privacy." In the tract, Brandeis and his coauthor, Samuel Warren, argued the then–novel legal idea that individuals had a right not to be invaded by outside forces (i.e., the sensational-istic yellow journalism popular at the time). In other words, because of our property in ourselves, we have a "right to be let alone" (Warren and Brandeis 1890, 193). As a Supreme Court justice, Brandeis extended this notion further into the realms of Fourth Amendment (see, for example, *Olmstead v. U.S.*, 277 U.S. 438, at 478–79 (1928) (Brandeis, J., dissenting)) and First Amendment law (see, for example, *Gilbert v. Minnesota*, 254 U.S. 325, at 336 (1920) (Brandeis, J., dissenting)). Although dissents at the time, his notions of privacy were later to become majority doctrine.

21. U.S. Constitution, Fifth Amendment (emphasis added). The Fourth Amendment also gives the nod to the sanctity of property: "The right of the people to be secure in their persons, houses, papers, and effects, against unreasonable searches and seizures, shall not be violated . . ."

22. All of this clearly has carried over into contemporary jurisprudence. Thus, American lawmakers, over the course of the twentieth century and like those in no other country, have acted to encourage widespread home ownership, notably through the mortgage-tax deduction and through government-underwritten loan programs.

23. *Coppage* was one of many cases reflecting Supreme Court doctrine during what has come to be called the "*Lochner* era," a period of legal history stretching roughly from the late 1890s through the mid-1930s in which the Court employed particular interpretations of the contract clause, the due process clause of the Fourteenth Amendment, Article I grants of congressional power, and the Tenth Amendment to invalidate progressive legislative policies, including policies designed to level the playing field between workers and employers.

24. De Tocqueville, "Causes Which Mitigate the Tyranny of the Majority in the United States" (1835; available at xroads.virginia.edu/~HYPER/DETOC/toc_indx.html).

25. Since about the mid-1970s, it has become commonplace to complain about the so-called "hyperlitigiousness" of American society. During the 1970s and early to mid-1980s, this type of complaint tended to come from judges (e.g., Burger 1982), law professors (e.g., Kurland 1979), and political scientists (e.g., Glazer 1975). Over the course of the past decade, allegations about the overlitigiousness of American society have tended to come from corporate concerns, doctors, and conservative legislators.

26. Indeed, without the vast array of entertainment choices at their fingertips that we enjoy today, our forebears may actually have treated trials more as diversion than we do. Moreover, throughout much of the eighteenth century, lawyers and judges traveled from town to town and county to county ("riding the circuit") and lawyers specifically aimed the flowery rhetoric popular at the time to audiences, all adding to the entertainment value of the trial.

27. For more contemporary lawyer humor, see chapter 5.

28. Indeed, because contracts were viewed in individualistic terms, it was considered unfair (and thus illegal) for workers to band together in order to negotiate common contracts with an employer.

29. In that case, Dred Scott, a slave, sued his owner for freedom, claiming that because his previous owner had taken him into a free state, under the terms of the Missouri Compromise, he should be considered a free man. The Supreme Court rejected his claim, however, stating that no Black person could be considered a constitutional citizen, empowered to make a legal claim under federal jurisdiction.

30. U.S. Bureau of the Census, *Statistical Abstract of the United States, 1996*, 116th ed., 1996, 405, cited in Abraham (1997, 16).

31. Ibid.

32. For a discussion of race, class, and gender in the legal profession, see chapter 5.

33. *Mitchell v. the Superior Court of the City and County of San Francisco*, 43 Cal. 3d 107; 729 P.2d 212, at 228 (S. Ct. CA 1987) (Bird, C.J. concurring).

34. In May 1998, PanAmSat's Galaxy 4 satellite spun out of control, disrupting service to tens of millions of paging and other customers.

35. In 1989, the tanker Exxon Valdez spilled oil along the coastline of Alaska, killing and maiming untold numbers of animals and resulting in billions of dollars of clean-up and compensation costs.

36. In a speech before a New York forum on Chernobyl in 1997, Ukranian President Kuchma said of the continuing effects of the 1986 disaster: "The social rehabilitation of 800,000 people affected by the accident has cost almost 4bn US dollars. That number includes 70,000 invalids. Their number rises annually by an average of 10,000. Consolidated expenditure on the elimination of the Chernobyl aftermath in Ukraine to the year 2005 is projected to reach a total of 600m dollars" (British Broadcasting Corporation 24 November 1997).

37. In 1984, in Bophal, India, forty-three tons of methyl isocyanate and other gases escaped from a Union Carbide factory, killing two thousand people within just a few weeks. In the aftermath, many more died or were seriously impaired.

38. During the 1960s, a number of congressional acts and executive orders addressing racial discrimination were promulgated. See, for example, the *Civil Rights Act of 1964*, the *Voting Rights Act of 1965*, and the *Fair Housing Act of 1968*.

39. See the *Age Discrimination in Employment Act of 1967*.

40. The *Civil Rights Act* has been amended to include, for example, Title V, which denies federal funding for programs that discriminate on the basis of gender; Title VII, which forbids discrimination in employment (including harassment) because of sex; and Title IX, which mandates equal school athletic opportunities for women.

41. See the *Americans with Disabilities Act of 1990*, which prohibits discrimination against any individual "on the basis of disability in the . . . enjoyment of the . . . services . . . of any place of public accommodation by any person who . . . operates [such] a place. . . ."

42. See, from among numerous examples of congressional legislation that have created judicial causes of action, the *Clean Water Act of 1972*, the *Resource Conservation and Recovery Act of 1976*, and the *Endangered Species Act of 1973*.

43. See the *Occupational Safety and Health Act of 1970*.

44. The *Social Security Act* created numerous populations entitled to income and medical support from the government, including retirees, those with disabilities, and the poor. But see, for a reversal in this tendency as it applies to the poor, the *Personal Responsibility and Work Opportunity Reconciliation Act (Welfare Reform) of 1996*.

45. In March 1998 during congressional testimony, Justice Kennedy bemoaned the congressional tendency to "federalize every single social problem," turning, in his words, "federal judges into police-court judges" (Lash 1998, A8).

46. Because of constitutional and statutory speedy trial requirements, criminal cases must take precedence over civil trials.

47. Among critics of the presidential–senatorial impasse has been Chief Justice Rehnquist who specifically chided the senators in his 1997 annual year-end report on the state of the judiciary, noting that "vacancies cannot remain at such high levels indefinitely without eroding the quality of justice" (cited in Cushman 1998, but see also "Hatch Defends Approval Rate for U.S. Bench," *Washington Post*, 2 January 1998, A21).

48. In 1995, ex-Mousketeer Billy Jean Matay was mugged in a Disneyland parking lot while on an outing with her grandchildren. Theme park staff brought Ms. Matay into a character changing area so that she and the children could compose themselves and give their statements. While in the area, Ms. Matay's grandchildren saw a staffer remove his Mickey headdress. Ms. Matay sued, alleging the sight traumatized her grandchildren (see, e.g., Ringle 1996; Belk 1997).

49. In 1998, the parents of twelve-year-old Anthea J. Kamalnath sued the sponsors of a regional spelling bee when their daughter lost in the final round after misspelling "impugn." The parents claimed that the word was unfairly inserted in the contest (see, e.g., National Public Radio 1998; Pulfer 1998).

50. In 1998, Melissa Jacklovich sued her ex-boyfriend for the cost of her prom dress ($224) after he broke up with her before taking her to the dance (see, e.g., "Miss Manners, Not Court Forum for Spurned Date," *National Law Journal*, 22 June 1998; Meryhew 1998).

51. One could argue that such is the case of Stella Liebach, a.k.a. "The McDonald's Coffee Lady." In fact, Ms. Liebach was very seriously burned and had tried to settle modestly with McDonald's before taking the company to court, and McDonald's had received many previous complaints about the temperature of their coffee before Ms. Liebach's mishap.

52. All three of the other cases cited—the Mouseketeer, the spelling bee, and the prom dress cases—were dismissed (thrown out of court) by judges.

53. For example, in the 105th Congress, at least forty-seven senators were lawyers, and attorneys made up roughly 35 percent of the House of Representatives. Indeed, these are conservative figures because members frequently list more than one occupation and some lawyers list their occupations as something else (Herrnson 1998, 48).

54. U.S. Chamber of Commerce, "Policy and Issue Information: Regulatory and Legal Impediments Issues—Issue: Tort Reform," available at www.uschamber.com/policy/d-reg.html (accessed 2 July 1998). Businesses, their political allies, and their associations, such as the U.S. Chamber of Commerce, the National Association of Manufacturers, the Business Roundtable, and the National Federation of Independent Business, have been in the forefront of efforts to curb litigation. They claim that the burden of lawsuits hurts businesses (and thus consumers), forcing "many companies . . . out of business." See Larry Fineran, National Association of Manufacturers, interview by Monica Brady, *Weekend All Things Considered*, National Public Radio, 9 August 1997 (transcript # 97080903-216). They are countered by such groups as the Association of Trial Lawyers and self-styled consumer groups such as Ralph Nader's "Public Citizen." Each side cites wildly disparate statistics to support its claims.

55. Representative John Kasich (R-OH), in *Congressional Record*, 103d Cong., 2d sess., 1994, 140. In the same statement, Kasich went on immediately to refer to the McDonald's coffee case.

Chapter 4

1. Simpson's one-time friend, Ron Shipp, was allowed to testify that Simpson had confessed to him of having dreams of killing his ex-wife (Associated Press 1996).

2. All of his grounds were dismissed and his conviction upheld unanimously by the Tenth Circuit Court of Appeals.

3. An exception to the *en banc* rule is the giant U.S. Court of Appeals for the Ninth Circuit. That court, which covers California, Alaska, Arizona, California, Hawaii, Idaho, Montana, Nevada, Oregon, Washington, Guam, and the Northern Mariana Islands, employs twenty-eight judges, far too unwieldy a number for collective decision making. Thus, when a Ninth Circuit case is deemed *en banc*–worthy, a panel of eleven judges is randomly drawn to serve the purpose (Smith 1997, 39).

4. The framers of the Constitution named only three felony violations as *federal* crimes. Over two centuries later in 1999, that list has grown to some three thousand federal felonies (Powell 1999, C1). An American Bar Association task force recently released a highly critical report on the "federalization of criminal law," urging Congress to refrain from "'[i]nappropriate federalization' which can contribute to 'long-range damage to real crime control'" by diverting federal money better spent on state law enforcement systems, and can "deplete funding of federal law enforcement efforts not duplicated by the states" ("AABA Task Force Urges Congress to Resist Pressure to 'Federalize' Crime," *Washington Post*, 16 February 1999, A3, available at www.washingtonpost.com/wp-srv/WPlate/1999-02/16/118l-021699-idx.html).

5. In 1998 alone, the number of criminal case filings in federal courts increased by 15 percent to 57,691 cases, "the biggest increase in 26 years and that came on top of steady growth in previous years" (Suro 1999, A2).

6. For example, Maryland's lower trial courts have exclusive civil jurisdiction over all landlord and tenant cases, replevin actions (recovery of property), and other cases involving amounts not exceeding $2,500. "Maryland Judicial Branch Overview," available at www.courts.state.md.us/overview.html#The District Court (accessed 9 September 1999).

7. For example, in Maryland, the District Court was created as a result of the 1970 ratification of a constitutional amendment, consolidating a miscellaneous system of trial magistrates, people's courts, and municipal courts into a fully state-funded court of record possessing statewide jurisdiction (District Court of Maryland, available at www.courts.state.md.us/district/dctpage.htm [accessed 9 September 1999]).

8. New York's courts of general jurisdiction are functionally and geographically divided into courts of claims, surrogate's courts, family courts, and, outside of New York City, county courts (Abadinsky 1995, 149).

9. In relevant part, Article III, § 1 reads: "The judicial Power of the United States, shall be vested in one Supreme Court, and in such inferior Courts as the Congress may from time to time ordain and establish."

10. U.S. District and Bankruptcy Court for the District of Idaho, available at www.id.uscourts.gov/ (accessed 9 September 1999).

11. U.S. District Court, Southern District of New York, U.S. District Judges, available at www.nysd.uscourts.gov/judges/USDJ.htm (accessed 9 September 1999).

12. In the twelve-month period from 1 July 1997 to 30 June 1998, bankruptcy filings totaled 1,429,451, an all-time high and a significant increase of about 100,000 over the previous twelve months (*National Law Journal*, 31 August 1998, A10).

13. The federal bankruptcy code recognizes four categories of bankruptcy and these constitute the workload of the courts: Chapter 7 liquidation, suitable for giving individuals and businesses a fresh start; Chapter 11 reorganization, suitable for large corporate debtors; Chapter 13 reorganization, suitable for individual wage earners; and Chapter 12 reorganization, suitable for family farmers (U.S. Courts, The Federal Judiciary Homepage, "Understanding the Courts," available at www.uscourts.gov/understanding_courts/89913.htm [accessed 1 October 1998]).

14. During the 1993–97 period, three-judge district panels considered forty-seven reapportionment cases, forty-three voting and election law cases, one employment discrimination case, and six additional civil rights cases (U.S. Courts, "Three-Judge District Court Hearings, By Nature of Suit," Table S-20, The Federal Judiciary Homepage, 1997a, available at www.uscourts.gov [accessed 19 March 2001]). More recently, as an example, a three-judge District Court, including Circuit Judge Douglas H. Ginsburg, and District Judges Ricardo Urbina and Royce Lamberth, ruled that the Census Bureau may not use statistical sampling in its 2000 population count (*U.S. House of Representatives v. U.S. Department of Commerce*, 11 F. Supp. 2d 76; 1998 U.S. Dist. LEXIS 13133 (1998)). That case went directly to the Supreme Court which, in 1999, upheld the ruling of the three-judge court (*U.S. Department of Commerce v. U.S. House of Representatives*, 525 U.S. 316 (1999)).

15. In 1993, 16 cases were heard by three-judge courts, 25 in 1994, 19 in 1995, 27 in 1996, and 14 in 1997 (U.S. Courts, "Three-Judge District Court Hearings, By Nature of Suit," Table S-20, The Federal Judiciary Homepage, 1997a, available at www.uscourts.gov [accessed 19 March 2001]).

16. Currently, plenary (full) review with oral arguments by attorneys is granted in roughly one hundred cases per term. The justices deliver formal written opinions in eighty to ninety of these cases. An additional fifty to sixty cases are disposed of without granting plenary review (U.S. Courts, "About the Supreme Court, 2000," The Supreme Court of the United States, available at www.supremecourtus.gov/about/about.htm [accessed 19 March 2001]).

17. The Court employed special masters in both of the abovementioned cases. For the record, Illinois won the bulk of its claim and New Jersey won most of what it wanted.

18. For an excellent general review of Court procedure, see Perry (1991, 23–39).

19. In *Flast v. Cohen* (392 U.S. 83, at 95 (1968); footnotes and citations omitted), the Court determined that "[j]usticiability is itself a concept of uncertain meaning and scope. Its reach is illustrated by the various grounds upon which questions sought to be adjudicated in federal courts have been held not to be justiciable. Thus, no justiciable controversy is presented when the parties seek adjudication of only a political question, when the parties are asking for an advisory opinion, when the question sought to be adjudicated has been mooted by subsequent developments, and when there is no standing to maintain the action. Yet it remains true that 'justiciability is . . . not a legal concept with a fixed content or susceptible of scientific verification. Its utilization is the resultant of many subtle pressures. . . .'"

20. At rare times, the Court has played rather fast and loose with the concept. In *Pollock v. Farmer's Loan & Trust*, 158 U.S. 601 (1895), a case testing the constitutionality of a federal tax, the litigants, a bank versus a stockholder, both wanted the same outcome.

21. In 1992, the Supreme Court refused to become substantively involved in the case of *Nixon v. United States*, 506 U.S. 224. In that case, involving the impeachment of federal judge Walter Nixon, the Court reasoned that the Judge Nixon's suit was nonjusticiable in part because judicial involvement in impeachment proceedings was counterintuitive, judicial review of Senate impeachment procedures would expose the country to months or years of political chaos, and it was uncertain what relief a court could give in such a case other than simply setting aside the political judgment of conviction. In other words, it determined that this was a "political question."

22. In fact, today very few cases accepted for review are dismissed on political question grounds. More frequently, dissenting justices will make the political question claim. For

example, Justice Scalia believes that party patronage employment "is a political question if there ever was one, and we should give it back to the voters of the various political units to decide, through civil service legislation crafted to suit the time and place, which mix is best." See for example, *Rutan v. Republican Party of Illinois*, 497 U.S. 62, at 114 (1990) (Scalia, J., dissenting).

23. The district courts, however, retain exclusive jurisdiction over tort claims and concurrent jurisdiction over tax refunds.

24. "Araneae: Spiders," available at www.ucmp.berkeley.edu/arthropoda/arachnida/araneae.html (accessed 3 August 1998).

25. "Reasonable doubt" may be defined as "The level of certainty a juror must have to find a defendant guilty of a crime. A real doubt, based upon reason and common sense after careful and impartial consideration of all the evidence, or lack of evidence, in a case. Proof beyond a reasonable doubt, therefore, is proof of such a convincing character that you would be willing to rely and act upon it without hesitation in the most important of your own affairs. However, it does not mean an absolute certainty" (The 'Lectric Law Lexicon, a service of *'Lectric Law Library*, available at www.lectlaw.com/def2/q016 [accessed 24 September 1998]).

26. "Preponderance of the evidence" may be defined as "The level of proof required to prevail in most civil cases. The judge or jury must be persuaded that the facts are more probably one way (the plaintiff's way) than another (the defendant's) (Ibid., available at www.leclaw.com/def2/p076 [accessed 24 September 1998]).

27. Louima filed his civil suit almost immediately. However, Judge Sterling Johnson, Jr., of the district court ordered it held in abeyance until the completion of the criminal case. Louima's case is also an example of the geographic jurisdictional confusion that sometimes arises in the law. The criminal case was delayed for months as parties wrangled over a switch from state to federal prosecution (Joseph P. Fried, "Judge Sets Tentative Trial Date for Five Policemen in Louima Brutality Case," *New York Times*, 19 September 1998, p. B3; John Marzulli, "Louima Lawyers Sue, Cite PBA Obstruction," *New York Daily News*, 7 August 1998, p. 30).

28. The Bureau of Justice Statistics (Brown and Langan 1998) reports a slight decline in plea bargain dispositions, down from 91 percent of all felony convictions in 1988.

29. The *U.S. Constitution*, Amendment VI, reads: "In all criminal prosecutions, the accused shall enjoy the right to a speedy and public trial, by an impartial jury of the state and district wherein the crime shall have been committed, which district shall have been previously ascertained by law, and to be informed of the nature and cause of the accusation; to be confronted with the witnesses against him; to have compulsory process for obtaining witnesses in his favor, and to have the assistance of counsel for his defense." Most state constitutions contain similar provisions. For example, *The California Declaration of Rights*, Article 1, § 15 reads: "The defendant in a criminal cause has the right to a speedy public trial, to compel attendance of witnesses in the defendant's behalf, to have the assistance of counsel for the defendant's defense, to be personally present with counsel, and to be confronted with the witnesses against the defendant. The Legislature may provide for the deposition of a witness in the presence of the defendant and the defendant's counsel. Persons may not twice be put in jeopardy for the same offense, be compelled in a criminal cause to be a witness against themselves, or be deprived of life, liberty, or property without due process of law."

30. Court TV features daily broadcasts of trials, often aired live. In addition, it features categorized special-interest series such as "Teens on Trial," "Police on Trial," and "The Greatest Trials of All Time." (See www.courttv.com/.)

31. California's law was passed as the result of a popular initiative, Ballot Proposition 184. The law is codified at *California Penal Code* Section 667 (b) through (i).

32. Legislative Analyst's Office (California), "The 'Three Strikes and You're Out' Law: A Preliminary Assessment," 6 January 1995 (available at www.lao.ca.gov/sc010695.html [accessed 19 March 2001]).

33. 'Lectric Law Library *Lexicon*, available at www.lectlaw.com/d-b.htm.

34. Ibid., www.lectlaw.com/def/e066.

35. Expert witnesses do present some difficult issues and the U.S. Supreme Court has laid down some general rules for federal judges to follow. See *Daubert v. Merrell Dow Pharmaceuticals*, 509 U.S. 579 (1993).

36. In relevant part, the Fifth Amendment reads, ". . . nor shall [any person] be compelled in any criminal case to be a witness against himself."

37. If a jury is hung, the prosecutor may decide to retry or simply to abandon the case.

38. The Bureau of Justice Statistics reports the following: "1996 was the first year State and Federal courts convicted a combined total of over 1 million adults of felonies—State convicted 997,970 adults and Federal convicted 43,839 adults (accounting for 4% of the national total). In 1996, 69% of all convicted felons were sentenced to a period of confinement—38% to State prisons and 31% to local jails. Jail sentences are for short-term confinement (usually for a year or less) in a county or city facility, while prison sentences are for long-term confinement (usually for over a year) in a State facility. State courts sentenced 38% of convicted felons to a State prison, 31% to a local jail, and 31% to straight probation with no jail or prison time to serve. Felons sentenced to a State prison in 1996 had an average sentence of 5 years but were likely to serve almost a half (45%) of that sentence—or just over 2 years—before release, assuming that 1996 release policies continue in effect. The average sentence to local jail was 6 months. The average probation sentence was about 3-1/2 years. Besides being sentenced to incarceration or probation, 32% or more of convicted felons also were ordered to pay a fine, pay victim restitution, receive treatment, perform community service, or comply with some other additional penalty. A fine was imposed on at least 20% of convicted felons" (Bureau of Justice Statistics 2000).

39. See especially, *Griffin v. Illinois*, 351 U.S. 12 (1956), granting indigent convicts the right to obtain trial transcripts free of charge; *Douglas v. California*, 372 U.S. 353 (1963), entitling indigent convicts to a court-appointed lawyer in their first appeal; and *North Carolina v. Pearce*, 395 U.S. 711 (1969), prohibiting judges from increasing sentences out of vindictiveness when a winning appellant is retried and found guilty.

40. Of the total number of appeals, 80 percent were terminated on the merits and, of those, 80 percent were fully affirmed the judgment of the trial court (Bureau of Justice Statistics 1995, 61).

41. Petitions claiming ineffective assistance of counsel are the most commonly cited errors, making up roughly 25% of habeas claims. Alleged trial court errors account for another 15%; Fourteenth Amendment violations, 14%; Fifth Amendment violations, 12%; Sixth Amendment, 7%; Eighth Amendment, 7%; prosecutorial misconduct, 6%; Fourth Amendment, 5%; and other complaints, 9% (Hanson and Daley 1995).

42. Indeed, it is much older. Habeas corpus comes to us via the English common law. It is believed that the first habeas writ was issued *before* the signing of the *Magna Carta*, so the origins of the writ go back at least to the twelfth century.

43. Although involving criminally adjudicated cases, habeas petitions are actually civil complaints and are counted as such by the Administrative Office of the U.S. Courts.

44. While such people are surely unusual, they are common enough to pose at least minor headaches in the judicial process. Thus, California and other states have attempted to deal with them legislatively. In California, for example, they are known as "vexatious litigants," individuals or institutions who, by law, are considered "persistent and obsessive litigant[s] who constantly [have] pending a number of groundless actions [which] abuse ... the judicial process." A person found, in judicial proceedings, to be a vexatious litigant is required "to post security for the reasonable expenses of a defendant who becomes the target of that person" (*Cal Code Civ Proc*, prec at 391 (1997)).

45. A contingency fee is an agreement between an attorney and his or her client that the attorney will only be paid if the case is successfully resolved in the client's favor. Generally, the agreement stipulates that the attorney will receive a percentage of the client's award.

46. In the same statement, Kasich went on immediately to refer to the McDonald's coffee case (*Congressional Record*, 103d Cong., 2d sess., 1994, 140; *Cong. Rec. H.* 9765, 27 September 1994).

47. American Tort Reform Association, available at www. atra.org/ (accessed 10 January 1999).

48. U.S. Chamber of Commerce, "Policy and Issues," available at www.uschamber.org/policy/d-reg.html (accessed 10 January 1999).

49. Public Citizen, Congress Watch, "Justice/Legal Rights," available at www.citizen.org/congress/civjus/home.html (accessed 10 January 1999).

50. The Association of American Trial Lawyers, available at www.atlanet.org/homepage/trmp1028.html (accessed 10 January 1999).

51. In general, damages may be defined as "financial compensation awarded to someone who suffered an injury or was harmed by someone else's wrongful act." Tort damages may be either compensatory or punitive. "By compensatory damages is meant such as are given . . . to recompense a party who has sustained a loss in consequence of the acts of the defendant. . . ." For example, if an injured plaintiff is unable to work for a year following his injury, he may be compensated for that lost income. Punitive damages, on the other hand, may be awarded over and above compensatory damages in order "to punish a defendant and to deter a defendant and others from committing similar acts in the future" ('Lectric Law Library, "Legal Lexicon," available at www.lectlaw. com/def.htm [accessed 10 January 1999]).

52. The estimated 378,000 tort cases were disposed from 1 July 1991 to 30 June 1992 in state general-jurisdiction courts. A representative sample of 18,000 tort cases was drawn from court files in forty-five of the nation's seventy-five largest counties. The forty-five are located in twenty-one states (Smith et al. 1995).

53. Available at www.atra.org/atra/ath.htm (accessed 10 January 1999).

54. For example, the Associated Press Online Newsfeed (1 July 1998, available through LEXIS-NEXIS, accessed 19 March 2001) reported the following: "A Florida man has filed suit against a nightclub, claiming he suffered whiplash when a topless dancer knocked him out with her oversized breasts. ... 'Apparently she jumped up and slammed her breasts on my head and just about knocked me out,' plaintiff Paul Shimkonis [is quoted] as saying. 'It was like two cement blocks hit me. I saw stars. I've never been right since.' Shimkonis, 38, filed suit in Pinellas County Court seeking more than $15,000 in damages from the Diamond Dolls club. The dancer, known as Tawny

Peaks, was not named in the lawsuit. Shimkonis suffered head, neck and other injuries that caused bodily injury, disability, pain and suffering, disfigurement, mental anguish and loss of capacity for the enjoyment of life, the suit said."

55. Under the heading, "Pickled Justice," ATRA cites a West Virginia case in which, according to the tort reform group, "convenience store worker Cheryl [Vandevender] was awarded an astonishing $2,699,000 in punitive damages after she injured her back when she opened a pickle jar. ..." On the face of it, given ATRA's spin, the case is made to seem absolutely asinine. However, Ms. Vandevender's case, which was ultimately considered by the state's supreme court, had to do with the store's unjust firing of her and not with suing it over a pickle jar (*Vandevender v. Sheetz*, 200 W. Va. 591; 490 S.E.2d 678 (1997)). For the record, ATRA even spelled the plaintiff's name wrong.

56. ATRA reports the case of David Schlessinger, who sued a steak house for overcooking his steak, along with the Town of Lake Geneva, Wisconsin, for failing to take his complaint seriously. ATRA does note that an appeals court ordered him to "show just cause . . . why [he] should not be penalized for pursuing a frivolous appeal." However, it neglects to note that the lower court had tossed his case out entirely and that the appeals court went so far as to deem his a "goofy lawsuit [which] deservedly met an abrupt end in the district court [and which was] frivolous at the outset, and likely maliciously retaliatory as well . . ." (*Schlessinger v. Salimes*, 100 F.3d 519 (7th cir) (1996)). No equivocation here!

57. Steven H. Gifis, *Law Dictionary*, 3d ed. (New York: Barron's Educational Series, 1991), 366.

58. As we noted above, habeas is technically a civil suit.

59. The figure excludes bankruptcy and administrative appeals (Commission on Structural Alternatives 1998).

60. Civil filings in the circuit courts (excluding prisoner-related filings, bankruptcy filings, and administrative complaints) now account for only 37 percent of all federal appellate filings, down significantly from 62 percent in 1960. This is due primarily to the huge increase in criminal and prisoner filings (Commission on Structural Alternatives 1998).

61. See, for example, American Civil Liberties Union, "Criminal Justice Issues," available at www.aclu.org/issues/criminal/hmcj.html (accessed 2 March 2000).

62. See, for example, Crime Victims' Rights, available at www.mcn.net/~smh264/ (accessed 2 March 2000) and National Victims' Constitutional Amendment Network, available at www.nvcan.org/ (accessed 2 March 2000). As a result of political pressure, most states and the federal government have launched "crime victims" programs. See, for example, U.S. Department of Justice, Office for Victims of Crime, available at www.ojp.usdoj.gov/ovc/ (accessed 2 March 2000).

Chapter 5

1. Public opinion polls indicate that Americans tend to have an unfavorable opinion of the Independent Counsel. For example, a CBS poll found that 48 percent of Americans held an unfavorable opinion of Kenneth Starr, while only 26 percent held a favorable opinion (*CBS Evening News with Dan Rather*, 20 November 1998). An NBC/*Wall Street Journal* poll found slightly higher "positives" for Starr (30 percent), but slightly higher "negatives" (50 percent) as well ("Poll Update," *The Hotline*, The National Journal Group, Inc., 11 December 1998).

2. This is a gross calculation based on the number of lawyers listed in the 1998 *Statistical Abstract*, compared to the current U.S. population of 271,712,680 (U.S. Census Bureau, "U.S.

POPClock Projection," available at www.census.gov/cgi-bin/popclock (accessed 13 January 1999).

3. Most of these schools are in California (Baum 1998, 61).

4. California is the only state that currently accepts the study of law by correspondence as a means of qualifying for the bar exam (Ibid.).

5. A number of law schools offer night or part-time courses of study that usually run for a four-year period. About one in ten graduates from ABA-approved schools attends part-time (Ibid.).

6. Reputation, the single largest weighted measure at 40 percent, "involves two *U.S. News* surveys conducted in [the] fall. . . . In one, the dean and other faculty members at each school were asked to rate the reputation of each accredited school using a five-point scale. This accounts for 25 percent of the total in the overall rankings. In the second survey, accounting for 15 percent of the total in the overall rankings, practicing lawyers, hiring partners, and senior judges were asked to rate each school on a five-point scale based on their appraisals of the work of recent graduates of that school" (*U.S. News and World Report* 1998).

7. "Selectivity" is weighted at 25 percent. "This combines median Law School Admission Test score (50 percent of this measure), median undergraduate GPA (40 percent), and proportion of applicants accepted as full-time J.D. students in the fall . . . entering class (10 percent)" (*U.S. News and World Report* 1998).

8. "Placement success (20 percent) [for the 1998 rankings involved] the proportion of the class of 1996 employed full and part time as of Feb. 15, 1997, including all those pursuing graduate degrees and one fourth of those whose employment status was unknown, but excluding those not looking for employment (60 percent of this measure) and the proportion of the class of 1996 employed full or part time at graduation, including those pursuing graduate degrees (30 percent). The final component (10 percent) takes into account the school's overall bar passage rate for the summer 1996 and winter 1997 tests in the jurisdiction where the largest number of its 1996 graduates took the test for the first time. This rate was divided by the overall passage rate for first-time test takers in that jurisdiction in the same time period, and the resulting ratio used for the rankings" (*U.S. News and World Report* 1998).

9. "Faculty resources (15 percent) [for the 1998 survey were] based on average total expenditures per student for instruction, library, and supporting student services in the years beginning in fall 1995 and 1996 (65 percent of this measure); student-to-teacher ratio (20 percent), average financial aid, indirect expenditures, and overhead expenditures per student in the years beginning in fall 1995 and 1996 (10 percent); and total number of volumes, microfilm, microfiche, and titles in the law library (5 percent)" (*U.S. News and World Report* 1998).

10. The *U.S. News* survey is inevitably a matter of great concern to school administrators, faculty, future employers, and current and prospective students. A number of alternatives have been devised over the years. Recently, for example, Brian Leiter, a professor of law and philosophy at the University of Texas School of Law, created a "Ranking of U.S. Law Schools by Educational Quality," a blend of his own work and other published studies, with an emphasis on law faculties' scholarly distinction. Leiter's new survey claims to almost entirely disregard the kind of reputational and financial criteria used by *U.S. News*. Despite, however, what he claims to be a more balanced, less elitist orientation, Leiter's rankings capture the "usual suspects." Thus, in his survey, the top contenders are Yale, Chicago, Harvard, Stanford, Columbia, the University of Virginia, New York University (NYU), Berkeley,

University of Texas (Austin), University of Michigan (Ann Arbor), Cornell, Georgetown, the University of Pennsylvania, Northwestern University, and Duke (Rovella 1997, A1). Big difference!

11. Although the structure of legal education was much different, de Tocqueville, writing about 170 years ago, noted that the "aristocratic character" of American lawyers stemmed in part "from [their] legal studies. . . ." (de Tocqueville, "Causes Which Mitigate the Tyranny of the Majority in the United States," volume 1, chapter XVI, *Democracy in America*, available at C-SPAN, xroads.virginia.edu/~HYPER/DETOC/1_ ch16.htm.).

12. In 1996, the Fifth Circuit Court of Appeals sent shock waves through the law school community when it ruled that a preferential admissions program at the University of Texas School of Law violated the equal protection clause of the Fourteenth Amendment (*Hopwood v. Texas*, 78 F.3d 932 (1996)). The U.S. Supreme Court later denied cert. in 518 U.S. 1033 (1996) and upon reconsideration by a district court awarding substantial damages to Hopwood and other plaintiffs, Texas Attorney General Dan Morales declined further appeal. Moreover, in the same year, California voters approved Ballot Proposition 209, which eliminated state affirmative action programs. A major ramification of the new law was significantly diminished minority enrollments in 1997 at Boalt Hall, the prestigious University of California–Berkeley law school.

13. The total includes $9,040 in annual in-state tuition, $5,850 for on-campus housing, and $1,500 for books (available at www.law.umaryland.edu/admiss/expense.htm [accessed 14 January 1999]).

14. The total includes $25,550 in yearly tuition, $8,980 in housing costs, and $780 for books (available at www.yale.edu/lawweb/lawschool/finaid/ [accessed 14 January 1999]).

15. Although we sometimes attribute this aspect of law to the "L.A. Syndrome" and bullish stock markets of the 1980s, please note the following complaint published in *American Lawyer* in 1895: "[The bar] has allowed itself to lose, in large measure, the lofty independence, the genuine learning, the fine sense of professional dignity and honor. . . . For the past thirty years it has become increasingly contaminated with the spirit of commerce which looks primarily to the financial value and recompense of every undertaking" ("The Commercialization of the Profession," *American Lawyer*, March 1895, p. 84, cited in Galanter 1996).

16. Karl Llewellyn, "The Bar Specializes—With What Results?," *Annals of the American Academy* 167 (1933): 177, cited in Galanter (1996, 557).

17. A rarely employed method of legislative selection in which the state legislature elects judges is employed in only two states, South Carolina and Virginia.

18. Justice Anthony Kennedy, speaking before an American Bar Association conference (Biskupic 1998b, A2).

19. The Ritchie letter is especially indicative of Jefferson's utter contempt for the judiciary in general and Marshall's Supreme Court in particular. For example, Jefferson calls the judiciary "the subtle corps of sappers and miners constantly working underground to undermine the foundation of our confederated fabric. They are construing our Constitution from a coordination of a general and special government to a general and supreme one alone. This will lay all things at their feet. . . ." With respect to Marshall, he goes on to allege that "[a]n opinion is huddled up in conclave, perhaps by a majority of one, delivered as if unanimous, and with the silent acquiescence of lazy or timid associates, by a crafty chief judge, who sophisticates the law to his mind, by the turn of his own reasoning. . . ." Earlier, in 1810, Jefferson wrote to John Tyler that as far as Marshall was concerned, the Constitution was

"nothing more than an ambiguous text, to be explained by his sophistry into any meaning which may subserve his personal malice" (cited in McDowell 1988, 1).

20. See, for example, Bradley C. Canon, "The Impact of Formal Selection Processes on the Characteristics of Judges," *Law and Society Review* 6 (1972): 579, cited in Baum 1998, 129.

21. The "due process revolution" refers to any number of landmark decisions made by the Court extending rights and liberties on Bill of Rights and Fourteenth Amendment grounds. The most controversial of these, however, were the Court's decisions in the area of criminal law, particularly rights of the accused. For a few of many familiar examples, this was the era in which the Court handed down *Mapp v. Ohio*, 367 U.S. 643 (1961), extending the Fourth Amendment–based exclusionary rule to state prosecutions; *Gideon v. Wainwright*, 372 U.S. 335 (1963), extending the Sixth Amendment's guarantee of counsel to state defendants, and *Miranda v. Arizona*, 384 U.S. 436 (1966), extending the Fifth Amendment's right against self-incrimination.

22. In 1966, the Court consisted of Earl Warren (R-Eisenhower), Hugo Black (D-FDR), William O. Douglas (D-FDR), Tom Clark (D-Truman), William Brennan (D-Eisenhower), John Harlan (R-Eisenhower), Potter Stewart (R-Eisenhower), Byron White (D-Kennedy), and Abe Fortas (D-LBJ).

23. Over the course of the 1980s and 1990s, the Court has created so many exceptions to the exclusionary rule that some constitutional scholars have called it effectively meaningless. See especially, the "good faith exception," in *U.S. v. Leon*, 468 U.S. 897 (1984). Similarly, *Miranda* has been effectively watered down over the course of the past two decades.

24. The current Court consists of Chief Justice William Rehnquist (R-Nixon), John Paul Stevens (R-Ford), Sandra Day O'Connor (R-Reagan), Antonin Scalia (R-Reagan), William Kennedy (R-Reagan), David Souter (R-Bush), Clarence Thomas (R-Bush), Ruth Bader Ginsburg (D-Clinton), and Steven Breyer (D-Clinton).

25. Members of Congress—particularly conservative Republicans—regularly rail against judicial activism. Indeed, Majority Whip Tom DeLay (R-TX) had an entire web page devoted to the perceived evils of an activist judiciary (DeLay 1998; no longer extant).

26. Very occasionally, even judges may be caught with their hands in the till. For one very notable example during the early 1990s, federal prosecutors tried four Dade County, Florida, judges on money laundering, bribery, and extortion charges in what came to be known as "Operation Court Broom."

27. In 1986, California voters ousted three members of their supreme court, including Chief Judge Rose Byrd. The judges' opponents waged a highly public campaign for the removal of the three who had been appointed by liberal Governor Jerry Brown.

28. Judge Ilana Diamond Rovner of the Seventh Circuit quoted in Holden (1997, 8).

29. The Framers had good experiential reason to believe so strongly in the liberty-enhancing properties of juries. Colonial juries often refused to convict defendants under what they deemed oppressive British law. In the most celebrated such case, that of dissident printer Peter Zenger, a New York jury in 1735 refused to convict on British seditious libel charges.

30. Note, for example, the considerable invective laid upon the poor jurors impaneled on the O. J. Simpson criminal trial.

31. A very telling indication of the vastly reduced status of the jury came during the Senate trial of President Clinton on 15 January 1999. During his presentation, Congressman and House Manager Bob Barr (R-GA) repeatedly referred to the Senators as "jurors." Ultimately, Senator Tom Harkin (D-IA) objected to the repeated, apparently insulting, references, noting that Senators, in these circumstances, are much more than ordinary jurors, for Senators determine the law as well as the facts. Chief Justice Rehnquist upheld Harkin's objection, admonishing Barr to "refrain from referring" to Senators as jurors (Keller 1999).

32. See, for example, *U.S. v. Addison*, 498 F.2d 741, at 744 (D.C. Cir. 1974), wherein complex scientific evidence may "assume a posture of mystic infallibility in the eyes of a jury of layman"; *U.S. v. Wilson*, 361 F. Supp. 510, 513 (D. Md. 1973), wherein given the complex nature of polygraph evidence, juries may be misled by its admission; and *State v. Schwartz*, 447 N.W.2d 422, 428 (Minn. 1989), wherein "In dealing with complex technology, like DNA testing, we remain convinced that juries in criminal cases may give undue weight and deference" to the evidence (cited in Petrosinelli 1990, 356). The late former Chief Justice Warren Burger once advised that "the masses of complicated technical information adduced [in complex trials], combined with the often difficult legal issues involved, strain the abilities of the juries to find the facts competently"(cited in Gildea 1994, 456).

33. With a general verdict, a jury declares which party prevails overall. A special verdict requires juries to make findings on specific factual issues (Brodin 1990, 17).

34. The role of interest groups in politics has long been a mainstay of political theory. Notwithstanding James Madison, political scientists and observers have continually noted the importance of groups to the American political enterprise. See, for examples of some of the more classic studies spanning the history of the United States, de Tocqueville (1835); Dahl (1956); Schattschneider (1960); Key (1964); and Lowi (1969), among many others.

35. The Supreme Court itself acknowledged and encouraged a court role for political "outs" in *U.S. v. Carolene Products*, 304 U.S. 144 (1938). In its famous footnote 4 to that opinion, the Court wrote:

> There may be narrower scope for operation of the presumption of constitutionality when legislation appears on its face to be within a specific prohibition of the Constitution, such as those of the first ten amendments, which are deemed equally specific when held to be embraced within the Fourteenth [Amendment].
>
> It is unnecessary to consider now whether *legislation that restricts those political processes which can ordinarily be expected to bring about repeal of undesirable legislation is to be subjected to more exacting scrutiny under the general prohibitions of the Fourteenth Amendment than are most other types of legislation.* On restrictions upon the right to vote, on restraints upon the dissemination of information, on interferences with political organizations, as to prohibition of peaceable assembly.
>
> Nor need we enquire whether similar considerations enter into the review of statutes directed at particular religious, or national, or racial minorities, whether *prejudice against discrete and insular minorities may be a special condition, which tends seriously to curtail the operation of those political processes ordinarily to be relied upon to protect minorities, and which may call for a correspondingly more searching judicial inquiry* [emphasis added].

36. The court-based strategy created by the NAACP has been copied by other groups, particularly over the course of the past thirty years. For example, women, Latinos, the disabled, and gays have employed court-based strategies with varying degrees of success.

37. For the most obvious example, *Roe v. Wade*, far from settling the abortion issue, set off a chain of litigation, legisla-

tive reaction, and interest group activity that persists to this day.

38. After all, as Chief Justice Marshall said as far back as 1803, "It is emphatically the province and duty of the judicial department to say what the law is" (*Marbury v. Madison*, 5 U.S. 137, at 178 (1803)).

39. Many good judicial process books are devoted entirely to the subject of this chapter. For one excellent example, see Baum (1998).

Part II, Introduction

1. "Quickening" is defined as "the first recognizable movement of the fetus in utero, appearing usually from the 16th to the 18th week of pregnancy" (*Roe v. Wade*, 410 U.S. 113, at 132 (1973)).

2. "Viability" is the "point at which there is a reasonable likelihood of the fetus' sustained survival outside the womb, with or without artificial support. [T]his point may differ with each pregnancy.... [I]t may be measured by weeks of gestation or fetal weight or [other factors]" (*Colautti v. Franklin*, 439 U.S. 379, at 388 (1979)).

3. Historically, this has involved a close physical relationship between mother and father. Even today, this is the way most of us come into being. Technological advancements, however, such as sperm and egg banks and surrogacy, have made possible more attenuated relationships between mothers and fathers. These technologies, which have left law reeling in their wake, are discussed in this book as well.

Chapter 6

1. Ten years later, in *Maynard v. Hill*, 125 U.S. 190, at 194 (1888) (examining a property dispute between spouses where the wife was notified that her husband had been granted a legislative divorce), the Supreme Court stated that marriage is "the most important relation in life" and "the foundation of the family and of society, without which there would be neither civilization nor progress." In 1923, the Court in *Meyer v. Nebraska*, 262 U.S. 390, at 399 (1923) (striking down a state law prohibiting teaching of a foreign language to children) described marriage as "essential to the orderly pursuit of happiness by free men." Then, in 1942, the Court in *Skinner v. Oklahoma*, 316 U.S. 535, at 541 (1942) (invalidating an Oklahoma statute providing for sterilization of habitual criminals) described marriage as "fundamental to the very existence and survival of the race."

2. There are indications that more than a century after it was outlawed, polygamy is flourishing in parts of Utah and several other western states (see, e.g., Egan 1999).

3. Eighteen state legislatures have enacted legislation that forbids the granting of marriage right to same-sex couples: 1996 Alaska Sess. Laws 21; Ariz. Rev. Stat. Ann. 25-101(c) (West 1996); Conn. Gen. Stat. 46a-91r (West 1995); H.B. 503, 138th Leg. (Del. 1995); Ga. Code Ann. 19-3-3.1 (1996); Haw. Rev. Stat. Ann. 572-1 (Michie 1997); Idaho Code 32-209 (1996); 750 Ill. Comp. Stat. 5/212 (West 1996); Ind. Code 31-7-1-2 (1995); S.B. 515, 76th Leg. (Kan. 1996); H.B. 5662, 88th Leg. (Mich. 1995); S.B. 937, 88th Leg. (Mich. 1995); 1995 N.C. Sess. Laws 588; S.B. 73, 45th Leg. (Okla. 1996); 23 Pa. C.S.A. 1704 (1996); H.B. 4502, 111th Leg. (S.C. 1996); S.D. Codified Laws 25-1-1 (Michie 1996); Tenn. Code Ann. 336-3-113 (1996); Tex. Code Ann. 68-11-90 (West 1996); Utah Code Ann. 30-1-4 (1995); Utah Code Ann.

30-1-2 (1994); and Va. Code Ann. 20-45.2 (Michie 1994). In addition, the case law of five states and Washington, D.C., indicates that the right to marry within the state does not extend to same-sex couples: *Dean v. District of Columbia*, 653 A.2d 307 (D.C. 1995); *Jones v. Hallahan*, 501 S.W. 2d 588 (Ky. 1973); *Baker v. Nelson*, 191 N.W.2d 185 (Minn. 1971); *Anonymous v. Anonymous*, 325 N.Y.S.2d 499 (1971); *De Santo v. Barnsley*, 476 A.2d 952 (Pa. Super. Ct. 1984); and *Singer v. Hara*, 522 P.2d 1187 (Wash. Ct. App. 1974). See also *Adams v. Howerton*, 673 F.2d 1036 (9th Cir. 1982) (holding that homosexual marriage is not recognized for citizenship purposes under Immigration and Naturalization Service provisions).

4. See footnotes 16 and 17 and accompanying text.

5. In *Pennoyer v. Neff*, 95 U.S. 714, at 734–35 (1878), the Court observed that a state "has the absolute right to prescribe the conditions upon which the marriage relation between its own citizens shall be created, and the causes for which it may be dissolved." This division of authority has been repeatedly affirmed. See *United States v. Lopez*, 514 U.S. 549, at 564 (1995) (rejecting the argument that the Commerce Clause might support a finding of federal legislative jurisdiction over "family law (including marriage, divorce, and child custody)").

6. Domestic relations issues and personal injury torts constitute two of the largest categories of civil litigation, nearly all of which is filed in state courts. For recent data and historical caseload trends, see, for example, National Center for State Courts (1994a, 1994b).

7. Powell also noted that "[i]n *Ginsberg v. New York*, 390 U.S. 629, at 639 (1968), the Court spoke of the rights of family members to make critical decisions for themselves as "basic in the structure of our society." *Griswold* . . . struck down Connecticut's anticontraception statute. Three concurring justices, relying on both the Ninth and Fourteenth Amendments, emphasized that 'the traditional relation of the family' is 'a relation as old and as fundamental as our entire civilization.'"

8. See 28 U.S.C. 1738B (1994). The purpose of the statute is to ensure that a child support order entered in one state will be honored by sister states.

9. *Defense of Marriage Act*, Pub. L. No. 104-199, 110 Stat. 2419 (codified at 1 U.S.C. 7 (1997); 28 U.S.C. 1738C (1997)). Section 1 states: "In determining the meaning of any Act of Congress, or of any ruling, regulation, or interpretation of the various administrative bureaus and agencies of the United States, the word 'marriage' means only a legal union between one man and one woman as husband and wife, and the word 'spouse' refers only to a person of the opposite sex who is a husband or a wife."

10. In addition, a plethora of benefits granted by state governments are tied to the marital status of citizens, such as inheritance rights, health benefits, insurance coverage, post-divorce rights regarding spousal support and property division, and the right to bring a wrongful-death suit (see, e.g., Cordell 1994).

11. For an excellent analysis of the developing role of the family from a sociological perspective, see Skolnick and Skolnick (1971).

12. The full text of de Tocqueville's *Democracy In America*, first published in 1835, is available online at the C-SPAN website, available at www.cspan.org/alexis (accessed 11 January 1999). See especially Book 3, chapters 8–10. The passages quoted next are taken from chapter 8.

13. In fact, polygamy was made illegal by federal law.

14. The opinion can be viewed at www.ftm.org/archive/miike.html (accessed 10 August 1998).

15. It did not take long for opponents to rally their troops and successfully amend the state's constitution (Hawaii Const., Art. I, §§ 23; state constitutional amendment over-

turned the same-sex marriage decision in *Baehr* by returning power to the legislature "to reserve marriage to opposite-sex couples"). As a consequence, when the case came back before the state supreme court, the justices found that the issues were now moot (*Baehr v. Miike*, Civ. No. 91-1394-05, 9 December 1999). Also, compare *Shahar v. Bowers*, 114 F.3d 1097 (11th Cir. 1997) (rejecting the contention that there is a "right to marry" a person of the same sex), and *In re Ladrach*, 32 Ohio Misc.2d 6, 513 N.E.2d 828 (1987) (rejecting an application for a marriage license to allow postoperative male to female transsexual to marry a male), with *Brause v. Bureau of Vital Statistics*, No. 3AN-95-6562 CI (Superior Ct. 3d Dist. Alaska, Feb 27, 1998) (holding that the state must "have a compelling purpose before it can define marriage to exclude partners of the same sex." The Alaska Supreme Court declined to rule on an appeal filed by the state, sending it back to the Superior Court for a full trial whether the state can justify the classification scheme. The case is now in the discovery phase.).

16. *Baker v. Vermont*, Chittenden (Vt) Superior Court (1009-97CnC, 1997), available online at Vermont Freedom to Marry, www.vtfreetomarry.org/ (accessed 6 July 1999). Also, cf. Eskridge (1993), Polikoff (1993), and Wardle (1996).

17. The legislature was careful not to refer to the newly recognized status as "marriage" (Act 91, An Act Relating to Civil Unions (H847 2000)). For a full-text account of all legislative proceedings in this matter, see The Vermont Legislative Bill Tracking System, available at www.leg.state.vt.us/baker/baker.cfm.

18. Indeed, according to the National Center for Health Statistics, the average expected family size was 2.2 children per woman in 1995 (available at www.cdc.gov/nchswww/releases/97facts/97sheets/nsfgfact.htm [accessed 13 January 1999]).

19. See footnote 13 and accompanying text.

20. California was the first to adopt "no fault" divorce in 1970. By 1980, only Illinois and South Dakota had not followed suit (see, e.g., Weitzman 1985; Jacob 1988).

21. The Rutgers University National Marriage Project reports that the marriage rate reached its lowest point in recorded history in 1996, plummeting from 87.5 marriages per 1,000 unmarried women in 1960 to 49.7 marriages in 1996. Moreover, the percentage of married people who indicate being "very happy" in their marriage dropped from 53.5 percent in 1973–76 to 37.8 percent in 1996. The report also cites an upsurge in unmarried couples living together and increased acceptance among young adults of unmarried cohabitation and single parenthood than ever before (Popenoe and Whitehead 1999).

22. Even with no-fault, some states continue to implement some restrictions. For example, Maryland imposes a mandatory period of separation prior to the divorce proceeding. Presumably, this is the state's way of having the couple "think it over."

23. The statute also allows already-married couples to convert to a "covenant marriage" (Act 1380, "Covenant Marriage Act," of 1997, available online at www.lafayetteparishclerk.com/covenantmarriage.html). According to one source, a coalition of twenty-four organizations has joined forces to push the covenant marriage idea in state legislatures across the country. See *Maranatha Christian Journal*, "Groups Launch Covenant Marriage Movement," 23 May 2000, available at www.mcjonline.com/news/news3109.htm.

24. States can impose other kinds of restrictions, however, such as mandatory waiting periods. See, for example, *Sosna v. Iowa*, 419 U.S. 393 (1975).

25. There are quite a few such cases in the state law archives. See, for example, *Paul v. Frazier* 3 Mass 71 (1807), and *Wightman v. Coates* 15 Mass. 2 (1918).

26. See, for example, *Wildey v. Springs*, 1995 U.S.App. LEXIS 4943 (7th Cir. 1995); *Michigan Law Review* (1985); and Kruckenberg (1998).

27. See also, e.g., *Pavlicic v. Vogtsberger*, 136 A.2d 127 (Pa. 1957).

28. See also, e.g., *Fierro v. Hoel*, 465 N.W.2d 669 (Ct App. IA, 1990); *Heiman v. Parrish*, 262 Kan. 926 (S Ct. KS, 1997); *Vigil v. Haber*, 888 P.2d 455 (N.M. 1994); *Luindh v. Surman*, 702 A.2d 560 (Superior Ct. PA, 1997); and *Fanning v. Iverson*, 1995 S.D. LEXIS 100 (S.Ct SD, 1995).

29. However, family members have established a time-honored tradition of squabbling over and litigating inheritance and estate division issues by contesting wills and business contracts.

30. For example, Regan (1993, 128–131) notes the continued virulence of the "marital rape exception" in criminal prosecutions. Accordingly, many states treat a husband's rape of his wife as a less serious offense than a comparable assault on another woman.

31. Juvenile justice issues are addressed in chapter 7.

32. See, for example, *Burnette v. Wahl*, 588 P.2d 1105 (Or. 1978); *Anderson v. Stream*, 295 N.W.2d 595 (Minn. 1980); and *Gibson v. Gibson*, 479 P.2d 648 (Cal. 1971).

33. *Pierce v. Society of Sisters*, 268 U.S. 510, at 534 (1925).

34. *Wisconsin v. Yoder*, 406 U.S. 205, at 231 (1972).

35. However, states do provide exemptions to vaccination requirements for religious reasons.

36. These and related issues will be discussed in more detail in chapter 7.

37. *Twigg v. Mays*, No. 88-4489-CA-01, 1993 WL 330624 (Fla. Cir. Ct. Aug. 18, 1993).

38. See chapter 7.

39. Cultural issues have also arisen in Immigration and Naturalization Service cases. For example, see *In Re: Fauziya Kasinga*, U.S. Board of Immigration Appeals, 2 May 1996, "Hearing Transcript re Whether Togo Citizen Fauziya Kasinga Should Be Granted Political Asylum Due to Her Fear of Female Circumcision Should She Return to Togo" (see 'Lectric Law Library 1999).

40. *Stanley* at 651, citing *Meyer v. Nebraska*, 262 U.S. 390, at 399 (1923); *Skinner v. Oklahoma*, 316 U.S. 535, at 541 (1942); *May v. Anderson*, 345 U.S. 528, at 533 (1953); and *Prince v. Massachusetts*, 321 U.S. 158, at 166 (1944).

41. According to Luker (1996, 33–34), Indiana was the first state to enact such a forced sterilization law in 1907, and by 1931 twenty-six sister states had followed suit.

42. Although the reasoning expressed in this case has been subsequently discredited, *Buck v. Bell* has not been overturned.

43. The line of cases in this area also demonstrates one of the hallmarks of legal development through the courts. It is usually a slow, plodding, piecemeal process. Indeed, more than forty years separate *Meyer*, where the Court pronounced the constitutional right "to marry, establish a home and bring up children" (262 U.S. 390, at 399 (1923)), and *Griswold*.

44. By 1999, two additional state legislatures and the District of Columbia had also done so. See ACLU, "Status of U.S. Sodomy Laws," available at www.aclu.org/issues/gay/hgml/sodomy.html (accessed 23 June 1999).

45. See, for example, *Commonwealth v. Wasson*, 842 S.W. 2d 487 (Ky. 1992); *People v. Onofre*, 415 N.E.2d 936 (N.Y. 1980); *Commonwealth v. Bonadio*, 415 A.2d 47 (Pa. 1980); *Gryczan v. Montana*, 942 P.2d 112 (Montana 1997); and *Campbell v. Sundquist*, 926 S.W. 2d 250 (Tenn. App. 1996).

46. Arkansas, Kansas, Missouri, Oklahoma, and Texas.

47. Alabama, Arizona, Florida, Idaho, Louisiana, Michigan, Massachusetts, Minnesota, Mississippi, North Carolina, South Carolina, Utah, and Virginia.

48. Also see Lambda Legal Defense and Education Fund, available at www.lambdalegal.org/cgi-bin/pages/ (accessed 25 June 1999); and Human Rights Campaign, available at www.hrcusa.org/ (accessed 25 June 1999).

49. See, for example, American Center for Law and Justice, available at www.aclj.org/index.html (accessed 25 June 1999); and Christian Legal Society, available at clsnet.com/clspage. html (accessed 25 June 1999). For related discussion, see footnote 13, *supra*, and accompanying text.

50. For a discussion of some of the grim realities, see, for example, *People v. Belous*, 458 P.2d 194 (1969).

51. Colorado actually was the first state to do so in 1967, followed by New York, Alaska, Hawaii, and Washington in 1970.

52. The case was initially argued on 13 December 1971, but because of pending personnel changes on the Court, it was reargued on 11 October 1972.

53. This process has been thoroughly investigated and reported. See, for example, O'Brien (1996). Moreover, composition of the bench at the U.S. District and Circuit levels is extremely important in shaping the contours of constitutional law, and presidents have many more opportunities to fill positions. See, for example, Goldman (1989a, 1989b, 1995).

54. Chief Justice Rehnquist and Justices White and Kennedy were also prepared to overturn *Roe*.

55. See chapter 2 for extensive opinion excerpts and related discussion.

56. For example, Alabama, 1997 Alabama Laws Act 97-485 (S.B. 314); Alaska, AK Statutes § 18.16.050; Arizona, Criminal Code § 13-3603.01; Arkansas, AR Code Annotated § 5-61-203; Florida, FS § 390.001; Georgia, GC 16-12-144; Illinois, IL Statutes Chapt. 720, § 513; Indiana, IC 16-34-2-1; Louisiana, LA R.S. 14: 32.9; Michigan, MCL 333.17016 and MCL 33.17516; Mississippi, Miss. Code 1972, § 41-41-73; Montana, MC § 50-20-109; Nebraska, NE ST § 28-326; New Jersey, NJ Statutes Title 2A, Chapt. 65A; Ohio, Ohio Revised Code § 2919.15; Rhode Island, RI Statutes § 23-4.12; South Carolina, SC Code 1976 § 44-41-85; South Dakota, SDCL 34-23A-27; Tennessee, TC § 39-15-209; Utah, UC 1953 § 76-7-310.5; and Virginia, VC § 18.2-74.2.

57. Supporters of the ban highlight the gruesomeness of the procedure and compare it to "infanticide." Challengers counter, however, that legislation on the matter is unconstitutionally vague and fails to meet the "undue burden" standard set forth in *Casey*. See, for example, *Women's Medical Professional Corp. v. Voinovich*, 130 F.3d 187 (6th Cir. 1997) (voiding Ohio's statute); and *Evans v. Kelly*, 977 F. Supp. 1283 (E.D. Mich. 1997) (enjoining enforcement of the Michigan statute).

58. See, e.g., "Clinton Veto Holds in Latest Abortion Battle," *Atlanta Journal and Constitution*, 19 September 1998, p. 07A. Supporters of the ban have vowed to continue the effort ("Ashcroft Co-sponsors Bill to Ban 'Partial-birth' Abortion Nationwide; Senator Blasts Clinton for Vetoing Previous Bans," *St. Louis Post-Dispatch*, 30 April 1999, p. B3).

59. From Twain's *Notebook*, in Barbara Schmidt, "Mark Twain Quotations, Newspaper Collections, & Related Resources," available online at www.tarleton.edu/~schmidt/Familiarity.html (accessed 6 July 1999).

60. Everett (1987, 559) argues that a contract's emphasis on the free will of individuals inevitably leads us to understand human life in terms of atomized persons who construct artificial, secondary relationships to pursue their individual choices. See also Glendon (1991, 121–30).

61. See, for example, *Kingsley v. Kingsley*, 623 So. 2d 780 (Fla. 1993); and *Twigg v. Mays*, No. 88-4489-CA-01, 1993 WL 330624 (Fla. Cir. Ct. Aug. 18, 1993).

Chapter 7

1. In addition to child welfare types of issues, the doctrine has been employed generally when the state steps in to protect health and welfare, such as in the enforcement of environmental law.

2. Although multiple births remain relatively rare, their occurrence is increasing with the use of fertility treatments. According to the Centers for Disease Control (CDC), in 1997, there were 110,874 live multiple births with twins accounting for 104,137, triplets accounting for 6,148, and quadruplets accounting for 560 (CDC 1997).

3. Andrews cites a telling example from her own experience: "Four years ago, I got a call from an infertility specialist who was in the midst of a procedure. He was just about to transfer an embryo created by a childless couple's egg and sperm to the woman who had volunteered to carry the baby for them. But he suddenly had second thoughts. 'I've got an embryo from a couple in a catheter,' he told me hurriedly. I pictured him, catheter in one hand, telephone receiver in the other. 'I'm about to implant it in the surrogate, who is the husband's sister,' he explained, and wanted to know if it would violate his state's ban on incest. If he decided not to go through with the implantation and the embryo died, he asked, could he be found guilty of murder? As a lawyer specializing in reproductive technologies for the past two decades, I've become used to such calls, and I shared this doctor's frustration about how little law there was to guide him. No, I told him, this probably wouldn't be incest. But the question of murder was more complicated. In some states, such as Louisiana, embryos that are created in vitro are viewed as people and cannot be destroyed. The incident reminded me once again that the United States lacks a national policy for dealing with reproductive technology—and is the only technologically sophisticated nation without one" (Andrews 1999).

4. According to the Tennessee Supreme Court, "The policy of the state on the subject matter before us may be gleaned from the state's treatment of fetuses in the womb. . . . The state's Wrongful Death Statute, Tenn. Code Ann. § 20-5-106 does not allow a wrongful death for a viable fetus that is not first born alive. Without live birth, the Supreme Court has said, a fetus is not a "person" within the meaning of the statute" (842 S.W. 2d 588, at 594 op. cit.).

5. Internal citations to case filing numbers are omitted.

6. During the initial appellate go-round in 1995, the Fourth Court of Appeals issued a peremptory writ issue directing the family law court to hold a hearing on Luanne's order to show cause for temporary child support and further directing it to issue an appropriate child support order (*Jaycee B. v. Superior Court of Orange County*, 42 Cal. App. 4th 718; 1996 Cal. App. LEXIS 101; 49 Cal. Rptr. 2d 694 (Court of Appeal of California, Fourth Appellate District, Division Three, 1996)).

7. On 10 June 1998, the California Supreme Court let stand, without opinion, the appellate court ruling (*In re Buzzanca*, S069696, 1998 Cal. LEXIS 3830 (Supreme Court of California, 1998)).

8. Reports of the Commission may be accessed at bioethics.gov/nbac.html.

9. Current law prohibits federal funding of embryonic stem cell research. In 2000, Senators Arlen Specter (R-PA) and Tom Harkin (D-IA), with substantial backing from the disability lobby, introduced *The Stem Cell Research Act*, S2015. If passed, the act would broaden the ability of federally funded researchers to pursue stem cell research.

10. In *Levy* the Court said: "We start from the premise that illegitimate children are not 'nonpersons.' They are humans,

live, and have their being. They are clearly 'persons' within the meaning of the Equal Protection Clause of the Fourteenth Amendment" (391 U.S. 68, at 70 (1968)).

11. Other state courts have similarly adopted standards requiring that before removing custody, a showing must be made that the gay parent's sexual orientation is deterimental to the child. See, for example, *S.N.E. v. R.L.B.*, 699 P.2d 875 (Alaska 1985); *In re: Marriage of Birdsall*, 197 Cal. App. 3d 1024, 243 Cal. Rptr. 287 (Cal. Ct. App. 1988); *R.S. v. S.S.*, 677 N.E.2d 1297 (Ill. App. Ct. 1996); *Doe v. Doe*, 16 Mass. App. Ct. 499, 452 N.E.2d 293 (Mass. App.Ct. 1983); *White v. Thompson*, 569 So. 2d 1181 (Miss. 1990); *M.P. v. S.P.*, 404 A.2d 1256 (N.J. Super. Ct. App. Div. 1979); *A.C. v. C.B.*, 113 N.M. 581, 829 P.2d 660 (N.M. Ct. App. 1992); *Anonymous v. Anonymous*, 120 A.D.2d 983, 503 N.Y.S.2d 466 (N.Y. 1986); *Pulliam v. Smith*, 124 N.C. App. 144, 476 S.E.2d 446 (N.C. Ct. App. 1996); *Whaley v. Whaley*, 61 Ohio App. 2d 111, 399 N.E.2d 1270 (Ohio Ct. App. 1978); *Fox v. Fox*, 904 P.2d 66 (Okla. 1995); *A. v. A.*, 514 P.2d 358 (Or. Ct. App. 1973); *Blew v. Verta*, 420 Pa. Super. 528, 617 A.2d 31 (Pa. Super. Ct. 1992); *Stroman v. Williams*, 291 S.C.76, 353 S.E.2d 704 (S.C. Ct. App. 1987); *Van Driel v. Van Driel*, 525 N.W.2d 37 (S.D. 1994); *Tucker v. Tucker*, 910 P.2d 1209 (Utah 1996); *Nickerson v. Nickerson*, 158 Vt. 85, 605 A.2d 1331 (Vt. 1992); *Schuster v. Schuster*, 90 Wash. 2d 626, 585 P.2d 130 (Wash. 1978); and *M.S.P. v. P.E.P.*, 178 W. Va. 183, 358 S.E.2d 442 (W. Va.1987).

12. There are three kinds of domestic adoption: adoptions through state or locally run and licensed public agencies, adoptions through state-licensed but privately run agencies, and independent adoptions, facilitated by doctors, lawyers, and, in some cases, by biological parents.

13. The state of Florida continues to bar gay and lesbian adoptions, although it is currently the only jurisdiction with so complete a ban. On 26 May 1999, the ACLU and Children First Project filed a complaint in U.S. District Court in Key West, claiming that Florida's 1977 law banning gay and lesbian adoptions "ignores the best interests of children by precluding an entire class of qualified adults from adopting, rather than making adoption decisions on a case-by-case basis" ("ACLU Challenges Florida Ban On Lesbian and Gay Adoption," available at www.aclu.org/features/f052699a.html [accessed 2 June 1999]).

14. Memorandum from David Chavkin, Deputy Director for Program Development, U.S. Department of Health and Human Services, to Virginia Apodaca, Region X Director, the Office for Civil Rights (19 January 1981), quoted in Perez 1998, 217.

15. Adoptions of Native American children have also been legally controversial. *The Indian Child Welfare Act of 1978* essentially permits tribes to intervene in adoption placements to outsiders. See, for example, *In the Matter of the Adoption of F.H.*, 851 P.2d 1361; 1993 Alas. LEXIS 42 (Supreme Court of Alaska, 1993).

16. Over half the children come from three countries: Russia, China, and South Korea.

17. International adoptions presumably have grown in popularity because of the increasing prevalence domestically of "open adoptions" (those in which the birth parent shares somehow in the family arrangement) and because of the perceived lack of "adoptable" children (preferably infants) in the United States.

18. See, for example, *Michael J. v. County of Los Angeles Department of Adoptions*, 247 Cal. Rptr. 504, at 513 (Ct. App. 1988); *Meracle v. Children's Service Society*, 437 N.W.2d 532, at 537 (Wis. 1989); *M.H. & J.L.H. v. Caritas Family Services*, 488 N.W.2d 282, at 288 (Minn. 1992); *Roe v. Catholic Charities*, 588 N.E.2d 354, at 365 (Ill. App. Ct. 1992); *Gibbs v. Ernst*, 647 A.2d 882, at 888 (Pa. 1994); *Mallette v. Children's Friend & Serv.*, 661

A.2d 67, 69 (R.I.1995); and *Mohr v. Commonwealth*, 653 N.E.2d 1104, at 1110–11 (Mass. 1995). Cases are cited in Fields (1996, 984–96).

19. So-called adoption "annulments" have been recognized by state law since the 1920s.

20. According to experts, unrelated to the tort of wrongful adoption, one reason for the growing number of annulments or attempts to return adopted children is the recent increase in adoptions of older children from former Soviet bloc nations (Seelye 1998).

21. On 19 November 1997, President Clinton signed the federal *Adoption and Safe Families Act* (Pub. L. 105-89).

22. Federal law requires larger companies to permit employees to take unpaid leave for certain family-related reasons (*The Family and Medical Leave Act of 1993* (29 U.S.C. 2601 et seq.)).

23. Most states require vaccinations against diphtheria, tetanus, pertussis, measles, mumps, rubella, and polio (Aspinwall 1997, 110).

24. As every horrified first-time parent learns when she signs her initial immunization release form, vaccinations are not without risk. However, the Centers for Disease Control and Prevention report that "vaccines cause so few ill effects that the risks cannot be reliably measured. The agency says that the risk of encephalitis or severe allergic reaction from mumps-measles-rubella vaccine is 1 in 1 million. [On the other hand], it says the risk to unvaccinated children is 1 death in 3,000 measles cases, 1 encephalitis case in 300 cases of mumps, and 1 case of congenital rubella syndrome for every 4 mothers infected early in pregnancy" (cited in Pollak 1999, F7). According to the American Academy of Pediatrics, "Reactions to the vaccines may occur, but they are usually mild. Serious reactions are rare but may occur. Remember, the risks should your child get one of these dangerous childhood diseases are far greater than the risk of a serious reaction from a vaccination" (available at www.aap.org/family/parents/vaccine.htm#8 [accessed 17 June 1999]).

25. See, for some of many examples, The National Vaccine Information Center, an organizational site dedicated to disseminating the risks of immunization, available at www.909shot. com/; Concerned Parents for Vaccine Safety, available at home.sprynet.com/~noshots/index.htm; "The Tragedy of Vaccinations," available at home.unicomp.net/~lschiele/vaccine. htm; and "Vaccines: The Truth Revealed," available at www. odomnet.com/vaccines/ (all sites accessed 18 June 1999). Of course, supporters of widespread immunization are also prominent on the web. See, for example, The Children's Vaccine Initiative, available at www.vaccines.ch/; The Vaccine Page, available at www.vaccines.com/; The Bill and Melinda Gates Children's Vaccine Program, available at www.path.org/childvac/home.htm; and the Centers for Disease Control and Prevention, available at www.cdc.gov/ (all sites accessed 18 June 1999).

26. See, for example, "Maryland's Tobacco Lead," *Washington Post*, 6 June 1999, p. B6.

27. See, for example, *Johnson v. State*, 602 So. 2d 1288 (Fla. 1992); *Commonwealth v. Welch*, 864 S.W. 2d 280 (Ky. 1993); *State v. Gray*, 62 Ohio St. 3d 514, 584 N.E.2d 710 (Ohio 1992); *Reyes v. Superior Court*, 75 Cal. App. 3d 214, 141 Cal. Rptr. 912 (1977); *State v.Carter*, 602 So. 2d 995 (Fla. Ct. App. 1992); *State v. Gethers*, 585 So. 2d 1140 (Fla. Ct. App. 1991); *State v. Luster*, 204 Ga. App. 156, 419 S.E.2d 32 (Ga. Ct. App. 1992), cert. denied (Ga. 1992); *Commonwealth v. Pellegrini*, No. 87970, slip op. (Mass. Super. Ct. Oct. 15, 1990); *People v. Hardy*, 188 Mich. App. 305, 469 N.W.2d 50 (Mich. Ct. App.), app. denied, 437 Mich. 1046 (Mich. 1991); and *Commonwealth v. Kemp*, 434 Pa.Super. 719, 643 A.2d 705 (Pa. Super. Ct. 1994).

28. See also, e.g., *Taylor v. Kurapati*, 600 N.W. 2d 670 (Mich. App. 1999).

29. For example, Maryland requires school attendance of all children from five through seventeen years of age (*Md. EDUCATION Code Ann.* § 7-301 (1998)). North Carolina compels attendance of those between the ages of seven and sixteen (*N.C. Gen. Stat.* § 115C-378 (1999)).

30. According to Brian D. Ray of the Home School Legal Defense Association, approximately 1.23 million American children were home schooled in 1996 (Ray, "Home Education Across the United States: Family Characteristics, Student Achievement, and Longitudinal Traits," Home School Legal Defense Association, available at www.hslda.org/central/statsandreports/ray1997/03.stm [accessed 17 June 1999]). The Educational Resources Information Center, U.S. Department of Education, citing several studies, including Ray's, estimates the number of home schoolers to be between 500,000 to 1.2 million students (Jacque Ensign, "Homeschooling Gifted Students: An Introductory Guide for Parents," ED414683 97, available at www.ed.gov/databases/ERIC_Digests/ed414683.html [accessed 17 June 1999]).

31. North Dakota, for example, requires home educators to "possess either: 1) a teaching certificate, or 2) a baccalaureate degree, 3) a high school diploma or GED and be monitored by a certified teacher during first two years or until child completes 3rd grade, whichever is later; monitoring must continue thereafter if child scores below the 50th percentile on required standardized achievement test, or 4) proof of meeting or exceeding the cut-off score of the national teacher exam." All state requirements are available at www.hslda.org/ (accessed 17 June 1999).

32. The state of Maryland, for example, mandates no particular education for home schooling parents (Ibid.).

33. For example, in Massachusetts, parents must "Annually, either: 1) administer a standardized test; must be administered by a neutral party, or 2) submit progress reports to the school district." In Maryland, home school instructors must maintain a portfolio of 'relevant materials,' reviewable by the local superintendent up to 3 times per year" (Ibid.).

34. In California, home-schooling parents are required only to keep an "attendance record," while the state of Michigan apparently has no record-keeping or testing requirements (Ibid.).

35. States may create other exemptions. Notably, children may be expelled from school for extremely disruptive, violent behavior. Many states and local school boards today, for example, maintain so-called "zero tolerance" policies, mandating expulsion for children caught bringing guns to school. Often, the state will first make an attempt to place the problem child in an alternative school setting away from the general population.

36. In response to a perceived sense that public schools are failing, legislative bodies across the country increasingly order achievement testing on a regular basis. For one of many examples, the state of Maryland mandates a statewide "Maryland School Performance Assessment Program" (MPSAP) test to be given to all third, fifth, and eighth graders. MSPAP supposedly "measures how well schools are teaching students the knowledge and skills they need to solve real-life problems" ("A Guide to MSPAP," available at www.carr.lib.md.us/ccps/mspap/index.htm [accessed 22 March 2000]).

37. For a much more thorough treatment of the case law, see Reutter (1994).

38. In relevant part, the First Amendment reads: "Congress shall make no law respecting an establishment of religion, or prohibiting the free exercise thereof. . . ." (U.S. Constitution, Amendment I).

39. Holding that religious instruction in tax-supported public schools violates the First Amendment.

40. Allowing release programs for religious instruction.

41. In which the Court held that "state officials may not compose an official state prayer and require that it be recited in the public schools of the State at the beginning of each school day—even if the prayer is denominationally neutral and pupils who wish to do so may remain silent or be excused from the room while the prayer is being recited."

42. Holding that "no state law or school board may require that passages from the Bible be read or that the Lord's Prayer be recited in the public schools of a State at the beginning of each school day—even if individual students may be excused from attending or participating in such exercises upon written request of their parents."

43. While social and religious conservatives have long legislated, lobbied, and litigated for the return of religion to public schools, a series of school shootings during the latter part of the 1990s intensified the movement. Among the more sensational incidents: On 1 October 1997, nine pupils were shot in Pearl, Mississippi, by a sixteen-year-old who killed his mother earlier in the day. On that same day, three students were killed in a school hallway in Paducah, Kentucky. In March 1998, eleven-year-old Andrew Golden killed five and wounded ten at Westside Middle School in Jonesboro, Arkansas. In May 1998, fifteen-year-old Kip Kinkel of Springfield, Oregon, killed both his parents before opening fire in his school cafeteria with a semi-automatic rifle, killing two students and injuring twenty-four others. Most dramatic, in April 1999, self-proclaimed student outcasts, Eric Harris and Dylan Kliebold, killed twelve of their fellow students and a teacher at Columbine High School in Littleton, Colorado.

44. *Santa Fe* available at supct.law.cornell.edu/supct/html/99-62.ZO.html. See also *Lee v. Weisman*, 505 U.S. 577 (1992).

45. See note 35.

46. Vermont's constitutional religious freedom provision reads: "That all persons have a natural and unalienable right, to worship Almighty God, according to the dictates of their own consciences and understandings, as in their opinion shall be regulated by the word of God; and that no person ought to, or of right can be compelled to attend any religious worship, or erect or support any place of worship, or maintain any minister, contrary to the dictates of conscience, nor can any person be justly deprived or abridged of any civil right as a citizen, on account of religious sentiments, or peculiar mode of religious worship; and that no authority can, or ought to be vested in, or assumed by, any power whatever, that shall in any case interfere with, or in any manner control the rights of conscience, in the free exercise of religious worship. Nevertheless, every sect or denomination of Christians ought to observe the Sabbath or Lord's day, and keep up some sort of religious worship, which to them shall seem most agreeable to the revealed will of God" (*Vt. Const.* ch I, art. 3, cited in *Chittenden Town School District v. Vermont Department of Education*, 1999 Vt. LEXIS 98, at LEXIS *20 (Supreme Court of Vermont, 1999)).

47. "School Voucher Program Becomes Law in Florida," *New York Times*, 22 June 1999, A23.

48. Children who, for religious or other reasons, do not wish to participate in the recital of the Pledge may not be forced to nor punished for their refusal. *West Virginia State Board of Education v. Barnette*, 319 U.S. 624 (1943).

49. The Department of Health Education, and Welfare, the predecessor of the present Department of Health and Human Services, issued regulations prohibiting discrimination in federally funded institutions, including "discrimination . . . in the

availability or use of any academic . . . or other facilities of the grantee or other recipient" (45 *CFR* § 80.5 (b)).

50. There are at least three methods of bilingual education: immersion, transitional, and maintenance or developmental. "Under the immersion method, limited English proficient (LEP) students are taught entirely in English, ideally in simple language, to allow for the internalization of the English language. The transitional method provides for instruction of students partially in English and partially in their native languages, with the goal of moving the students into mainstream English classes. The maintenance, or developmental, education method allows students to acquire English while maintaining their native-language skills. During the past thirty years, each type of bilingual education has developed its own followers and each group propounds research that suggests its teaching methodology works best" (Felton 1999, 845; footnotes omitted).

51. In November 2000, bilingual education opponents won a landslide victory in Arizona with the passage of Proposition 203, which requires public schools to end traditional bilingual education (Gonzalez 2000, A1).

52. In 1999, Gary Orfield and John T. Yun of the Harvard School of Graduate Education reported a series of trends in the nation's schools pointing to rapid resegregation: "First, the American South is resegregating, after two and a half decades in which civil rights law broke the tradition of apartheid in the region's schools and made it the section of the country with the highest levels of integration in its schools. Second, the data shows continuously increasing segregation for Latino students, who are rapidly becoming our largest minority group and have been more segregated than African Americans for several years. Third, the report shows large and increasing numbers of African American and Latino students enrolled in suburban schools, but serious segregation within these communities, particularly in the nation's large metropolitan areas. Since trends suggest that we will face a vast increase in suburban diversity, this raises challenges for thousands of communities. Fourth, we report a rapid ongoing change in the racial composition of American schools and the emergence of many schools with three or more racial groups. The report shows that all racial groups except whites experience considerable diversity in their schools but whites are remaining in overwhelmingly white schools even in regions with very large non-white enrollments" (Orfield and Yun 1999).

53. "Oakland Group Retreats on 'Ebonics'," *Washington Post*, 6 May 1997, p. A4.

54. In dissent, Justice Kennedy complained that "The majority's limitations on peer sexual harassment suits cannot hope to contain the flood of liability the Court today begins" (119 S. Ct. 1661; 1999 U.S. LEXIS 3452 (1999) at *89 (Kennedy, J., dissenting)).

55. Indeed, in 1993, G. F. "was charged with, and pleaded guilty to, sexual battery for his misconduct" (119 S. Ct. 1661; 1999 U.S. LEXIS 3452 (1999), op. cit. at *11).

56. Much of this has been based more in perception than in reality. "Although the number of arrests for violent crimes has increased, the data also reveal that juveniles are not responsible for most violent crimes. In 1994 juveniles accounted for just 19 percent of all violent crime arrests. This means that slightly fewer than one-fifth of all persons entering the justice system on a violent crime charge were juveniles. Moreover, fewer than one-half of 1 percent of juveniles in the United States were arrested for a violent offense in 1994. That represents fewer than 1 in 200 juveniles, yet these juveniles are driving national juvenile justice policy concerns. Although violence committed by juveniles is on the increase, adults were responsible for 74 percent of the increase in violent crimes from 1985 to 1994" (Torbet 1996).

57. During the 1990s, at least five states established exclusion provisions, twenty-four states expanded the list of crimes eligible for exclusion, and six states lowered age limits for exclusion (Sickmund 1997b).

58. The ability to waive youngsters out of the juvenile justice system and into the criminal courts may even result in execution of the very young. Although the Supreme Court has ruled that states may not execute individuals who were younger than 16 when they committed their crimes (see *Thompson v. Oklahoma*, 487 U.S. 815 (1988)), according to DeathPenalty.Net, "At present, 51 death row inmates, all male, were less than 18 when they committed the crime. Three-fourth [*sic*] of them were 17, a quarter were 16 years old. Texas' death row holds 20 of the 51, nine are in Alabama. Since 1976, nine men have been executed for crimes committed at age 17; none since 1993. In 1997, at least 6 juveniles aged 16 or 17 when they killed were condemned to death. In February 1999, Oklahoma executed Sean Sellers for a horrendus [*sic*] crime he committed when he was 16. In 1992, a defense-sponsored psychiatric evaluation concluded Sellers had multiple personality disorder. But the Tenth U.S. Circuit Court of Appeals, based on a technicality (the issue had not been raised in the lower courts) said it could not grant relief. Thus Sean Sellers was executed because of a horrible mistake he made as a child" (DeathPenalty.Net, available at www. deathpenalty.net/juveniles.html [accessed 8 July 1999]).

59. U.S. Selective Service System, available at www.sss.gov/ (accessed 5 July 1999).

60. Continuously between 1948 and 1973, during both peacetime and periods of conflict, men were drafted to fill vacancies in the armed forces that could not be filled through voluntary means. Throughout the latter years of the Vietnam War, the late 1960s and early 1970s, the mandatory draft became one of the most divisive issues facing the United States. As a result, in 1973, the draft ended, although registration continued. In 1975, even the registration requirement was suspended. However, in 1980, in response to the Soviet invasion of Afghanistan, President Carter resumed the registration requirement (Ibid.).

61. There is a minimum age requirement of fourteen years generally for employment in agriculture outside school hours. However, a minor twelve or thirteen years of age may be so employed with written consent of his parent or guardian, or may work on a farm where his or her parent or guardian is also employed, and a minor under twelve years of age may be employed by his parent or guardian on a farm owned or operated by the parent or guardian (29 *CFR* 570, subpart A). Regulation accessed at U.S. Department of Labor, "Child Labor Regulations, Orders and Statements of Interpretation," www.dol.gov/dol/esa/public/regs/cfr/29cfr/toc_Part500-899/0570_toc.htm (accessed 7 July 1999).

62. Employment of those fourteen to sixteen years of age "is confined to periods which will not interfere with their schooling and to conditions which will not interfere with their health and well-being" (Ibid.).

63. Ibid.

64. "Even if Congress, in view of the Twenty-first Amendment, might lack the power to impose directly a national minimum drinking age (a question not decided here), . . . indirect encouragement of state action to obtain uniformity in the States' drinking ages is a valid use of the spending power" (*South Dakota v. Dole*, 483 U.S. 203 (1987)).

65. Ratings in general and their application to individual films are set by the Motion Picture Association of America (MPAA). The rating system is familiar to most American movie-goers: "G" indicates movies acceptable for a general audience, "PG" is set for movies containing some material that may not be suitable for children, "PG-13" denotes movies that

may be unacceptable for children under the age of thirteen, "R" movies are restricted such that those under seventeen must be accompanied by an adult, and "NC-17" films are supposedly out of reach to those under eighteen years of age whether or not they bring along an adult (MPAA, "Movie Ratings," available at www.mpaa.org/movieratings/ [accessed 7 July 1999]). According to the MPAA, "The ratings are decided by a full-time Rating Board located in Los Angeles. There are 8–13 members of the Board who serve for periods of varying length. They work for the Classification and Rating Administration, which is funded by fees charged to producers/distributors for the rating of their films. The MPAA President chooses the Chairman of the Rating Board, thereby insulating the Board from industry or other group pressure. No one in the movie industry has the authority or the power to push the Board in any direction or otherwise influence it.... There are no special qualifications for Board membership, except the members must have a shared parenthood experience, must be possessed of an intelligent maturity, and most of all, have the capacity to put themselves in the role of most American parents so they can view a film and apply a rating that most parents would find suitable and helpful in aiding their decisions about their children's moviegoing" (MPAA, "How Ratings are Decided," available at www.mpaa.org/movieratings/about/index.htm [accessed 7 July 1999]).

66. In June 1999, a House bill that "would have made it possible to ban any form of entertainment that courts found harmful to children" was defeated (Schaefer 1999, 37).

67. Since the new efforts have gone into effect, interviews with teens suggest that they intend to find ways to get into such movies, while interviews with theater managers suggest numerous ways that kids can still get around the rating restrictions. See, for example, Babbington (1999, A1); Stetz (1999, A1); Dodge (1999, 1999); and Ng (1999, E8).

Chapter 8

1. Abraham Lincoln, *The Emancipation Proclamation*, 22 September 1862, available at www.nps.gov/ncro/anti/emancipation.html (accessed 20 July 1999). Ironically, the Emancipation Proclamation only freed slaves within the rebel territories. Slaves held in states loyal to the Union were not liberated.

2. The phrase first appeared in 1890 in a *Harvard Law Review* article penned by lawyer Brandeis and his partner Samuel Warren. Here, the concern was explicitly with private tort action and was aimed at the yellow, sensationalistic journalism of the time (Warren and Brandeis 1890). Later, wielding the pen as Justice Brandeis, he expanded the phrase to cover invasive governmental action, noting that "[t]he protection guaranteed by the [Fourth and Fifth] Amendments is much broader in scope. The makers of our Constitution undertook to secure conditions favorable to the pursuit of happiness. They recognized the significance of man's spiritual nature, of his feelings and of his intellect. They knew that only part of the pain, pleasure and satisfactions of life are to be found in material things. They sought to protect Americans in their beliefs, their thoughts, their emotions and their sensations. They conferred against the Government, *the right to be let alone*—the most comprehensive of rights and the right most valued by civilized men. To protect that right, every unjustifiable intrusion by the Government upon the privacy of the individual, whatever the means employed, must be deemed a violation of the Fourth Amendment. And the use, as evidence in a criminal proceeding, of facts ascertained by such intrusion must be

deemed a violation of the Fifth" (*Olmstead v. United States,* 277 U.S.438, at 478–79 (Brandeis, J., dissenting); emphasis added).

3. As Friedman (1998, 169) notes, "[T]he railroad created the law of torts. Not a single treatise on the law of torts was published before 1850, either in England or in the United States. Early tort cases often came out of railroad accidents."

4. In 1632, William Prynn published a book critical of actors. Because the queen herself had appeared in a play, the work was viewed as an affront to her royal majesty and Prynn was tried before the Star Chamber. Found guilty of libel, he was fined 10,000 pounds, sentenced to prison for life, branded, had his nose slit, and both ears cut off (*Trial of William Prynn*, 3 Howell's State Trials 561 (1632), cited in O'Brien 1995, 666).

5. Of course, as we all know, for a very brief time, libel—at least seditious libel—managed to trump the First Amendment. In 1798, John Adams' congressional friends (or, conversely, Thomas Jefferson's congressional enemies) passed the *Alien and Sedition Act*, making "it a crime, punishable by a $5,000 fine and five years in prison, 'if any person shall write, print, utter or publish ... any false, scandalous and malicious writing or writings against the government of the United States, or either house of the Congress ..., or the President ..., with intent to defame ... or to bring them, or either of them, into contempt or disrepute; or to excite against them, or either or any of them, the hatred of the good people of the United States.'" Still, although the statute was not tested in court until 166 years later—talk about legal lag time!—outrage against it was such and political tables were turned so dramatically that its effects were relatively short-lived. No less than Madison himself condemned the act; Jefferson, upon assuming the presidency, pardoned those convicted under it; and, in 1840, "[f]ines levied in its prosecution were repaid by Act of Congress on the ground that it was unconstitutional." Discussion and quotations are found in *New York Times v. Sullivan*, 376 U.S. 254, at 273–76 (1964).

6. A number of states do not recognize the false light tort, "because it adds so little to defamation that it is not worth the confusion it creates or because the social interest it supports does not justify its incursion on speech..." (Smolla 1992, 148).

7. For an excellent scholarly treatment and entertaining discussion, see Smolla (1990).

8. The sordid account, if not the principle itself, gained a much wider audience in the Oliver Stone production of *The People v. Larry Flynt*, a 1996 film starring Woody Harrelson and Courtney Love.

9. In 1986, Congress increased the coverage of wiretapping limitation laws to include digital communications. In addition, it prohibited unauthorized eavesdropping, not only by government, but by other individuals and businesses. Significantly, however, if any party to a communication consents to eavesdropping and disclosure it is legally okay (*Electronic Communications Privacy Act of 1986*, 18 U.S.C. §§ 2510–21, 2701–10, 3121–26, Pub. L. No. 99-508, 100 Stat. 1848). The limits of the law are evident as in the Fifth Circuit holding that "the seizure of a computer, used to operate an electronic bulletin board system, and containing private electronic mail which had been sent to (stored on) the bulletin board, but not read (retrieved) by the intended recipients, [does not] constitute ... an unlawful intercept" (*Steve Jackson Games, Inc. v. United States Secret Service*, 36 F.3d 457 (United States Court of Appeals for the Fifth Circuit, 1994)).

10. America Online has even been known to turn over very personal information *without* being served a subpoena. For example, in what it later admitted was a mistake, the company recently turned over the name of a Navy officer who had participated in a gay chat room. The Navy considered such chatting a violation of the military's "don't ask, don't tell"

policy and sought to discharge the officer from the service. As of this writing, the dismissal has been temporarily enjoined by U.S. District Court Judge Sporkin. See *McVeigh v. Cohen*, 983 F. Supp. 215 (U.S. District Court for the District of Columbia, 1998).

11. The many data banks available on any one of us can, of course, be mined toward the aim of creating profiles and snooping into the lives of nearly everyone. For example, 1800USSEARCH.com, which bills itself as "The Worldwide Leader in Public Record Information," will conduct for $39.98 a so-called "Super Search" providing for anyone, on anyone the following data: "Current and previous addresses going back 10 years; Any additional phone numbers available; Driver's License physical descriptions in Florida and Texas; Family members of individual; Other people at the same address; Neighbors with listed phone numbers; Spouses (if individual currently lives in Florida or Texas); Summary of Assets; Professional Licenses; Property Ownership and value; Vehicle Ownership and value; Lien Filings; Civil Judgments; and Bankruptcies" (available at http: //www.1800ussearch.com/ 1800ussearch-78/mck-cgi/bsdhome.pl [accessed 29 July 1999]).

12. AND Identification Systems puts it rather chillingly in its logo, which contends that "Electronic Business Determines the Worldview of the 21st Century," and in its description of biometric identification products: "The need to identify people is as old as humankind. People recognise each other by sight and sound. However in today's complex society, it's impossible to personally know everyone. Biometric devices automate the personal recognition process. Each of us is unique from every other human being. We have unique physical characteristics, such as hand shape, fingerprint, iris. Biometric devices measure and record these characteristics for automated comparison and verification." For a description of biometric identification technologies from hand geometry to retinal patterning, see AND Identification, available at www.and. com/id/home/home.html (accessed 28 July 1999).

13. See Cho (1999).

14. Some private company researchers have put themselves in competition with the federal Genome Project. Most notable among these is the privately funded and operated Celera Genomics Corporation, available at www.celera.com/index2. html (accessed 2 August 1999). In February 2001, the Genome Project and Celera jointly announced their initial findings. The public findings (Genome Project) are widely available. It is unclear what Celera intends to do with its findings, but potentially they will be available *only* for private sale and access. See, for example, Wheeler 1999, A18, and Johnson 1999, A13.

15. "About the Human Genome Project," Human Genome Project Information, available at www.ornl.gov/ TechResources/Human_Genome/about.html (accessed 29 July 1999). The project is a joint venture of the U.S. Department of Energy (DOE) and the National Institutes of Health (NIH). Begun in 1990, it now has an expected completion date of 2003. Both DOE and NIH have set aside a portion of their genomic budgets for the study of ethical, legal, and social implications of advanced genetic discovery and testing. To date, they have identified many of the same concerns as those voiced by Dr. Cho above, including: "[1] Fairness in the use of genetic information by insurers, employers, courts, schools, adoption agencies, and the military, among others. Who should have access and how will it be used? [2] Privacy and confidentiality of genetic information. Who owns and controls it? [3] Psychological impact and stigmatization due to an individual's genetic differences. How does the information affect an individual, and society's perceptions of that individual? [4] Genetic testing of an individual for a specific condition due to family history (prenatal, carrier, and presymptomatic testing)

and population screening (newborn, premarital, and occupational). Should testing be performed when no treatment is available? Should parents have the right to have their minor children tested for adult-onset diseases? Are genetic tests reliable and interpretable by the medical community? [5] Reproductive issues including informed consent for procedures, use of genetic information in decision making, and reproductive rights. [6] Clinical issues including education of health service providers, patients, and the general public; and implementation of standards and quality control measures in testing procedures. [7] Commercialization of products: issues include property rights (patents, copyrights, and trade secrets) and accessibility of data and materials. [8] Conceptual and philosophical implications regarding human responsibility, free will versus genetic determinism, and concepts of disease and health 'Ethical, Legal, and Social Issues (ELSI) of the Human Genome Project,'" available at www.ornl.gov/hgmis/resource/ elsi.html [accessed 29 July 1999]).

16. "Use of Genetic Testing in Employment Situations," RSA 141-H: 3 (1999), Title X, Public Health, Chapter 141-h. New Hampshire law provides for the following exceptions: "IV. This section shall not prohibit the genetic testing of an employee who requests to undergo genetic testing and who provides written and informed consent to genetic testing for any of the following purposes: (a) Investigating a worker's compensation claim under RSA 281-A. (b) Determining the employee's susceptibility or level of exposure to potentially toxic chemicals or potentially toxic substances in the workplace, if the employer does not terminate the employee, or take any other action that adversely affects any term, condition, or privilege of the employee's employment, as a result of genetic testing. V. This section shall not prohibit or limit genetic testing for evidence of insurability with respect to life, disability income, or long-term care insurance under the terms of an employee benefit plan."

17. Lawrence discontinued syphilis testing in April 1993, pregnancy testing in December 1994, and sickle-cell trait testing in June 1995 (*Norman-Bloodsaw*, at 1265).

18. The Circuit Court agreed with the district court in dismissing the ADA portion of the claim because (1) most of the plaintiffs' tests had occurred before the effective date of the law and (2) because the two remaining plaintiffs failed to articulate an actionable ADA claim.

19. Jones may want to think twice about it. In May 1999, a Michigan jury ordered the "The Jenny Jones Show" to pay $25 million to the family of a gay man who was murdered by another participant after a show on "secret admirers." Jonathan Schmitz was apparently humiliated when fellow guest, Scott Amedure, revealed on-air, that he had a homosexual crush on Schmitz. Thereafter, Schmitz shot Amedure twice in the chest, killing him. The Michigan jury found the "Jones Show" partly responsible for Amedure's death. As of this writing, the case is currently on appeal (Calvert 2000).

20. The Supreme Court has said that the Amendment is violated in "all situations in which labor is compelled by physical coercion or force of law. . . ." (*U.S. v. Kozminski*, 487 U.S. 931, at 943 (1988)). So, for example, you may not sell yourself into a state of peonage in order to work off a debt (*Clyatt v. United States*, 197 U.S. 207 (1905)). There are, however, well-recognized exceptions to the rule. Notably, of course, the plain language of the Amendment itself excludes forced labor or confinement as punishment for a crime. Moreover, "the Court has recognized that the prohibition against involuntary servitude does not prevent the State or Federal Governments from compelling their citizens, by threat of criminal sanction, to perform certain civic duties [i.e., jury duty or military service]. . . . Moreover, . . . the Thirteenth Amendment was not intended to apply to 'excep-

tional' cases well established in the common law at the time of the [ratification of the] Thirteenth Amendment, such as 'the right of parents and guardians to the custody of their minor children or wards,' ... or laws preventing sailors who contracted to work on vessels from deserting their ships" (*Kozminski* at 943–44; citations omitted). Notably, also, the Court has said that "[t]he guarantee of freedom from involuntary servitude has never been interpreted specifically to prohibit compulsion of labor by other means, such as psychological coercion" (at 943).

21. In Nevada, brothels may be licensed and operated in counties with populations under 400,000 (*Nev. Rev. Stat.* Ann. § 244.345 (1998)).

22. Presently, payment for sexual acts is explicitly banned in thirty-eight states and "solicitation laws" exist in forty-four states and the District of Columbia. "Other states use vagrancy and loitering statutes to control prostitution" (Drexler 1996, 205).

23. Holding that restrictions on "indecent" (though not "obscene") telephone messages (i.e., "dial-a-porn" systems) that restrict adult access violate the First Amendment. See also, *Reno v. ACLU*, 521 U.S. 844 (1997), holding that restrictions on "indecent" or "patently offensive" Internet sites violate the First Amendment.

24. We defer any discussion of suicide for the subsequent chapter on law and the end of life. Suffice it to say at this point, however, that the movement toward physician-assisted suicide has had a number of legal ramifications over the course of the 1990s.

25. Feiler (1998, 2455).

26. See www.ronsangels.com/ (accessed 28 October 1999).

27. D.C. Code Ann. 6-2601(b) (1995); Fla. Stat. Ann. 873.05(1)–(3) (LEXIS 1998); 755 Ill. Comp. Stat. 50/8.1 (West 1992); La. Rev. Stat. Ann. 9: 122 (West 1991); Minn. Stat. Ann. 145.422(3) (West 1989); 18 Pa. Cons. Stat. Ann. 3216(b)(3) (West Supp. 1997); Tex. Penal Code Ann. 48.02 (West Supp. 1994); Utah Code Ann. 76-7-311 (1997); Va. Code Ann. 32.1-289.1 (Michie 1997); see GA Code Ann.16-12- 160(b)(5) (1996) (allowing payment for embryos to be used for health services education); Mich. Comp. Laws Ann. 333.2690 (West 1992) (prohibiting payment for embryos used for illegal purposes); R.I. Gen. Laws. 11-54-1(f) (1994) (disallowing commercialization of unlawful embryo transfers). Four states specifically prohibit the sale of embryos for research purposes. See Me. Rev. Stat. tit. 22, 1593 (West 1992); Mass. Ann. Laws ch. 112, 12(J)(a)(IV) (Law Co-op 1991); Mich. Comp. Laws Ann. 333.10204(1) (West 1992); N.D. Cent. Code 14-02.2-02(4) (1991) (Feiler 1998, 2462).

28. In addition to the huge variety of state laws, the federal *Organ Procurement and Transplantation Act of 1984* (Pub. L. 98-507) prohibits the purchase or sale of human organs in interstate commerce.

29. According to the National Academy of Sciences, Institute of Medicine, "Roughly 4,000 Americans die each year (11 people per day) waiting for organs" (Committee on Organ Procurement and Transplantation Policy, Division of Health Sciences Policy, Institute of Medicine, National Academy of Sciences, *Organ Procurement and Transplantation: Assessing Current Policies and the Potential Impact of the DHHS Final Rule*, 1999, p. 16, available at books.nap.edu/books/030906578X/html/16.html#16 [accessed 3 August 1999]). The U.S. Department of Health and Human Services oversees the Organ Procurement and Transplantation Network and Scientific Registry of Information on Transplant Recipients, which keep records for a loose conglomeration of private organizations that distribute organs. "Patients are matched to organs based on a number of factors including blood and tissue typing, medical urgency, time on the waiting list, and geographical

location" (available at organdonor.gov/faq.html#12 [accessed 3 August 1999]).

30. Definition at The 'Lectric Law Library's Lexicon, available at www.lectlaw.com/def/i051.htm (accessed 3 August 1999).

31. The *Copyright Act* generally gives the owner of copyright the exclusive right to do and to authorize others to do the following: "To reproduce the work in copies or phonorecords; To prepare derivative works based upon the work; To distribute copies or phonorecords of the work to the public by sale or other transfer of ownership, or by rental, lease, or lending; To perform the work publicly, in the case of literary, musical, dramatic, and choreographic works, pantomimes, and motion pictures and other audiovisual works; To display the work publicly, in the case of literary, musical, dramatic, and choreographic works, pantomimes, and pictorial, graphic, or sculptural works, including the individual images of a motion picture or other audiovisual work; and In the case of sound recordings, to perform the work publicly by means of a digital audio transmission. In addition, certain authors of works of visual art have the rights of attribution and integrity" (U.S. Copyright Office 1999, 1–2).

32. See www.uspto.gov/web/offices/pac/doc/general/whatis.htm (accessed 4 August 1999). The congressional patent authority derives, like copyright, from Article I, § 8.

33. An exception is provided by *The Atomic Energy Act of 1954*, which excludes the patenting of inventions useful solely in the utilization of special nuclear material or atomic energy for atomic weapons (see www.uspto.gov/web/offices/pac/doc/general/what.htm [accessed 4 August 1999]).

34. The federal registration of trademarks is governed by the *Trademark Act of 1946*, as amended, 15 U.S.C. § 1051 et seq.; the Trademark Rules, 37 C.F.R. Part 2; and the *Trademark Manual of Examining Procedure*, 2d ed. (Washington, D.C.: GPO, 1993) (see U.S. Patent and Trademark Office, available at www.uspto.gov/web/offices/tac/doc/basic/basic_facts.html [accessed 4 August 1999]).

35. McDonald's has even gone so far as to formally register McWorld! McWorld is the term it uses for a series of children-oriented "games, polls, and cool stuff." See www.mcworld.com/index_frame.html (accessed 4 August 1999). McDonald's has been in involved in numerous trademark infringement litigations over the years, mostly involving recalcitrant or renegade franchisees. But, McDonald's has also gone after less likely foe. For example, it won a legal battle in 1986 against a single bagel bakery in New York that had the nerve to name itself "McBagel" (*McDonald's v. McBagel's Inc.*, 49 F. Supp. 1268 (U.S. District Court for the Southern District of New York, 1986)). The giant burger chain has, however, lost some cases. In 1966, it lost to a small Alabama chain that employed arch-like designs in its edifices (*McDonald's v. McBagel's Inc.*, 49 F. Supp. 1268 (U.S. District Court for the Southern District of New York, 1986)).

36. For a truly outstanding web-based source of information on intellectual property, you may want to check out the homepage of James Boyle, Professor of Law at the American University. Professor Boyle's page, including his course syllabus and materials, is a treasure trove of copyright, patent, and trademark law and analysis (available at james-boyle.com/). Boyle is also the author of a very useful and well-written work on law in the information age (see Boyle 1996). Many weighty (both literally and figuratively) treatises have been published in the area of intellectual property. For a relatively accessible treatment, see Miller and Davis (1990).

37. For example, in the Orbison version, the woman is "lovely as can be." In the Campbell version, the "[b]ig hairy woman" needs "to shave that stuff." And where Orbison

promises that if the woman will simply look his way, he'll "treat [her] right," Campbell threatens to "let the boys [j]ump in" (*Campbell v. Acuff-Rose Music*, 510 U.S. 569, at 595–96, Appendices A and B (1994)).

38. Ibid. The limits of fair use have been at the heart of a number of important intellectual property battles in recent years. Several have been particularly noteworthy. For example, in *Princeton University Press v. Michigan Document Services*, 99 F.3d 1381 (U.S. Court of Appeals for the 6th Circuit, 1996), the Sixth Circuit threw academia into a tailspin when it announced that the copying of portions of copyrighted materials by commercial copying centers for college professors and their students is *not* a fair use. The decision has vastly increased the time and effort that professors and copiers must put into course packs and the cost to students. In *American Geophysical Union v. Texaco*, 60 F.3d 913 (U.S. Court of Appeals for the 2d Circuit, 1994), the Second Circuit determined that the photocopying of full journal articles by an institutional, for-profit concern was not fair use and thus violated copyright. See also, *Sony Corp. v. Universal City Studios Inc.*, 464 U.S. 417 (1984) (refusing to hold the manufacturer of video recorders liable for copyright infringement if the recorders could be used for substantial noninfringing purposes).

39. In general, digital audio-recording devices or digital audio-interface devices are required to conform to the Serial Copyright Management System (SCMS) or similar certified systems that send, receive, and act upon information about the generation and copyright status of the files that they play (17 U.S.C.S., at 1002 (1999)). In effect, SCMS prevents consumers from making repeated copies of recordings.

40. According to the court, "The typical computer hard drive from which a Rio directly records is, of course, a material object. However, hard drives ordinarily contain much more than 'only sounds, and material, statements, or instructions incidental to those fixed sounds' [citing AHRA, op. cit.]. Indeed, almost all hard drives contain numerous programs (e.g., for word processing, scheduling appointments, etc.) and databases that are not incidental to any sound files that may be stored on the hard drive. Thus, the Rio appears not to make copies from digital music recordings, and thus would not be a digital audio recording device under the act's basic definition unless it makes copies from transmissions (*Recording Industry of America v. Diamond Multimedia Systems*, 1999 U.S. App. LEXIS 13131, at LEXIS *11 (United States Court of Appeals for the Ninth Circuit, 1999).

41. In August 1999, RIAA agreed not pursue any further appeals. The industry and MP3 manufacturers apparently cooperated in an effort to establish guidelines for Internet music by 2000 ("Dispute Over On-Line Music Is Settled," *New York Times*, 5 August 1999, C11). A new MP3 battle may be looming over 1999's disastrous re-make of Woodstock. Hence, not only did the latest permutation of the festival differ from its 1969 progenitor in its violent ending, but where "[i]t took 11 months for the music of the original Woodstock to make it onto six sides of vinyl" before the 1999 event was even over, "technologically facile fans had converted live pay-per-view transmissions into near-CD-quality copies of performances by bands such as Korn, Live, Tragically Hip, and Rage Against the Machine." Shortly thereafter the bootlegs found their way onto such Internet auction sites as eBay, Yahoo, and Amazon.com. See "Woodstock Is Boarded by Digital Pirates: Bootlegs of the Festival Arrive on the Internet," *Washington Post*, 4 August 1999, p. C5, available at search.washingtonpost.com/wp-srv/WPlate/1999-08/04/151l-080499-idx.html (accessed 6 August 1999).

42. Arguments over interpretation of relatively recently passed law are adding to the confused legal state of affairs. In 1998, Congress passed the *Digital Millennium Copyright Act* (DMCA) (Pub. L. No. 105-304, 112 Stat. 2877 (1998)). The law was seen as a victory for industry and artists, tightening online copyright protection. The act, however, provides so-called "safe harbor provisions," designed to shield Internet access providers from liability when their users engage in copyright infringement. The problem has become how to define "providers." Thus, Napster claims that it is a "provider" under the law and cannot be found liable for any copyright violations of its users. Its assertion is being tested in the courts. See Jacobus (2000).

43. There are seven general top-level domains: "com" (commercial organizations), "edu" (educational), "gov" (government), "mil" (military), "org" (other organizations), "int" (organizations established by international treaties), and "net" (network providers). Because of the global character of the Internet, a two-character code is often appended to the end of an address, indicating national origin (e.g., "us" for United States, "uk" for the United Kingdom, and "au" for Australia).

44. Domains are registered through InterNIC, a cooperative activity between the U.S. government and Network Solutions, Inc., available at www.networksolutions.com/.

45. Take the real-life (and far more enterprising) case of Jim Cashel, who in 1994 snatched up such domain names as esquire.com, hertz.com, and trump.com (Ugelow 1994, A1). Later, Cashel voluntarily relinquished rights to the name (Corcoran 1994, B11).

46. According to the court record, Toeppen had registered domain names for a number of other companies including Delta Airlines, Neiman Marcus, Eddie Bauer, Lufthansa, and over one hundred other marks. Some of those have been the subjects of subsequent litigation against him.

47. A particularly egregious form of squatting is frequently done by pornographers, seeking to exploit brand names, often as a way of enticing children to their sites. One such case involved the use of candyland.com by a sexually explicit site. Candyland is more commonly known as a popular children's board game produced by Hasbro. In 1996, Hasbro was granted an injunction against the pornographic site (*Hasbro v. Internet Entertainment Group*, 1996 U.S. Dist. LEXIS 11626 (U.S. District Court for the Western District of Washington, 1996)).

48. While many in Congress are seeking to make litigation against corporations by individuals more difficult, here note that they are seeking to make litigation against individuals by corporations easier.

49. Historically, one means of oppression has been to rob subjugated peoples of their individual names as a way of reidentifying them as subjects or property of the oppressor. This, of course, was widely done by slave traders and holders. Even today, we feel great sadness when police and public mortuaries are able only to characterize an individual as "John Doe"—a person who has died without an identity.

50. The law has had much to do both with discrimination based on gender and, more recently, with antidiscrimination. Many books and hundreds of articles trace the development of gender law. For one relatively accessible treatment, see Thomas (1991).

51. American society has long accepted the myth of classlessness. Indeed, even when the existence of class is grudgingly acknowledged, we tend to believe that the boundaries between economic strata are extremely porous. Thus, in our grand mythology the poor, through hard work and plucky perseverance, can presumably move into the upper classes. While American law, like American society, is loathe to employ the word "class," it, too, has long, and in many ways, accepted the myth. Note, for example, nineteenth-century contract law (see chapter 3), which placed wealthy employer and impoverished employee on equal legal footing. (The result, of

course, was enormously beneficial to the wealthy employer!) Although modern law accepts (indeed defines) poverty as a classification, in many respects it continues, for better or worse, the mythology. For example, the sweeping welfare reform, signed into law in the late 1990s (*The Personal Responsibility and Work Opportunity Reconciliation Act*, § 101, Pub. L. No. 104-193, 110 Stat. 2105, 2110 (1996) (codified as amended at 42 U.S.C. § 601 note (1997)) is premised on the philosophy that hard work—not "handouts"—will result in the realization of the American dream for the nation's millions of poor.

52. Millions of Americans suffer physical or mental disabilities and, for much of our history, this broad and very diverse group has suffered discrimination as well. In 1992, the *Americans with Disabilities Act* (ADA) (42 U.S.C.S. § 12101 (1999)) took effect. The purpose of the act was to end discrimination against the disabled in employment and public accommodation. Since its implementation, the ADA has generated literally thousands of legal actions. In many cases, it has fallen to the courts to determine the scope of the law, including identifying those individuals who are disabled for the purposes of the ADA. See for example, *Murphy v. UPS*, 527 U.S. 516 (1999) (holding that "Under the ADA, the determination whether petitioner's impairment 'substantially limits' one or more major life activities is made with reference to the mitigating measures he employs"); *Sutton v. United Airlines*, 527 U.S. 471 (1999) (holding that "A 'disability' exists only where an impairment 'substantially limits' a major life activity, not where it 'might,' 'could,' or 'would' be substantially limiting if corrective measures were not taken); *Albertsons, Inc., v. Kirkingburg*, 527 U.S. 555 (1999) (holding that "The ADA requires monocular individuals, like others claiming the act's protection, to prove a disability by offering evidence that the extent of the limitation on a major life activity caused by their impairment is substantial"); and *Olmstead v. L.C.*, 527 U.S. 581 (1999) (holding that "Undue institutionalization qualifies as discrimination 'by reason of ... disability'").

53. In many ways, as illustrated by the military's "don't ask, don't tell" rule, the law depends on self-identification in the realm of sexual preference. Once "told," however, civil rights laws that apply to other groups do not necessarily apply to discrimination against gays and lesbians. See for example, Rubenstein (1996).

54. In relevant part, the Fourteenth Amendment reads: "All persons born or naturalized in the United States, and subject to the jurisdiction thereof, are citizens of the United States and of the State wherein they reside. No State shall make or enforce any law which shall abridge the privileges or immunities of citizens of the United States; nor shall any State deprive any person of life, liberty, or property, without due process of law; nor deny to any person within its jurisdiction the equal protection of the laws" (§ 1). Over the course of the twentieth century, both the due process and equal protection clauses have been crucial for expanding liberties and rights. Litigants, lawyers, and courts have used the due process clause as a means of extending most of the protections in the Bill of Rights to state governmental actions through the process of "selective incorporation." The equal protection clause has been employed as a means of securing civil rights for racial and ethnic minorities, as well as women, and other traditionally disadvantaged groups. Hundreds of books have been written about the Fourteenth Amendment. See, for example, Perry (1999) and Nelson (1988).

55. Holding that "a negro, whose ancestors were imported into this country and sold as slaves ... [cannot be] included, and were not intended to be included, under the word 'citizens' in the Constitution, and can, therefore, claim none of the rights and privileges which that instrument provides for and

secures for citizens of the United States [including] ... the privilege of suing in a court of the United States ... " (*Dred Scott v. Sanford*, 60 U.S. 393 at 403 (1857)).

56. Upholding Louisiana's system of segregated transportation (*Plessy v. Ferguson*, 163 U.S. 537 (1896).

57. Standing is the legal right to bring a lawsuit. Traditionally, the rules of standing are such that an individual has to demonstrate that she has been personally injured as a result of the matter before the court and that the matter can be resolved by a court. According to the Supreme Court, "the irreducible constitutional minimum of standing contains three elements. First, the plaintiff must have suffered an 'injury in fact'—an invasion of a legally protected interest which is (a) concrete and particularized, ... and (b) 'actual' or imminent, not 'conjectural' or 'hypothetical.'... Second, there must be a causal connection between the injury and the conduct complained of—the injury has to be 'fairly ... trace[able] to the challenged action of the defendant, and not ... the result [of] the independent action of some third party not before the court.' ... Third, it must be 'likely,' as opposed to merely 'speculative, that the injury will be 'redressed by a favorable decision'" (*Lujan v. Defenders of Wildlife*, 504 U.S. 555, at 560 (1992); internal citations omitted). During the 1960s and 1970s, the courts loosened the rules somewhat, making it easier for groups to have standing. See, for example, Office of Communication of the *United Church of Christ v. FCC*, 123 U.S. App. D.C. 328; 359 F.2d 994; 1966 U.S. App. LEXIS 6756 (1966).

58. The idea was reiterated roughly seven decades later by Chief Justice Taney in his infamous *Dred Scott* opinion:

[T]he men who framed [the] Declaration [of Independence] were great men—high in literary acquirements—high in their sense of honor, and incapable of asserting principles inconsistent with those on which they were acting. They perfectly understood the meaning of the language they used, and how it would be understood by others; and they knew that it would not in any part of the civilized world be supposed to embrace the negro race, which, by common consent, had been excluded from civilized Governments and the family of nations, and doomed to slavery. They spoke and acted according to the then established doctrines and principles, and in the ordinary language of the day, no one misunderstood them. The unhappy black race were separated from the white by indelible marks, and laws long before established, and were never thought of or spoken of except as property, and when the claims of the owner or the profit of the trader were supposed to need protection. This state of public opinion had undergone no change when the Constitution was adopted, as is equally evident from its provisions and language. The brief preamble sets forth by whom it was formed, for what purposes, and for whose benefit and protection. It declares that it is formed by the people of the United States; that is to say, by those who were members of the different political communities in the several States; and its great object is declared to be to secure the blessings of liberty to themselves and their posterity. It speaks in general terms of the people of the United States, and of citizens of the several States, when it is providing for the exercise of the powers granted or the privileges secured to the citizen. It does not define what description of persons are intended to be included under these terms, or who shall be regarded as a citizen and one of the people. It uses them as terms so well understood, that no further description or definition was necessary. But there are two clauses in the Constitution which point directly and specifically to the negro race as a separate class of persons, and show clearly that they were not regarded as a portion of the people or citizens of the Government then formed. One of these clauses reserves to each of the thirteen States the right to import slaves until the year 1808, if it thinks proper. And the importation which it thus sanctions was unquestionably of persons of the race of which we are speaking, as the traffic in slaves in the United States had always been confined to them. And by the other provision the States pledge themselves to each other to maintain the right of property of the master, by delivering up to him any slave who may have escaped from his service, and be found within their respective territories. By the first above-mentioned clause, therefore, the right to purchase and hold this property is directly sanctioned and authorized for twenty years by the people who framed the Constitution. And by the second, they pledge themselves to maintain and uphold the right of the master in the manner specified, as long as the Government they then formed should endure. And these two provisions show, conclusively, that neither the description of persons therein referred to, not their descendants, were embraced in any of the other provisions of the Constitution; for certainly these two clauses were not intended to confer on them or their posterity the blessings of liberty, or any of the personal rights so carefully provided for the citizen (*Dred Scott v. Sanford*, at 410–12).

59. In *Brown II*, the Court remanded all of the desegregation cases to the appropriate "District Courts to take such proceedings and enter such orders and decrees consistent with this opinion as are necessary and proper to admit to public schools on a racially nondiscriminatory basis with all deliberate speed the parties to these cases" (*Brown v. Board of Education* (*Brown II*), 349 U.S. 294, at 301 (1955)).

60. The first such instance occurred when President Eisenhower sent troops to Little Rock in 1958 to enforce the Court's desegregation order there against the strong resistance of Arkansas Governor Orval Faubus.

61. Title VI of the *Civil Rights Act of 1964* authorizes the withdrawal of federal funds to educational facilities or programs that discriminate (42 *U.S.C.* 2000d (1999)).

62. Upholding busing plans where there was evidence of past state-sponsored segregation. In September of 1999 U.S. District Court Judge Robert Potter determined that the Charlotte-Mecklenburg school system had "eliminated, to the extent practicable, the vestiges of past discrimination in the traditional areas of school operations," putting an end to nearly three decades of race-based busing in the region ("North Carolina City Told to End Race-based Busing," Reuters News Service, 10 September 1999, available at LegalNews.Find-Law.com/ [accessed 15 September 1999]). However, see *Milliken v. Bradley*, 418 U.S. 717 (1974) (forced busing not required where there has been no evidence of past legally imposed segregation).

63. But, see *Missouri v. Jenkins*, 495 U.S. 33 (1990) (holding that courts may not impose tax increases in order to pay for desegregation programs).

64. Titles II and III of the *Civil Rights Act of 1964* prohibit discrimination in public accommodations and facilities (42 U.S.C. 2000a(b) (1999)).

65. Title VII of the *Civil Rights Act of 1964* (2000d).

66. *The Fair Housing Act of 1968* outlawed discrimination in the sale or rental of housing.

67. *The Voting Rights Act of 1965* outlawed discrimination in voting.

68. President Johnson first used the term in Executive Order 11,246, requiring federal contractors to take "affirmative action" in the hiring and promotion of minorities. Later, President Nixon's "Philadelphia Plan" required contractors to set goals and timetables in hiring. See, generally, Jones (1982).

69. Many litigants have challenged affirmative action programs. See especially, *Regents of the University of California v. Bakke*, 438 U.S. 265 (1978) (striking down the affirmative ac-

tion admission program of the University of California, but approving minority preference programs in some circumstances); *Richmond v. J.A. Croson*, 488 U.S. 469 (1989) (striking down Richmond's minority set-aside plan for city contracts); and *Hopwood v. Texas*, 84 F.3d 720, cert. denied, 518 U.S. 1033 (U.S. Court of Appeals for the 5th Circuit, 1996) (striking down the affirmative action program of the University of Texas Law School).

70. Citation and discussion found at Ford (1994, 1232ff).

71. North Carolina: *State v. Chavers*, 5 Jones, [N.C.] 1, at 11, cited in *Plessy v. Ferguson*, 163 U.S. 537, at 552 (1896) (Brown, J., concurring).

72. Ohio: *Gray v. State*, 4 Ohio, 354; *Monroe v. Collins*, 17 Ohio St. 665, cited in *Plessy*, at 552.

73. Michigan and Virginia: *People v. Dean*, 14 Michigan 406 (1866); *Jones v. Commonwealth*, 80 Virginia, 538, cited in *Plessy*, at 552.

74. Most other tribes require some blood connection as well. See, for example, the Constitution of the Chickasaw Nation, available at www.chickasaw.net/government/constitution.html (accessed 12 April 2000) and the Constitution and By-Laws of the Cheyenne River Sioux Tribe, available at www.sioux.org/constitution_and_by.htm (accessed 12 April 2000).

75. See, for example, Project RACE, available at projectrace. home.mindspring.com/, and the Association of MultiEthnic Americans, available at www.ameasite.org/ (both sites accessed 16 August 1999).

76. Over the past several years, a number of states have revised their records and form management procedures to allow for multiracial identifications. For example, a 1998 revision to Maryland's form management law stipulates: "A form that requires identification of individuals by race shall include instructions that multiracial respondents may select all applicable racial categories" (Md. State Government Code Ann. § 10-606 (1998)).

Chapter 9

1. According to the Administration on Aging, Department of Health and Human Services: "The older population—persons 65 years or older—numbered 34.1 million in 1997. They represented 12.7% of the U.S. population, about one in every eight Americans. The number of older Americans increased by 2.8 million or 9.1% since 1990, compared to an increase of 7.0% for the under-65 population.... Since 1900, the percentage of Americans 65+ has more than tripled (4.1% in 1900 to 12.7% in1997), and the number has increased eleven times (from 3.1 million to 34.1 million). The older population itself is getting older. In 1997 the 65–74 age group (18.5 million) was eight times larger than in 1900, but the 75–84 group (11.7 million) was 16 times larger and the 85+ group (3.9 million) was 31 times larger.... [T]he older population will burgeon between the years 2010 and 2030 when the 'baby boom' generation reaches age 65.

By 2030, there will be about 70 million older persons, more than twice their number in 1997. People 65+ are projected to represent 13% of population in the year 2000 but will be 20% by 2030" ("Profile of Older Americans: 1998," available at www.aoa.dhhs.gov/aoa/stats/profile/#table1 [accessed 26 October 1999]).

2. The Court had addressed the question of whether age distinctions violate the equal protection requirements of the Fourteenth Amendment on one other occasion, reaching a similar conclusion: *Vance v. Bradley*, 440 U.S. 93 (1979) (up-

holding constitutionality of State Department regulation mandating retirement of Foreign Service employees at age sixty).

3. At issue here was whether Congress, in extending age discrimination protection to state employees, had violated the states' immunity from prosecution under the Eleventh Amendment. The 5–4 majority declared that Congress had overstepped its authority and restated its understanding that age is not a suspect classification.

4. See 49 Stats. 623. For a thorough account of the committee's actions and the legislative history of the *Social Security Act*, see Witte (1962). Also see Weaver (1982), Altmeyer (1968), and Nash, Pugach, and Thomasson (1988).

5. *Helvering v. Davis*, 301 U.S. 619 (1937) represented a frontal assault on the general policy, while *Steward Machine Company v. Davis*, 301 U.S. 548 (1937) challenged the taxation and employer contribution scheme.

6. The depression era Townsend Movement in California, led by Dr. Francis E. Townsend, was actually the first effort to organize elderly people for the purpose of political action. The primary thrust of the movement was that every citizen should, at age sixty, get $200 per month from the government with the requirement that it be spent, thereby both providing for old age and stimulating the economy. Older folks would also be taken care of, and they would immediately put their stipends into circulation, which would serve as an economic stimulus (Holtzman 1963). In addition, Abraham Epstein organized the American Association for Old Age Security in 1927 (which became the Association for Social Security in 1933) for the purpose of promoting old-age assistance laws (e.g., Lubove 1968).

7. See www.aarp.org for a full analysis of the organization's lobbying and litigation efforts on behalf of senior citizens (accessed 13 January 2000).

8. See NY Exec. Law, § 296 (1958); Laws Cal. 1961, ch. 1623.

9. See 79 Stat. 218, July 14, 1965.

10. See 81 Stat. 602, December 15, 1967; 29 U.S.C. 621. The ADEA covered all individuals between the ages of forty and sixty-five, and was amended in 1978 to increase the upper age to seventy (92 Stat. 189, April 6, 1978).

11. There have been a number of such cases that have worked their way through the federal courts under ADEA. *Waggoner v. City of Garland*, 987 F.2d 1160 (5th Cir. 1993) (finding supervisor's stray remarks insufficient to prove age discrimination in employment) is an often-cited and pivotal case. Also see *Bolton v. Scrivner, Inc.*, 36 F.3d 939, 944–45 (10th Cir. 1994), cert. denied, 115 S. Ct. 1104 (1995).

12. Medicare and Medicaid were parts of the *Health Insurance for the Aged Act* (79 Stat. 290, July 20, 1965).

13. For an extensive summary of both the Medicare and Medicaid programs, see Waid (1998).

14. Thus, a person who is eligible for Medicaid in one state might not be eligible in another state; and the services provided by one state may differ considerably in amount, duration, or scope from services provided in a similar or neighboring state. In addition, Medicaid eligibility and/or services within a state can change during the year.

15. See *Goldberg v. Kelly*, 405 U.S. 134 (1972) (holding that states cannot terminate benefits without a formal hearing on the recipient's eligibility); and *Shapiro v. Thompson*, 394 U.S. 618 (1969) (invalidating residency requirements for receipt of benefits in light of the constitutional "right to travel").

16. It was estimated that by the year 2000 the average life expectancy would rise to eighty years of age. Indeed, if medical research into such technologies as stem cell replacement continues to progress, the Census Bureau predicts that within a century, more than 5,000,000 Americans will be living past 100! (Hall 2000).

17. Agriculture is heavily regulated and subsidized by law, both state and federal. Law covers a wide variety of loan programs, production assistance, disaster aid, crop insurance, pricing, trade agreements, and special labor regulations, to name a few. For more information, see U.S. House of Representatives, Committee on Agriculture, available at agriculture.house.gov/ (accessed 26 October 1999); U.S. Senate, Committee on Agriculture, Nutrition, and Forestry, available at www.senate.gov/~agriculture/ (accessed 26 October 1999); and Farm Services Administration, U.S. Department of Agriculture, available at www.fsa.usda.gov/pas/default.asp (accessed 26 October 1999).

18. See U.S. Food and Drug Administration, Center for Food Safety and Applied Nutrition, available at vm.cfsan.fda.gov/list.html (accessed 26 October 1999); and "Food Safety" site, available at www.foodsafety.gov/ (accessed 26 October 1999).

19. See, for example, U.S. Centers for Disease Control and Prevention, available at www.cdc.gov/ (accessed 26 October 1999); U.S. Department of Health and Human Services, Health Resources and Services Administration, available at www.hrsa.dhhs.gov/ (accessed 26 October 1999); and National Institutes of Health, available at www.nih.gov/ (accessed 26 October 1999).

20. Yes, there's even a President's Council on Physical Fitness and Sports. See www.indiana.edu/~preschal/council.html (accessed 26 October 1999).

21. See, for example, the U.S. Consumer Product Safety Commission, available at www.cpsc.gov/ (accessed 26 October 1999).

22. See U.S. Department of Labor, Occupational Health and Safety Administration, available at www.osha.gov/ (accessed 26 October 1999).

23. *Black's Law Dictionary*, 5th ed. (1979), 361, cited in Banks (1995).

24. 381 U.S. 479 (1965). For a discussion of *Griswold*, see chapter 5.

25. 410 U.S. 113 (1973). For a discussion of *Roe*, see chapter 5.

26. Notably, the withdrawal of the life-sustaining apparatus did not bring on Karen's death. She persisted in her vegetative coma for a full nine years before her death in 1985. See, for example, Malcolm (1985, 22).

27. From 1976 through 1988, at least fifty-four such cases were reported, marking a substantial increase over previous years (760 S.W. 2d at 412, n. 4, cited in *Cruzan v. Missouri Department of Health*, 497 U.S. 261, at 269 (1989)).

28. *App. to Pet. for Cert.* A99, cited in *Cruzan*, at 267.

29. The 5–4 decision included a majority consisting of the chief justice and Justices White, O'Connor, Scalia, and Kennedy (O'Connor and Scalia wrote concurrences). The dissent, led by Justice Brennan, included Justices Marshall, Blackmun and Stevens, with Stevens writing separately.

30. "Kevorkian's Patients," The Kevorkian File, available at www.rights.org/deathnet/Kfiles_details.html (accessed 5 January 2000).

31. On 14 March 1998, Kevorkian assisted in his hundredth suicide. See Public Broadcasting System (1998).

32. On 13 April 1999, Kevorkian was convicted of second-degree murder and delivery of a controlled substance in the death of Thomas Youk. Kevorkian was sentenced to ten to twenty-five years in prison for delivery of a lethal injection to Youk. Kevorkian had videotaped this particular death, which was aired on *60 Minutes* by CBS the previous November. Prior to his conviction, Kevorkian had been tried and acquitted several times by Michigan juries and had been the impetus for two state laws outlawing assisted suicide, the first of which was

declared unconstitutional by the Michigan Supreme Court. For a complete chronology of Kevorkian's activities and the legal responses to those exploits, see Public Broadcasting System (1998). See also Lessenberry (1994).

33. Or. Rev. Stat.127.800 *et seq.* Although some states, such as Maine, are considering measures similar to that of Oregon, the trend in recent years has been in the opposite direction, with more states acting to explicitly ban assisted suicide. See Choice in Dying, "Legal Developments: Recent Legislation," available at www.choices.org/legal.htm#Legislation (accessed 6 January 2000).

34. Oregon Department of Human Resources, Health Division, "Oregon's Death with Dignity Act," available at www.ohd. hr.state.or.us/cdpe/chs/pas/pas.htm (accessed 6 January 2000).

35. Oregon Deptartment of Human Resources, Health Division, Annual Report: "Oregon's Death with Dignity Act: The First Year's Experience," available at www.ohd.hr.state.or.us/cdpe/chs/pas/arresult.htm (accessed 6 January 2000).

36. Chief Justice Burger and Justices White and Rehnquist would have upheld, in addition, the Louisiana and North Carolina Laws. See *Roberts v. Louisiana*, 428 U.S. 325, at 337ff (1976) (White, J., dissenting). Justices Brennan and Marshall continued to maintain that the death penalty is always unconstitutional. See *Gregg*, Brennan, J., dissenting at 227ff; Marshall, J., dissenting at 231ff.

37. Not a single member of the Court today views the death penalty as unconstitutional per se.

38. *Thompson v. Oklahoma*, 487 U.S. 815 (1988) (ruling unconstitutional the execution of anyone under the age of sixteen). In *Stanford v. Kentucky*, 492 U.S. 361 (1989), the Court ruled permissible executions of sixteen- and seventeen-year-olds.

39. *Penry v. Lynaugh*, 492 U.S. 302 (1989). The Court, however, determined that juries must be instructed as to the mental retardation of the defendant.

40. ACLU, "The Poverty Connection," ACLU Execution Watch, available at www.aclu.org/executionwatch.html (accessed 3 January 2000).

41. See, for example, *Powell v. Alabama*, 287 U.S. 45 (1932); *Gideon v. Wainwright*, 372 U.S. 335 (1963); and *Douglas v. California*, 372 U.S. 535 (1963).

42. The term was quoted and accepted by the ABA in a 1997 report (ABA 1998, 224).

43. In spite of all the negligence, "both the Alabama Court of Criminal Appeals, *Haney v. State*, 603 So. 2d 368 (Ala. Crim. App. 1991), and the Alabama Supreme Court, *Ex parte Haney*, 603 So. 2d 412 (Ala. 1992), upheld the conviction and death sentence in the case" (Bright 1994, 1836, fn. 2).

44. See Baldus et al. (1980), Baldus et al. (1983); Baldus et al. (1985); and Baldus et al. (1986).

45. Justice Powell was joined by Chief Justice Rehnquist and by Justices White, O'Connor, and Scalia.

46. Justice Brennan was joined in full by Justice Marshall and in part by Justices Blackmun and Stevens.

47. Dennis Culloton, press secretary to Governor Ryan, quoted in Claiborne (2000, 1).

48. See, for example, *Herrera v. Collins*, 506 U.S. 390 (1993) (holding that a claim of actual innocence does not entitle a defendant to federal habeas relief where he has been afforded a fair trial and appeals) and *Felker v. Turpin*, 518 U.S. 651 (1996) (upholding congressional restrictions on habeas passed as part of the *Antiterrorism and Effective Death Penalty Act of 1996*).

49. See generally, Md. HEALTH OCCUPATIONS Code Ann. § 7-101ff (1999).

50. The FTC attempts to be solicitous of state prerogatives here, exempting any state that "affords an overall level of protection to consumers which is as great as, or greater than, the protection afforded by [the FTC rule]" (16 C.F.R. 453.9).

51. *Magna Carta*, chapters 26 and 27 (1215 A.D.), posted by The University of Oklahoma Law Center, available at www.law.ou.edu//hist/magna.html (accessed 4 August 1998).

52. Generally, this would mean that the spouse gets some portion of the estate, while the children get the remainder. However, if there are no children, the spouse may have to split the estate with her dearly departed's parents or siblings.

53. "A Trust is a creature of the law in which one party—the Trustee—has legal ownership of any form of property that has been transferred to him/her or 'it' (e.g., a bank) by the person establishing the Trust. That 'establishing' person is called the Grantor (or Settlor, or Trustor). The property is known as the Trust 'principal,' or 'corpus.' These Trust assets are invested and/or managed for the benefit of one or more beneficiaries. Sometimes, the Grantor also wears the hats of Trustee and beneficiary. Generally, however, if the Grantor is the Trustee, he/she cannot be the only beneficiary. . . . [A] 'living' [trust is one] established during the Grantor's lifetime" (Palermo 1996).

54. Joint tenancy is the legal term for joint ownership of property. For example, most husbands and wives jointly hold title to the couple's house.

55. Cornell Law School, Legal Information Institute (LLI), "Estate and Gift Tax: an Overview," available at www.law.cornell.edu/topics/estate_gift_tax.html (accessed 30 September 1999).

56. "A gift tax is imposed on lifetime transfers and an estate tax is imposed on transfers at death. Since 1976, the gift tax and the estate tax have been unified so that a single graduated rate schedule applies to cumulative taxable transfers made by a taxpayer during his or her lifetime and at death. Under this rate schedule, the unified estate and gift tax rates begin at 18 percent on the first $10,000 in cumulative taxable transfers and reach 55 percent on cumulative taxable transfers over $3 million. In addition, a 5-percent surtax is imposed upon cumulative taxable transfers between $10 million and the amount necessary to phase out the benefits of the graduated rates and the unified credit (U.S. Congress 1998).

57. See, for example, the *Estate and Gift Tax Rate Reduction Act*, H.R. 8, and the *Family Heritage Preservation Act*, H.R. 86.

Chapter 10

1. Indeed, these connections have been aggressively investigated by historians, anthropologists, sociologists, psychologists, linguists, philosophers, and theorists (see, e.g., R. Clark 1981).

2. See, especially, Nedelsky (1990) on Madison's efforts to resolve the tensions between liberty and property rights.

3. In addition, in *Federalist* #23, Hamilton states that one of the primary reasons for discarding the confederate model in favor of a strong central government is to provide for a unified regulation of commerce. In *Federalist* #7, he argues that economic and commercial competitions among the states, if not held in check by a strong central authority, could well lead to war.

4. See chapter 3 for more in-depth consideration of these issues.

5. Most torts involved issues such as property damage, libel, and slander. The propertied class had more to lose, and their claims dominated this field. In addition, as we discussed in chapter 7, libel and slander law was generally out of reach to the average citizen. According to common law principles, only

the wealthy, propertied elite had reputations that could be damaged.

6. According to the laissez faire principle, as developed in the influential political economic theory of Adam Smith ([1776] 1937), people should be free to make their own decisions, particularly in business dealings. Freedom of contract is not only essential to economic prosperity, but it is also critical to a system of social justice. Government must resist the temptation to interfere with a contractual system, except to assist with enforcement of agreements. In the long run individuals' pursuit of their own selfish interests will serve the larger community interest. This sentiment largely governed the legal approach to family relationships as well (see chapter 6). The full text of Smith's treatise is available online at Maytech Publishing Ltd, *Bibliomania, The Network Library*, www.bibliomania.com/NonFiction/Smith/Wealth/index.html (accessed 26 July 1999).

7. Bourgin (1989), reconsidering the writings and policies of the Founders and early era of the republic, argues that laissez faire principles were not as dominant as most scholars assume.

8. The U.S. Congress did issue some charters, as they did in creating the second Bank of the United States. The constitutional authority to do so was challenged and subsequently upheld by the Supreme Court in *McCulloch v. Maryland*, 17 U.S. 316 (1819).

9. In many cases, the franchise was authorized to operate for a fixed number of years, after which the facility would convert to public ownership.

10. See Horwitz (1977, 130–39). For a thorough discussion of this case see Kutler (1971).

11. The Court heard arguments in the case twice. It was originally heard in 1831, but no majority surfaced, and the justices put the case off for future consideration. It was finally re-heard in 1837. The key that ultimately allowed a majority to unlock themselves from the contractual issues was that the Charles River Bridge charter was silent on its monopoly status. That the bridge would operate as a monopoly was simply implied, no doubt clearly understood by the authors of the 1785 charter. But the fact that it was not made explicit provided the Court with sufficient room to find against the claimants.

12. In addition, Congress created two new Supreme Court seats in 1836, expanding the membership to nine. Jackson filled one of these new positions, and his successor, Martin Van Buren, the other.

13. For more comprehensive discussion of these matters, see, for example, White (1991) and Kutler (1971).

14. Indeed, there are many examples where law is used to create sets of incentives and disincentives, encouraging some and discouraging other types of activities. Systems of taxation, regulatory laws, and local zoning ordinances all tend to have this effect.

15. Indeed, appeals cases, particularly those decided by the Supreme Court, have attracted the lion's share of research attention. Moreover, the law school curriculum consists in large part of the study of landmark case law.

16. See, for example, *Dred Scott v. Sanford*, 60 U.S. 393 (1856).

17. *Santa Clara County v. Southern Pacific Railroad*, 118 U.S. 394, at 396 (1886). Also see Tushnet (1982, 255–56) and Rivard (1992).

18. The *Hale* Court raised and answered the Fourth Amendment question on its own. The corporate parties had argued they should be granted Fifth Amendment protection against self-incrimination, but the justices balked at that one. Also, see *Federal Trade Commission v. American Tobacco Co.*, 264 U.S. 298 (1924) (following *Hale*).

19. Gillman (1993) argues that the Court was attempting to maintain the principle of state neutrality.

20. See, for example, Mayer (1990) and Samuels and Miller (1987). For an excellent discussion and analysis of *Lochner*, see Kens (1990).

21. Like the property and other economic issues that dominated the courts in the nineteenth century, torts and criminal cases nearly always involve status unequals. Tort plaintiffs are usually individuals, while an insurance company is the typical tort defendant. Criminal prosecutions are brought by the state against an individual defendant. The resource and power discrepancy between the parties is generally fairly obvious.

22. See, for example, McIntosh (1990); Kagan, Cartwright, Friedman, and Wheeler (1977); and D. Clark (1981).

23. Dormant commerce clause questions arise under the rationale that Congress does not have to act in an area to preclude state action. For example, three years after *Gibbons*, the Court held that states were prohibited from licensing and taxing importers, because Article I, Section 8 granted the power to regulate foreign commerce exclusively to Congress (*Brown v. Maryland*, 25 U.S. 419 (1827)).

24. Although *Munn* actually upheld Illinois' regulation of grain elevator charges, the Court noted that state actions would receive thorough judicial scrutiny and be carefully compared to common law principles.

25. Also see *Wickard v. Filburn*, 317 U.S. 111 (1942) (describing development of commerce clause jurisprudence).

26. For example, compare *National League of Cities v. Usery*, 426 U.S. 833 (1976), overruled by *Garcia v. San Antonio Metropolitan Transit Authority*, 469 U.S. 528 (1985).

27. See John (1995) for an excellent account of the establishment and development of the U.S. Postal Service.

28. He was also impressed with the communication system that had been established connecting the most remote areas to the main currents of "intellectual movement." For example, in his journal entries from Kentucky and Tennessee, he noted:

> There is an astonishing circulation of letters and newspapers among these savage woods. We traveled with the mail. From time to time we stopped at what is called the post office; almost always it was an isolated house in the depths of a wood. There we dropped a large parcel from which no doubt each inhabitant of the neighborhood came to take his share. I do not think that in the most enlightened rural districts of France there is intellectual movement either so rapid or on such a scale as this in this wilderness (available at www.c-span.org/alexis/tn3.htm (accessed 18 August 1999)).

29. de Tocqueville, *Democracy in America*, Book 2, Chapter 6, available online at C-SPAN, "In Search of de Tocqueville's Democracy in America," xroads.virginia.edu/~HYPER/DETOC/ch2_06.htm (accessed 18 August 1999).

30. For a much more in-depth discussion of these developments, see, for example, Douglas (1987) and Barnouw (1968).

31. As a rule, courts address new media by analogizing to existing technologies. As a rule, they have been reluctant to extend analytical models and the constitutional principles derived from them into unfamiliar terrain. For example, when the U.S. Supreme Court first encountered electronic surveillance (*Olmstead v. U.S.*, 277 U.S. 438) in 1928, the Court found that because there was no physical intrusion nor anything tangible seized, a telephone wiretap did not implicate the Fourth Amendment. Four decades later (*Katz v. U.S.*, 389 U.S. 347, at 351 (1967)) the Court reversed itself, finding that "the Fourth Amendment protects people not places."

32. Congressman Ernest W. Roberts of Massachusetts, quoted in Douglas (1987, 218).

33. As of 1994, 60 percent of all homes were cable connected. See *Turner Broadcasting System, Inc. v. FCC*, 114 S. Ct.

2445, at 2451 (1994). For a discussion of satellite communications see, for example, Gibbons 1995, 1391ff).

34. Meyrowitz (1985, 143–144), for example, argues that the revolution in information technology will have a democratizing influence and will actually draw people together: "Many categories of people [such as] women, ghetto dwellers, prisoners, [and] children were once 'naturally' restricted from much social information by being isolated in particular places. The identity and cohesion of many groupings and associations were fostered by the fact that members were 'isolated together' in the same or similar locations. . . . Now, however, electronic messages . . . democratize and homogenize places by allowing people to experience and interact with others in spite of physical isolation. As a result, physical location now creates only one type of information-system, only one type of shared but special group experience."

35. For an excellent discussion of these dynamics, see Merry (1981).

36. With protracted division of labor, differences among people multiply, and Durkheim posited that "the moment approaches when the only remaining bond among members of a single human group will be that they are all men" (cited by Lukes and Scull 1983, 143). We discussed some of these issues in chapter 8.

37. For those very few individuals running the large corporations, compensation rates in the 1990s were apparently unprecedented. Is Eisener really so essential to Disney that he should be half a billion dollars annually?

38. See, for example, Ellul (1964, 1973) for an extensive theoretical discussion of the influences of technology on society, displacement of custom and morality systems, and the conversion of means to ends.

39. Moreover, Republicans in Congress raised some questions about the continued government support of the Public Broadcasting System when it was revealed in July 1999 that several stations in major markets had sold or exchanged their donor lists with Democrat fund-raising groups (Seelye 1999). By September 1999, according to an internal investigation by the Corporation for Public Broadcasting, the number of public stations that swapped donor lists with political organizations had risen to fifty-three, including twenty-nine television and twenty-four radio stations. Although a few Republican groups were involved, most of the activity occurred with Democrat organizations (Robinson 1999).

40. Also see Blattberg, Glazer, and Little (1994), and Peppers and Rogers (1993). In addition, an Internet search in August 1999, using the term "narrowcasting," returned between 2,000 and 3,000 web page "hits" depending upon the search engine used.

41. A growing number of marketers involved in the emerging e-commerce industry are employing a device dubbed "opt-in" e-mail, which online customers agree to receive. Accordingly, e-mail sales and product announcements can be personalized and customized to the tastes of each individual. See, for example, Tedeschi (1999). At the same time, service and merchandise businesses have stepped up their use of direct telephone contacts.

42. In a computer-mediated world, the issue of individual privacy is reflected in at least two important phenomena: anonymity and encryption. As Lawrence Lessig (1995, 1749) notes, "anonymity . . . enables individuals to control what about themselves is known by those with whom they interact—control, for example, whether others know a user's name or association or, more generally, any feature of that individual. . . . [E]ncryption [enables] users . . . to speak a language that only intended recipients can understand." See chapter 8 for a discussion of privacy issues.

43. Often a great deal can be found out about an individual user (e.g., name, home address, birth date, and so on) if one knows the right commands.

44. Internet activities leave traces that can be reconstructed into a log, much like the pen registers associated with telephone use.

45. The U.S. government is concerned about encryption technology and the capability that it would give to criminals. Hence, steps are being taken to ensure that top-secret government files can be securely locked but that all others can be decoded. Indeed, the "Clipper Chip" standard, proposed by the Clinton administration, created considerable controversy. See, for example, Froomkin (1995). Some employers, concerned that employees are wasting company time frivolously surfing the web and/or using the corporate system for personal correspondence (e-mail technically belongs to the corporate owner, not the individual recipient), are periodically checking all electronic activities of their workforce.

46. For some, particularly those involved in litigation, the process can be very frustrating. To see their rawest passions translated into the dull, placid language of law can be dispiriting. See, for example, Conley and O'Barr (1990).

47. Science fiction author William Gibson (1995) is credited with coining the term in his novel *Neuromancer*. Cyberspace, as it is currently understood, "is the conceptual 'location' of the electronic interactivity available using one's computer" (Byassee 1995, 199, n5). It has also been characterized as the "words, human relationships, data, wealth, and power . . . by people using computer-mediated communications" (Rheingold 1993, 5). For an excellent and thorough discussion see Kroll (1994).

48. Although entirely dependent upon actions in real time in the concrete real world, cyberspace constitutes a "virtual reality." See, for example, Tribe (1991, 15). Computer-mediated activities likely to produce litigation in the near term (some already have) are difficult even to categorize, but can be tentatively differentiated by their distinct communications protocols, such as e-mail, Usenet, FTP, Telnet, and the World Wide Web (this list is admittedly not complete).

Chapter 11

1. For readers who came of television age after the mid-1980s, Winkler starred for ten years (1974–84) in the popular sitcom *Happy Days*. His leather-jacketed character, "the Fonz," was something of a "rebel-without-a-cause" type who ultimately became the show's most recognizable and favorite personality.

2. Nancy, although still suffering from her injuries, did emerge from the coma, and lives today in Florida with her parents.

References

Abadinsky, Howard. 1995. *Law and Justice: An Introduction to the American Legal System.* 2d ed. Chicago: Nelson-Hall.

Abraham, Henry J. 1997. "Reflections on the Contemporary Status of Our Civil Rights and Liberties and the Bill of Rights." *Journal of Law and Politics* 13: 7–20.

Abramson, Jeffrey. 1994. *We, The Jury: The Jury System and the Ideal of Democracy.* New York: Basic Books.

Administration on Aging, Department of Health and Human Services. [1998?]. "Profile of Older Americans, 1998." Available at www.aoa.dhhs.gov/aoa/stats/profile/#table1 (accessed 26 October 1999).

Administrative Office of the U.S. Courts, U.S. Department of Justice. 1999. *The Federal Judicial Caseload: A Five-Year Retrospective.* Available at www.uscourts.gov/publications.html (accessed 10 September 1999).

Alexander, Michael. 1994. "Klein Relinquishes Role As Wife's Conservator." *Newsday,* 8 June 1994, p. 24.

Altmeyer, Arthur J. 1968. *The Formative Years of Social Security.* Madison: The University of Wisconsin Press.

American Bar Association. 1998. "Resolution and Report on the Death Penalty." *Law and Contemporary Problems* 61: Appendix.

American Civil Liberties Union. [1999?]. "ACLU Challenges Florida Ban On Lesbian and Gay Adoption." Available at www.aclu.org/features/f052699a.html (accessed 2 June 1999).

———. 1999. "Status of U.S. Sodomy Laws," 23 June. Available at www.aclu.org/issues/gay/hgml/sodomy.html (accessed 23 June 1999).

———. [2000?]. "Criminal Justice Issues." Available at www.aclu.org/issues/criminal/hmcj.html (accessed 2 March 2000).

Anderson, Nick, and Louis Sahagun. 1998. "Bilingual Classes Still Thriving in Wake of Prop. 227." *Los Angeles Times,* 22 October, p. A1.

Andrews, Lori B. 1999. "Embryonic Confusion When You Think Conception, You Don't Think Product Liability: Think Again." *Washington Post,* 2 May, p. B1.

Annin, Peter. 1994. "Looking for a Piece of the Action." *Newsweek,* 13 June, p. 44.

Aquinas, St. Thomas. 1988. *On Law, Morality and Politics.* Edited by William P. Baumgarth and Richard J. Regan. Indianapolis: Hackett Publishing Company, 1988.

Archer, Dane, Rosemary Gartner, and Marc Beittel. 1983. "Homicide and the Death Penalty: A Cross-National Test of a Deterrence Hypothesis." *Journal of Criminal Law and Criminology* 74: 991–1013.

Asher, Herb, and Mike Barr. 1994. "Popular Support for Congress and Its Members." In *Congress, the Press, and the Public,* edited by Thomas E. Mann and Norman J. Ornstein, 15–28. Washington, D.C.: American Enterprise Institute and Brookings Institution.

Aspinwall, Timothy J. 1997. "Religious Exemptions to Childhood Immunization Statutes: Reaching for a More Optimal Balance Between Religious Freedom and Public Health." *Loyola University Chicago Law Journal* 29: 109–39.

Associated Press. 1996. "O.J. Friends May Become Foes/Pals Slated to Testify for Plaintiffs in Trial." *Newsday,* 29 November, p. A6.

Associated Press Online Newsfeed, 1 July 1998. Available through LEXIS-NEXIS (accessed 19 March 2001).

Atlanta Journal and Constitution, 19 September 1998.

Auerbach, Jerold S. 1976. *Unequal Justice.* New York: Oxford University Press.

———. 1984. *Justice Without Law.* New York: Oxford University Press.

Babbington, Charles. 1999. "Theaters to Require Picture IDs for R Films; Effect of Post-Littleton Move Is Questioned." *Washington Post,* 9 June, p. A1.

Baddeley, Jeffrey. 1983. "Parens Patriae Suits by a State Under 42 U.S.C. § 1983." *Case Western Reserve Law Journal* 33: 431–57.

Bailyn, Bernard. 1967. *The Ideological Origins of the American Revolution.* Cambridge, Mass.: Belknap Press.

Baldus, David C., Charles Pulaski, George Woodworth, and Frederick D. Kyle. 1980. "Identifying Comparatively Excessive Sentences of Death: A Quantitative Approach." *Stanford Law Review* 33: 1–75.

Baldus, David C., Charles Pulaski, and George Woodworth. 1983. "Comparative Review of Death Sentences: An Empirical Study of the Georgia Experience." *Journal of Criminal Law and Criminology* 74: 661–753.

Baldus, David C., George Woodworth, and Charles Pulaski. 1985. "Monitoring and Evaluating Contemporary Death Sentencing Systems: Lessons from Georgia." *University of California, Davis Law Review* 18: 1375–1417.

———. 1986. "Arbitrariness and Discrimination in the Administration of the Death Penalty: A Challenge to State Supreme Courts." *Stetson Law Review* 15: 133–262.

Baldus, David C., George Woodworth, David Zuckerman, Neil Alan Weiner, and Barbara Broffitt. 1998. "Symposium: Racial Discrimination and the Death Penalty in the Post-Furman Era: An Empirical and Legal Overview, with Recent Findings from Philadelphia." *Cornell Law Review* 83: 1638–1770.

Banks, Gloria J. 1995. "Legal and Ethical Safeguards: Protection of Society's Most Vulnerable Participants in a Commercialized Organ Transplantation System." *American Journal of Law and Medicine* 21: 45–110.

Banks, Russell. 1998. *Cloudsplitter.* New York: Harper Flamingo.

Barber, Benjamin R. 1996. *Jihad vs. McWorld.* New York: Ballentine Books.

Barber, Sotirious. 1988. "Judicial Review and the Federalist." *University of Chicago Law Review* 55: 836–87.

Barnouw, Erik. 1968. *The Golden Web, 1933 to 1953.* Vol. 2 of *A History of Broadcasting in the United States.* New York: Oxford University Press.

Bartholet, Elizabeth. 1991. "Where Do Black Children Belong? The Politics of Race Matching in Adoption." *University of Pennsylvania Law Review* 139: 1163–1256.

———. 1998. "Correspondence: Private Race Preferences in Family Formation." *Yale Law Journal* 107: 2351–56.

Bartlett's Familiar Quotations. 14th ed. 1968. Boston: Little, Brown.

Baum, Lawrence. 1998. *American Courts: Process and Policy.* Boston: Houghton Mifflin.

Becker, Carl Lotus. 1922. *The Declaration of Independence, A Study in the History of Political Ideas.* New York: Harcourt, Brace.

Belk, Diana. 1997. "Fantasy vs. Reality? Grow Up." *The Orlando Sentinel,* 31 August 1997.

Bentley, Arthur F. 1908. *The Process of Government.* Chicago: Univeristy of Chicago Press.

Berger, Raoul. 1977. *Government By Judiciary.* Cambridge: Harvard University Press.

———. 1986. "New Theories of 'Interpretation'." *Ohio State Law Journal* 47: 1–45.

Berry, Jeffrey M. 1989. *The Interest Group Society.* 2d ed. Glenview, Ill.: Scott, Foresman/Little, Brown.

Bickel, Alexander. 1962. *The Least Dangerous Branch: The Supreme Court at the Bar of Politics.* Indianapolis: Bobbs-Merrill.

Biskupic, Joan. 1996. "A Declaration of Independence; Though Open to Criticism, Judges' Rulings Must Not Jeopardize Their Jobs, Rehnquist Says." *Washington Post,* 10 April, p. A17.

———. 1998a. "Despite Ruling, Smoking Bans Are Here to Stay, Officials Say." *Washington Post,* 20 July, p. A4.

———. 1998b. "2 Justices Concur Against Threats to Neutrality." *Washington Post,* 6 December.

Blackstone, William. 1765. *Commentaries on the Law of England.* Vol. 1. Oxford: Clarendon.

———. 1769. *Commentaries on the Law of England.* Vol. 3. Oxford: Clarendon.

Blake, Judith. 1971. "Abortion and Public Opinion: The 1960–1970 Decade." *Science* 171: 540–549.

Blake, Nelson Manfred. 1962. *The Road to Reno: A History of Divorce in the United States.* New York: Macmillan.

Blattberg, Richard, Rashi Glazer, and John D. C. Little. 1994. *The Marketing Information Revolution.* Boston: Harvard Business School Press.

Bonsignore, John J., et al., eds. 1994. *Before the Law: An Introduction to the Legal Process.* 5th ed. Boston: Houghton Mifflin Company.

Booth, William. 2000. "Tribes Ride a Casino Dream." *Washington Post,* 9 May, pp. A1, 18.

Bork, Robert. 1990. *The Tempting of America.* New York: Simon and Schuster.

Borman, Karlyn, and Everett Carll Ladd. 1994. "Public Opinion toward Congress: A Historical Look." In *Congress, the Press, and the Public,* edited by Thomas E. Mann and Norman J. Ornstein, 28–41. Washington, D.C.: American Enterprise Institute and Brookings Institution.

Bourgin, Frank. 1989. *The Great Challenge: The Myth of Laissez-Faire in the Early Republic.* New York: Harper and Row.

Boyle, James. 1996. *Shamans, Software, and Spleens: Law and the Construction of the Information Society.* Cambridge, Mass.: Harvard University Press.

Bright, Stephen. 1994. "Counsel for the Poor: The Death Sentence Not for the Worst Crime but for the Worst Lawyer." *Yale Law Journal* 103: 1835–83.

British Broadcasting Corporation, 24 November 1997.

Brodin, Mark S. 1990. "Accuracy, Efficiency, and Accountability in the Litigation Process—The Case for the Fact Verdict." *University of Cincinnati Law Review* 59: 15–111.

Brown, Jodie M., and Patrick A. Langan. 1998. *State Court Sentencing of Convicted Felons, 1994.* Report # NCJ-164615. Washington, D.C.: Bureau of Justice Statistics, U.S. Department of Justice.

Brown, Leslie F. 1999. "I. Intellectual Property: C. Trademark: 2. Domain Name: a) Dilution: *Avery Dennison Corp. v. Sumpton.*" *Berkeley Technology Law Journal* 14: 247–66.

Brumas, Michael. 2000. "Eight States Seek to Post 10 Commandments." *Times Picayune,* 8 February, p. A12.

Bruno, Robert J. 1989. "Constitutional Analysis of Educational Vouchers in Minnesota." *Education Law* 53: 9–28.

Bureau of Indian Affairs, U.S. Department of the Interior. 1999. "Tribal-State Gaming Compacts as of July 30, 1999."

Available at www.doi.gov/bia/gaming/complist/ gamingcmptindex.htm (accessed 5 April 2000).

———. 2000. "Indian Entities Recognized and Eligible to Receive Services From the U.S. Bureau of Indian Affairs." Federal Register, Vol. 65, No. 49, 13 March; Notices, FR Doc. 00-6064. Available at www.doi.gov/bia/tribes/ FRLIST2000. htm (accessed 5 April 2000).

Bureau of Justice Statistics, U.S. Department of Justice. 1995. *Compendium of Federal Justice Statistics,* 1995. Available at www.ojp.usdog.gov/bjs/.

———. 1997. *Capital Punishment 1996 Bulletin.* Updated by Death Penalty Information Center, 27 July 1998. Available at www.essential.org/dpic/methods.html (accessed 5 August 1998).

———. 2000. *Criminal Sentencing Statistics: Summary Findings.* Available at www.ojp.usdoj.gov/bjs/sent.htm.

Bureau of Labor Statistics. 1998. "Lawyers and Judges," in *1998–99 Occupational Outlook Handbook.* Available at stats.bls.gov/oco/ocos053.htm#outlook (accessed 13 January 1999).

Burger, Warren. 1982. "Isn't There a Better Way?" *American Bar Association Journal* 68. Available through LEXIS-NEXIS (accessed 21 March 2001).

Burns, W. Haywood. 1998. "Law and Race in Early America." In *The Politics of Law,* 3d ed., edited by David Kairys, 279–84. New York: Pantheon Books.

Burt, Robert A. 1979. "The Constitution of the Family." *Supreme Court Review* 1979: 329–95.

Butts, J. 1997. "Prosecuting Juveniles in Criminal Court." NCJJ In Brief 1(4). Pittsburgh, Pa.: National Center for Juvenile Justice. Available at brendan.ncjfcj.unr.edu/ homepage/ncjj/homepage-revised/freq-quest.html#anchor 48562 (accessed 2 July 1999).

Butty, David C. 1996. "Afrocentrism Generates Mixed Results in Detroit and Debate Across Nation." *Detroit News,* 19 May.

Byassee, William S. 1995. "Jurisdiction of Cyberspace: Applying Real World Precedent to the Virtual Community." *Wake Forest Law Review* 30: 197–220.

Caldeira, Gregory, and John R. Wright. 1988. "Organized Interests and Agenda Setting in the U.S. Supreme Court." *American Political Science Review* 82: 1109–28.

Calvert, Clay. 2000. "Media Bashing at the Turn of the Century: The Threat to Free Speech after Columbine High and Jenny Jones." *Detroit College of Law Review* 2000: 151–63.

Canby, William C., Jr. 1987. "The Status of Indian Tribes in American Law Today." *Washington Law Review* 62: 1–22.

Cardozo, Benjamin N. 1924. *The Nature of the Judicial Process.* New Haven: Yale University Press.

Carlson, Peter. 1999. "(THE LAST) TRIAL OF THE CENTURY! Will Bill Clinton's Day in Court Live Up to Its Billing? Let's Look at the Legal Precedent." *Washington Post,* 4 January, p. C1.

Carter, James Coolige. 1907. *Law: Its Origin, Growth and Function.* New York: Knickerbocker Press.

Cate, Fred H. 1997. *Privacy in the Information Age.* Washington, D.C.: The Brookings Institution.

Cawley, Janet. 1987. "Jurist's Job Is to Interpret Law, Not Make It, Bork Says in Last Testimony." *Chicago Tribune,* 20 September, p. 3.

CBS Evening News with Dan Rather, 20 November 1998.

Centers for Disease Control and Prevention. 1997. *National Vital Statistics Reports**check notes,* Vol. 47, No. 18. Available at www.cdc.gov/nchswww/fastats/multiple.htm (accessed 7 July 1999).

Chambers, David L. 1985. "The 'Legalization' of the Family: Toward a Policy of Supportive Neutrality." *University of Michigan Journal of Law Reform* 18: 805–31.

Chase, Adam. 1998. "A Primer on Recent Domain Name Disputes." *Virginia Journal of Law and Technology* 3, Article 3.

Cho, Mildred K. 1999. "Genetic Technologies: Issues for Ethics Committees." *The Mid-Atlantic Ethics Committee Newsletter*, reprinted by The University of Pennsylvania, Center for Bioethics. Available at www.med.upenn.edu/bioethic/library/papers/mildred/ChoMidAtlanticEthics.html (accessed 28 July 1999).

Cirelli, Dominick, Jr. 1997. "Utilizing School Voucher Programs to Remedy School Financing Problems." *Akron Law Review* 30: 469–500.

Claiborne, William. 2000. "Illinois Governor, Citing Errors, Will Block Executions." *Washington Post*, 31 January, p. A1.

Clark, David S. 1981. "Adjudication to Administration: A Statistical Analysis of Federal District Courts in the Twentieth Century." *Southern California Law Review* 55: 65–152.

Clark, Robert C. 1981. The Interdisciplinary Study of Legal Evolution." *Yale Law Journal* 90: 1238–74.

Clinton, William. 1997. "President's Memorandum on the Prohibition on Federal Funding for Cloning of Human Beings." *Weekly Compilation of Presidential Documents* 33, No. 281, 4 March. Available at frwebgate.access.gpo.gov/cgi-bin/multidb.cgi (accessed 7 July 1999).

Cohen, Lloyd R. 1995. *Increasing the Supply of Transplant Organs: The Virtues of a Futures Market*. New York: Springer; Austin, Texas: R. G. Landes.

Coleman, Doriane L. 1996. "Individualizing Justice Through Multiculturalism: The Liberals' Dilemma." *Columbia Law Review* 96: 1093–1167.

Coleman, James S. 1974. *Power and the Structure of Society*. New York: Norton.

———. 1982a. *The Asymmetric Society*. Syracuse, N.Y.: Syracuse University Press.

———. 1982b. *The Foundations of Social Theory*. Cambridge: Harvard University Press.

Collins, Francis S., Director, National Human Genome Research Institute, National Institutes of Health. 1997. "Preventing Genetic Discrimination In Health Insurance." Prepared Statement Before the House Commerce Committee Task Force on Health Records and Genetic Privacy, *Federal News Service*, 22 July.

Collins, Senator Susan M. 2000. "Opening Statement: Hearings on Phony Ids and Credentials via the Internet." U.S. Senate, Permanent Subcommittee on Investigations, 19 May. Available at www.senate.gov/~gov_affairs/051900_coillins.htm (accessed 21 May 2000).

Commission on Structural Alternatives for the Federal Courts of Appeal. 1998. *Final Report*. Submitted to the President and the Congress pursuant to Pub. Law No. 105-119, 18 December. Available at app.comm.uscourts.gov/ (accessed 12 January 1999).

Committee on Organ Procurement and Transplantation Policy, Division of Health Sciences Policy, Institute of Medicine, National Academy of Sciences. 1999. *Organ Procurement and Transplantation: Assessing Current Policies and the Potential Impact of the DHHS Final Rule*. Available at books.nap.edu/books/030906578X/html/16.html#16 (accessed 3 August 1999).

Concise Columbia Encyclopedia, The. 1991. New York: Columbia University Press. Available at daemon.ilt.columbia.edu/academic/digitexts/notes/empiricism.html (accessed 28 January 1998).

Conley, John M., and William M. O'Barr. 1990. *Rules Versus Relationships: The Ethnography of Legal Discourse*. Chicago: University of Chicago Press.

Conrad, Clay S. 1998. *Jury Nullification: The Evolution of a Doctrine*. Durham, N.C.: Carolina Academic Press.

Corcoran, Elizabeth. 1994. "For D.C. Man, a Flier on E-Mail Addresses Yields a 'Net Loss." *Washington Post*, 8 September, p. B11.

Cordell, Robert L. 1994. "Same-Sex Marriage: The Fundamental Right of Marriage and an Examination of Conflict of Laws and the Full Faith and Credit Clause." *Columbia Human Rights Law Review* 26: 247–93.

Corwin, Edward S. 1929. *The Higher Law Background of American Constitutional Law*. Ithaca, N.Y.: Cornell University Press.

Cover, Robert M. 1975. *Justice Accused: Antislavery and the Judicial Process*. New Haven, Conn.: Yale University Press.

Coyle, Marcia, Marianne Lavelle, and Fred Strasser. 1990. "Fatally Flawed." *National Law Journal*, 19 November, pp. 1–2.

Crawshaw-Lewis, Stacey. 1996. "Note and Comment: 'Overpaid' Older Workers and the Age Discrimination in Employment Act." *Washington Law Review* 71: 769–96.

Crespi, Gregory S. 1994. "Overcoming the Legal Obstacles to the Creation of a Futures Market in Bodily Organs." *Ohio State Law Journal* 55: 1–77.

Crimmins, Eileen M., and Dominique G. Ingegneri. 1993. "Trends in Health Among the American Population." In *Demography and Retirement: The Twenty-First Century*, edited by Anna M. Rappaport and Sylvester J. Schieber, 275–96. Westport, Conn.: Praeger.

Curtis, George B. 1977. "The Colonial County Court, Social Forum and Legislative Precedent: Accomack County, Virginia, 1633–1639." *Virginia Magazine of History & Biography* 85: 274–88.

Cushman, John H. 1998. "Senate Imperils Judicial System, Rehnquist Says." *New York Times*, 1 January, p. A1.

Dahl, Robert A. 1956. *A Preface to Democratic Theory*. Chicago: University of Chicago Press.

———. 1957. "Decision-Making in a Democracy: The Supreme Court as a National Policy-Maker." *Journal of Public Law* 6: 279–95.

———. 1961. *Who Governs?* New Haven, Conn.: Yale University Press.

Dahrendorf, Ralf. 1959. *Class and Class Conflict in Industrial Society*. London: Routledge.

Dao, James. 1998. "$200 Billion Bill For Public Works Passed by Congress." *New York Times*, 22 May, p. A1.

Davis, David Brion. 1975. *The Problem of Slavery in the Age of Revolution 1770–1823*. Ithaca, N.Y.: Cornell University Press.

Davis, Peggy C. 1989. "Popular Legal Culture: Law As Microaggression." *Yale Law Journal* 98: 1559–77.

Dawson, Michael, and John Bellamy Foster. 1998. "Virtual Capitalism." In *Capitalism and the Information Age: The Political Economy of the Global Communication Revolution*, edited by Robert W. McChesney, Ellen Meiksins Wood, and John Bellamy Foster, 66–91. New York: Monthly Review Press.

DeLay, Tom. 1998. "Tom DeLay's Judicial Activism Website." Former Web address, www.majoritywhip.house.gov/judges2/ (accessed 3 December 1998).

Denver Post, 6 May 1997.

Dieter, Richard C. 1997. "Innocence and the Death Penalty." Death Penalty Information Center. Available at www.essential.org/dpic/innoc.html (accessed 31 January 2000).

———. 1998. "The Death Penalty in Black and White: Who Lives, Who Dies, Who Decides." Death Penalty Information Center. Available at www.essential.org/dpic/racerpt.html (accessed 10 January 2000).

Dodge, Susan. 1999. "Teens Put Theaters to Test; 3 of 8 Cinemas Let Underage Girls In." *Chicago Sun-Times*, 13 June, p. 4.

Doernberg, Donald. 1985. "'We the People': John Locke, Collective Constitutional Rights, and Standing to Challenge Government Action." *California Law Review* 73: 52–118.

Dolbeare, Kenneth, and Phillip E. Hammond. 1971. *The School Prayer Decision: From Court Policy to Local Practice.* Chicago: University of Chicago Press.

Douglas, Susan J. 1987. *Inventing American Broadcasting, 1899–1922.* Baltimore: Johns Hopkins University Press.

Drexler, Jessica N. 1996. "Governments' Role in Turning Tricks: The World's Oldest Profession in the Netherlands and the United States." *Dickinson Journal of International Law* 15: 201–36.

Dubois, Philip. 1980. *From Ballot to Bench: Judicial Election and the Quest for Accountability.* Austin: University of Texas Press.

Durkheim, Emile. 1951. *Suicide.* New York: Free Press.

Egan, Timothy. 1999. "The Persistence of Polygamy." *New York Times,* 28 February, sec. 6, p. 51.

Ellul, Jacques. 1964. *The Technological Society.* New York: Knopf.

———. 1973. *Propaganda: The Formation of Men's Attitudes.* New York: Random House.

Ely, James W., Jr. 1992. *The Guardian of Every Other Right.* New York: Oxford University Press.

———. 1997. *Property Rights in American History.* New York: Garland Publishing.

Ely, Margo. 1999. "Students Win Narrow Protection in Narrow Victory." *Chicago Daily Law Bulletin,* 14 June 1999, p. 5.

Emswiler, Thomas Keith. 1994. "Defying Precedent: The Army Writing Style." *Military Law Review* 143: 224–49.

Ensign, Jacque. [1997?]. "Homeschooling Gifted Students: An Introductory Guide for Parents." Educational Resources Information Center, U.S. Department of Education, ED414683 97. Available at www.ed.gov/databases/ ERIC_Digests/ed414683.html (accessed 17 June 1999).

Epstein, Lee. 1985. *Conservatives in Court.* Knoxville: University of Tennessee Press.

———. 1991. "Courts and Interest Groups." In *The American Courts: A Critical Assessment,* edited by John B. Gates and Charles A. Johnson, 348–64. Washington, D.C.: Congressional Quarterly Press.

Epstein, Lee, and Jack Knight. 1998. *The Choices Justices Make.* Washington, D.C.: Congressional Quarterly Press.

Eskridge, William N, Jr. 1993. "A History of Same Sex Marriage." *Virginia Law Review* 79: 1419–1513.

Everett, William J. 1987. "Contract and Covenant in Human Community." *Emory Law Journal* 36: 557–68.

Fairfield, Roy P., ed. 1966. *The Federalist Papers.* 2d ed. Garden City, N.Y.: Anchor Books.

Federalist Papers. Emory University School of Law, Public Interest Projects. "The Federalist." Available at www.law.emory.edu/FEDERAL/federalist/federser.html (accessed June/July 1998).

Federal Trade Commission. 1998. "FTC Announces Results of Compliance Testing of over 300 Funeral Homes in the Second Year of the Funeral Rule Offenders Program." FTC Press Release, 25 February. Available at www.ftc.gov/opa/1998/9802/frop-97.htm (accessed 31 January 2000).

Feiler, Christine L. 1998. "Human Embryo Experimentation: Regulation and Relative Rights." *Fordham Law Review* 66: 2435–67.

Felstiner, William L. F. 1974. "Influences of Social Organization on Dispute Processing." *Law and Society Review* 9: 63–94.

Felstiner, William L. F., Richard Abel, and Austin Sarat. 1980–81. "The Emergence and Transformation of Disputes: Naming, Blaming, Claiming..." *Law and Society Review* 15: 631–54.

Felton, Thomas F. 1999. "Sink or Swim? The State of Bilingual Education in the Wake of California Proposition 227." *Catholic University Law Review* 48: 843–79.

Ferdinand, Pamela. 2001. "Vt. House Votes to Outlaw Gay Marriage: Action Is Backlash Against Approval of Civil Unions." *Washington Post,* 17 March, p. A3.

Fields, Thanda A. 1996. "Declaring a Policy of Truth: Recognizing the Wrongful Adoption Claim." *Boston College Law Review* 37: 975–1018.

Fineran, Larry. 1997. Interview by Monica Brady. *Weekend All Things Considered.* National Public Radio, 9 August (transcript # 97080903-216).

Fiore, Faye. 1997. "Multiple Race Choices to Be Allowed on 2000 Census; Demographics: People of Mixed Heritage Will No Longer Be Held to One Label. Policy Will Expand to Other Forms." *Los Angeles Times,* 30 October, p. A1.

Fisk, Margaret Cronin. 1998. "Stratospheric Salary Gap Reflects National Trend: The 'Haves' of Private Law Soar; Public Sector Lawyers Trail Below; 10th Annual Survey of Salaries in the Legal Profession—What Lawyers Earn." *National Law Journal,* 1 June, p. B8.

———. 1999. "School Harassment Suit Boom?" *National Law Journal,* 7 June, p. B19.

Ford, Christopher A. 1994. "Administering Identity: The Determination of 'Race' in Race-Conscious Law." *California Law Review* 82: 1231–56.

Frank, Jerome. 1930. *Law and the Modern Mind.* New York: Coward-McCann.

Frankel, Alison. 1997. "Tale of the Tapes." *American Lawyer,* March, p. 64.

Fried, Joseph P. 1998. "Judge Sets Tentative Trial Date for Five Policemen in Louima Brutality Case." *New York Times,* 19 September, p. B3.

Friedenwald, Herbert. 1974. *The Declaration of Independence, an Interpretation and an Analysis.* New York: Da Capo Press.

Friedman, Lawrence M. 1973. *A History of American Law.* New York: Simon and Schuster.

Friedman, Lawrence M., and Robert V. Percival. 1976. "A Tale of Two Courts: Litigation in Alameda and San Benito Counties." *Law and Society Review* 10: 267–301.

Friedman, Lawrence M. 1984a. *American Law: An Introduction.* New York: W. W. Norton.

———. 1984b. "Rights of Passage: Divorce Law in Historical Perspective." *Oregon Law Review* 63: 666–69.

———. 1984c. *Your Time Will Come: The Law of Age Discrimination and Mandatory Retirement.* New York: Russell Sage Foundation.

———. 1985. *A History of American Law.* 2d ed. New York: Simon and Schuster.

———. 1989. "Popular Legal Culture: Law, Lawyers, and Popular Culture." *Yale Law Journal* 98: 1579–1605.

———. 1998. *American Law.* 2d ed. New York: W. W. Norton.

Frohock, Fred M. 1983. *Abortion: A Case Study in Law and Morals.* Westport, Conn.: Greenwood Press.

Froomkin, A. Michael. 1995. "The Metaphor Is the Key: Cryptography, the Clipper Chip and the Constitution." *University of Pennsylvania Law Review* 143: 709–897.

Gaddis, William. 1994. *A Frolic of His Own.* New York: Poseidon Press.

Galanter, Marc. 1974. "Why the 'Haves' Come Out Ahead: Speculations on the Limits of Legal Change." *Law and Society Review* 9: 95–160.

———. 1983a. "Mega-Law and Mega-Lawyering in the Contemporary United States." In *The Sociology of the Profes-*

sionals: Lawyers, Doctors, and Others, edited by R. Dingwall and P. Lewis, 152–76. New York: St. Martin's Press.

———. 1983b. "Reading the Landscape of Disputes: What We Know and Don't Know (And Think We Know) about Our Allegedly Contentious and Litigious Society." *UCLA Law Review* 31: 4–71.

———. 1994. "Why the 'Haves' Come Out Ahead: Speculations on the Limits of Legal Change." In *Before the Law: An Introduction to the Legal Process*, 5th ed., edited by John J. Bonsignore, et al., 357–68. Boston: Houghton Mifflin Company.

———. 1996. "A Nation Under Lost Lawyers: The Legal Profession at the Close of the Twentieth Century: Lawyers in the Mist: The Golden Age of Legal Nostalgia." *Dickinson Law Review* 100: 549–62.

Gates, Bill. 1995. *The Road Ahead*. New York: Viking.

"Genetic Discrimination: The Next Civil Rights Issue?" 1999. *Health Line* 6. Available through LEXIS-NEXIS (accessed 21 March 2001).

George, Tracey E., and Lee Epstein. 1992. "On the Nature of Supreme Court Decision Making." *American Political Science Review* 86: 323–37.

Gibbons, John J. 1995. "Convergence in Communications Technology and the First Amendment." *Seton Hall Law Review* 25: 1375–96.

Gibson, James L., Gregory A. Caldeira, and Vanessa Baird. 1998. "On the Legitimacy of National High Courts." *American Political Science Review* 92: 343–58.

Gibson, William. 1995. *Neuromancer*. New York: Ace Books.

Gifis, Steven H. 1991. *Law Dictionary*. 3d ed. New York: Barron's Educational Series.

Gildea, Andrew J. 1994. "The Future of the American Jury Trial." In *Before the Law*, 5th ed., edited by John J. Bonsignore, et al., 456–57. Boston: Houghton Mifflin.

Gilder, George. 1989. *Microcosm*. New York: Simon and Schuster.

Gillman, Howard. 1993. *The Constitution Besieged: The Rise and Demise of Lochner Era Police Powers Jurisprudence*. Durham, N.C.: Duke University Press.

Glaberson, William. 2001. "Juries Find Their Central Role in Courts Fading." *New York Times*, 2 March. Available at www.nyt.com (accessed 2 March 2001).

Glassner, Barry. 1999. *The Culture of Fear: Why Americans are Afraid of the Wrong Things*. New York: Basic Books.

Glazer, Nathan. 1975. "Towards An Imperial Judiciary." *The Public Interest* 41: 104–23.

Gleick, James. 1996. "Behind Closed Doors; Big Brother Is Us." *New York Times Sunday Magazine*, 29 September, sec. 6, p. 130.

Glendon, Mary Ann. 1989. *The Transformation of Family Law*. Chicago: University of Chicago Press.

———. 1991. *Rights Talk: The Impoverishment of Political Discourse*. New York: Free Press.

Glod, Maria. 1999. "When Marriage Is Deleted, E-Mail Can Be Evidence; Spouses Taking Cyber-Chat to Court." *Washington Post*, 27 April, p. A1.

Gold, Lisa K. 1998. "Who's Afraid of Big Government? The Federalization of Intercountry Adoption: It's Not as Scary as it Sounds." *Tulsa Law Journal* 34: 109–31.

Goldhaber, Michael D. 1998. "Women's Numbers Rise at the Bigger Law Firms Nationwide." *Legal Intelligencer*, 21 December.

Goldman, Sheldon. 1989a. "Judicial Appointments and the Presidential Agenda." In *The Presidency in American Politics*, edited by Paul Brace, Christine B. Harrington, and Gary King, 120–32. New York: New York University Press.

———. 1989b. "Reagan's Judicial Legacy: Completing the Puzzle and Summing Up." *Judicature* 72: 318–21.

———. 1995. "Judicial Selection Under Clinton: A Midterm Examination." *Judicature* 78: 276–91.

Goldstein, Amy. 1998. "Clinton Orders Better Nursing Home Care." *Washington Post*, 22 July, p. A3.

Gonzalez, Daniel. 2000. "Arizona Win Encourages Bilingual-Ed Opponents." *Arizona Republic* 20 November, p. A1.

Gordon, Robert W. 1984. "Critical Legal Histories." *Stanford Law Review* 36: 57–125.

Gorney, Cynthia. 1999. "Teaching Johnny the Appropriate Way to Flirt." *New York Times Sunday Magazine*, 13 June, sec. 6.

Gostin, Lawrence O., Scott Burris, and Zita Lazzarini. 1999. "The Law and the Public's Health: A Study of Infectious Disease Law in the United States." *Columbia Law Review* 99: 59–128.

Graham, Howard Jay. 1968. *Everyman's Constitution*. Madison: State Historical Society of Wisconsin.

Grant, George. 1969. *Technology and Empire*. Concord, Ontario (Canada): House of Anansi Press Limited.

———. 1986. *Technology and Justice*. Notre Dame, Ind.: Notre Dame University Press.

Greenawalt, Kent. 1995. *Private Consciences and Public Reasons*. New York: Oxford University Press.

Greenhouse, Linda. 2000. "Case on Visitation Rights Hinges on Defining Family." *New York Times on the Web*, 4 January. Available at www.nytimes.com.

Grisham, John. 1992. "The Rise of the Legal Thriller: Why Lawyers Are Throwing the Books at Us." *New York Times* (essay), 18 October, p. 33.

Grunwald, Michael. 1999. "In Vitro, in Error—and Now, in Court." *Washington Post*, 31 March, p. A1.

Hall, Kermit L. 1989. *The Magic Mirror: Law in American History*. New York: Oxford University Press.

Hall, Stephen S. 2000. "Racing Toward Immortality: The Spectacular—And Scary—Promise of Embryonic Cell Research." *New York Times Magazine*, 30 January, p. 33.

Hallifax, Jackie. 2000. "Judge Throws Out Florida's School Voucher Law." *Legal Intelligencer*, 13 March, p. 4.

Halpern, Stephen C., and Charles M. Lamb, eds. 1982. *Supreme Court Activism and Restraint*. Lexington, Mass.: Lexington Books.

Hamblett, Mark. 1999. "Danish Parents' Suit Against NYC Survives." *New York Law Journal*, 22 July. Available at www.nylj.com/stories/99/07/072299a1.htm (accessed 26 May 2000).

Hames, Joanne Banker, and Yvonne Ekern. 1998. *Introduction to Law*. Upper Saddle River, N.J.: Prentice-Hall.

Hanson, Roger A., and Henry W. K. Daley. 1995. Bureau of Justice Statistics, U.S. Department of Justice, "Federal Habeas Corpus Review Challenging State Court Criminal Convictions." September 1995, NCJ-155504. Available at www.ojp.usdoj.gov/bjs/.

Heinz, John P., and Edward O. Laumann. 1982. *Chicago Lawyers: The Social Structure of the Bar*. New York: Russell Sage Foundation; Chicago: American Bar Foundation.

Henry, Patrick. 1788. "In the Ratifying Convention of Virginia, 4–12 June 1788." *The Debates in the Several State Conventions on the Adoption of the Federal Constitution, Elliot's Debates, Vol. 3*. Available at memory.loc.gov./ammem/amlaw/lwed.html (accessed 21 March 2001).

Herrnson, Paul. 1998. *Congressional Elections: Campaigning at Home and in Washington*. Washington, D.C.: Congressional Quarterly Press.

Herrnson, Paul S., Ronald G. Shaiko, and Clyde Wilcox, eds. 1998. *The Interest Group Connection*. Chatham, N.J.: Chatham House Publishers, 1998.

Higgenbotham, A. Leon, Jr. 1978. *In the Matter of Color*. New York: Oxford University Press.

Hirsch, Adam J. 1996. "Inheritance and Inconsistency." *Ohio State Law Journal* 57: 1057–162.

Hoekstra, Valerie J., and Jeffrey A. Segal. 1996. "The Shepherding of Local Public Opinion: The Supreme Court and *Lambs Chapel*." *Journal of Politics* 58: 1079–102.

Holden, Mary Wisniewski. 1997. "Questions Remain after 10 Years of Sentencing Guidelines." *Chicago Lawyer* December: 8–10.

Holland, Kenneth M., ed. 1991. *Judicial Activism in Comparative Perspective*. New York: St. Martin's Press.

Holmes, Oliver Wendell, Jr. 1918. "Natural Law." *Harvard Law Review* 32: 40–76.

Holtzman, Abraham. 1963. *The Townsend Movement: A Political Study*. New York: Octagon Books.

Horowitz, Donald L. 1977. *The Courts and Social Policy*. Washington, D.C.: The Brookings Institution Press.

Horsley, Lynn. 1997. "Crowd Backs Afrocentric Curriculum: School Board Is Urged to Counter Desegregation Lawyer's Opposition." *Kansas City Star*, 9 December, p. B1.

Horwitz, Morton J. 1977. *The Transformation of American Law: 1780–1860*. Cambridge, Mass.: Harvard University Press.

———. 1992. *The Transformation of American Law, 1870–1960: The Crisis of Legal Orthodoxy*. New York: Oxford University Press.

Hughes, Langston. 1953. *Simple Takes a Wife*. New York: Simon and Schuster.

Hume, David. [1751] 1957. *Enquiry Concerning the Principles of Morals*. New York: Liberal Arts Press.

Hurst, James Willard. 1950. *The Growth of American Law: The Law Makers*. Boston: Little, Brown.

———. 1982. *Law and Markets in United States History*. Madison: University of Wisconsin Press.

Jacob, Herbert. 1988. *Silent Revolution: The Transformation of Divorce Law in the United States*. Chicago: University of Chicago Press.

Jacobus, Patricia. 2000. "Napster Suit Tests New Copyright Law." *CNET News.com*, 11 April. Available at news.cnet.com/news/0-1005-200-1679581.html.

Jefferson, Thomas. 1787. *Notes on the State of Virginia*. Available at www.pbs.org/jefferson/archives/documents (accessed 5 May 2000).

———. 1905. *The Writings of Thomas Jefferson*. Vol. 15. Edited by Andrew A. Lipscomb and Albert Ellery Bergh. Washington, D.C.: Thomas Jefferson Memorial Association of the United States.

———. 1924. *The Works of Thomas Jefferson*. 12 vols. Edited by Paul Leicester Ford. New York: G. P. Putnam and Sons.

John, Richard R. 1995. *Spreading the News: The American Postal System from Franklin to Morse*. Cambridge, Mass.: Harvard University Press.

Johnson, George. 1999. "The Genome Race." *Washington Times*, 6 July, p. A13.

Jimenez, Ralph. 1998. "Marriage Age Remains 13 for Girls, 14 for Boys." *Boston Globe*, 12 April, p. 7.

Joint Economic Committee. 1998. "The Economics of the Estate Tax." U.S. Congress. Available at www.house.gov/jec/fiscal/tx-grwth/estattax/estattax.htm (accessed 30 September 1999).

Jones, James E., Jr. 1982. "Reverse Discrimination in Employment: Judicial Treatment of Affirmative Action Programs in the United States." *Harvard Law Journal* 25: 217–45.

Kagan, Robert A., Bliss Cartwright, Lawrence M. Friedman, and Stanton Wheeler. 1977. "The Business of State Supreme Courts: 1870–1970." *Stanford Law Review* 30: 121–56.

Kairys, David, ed. 1990. *The Politics of Law: A Progressive Critique*. New York: Pantheon.

Katsch, M. Ethan. 1989. *The Electronic Media and the Transformation of Law*. New York: Oxford University Press.

Kaufmann, Melinda B. 1999. "Genetic Discrimination in the Workplace: An Overview of Existing Protections." *Loyola University Chicago Law Journal* 30: 393–438.

Keller, Amy. 1999. "President, Lawyers Ready for Their Turn House Managers Say Clinton Should Be Convicted." *Roll Call*, 18 January.

Kennedy, Duncan. 1983. "The Political Significance of the Structure of the Law School Curriculum." *Seton Hall Law Review* 14: 1–16.

———. 1990. "Legal Education as Training for Hierarchy." In *The Politics of Law: A Progressive Critique*, edited by David Kairys, 54–75. New York: Pantheon Books.

Kens, Paul. 1990. *Judicial Power and Reform Politics: The Anatomy of* Lochner v. New York. Lawrence: University of Kansas Press.

Kerwin, Cornelius. 1994. *Rulemaking: How Government Agencies Write Law and Make Policy*. Washington, D.C.: Congressional Quarterly Press.

Kevorkian, Jack. 1991. *Prescription Medicide: The Goodness of Planned Death*. Amherst, N.Y.: Prometheus Books.

Key, V. O. 1964. *Politics, Parties, and Pressure Groups*. New York: Cromwell.

Kibble-Smith, Brian. 1985. "Can Good Medicine Be Bad Law?" *Chicago-Kent Law Review* 61: 151–64.

Kleiman, Erika Lynn. 1997. "Caring for Our Own: Why American Adoption Law and Policy Must Change." *Columbia Journal of Law & Social Problems*, 30: 327–68.

Klein, Chris. 1997. "Minorities Up At Law Schools." *National Law Journal* 20 October, p. A6.

Kluger, Richard. 1976. *Simple Justice*. New York: Knopf.

Knight, Jack, and Lee Epstein. 1996a. "The Norm of Stare Decisis." *American Journal of Political Science* 40: 1018–35.

———. 1996b. "On the Struggle for Judicial Supremacy." *Law and Society Review* 30: 87–120.

Koch, Wendy. 1999. "Bill Would Overturn Suicide Law." *USA Today*, 28 October, p. A1.

Korman, Richard. 1998. "Lo! Here Come the Technology Patents. Lo! Here Come the Lawsuits!" *New York Times*, 27 December.

Kritzer, Herbert. 1990. *The Justice Broker*. New York: Oxford University Press.

———. 1998. "The Wages of Risk: The Returns of Contingency Fee Legal Practice." *DePaul Law Review* 47: 267–315.

Kroll, Ed. 1994. *The Whole Internet*. 2d ed. Sebastopol, Calif.: O'Reilly and Associates.

Kruckenberg, Brian L. 1998. "'I Don't': Determining Ownership of the Engagement Ring When the Engagement Terminates." *Washburn Law Journal* 37: 425–38.

Kurland, Phillip. 1979. "Government By Judiciary." *University of Arkansas, Little Rock Law Journal* 2: 307–25.

Kutler, Stanley. 1971. *Privilege and Creative Destruction: The Charles River Bridge Case*. Philadelphia: Lippincott.

Lash, Steve. 1998. "Two Justices Assail Federal Criminal Code: Too Many Laws Cause Overload for Judges." *Cincinnati Enquirer*, 12 March, p. A8.

Laslett, Peter. 1960. *Two Treatises of Government: A Critical Edition with an Introduction and Apparatus Criticus*. Cambridge: Cambridge University Press.

Lawrence, Curtis. 1996. "Cultural Immersion Programs Face Review: MPS Board Takes Action after Ban on Teaching of Afrocentrism Fails." *Milwaukee Journal Sentinel*, 19 December, p. 1.

'Lectric Law Library. 1999. "Newsworthy Litigation Documents." Available at www.lectlaw.com/top1.htm (accessed 15 June 1999).

LeDuc, Daniel. 2000. "With President on Hand, Gun Locks Become Law; Glendening Signs Measure Requiring Child-proof Devices." *Washington Post*, 12 April, p. B4.

Lee, Harper. 1960. *To Kill A Mockingbird*. New York: Warner Books.

Legislative Analyst's Office (California). 1995. "The 'Three Strikes and You're Out' Law: A Preliminary Assessment." 6 January. Available at www.lao.ca.gov/sc010695.html (accessed 19 March 2001).

Lempert, Richard, and Joseph Sanders. 1986. *An Invitation to Law and Social Science*. New York: Longman.

Lessenberry, Jack. 1994. "Death Becomes Him." *Vanity Fair* July, pp. 108–12.

Lessig, Lawrence. 1995. "The Path of Cyberlaw." *Yale Law Journal* 104: 1743–55.

Locke, John. [1690] 1960. "The Second Treatise of Government: An Essay Concerning the True Original, Extent, and End of Civil Government." In *Two Treatises of Government: A Critical Edition with an Introduction and Apparatus Criticus* by Peter Laslett. Cambridge: Cambridge University Press. Also available at www.swan.ac.uk/poli/texts/index.htm (accessed 5 May 2000) and history.hanover.edu/early/locke/ j-12-001.htm (accessed 14 June 2000).

Lowi, Theodore J. 1969. *The End of Liberalism: The Second Republic of the United States*. New York: Norton.

Lowy, Joan. 1999. "Opposition to Vaccinations Is Worrisome to Physicians; Outbreaks of Kids' Diseases Are Feared; Critics' Rhetoric Is Taking a Hard Edge." *San Diego Union-Tribune*, 26 May, p. A-25.

Lubove, Roy. 1968. *The Struggle for Social Security 1900–1935*. Cambridge, Mass.: Harvard University Press.

Luke, Timothy W. 1991. "Community and Ecology." *Telos* 8: 69–79.

Luker, Kristin. 1984. *Abortion and the Politics of Motherhood*. Berkeley: University of California Press.

———. 1996. *Dubious Conceptions: The Politics of Teenage Pregnancy*. Cambridge, Mass. Harvard University Press.

Lukes, Steven, and Andrew Scull, eds. 1983. *Durkheim and the Law*. New York: St. Martin's Press.

Maier, Pauline. 1997. *American Scripture: Making the Declaration of Independence*. New York: Knopf.

Maine, Henry Sumner. 1861. *Ancient Law*. London: J. Murray.

Malcolm, Andrew H. 1985. "The End of the Quinlan Case, but Not the Issue It Raised." *New York Times*, 16 June, sec. 4, p. 22.

Malone, Dumas. 1975. *The Story of the Declaration of Independence*. New York: Oxford University Press.

Maltz, Earl. 1983. "Some New Thoughts on an Old Problem: The Role of the Intent of the Framers." *Boston University Law Review* 63: 811–50.

Mann, Bruce H. 1994. "Essay: Formalities and Formalism in the Uniform Probate Code." *University of Pennsylvania Law Review* 142: 1033–62.

Mannies, Jo. 1999. "Ashcroft Co-sponsors Bill to Ban 'Partial-birth' Abortion Nationwide; Senator Blasts Clinton for Vetoing Previous Bans." *St. Louis Post-Dispatch*, 30 April, p. B3.

Manwaring, David. 1962. *Render Unto Caesar: The Flag Salute Controversy*. Chicago: University of Chicago Press.

Maranatha Christian Journal, 23 May 2000. Available at www.mcjonline.com/news/news3109.htm.

Margolick, David. 1989. "The Lonely View from the Bench for the New Judge Who Must Undergo a Rite of Passage." *New York Times*, 6 January, pp. B9–10.

Marshall, Thomas. 1989. *Public Opinion and the Supreme Court*. New York: Longman.

Marzulli, John. 1998. "Louima Lawyers Sue, Cite PBA Obstruction." *New York Daily News*, 7 August, p. 30.

Masters, Brooke A., and Michael D. Shear. 2000. "Potomac Pipe Fight Heads for High Court." *Washington Post*, 31 May, p. B1.

Mayer, Carl J. 1990. "Personalizing the Impersonal: Corporations and the Bill of Rights." *Hastings Law Journal* 41: 577–667.

Mayer, Caroline E. 2000. "Web Also Revolutionizing ID Fakery." *Washington Post*, 19 May, available at www.washingtonpost.com/wp-dyn/articles/A29724-2000May18.html (accessed 23 May 2000).

McCann, Michael W. 1994. *Rights At Work*. Chicago: University of Chicago Press.

McClintock, Pamela. 2000. "Gibson Hikes Summer Associate Pay." *The Recorder*, 6 April 2000, p. 1.

McDowell, Gary L. 1988. *Curbing the Courts*. Baton Rouge: Louisiana State University Press.

McGuire, Kevin T. 1993. *The Supreme Court Bar: Legal Elites in the Washington Community*. Charlottesville: University of Virginia Press.

McIntosh, Wayne V. 1990. *The Appeal of Civil Law: A Political-Economic Analysis of Litigation*. Urbana: University of Illinois Press.

McIntosh, Wayne V., and Cynthia L. Cates. 1997. *Judicial Entrepreneurship: The Role of the Judge in the Marketplace of Ideas*. Westport, Conn.: Greenwood Press.

"McVeigh Conviction, Sentence Upheld." 1998. *Washington Post*, 9 September, p. A5.

Melton, Gary B. 1993. "Children, Families, and the Courts in the Twenty-First Century." *Southern California Law Review* 66: 1993–2047.

Merrill, Thomas W. 1987. "The Individual Liberties Within the Body of the Constitution." *Case Western Reserve Law Review* 37: 597–630.

Merry, Sally Engle. 1981. *Urban Danger: Life in a Neighborhood of Strangers*. Philadelphia: Temple University Press.

———. 1990. *Getting Justice and Getting Even*. Chicago: University of Chicago Press.

Meryhew, Richard. 1998. "When Teen Reneged on Taking Girl to Prom, She Took Him to Court." *Minneapolis Star Tribune*, 3 June, p. 1B.

Meyrowitz, Joshua. 1985. *No Sense of Place: The Impact of Electronic Media on Social Behavior*. New York: Oxford University Press.

Michigan Law Review. 1985. "Heartbalm Statutes and Deceit Actions." *Michigan Law Review* 83: 1770–97.

Miller, Arthur R., and Michael H. Davis. 1990. *Intellectual Property: Patents, Trademarks, and Copyrights in a Nutshell*. 2d ed. St. Paul, Minn.: West Publishing.

Mills, Michelle D. 1998. "Fetal Abuse Prosecutions: The Triumph of Reaction over Reason." *DePaul Law Review* 47: 989–1040.

Mohr, James C. 1978. *Abortion in America*. New York: Oxford University Press.

Mullenix, Linda. 1986. "A Branch Too Far." *Georgetown Law Journal* 75: 99–157.

Nash, Gerald D., Noel H. Pugach, and Richard F. Tomasson, eds. 1988. *Social Security: The First Half-Century*. Albuquerque: University of New Mexico Press.

National Center for Juvenile Justice. 2000. "Q&A." Available at www.ncjfcj.unr.edu/homepage/ncjj/homepage—revised/freq-quest.html (accessed 14 June 2000).

National Center for State Courts. 1994a. "Caseload Highlights: Tort Filings in the Nation's State Courts, 1974–1994." Available at www.ncsc.dni.us/research/csp/tortfile.htm (accessed 10 June 2000).

———. 1994b. "National State Court Caseload Trends, 1984–1994 Caseload Highlights." Available at www.ncsc. dni.us/research/csp/csphigh1.htm (accessed 2 June 2000).

National Journal Group, *The Hotline*, 11 December 1998.

National Highway Traffic Safety Administration, U.S. Department of Transportation. 1999. "Saving Teenage Lives." Appendix B, "Characteristics of Selected U.S. Licensing Laws." Available at: www.nhtsa.dot.gov/people/injury/newdriver/ SaveTeens/append_b.html (accessed 5 July 1999).

National Law Journal. 1 June, 22 June, 31 August 1998. Available through LEXIS-NEXIS (accessed 21 March 2001).

National Public Radio, *Morning Edition*, 11 March 1995, 30 June 1998 (transcript #98063016-210).

Neath, Mark. 1995. "American Indian Gaming Enterprises and Tribal Membership: Race, Exclusivity, and a Perilous Future." *University of Chicago Law School Roundtable* 2. Available through LEXIS-NEXIS (accessed 21 March 2001).

Nedelsky, Jennifer. 1990. *Private Property and the Limits of American Constitutionalism: The Madisonian Framework and Its Legacy*. Chicago: University of Chicago Press.

Neely, David E. 1994. "Pedagogy of Culturally Biased Curriculum in Public Education: An Emancipatory Paradigm for Afrocentric Educational Initiatives." *Capital University Law Review* 23: 131–50.

Negroponte, Nicholas. 1995. *Being Digital*. New York: Knopf.

Nelson, Robert L. 1994. "The Futures of American Lawyers: A Demographic Profile of a Changing Profession in a Changing Society." *Case Western Reserve Law Review* 44: 345–406.

Nelson, William E. 1988. *The Fourteenth Amendment: From Political Principle to Judicial Doctrine*. Cambridge: Harvard University Press.

Neubauer, David W. 1997. *Judicial Process: Law, Courts and Politics in the United States*. Fort Worth, Tex.: Harcourt Brace.

New York Times, 4 June 1998, 22 June 1999, 5 August 1999.

Ng, Jonathan. 1999. "Rated H (As in 'Ha!') That's What Most Teens Think about Efforts to Keep Them Out of R-rated Films." *Kansas City Star*, 25 June, p. E8.

Norgren, Jill, and Serena Nanda. 1988. *American Cultural Pluralism and Law*. New York: Praeger.

O'Brien, David M. 1995. *Constitutional Law and Politics*. 2d ed. New York: W. W. Norton.

———. 1996. *Storm Center: The Supreme Court in American Politics*. 4th ed. New York: W. W. Norton.

O'Connor, Karen. 1980. *Women's Organizations' Use of the Courts*. Lexington, Mass.: Lexington Books.

———. 1998. "Lobbying the Justices or Lobbying for Justice?" In *The Interest Group Connection*, edited by Paul Herrnson, et al., 267–88. Chatham, N.J.: Chatham House Publishers.

Office of Management and Budget. 1999. "Draft Provisional Guidance on the Implementation of the 1997 Standards for Federal Data on Race and Ethnicity," prepared by the Tabulation Working Group, Interagency Committee for the Review of Standards for Data on Race and Ethnicity. Washington, D.C., 17 February. Available at U.S. Census Bureau, Race Data, "Issues for 2000 Census," www.census. gov/population/ www/socdemo/race.html (accessed 15 August 1999).

Olson, Mancur. 1971. *The Logic of Collective Action*. Cambridge, Mass.: Harvard University Press.

Orfield, Gary, and John T. Yun. 1999. "Resegregation in American Schools." *The Civil Rights Project*, Harvard University, June. Available at www.law.harvard.edu/groups/ civilrights/publications/resegregation99.html (accessed 30 June 1999).

Pace, Kimberly A. 1997. "Recalibrating the Scales of Justice Through National Punitive Damage Reform." *American University Law Review* 46: 1573–638.

Padget, Cindy D. 1997. "The Lost Indians of the Lost Colony: A Critical Legal Study of the Lumbee Indians of North Carolina." *American Indian Law Review* 21: 391–424.

Palermo, Michael T. 1996. "Trust Basics." Available at www. mtpalermo.com/SEC-3.HTM#I2 (accessed 30 September 1999).

Paltrow, Lynn M. 1999. "Pregnant Drug Users, Fetal Persons, and the Threat to *Roe v. Wade*." *Albany Law Review* 62: 999–1055.

Peller, Gary. 1990. "Race Consciousness." *Duke Law Journal* 1990: 758–847.

Peppers, Don, and Martha Rogers. 1993. *The One to One Future*. New York: Doubleday.

Perez, Amanda T. 1998. "Transracial Adoption and the Federal Adoption Subsidy." *Yale Law and Policy Review* 17: 201–47.

Perry, H. W. 1991. *Deciding to Decide: Agenda Setting in the United States Supreme Court*. Cambridge, Mass.: Harvard University Press.

Perry, Michael J. 1999. *We the People: The Fourteenth Amendment and the Supreme Court*. New York: Oxford University Press.

Petrosinelli, Joseph G. 1990. "Note and Comment—The Admissibility of DNA Typing: A New Methodology." *Georgetown Law Journal* 79: 313–35.

Pokorak, Jeffrey J. 1998. "Symposium: Probing the Capital Prosecutor's Perspective: Race of the Discretionary Actors." *Cornell Law Review* 83: 1811–20.

Polikoff, Nancy D. 1993. "We Will Get What We Ask For: Why Legalizing Gay and Lesbian Marriage Will Not 'Dismantle the Legal Structure of Gender in Every Marriage.'" *Virginia Law Review* 79: 1535–99.

Pollak, Michael. 1999. "Doctors Fighting Backlash over Vaccines." *New York Times*, 27 April, p. F7.

Polsby, Nelson W. 1963. *Community Power and Political Theory*. New Haven, Conn.: Yale University Press.

Popenoe, David, and Barbara Dafoe Whitehead. 1999. *The State of Our Unions: The Social Health of Marriage in America*. Publication of The National Marriage Project, Rutgers University. Available at ur.rutgers.edu/medrel/news/ healthandbs/marry.html (accessed 2 July 1999).

Post, Robert C. 1987. "On the Popular Image of the Lawyer: Reflections in a Dark Glass." *California Law Review* 75: 379–89.

Powe, Lucas A., Jr. 1987. *American Broadcasting and the First Amendment*. Berkeley: University of California Press.

Powell, Michael. 1999. "Private Acts, Public Crimes." *Washington Post*, 18 January, p. C1.

Pratt, David A. 1999. "Too Many Physicians: Physician-Assisted Suicide After *Glucksberg/Quill*." *Albany Law Journal of Science and Technology* 9: 161–234.

du Preez, Peter. 1980. *The Politics of Identity*. New York: St. Martin's Press.

Probert, Walter. 1972. *Law, Language and Communication*. Springfield, Ill.: Charles C. Thomas.

Provine, Doris Marie. 1980. *Case Selection in the United States Supreme Court*. Chicago: University of Chicago Press.

Public Broadcasting System. 1998. "Chronology of Dr. Jack Kevorkian's Life and Assisted Suicide Campaign." *The Kevorkian Verdict: The Life and Legacy of the Suicide Doctor*. Aired on *Frontline*. Available at www.pbs.org/wgbh/pages/ frontline/kevorkian/ (accessed 4 January 2000).

Public Citizen, Congress Watch. [1999?]. "Justice/Legal Rights." Available at www.citizen.org/congress/civjus/ home.html (accessed 10 January 1999).

Pulfer, Laura. 1998. "Can You Spell Sour Grapes? Or Litigate?" *Cincinnati Enquirer*, 9 June. Available through LEXIS-NEXIS (accessed 21 March 2001).

Putnam, Robert D. 1995. "Bowling Alone." *Journal of Democracy* 6: 65–78.

Putzel, Michael. 1995. "A Personal Journal from Dow Jones." *Boston Globe*, 6 February, p. 19.

Rao, Radhika. 1998. "Reconceiving Privacy: Relationships and Reproductive Technology." *UCLA Law Review* 45: 1077–123.

Ray, Brian D. 1997. "Home Education Across the United States: Family Characteristics, Student Achievement, and Longitudinal Traits." Home School Legal Defense Association. Available at www.hslda.org/central/statsandreports/ray1997/03.stm (accessed 17 June 1999).

Recording Industry Association of America. 1999. "Online Piracy." Available at www.riaa.com/piracy/pir_op.htm (accessed 5 August 1999).

Redhead, Steve. 1995. *Unpopular Cultures: The Birth of Law and Popular Culture*. New York: Manchester University Press.

Regan, Milton C., Jr. 1993. *Family Law and the Pursuit of Intimacy*. New York: New York University Press.

Rehnquist, William H. 2000. "Panel Attorney Compensation." The 1999 Year-End Report on the Federal Judiciary. Available at www.uscourts.gov/ttb/jan00ttb/jan2000.html (accessed 5 May 2000.).

Reuters News Service, 10 September 1999, 4 April 2000. Available at "Findlaw News," legalnews.findlaw.com/legalnews/s/20000414/n14621403.html.

Reutter, E. Edmund, Jr. 1994. *The Law of Public Education*. 4th ed. Westbury, N.Y.: Foundation Press.

Rheingold, Howard. 1993. *The Virtual Community: Homesteading the Electronic Frontier*. New York: Addison-Wesley.

Rheinstein, Max. 1972. *Marriage Stability, Divorce, and the Law*. Chicago: University of Chicago Press.

Riley, Glenda. 1991. *Divorce: An American Tradition*. New York: Oxford University Press.

Ringle, Ken. 1996. "Beyond the Beltway: You Thought Things Were Strange Here." *Washington Post*, 1 January. Available through LEXIS-NEXIS (accessed 21 March 2001).

Rivard, Michael D. 1992. "Symposium: Contemporary Issues in Administrative Adjudication. Comment: Toward a General Theory of Constitutional Personhood: A Theory of Constitutional Personhood for Transgenic Humanoid Species." *UCLA Law Review* 39: 1425–510.

Robb, Barbara A. 1997. "The Constitutionality of the Defense of Marriage Act in the Wake of *Romer v. Evans*." *New England Law Review* 32: 263–348.

Robinson, Marlyn. 1998. "Law and Popular Culture: Collins to Grisham: A Brief History of the Legal Thriller." *Legal Studies Forum* 22: 21–34.

Robinson, Melissa B. 1999. "53 PBS Stations Did List-Swapping." *Washingtonpost.com*, 10 September. Available at search.washingtonpost.com/wp-srv/WAPO/19990910/V000868-091099-idx.html (accessed 11 September 1999).

Robinson, Shelby E. 1999. "Organs for Sale? An Analysis of Proposed Systems for Compensating Organ Providers." *University of Colorado Law Review* 70: 1019–50.

Rosen, Jeffrey. 1998. "Is Nothing Private." Annals of Law, *New Yorker*, 1 June, pp. 41–51.

———. 1999. "Rehnquist's Choice." *New Yorker*, 11 January, pp. 32–35.

Rosenberg, Gerald N. 1991. *The Hollow Hope: Can Courts Bring About Social Change?* Chicago: University of Chicago Press.

Rothstein, Mark A., Betsy D. Gelb, and Steven G. Craig. 1998. "Protecting Genetic Privacy by Permitting Employer Access Only to Job-Related Employee Medical Information: Analysis of a Unique Minnesota Law." *American Journal of Law and Medicine* 24: 399–416.

Rotunda, Roland. 1988. "Not Much Bang in Litigation Explosion; Race to Courthouse—Or Walk?" *Legal Times*, 15 August, p. 14.

Rovella, David E. 1997. "A Survey of Surveys Ranks the Top U.S. Law Schools." *National Law Journal*, 2 June. Available through LEXIS-NEXIS (accessed 21 March 2001).

Rubenstein, William B. 1996. *Cases and Materials on Sexual Orientation and the Law: Lesbians, Gay Men, and the Law*. St. Paul, Minn.: West Publishing.

Rubin, Eva R. 1982. *Abortion, Politics and the Courts*. Westport, Conn.: Greenwood Press.

———. 1986. *The Supreme Court and the American Family: Ideology and Issues*. Westport, Conn.: Greenwood Press.

Samuels, Warren J., and Arthur S. Miller, eds. 1987. *Corporations and Society*. Westport, Conn.: Greenwood Press.

Sarat, Austin, and William Felstiner. 1995. *Divorce Lawyers and Their Clients: Power and Meaning in the Legal Process*. New York: Oxford University Press.

Schaefer, Stephen. 1999. "Natural Born Scapegoats? Hollywood Takes it on the Chops in Wake of High School Shootings." *Boston Globe*, 28 June, p. 37.

Schattschneider, E. E. 1960. *The Semi-Sovereign People: A Realist's View of Democracy in America*. New York: Holt, Rinehart, and Winston.

Scheingold, Stuart A. 1974. *The Politics of Rights: Lawyers, Public Policy, and Political Change*. New Haven, Conn.: Yale University Press.

Schlozman, Kay Lehman, and John T. Tierney. 1986. *Organized Interests and American Democracy*. New York: Harper and Row.

Schmidt, Barbara. [1999?]. "Mark Twain Quotations, Newspaper Collections, and Related Resources." Available online at www.tarleton.edu/~schmidt/Familiarity.html (accessed 6 July 1999).

Schmitt, Ben. 1999a. "Judge Must Decide if Jewell Was Public or Private Figure." *Law News Network.com*, 26 July. Available at www.lawnewsnet.com/stories/A3773-1999Jul23.html (accessed 27 July 1999).

———. 1999b. "Appeals Court Will Consider Jewell Public Figure Ruling." *Fulton County Daily Report*, 18 November. Available through LEXIS-NEXIS (accessed 21 March 2001).

Schmitt, Eric. 1989. "Appeal on Abortion Refused; Woman in Coma Is Readied." *New York Times*, 11 February, p. 26.

Schubert, Glendon. 1972. "Judicial Policymaking." In *The Supreme Court in American Politics: Judicial Activism vs. Judicial Restraint*, edited by David F. Forte, 112–25. Lexington, Mass.: Heath.

Sconiers, Nicole D. 1994. "The Multicultural Whirl of Racial Identity." *Baltimore Sun*, 15 September, p. 15A.

Seelye, Katharine Q. 1999. "PBS Stations Admit Swaps of Donor Lists since 1981." *New York Times*, 21 July, p. A18.

———. "Specialists Report Rise in Adoptions That Fail." *New York Times*, 24 March. Available through LEXIS-NEXIS (accessed 21 March 2001).

Segal, David. 1998. "Pursuing Clinton Suits Him Just Fine: Using Subpoenas to Attack, Larry Klayman Moves into Scandal Spotlight." *Washington Post*, 30 May. Available through LEXIS-NEXIS (accessed 21 March 2001).

Segal, Jeffrey A. 1991. "Courts, Executives, and Legislatures." In *The American Courts: A Critical Assessment*, edited by

John B. Gates and Charles A. Johnson, 373–93. Washington, D.C.: Congressional Quarterly Press.

Segal, Jeffrey A., and Harold J. Spaeth. 1993. *The Supreme Court and the Attitudinal Model*. New York: Cambridge University Press.

Segal, Jeffrey A., and Harold J. Spaeth. 1996a. "The Influence of *Stare Decisis* on the Votes of U.S. Supreme Court Justices." *American Journal of Political Science* 40: 971–1003.

———. 1996b. "Norms, Dragons, and *Stare Decisis*: A Response." *American Journal of Political Science* 40: 1064–82.

Segal, Jeffrey A., Lee Epstein, Charles M. Cameron, and Harold J. Spaeth. 1995. "Ideological Values and the Votes of U.S. Supreme Court Justices Revisited." *Journal of Politics* 57: 812–20.

Sege, Irene. 1999. "A $50,000 Dilemma on Campus; Top Students Wrestle with Egg Donor Lure." *Boston Globe*, 6 March, p. A1.

Sennett, Richard. 1978. *The Fall of Public Man*. New York: Alfred A. Knopf.

Seron, Caroll. 1996. *The Business of Practicing Law: The Work Lives of Solo and Small-Firm Attorneys*. Philadelphia: Temple University Press.

Shelley, Percy Bysshe. 1820. *Prometheus Unbound: A Lyrical Drama in Four Acts*, Act IV. Available at www.english.upenn.edu/~jlynch/Frank/PShelley/prom4.html (accessed 4 August 1998).

Sickmund, Melissa. 1997a. "Delinquency Cases, 1995." Adapted from Sickmund, *Offenders in Juvenile Court, 1995* (Washington, D.C.: Office of Juvenile Justice and Delinquency Prevention, 1997). Available at ojjdp.ncjrs.org/ojstatbb/qa031.html (accessed 2 July 1999).

———. 1997b. "States That Changed Their Transfer Laws, 1992–1995." Adapted from Sickmund, H. Snyder, and E. Poe-Yamagata, "Juvenile Offenders and Victims: 1997 Update on Violence" in *OJJDP Statistical Briefing Book* (Washington, D.C.: Office of Juvenile Justice and Delinquency Prevention, 1997). Available at ojjdp.ncjrs.org/ojstatbb/qa068.html (accessed 2 July 1999).

———. 1998. "Upper Age of Original Juvenile Court Jurisdiction, 1997." Adapted from P. Torbet and L. Szymanski, "State Legislative Responses to Violent Juvenile Crime: 1996–97 Update," in *OJJDP Statistical Briefing Book* (Washington, D.C.: Office of Juvenile Justice and Delinquency Prevention, 1998). Available at www.ojjdp.ncjrs.org/ojstatbb/qa085.html (accessed 21 March 2001).

Silver, Jay Sterling. 1994. "Professionalism and the Hidden Assault on the Adversarial Process." *Ohio State Law Journal* 55: 855–87.

Skolnick, Arlene S., and Jerome H. Skolnick, eds. 1971. *Family in Transition*. Boston: Little, Brown.

Skorownek, Stephen. 1982. *Building a New American State: The Expansion of Administrative Capacities, 1877–1920*. New York: Cambridge University Press.

Sloan, Eugene. 1991. "Pro-choice Forces Rally in Support of TV Movie." *USA Today*, 11 April. Available through LEXIS-NEXIS (accessed 21 March 2001).

Smith, Adam. 1776. *An Inquiry into the Nature and Causes of the Wealth of Nations*. Available at www.bibliomania.com/NonFiction/Smith/Wealth (accessed 26 July 1999).

———. [1776] 1937. *The Wealth of Nations*. New York: Random House.

Smith, Christopher E. 1997. *Courts, Politics, and Judicial Process*. New York: Nelson Hall.

Smith, Steven K., Carol J. DeFrances, Patrick A. Langan, and John Goerdt. 1995. *Tort Cases in Large Counties*. Bulletin NCJ-153177. Washington, D.C.: Bureau of Justice Statistics, U.S. Department of Justice.

Smolla, Rodney A. 1990. *Jerry Falwell v. Larry Flynt: The First Amendment on Trial*. Urbana: University of Illinois Press.

———. 1992. *Free Speech in an Open Society*. New York: Knopf.

Snell, Tracy L. 1999. *Capital Punishment 1998*. Bulletin NCJ 179012. Washington, D.C.: U.S. Department of Justice, Bureau of Justice Statistics, December. Available at www.ojp.usdoj.gov/bjs/pubalp2.htm#Capital Punishment (accessed 6 January 2000).

Snyder, Howard. 1997. "Estimated Number of Juvenile Arrests, 1997." Adapted from H. Snyder, "Juvenile Arrests in 1997." In *Statistical Briefing Book* (Washington, D.C.: Office of Juvenile Justice and Delinquency Prevention, Office of Justice Programs, U.S. Department of Justice). Available at ojjdp.ncjrs.org/ojstatbb/qa001.html (accessed 2 July 1999).

Songer, Donald, and Reginald S. Sheehan. 1993. "Interest Group Success in the Courts: Amicus Participation in the Supreme Court." *Political Research Quarterly* 46: 339–54.

Steele, Walter W., Jr., and Elizabeth G. Thornburg. 1988. "Jury Instructions: A Persistent Failure to Communicate." *North Carolina Law Review* 67: 77–119.

Steinhauer, Jennifer. 1994. "3 Million Points of Light Waiting to Be Turned On." *New York Times*, 18 December, Sunday, final ed., sec. 1, p. 26.

Stetz, Michael. 1999. "Entry to R-rated Films Gets Tougher; But S.D. Teens Scoff at Clinton Crackdown." *San Diego Union-Tribune*, 9 June, p. A1.

Strossen, Nadine. 1993. "Pro Bono Legal Work: For the Good of Not Only the Public, but Also the Lawyer and the Legal Profession." *Michigan Law Review* 91: 2122–49.

Sunstein, Cass R. 1995. "The First Amendment in Cyberspace." *Yale Law Journal* 104: 1757–804.

Suro, Robert. 1999. "Rehnquist: Too Many Offenses Are Becoming Federal Crimes." *Washington Post*, 1 January, p. A2.

Tajfel, Henri, ed. 1978. *Differentiation Between Social Groups*. London: Academic Press.

Taylor, Stuart. 1999. "Title IX's Undreamed of Reach." *The Connecticut Law Tribune*, 7 June.

Tedeschi, Bob. 1999. "Personalized E-Mail Ads: Low Cost, High Response Rate." *New York Times on the Web*. Available at www.nytimes.com/library/tech/99/08/cyber/commerce/09commerce.html (accessed 9 August 1999).

Thomas, Claire. 1991. *Sex Discrimination in a Nutshell*. 2d ed. St. Paul Minn.: West Publishing.

Thoreau, Henry David. [1849] 1975. "Civil Disobedience." In *The Selected Works of Thoreau*. Revised, with a new introduction by Walter Harding. Boston: Houghton Mifflin.

Times Union (Albany), 21 October 1997.

de Tocqueville, Alexis. 1835. *Democracy in America*. Available at xroads.virginia.edu/~HYPER/DETOC/toc_indx.html.

———. [1835] 1945. *Democracy in America*. Vol. 1. New York: Alfred A. Knopf.

Tönnies, Ferdinand. [1887] 1957. *Community and Society (Gemeinschaft und Gesellschaft)*. East Lansing: Michigan State University Press.

Torbet, Patricia. 1996. *State Responses to Serious and Violent Juvenile Crime*. Washington, D.C.: Office of Juvenile Justice and Delinquency Prevention. Available at www.ncjrs.org/txtfiles/statresp.txt (accessed 5 July 1999).

Totenberg, Nina. 1997. "Judicial Intimidation." In *Morning Edition*. National Public Radio, 26 September (transcript # 97092615-210).

Tribe, Lawrence H. 1991. "The Constitution in Cyberspace: Law and Liberty Beyond the Electronic Frontier." *The Humanist*, 26 March. Available at www.sjgames.com/ss/tribe.html (accessed 20 March 2000).

Truman, David. 1951. *The Governmental Process*. New York: Knopf.

Turow, Scott. 1977. *One L*. New York: Farrar, Straus, and Giroux.

Tushnet, Mark. 1982. "Corporations and Free Speech." In *The Politics of Law: A Progressive Critique*, edited by David Kairys, 253–61. New York: Pantheon.

Twiss, Benjamin. 1942. *Lawyers and the Constitution: How Laissez Faire Came to the Supreme Court*. Princeton, N.J.: Princeton University Press.

Tyler, Tom R. 1990. *Why People Obey the Law*. New Haven, Conn.: Yale University Press.

———. 1997. "Citizen Discontent with Legal Procedures: A Social Science Perspective on Civil Procedure Reform." *American Journal of Comparative Law* 45: 871–900.

Ugelow, Stewart. 1994. "Address for Success: Internet Name Game; Individuals Snap Up Potentially Valuable Corporate E-Mail IDs." *Washington Post*, 11 August, p. A1.

Uhlman, Thomas, and Darlene Walker. 1980. "He Takes Some of My Time, I Take Some of His: An Analysis of Judicial Sentencing Patterns in Jury Cases." *Law and Society Review* 14.

Ulmer, S. Sidney. 1984. "The Supreme Court's Certiorari Decisions: Conflict as a Predictive Variable." *American Political Science Review* 78: 901–18.

Unger, Roberto Mangabeira. 1976. *Law in Modern Society: Toward a Criticism of Social Theory*. New York: Free Press.

United Press International, 27 September 1997.

Updike, John. 1997. *Toward the End of Time*. New York: Alfred A. Knopf.

USA Today, 22 July 1998.

U.S. Census Bureau. 1998. "Employed Civilians, by Occupation, Sex, Race, and Hispanic Origin: 1983 and 1997." In *Statistical Abstract of the United States*, 1997. Available at www.census.gov/prod/3/98pubs/98statab/cc98stab.htm (accessed 12 January 1999).

———. [1999?]. "U.S. POPClock Projection." Available at www.census.gov/cgi-bin/popclock (accessed 13 January 1999).

U.S. Chamber of Commerce. [1999?]. "Policy and Issues." Available at www.uschamber.org/policy/d-reg.html (accessed 10 January 1999).

U.S. Congress. 1998. Joint Committee on Taxation. *Present Law and Background Relating to Estate and Gift Taxes: Hearing before the House Committee on Ways and Means*. JCX-2-98, 28 January.

U.S. Copyright Office. 1998. "Fair Use," Form Letter 102. Available at www.loc.gov/copyright/circs/index.html#circ1 (accessed 4 August 1999).

———. 1999. "Circular 1." Available at lcweb.loc.gov/copyright/ (accessed 4 August 1999).

U.S. Courts. 1997a. "Three-Judge District Court Hearings, by Nature of Suit," Table S-20. The Federal Judiciary Homepage. Available at www.uscourts.gov (accessed 19 March 2001).

———. 1997b. "Understanding the Federal Courts." The Federal Judiciary Homepage. Available at www.uscourts gov/understanding_courts/8997.htm, www.uscourts.gov/understanding_courts/89920.htm, and www.uscourts.gov/understanding_courts/89922.htm (accessed 1 October 1998).

———. 1998a. "Judicial Business of the United States Courts, U.S. District Courts: Criminal Defendants Disposed of, by Type of Disposition and Offense, During the Twelve-Month Period Ending September 30, 1997." Available at www.uscourts.gov/dirrpt98/contents.html.

———. 1998b. "Understanding the Federal Courts." The Federal Judiciary Homepage. Available at www.uscourts.gov/understanding_courts/89912.htm, www.uscourts.gov/

understanding_courts/89919.htm, and www.uscourts.gov/understanding_courts/89921.htm.

U.S. Food and Drug Administration, Center for Food Safety and Applied Nutrition. [2000?]. "Office of Cosmetics Fact Sheet." Available at vm.cfsan.fda.gov/~dms/cos-215.html (accessed 21 March 2000).

U.S. News and World Report. 1998. "1998 Annual Guide; Best Graduate Schools, Law School." Available at www.usnews.com/usnews/edu/beyond/gradrank/law/gdlawt1.htm (accessed 14 January 1999).

U.S. Patent and Trademark Office. 1993. *Trademark Manual of Examining Procedure*. 2d ed. Washington, D.C.: GPO.

———. 1995. "Basic Facts About Registering a Trademark." Available at www.uspto.gov/web/offices/tac/doc/basic/basic_facts.html.

U.S. Supreme Court. 2000. "About the Supreme Court." Available at www.supremecourtus.gov/about/about.htm.

Vinson, Ken. 1996. "Fred Rodell's Case Against the Law." *Florida State University Law Review* 24: 107–19.

Vobejda, Barbara. 1998. "Billy's Story: Adopting a Child and His Demons: Pressure to Place Foster Children Raises Fears about Disclosure, Toll on Families." *Washington Post*, 28 November, p. A1.

———. 1999. "Egg Donation: A Growing Business; Fertility Successes Raise Demand, Price." *Washington Post*, 7 March, p. A1.

Waid, Mary Onnis. 1998. *Brief Summaries of Medicare and Medicaid: Title VIII and Title XIX of the Social Security Act*. Washington, D.C.: Health Care Financing Administration, Department of Health and Human Services. Available at www.hcfa.gov/medicare/ormedmed.htm#Medicaid (accessed 8 March 2000).

Walsh, Edward, and David A. Vise. 2000. "U.S., Gunmaker Strike a Deal; Smith & Wesson Plans Safety, Sales Steps; Suit Threats Dropped." *Washington Post*, 16 March, p. A1.

Wardle, Lynn D. 1996. "A Critical Analysis of Constitutional Claims for Same-Sex Marriage." *Brigham Young University Law Review* 1996: 1–101.

Warren, Samuel D., and Louis D. Brandeis. 1890. "The Right to Privacy." *Harvard Law Review* 4. Available at www.lawrence.edu/fac/boardmaw/Privacy_brand_warr2.html (accessed 21 March 2001).

Washington Post, 6 May 1997, 2 January 1998, 16 February 1999, 6 June 1999, 4 August 1999.

Weaver, Carolyn L. 1982. *The Crisis in Social Security: Economic and Political Origins*. Durham, N.C.: Duke University Press.

Wechsler, Herbert. 1961. *Principles, Politics, and Fundamental Law*. Cambridge, Mass.: Harvard University Press.

Weise, Elizabeth. 1999. "Electronic Evidence Hot New Tactic." *USA Today*, 10 May, p. A1.

Weiss, Rick. 1999. "Embryo Work Raises Specter of Human Harvesting." *Washington Post*, 14 June, p. A1.

Weitzman, Lenore J. 1985. *The Divorce Revolution: The Unexpected Social and Economic Consequences for Women and Children in America*. New York: Free Press; London: Collier Macmillan.

West, Darrell and Burdett Loomis. 1998. *The Sound of Money: How Political Interests Get What They Want*. New York: Norton.

Wheeler, David L. 1999. "The Real Impact of the Race to Sequence the Human Genome." *The Chronicle of Higher Education*, 16 July, p. A18.

White, E. B. 1952. *Charlotte's Web*. New York: Harper and Row.

White, G. Edward. 1991. *The Marshall Court and Cultural Change, 1815–1835*. New York: Oxford University Press.

———. 1988. *The American Judicial Tradition*. New York: Oxford University Press.

Wice, Paul. 1991. *Judges and Lawyers: The Human Side of Justice*. New York: Harper-Collins.

Williams, Neil G. 1995. "What to Do When There's No 'I Do': A Model for Awarding Damages Under Promissory Estoppel." *Washington Law Review* 70: 1019–69.

Williamson, Judith. 1978. *Decoding Advertisements: Ideology and Meaning in Advertising*. New York: Marion Boyers.

Wills, Garry. 1979. *Inventing America: Jefferson's Declaration of Independence*. New York: Vintage Books.

Withers, Kenneth J. 1999. "Third-Party Electronic Discovery: New Strategies for a New Technology." *Federal Discovery News* 5. Available at LEXIS-NEXIS (accessed 21 March 2001).

Witte, Edwin E. 1962. *The Development of the Social Security Act*. Madison: University of Wisconsin Press.

Wold, John, and John Culver. 1987. "The Defeat of the California Justices: The Campaign, the Electorate, and the Issue of Judicial Accountability." *Judicature* 70: 348–54.

Wolfe, Christopher. 1991. *Judicial Activism: Bulwark of Freedom or Precarious Security*. Pacific Grove, Calif.: Brooks/Cole Publishing.

Wolfskill, George. 1962. *The Revolt of the Conservatives: A History of the American Liberty League, 1934–1940*. Boston: Houghton Mifflin.

Wright, Richard. [1947] 1993. *Native Son*. Rep. ed. New York: Harper Perennial Library.

Yesley, Michael S. 1998. "Protecting Genetic Difference." *Berkeley Technology Law Journal* 13: 653–65.

Cases Cited

A & M Records v. Napster, Inc., No. 00-16401 (U.S. Court of Appeals for the 9th Circuit, 2001): 142

A. v. A., 514 P.2d 358 (Or. Ct. App. 1973): 206n11

A.C. v. C.B., 113 N.M. 581, 829 P.2d 660 (N.M. Ct. App. 1992): 206n11

Adams v. Howerton, 673 F.2d 1036 (9th Cir. 1982): 203n3

Adoption of F.H., In re, 851 P.2d 1361; 1993 Alas. LEXIS 42 (Supreme Court of Alaska, 1993): 206n15

Albertsons, Inc., v. Kirkingburg, 527 U.S. 555 (1999): 213n52

American College of Obstetricians v. Thornburgh, 699 F.2d 644 (3d Cir. 1983): 192n1

American Geophysical Union v. Texaco, 60 F.3d 913 (2d Cir., 1994): 212n38

American Trucking Association v. Smith, 496 U.S. 167 (1990): 194n37

Anderson v. Stream, 295 N.W.2d 595 (Minn. 1980): 204n32

Anonymous v. Anonymous, 325 N.Y.S.2d 499 (1971): 206n11

Anonymous v. Anonymous, 120 A.D.2d 983, 503 N.Y.S. 2d 466 (N.Y. 1986): 203n3

Aronow v. Silver, 223 N.J. Super. 344 (1987): 94

Avery Dennison Corporation v. Sumpton, 999 F. Supp. 1337 (United States District Court for the Central District of California, 1998): 143

Baby M, In re, 109 N.J. 396; 537 A.2d 1227 (1988): 195n2

Baehr v. Miike, 910 P.2d 112 (1st Cir. Ct. HI, 1996): 89, 204n15

Baker v. Carr, 369 U.S. 186 (1962): 55

Baker v. Nelson, 191 N.W.2d 185 (Minn. 1971): 203n3

Baker v. Vermont, 744 A.2d 864 (S Ct VT 1999): 191n17, 204n15

Bauchman v. West High School, 132 F.3d 542 (10th Cir., 1997) (cert. denied, June 26, 1998): 118

Beauharnais v. Illinois, 343 U.S. 250 (1952): 131

Bernstein v. U.S. Department of Justice, No. 97-16686 (9th Cir. 1999): 181

Blew v. Verta, 420 Pa. Super. 528, 617 A.2d 31 (Pa. Super. Ct. 1992): 206n11

Boddie v. Connecticut, 401 U.S. 371 (1971): 92

Bolton v. Scrivner, Inc., 36 F.3d 939 (10th Cir. 1994), cert. denied, 115 S. Ct. 1104 (1995): 215n11

Bottoms v. Bottoms, 249 Va. 410; 1995 Va. LEXIS 43; 457 S.E.2d 102 (Supreme Court of Virginia, 1995): 111

Bourke v. Nissan Motor Corporation in U.S.A., California Court of Appeals, Second Appellate District, Case No. B068705 (July 26, 1993): 135

Bowers v. Hardwick, 478 U.S. 186 (1986): 14, 99

Brause v. Bureau of Vital Statistics, No. 3AN-95-6562 CI (Superior Ct. 3d Dist. Alaska, Feb. 27, 1998): 204n15

Brooks v. Beto, 366 F.2d 1 (U.S. Court of Appeals for the 5th Circuit, 1966): 148

Brown v. Board of Education, 347 U.S. 483 (1954): 147

Brown v. Board of Education (Brown II), 349 U.S. 294 (1955): 147, 214n59

Brown v. Maryland, 25 U.S. 419 (1827): 217n23

Buck v. Bell, 274 U.S. 200 (1927): 98

Burlington Industries v. Ellerth, 524 U.S. 742 (1998): 191n15

Burnette v. Wahl, 588 P.2d 1105 (Or. 1978): 95, 204n32

Burr v. Board of Stark County Commissioners, 23 Ohio St. 3d 69; 491 N.E.2d 1101 (Supreme Court of Ohio, 1986): 113

Bush v. Gore, 121 S.Ct. 525 (2000): 76

Byrn v. New York City Health & Hospitals Corp., 286 N.E.2d 887 (1972): 100

California v. Ciraolo, 476 U.S. 207 (1986): 134

California v. Greenwood, 486 U.S. 35 (1988): 134

Campbell v. Acuff-Rose Music, 510 U.S. 569 (1994): 141

Campbell v. Sundquist, 926 S.W. 2d 250 (Tenn. App. 1996): 204n45

Canesi v. Wilson, 730 A.2d 805 (N.J. 1999): 116

Cantrell v. Forest City Publishing, 419 U.S. 245 (1974): 133

Carey v. Population Services International, 431 U.S. 678 (1977): 99, 107

Carson v. Here's Johnny Portable Toilets, Inc., 698 F.2d 831 (6th Cir., 1982): 132

Chandler v. James, 958 F. Supp. 1550; 1997 U.S. Dist. LEXIS 4603 (1997): 118

Chandler v. James, 180 F.3d 1254 (U.S. Court of Appeals for the 11th Circuit, 1999): 118

Chittenden Town School District v. Vermont Department of Education, 1999 Vt. LEXIS 98 (Supreme Court of Vermont, 1999): 119, 207n46

Clinton v. Jones, 520 U.S. 681 (1997): 55

Clyatt v. United States, 197 U.S. 207 (1905): 210n20

Coker v. Georgia, 433 U.S. 584 (1977): 162

Colautti v. Franklin, 439 U.S. 379 (1979): 203n2

Colegrove v. Green, 328 U.S. 549 (1946): 55

Commonwealth v. Bonadio, 415 Pa. 47 (Pa. 1980): 204n45

Commonwealth v. Kemp, 434 Pa. Super. 719, 643 A.2d 705 (Pa. Super. Ct. 1994): 206n27

Commonwealth v. Pellegrini, No. 87970, slip op. (Mass. Super. Ct. Oct. 15, 1990): 206n27

Commonwealth v. Wasson, 842 S.W. 2d 487 (Ky. 1992): 204n45

Commonwealth v. Welch, 864 S.W. 2d 280 (Ky. 1993): 206n27

Compassion in Dying v. Washington, 850 F. Supp. 1454 (WD Wash. 1994): 158

Compassion in Dying v. Washington, 79 F.3d 790 (1996) (9th U.S. Circuit Court of Appeals, *en banc*, 1996): 158

Cook v. Cook, 124 S.W. 2d 675 (Mo. Ct. App. 1939): 94

Coppage v. Kansas, 236 U.S. 1 (1915): 37

Cruzan v. Director, Missouri Department of Health, 497 U.S. 261 (1990): 157, 215nn27, 28

Recording Industry of America v. Diamond Multimedia Systems, 1999 U.S. App. LEXIS 13131 (United States Court of Appeals for the 9th Circuit, 1999): 142

Regents of the University of California v. Bakke, 438 U.S. 265 (1978): 192n1, 214n69

Reno v. ACLU, 521 U.S. 844 (1997): 17, 42, 78

Reyes v. Superior Court, 75 Cal. App. 3d 214, 141 Cal. Rptr. 912 (1977): 206n27

Reynolds v. U.S. 98 U.S. 145 (1878): 87, 89

Richmond v. J.A. Croson, 488 U.S. 469 (1989): 214n69

Rivers v. Roadway Express, Inc., 511 U.S. 298 (1994): 26

Roberts v. Louisiana, 428 U.S. 325 (1976): 216n36

Roe v. Catholic Charities, 588 N.E.2d 354 (Ill. App. Ct. 1992): 206n18

Roe v. Wade, 410 U.S. 113 (1973): 100–101, 107, 108, 129, 156

Roller v. Roller, 79 P. 788 (Wash. 1905): 94

Rutan v. Republican Party of Illinois, 497 U.S. 62 (1990): 198n22

R.S. v. S.S., 677 N.E.2d 1297 (Ill. App. Ct. 1996): 206n11

Sable Communications v. FCC, 492 U.S. 115 (1989): 138

San Antonio Metropolitan Transit Authority, 469 U.S. 528 (1985): 217n26

Sanders v. United States, 373 U.S. 1 (1963): 62

Santa Clara County v. Southern Pacific Railroad, 118 U.S. 394 (1886): 143, 217n17

Santa Fe Independent School District v. Doe, U.S. Supreme Court, No. 99-62 (2000): 118

Schall v. Martin, 467 U.S. 253 (1984): 106, 124

Schlessinger v. Salimes, 100 F.3d 519 (7th Cir) (1996): 200n56

School District v. Schempp, 374 U.S. 203 (1963): 117

Schuster v. Schuster, 90 Wash. 2d 626, 585 P.2d 130 (Wash. 1978): 206n11

S.E.G. v. R.A.G., 735 S.W. 2d 164 (Mo. Ct. App. 1987): 111

Senate Select Committee on Ethics v. Packwood, 845 F. Supp. 17 (U.S. District Court for the District of Columbia, 1994): 134

Shahar v. Bowers, 114 F.3d 1097 (11th Cir. 1997): 204n15

Shapiro v. Thompson, 394 U.S. 618 (1969): 215n15

Simmons-Harris v. Goff, 86 Ohio St. 3d 1; 711 N.E.2d 203 (Supreme Court of Ohio 1999): 119

Simmons-Harris v. Zelman, 72 F. Supp. 2d 834 (United States District Court for the Northern District of Ohio, Eastern Division, 1999): 119

Singer v. Hara, 522 P.2d 1187 (Wash. Ct. App. 1974): 203n3

Skinner v. Oklahoma, 316 U.S. 535 (1942): 98, 107, 203n1

Smyth v. Pillsbury Company, 914 F. Supp. 97 (U.S. District Court for the Eastern District of Pennsylvania, 1996): 135

S.N.E. v. R.L.B., 699 P.2d 875 (Alaska 1985): 206n11

Sommersett v. Stuart, 1 Lofft 1, 98 Eng. Rep. 499, 20 Howell's State Trials 1, 80-81 (KB 1772): 11

Sony Corp. v. Universal City Studios Inc., 464 U.S. 417 (1984): 212n38

Sosna v. Iowa, 419 U.S. 393 (1975): 204n24

South Dakota v. Dole, 483 U.S. 203 (1987): 126

Sparf and Hansen v. United States, 156 U.S. 51 (1895): 77

Stanford v. Kentucky, 492 U.S. 361 (1989): 216n38

Stanley v. Illinois, 405 U.S. 645 (1972): 97

State v. Carter, 602 So. 2d 995 (Fla. Ct. App. 1992): 206n27

State v. Chong Sun France, 379 S.E.2d 701 (N.C. Ct. App. 1989): 97

State v. Deborah J.Z., 1999 Wisc. App. LEXIS 581 *2 (Court of Appeals of Wisconsin, District Two, 1999): 116

State v. Gethers, 585 So. 2d 1140 (Fla. Ct. App. 1991): 206n27

State v. Gray, 62 Ohio St. 3d 514, 584 N.E.2d 710 (Ohio 1992): 206n27

State v. Luster, 204 Ga. App. 156, 419 S.E.2d 32 (Ga. Ct. App. 1992), cert. denied (Ga. 1992): 206n27

State v. Schwartz, 447 N.W.2d 422 (Minn. 1989): 202n32

Stenberg v. Carhart, No. 99-830 (2000): 102

Steve Jackson Games, Inc. v. United States Secret Service, 36 F.3d 457 (United States Court of Appeals for the 5th Circuit, 1994): 209n9

Steward Machine Company v. Davis, 301 U.S. 548 (1937): 215n5

Stone v. Powell, 428 U.S. 465 (1976): 62

Stroman v. Williams, 291 S.C. 76, 353 S.E.2d 704 (S.C. Ct. App. 1987): 206n11

Sutton v. United Airlines, 527 U.S. 471 (1999): 213n52

Swann v. Charlotte-Mecklenburg Board of Education, 402 U.S. 1 (1971): 147

Taylor v. Kurapati, 600 N.W.2d 670 (Mich. App. 1999): 207n28

Teague v. Lane, 489 U.S. 288 (1990): 62

Texas v. Johnson, 491 U.S. 397 (1989): 192n27, 195n3

Thompson v. Oklahoma, 487 U.S. 815 (1988): 208n58, 216n38

Thornburg v. American College of Obstetricians and Gynecologists, 476 U.S. 747 (1986): 101

Tilton v. Richardson, 403 U.S. 672 (1971): 119

Townsend v. Sain, 372 U.S. 745 (1963): 52

Troxel v. Granville, No. 99-138 (2000): 96

Tucker v. Tucker, 910 P.2d 1209 (Utah 1996): 206n11

Turner Broadcasting System, Inc. v. FCC, 114 S. Ct. 2445 (1994): 217n33

Twigg v. Mays, No. 88-4489-CA-01, 1993 WL 330624 (Fla. Cir. Ct. Aug. 18, 1993): 204n37, 205n61

United Church of Christ v. FCC, 123 U.S. App. D.C. 328; 359 F.2d 994 (1966): 213n57

U.S. v. Addison, 498 F.2d 741 (D.C. Cir. 1974): 202n32

U.S. v. Bayless, 913 F. Supp. 232 (S.D.N.Y. 1996): 19, 193n24

U.S. v. Carolene Products, 304 U.S. 144 (1938): 146, 202n35

U.S. v. Darby, 312 U.S. 100 (1941): 177

U.S. v. Eichman, 496 U.S. 310 (1990): 192n27, 195n3

U.S. v. Georgia, 171 F.3d 1333; 1999 U.S. App. LEXIS 6306 (11th Cir. 1999): 78

U.S. v. Kozminski, 487 U.S. 931 (1988): 210n20

U.S. v. Leon, 468 U.S. 897 (1984): 202n23

U.S. v. Lopez, 514 U.S. 549 (1995): 178–79, 180, 203n5

U.S. v. McVeigh, 153 F.3d 1166; 1998 U.S. App. LEXIS 21877 (10th Circuit Court of Appeals, 1998): 57

U.S. v. Microsoft, 65 F. Supp. 2d 1; 1999 U.S. Dist. LEXIS 17110 (U.S. District Court for the District of Columbia, 1999): 76

U.S. v. Morrison, 120 S.Ct. 1740 (2000): 179, 180

U.S. v. Wilson, 361 F. Supp. 510 (D. Md. 1973): 202n32

U.S. Department of Commerce v. U.S. House of Representatives, 525 U.S. 316 (1999): 198n14

U.S. House of Representatives v. U.S. Department of Commerce, 11 F. Supp. 2d 76; 1998 U.S. Dist. LEXIS 13133 (1998): 198n14

U.S. Term Limits, Inc. v. Thornton, 514 U.S. 779 (1995): 12

Utah Pie Co. v. Continental Baking Co., 386 U.S. 685 (1967): 195n5

Vacco v. Quill, 521 U.S. 793 (1997): 158

Valeria G. v. Wilson, 12 F. Supp. 2d 1007; 1998 U.S. Dist. LEXIS 10675 (U.S. District Court for the Northern District of California, 1998): 121

Vance v. Bradley, 440 U.S. 93 (1979): 214n2

Vandevender v. Sheetz, 200 W. Va. 591; 490 S.E.2d 678 (1997): 200n55

Van Driel v. Van Driel, 525 N.W.2d 37 (S.D. 1994): 206n11

Vaughns v. Board of Education of Prince George's County, 574 F. Supp. 1280 (U.S. District Court for the District of Maryland, 1983): 147

Vernonia School District 47j v. Acton, 515 U.S. 646 (1995): 187–88

Vigil v. Haber, 888 P.2d 455 (N.M. 1994): 204n28

Wabash, St. Louis & Pacific Ry. Co. v. Illinois, 118 U.S. 557 (1886): 177

Waggoner v. City of Garland, 987 F.2d 1160 (5th Cir. 1993): 215n11

Wainwright v. Sykes, 433 U.S. 72 (1977): 62

Washington v. Glucksberg, 521 U.S. 702 (1997): 158

Webster v. Reproductive Health Services, 492 U.S. 490 (1989): 101

West Virginia State Board of Education v. Barnette, 319 U.S. 624 (1943): 207n48

Whaley v. Whaley, 61 Ohio App. 2d 111, 399 N.E.2d 1270 (Ohio Ct. App. 1978): 206n11

White v. Thompson, 569 So. 2d 1181 (Miss. 1990): 206n11

Whitner v. South Carolina, 328 S.C. 1; 492 S.E.2d 777; Rehearing Denied November 19, 1997, cert. denied, May 26, 1998, Reported at 523 U.S. 1145 (1998): 115, 192n26

Wickard v. Filburn, 317 U.S. 111 (1942): 217n25

Wightman v. Coates, 15 Mass. 2 (1918): 204n25

Wildey v. Springs, 1995 U.S. App. LEXIS 4943 (7th Cir. 1995): 204n26

Winship, In re, 397 U.S. 358 (1970): 124

Wisconsin v. Yoder, 406 U.S. 205 (1972): 117, 204n34

Women's Medical Professional Corp. v. Voinovich, 130 F.3d 187 (6th Cir. 1997): 205n57

Zablocki v. Redhail 434 U.S. 374 (1978): 91

Zorach v. Clauson, 343 U.S. 306 (1952): 117

Index